Insuring the Industrial Revolution

Insuring the Industrial Revolution

Fire Insurance in Great Britain, 1700-1850

ROBIN PEARSON

ASHGATE

Published by
Ashgate Publishing Limited
Gower House
Croft Road
Aldershot
Hampshire GU11 3HR
England

Ashgate Publishing Company
Suite 420
101 Cherry Street
Burlington, VT 05401-4405
USA

Ashgate website: http//www.ashgate.com

British Library Cataloguing in Publication Data
Pearson, Robin
    Insuring the Industrial Revolution : fire insurance in
    Great Britain, 1700-1850. - (Modern economic and social
    history)
    1.Insurance, Fire - Great Britain - History - 18th century
    2.Insurance, Fire - Great Britain - History - 19th century
    3.Insurance companies - Great Britain - History - 18th century
    4.Insurance companies - Great Britain - History - 19th century
    I.Title
    368.1'1'00941'0903

Library of Congress Control Number: 2003045151

ISBN 0 7546 3363 2

Printed and bound in Great Britain by MPG Books Ltd, Bodmin, Cornwall

Contents

List of Figures

List of Tables

List of Maps

Acknowledgements

The germination of this book commenced over a decade ago and it has been pretty much a solitary effort on my part since then. Nevertheless along the way I have benefited from the support of several institutions without which this project could not have been completed. I am most grateful for small grants from the Twenty-Seven Foundation and the Nuffield Foundation (SOC/100[284]) which aided the early stages of the research, and to the University of Hull for granting sabbatical terms in 1995 and 1999 to devote to writing. The Philipps-Universität Marburg, Germany, appointed me visiting professor to the Department of History for the summer semester 1998, which allowed me to make substantial progress with the text. I am grateful to the University of Hull for permission to take up that opportunity, to the British Council for a grant towards the visit, and to Professor Dr Peter Borscheid for extending the invitation and for the kindness and hospitality of himself and his colleagues during my stay in Marburg.

Much of the research upon which this book is based has been conducted in corporate archives. I wish to thank the following institutions for their permission to consult their records and the following individuals for their help: Sun Alliance plc, Brian Sole, John Read and the late David Hill; Phoenix Assurance plc and their former archivist Ray Tye; GRE (UK) Ltd and their archivist, Miss C.B. Lillystone; Royal Insurance (UK) Ltd and Phil Turner of their Leeds office. I am also grateful to Arthur Owen and Mark Nicholls of the Department of Manuscripts, Cambridge University Library, for making available to me the newly deposited records of the Phoenix Assurance before they had been catalogued, and to Stephen Freeth, Keeper of Archives at the Guildhall Library, London, and his team, for their friendly and professional assistance over the years.

I have also incurred debts of gratitude to a number of colleagues and friends. Former students of economic and social history at the University of Hull, Caroline Ashton, Julia Lane, Angela McCabe and Liam Mogan, provided references and some research assistance. During my stay in Marburg, Anja Hauer kindly processed much of the data presented in chapters four and five. Harold Blakey, Martin Daunton, Edwin Green, Kevin Grady, T.V. Jackson, David Jenkins, David Jeremy, Clive Trebilcock, Oliver Westall and John Wilson generously supplied me with material or references. I have benefited from discussions with Bob Gibbons, David Richardson and Michael Turner, and Mike also kindly read and commented upon a draft of chapter one. My greatest thanks must go to John Peterson who has read and commented upon the whole manuscript and rescued me from several errors. Any that remain are of course entirely my responsibility. I would also like to thank the series editor, Derek Aldcroft, for his enthusiastic support for this project, and the commissioning editor, Tom Gray, and his colleagues at Ashgate, for their efforts in bringing it forward to publication.

My wife Sarah and our children, Henri, Susanna and Liam, have been a source of love and support, as well as considerable distraction from the work in hand. This book is dedicated to my parents, John and Elizabeth, who have always believed in the value of education and intellectual endeavour. I hope this book confirms that belief and helps repay their patience and their love.

Robin Pearson

List of Abbreviations

AR	Annual Register
CCM	Country Committee Minutes, Sun Fire Office
CKS	Centre for Kentish Studies, Maidstone
CMM	Committee of Management Minutes, Sun Fire Office
CUL	Cambridge University Library
DM	Board of Directors Minutes
FCM	Fire Committee Minutes
GCA	Glasgow City Archives
GCM	General Court (of Directors) Minutes
GCM	General Committee Minutes, Sun Fire Office
GL	Guildhall Library, London
GM	Gentleman's Magazine
GPL	Gateshead Public Library
GRE	Guardian Royal Exchange
LCA	Leeds City Archives
LM	London Magazine
LRO	Liverpool Record Office
MFLAC	Manchester Fire & Life Assurance Company
PAA	Phoenix Assurance Archive (CUL)
PP	Parliamentary Papers
PRO	Public Record Office
REA	Royal Exchange Assurance
SC	Select Committee of the House of Commons
SRO	Shropshire Record Office
VCH	Victoria County History
WCA	Westminster City Archives

Modern Economic and Social History Series
General Editor's Preface

Economic and social history has been a flourishing subject of scholarly study during recent decades. Not only has the volume of literature increased enormously but the range of interest in time, space and subject matter has broadened considerably so that today there are many more sub-branches of the subject which have developed considerable status in their own right.

One of the aims of this new series is to encourage the publication of scholarly monographs of any aspect of modern economic and social history. The geographical coverage is world-wide and contributions on non-British themes will be especially welcome. While emphasis will be placed on works embodying original research, it is also intended that the series should provide the opportunity to publish studies of a more general and thematic nature which offer a reappraisal or critical analysis of major issues of debate.

Derek H. Aldcroft

University of Leicester

Introduction

Fire insurance and perceptions of risk

One summer morning in 1731 a farmer in Devon sent out his servants to burn some rubbish. The fire they lit destroyed two fields of corn and peas worth £50. On a winter's day in 1754 the keeper of the Earl of Tilney's house at Wanstead forgot about a dish of hot coals which she had used to dry sweetmeats. A fire resulted which burned most of the Earl's linen, china and pewter worth over £1000. In the following year a boy took a candle into the loft of a stable at Walker's wharf, by the Thames in London. Within minutes the loft was ablaze. Four warehouses adjacent to the wharf were burnt down, plus a further eight warehouses across the street. The total damage was estimated at £20000.[1]

The outbreak of fire was invariably calamitous to eighteenth-century Britons, as it always had been in the past. Chimneys caught fire, coals fell out of hearths, ovens and copper wash tubs overheated when left alone by servants, tar kettles boiled over (one such fire destroyed the Royal rope yard at Woolwich during the Seven Years War, 'to the almost irreparable damage of this nation'),[2] lids blew off stills, burning candles touched bedsheets and curtains, and toppled into casks of oil and spirits or onto straw and hay in stables, hot ashes were thrown into back yards setting household rubbish alight, and sparks from burning warehouses blew across docks to set alight the rigging of ships. Such events were commonly regarded as acts of God or, by many, as unlucky accidents with astrological causes. Across Britain and Europe prayers continued to be offered and magic invoked to prevent or put out fires, as they had been for centuries.[3] Popular perceptions of fire hazard, however, also came to reflect the paradoxical alliance of science and providence which emerged during the seventeenth and early eighteenth centuries. As the laws which governed natural phenomena were gradually revealed by science, the immediacy of God's will was replaced by claims for its indirect revelation through the workings of nature. Natural disasters could thus be interpreted as the result of imprudence from which moral lessons could be drawn. Virtuous and careful behaviour might have its rewards in a safer, healthier life on earth, as well as securing entry into Heaven.

In this period perceptions of risk began to be informed by scientific debates about rationality. In turn, the latter found their reference point in social values and expectations, resulting in a difficult coexistence between optimism about technological progress and fatalism when confronted with the uncertainties of the social and physical world.[4] This tension underpinned the eighteenth-century fascination with natural disasters. On the one hand, earthquakes, famine and plague in foreign places helped the patriotic advocates of 'progress' and colonialisation to define the alterity and superiority of Britain over 'less developed' societies or declining Empires. On the other hand, the destructive power and apparent randomness of catastrophic events challenged the claims of western science to categorise and subordinate the natural world, and gave a fillip to evangelical preaching.[5] In Britain fire was a more immediate calamity than the greater types of catastrophe, but large conflagrations were terrible and frequent enough to heighten a sense of precarious living and expose the shallowness of technological and cultural pretensions.[6] The shocking accounts of the disaster at Blandford, Dorset, in 1731 - where 3000 people lay in the fields without shelter, food or clothing, and where smallpox victims 'were carried out of their beds into the meadows, and several dy'd and remain'd unbury'd...' - evoked Asiatic images of a society enmeshed in poverty and disease, without the governance structures which could deliver an adequate protection against the elements.[7]

For many Britons below the middling classes fire events remained largely the result of the confluence of chance and/or God's providence. This was a reflection of the narrow margins by which most people subsisted and the 'careless stoicism' to which many subscribed.[8] Yet this belief in the providential and capricious nature of fire was weakening in the most affluent societies in Europe. There were still places where it was thought an affront to the divine will to interfere with the workings of providence, such as Düsseldorf, whose inhabitants rioted in 1783 in order to destroy the lightning rods newly erected on public buildings.[9] In Britain, however, the fear of fire was being domesticated and managed by the process of identifying and categorising its material causes, and by the practical measures taken to prevent and contain fires and to save lives and property. While fire, to its immediate victims, frequently seemed to strike at random, with the benefit of hindsight it was increasingly viewed as predictable and preventable. The direction, ferocity, duration and destructiveness of conflagrations varied with the chance combination of familiar, potentially measurable, variables - wind direction and speed, weather, construction materials and building design, the position and density of the structures in their path, the efficiency of fire alarm and fire-fighting systems, the availability of equipment and water supplies. Fire prevention had a provenance dating back to at least the fifteenth century. By the early seventeenth century it was receiving increasing attention in the wake of population growth, urban expansion and the rise in property values. The Great Fire of London stimulated the most concerted attempt to apply science and the law to the problem.[10] During the half-century following the Fire there were attempts to regulate the rebuilding of the City in brick, to reduce the risk of fire and to improve facilities for fighting it. After a period of inactivity in the second quarter of the eighteenth century, further major fires, such as that which destroyed Cornhill in 1748, provoked renewed investigations into the nature of fire and combustion, the invention of new types of fire escapes and fire extinguishers, public demonstrations of fireproofing systems, and, from the 1760s, a new cycle of building legislation.[11]

As Thomas has pointed out, Protestantism taught men and women to try such methods of self help in the face of calamities, before invoking supernatural aid. From this developed a 'nascent statistical sense', an awareness of patterns in apparently random behaviour.[12] The search for quantifiable patterns in nature was reinforced by a burgeoning reportage. Bernstein has remarked that probability judgements are attached not to events but to descriptions of events. The more vivid and accurate the account, the greater the propensity to assign a probability value to the event described.[13] The eyewitness reports of earthquakes, floods and fires, given wide publicity by a growing pamphlet and newspaper press from the late seventeenth century, drove these events into the popular consciousness, as well as raising awareness among the educated and propertied classes of the need for preventive or remedial action.

The ideology of private property, whose primacy was acknowledged in the constitutional settlement of 1688, underlined this search for pattern and predictability, by emphasising the need to reduce uncertainty for the property-owning classes and to bolster the social order. The rise of humanitarianism was also a factor, for efforts at fire prevention can be seen as part of a wider movement which included projects for reviving victims of drowning accidents and suicide attempts, the building of hospitals and dispensaries, and schemes for rescuing destitute children and 'penitent' prostitutes.[14] Fire, of course, frequently provided a tool for individual vengeance, a means of collective social protest, and a vehicle for social discipline. Arson had long been associated with malevolent spirits, most notably witches, and with society's marginal groups, vagrants, beggars, and the economically and politically disaffected. Deliberate fires were commonly started by burglars and aggrieved employees.[15] During the second half of the eighteenth century the incidence of arson rose in conjunction with growing labour unrest, especially during wartime, and there was a tangible increase in the sense of the threat to property, which made the search for protection from fire more urgent. Indeed, it has been suggested that one of the characteristic institutions of this period, the associations for prosecuting felons, may have helped spread the fire insurance habit in their local areas.[16]

Despite the obvious danger it posed to property and order, however, the political and social impact of fire remained ambiguous. Large fires were presented as brief but recurring instances of social levelling which revealed the fragility and pathos of naked humanity. Fire was commonly perceived as failing to discriminate between the cottages of the poor and the mansions of the rich, notwithstanding the investment made in private fire-fighting equipment by many of the gentry and aristocracy. Conflagrations were reported as displays of social harmony in the face of calamity, which offered opportunities for patricians to exercise an idealised paternalism and, in doing so, to highlight the advantages of retaining the established divisions of wealth and status. Municipal leaders commonly led the collective effort to fight fires which threatened their towns, and successive members of the Royal household from Charles II to George III visited the scene of many London fires in person, distributing largesse to encourage firefighters.

British fire insurance was born into this mental world, in which the meaning of fire and its impact upon society was ambiguous, and its predictability still uncertain. It was a world in which scientific and political opinion placed an increasing, if often fitful, attention to building regulation and fire prevention, but where older attitudes of resignation to chance and habits such as the careless handling of fire were still widely found. Although there were a few abortive attempts to form insurance societies under the early Stuarts, the shock of 1666 resulted, within 20 years of the Great Fire, in the creation of the first permanent fire insurance institutions.[17] In the face of this and other large fires, the old system of raising charitable subscriptions through churchwardens' briefs to relieve victims of fires proved inadequate and increasingly burdensome to parish ratepayers. It was also criticised for permitting frauds to be committed too easily. This type of *ex-post* risk distribution, carrying a high moral hazard, gave way to several different forms of *ex-ante* risk pooling, which, it was reasoned, were better able to cope with the problems of aggregate uncertainty and adverse selection. Crucially, these forms of risk pooling also opened up entrepreneurial opportunities for profit. Early British fire insurance was characterised by low entry barriers, by a lack of regulation and monopoly privileges, by a diversity of organisational forms, and by large, but widely held, amounts of private capital. This contrasted sharply with continental Europe, where state and municipal insurance monopolies or small local mutual and cooperative societies were predominant well into the nineteenth century.[18] In Britain fire insurance appeared almost from its inception as a 'modern', large-scale, capital intensive, organisationally advanced form of business, which at the time could only be found among a few great corporations, most notably the East India Company and the Bank of England.

Yet, as this book will demonstrate, fire insurance was not entirely 'modern', rational or optimally efficient in its business practices, nor was it a consistently innovative and dynamic sector of the economy. The industry achieved no major productivity gains in this period. There was little product or process innovation within fire insurance, and almost no diversification by large wealthy fire offices into new branches of insurance. For much of this period these offices also failed to introduce the systematic analysis of their own underwriting data upon which more accurate and differentiated premium rates might have been based, and they failed to design more complex financial structures and systems of accounting, which might have offset the increasing volatility of the industry as it expanded and became more competitive. What Daston has called the 'anti-statistical bias' of eighteenth-century insurance was the product of an age which did not yet reject pre-probabilistic practices, or the legal notion of risk as a 'genuine' and unquantifiable uncertainty.[19] This changed only slowly. As the century progressed, new sources of combustion hazard appeared and there were novel, larger and more complex risks in the shape of new machinery, processes and materials to insure. This increased the pressure on underwriters to discriminate between risks with greater precision, to spread risk across regional and national boundaries, and to put fire insurance on a more scientific and financially sound footing. Furthermore, as the industry expanded and its demand for capital grew, the joint-stock form of organisation came to predominate. Where there had been 10 offices in Britain and Ireland in 1730, half of them mutual, insuring about £40m, by 1850 there were 70 companies, mostly joint-stock, insuring £731m. This expansion outstripped the growth of the economy as a whole. The estimates presented in Chapter 1 below suggest that by the middle of the nineteenth century well over half of all insurable property in Great Britain was insured against fire.

Historiography

Fire insurance, therefore, was a major business, expanding rapidly, though unevenly, throughout the course of Britain's industrial revolution. Yet, notwithstanding a growing body of research, insurance has seldom found its way into the standard economic histories of this period. Mathias makes three brief references to it in over 400 pages of text, while in the first volume of Floud and McCloskey, there is only one reference, characteristically in a chapter entitled 'the finance of business'. Similarly, in Daunton's recent textbook insurance is mentioned just twice in 565 pages, again in a chapter dealing with the finance of industrialisation.[20]

This neglect might in part be attributed to the influence of modern theories about the relationship between services and economic growth.[21] For some economists, services are inimical to the growth of national product, for this is largely determined by the growth of output in manufacturing. Productivity growth in services is held to be dependent upon an expansion of manufacturing helping to draw off underutilised labour. Thus services, including financial institutions, are accorded an entirely passive role. Indeed, any concentration of resources in this sector, it is claimed, will inhibit growth. A still more pessimistic view is that manufacturing growth generates increases in income which in turn create a rising demand for services, sucking labour into this less productive sector. In this view, service growth undermines aggregate productivity growth, and thus the growth of the economy as a whole. The continued expansion of labour in the service sector at the expense of manufacturing leads eventually to economic *stasis*. The intellectual origins of both these views can be found in the classical division of labour into productive and unproductive sectors. A service such as insurance, by definition is consumed at the point of production, or, as Smith put it, 'perishes at the very instant of [its] performance', and therefore it can add no permanent value to the wealth of nations.[22]

Some authors, however, have emphasised the risk pooling aspect of insurance and argue that this enables the production of goods which would otherwise not be produced. In this way insurance is seen as achieving net welfare gains for the benefit of the economy as a whole, although such gains have yet to be measured.[23]

Modern international studies have demonstrated the high income elasticity of insurance demand and the existence of insurance multipliers. For the most advanced economies, this multiplier proves to be close to one, so that for each percentage increase in GNP, insurance premiums increase by a similar amount. In developing economies the multiplier is higher, up to five or six. Thus as a country develops, its insurance industry outpaces the growth of the economy as a whole.[24] Hitherto, these results have not been tested against long-run historical data for any nation's insurance industry. A tentative start is made for Britain in Chapter 1 below.

Most applications of economic theory have focused not upon the macro-economic gains of insurance or the workings of the insurance market, but upon the process of decision making under uncertainty. Since the 1950s numerous authors have applied game theory and decision theory to problems in insurance, so that the latter has become central to the development of the economics of uncertainty. Insurance had been largely ignored by classical economics, because the latter assumed away uncertainty, making insurance unnecessary or irrational. The renewed interest in Bernouilli's solution to the St Petersburg paradox - namely that it is expected utility not expected wealth which is maximised by economic actors - and the recognition by Knight and others that utility can be non-linear and perceptions fallible, opened the way for insurance to be integrated into more sophisticated theories of economic behaviour than those permitted by *homo economicus*.[25] In this expanding literature, the economics of insurance became largely about finding the optimal levels of insurance in order to maximise different utility functions which vary according to the risk aversion of different players and the riskiness of their endowments.[26] Other insurance problems which have received attention from mathematical economists include moral hazard, where the search has been to find the optimal incentive and monitoring contracts, and adverse selection, where solutions have been sought to the problem of asymmetric information.[27] In turn, within the field of financial economics, these problems have generated a considerable literature on the relative efficiency of stock and mutual forms of corporate organisation, where the principal focus has been on the insurance industry.[28]

Hitherto there has been virtually no application of these areas of economics to insurance history. There are obvious difficulties in reconciling the algorithms in the micro-models of choice, risk and uncertainty to the fragmentary data and macro-historical accounts which insurance records offer. The path which most insurance theory has taken, out of actuarial science and into mathematical and behavioural economics, has left a large gap between theory and history which is beyond the scope of this book to fill. Another developing area of economics, however, presents more immediate possibilities for its application to the history of insurance. Institutional economics emphasises the role of institutions - in the sense both of formal rules and organisations, and informal norms and customs - in providing incentives for, or imposing constraints upon, economic growth. The 'institutional matrix' of a society - which is itself a product of the dominant belief system - creates path dependency that typically makes change incremental. Belief systems, however, can change, sometimes radically, which in turn leads to institutional change and the release of constraints on growth.[29] Fire insurance might be regarded as an institutional product of changing attitudes to providence and hazard during the seventeenth and eighteenth centuries. By reducing uncertainty and the fear of loss, insurance safeguarded the value of property and acted as an incentive for accumulation, investment and innovation. A tentative start is made in this book to view insurance in this way, and to explore the relationship between perceptions of risk and the development of the industry. In Chapter 6 the embeddedness of trust in the social and business networks of those who established provincial insurance companies is found to be critical to their proliferation during the late eighteenth and early nineteenth centuries. Chapter 7 examines the more direct costs and benefits of insurance for textile manufacturers.

Until recently the traditional nature of much writing on insurance history has not encouraged historians to think conceptually of the relationship between insurance and economic growth. Insurance historiography has its origins in the rise of insurance journalism from the middle of the nineteenth century. The systematic collection of data and the interest taken in the development of insurance law and underwriting practice, was reflected in the content of numerous articles appearing in the early insurance press, in the reports of Brown and Coode and the works of Relton and Walford.[30] The first general history of British insurance, published by the actuary Harold Raynes in 1948, fitted into the existing mould of historiography dating back to Walford, which placed the primary emphasis on the development of institutions, the technology of underwriting, and the regulatory framework within which insurance operated.[31]

This began to change in 1960 with the publication of the first of three outstanding histories of major companies by professional historians. Peter Dickson provided a masterful synopsis of the first two and a half centuries of the Sun Insurance, the biggest fire insurer in Britain during the industrial revolution, without ever fully excavating the vast archives of that office. This was followed ten years later by Barry Supple's history of the Royal Exchange Assurance, and fifteen years after that by the first volume of Clive Trebilcock's history of the Phoenix Assurance. In their different ways, each of these authors moved beyond the confines of the in-house company history to write wider histories of British insurance. My debt to their pioneering work is apparent throughout the footnotes of this book.[32] Together, these three texts described a generally unregulated industry, which expanded from a metropolitan base to national and international markets during the course of the eighteenth and nineteenth centuries, and which was characterised by recurrent periods of cooperation, interrupted by cycles of fierce competition, high levels of market entry, and a high attrition rate. Competition mostly took place in the arena of marketing rather than through product differentiation or price cuts, although there were intermittent periods of savage price warfare. Informal oligopolistic collusion flourished during the 1790s between the three largest offices, the Sun, the Royal Exchange and the Phoenix, and was revived on a wider and more permanent basis after 1840. Underwriting techniques developed relatively slowly in response to accelerating commercial and industrial growth and technological change after 1780, but higher levels of uncertainty did not prevent the largest insurance offices from entering the market to insure mills, warehouses, docks, breweries and sugar refineries with energy, if not always enthusiasm. The Phoenix also pioneered a path into overseas markets.

Since the 1970s, apart from the company histories, insurance history has developed in several new directions. Cockerell and Green's comprehensive guide to British insurance archives has helped to make the industry more accessible for historical research.[33] Industrial and urban historians have made use of the policy registers of the Sun and the Royal Exchange to reconstruct data on capital formation, firm size and property values, and this has given rise to a debate about the meaning and accuracy of the valuations in these registers.[34] A collection of essays, published in 1984, marked a diversification of interests, though some of the paths explored there, notably brokerage and the marine market, remain relatively undeveloped.[35] During the last decade, insurance history has also made some progress towards a greater engagement with economic theory and with central themes in economic and business history. Westall has contributed several important essays which have applied concepts drawn from new institutional economics.[36] His view of insurance as an industry characterised by corporate cultural rigidities, by a tension between collusive practices and the problems caused by porous barriers to entry, and by the impact of marketing and agency problems on organisational change, finds several echoes in this book. Among my own articles, an examination of the motives for Manchester cotton merchants moving into fire insurance was set within the literature on entrepreneurial diversification. An analysis of competition in nineteenth-century fire insurance drew on oligopoly theory, and modern theories of financial innovation were applied to a general model of innovation in insurance before 1914. Finally, Clark's recent book on early life insurance has questioned orthodox accounts of the speculative nature of the business during the eighteenth century, and shown how gambling and prudential motives could coexist.[37]

The purpose and structure of this book

Despite the extent of this literature and its increasing orientation away from a focus on corporate histories, insurance is still regarded by many as a specialist, technical and rather arcane subject of only marginal interest. Recently the works of Neal, Michie and others have done much to raise the profile of the stock market, and Kynaston has reminded us of the complexity and variety of the elements which comprised the City of London.[38] In general, however, there is still a tendency to define the growth of financial services and their role in the British economy largely as the history of banking. Banking, in contrast to insurance, has already developed a critical mass in terms of the volume of active researchers, international associations and regular conferences.

Thus, a problem for the insurance historian is that there remains not only a deficit of knowledge but also a deficit of attention. One aim of this book is to pull insurance, or at least its major branch, out of its backwater as a subset of business or financial history, and to provide a foundation for future comparative international studies and a greater level of theorising about the historical relationship between insurance, economic development and social change. The book succeeds if it presents a comprehensive picture of early fire insurance in Britain, and also if it demonstrates ways in which this industry can be linked into wider questions about British economy and society during the first industrial revolution.

How is this book different from the major company histories which have defined the subject for the past four decades? First, unconstrained by the limits of official in-house histories, this book adopts a market-oriented rather than corporate-oriented approach, to reveal the full diversity of organisational structures, underwriting and marketing practices in fire insurance across eighteenth- and early nineteenth-century Britain. Fire insurance generated relatively little public debate during this period. Its history can only be followed by going behind closed doors - to the internal archives of the companies themselves - the minute and letter books, ledgers, registers and accounts. The surviving records of several dozen English and Scottish insurance offices founded between 1696 and 1850 - most of the records currently available - have been analysed in detail to produce the most complete history yet of any financial service. Second, attention has been paid to the smaller provincial as well as the larger metropolitan insurers, placing both in their local and national contexts. The result is a new emphasis on the market power and comparative advantage of provincial offices in their own areas in the face of metropolitan competition. Third, this book takes the region and the locality, as well as national aggregates, as units within which to analyse the relationship between insurance and economic growth. New regional and urban data sets are constructed, for instance, to measure insurance penetration and the distribution of wealth and population, or to examine the share of competing firms in local markets. Fourth, several other new aspects of the industry are explored, such as the chronology and pace of insurance growth in comparison to other sectors of the economy; volume estimates of fire insurance during the eighteenth century, which reveal the relative importance of the London mutual offices; the timing and intensity of different phases of cooperation and competition, which give new emphasis to the persistence of collusive practices; the competitive strategies and sophisticated negotiating techniques employed in the first merger and acquisition waves of the 1820s and 1830s, which underline the 'modernity' of the insurance industry by this period; the close-knit, high-trust business and social networks behind the foundation of provincial offices.

Much of this is new, and much of it converges with current themes in the economic and business history of the British industrial revolution. Notwithstanding the attempt to be comprehensive, it must be acknowledged that certain areas have not received the attention they deserve. Scotland and Ireland are largely, though not entirely, viewed through the records of the English fire offices which operated there. The development of the native insurance industries in both countries remains to be properly researched. Furthermore, although Chapter 9 below captures the diversity of insurance investment, it was beyond the scope of this book systematically to reconstruct the portfolios of a large number of offices from surviving ledgers, a labour which might in the future yield dividends, particularly for historians interested in intra-regional capital flows.

What follows is organised into two parts, the first chronological, and the second thematic. These are preceded by an opening chapter which presents the results of the aggregate data analysis for the entire period covered by this book. Estimates are made of the number of firms, labour employed and capital invested in the industry, and time series are constructed for sums insured, premium income, average premium rate (price), and real per caput sums insured. These enable comparisons to be made between fire insurance and the growth of other economic sectors, of population and national product. Estimates are also made of the proportion of insurable property insured, and of insurance 'penetration' in early nineteenth-century Britain relative to that in the contemporary developing world. Factors that may have determined the growth of fire insurance are examined. These include levels of fire damage and construction activity, and the cost of insurance relative to purchasing power. The overall picture emerging from Chapter 1 is of a financial service whose development is highly volatile and uneven, either racing ahead of, or lagging behind the growth of the economy as a whole, and whose relationship with the building cycle weakened as its market expanded and diversified.

Part I contains four chapters which provide an account of the development of the industry between 1700 and 1850. Chapter 2 examines the growth and segmentation of the market for fire insurance in eighteenth-century London, and the organisation, strategies and performance of the companies that operated there between 1720 and 1782. Estimates are made of the proportion of property insured and the frequency of fires, and there is a discussion of the efficiency of firefighting in the capital. Chapter 3 examines the development of fire insurance outside London during the same period, and explores some of the reasons for its slow rate of diffusion. It reconstructs the provincial business of the London mutual and stock offices, and in particular the agency system of the Sun Fire Office, and discusses their monitoring problems and the difficulties presented by urban and industrial growth and competition from the first local fire offices. Chapter 4 covers the period between the end of the American War of Independence and the end of the Napoleonic war in 1815. The increasing burden of taxation upon the industry is examined, together with the strategies adopted by insurance companies to deal with the subsequent slowdown in real growth, and their underwriting performance and profitability. This period witnessed the rise and fall of a powerful cartel organise by the three principal London offices, followed by a phase of bilateral cooperation among several of the new offices founded during the war. Chapter 5 deals with a period, 1815-50, when the industry accelerated out of its long wartime stagnation, growing larger and more diverse than ever before. Sums insured more than doubled in real terms, the proportion of property insured against fire rose from below 40 to over 56 per cent, and competition rose to new heights. The sources of competition and the various strategies for dealing with them - price-cutting, retrenchment, corporate acquisitions, collusive practices - are examined. By the 1840s fire insurance had begun to abandon open warfare and move towards the formal cooperation which was to characterise the industry into the second half of the twentieth century.

Part II analyses central aspects of fire insurance in four thematic chapters. Chapter 6 explores the process by which unincorporated stock companies - who comprised the great majority of all insurance companies during this period - were founded. The nature of share ownership is examined, as is the relationship between owners, directors and officers. In this context, an analysis is also made of the social, political and economic networks behind the founders of the first fire office in Newcastle, which expands upon my previous studies of businessmen diversifying into fire insurance in Lancashire, Yorkshire and Wiltshire.[39] Chapter 7 looks at the size and distribution of company sales forces, at trends in marketing, at the problems involved in establishing and monitoring agencies, and at relations between policyholders and their insurers. Chapter 8 focuses on the practice of underwriting. It resolves the debate about the meaning of property valuations in policy registers through an analysis of the process of risk assessment and the problems of underinsurance and coinsurance. It also examines the impact of changes in underwriting practice both on policyholders' perceptions of fire hazard and on the insurance companies themselves. Chapter 9 explores the changing trends in insurance investment over the period. The contribution of investment income to total income, profits and dividends is analysed for several firms, and returns on capital are compared with profit levels in other sectors of the economy. Profitability is also explored from the perspective of the individual investor, through an examination of average dividends and share price movements. The final chapter summarises the main findings and draws conclusions about the significance of fire insurance to Britain's industrial revolution.

This book has been many years in the making. It is hoped that it will be regarded as an important contribution to British economic and social history and realise most of the goals set out above. It is also hoped that it will prove engaging to a wide audience, for, in an optimistic vein, one might cite the proverbial Dr Johnson, that 'what is written without effort is in general read without pleasure'.[40]

Notes

1   *GM*, 1 (1731); *LM*, 23 (1754), p.427, 24 (1755), p.249.

2   *GM*, 29 (1759), p.143. All the references in this paragraph are to fires described in *Gentleman's Magazine* 1731-80, *London Magazine* 1732- 80, a nd *Annu al Register* 1758-80.

3   For English prayers to St Osyth for deliverance from fire, and for the use of holy water, agnus dei and St Agatha's letters to protect against lightning and fire, see Thomas, *Religion and the Decline of Magic*, pp.31, 33-5, 60, 85, 135. For prayers to saints to quench fires in sixteenth-century France, see Roberts, 'Agencies Human and Divine', p.21.

4   Beck, *Risikogesellschaft*, pp.38-40.

5   Arnold, 'Hunger in the Garden of Plenty'; Walker, 'Shaking the Unstable Empire'; Kendrick, *Lisbon Earthquake*.

6   Cf. Jones, Porter and Turner, *Gazetteer*, and see the discussion in Chapters 1 and 2 below. With the extremes of climate in eighteenth-century Britain, there were also numerous other disasters to enhance such sensibilities. Davison has catalogued nearly 150 earthquakes for the century, Davison, *History of British Earthquakes*, pp.12-34. The earthquake of March 1750 caused a panic and exodus from London. Kendrick, *Lisbon Earthquake*, pp.11-14. There were widespread reports of storms, hurricanes, floods, and frost, for example, *GM*, 9 (1739), p.45, 10 (1740), p .569, 11 (1741), p.498. The existence of famine in Britain, however, has been the subject of debate: Stevenson, 'Food Riots in England'; Williams, 'Were "Hunger Rioters" Really Hungry?'; Wells, *Wretched Faces*; Turner, 'Corn Crises in Britain'.

7   *GM*, 1 (1731). Cf. Frost, 'Coping In Their Own Way'. Constantinople was widely regarded by contemporaries as the most flammable city outside Christendom, with some justification. Cf. Mansel, *Constantinople*, pp.224-5.

8   Thomas, *Religion and the Decline of Magic*, p.20. On the pugnacious, rumbustious character of the English, see Porter, *English Society in the Eighteenth Century*, pp.23-34.

9   Arps, *Auf Sicheren Pfeilern*, p.19.

10   Ordinances against lighting fires beneath wooden chimneys, and municipal provisions for firefighting can be found before 1500, for example, in London, Cambridge and Worcester. Blackstone, *History of the British Fire Service*, pp.15-16.

11   Knowles and Pitt, *History of Building Regulation*, pp.28-54; Blackstone, *History of the British Fire Service*, pp.35-64, 78-93.

12   Thomas, *Religion and the Decline of Magic*, pp.784-94. One aspect of this was the emergence of 'political arithmetic' in areas of public policy, Hoppit, 'Political Arithmetic'. Another was the increase in popular mathematical and accounting manuals serving a range of needs from those of shopkeepers and merchants to schoolteachers and cardsters. Among numerous examples, see Dodson, *Arithmetique Made Easie*; Gordon, *The Universal Accountant*; Hoyle, *Doctrine of Chances*; Hutton, *The Schoolmaster's Guide*.

13   Bernstein, *Against the Gods*, p.279.

14   Langford, *Polite and Commercial People*, p.490; Lloyd, '"Pleasure's Golden Bait"'. On the primacy of property, see Langford, *Public Life and the Propertied Englishman*, pp.1-70.

15 For examples of young maidservants setting fire to their employers' houses after theft, see *GM*, 33 (1763), pp.358, 360.

16 King, 'Prosecution Associations', p.203 n115; Philips, 'Good Men to Associate'.

17 For the origins of fire insurance in Britain, see Raynes, *History of British Insurance*, pp.76-96; Dickson, *Sun Insurance*, pp.1-16; Supple, *Royal Exchange*, pp.6-12.

18 For the multiplicity of company forms in early British insurance, see Harris, *Industrializing English Law*, pp.100-7. Most authors date the rise of private joint-stock insurance companies in Germany to the Hardenberg reforms of 1811, although a stock company for marine and fire insurance was founded in Hamburg as early as 1765. Arps, *Auf Sicheren Pfeilern*, pp.40-41; Gesellschaft für feuerversicherungs-geschichtliche Forschung, *Das Deutsche Feuerversicherungswesen*, I, pp.451-4. The first private stock fire insurance company in France was founded in 1819. Walford, *Insurance Cyclopedia*, vol.IV, p.266.

19 Daston, 'Domestication of Risk', p.240.

20 Mathias, *First Industrial Nation*, pp.308, 310, 314; Neal, 'Finance of Business during the Industrial Revolution', p.152; Daunton, *Progress and Poverty*, pp.240-41. One exception to this pattern is Lee, *British Economy since 1700*, ch.3, who pays some attention to the institutional growth of insurance, though his primary focus is also on insurers as investors.

21 The following draws on the discussion in Lee, 'Service Industries', pp.117-8.

22 Smith, *Wealth of Nations*, vol.1, pp.330-31.

23 Carter, 'Economics of Insurance', p.197; Clayton and Osborn, *Insurance Company Investment*, p.11; Dunning, *Insurance in the Economy*, p.38.

24 Baker, 'Liberalization of Trade in Services'; Wasow, 'Determinants of Insurance Penetration', p.160.

25 Borch, *Mathematical Theory*, pp.179-95; Knight, *Risk, Uncertainty and Profit*. On the St Petersburg paradox, see Daston, *Classical Probability*, pp.68-76. For an entertaining account of the development of the concepts of utility and uncertainty, see Bernstein, *Against the Gods*.

26 A simple illustration can be found in Smith, *Economics of Financial Institutions*, pp.42-3. Greater sophistication can be found in Borch's famous theorem on optimal risk exchange, which explores the basis for Pareto-optimality with risk pooling, see Lemaire, 'Borch's Theorem'; Borch, *Economics of Insurance*, pp.211-28.

27 Lippman and McCall, 'Economics of Uncertainty'. The literature is vast, but see the exchange between Pauly and Arrow on the economics of moral hazard, in *American Economic Review*, 58 (1968), pp.531-9, and also Pauly, ' Overinsurance'; Shavell, 'Moral Hazard'.

28 Here too the literature is extensive. A recent summary can be found in Smith and Stutzer, 'Theory of Mutual Formation'. See also Marshall, 'Insurance Theory'.

29 North, *Economic Change*, pp.10-15. I am grateful to David Richardson for drawing my attention to this reference, and for many discussions on these ideas. See also North, *Institutions*.

30 Brown, 'Progress of Fire Insurance'; Coode, 'Revised Report'; Relton, *Account of the Fire Insurance Companies*; Walford, *Insurance Cyclopedia*; *idem.*, 'Fires and Fire Insurance Considered'. Similar efforts were made abroad before the First World War, for example, Hamon, *Histoire Générale de l'Assurance en France*; Gesellschaft für

feuerversicherungsgeschichtliche Forschung, *Das Deutsche Feuerversicherungs-wesen*.

31   Raynes, *History of British Insurance*. The only other general history was that by Clayton, *British Insurance*, published in 1971, but this was heavily derivative of secondary sources.

32   Dickson, *Sun Insurance*; Supple, *Royal Exchange*; Trebilcock, *Phoenix Assurance*, vol.I. I should also note my debt to the excellent but unpublished doctoral thesis of Roger Ryan on Britain's largest provincial insurer during this period. Ryan, 'History of Norwich Union'.

33   Cockerell and Green, *British Insurance Business*.

34   Pearson, 'Capital Formation'.

35   Westall, *Historian and the Business of Insurance*.

36   Westall, 'Assumptions of Regulation'; *idem.*, 'Marketing Strategy', *idem.*, 'Invisible, Visible and "Direct" Hands'.

37   Pearson, 'Collective Diversification'; *idem.*, 'Taking Risks'; *idem.*, 'Towards an Historical Model of Services Innovation'; Clark, *Betting on Lives*.

38   Neal, *Financial Capitalism*; Michie, *London and New York Stock Exchanges*; Kynaston, *City of London*; Mirowski, 'The Rise (and Retreat) of a Market'.

39   Pearson, 'Collective Diversification'; Pearson and Richardson, 'Business Networking'.

40   Boswell, *Life of Samuel Johnson*, p.19.

Chapter 1

Fire Insurance and British Economic Growth, 1700-1850

That, Sir, is the good of counting. It brings everything to a certainty, which before floated in the mind indefinitely.

Samuel Johnson.[1]

This chapter examines the growth of fire insurance in eighteenth- and early nineteenth-century Britain, places the industry in its economic context and explores some of the likely determinants of its growth. Necessarily it is concerned with national aggregates rather than with the local or regional variations which are the subject of subsequent chapters. Two obvious ways to measure growth are to examine the number of policies issued or the number of properties insured. Unfortunately these data were rarely recorded by the insurance offices of the period or have failed to survive. However, we are able to construct, for the first time, annual time series for sums insured and premium income for the period 1720-1850. Without taking Johnson's apothegm too seriously, this data should interest everyone concerned with the relationship between British economic development and the growth of financial services. One of the deficiencies of the various national income accounts constructed for this period has been the service sector. Deane and Cole noted the 'absence of information', and Crafts, when attempting to calculate the real output growth of the British economy, commented that services constituted 'the most problematic part of the measurement'.[2] The usual solution has been to assume that this sector grew at the same rate as population. This assumption must now be questioned in the light of the estimates presented below. They provide the most accurate and detailed quantitative account yet of the development of any major service industry during the Industrial Revolution.

The contours of the industry: numbers, employment and capital

Counting British insurance offices is not an exact science. This is true even for the period after 1782 when annual returns of stamp duty on fire insurance were first made. A published breakdown of the duty paid by individual offices in England and Wales is first available from 1821, and for offices in Ireland and Scotland from 1824.[3] Furthermore, collection of the duty was never exact, and some insurers,

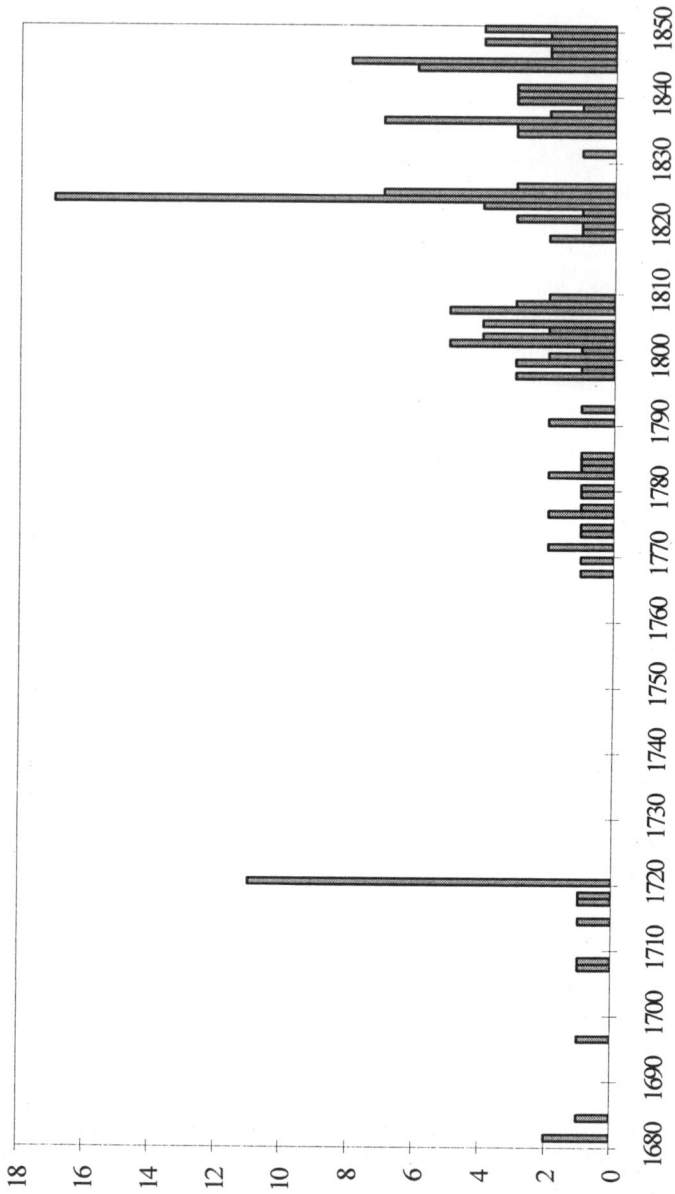

Figure 1.1 New fire offices established in Britain and Ireland, 1680-1850
Source: see text.

mostly small, short-lived offices, failed to appear in the returns. Nevertheless, using these returns, supplemented by a range of other sources, we have identified 169 fire offices established in Britain and Ireland between 1681 and 1850. These are shown in figure 1.1.[4]

The graph indicates that company formation was highly cyclical and concentrated over time. Eighty-four per cent of all offices were established during five distinct periods - 1717-20, 1797-1809, 1818-26, 1834-41, 1844-50. Seventy-seven offices were founded in just 11 years (1720, 1802-3, 1807-8, 1824-5, 1835-6, 1844-5). Table 1.1 shows end-of-decade totals for Britain and Ireland. Throughout this period the population of fire offices remained small compared with other sectors in which corporate or partnership forms of business organisation predominated. In the early 1780s there were over 100 banks in existence and just 18 fire insurance companies. By 1800 there were about 30 country banks in England and Wales for every country fire office. In 1814 there were over 160 river and canal navigations, compared to the 70 fire offices established by that date. One hundred and forty gas companies existed in 1826, but fewer than 60 fire offices. The railway mania of the 1840s produced 25 new railway companies for every new fire office established during that decade.[5] With the largest manufacturing industries the differential was greater still. Around 1800 there were over 1300 common brewers in England and Wales, and in 1838 there were over 4200 factory-based textile firms in Britain. Such numbers highlight how rare a sight was an insurance company on the British economic landscape.[6]

General patterns in the geography of company formation are also evident from table 1.1. The promotions of 1720, associated with the speculative boom which led to the South Sea Bubble crisis of that year, were almost exclusively London-based. By contrast, the steady growth in the number of offices after 1760 took place exclusively outside London. By 1780 provincial offices were in the majority, and this remained the case until the 1840s. The numerical gap between London offices and the rest was widest after the boom of the early 1820s. Just nine of the 37 offices established between 1819 and 1826 were located in London. By 1830 only about one in four British fire insurance companies were metropolitan. Because of corporate takeovers and new company foundations, this trend was subsequently reversed so that by 1850 the ratio was nearly one in two. Most provincial offices, however, were relatively small. The proportion of UK insurances sold by non-London offices was just 13 per cent in 1810, rising to 33 per cent by 1850.

Although the number of fire insurance offices was modest, how important were they in terms of employment creation and capital accumulation? The financial sector has always been regarded as having a poor capacity to generate jobs by comparison with primary or secondary industries. This may explain why historians have largely ignored the labour question when discussing financial services. At first glance, the orthodox view seems to hold for fire insurance. The number of salaried and waged employees of insurance offices remained tiny in relation to their 'output' and 'income', measured by sums insured and premiums received. The largest

Table 1.1 Fire insurance offices in Britain and Ireland, 1690-1850

Year	London	Current Offices English Provincial	Scottish	Irish	Current Total
1690	2				2
1700	3				3
1710	5				5
1720	14	1	2	2	19
1730	6	1	2	1	10
1740	6	1	2	1	10
1750	6	1	2	1	10
1760	6	1	2	1	10
1770	6	3	2	1	12
1780	7	8	2	3	20
1790	7	11	2	4	24
1800	8	12	4	6	30
1810	15	23	8	7	53
1820	16	22	7	6	51
1830	16	26	11	4	57
1840	22	24	14	3	63
1850	33	26	9	2	70

Notes: For the purposes of counting current totals, where the fate of an office is unknown, it is presumed to have ceased underwriting in the decade following its establishment. The Suffolk & General (established 1802) had two divisions, 'east' and 'west', which were listed separately in the duty returns before 1837. This is counted as one office in the above table.

Sources: Duty returns 1822-50; Trebilcock, *Phoenix Assurance*, pp.451, 495, tab.8.4; *Insurance Yearbook 1981/2*; Walford, *Insurance Cyclopaedia*; Walford, 'Fires and Fire Insurance Considered'; Raynes, *History of British Insurance*; Ryan, 'History of the Norwich Union'; Jenkins, 'Practice of Insurance against Fire', pp.19-20; GL Ms 16170/2, Atlas, DM, 27 May 1813.

London offices had permanent staffs of no more than 15 for most of the eighteenth century, 20 to 30 during the early nineteenth century, and still fewer than 50 by midcentury. Using the data in table 1.1 and the records of 16 companies, it is estimated that there were only about 80 permanent full-time staff employed by all British fire offices c.1750, about 250 in 1800 and nearly 800 by 1850.

Beyond the small numbers of clerical staff many others gleaned an income from insurance offices. Housekeepers, doorkeepers, cleaners, watchmen, porters, messengers and collectors could be found either among the permanent establishment or the casual staff. Solicitors, printers and stationers, metal and leather workers, tailors, buttonmakers, painters, carpenters, carvers, plumbers, bricklayers, glaziers and smiths provided the fire offices with a range of services and equipment by fee or retainer. Teams of building workers were contracted to repair and rebuild insured property which had been damaged or destroyed. Fire 'preventers', caps and hooks for firefighters were supplied by numerous small artisans, mostly in London, as well as fire engines and leather hose by the better known firms such as Newsham & Ragg. Firemen's uniforms, hats and boots were manufactured, leather buckets cut, sewn, and lacquered by the dozen, firemarks cast and gilded by the hundred. Many suppliers of smaller items were women, including six of the twelve individuals paid through the Sun's petty accounts between the 1730s and 1750s for firemarks, buckets, preventers, buttons and rolling press work. Ann Humphreys earned over £22 in 1739 for supplying and mending buckets. Mary Taylor succeeded her late husband as painter to the Sun in 1740, and earned over £60 that year for painting the office and gilding 1500 firemarks. Over the period 1739-59 Ann Bagley earned an annual average of £15 for casting thousands of lead firemarks for the Sun.[7]

It is impossible to reconstruct the numbers earning a crust in these ways. However, some idea of the size of two groups of part-time employees, firemen and agents, can be obtained from scattered references in company records.[8] During the eighteenth century most London offices maintained brigades of between 24 and 50 firemen and auxiliaries. Some provincial offices also had fire brigades. The Kent Fire Office employed at least 63 firemen in several Kentish towns in 1809. Estimates suggest about 250 employed by British insurers in 1750, over 500 in 1800, and about 1000 in the 1810s and 1820s, before numbers fell rapidly with the advent of the London Fire Engine Establishment in 1833 and the municipal fire brigades which followed. The population of insurance agents, on the other hand, rose rapidly from over 100 in 1750, to over 800 in 1800 and 13000 by 1850. The numbers are crude, but aggregating the three major groups of permanent and part-time staff, we arrive at the following totals; nearly 500 in 1750, 1600 in 1800, 4000 in 1810, 5300 in 1820, and 14100 by 1850.[9] According to these estimates, total insurance employment remained a tiny fraction of the occupied population of Great Britain - about 0.02 per cent in 1750, and 0.15 per cent a century later.[10] Yet the absolute numbers employed may surprise those who have dismissed labour creation by the financial sector during the Industrial Revolution. Moreover, the above estimates suggest that employment in fire insurance grew ten times faster than the growth of the occupied population.

Using these figures, and the series for real sums insured discussed below, we can make a crude estimate of labour productivity.[11] The results suggest that per caput real output fell by 60 per cent between 1750 and 1810, from £0.17m to £0.07m. This was an effect of the expansion of agency networks by the London stock companies, of increasing levels of competition, and of the ever wider trawl for business, which frequently entailed appointing agents in locations which generated little insurance but plenty of monitoring problems. There was some recovery of productivity in the decade 1810-20, but thereafter little change is evident before 1850 when per caput real output amounted to £0.09m. The halting of the productivity decline suggests that the management of marketing was becoming more efficient during the first half of the nineteenth century - for the further very rapid expansion of agents, offset only to a small degree by the decline in the employment of firemen, was not accompanied by any reduction in the amount of real sums insured generated by each employee. It should also be noted that many of the new agencies, especially during the 1840s, were located in metropolitan London, where the volume and value of insurable property accessible to each agent may have been higher than elsewhere.

In an era largely devoid of reinsurance facilities, that is, where one insurer could lay off portions of large risks to another insurer, every insurance office had to commence business with relatively deep pockets.[12] So while they were few in number, they were, on average, very substantial enterprises. Data on share capital has been found for 37 fire offices established during this period. The nominal capitalisation of eighteenth-century insurers - the share capital advertised at foundation - ranged from the £1.2m of the two large corporations of 1720, the Royal Exchange Assurance (hereafter REA) and the London Assurance, to provincial offices established with a capital of between £20000 and £50000. After 1780 there was a tendency for nominal capital to increase, a tendency reinforced by wartime inflation. Of 14 provincial insurers established between 1783 and 1821, all but three began with a capital of £100000 or above. By the mid 1820s new offices in Edinburgh, Leeds and Manchester each had a capital of £1m, while a few metropolitan foundations such as the Alliance and the Protector boasted £5m. Generally, new London offices were larger than their provincial counterparts, but the range of capitalisation was considerable within both groups.

Fire insurers were large by comparison with firms in other tertiary sectors. An average paid-up capital - the amount actually paid into an office by its shareholders - of £25000 among nine provincial fire offices established by 1809 may be compared with an average of £10000 for country banks. Seven fire offices established in London between 1803 and 1808 had an average paid-up capital of £230000, compared with an average for London private banks of between £30000 and £50000. The average of £69000 for eight provincial insurance offices, 1818-48, contrasts with an average investment of £27000 in 50 north-west gas companies in 1847. Canals and railways were among the largest capital projects of the industrial revolution, but the biggest London insurance offices could match them for finance. The average amount raised by Ward's sample of 50 canal companies was £248000. Of 50 railway companies incorporated before 1830, only seven had authorised (nominal) capitals above £100000.[13] By comparison, five London fire insurers established in the 1820s had an average paid-up capital of £266000, with an average nominal capital of £2.8m. Moreover, insurance offices raised their share capital typically within 12 to 24 months, compared to the much longer period required by most canal finance. As a result, insurance company formation became a significant element in the periodic manias of company promotion. Among the joint-stock ventures to survive the boom and bust of 1824-6, (fire and life) insurance companies formed the largest group, accounting for 43 per cent of total share capital.[14]

Estimates can be made of the capital raised by British fire insurance in the first half of the nineteenth century. Assuming an average paid-up capital of £25000 for provincial and £100000 for London offices in 1800, the numbers in table 1.1 give a total capital of £1.5m for that year. A similar calculation for 1850, using averages of £70000 and £250000 respectively, gives £10.6m paid up.[15] These totals imply that while the number of offices more than doubled, their aggregate capital rose seven fold. This may be compared with estimates of banking capital at £5.5m in 1800 and £36m in 1850, making fire insurance rather more than one quarter of the size of private banking in England and Wales at both dates, and indicating that investment in insurance grew as rapidly as investment in banking over this period. We might also compare insurance capital with the £9m raised on canals and rivers by 1800, £4m invested in the gas industry by 1826, £3.5m invested in roads and bridges during the 1830s and 1840s, and £113m invested in railways by 1846.[16] Fixed capital in wool textile manufacturing and brewing in the mid 1830s, about £6m each, probably resembled the aggregate sum invested in fire insurance. A few other major industries were larger, for example cotton with over £15m in 1835, and corn milling with £11m by 1820.[17] The comparisons are crude, but by suggesting the relative capacity to absorb capital, they help to indicate the place occupied by fire insurance in the economy of industrialising Britain. In terms of capital accumulation, fire insurance lay behind the very largest sectors of manufacturing, finance and transport, but it did rank alongside a second group of important industries and services.

The above estimates also suggest that aggregate sums invested in English fire insurance represented 0.8 per cent of national income for England and Wales in 1800 and 2.4 per cent by 1850. Capital employed in English banking rose at a similar rate from 2.8 per cent to 8.2 per cent of national income in the same period. During the first half of the nineteenth century, therefore, capital in these two major financial services accumulated far more rapidly than the rate by which the economy grew.[18]

The contours of the industry: output and premium income

No aggregate data exist on the volume of fire insurance sold in Britain before 1782, when sums insured can first be calculated from the official returns of the stamp tax introduced that year. Annual estimates for this period have now been constructed from the records of individual fire offices (see appendix A). For the period after 1782, there are several, inconsistent, published accounts of sums insured. From these a revised series has been constructed. The consolidated data, covering 1723-1850, are presented as a five year moving annual average in appendix A,

Table 1.2 Sums insured and premium income: English fire offices, 1723-1850

Five year centred moving averages
(Deflators based on 1800 = 100, indices based on 1725 = 100)

	Sums insured		Premiums		Indices	
	current	real	current	real	current sums insured	current premiums
	£m	£m	£'000	£'000		
1725	31.4	52.0	35.9	92.2	100	100
1730	40.9	60.1	47.2	123.4	130	131
1740	45.8	74.1	59.0	143.7	146	164
1750	52.6	86.0	73.2	194.5	167	204
1760	72.2	101.9	101.9	249.0	230	284
1770	110.3	169.0	157.6	345.9	351	439
1780	135.5	172.7	196.5	421.7	431	547
1790	146.6	197.3	232.3	418.0	466	647
1800	206.1	206.1	375.9	375.9	656	1047
1810	339.2	282.1	587.3	551.1	1079	1635
1820	396.5	534.1	675.4	782.2	1261	1881
1830	486.8	844.2	741.4	1013.8	1549	2065
1840	638.1	904.5	1015.0	1236.7	2030	2826
1848	730.7	1294.6	1255.4	1780.3	2325	3496

Sources: Appendices A and B.

and in summary form in table 1.2. The choice of a five year moving average has nothing to do with detrending but reflects the fact that the annual data are distorted by non collection and arrears. This is fully explained in appendix A.3. Movements in property prices and building costs affected the value of sums insured. The latter, therefore, have been deflated using a composite price index of producers' goods from Schumpeter-Gilboy, spliced with industrial products from Rousseau. This composite index contains several commodities such as bricks, wood, lead, lime and tiles directly related to construction.[19] The resultant series of real sums insured is also presented in appendix A and summarised in table 1.2.

Thirty-one million pounds of fire insurance was sold annually in the mid 1720s, and £731m by the middle of the nineteenth century, a twenty-four fold increase over the period. In real terms, as figure 1.2 indicates, the industry grew in stages. Rapid early growth was interrupted twice, from 1738 to 1744 and from 1753 to 1758. From the late 1750s to the mid 1770s there was a powerful acceleration which added nearly 90 per cent to the volume of real sums insured. There followed a long irregular period of stagnation, short upswings and sharp downturns. This period, covering most of the American and French wars, saw a net addition of only

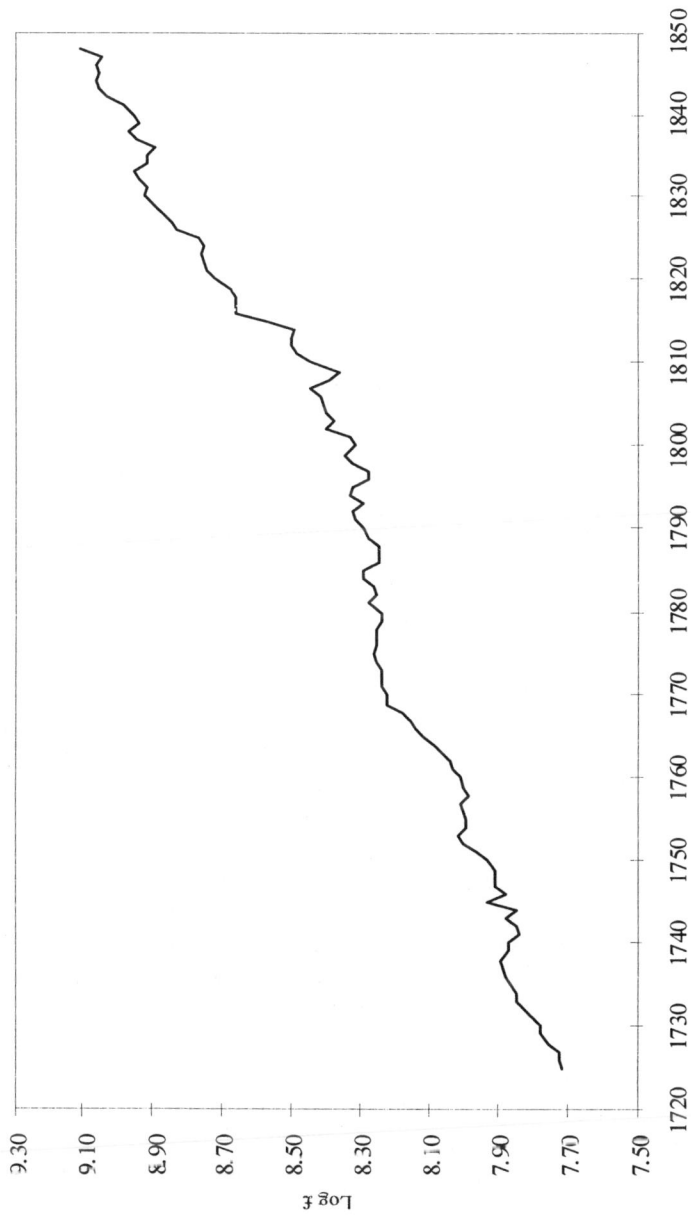

Figure 1.2 Real sums insured: English fire offices, 1723–1850
Source: see text.

26 per cent to the real value of fire insurance. From 1810 to 1833 there was a second long upswing in which nearly 300 per cent was added to real sums insured. Insurance stagnated during the later 1830s but then accelerated again to mid-century.

First, the results underline the decades after 1815 as witnessing the most rapid real growth in British fire insurance.[20] Second, they indicate that insurance struggled to expand in real terms during the last quarter of the eighteenth century, at the very time some regions of Britain were undergoing rapid urbanisation and industrialisation. Third, they suggest that fire insurance experienced its first important and sustained acceleration of real growth between the late 1750s and the early 1770s, on the eve of, rather than during, the classic period of the industrial revolution.

Sums insured are the best measure we have of insurance 'output'. Premiums, that is income earned from that output, reveal a similar but not identical pattern of growth. National estimates of premium income have not been produced before, probably because of the difficulty of collecting the data piecemeal from the surviving records of individual offices. The new estimates are presented in appendix B, where the method of estimation is given, and they are summarised in table 1.2. The solidity of the series rests upon the basis, first, that it contains original premium data from offices which together accounted for between 70 and 96 per cent of insurances sold in any one year, and, second, that the series comprises data from the entire range of small, medium and very large provincial and metropolitan insurers.

Fire insurance generated about £36000 annually in premiums for the handful of English offices at the beginning of our period. By 1840 fire insurance had become a million pound industry. The current premium totals were deflated using Phelps-Brown and Hopkins' price index of a basket of consumables, which provides a view of the real cost to policyholders, and the real value to insurers, of the premiums generated by fire insurance. Alternative price indices were also considered, including the spliced Schumpeter-Rousseaux index used above to deflate sums insured. There was generally little difference between the deflators, although the consumables index, not surprisingly given the volatility of food prices and their rapid inflation at the end of the eighteenth century, tended to suggest a less rapid but more fluctuating growth in real premiums (see appendix B.5).

Real premium growth was interrupted by sharp falls in 1739-41, 1746-8, 1757-8, the early 1780s, 1795-6 and 1799-1801, mostly coinciding with periods of wartime inflation, rising taxation or tight credit. Between 1759 and 1780 and between 1784 and 1793 real premiums surged forward with only minor interruptions. After stagnating during the Napoleonic wars, there was further rapid growth to the mid 1830s as consumer prices fell from their wartime peaks. This was interrupted only by a drop in real premiums between 1823 and 1825, which was probably the result of greater competition over premium rates from new entrants to the industry. After another period of stagnation in the late 1830s, real premiums again rose rapidly, aided by collusive pricing among the largest fire offices.

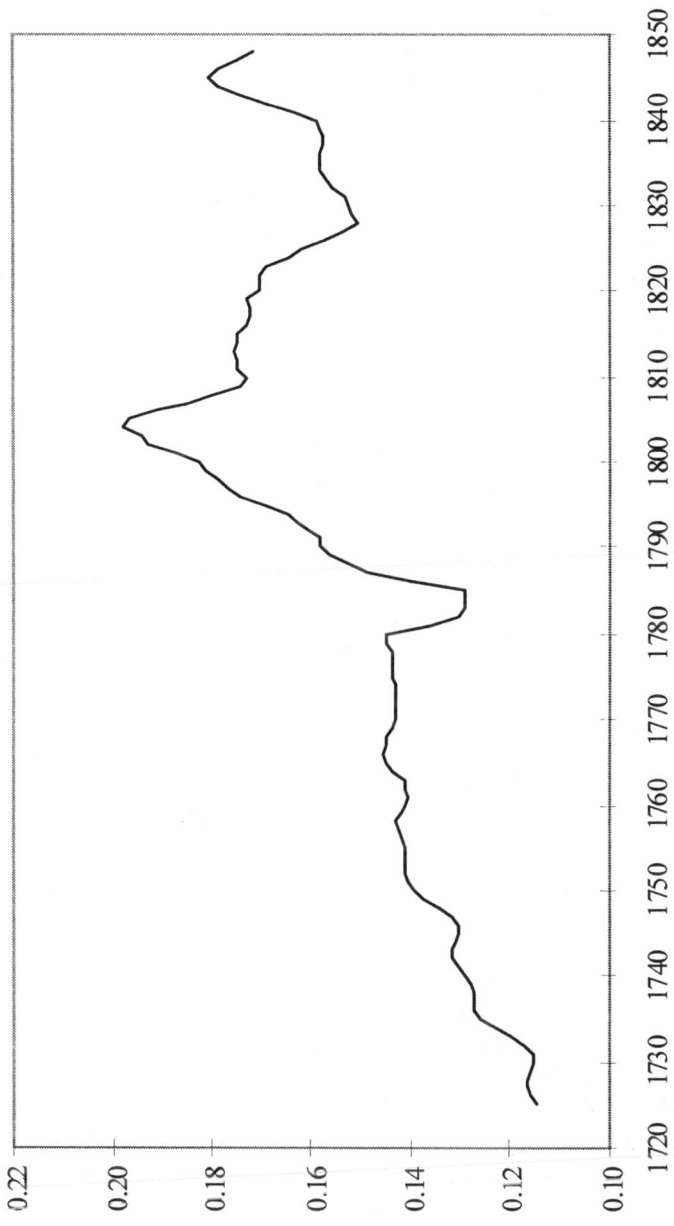

Figure 1.3   **Average premium rates (£%): English fire offices, 1723-1850**
Source: see text.

Figure 1.3 brings together the estimates of sums insured and premium income in current values to produce a series of average rates - that is the average premium generated per £100 of insurance sold. This provides, for the first time, a national price series for fire insurance during the eighteenth and nineteenth centuries. Although, as we shall see in subsequent chapters, premium rates varied greatly over time, between offices and for different categories of hazard, the average rate per £100 (or £ per cent) was the most important and widely used measure of the price/output ratio by contemporary underwriters.

Figure 1.3 paints a dramatic picture. After rising during the second quarter of the eighteenth century, the average price of insurance was stable during the great expansion of the 1760s and 1770s, perhaps encouraging sales. The collapse of the average premium rate during the early 1780s may be, in part, an aberration of the estimates. As explained in appendix A, the basis for estimating sums insured changed in 1782 from internal company accounts to the published returns of stamp duty on insurances. The sharp drop in the average rate, however, to an extent also reflected a real response of insurers to falling demand following the introduction of the punitive stamp duty. Premium rates on some categories of commercial and industrial property were cut in 1782-4. Thereafter, the stagnation and slow growth in sums insured between the 1780s and 1800s was accompanied by a 55 per cent increase in the price of fire insurance from the trough of 1784 to the peak of 1804. This period coincided almost precisely with the first phase of extensive collusion between the big three offices, the Sun, the REA and the Phoenix. The break down of this cartel around 1805 was followed immediately by falling prices. The average price of insurance continued to fall after the end of the French wars, and, while sums insured soared, by the end of the 1820s average premium rates had collapsed to levels which had not been seen for 40 years. This period was marked by increasingly fierce price competition, further market entry, and considerable customer pressure to reduce premium rates. Eventually, in 1826, the leading London offices responded with an agreement to increase rates on the worst loss-making industrial and mercantile risks, and to cut the price of insuring common residential property in an attempt to drive smaller companies to the wall. The recovery in premium income growth from 1830 was accompanied by a rapid recovery in the average price of insurance. Such powerful price movements would suggest that they not only reflected levels of competition within insurance, but that they also helped determine the rate at which the industry grew during its first century and a half. The final section in this chapter returns to this question of price as a determinant of insurance growth, while subsequent chapters explore some of the supply and demand factors which influenced the price of insurance itself.

Having outlined the dimensions and growth of fire insurance, we can begin to place the industry in its wider economic context. The first part of table 1.3 compares Crafts's estimates of industrial growth with sums insured and premium income. It suggests that insurance outpaced most industrial and commercial sectors for most of the eighteenth century, and again in the early nineteenth century. Only

Table 1.3   Comparative output growth: financial services, industry and national product, 1700-1844

(compound % p.a., real values)

	Sums Insured	Pre- miums	Cotton	Iron	Building	Coal	Can- dles
1700-60			1.37	0.60	0.74	0.64	0.49
1725-60	1.91	2.81					
1760-70	4.65	2.73	4.59	1.65	0.34	2.19	0.71
1770-80	0.43	1.76	6.20	4.47	4.24	2.48	1.15
1780-90	1.01	0.32	12.76	3.79	3.22	2.36	0.43
1790-1800	0.66	- 0.29	6.73	6.48	2.01	3.21	2.19
1801-11	2.73	2.74	4.49	7.45	2.05	2.53	1.34
1811-21	5.73	4.51	5.59	-0.28	3.61	2.76	1.80
1821-31	3.93	0.87	6.82	6.47	3.14	3.68	2.27

Sources: Appendices A and B; Crafts, *British Economic Growth*, p.23.

Note: Insurance figures here and below are based on three year centred averages of the data in appendices A and B.

(compound % p.a., real values)

	Sums Insured	Premiums	National product	Industry	Commerce
1700-60			0.69	0.71	0.69
1725-60	1.91	2.81			
1760-80	2.64	2.35	0.64	1.29	0.64
1780-1801	1.05	0.09	1.38	1.96	1.38
1801-31	4.40	2.87	1.90	2.78	2.13

Sources: Appendices A and B; Crafts and Harley, 'Output Growth', tab. 4.

(compound % p.a., current values)

	Sums Insured	Pre- miums	Bank Assets	National Income/ Cameron	National Income/ Lindert & Williamson	Population of England & Wales
1775-1800	1.97	2.94	3.85	1.50	2.02	0.98
1800-25	2.93	2.52	1.47	1.20		1.37
1825-44	2.26	2.75	2.80	2.10		1.20
1775-1844	2.47	2.78	2.77	1.58		1.21

Sources: Appendices A and B; Cameron, 'England', p.34; Crafts, *British Economic Growth*, p.13; Wrigley & Schofield, *Population History of England*.

the technologically revolutionised industries such as cotton and iron grew faster after 1815. For the last three decades of the eighteenth century, however, real insurance output and income lagged well behind the growth of industry and trade.

The insurance data also raise questions about the measurement of services within the historical national accounting framework. The estimates suggest that the assumption that service output rose by about the rate of population is misleading.[21] Table 1.3 compares the growth of population, sums insured, bank assets and national income, following the periodisation of Crafts-Harley and Cameron. Both insurance and banking grew faster than Cameron's national income estimates over the whole period 1775-1844.[22] These services also expanded at twice the rate of the English population. The GNP and national income estimates of Crafts-Harley (real values) and Lindert-Williamson (current values), however, both suggest that fire insurance fell behind the growth of the national economy during the last decades of the eighteenth century, but grew faster at other times, reinforcing the picture presented above of the stepped development of fire insurance.[23]

Using modern data, it is also possible to draw a comparison with the insurance industries of developing countries in the late twentieth century, in order to get some idea of where industrialising Britain lay in the development path for this financial service. Table 1.4 compares the volume of non-life (i.e. fire and marine) insurance premiums as a percentage of British GDP in 1801 and 1841, with non-life premiums as a percentage of GNP for a range of advanced and developing economies in 1971. For Britain the historical estimates for what modern statisticians call 'insurance penetration' are crude, in particular because we have no reliable data on marine premiums, and it is not easy to disaggregate the modern data into the different categories of non-life insurances. In order to arrive at a total for non-life premiums, I have simply assumed that the ratio of marine to fire insurance premiums was the same as the ratio of sums insured in marine and fire insurance. Nevertheless the estimates are as good as they can be with the available data, and are unlikely to be misleading. They suggest that at comparable levels of real per caput income, the insurance industry in early nineteenth-century Britain, after a century of growth, was still less developed than insurance in the emerging economies of the Third World. Despite a real per caput income in 1801 one-third higher than that of India in 1970, insurance penetration in Britain was lower. By 1841, real per caput income in Britain had already overtaken the levels reached by Pakistan and the Philippines in 1970, yet British non-life insurance as a proportion of GDP was about the same size as in modern Pakistan, and just one-third of the size of insurance in the Philippines.

A recent survey of world insurance in 1991 regressed per caput premium volume upon per caput GDP for over 70 countries, and found an income elasticity of demand for non-life insurance of 1.4.[24] If it is assumed, for the moment, that, *ceteris paribus*, modern countries follow a common development path, this coefficient suggests that for every one unit increase in GDP, premium volume will rise by 1.4. Many unaccounted factors, such as changes in the legal framework,

Table 1.4 Insurance penetration in selected countries

(Premium volume as % of GDP)

	1 Real per caput income in US$ 1970	2 Non-life premium volume as % of GNP in 1971	3 Great Britain Real per caput income US$ 1970	4 Great Britain Non-life premium volume as % of GDP	
India	290	0.32			
			399	0.27	in 1801
Pakistan	435	0.37			
Philippines	476	1.21			
			567	0.36	in 1841
Korea	632	0.62			
Brazil	1102	0.81			
Gt Britain	2994	1.76			
Germany	3569	2.82			
Canada	3923	2.63			
Sweden	4148	1.76			
USA	4790	4.44			

Notes: British non-life premiums were derived from the fire insurance premiums (current values) given in appendix B, plus estimates for marine insurance premiums, based upon the ratio of sums insured in marine to sums insured in fire insurance, from the data given in Pearson, 'Services Innovation', table 3, p.245.

Sources: Column 1: Kravis, Heston and Summers, 'Real GDP Per caput', table 4, column 5. Column 2: 'The World's Most Important Insurance Countries in 1971', *Sigma*, no.3 (1973), table 1. Column 3: Crafts, *British Economic Growth*, p.49. Column 4: appendix B; Pearson, 'Services Innovation', table 3, p.245; Deane and Cole, *British Economic Growth*, table 37, p.166.

could have a significant effect on the development of insurance in individual countries, so the result must be treated with caution. Nevertheless if we apply it to the Crafts-Harley estimates for the growth of British real GNP, real premiums in Britain should have increased annually by 0.90 per cent between 1760 and 1780, 1.93 per cent between 1780 and 1801, and by 2.66 per cent between 1801 and 1831. In fact, as table 1.3 shows, British fire insurance premiums grew in real terms by 2.35 per cent in the first period, slowing down to just 0.09 per cent in the second period, and then accelerating to 2.87 per cent between 1801 and 1831. Thus the experience of insurance in the modern world appears to provide a poor guide to the development of fire insurance in Britain during the industrial revolution.

The growth pattern of British insurance described above is reinforced when we explore the extent to which fire insurance kept pace with its potential market. Using Wrigley and Schofield's population estimates for England and Wales, figure 1.4 presents real per caput sums insured by English fire offices between 1723 and 1850. Here the stepped pattern is again marked. Per caput insurance rose by 56 per cent during the second quarter of the eighteenth century, at ten times the rate of population growth. Between 1758 and 1775 per caput sums insured increased by 70 per cent. This was followed by over 30 years of relative stagnation, when insurance barely kept pace with demographic expansion. By 1810 the amount of fire insurance sold per caput, about £28, was little different in real terms from the amount which had been sold in 1770. From 1810 to 1833 per caput sums insured leapt forward by 182 per cent. By 1850 about £80 of insurance was sold by English fire offices per caput, or eight times the amount sold in the 1720s in a market three times as large.

Population estimates are a crude proxy for market size. A measure of insurable property, including moveable goods as well as bricks and mortar, would be better. There are some contemporary estimates for the proportion of insurable property covered by fire insurance. The calculations of Eden and Brown suggested that this proportion rose from 36 per cent in 1802 to 49 per cent by 1855. Coode, writing in 1863, estimated that of £1767m insurable property, £1007m, or 57 per cent, was insured.[25]

We also have Feinstein's recent estimates of 'net domestic reproducible assets' for Great Britain. These comprise fixed capital stock (net of depreciation) plus net circulating capital of non-farm stock in trade and farm crops and livestock. Although not directly equivalent to 'insurable property', they might reasonably be assumed to bear a close relation to the latter, so that trends may be considered fairly reliable.[26] Table 1.5 presents sums insured as a percentage of Feinstein's estimates. These further underscore the pattern of development discussed above. The expansion of insurance outstripped property growth during the 1760s and 1770s so that over one-third of domestic assets were insured by the end of the third quarter of the eighteenth century. There followed three decades in which fire insurance largely failed to keep pace with the growth of fixed and circulating capital, although it should be noted that some of this capital was invested in large projects, such as canals, mines and iron works, deemed uninsurable by the fire offices. Between 1810 and 1830 expansion in market coverage was extremely rapid, from 30 to 50 per cent, followed by another slowdown during the 1830s and by renewed rapid growth in the 1840s. It is encouraging that these figures are not far from the contemporary estimates, though they suggest that Eden's percentage for 1802 may be rather high and Brown's for 1855 too low.

The proportion of property in Britain insured against fire by the 1770s was not seen again until the years after the Napoleonic wars. Remarkably, the first waves

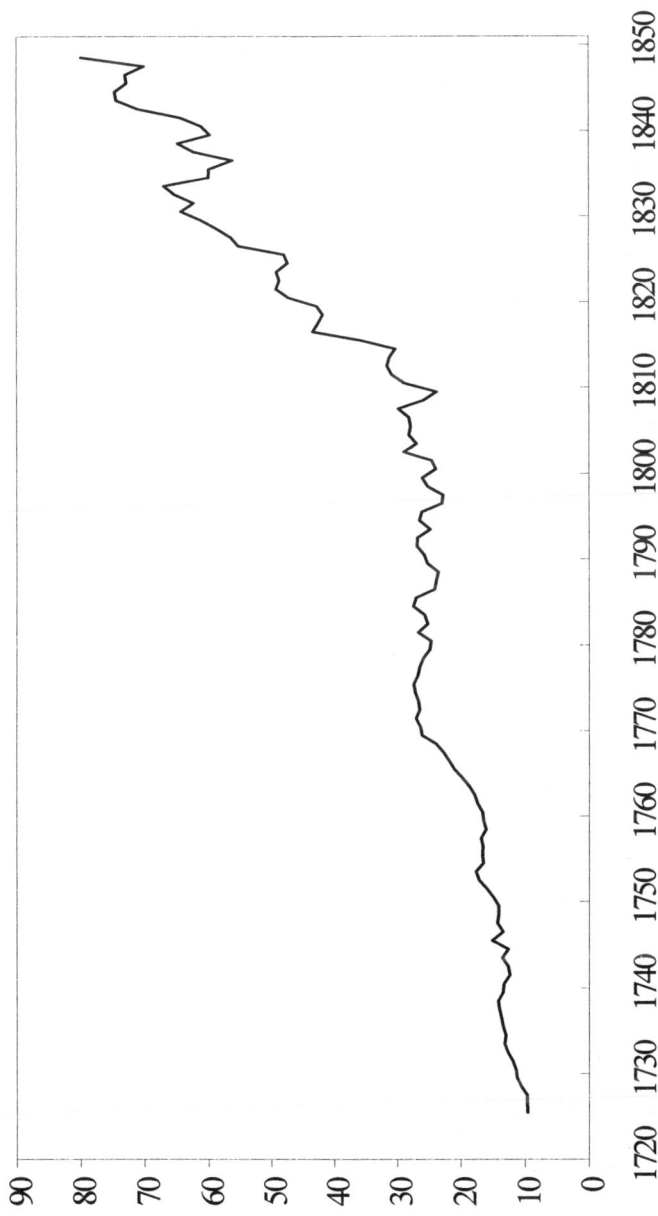

Figure 1.4 Real sums insured per caput: English fire offices, 1723-1850

Source: see text.

Table 1.5 Proportion of property insured against fire in Britain, 1760-1850

Current values

Year	Net Assets (£m)	£m Insured	% Assets Insured
1760	300	72	24.0
1770	320	110	34.4
1780	390	136	34.9
1790	430	147	34.2
1800	690	206	29.9
1810	1090	339	31.1
1820	960	397	41.4
1830	990	487	49.2
1840	1290	638	49.5
1850	1300	731	56.2

Note: £ insured are five year centred moving averages, except 1850, which is the average of 1846-50.

Sources: Net assets from Feinstein, 'National Statistics', table XIX; for £ insured see appendix A.

of company promotions towards the end of the century, and the greater competition which accompanied these, failed to help the insurance industry expand with its market. Explanations for this failure, whether on the demand or supply-side, are hard to find, but this is a task for the following sections which explore the determinants of insurance growth.

The determinants of growth

In this section we examine, first, the factors which may have most immediately influenced demand for insurance, namely the level of damage and loss by fire, and changing perceptions of fire risk. Second, we look at the relationship between construction activity and fire insurance. How closely did sales of property insurance follow the building cycle? Third, we examine the business cycle and other variables, such as the cost of borrowing and the relative cost of insurance, which may have influenced the propensity to purchase a policy. This discussion does not preclude the more detailed analysis of the relationship between regional insurance markets and regional economies conducted in subsequent chapters.

The impact of fire

During the eighteenth and nineteenth centuries fires occurred suddenly, frequently, and, although probably cyclical by nature, they were to all appearances random.

They laid waste to inner-city districts and destroyed entire villages and small towns. Creating uncertainty as well as material damage, they could deliver a considerable economic and psychological shock to a community. Despite their importance there have been few attempts by historians to measure trends in the number and cost of fires. The most serious effort was made by Jones, Porter and Turner, who constructed a gazetteer of English urban fire disasters.[27] Collecting references to large fires in provincial towns, where ten or more houses were destroyed, they counted 618 such fires for the period 1500-1900. They found peaks in the number of fires in the 1720s and 1760s, and also a reduction in multi-house fires after 1760, falling to a 'plateau' during the last quarter of the eighteenth century, which represented a decline in real terms given the rapid urbanisation of the period. Thereafter large town fires declined in an irregular way. This chronology has been followed by others such as Borsay, who argued that only after 1760 did 'a sharp and permanent decline (in the incidence of urban fires) set in'.[28] Jones, Porter and Turner qualified their conclusion by suggesting that, as property risks became smaller, more separated and more manageable, the reduction in the scale of urban fires was steeper than the decline in their incidence. They argued that from the last decades of the eighteenth century a higher proportion of total losses occurred through fires in single premises, as the values of stock and fixed capital in commercial and industrial buildings rose. In a later period, 1833-65, when there is official data available for London, multiple house fires certainly decreased, while the total number of fires increased at a similar rate to the growth of housing in the metropolis.[29]

These conclusions should be treated cautiously. First, only large multi-building fires in specific urban locations were included, and the gazetteer did not capture all of these.[30] Second, large village fires, which could be as destructive as those in towns, were ignored. Third, large single building fires were also not included. Jones, Porter and Turner speculated that the latter increased during the late eighteenth century. In an attempt to gain some idea of trends in the categories of fires excluded from the gazetteer, a survey was carried out of all fires recorded between 1730 and 1779 in three monthly publications, *Gentleman's Magazine* (from 1731), *London Magazine* (from 1732), and *Annual Register* (from 1758), but which were excluded from the gazetteer. The period was chosen to test the premiss that 1760 did indeed mark a watershed in the incidence of urban fires, for this may have had an impact on popular perceptions of fire hazard, with consequences for the propensity to buy fire insurance. The results are shown, together with the relevant data from the gazetteer, in table 1.6. This survey is clearly restricted by the sources, is strongly biased towards London, and faces the same problems of definition - notably that of a 'house' - which confronted Jones, Porter and Turner. Nevertheless, it adds 814 fires to the 126 urban fire disasters counted for this period in the gazetteer. The combined series peaks sharply in the 1760s, with 2443 houses destroyed in 423 fires. However, while the gazetteer's count of large fires declines from the 1730s to the 1750s, the reverse is true for my count of smaller

Table 1.6 Fires in England, Wales and Scotland, 1730-79

	English Urban Provincial			All other Fires			
	Fires	Fires with data on houses des-troyed	Houses des-troyed	Fires	Houses des-troyed	Other buildings des-troyed	No. dead
1730-39	30	18	1326	60	261	106	27
1740-49	23	17	1174	55	581	140	66
1750-59	16	12	341	194	506	94	39
1760-69	33	29	1337	390	1106	179	146
1770-79	24	21	627	115	373	161	98
1730-79	126	97	4805	814	2827	680	376

Aggregate Totals

	Fires	Houses destroyed	Average size of fires
1730-39	90	1587	18
1740-49	78	1755	23
1750-59	210	847	4
1760-69	423	2443	6
1770-79	139	1000	7
1730-79	940	7632	8

Sources: see text.

fires. One consequence is that the average size of a fire, measured by houses destroyed, fell substantially after 1750.[31]

These trends will be distorted by missing data. The level of reporting of fires was, not surprisingly, dependent upon the contemporary political scene and the impact of war. *London Magazine* all but evaporated as a source of fire reports after 1770 as news from America and stories about John Wilkes occupied more print columns. Notwithstanding these drawbacks, table 1.6 gives some impression of the scale of disaster. Over 8300 houses and other buildings were destroyed in these fires, plus an incalculable amount of agricultural produce and livestock - for example, over 100 horses died. Then there was the terrible human toll - at least 376 persons were burnt to death in the 940 fires recorded. While these losses represent only an unknown part of the actual total destruction, some proportions are suggested by other data. During the year ending Michaelmas 1806 the London insurance offices experienced 492 'fire accidents', of which 31 were 'serious fires', 306 did little damage, and 155 were chimney fires.[32] It is likely, though not certain, that these figures related to fires in London only. During the month of January 1763 32 fires were recorded as occurring in London. Allowing for fewer outbreaks in the summer, this suggests about 300 fires during that year.[33] Taking the midpoint of these estimates would give 400 as an annual average number of fires in the capital, which suggests a total of 20000 London fires for the period 1730-80. If, as in 1806, about six per cent of these were 'serious', burning eight houses each (the average from table 1.6), this would have resulted in the destruction of 9600 houses in London alone. Allowing for the greater fire risk in the capital, multiplying this figure by, say, half of London's share in the population gives a total of over 40000 houses burnt down across England and Wales in this period.[34] The 7600 houses recorded in table 1.6, therefore, may represent less than a quarter of the actual number destroyed by fire in mid-eighteenth-century Britain.

This is largely guesswork, but clearly the figures in table 1.6 are fractions of the total losses. Tens of thousands of properties were afflicted by fire in this half century and several hundred Britons died in the flames. Fire, therefore, was a major economic, social and existential problem. It may have been declining from the late 1760s, though the decline was probably only relative and concentrated in the category of large provincial town fires. It remained an important source of death and destruction, especially in the docklands and the more impoverished parts of London, and in the large villages of southern England.

The figures above support the picture of the 1760s as a decade of crisis, with the coincidence of peak levels of fires and long-term changes in their pattern. There is also evidence of an increase in public concern about fire hazards and fire protection at this time. During the half century following the Great Fire of London, there was a fairly regular stream of private projects and official measures to improve fire prevention, encouraged by the personal interest in these matters shown by the later Stuarts and the early Hanoverians. However, despite frequent devastating fires - Blandford, Dorset (1731), Crediton, Devon (1742), Honiton, Devon (1747), Cornhill, London (1748) to name a few - a hiatus occurred during the second quarter of the century. No significant London building acts with fire prevention measures were passed between the 1720s and 1760s, and some of the more promising experiments of the 1720s, such as David Hartley's fire-plating system or Ambrose Godfrey's water bomb, waited nearly four decades before public interest was renewed. Sir John Fielding led the way with his call in 1755 for an improved water supply and the provision in London's streets of turncocks for fire engines.[35] Numerous competitive experiments with water pumps, not only for draining collieries but also with firefighting in mind, were carried out during the following decades. Various fire-escape devices were 'invented'. The fire extinguishers of Godfrey and other inventors were demonstrated, and David Hartley junior took up patents for his father's fire plates, a method of fireproofing which Viscount Mahon, Third Earl of Stanhope, also investigated. Newspapers printed frequent warnings about the dangers of candles and open fires, and there was a perceptible increase in concern about incendiarism during the 1760s and 1770s, particularly involving rural property and the naval dockyards.[36]

Faced with a wave of accidental fires and the increasing threat of arson, attitudes towards fire hazards and fire protection shifted during the third quarter of the eighteenth century, possibly furthering the growth of insurance. Whether a proliferation in fire damage always stimulated a proportionate increase in the demand for insurance remains an open question. The long-run trend in fires is also partially reflected in the fire offices' own records of losses on insured property. Figure 1.5 presents, alongside the average premium rate series taken from figure 1.3, the average loss on fire insurance, expressed as a five year moving average of the amount paid out in claims per £100 insured, for 24 English fire offices between 1723 and 1850. This notion of 'average loss' was one of the two most common measurements used by contemporary underwriters to ascertain the performance of a company's business over time.[37] For the years to 1800 the series is an aggregate of the seven principal London offices, while data for 23 offices, including 11 provincial insurers, cover various periods after 1800. The basis of the calculation of sums insured is given in appendix A. Most large insurers are included in this series, so we may feel confident about the representativeness of its trends.[38]

The average loss rate in figure 1.5 is in effect an index of the burden of fire damage on that 25 to 50 per cent of British property which was insured during the eighteenth and early nineteenth centuries. Certainly the average loss would have been affected by other factors. Loss adjustment methods changed, rules applying to the valuation of salvage may have become more stringent or more generous in the aggregate. Insurers changed the categorisation of risks, and the overall rate at which claims were paid may also have been altered by new subdivisions within insurances and by the increasing use of the average clause. The overriding element, however, which drove the loss series in figure 1.5 up or down was the destructiveness of fire itself.

The series shows a number of strongly defined cycles with peaks in 1748, 1764, 1783, 1793, 1801, 1819 and 1844. It is striking that, peak to peak, these cycles average 17 years in duration, close to the 20 year cycle in urban fire disasters briefly noted, without explanation, by Jones, Porter and Turner.[39] There was also a temporary increase in the velocity of the fire cycle as losses peaked during the wartime riots and strife of the 1790s. Indeed it is noticeable that, from the 1790s, all the major and minor peaks of fire damage coincided with years of political turbulence and economic distress, including 1801, 1819 and 1832.[40] Figure 1.5 also confirms the 1750s and 1760s as a period of increasing destruction. The rate of loss by fire on insured property rose by nearly three fold between 1752 and 1764 (five year averages centred on these dates). This occurred over a period in which average premium rates rose only modestly. Allowing for a short time lag, this combination of stable prices, rising levels of fire damage, and increasing interest in methods of protection and prevention, may help explain why real sums insured grew by 90 per cent between the late 1750s and the mid 1770s, and in per caput terms by 70 per cent, the fastest expansion of the eighteenth century.

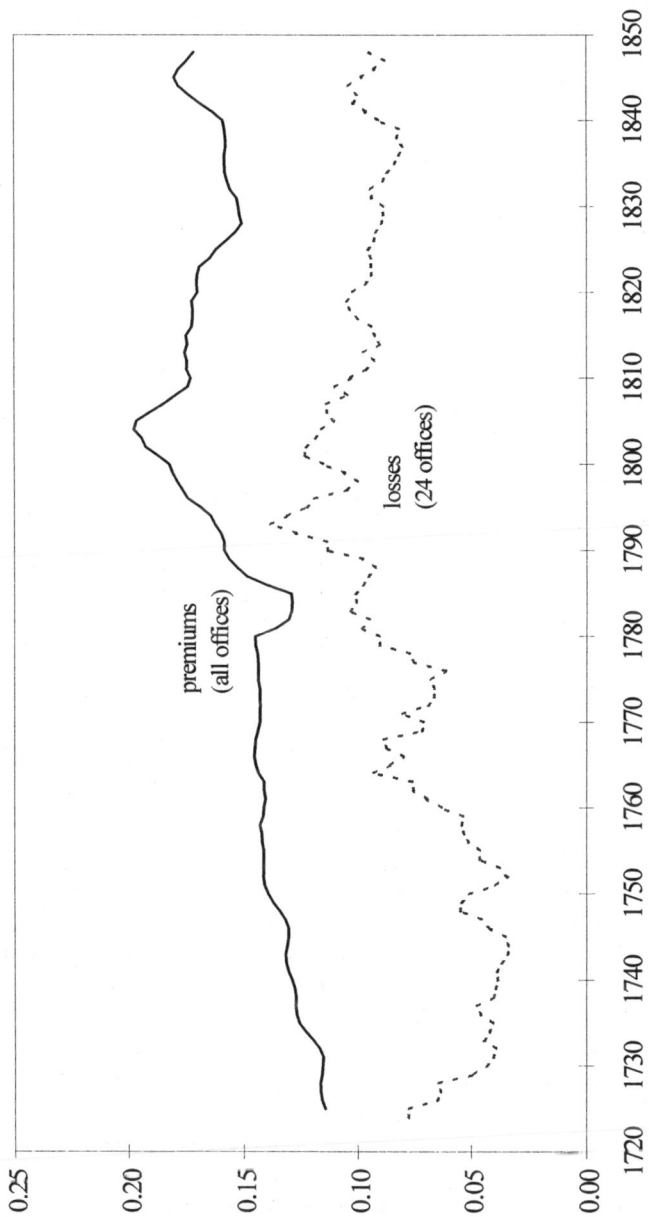

Figure 1.5 Average rates, 1723–1850

Source: see text.

The average loss rate grew again from the late 1770s and rose to new heights during the 1790s, without, however, stimulating a concomitant real increase in sums insured (cf. figure 1.2). This suggests, once more, that price may have been a factor affecting demand. In response to rising losses, especially on new warehouse and mill property in the urban docklands and the northern textile districts, insurers hiked their prices up to levels far in excess of what they paid out in claims, and they maintained these price levels for over a decade after loss rates began to fall. When prices did begin to fall from 1805, they continued downwards until the late 1820s, although the margin between average premiums and average losses altered very little during this period. Over the long run, the data suggest that the level of fire damage, though possibly providing an incentive to insure, was a less dominant factor than the cost of insurance.

Finally, the average rates of loss do not suggest that the incidence of fire damage, absolute or relative, was declining after 1760. At no point after 1764 do loss rates fall again to the levels of the 1730s and 1740s, and before 1850 rates never again drop to the level of 1776. While multi-house fires may have declined, the series indicates that this made little difference to the impact of fire damage on insured property. In this growing segment of the market, destruction by smaller fires more than compensated for the decline of the spectacular urban disasters.

The building cycle

While the incidence of fire may have had some impact on the propensity to insure, it is reasonable to assume that the demand for insurance was also influenced by the volume of building activity at any given time. Insurance business could be encouraged by offices maintaining a good relationship with the building industry. For much of the eighteenth century this relationship was close, especially in London. Most fire offices had surveyors on their staff, either as permanent salarymen, or employed on a casual basis. These men had to be intimately acquainted with building structures and processes, materials and labour costs. Their tasks varied, but they could include inspecting property before and after insurance, as well as viewing insured property damaged by fire. It was important for insurers to obtain the services of competent and knowledgeable men, for the accuracy of valuations and loss adjustments, and ultimately the level of underwriting profits, could depend upon their reports. Most offices contracted out the work of rebuilding insured houses destroyed by fire, and thus had to maintain a reliable pool of builders.[41] Classifying insured property by type of construction was also a task for which expertise was sought from the building trades. Another area of cooperation related to building regulations. Insurance offices were troubled by the shoddy work of speculative builders who failed to comply with the London building acts. As early as 1763 London insurers combined to promote regulation to prevent the spread of fires in the metropolis. In 1772 several offices supported the Committee of London Builders in their successful application to obtain a consolidated building

Table 1.7 Average sums insured by dwelling, 1760-1850

	Dwelling stock at end of decade	Average current £ insured per dwelling	Average real £ insured per dwelling - deflator based on 1800=100	Index of average real £ insured per dwelling - 1800=100
1760	1443000	50.02	70.62	66
1770	1500000	73.53	112.64	105
1780	1608000	84.27	107.38	100
1791	1739000	89.14	119.97	111
1800	1912000	107.79	107.79	100
1810	2160000	157.04	130.60	121
1820	2521000	157.28	211.87	197
1830	3027000	160.82	278.88	259
1840	3619000	176.33	249.92	232
1850	3985000	183.37	324.88	301

Sources: Sums insured from appendix A. Dwellings from Feinstein, 'National Statistics', table 17.5, p.389.

act for the capital.[42] For most of the eighteenth century such cooperation remained feasible because the number of competing insurance offices remained limited, and some overview was possible of the quality of new building, and the virtues and vices of different building contractors. By the early nineteenth century the old associations with the London building trades weakened as most major offices became preoccupied with the new problems of assessing large industrial risks in the provinces, and as the number of domestic property insurances multiplied. Fewer damaged houses were rebuilt by the fire offices, and fewer common residential properties were subjected to inspection.

There are no annual indices of house building in Britain during the Industrial Revolution, but Feinstein has estimated the stock of dwellings at the end of each decade between 1760 and 1850. Table 1.7 compares the growth of real sums insured with these estimates.[43] This suggests that fire insurance outpaced the increase in the national housing stock by three fold between 1800 and 1850, despite a setback in the 1830s. During the late eighteenth century the growth of insurance was less impressive. After outstripping house building during the 1760s, fire insurance fell behind during the 1770s and again in the 1790s. Feinstein's end of decade estimates, however, show a steadily increasing rate of construction from 1760 to the second quarter of the nineteenth century, and do not reflect the well-known cyclical fluctuations in the building industry.

Much attention has been paid by historians to the building cycle.[44] Parry Lewis has identified long cycles in building activity using data on timber imports

Table 1.8   Cycles of building activity and insurance growth, 1723-1850

The Building Cycle		Real Sums Insured	
Trough	Peak	Trough	Peak
1729*			
	1736		1738
1744		1741	
			1745
	1753		1753
1762		1758	
	1776		1775
1781		1780	
			1784
		1788	
	1792		1794
1798		1796	
	1805	1809	
1816			
	1825		
1832			1833
	1836/40**	1836	
1843			
	1847		

Notes: * corrected by Chalklin to 1729 (from 1727), Chalklin, *Provincial Towns*, p.258n19.
** twin peak.

Sources: see text.

before 1785 and brick output from 1785 to 1850. For comparative purposes, major peaks and troughs in the series of real sums insured were identified using Parry Lewis's n^{th} order method.[45] Table 1.8 compares the insurance cycle with Parry-Lewis's building cycles. This suggests, first, that the former remained fairly closely synchronised with the latter until the 1780s, and possibly until the late 1790s. The eighteenth-century peaks, with the exception of 1784, are nearly synchronous.[46] There is a small, irregular, time lag on the troughs, of between one and three years, but this may just reflect that fact that the insurance data are five year moving averages. Second, table 1.8 suggests that a disjunction occurred during the 1800s. A minor peak in 1807 was the last turning point in the insurance cycle to bear any correspondence to the building cycle.[47] Real sums insured slumped in 1809, with the next major trough occurring in 1836, a peak year for building. Fire insurance seems to have entirely bypassed the trough to trough building cycle of 1816 to 1832, and through the 1830s and 1840s the two cycles appear to be the obverse of each other. It is not obvious why the two cycles ceased to run concurrently after the 1800s. Before any explanations are offered, we might also consider both insurance and building cycles in conjunction with the business cycle.

The business cycle

Fisher has conveniently brought together several series relating to eighteenth- and early nineteenth-century business cycles, which may be examined in conjunction with the building and insurance data in order to compare the respective chronologies.[48] The so-called 'great depression' of the late 1720s appears to have had only a limited impact on fire insurance. There is some doubt about the course of the building cycle in this period. Ashton suggests that a building boom continued until 1730 and was inversely related to the flow of overseas trade. While some of the insurance offices were busy restructuring management, underwriting and accounting practices during these years, only in the Union Fire Office is there evidence of hard times. Otherwise there were two substantial entrants to the market, the London Assurance and the REA, both of whose shares doubled in value between 1724 and 1729, and plenty evidence of growth elsewhere to belie the notion of this as the 'worst decade of the century' as far as insurance was concerned.[49]

There was a business boom and crash in 1733-4, but the building cycle swung gently upwards, peaking in 1736. Between 1738 and the mid-1740s the economy experienced difficulties. There was a profit slump in 1739, bad harvests, a fuel crisis in London in 1740, low levels of timber imports, rising interest rates and a widespread depression in the building trades. Surviving insurance records offer little comment on this downturn, but it seems likely that insurance was also affected. The Hand-in-Hand, still Britain's largest fire office at this time, saw the current value of its sums insured stagnate throughout this period. Not until 1748 did they exceed the level attained in 1732.

Building recovered from the mid 1740s in provincial towns and rather later in London. According to Fisher, the business cycle recorded a double peak in 1743-5, and another peak in 1748, despite falling wheat exports 1744-6, falling share prices until 1748, and the financial crisis associated with the Jacobite invasion. There was a minor surge in insurance output in 1745, visible in figure 1.2, which suggests that this exogenous tartan shock had no negative impact on the demand for cover, just as it failed to alter the upward course of profits.[50] A sustained upturn in insurance output began after the outbreak of peace in 1748, when interest rates fell and there was an upswing in building. The Westminster and the Sun both remarked on the great increase of business at this time.[51] Building fell back to a low ebb in London and many provincial towns during the mid 1750s. Several insurance offices resorted to price reductions during this period, or deferred passing on increases in the duty on policies to their customers.[52] With rising interest rates and declining profits, building and business activity remained depressed until the end of the Seven Years War in 1763. Real insurance output however had already commenced its long upswing, and was greatly boosted by the national building boom of the mid

1760s. The increases in sums insured were reflected in additions to the clerical staff of the London offices as well as salary hikes and gratuities to employees.[53] Insurance growth remained rapid until 1775 despite troubles in the wider economy - rising prices, a financial crisis in 1772, an export collapse in 1773, rising bankruptcy rates and a slowdown in construction. In London, Manchester, Birmingham and Nottingham building experienced a second upswing between 1775 and 1778, but as the war intensified against the American colonies and their European allies, recession followed and the business cycle declined to a trough in 1781. A slowdown in the growth of insurance output also accompanied this wartime recession.

Ashton viewed the business cycle in the eighteenth century as endogenous of an inherently unstable economic system, in which the irregularity of fluctuations was due, in the main, to the importance of the harvest, the imperfect mobility of factors of production, the ineffectiveness of interest rates to act as a control on credit, and the scale of state intervention in the economy, above all in the area of war finance.[54] Surveying the period between the South Sea Bubble and the end of the American War of Independence, it is not clear that the growth of fire insurance depended greatly on any of these factors, although there may have been an indirect link to movements in interest rates via their impact on building activity. Generally it seems that the relationship between fire insurance and the economy before the 1780s was mediated through the building cycle. The descriptive data suggest that an important factor influencing the real growth of insurance in this period was the absolute volume of (insurable) property, above all residential building, available to insure. The stability in the nominal price of insurance, particularly during the third quarter of the century, coupled with sustained periods of rising losses through fire, may also have been significant. (See figure 1.5.) Other factors such as the availability of credit, the level of employment and earnings, trends in consumer prices, profits and interest rates appear to have been, at best, of secondary importance. Various determinants of demand, including the volume of building and the price of insurance, are considered more closely in the following section.

For the period 1790-1850 Fisher has brought together the business cycles identified by Gayer, Rostow and Schwarz (hereafter GRS) with the index of company profits constructed by Mirowski.[55] The GRS data show the business cycle to have been mostly on or above trend during the French wars, at least until 1810, and the profit series is also above trend in these years. Figure 1.2 shows real sums insured to have grown only slowly for most of this period. By 1815 insurance had lost any correspondence to the other series on building, business activity or profits, and none was restored before 1850. The troughs in building activity in 1816 and 1821 were accompanied by peak years for real insurance output, while neither the export collapse of 1832 nor the recession of 1837 were reflected in insurance sales.

Why then, from the first decades of the nineteenth century, did fire insurance cease to have any overt relationship to output in the building industry? One explanation might be that bricks became a less reliable proxy for building demand for insurance. Parry Lewis expressed doubts about bricks as an index for house building in the 1830s and 1840s and pointed out that the peak in brick production during the late 1840s was largely associated with railway construction, which would have generated little demand for fire insurance.[56] Another possibility is that demand for fire insurance on buildings was falling relative to the demand for insuring moveable property such as stock, goods, tools, furnishings, at least in the large residential and commercial insurance markets, if not on industrial property.[57] We have, however, no national series for consumer durables and other insurable domestic goods such as plate, pictures, jewellery and furniture, and no idea o f whether the value of household contents was rising or falling relative to the value of houses during this period.[58] Data from probate inventories cease around 1730, and though it seems probable that the range and volume of consumer goods continued to increase, we do not know whether the proportion of insurable household wealth invested in such goods rose or fell during the eighteenth century and the first half of the nineteenth century.[59]

It may be that the enormous, unprecedented, secular growth in insurance between the second and fourth decades of the nineteenth century itself destroyed any older connection between insurance output and building output. Some support for this explanation can be found in table 1.7 which compared the growth of insurance with Feinstein's estimates of the growth of the housing stock. If we view the rapid increase in the average real sum insured per dwelling during the 1760s as a catching up process by the insurance industry, particularly in its London market, the final quarter of the eighteenth century appears marked by insurance output more or less keeping pace with building. It is after 1800, and particularly from the 1810s that insurance began to leave housing stock behind in terms of its rate of growth. A close relationship between building and property insurance appears to fit not just the respective chronologies of upswings and downturns in the eighteenth century, but also the comparative data presented in table 1.7. From the early nineteenth century the relationship, if it continued at all, became much weaker.

Multiple determinants of demand

The determinants of insurance demand may also be explored by regression analysis. The variables examined depended on the time series available, but they included annual population estimates for England and Wales; the average real premium rate series, representing the real price of insurance; proxies for building activity, namely, timber imports and stained paper output (available for the period to 1782) and brick and glass output (available from 1785 and 1747 respectively); and various proxies for general economic and business activity, namely, bankruptcies, interest rates, and share price and profit indices (the latter covering 1728-1826 only).[60]

None of the building data, and only bankruptcies and share prices among the business data, cover the whole period from 1723 to 1850. It was therefore necessary, but also instructive, to examine two sub-periods 1723-82 and 1785-1850. The break between these sub-periods is appropriate in several ways. First, as noted above, 1782-5 marks the change in the major building proxy from timber imports to brick output. Theoretically, after the London building acts of the 1770s, the proportion of timber-built dwellings in the capital should have declined rapidly, and bricks should provide a better proxy than timber for the later period.[61] Second, the break reflects the introduction of stamp duty in 1782, and the different bases for estimating sums insured before and after that date, as explained in appendix A. By substantially raising the cost of an insurance policy, the duty may have had a longer run impact on the growth of insurance than the temporary downturn in sums insured immediately following its imposition. To take this into account, duty is included as a dummy variable in the regression equation below for 1785-1850.

From the discussion in the previous sections, the most important variables appear to be population and building, while price and interest rates also seem to be worth investigation. Consideration was given to stained paper output as an alternative proxy to timber imports for the period before 1782, in view of the very high correlation ($r = 0.96$) between insurance and stained paper production. Wallpaper block-printed with distemper colours was becoming more widely used from the 1750s, competing with the more expensive Chinese painted paper hangings which had been fashionable during the early to mid-Georgian period. Around this time some London insurance companies began to receive proposals to insure wallpaper in houses, suggesting that its use was becoming more common. The main surge in English wallpaper production, however, did not commence until the last two decades of the century, following the prohibition in 1779 of continental imports and the rise of factory production.[62] On the whole, given the limited scope of the market for wallpaper for most of the period 1725-82, building output is best represented by the timber series.

Multiple regressions were run for both sub-periods with the following forms; (1.1) for 1725-82:

$$\ln SUMINSD_t = \alpha_t + \beta \ln POP_t + \gamma \ln TIMBER_t + \delta \ln PRICE_t + \varepsilon \ln INT_t + e_t$$

(1.2) for 1785-1848:

$$\ln SUMINSD_t = \alpha_t + \beta \ln POP_t + \gamma \ln BRICKS_t + \delta \ln PRICE_t + \varepsilon \ln INT_t + \xi DUTY_t + e_t$$

where ln is the natural logarithm, SUMINSD is real sums insured, POP is population, PRICE is the average real premium rate, INT represents the yield on bank dividends for 1725-82, and on three per cent consols for 1785-1848. DUTY was a dummy using the actual rate per £100 insured. The data for the second regression commenced in 1785, because figures for brick output are unavailable before that year. In both cases the estimations in levels revealed a serial correlation problem with the Durbin-Watson statistics insignificant at 95 per cent. Equations 1.1 and 1.2 were therefore reestimated in first differences. The first difference

Table 1.9   Regression results for real sums insured

First difference estimations

1725-82			1785-1848		
ΔlnPOP	2.044	(0.844)	ΔlnPOP	2.225	(0.621)
ΔlnTIMBER	0.047*	(0.043)	ΔlnBRICKS	-0.237	(0.057)
ΔlnPRICE	-0.284	(0.079)	ΔlnPRICE	-0.320	(0.086)
ΔlnINTEREST	-0.216	(0.109)	ΔlnINTEREST	-0.146*	(0.102)
			ΔDUTY	2.291*	(1.482)
Adjusted R^2	0.189		Adjusted R^2	0.318	
N	57		N	63	
d.f.	3, 53		d.f.	4, 58	
F	5.36		F	8.22	
RSS	0.103		RSS	0.216	
DW	1.818		DW	1.807	

Note: * insignificant at 95 per cent confidence level. Standard errors in parentheses.

Sources: see text.

estimations proved better than those in levels, because they gave lower residual sums of squares (even after adjustment) and higher, significant, DW statistics.[63] The results are reported in table 1.9. These indicate that population growth had the greatest impact on the growth of fire insurance in the eighteenth and early nineteenth centuries. The population coefficients are considerably larger than those attached to the other variables in both sub-periods. The signs for price and interest rates are negative as expected, but the building proxies are puzzling. The timber coefficient is small and insignificant for the period to 1782, while the brick coefficient for the period from 1785 is negative. Taking the regressions at face value, building output played no part in determining the growth of fire insurance before the 1780s, and had a negative impact thereafter.

One may be suspicious of such results. Although first difference estimations will automatically produce lower R^2 statistics than estimations in levels, and although one should be cautious about attributing too much explanatory power to a high R^2, the very low R^2 figures in table 1.9 suggest that the above models are not well specified. This is unlikely to be due to inadequate data or omitted variables. The insurance series constructed here are reliable, and the other data series employed are all familiar sources, widely used by economic historians. There are no other series omitted which are obvious possible determinants of insurance growth. The inference would seem to be that the relationship between real sums insured and the variables jointly influencing the demand for insurance - population, building, cost of insurance, cost of credit - was a weak one throughout this period. If this is the case, supply-side factors, which are impossible to measure, may have been more important in determining the rate and fluctuations in insurance growth during the industrial revolution. Such factors may have included the relative profitability of fire insurance versus other investment opportunities, encouraging the establishment of new offices. Profitability itself was determined in part by the incidence of fires and by the ability of underwriters to measure risk, or, in other words, by the changing relationship between risk and uncertainty. Other immeasurable supply-side variables may have been the quality of insurance agents, the efficiency of advertising and marketing by fire offices, and the efficiency of management. These factors are examined more closely in subsequent chapters.

The cost of insurance

While one suspects that supply-side factors may have been important, the regressions are not so conclusive as to rule out demand as an influence on the growth of fire insurance. Figure 1.3 illustrates the large movements in the average price of insurance over the period, and in several places above it has been suggested that price may have been a factor in determining the level of demand.[64] In this final section, we explore the price of insurance and its relative cost to policyholders a little further. The Schumpeter-Gilboy consumer goods price index (including cereals) was spliced with Rousseau's overall index, at 1800 = 100, to obtain a general consumer price index for the whole period. The average premium rate series (current values) was also indexed at 1800 = 100. In figure 1.6 the latter has then been plotted as a proportion of the former to create a terms of trade lookalike index.[65] Amidst all the disturbance, caused mainly by the volatility of consumer prices - the average premium rate, as might be expected, was far more stable - three phases emerge over the period.[66] First, the price of fire insurance increased relative to consumer prices between the 1720s and the mid 1750s by about 30 per cent. Then, the relative cost of insurance fell by over 50 per cent to the end of the Napoleonic wars, as consumer prices rose more rapidly than premium rates. Third, between 1815 and mid-century insurance prices rose by nearly 100 per cent relative to consumer prices. While the average premium rate fell from its wartime peak in 1804-5 to 1830, this decline was not nearly as precipitous as the fall in the prices of consumables. Although both price series turned upwards during the 1830s, after 1840 premium rates continued to climb, more steeply than before under the impact of new tariff agreements among the fire offices, while consumer prices once again slid downwards.

In sum, figure 1.6 indicates that fire insurance was becoming much cheaper relative to the cost of necessities between 1760 and 1815, but thereafter it grew more expensive. It is also possible to examine the real price of fire insurance relative to the real earnings of some of those groups most likely to purchase cover. This provides a very different perspective. In table 1.10 the average real premium rate is indexed on a base of 1815 = 100, and divided into four series of earnings, all reindexed to the same base year, to produce an insurance purchasing power index

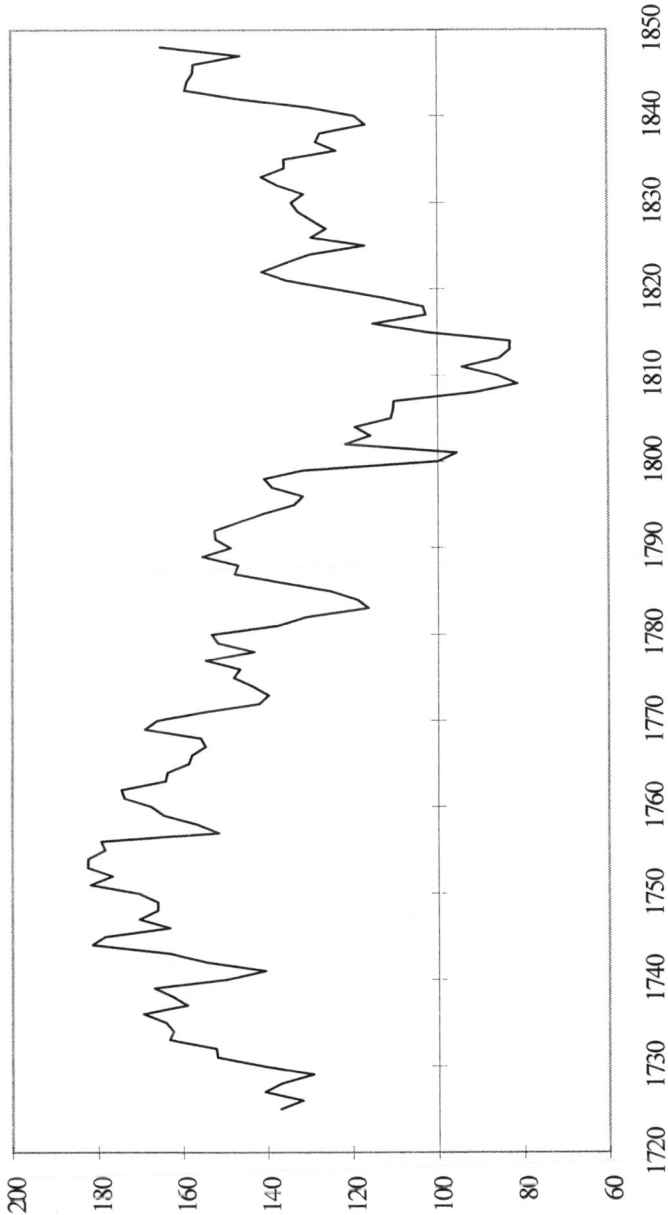

Figure 1.6 Average premium rates and consumer prices: terms of trade index (1800=100)
Source: see text.

Table 1.10   Real earnings and the cost of insurance, 1755-1850

	Average real premium rates index 1815=100	Insurance Purchasing Power Indices (1815 = 100)			
		'White collar workers'	East India Company clerks	Bank of Scotland clerks	Manual Workers
1755	129	65			
1780	130		48	47	75
1781	114	74			
1797	138	63			
1800	97		69	66	99
1805	110	70			
1810	104	70	67	63	96
1815	100	100	100	100	100
1819	79	136			
1825	72		160	147	152
1827	67	220			
1835	84	288			
1840	73		182	192	146
1848/51*	73	484			

Notes: Insurance years are centres of five year moving averages. * Real earnings end year is 1851, the insurance data end year is 1848 (the average of 1846-50).

Sources: Average rates (premium per £100 insured) calcuated from real sums insured and real premium income, as given in appendices A and B. Lindert and Williamson's index of 'white collar' real earnings from Mitchell, *British Historical Statistics*, p.152. Age-adjusted average real earnings of East India Company clerks and Bank of Scotland clerks, and Feinstein's estimates of manual workers' real earnings, from Boot, 'Real Incomes', table 5, p.659.

for each group of earners. The earnings indices are Boot's recent data on age-adjusted real earnings of clerks with the East India Company and the Bank of Scotland, Feinstein's estimates of the real income of manual workers (as given by Boot), and Lindert and Williamson's index of real earnings for white collar workers. 'White collar workers' here comprise messengers and porters, government employees, clergymen, lawyers, clerks, surgeons, teachers, engineers and surveyors.

The table shows that purchasing power of these heterogeneous 'white collar workers' relative to the average cost of insurance rose only modestly between 1755 and 1780. Between 1780 and 1800 the experience of the four groups varied. The insurance purchasing power of the clerks rose by over 40 per cent, while that of manual workers rose by 32 per cent. Lindert and Williamson's 'white collar workers', by contrast, were barely able to buy more insurance by the turn of the century, than they had 20 years earlier. A lack of growth in their capacity to purchase insurance may have contributed to the slowdown in the expansion of real sums insured from the 1770s and to the stagnation in real per caput sums insured (see figures 1.2 and 1.4), although the same cannot be said for the East India Company and Bank of Scotland employees. The indices agree, however, that purchasing power stood still for all groups during the first decade of the nineteenth century.

After 1810 the differential between the salaried and manual workers grew rapidly. By the 1840s the income power of 'white collar workers' to purchase fire insurance had risen nearly seven fold, and that of the two groups of clerks by three fold. By contrast, the insurance purchasing power of manual workers increased by a factor of just 1.6 until 1825, and then declined. So while the price of insurance relative to the price of daily necessities rose for most of this period, this increase was more than offset by the huge increase in real earnings for the salaried sector of the labour force. The massive cheapening of insurance cover for some of those groups below the landed classes with the greatest propensity to buy it may help explain the acceleration in the real growth of insurance during the first half of the nineteenth century. At this point we run into the insurmountable difficulty of differentiating between sectors of market demand for insurance. What is clear is that from the peak of nominal price levels in the 1800s, there was a multiplication of fire offices, a huge expansion in the numbers of agents and a rapid increase in the availability of fire insurance throughout the country. This may have been accompanied by either an increase in risk aversion among the swelling ranks of the rural and urban middle classes during politically and socially troubled times, or a widening perception among other social classes that property insurance had become a necessity rather than a luxury. The changing structure of demand, and its expanded and more stratified character after 1800, together with the great improvements in the supply of insurance, may help explain the curious coexistence of a rapid real growth in sums insured, a falling cost of insurance, both in terms of nominal premium rates and white collar real earnings, and a rise in the price of insurance relative to commodity prices. Customer perceptions of risk are generally hard to identify from the sources, but these, together with other supply-side and demand-side factors shaping the insurance markets in London and the provinces, are among the issues to be explored in the following chapters.

Notes

1   Boswell, *Life of Johnson*, p.295.
2   Deane and Cole, *British Economic Growth*, p.76; Crafts, *British Economic Growth*, p.34.
3   *PP* (1824) XVII, 495-502; *PP* (1825) XXI, 105-11. Cf. the inaccurate statements in Ryan, 'Percentage Duty on British Fire Insurance', and in Raynes, *History of British Insurance*, p.211, that 1831 was 'the first year of full publication'. A breakdown of returns for 1805 is also given by Walford, from data originally collected by Sir Frederick Eden from the Stamp Office, Walford, *Insurance Cyclopaedia*, vol.III, p.420. A partial printed list of returns for 1809 can also be found in County Fire Office, Bedford Agency Register. Another copy of the same return is in GL Ms 16206/1, Essex & Suffolk Fire Office, Minute Book no.1. The Phoenix kept their own manuscript record of the returns made by the major offices, but this was unavailable for consultation at the time of writing. Cf. Trebilcock, *Phoenix Assurance*, vol.I, note to table 1.1, p.12.
4   This graph, and table 1.1 below, cover 167 of these offices. Two offices, the Fife and the Yarmouth, are listed in the 1809 returns, but their date of establishment is unknown. They are not included in Jenkins's list of fire offices before 1840, which has several other inaccuracies, Jenkins, 'Practice of Insurance against Fire', pp.19-20.
5   Pressnell, *Country Banking*, table 1, p.11; Ward, *Finance of Canal Building*, table II, p.164; Wilson, *Lighting the Town*, p.29; Bagwell, *Transport Revolution*, pp.93-4. There were over 500 gas companies in the UK by 1850, compared with 70 fire offices, Falkus, 'British Gas Industry', p.500.
6   Mathias, *Transformation*, p.232; Jenkins, 'Validity of the Factory Returns', table 6.
7   Details from GL Ms 11932/2-6, Sun, CMM, 1730-59 *passim*.
8   Data was available, though seldom on an annual basis, on firemen for 15 fire offices, and on agents for 22 offices across the period.
9   For comparison, the 1851 census returned 808 'insurance agents and officers', which bore no resemblance to the true extent of part-time and full-time insurance employment. *PP* (1851) LXXXVIII, part I, table 53, p.cxxi.
10   Occupied population from Deane and Cole, *British Economic Growth*, p.143. I have estimated 3.1m for 1750, based upon the proportion of occupied to total population in 1801 and Wrigley and Schofield's estimate for the population of England and Wales in 1750, adjusted to include Scotland using Deane and Cole's estimate for 1751.
11   No adjustment, for instance, can be made for changes in hours worked.
12   Although the first tentative steps towards reinsurance between British fire offices were taken in the 1800s, the business did not take off until the later 1820s. Pearson, 'Reinsurance'.
13   Pressnell, *Country Banking*, p.227; Cameron, 'England', p.33 n; Wilson, *Lighting the Town*, p.47; Ward, *Finance of Canal Building*, table II, pp.26-73; Pollins, 'Marketing of Railway Shares'. Railways founded after 1830 were much larger, ranging from the Liverpool-Manchester at £300000 to the London-Birmingham at £2.5m.
14   English, *A Complete View*, p.32.
15   Average capital for 1800 from the average of seven provincial offices founded 1790-1809 (£24746), and from six London offices founded 1803-8 (£102000). I have excluded the Globe Fire Office of 1803 (£1m fully paid up) as an outlier. Average

capital for 1850 from eight provincial offices, 1818-1848 (£69250), and from five London offices, 1821-4 (£266000).

16   Cameron, 'England', p.33; Deane and Cole, *British Economic Growth*, pp.237-8; Wilson, *Lighting the Town*, p.29.

17   Pearson, 'Capital Formation'; Chapman and Butt, 'Cotton Industry'; Jenkins, 'Wool Textile Industry'; Mathias, *Transformation*, p.226; Orbell, 'Corn Milling', table 6.5, p.161.

18   National income calculated from Deane and Cole, *British Economic Growth*, p.166, adjusted for England and Wales using Cameron's method. Banking percentages from Cameron, 'England', p.33. An alternative perspective of fire insurance capital as a proportion of British net national wealth (current values), gives 0.1 per cent in 1800, and 0.4 per cent in 1850. Calculated from Feinstein, 'National Statistics', tables VI & XIX, pp.437, 465.

19   As explained in appendix A.4, O'Brien's indices of industrial and construction prices were tried as alternative deflators, but they made little difference to the shape or rate of growth of real sums insured.

20   Supple, *Royal Exchange*, pp.106-8; Trebilcock, *Phoenix Assurance*, vol.I, pp.11-14.

21   Crafts, *British Economic Growth*, pp.34-6; Deane and Cole, *British Economic Growth* p.77. This, of course, is not the same as stating that service output was not driven to some degree by population growth, a question explored below.

22   These estimates, however, might be questioned as they are based upon Deane and Cole's much criticised figures.

23   Calculated from Lindert and Williamson's figures as given by Crafts, *British Economic Growth*, p.13.

24   'World Insurance in 1991', *Sigma*, no.4 (1993).

25   Walford, 'Fires and Fire Insurance Considered', pp.403-5; Coode, 'Revised Report', p.33.

26   The greatest problem lies with the inclusion of farm crops and livestock in Feinstein's estimates, when an unknown, but probably very limited, proportion of these were insured. In turn, it is difficult to know whether insurable non-farming capital rose or fell as a proportion of total capital (including farming capital and uninsurable non-farm capital) over time.

27   Jones, Porter and Turner, *Gazetteer*. Cf. also Porter, 'Fires and Pre-industrial Towns'.

28   Borsay, *Urban Renaissance*, p.18.

29   Jones, Porter and Turner, *Gazetteer*, pp.58-9.

30   For instance the great fire of 1803 in the 'Goree' warehouse district of Liverpool is not included.

31   The terms 'house' and 'building' are inevitably used here rather loosely. The former simply replicates contemporary newspaper usage, while the latter covers 'non-residential' buildings such as those denoted as warehouses, sheds, barns, offices etc., although it is recognised that many of these may have also been part-occupied as dwellings.

32   *GM*, 77 ii (1807), p.821.

33   Estimation based upon 30 fires per month between October and March, and 20 per month between April and September.

34   About one in nine inhabitants of England and Wales at the end of the eighteenth century
      were Londoners. 4.5 x 9600 = 43200 houses. Green, *Artisans to Paupers*, p.1.

35   *LM*, (1755), p.185.

36   *AR*, (1777), pp.28-30, 245-9; *LM*, (1777), pp.109-10.

37   The other being the 'underwriting' or 'loss ratio', that is claims paid expressed as a
      percentage of gross premium income (before deduction of commission and expenses
      etc.).

38   For example, the Sun (1743-1850), the Phoenix (1788-1845), the REA (1732-1850),
      the London (1722-1850), the Globe (1804-50), the Norwich Union (1801-50), the
      County (1807-46), the Imperial (1803-50), the Alliance (1824-50), the Guardian
      (1822-45).

39   Jones, Porter and Turner, *Gazetteer*, p.63.

40   It should be remembered that, for the reasons given in appendix A, the insurance data
      are five year centred moving averages, so that 1801, for example, is the average of
      1799-1803, and encompassed policies current and losses recorded in the poor harvest
      years of 1799 and 1800, as well as 1802, the year of Colonel Despard's conspiracy.
      This introduces a certain inexactitude in locating insurance peaks and troughs to
      particular calendar years.

41   That is in cases where the cost of rebuilding was less than the value of the claims
      settlement, or where policyholders refused to accept the amount offered by the insurer
      for settlement.

42   GL Ms 8666/18, Hand-in-Hand, BM, 10 Nov. 1758; Ms 8670, Hand-in-Hand,
      General Letter Book, letter to Lord Warkworth, 20 Dec. 1763; Ms 8728/9, London
      Assurance, GCM, 1 July 1772; Ms 11932/10, Sun, CMM, 3 Nov. 1774.

43   Feinstein, 'National Statistics', table 17.5, p.389.

44   Parry Lewis, *Building Cycles*, remains the principal text, but see also Cairncross and
      Weber, 'Fluctuations in Building', and Chalklin, *Provincial Towns*.

45   Real sums insured are given in appendix A. The nth order method used here defines a
      major peak as an observation whose value is greater than those of the three previous
      and three succeeding observations. A major trough is defined as the obverse of this.
      Parry Lewis, *Building Cycles*, appendix 1.

46   The peak of 1784 may be affected by a clustering in the returns of the new stamp duty
      on fire insurance (introduced in 1782) upon which the estimates of sums insured from
      1783 are based. Initial difficulties in collection caused delays in remittances which
      particularly affected the annual returns at this time.

47   1807 is a minor peak because it does not fulfill the 2n+1 criterion of a major peak.
      Real sums insured in that year were greater than the values of the two (but not *three*)
      preceding and following years.

48   The discussion in this and following paragraphs draws on Fisher, *Industrial
      Revolution*; Ashton, *Economic Fluctuations*; Parry Lewis, *Building Cycles*; Mirowski,
      Birth of the Business Cycle; Chalklin, *Provincial Towns*. The series summarised by
      Fisher for the period to 1780 are those of Mirowski (profit index), Deane (business
      cycles), Ashton (business cycles), Hoffmann (index of industrial production), and
      Mirowski and Weiler (real interest rates).

49   Ashton, *Economic Fluctuations*, p.94; Mirowski, *Birth of the Business Cycle*, pp.232-
      3; GL Ms 4022/3-4, Union, DM, 1721-30 *passim*. For references to insurance growth,

see GL Ms 11931/4, Sun, GCM, 9 June 1726; WCA, Ms 343/75, Westminster, GCM, 13 Oct. 1726.

50   The Jacobite threat may indeed have encouraged the gentry, from the safety of their London residences, to seek increased cover on their country homes. I am grateful to Mike Turner for this suggestion.

51   WCA, Ms.343/75, Westminster Fire, GCM, 21 Apr. 1748; GL Ms 11932/4, S un, CMM, 5 July 1750.

52   GL Ms 11932/5, Sun, CMM, 13 May 1756; Ms 11931/5, Sun, GCM, 7 July, 13 Oct. 1757.

53   GL Ms 11931/5-6, Sun, GCM, 5 Apr. 1764, 3 Jan. 1765, 5 Jan. 1775; WCA, Ms 343/75, Westminster Fire, GCM, 16 Oct. 1760, 23 Oct. 1766, 19 Oct. 1769.

54   Ashton, *Economic Fluctuations*, pp.173-6.

55   Fisher, *Industrial Revolution.*, pp. 69-71 and fig.2.4. The original profit index is given in Mirowski, *Birth of the Business Cycle*, pp.209-10.

56   Parry Lewis, *Building Cycles*, p.81.

57   For a recent challenge to the orthodox view that fixed capital, from a subsidiary role in industrial capital formation, grew in significance during the early nineteenth century, see Richardson, 'The Structure of Capital'.

58   Feinstein explicitly excludes consumer durables from his estimates of 'non-farm stock' in his recent study of capital formation. His definition of the former (circulating capital) comprises stocks of raw material, semi-manufactured and finished products, and the value of work in progress on houses and ships. Feinstein, 'National Statistics', pp.393-4.

59   For the period before 1725, Shammas has shown how falling relative prices and the substitution of cheaper semi-durable goods could result in an increasing volume of goods purchased, but a static share of household wealth invested in such goods. But it is the relation between the insured values of goods and fixed capital which concerns us here. Shammas, 'Changes in English and Anglo-American Consumption'. For inventory evidence of the increasing possession of durables, see Weatherill, 'The Meaning of Consumer Behaviour'. Cf. also Stobart and Owens, *Urban Fortunes*; McKendrick, Brewer and Plumb, *Birth of a Consumer Society*.

60   Population from Wrigley and Schofield, *Population History*, table A3.3. Timber and stained paper from Ashton, *Economic Fluctuations*, p.188. Bricks from Shannon, 'Bricks'; glass (white glass) from Mitchell, *Abstract*, p.267. Bankruptcies to 1800 from Hoppit, *Risk and Failure*, appendix 1 (adjusted series), 1801-48 from Green, *Artisans to Paupers*, appendix 2.1. Green's series is preferred to those in Mitchell, *British Historical Statistics*, pp.694-5, because, being commissions gazetted rather than commissions sealed, it is more compatible with Hoppit's data. Interest rates to 1783 (annual averages of quarterly bank dividend yields) calculated from Weiler and Mirowski, 'Interest Rates', appendix II, 1785-1848 (three per cent consol yields) from Mitchell, *British Historical Statistics*, p.678. Share price index to 1810 from Mirowski, 'Rise (and Retreat) of a Market', p.572, and for 1811-48 (excluding mines) from Gayer, Rostow and Schwartz as reported in Mitchell, *British Historical Statistics*, p.687. The GRS series is spliced to Mirowski's by reindexing it as 1750=100. Adjusted profit index from Mirowski, *Birth of the Business Cycle*, pp.209-10.

61   The survival of timber buildings in late eighteenth-century London is discussed in Chapter 2.

62   GL Ms 14022/13, Union, DM, 17 Apr. 1765; WCA, Ms 343/76, Westminster, GCM, 16 Apr. 1772. Hussey gives the output of English wallpaper as 255730 pieces in 1770, rising to 12 million by 1800. Hussey, *English Country Houses*, p.28. On wallpaper, see also Jourdain, *English Interiors*, pp.135-6; Fowler and Cornforth, *English Decoration*, pp.122-4; Crick, 'Origins and Development of Wallpaper'.

63   The residual sums of squares of the equations 1.1 and 1.2 were adjusted to make them directly comparable with those of equations 1.3 and 1.4, using the procedure given in Maddala, *Introduction to Econometrics*, pp.233-4.

64   See above, pp.30, 41.

65   I am grateful to Mike Turner for this suggestion.

66   The standard deviation of the premium rate index was 11.3, compared to 19.3 for consumer prices.

PART I

Chapter 2

The Fire Insurance Markets of Georgian London

In the great Babylon - oppressed, engulfed
By crowds, and smoke, and vapour...

Caroline Bowles.[1]

At the beginning of the eighteenth century, London, with some 580000 inhabitants, was already the largest city in Europe, and nearly twenty times bigger than the next largest English town, Norwich. London grew by 100000 in the first half of the century, and by nearly 300000 during the second half. By 1801, despite the rapid rise of provincial centres, the capital's population of 960000 remained ten times greater than the largest of these, Manchester.[2] Raymond Williams once wrote that the sheer scale of eighteenth-century London 'provoked the sense of a new human dimension, a new kind of society' among contemporaries.[3] More prosaically its growth also created the biggest market for property insurance in the world.

Eighteenth-century London

London grew irregularly and unevenly in space and time. Although largely unnoticed by contemporaries, some areas became less populated. The City's population declined from over 208000 to 134000 during the course of the century, as warehouses and counting houses gradually replaced tenements.[4] Outside the City, in some of the oldest and poorest districts, the population may have also declined. Nevertheless, the common perception of London was of a frenetic and uncontrolled physical growth. In 1724 Defoe lamented the sprawl, seeing London as 'stretched out in buildings...in a most straggling, confused manner, out of all shape, uncompact and unequal'. Seventy years later Burke, who never much admired the metropolis, declared that London was 'but...an endless addition of littleness to littleness, extending itself over a great tract of land'.[5]

Some growth was the result of a westward drift of population as City families moved to newer areas, especially Marylebone and St Pancras, and as the fashionable world moved from Covent Garden to Hanover and Grosvenor Squares, or out to Chelsea and Kensington. Westminster's population rose from 130000 to 165000, while the five parishes of Marylebone, St Pancras, Hammersmith, Chelsea and Kensington together expanded from 9000 in 1700 to 123000 in 1801.[6]

Contrary to Defoe's perception of a haphazard sprawl, much of the development in the west was planned, as streets and squares were laid out on long leases, with building and design closely regulated by private and local acts. Ribbon development and suburban growth were also factors. Because of improvements to roads out of London and the survival of green spaces, many of the outer villages, such as Highgate, Hampstead, Hackney, Stratford and Walthamstow, became the retreats of 'wealthy Cits', tradesmen and professional men building substantial houses either as second homes or for retirement. These were the suburban villas lampooned by contemporaries and later by Cobbett as 'tax-eaters' showy, tea-garden like boxes'.[7] The metropolis itself became longer and fatter, some eight miles from west to east and six miles north to south. Walpole wrote in 1791 that 'the town is so extended the breed of chairs is almost lost, for Hercules and Atlas could not carry anybody from one end of this enormous capital to the other'.[8]

Within this vast cityscape the range of residential property was huge. There were the great palaces and larger town houses of the aristocracy in St James's, Piccadilly, Whitehall and Mayfair, designed and ornamented by the best architects, brick and stone built by master builders, with plasterwork ceilings, marble chimneypieces and wrought iron or mahogany hand rails.[9] There were the solid, brown-brick villas of the suburbs with good joinery, stucco and wrought-iron work, and some pretensions to fashionable design. But the tall narrow houses occupied by most Londoners were built by speculative small builders or were tenement conversions often of poor construction. Bricklayers or carpenters with a few guineas in their pocket would take a site on a long lease from a landowner at a peppercorn ground rent for the first year or two of the lease. The brick shells of houses would be thrown up quickly, in the hope of selling them before the period of low rent expired. The speed and cost of construction were critical to success or bankruptcy.[10] In 1757 the Hand-in-Hand Fire Office streamlined its surveying procedure to cope with the rising demand from builders for insurance on houses under construction.[11] In the summer of 1765 it was reported that

> the rage, or at least hurry, of building is so great at present that the bricks are often brought to the bricklayers before they are cold enough to be handled; so that some days ago the floor of a cart loaded with bricks took fire in Golden Lane, Old Street, and was consumed before the bricks could be unloaded.[12]

As demand for bricks surged during a building boom, and prices rose, there was a temptation to mix in ash or dirt to make the brick clay go further.[13] Such bricks were used for the unseen work in party walls, leaving structural weaknesses which often quickly became apparent. External walls were also made from the cheaper sorts of grey-yellow brick, just one row deep, while small, thin planks of deal took the place of internal beams. A common impression was that much housing was poorly built and some danger to its inhabitants and passers-by. Johnson regarded London as a place where 'falling houses thunder on your head'.[14] Between 1763 and 1774 at least 40 houses collapsed killing some 50 people.[15] All types of cheap houses, new as well as old, tumbled down without warning. In 1768 five newly built houses at Bethnal Green fell down the day before they were to be sold at auction. The previous year an empty house under repair in Cursitor Street, off Chancery Lane, collapsed, carrying with it part of the alehouse next door. Five lodgers in the tavern died, including three children and a pregnant woman. A baby was reported missing in the ruins.[16]

Attempts to regulate building in London were not new. From the late sixteenth century many acts had aimed at preventing the growth of housing, especially for the poor. Most legislation was evaded or ignored. Profits were to be made from patching up old buildings, digging cellars out of foundations, and constructing rickety extensions to existing houses to accommodate more tenants. In the wake of the Great Fire a new type of legislation appeared, which focused on improving structures by regulating party walls, limiting the use of wood, and standardising the size and quality of bricks. Much of this also failed. The Brick Act of 1727 was widely ignored by members of the Company of Tilers and Brickmakers who were given the task of implementing it. Insurers complained that fire damage was greater than it should have been, because builders ignored the regulations requiring them to continue party walls up through the roofs of houses.[17] For most of the reigns of the first two Georges little further was done to follow up earlier legislation. From the early 1750s the Common Council of the City began to discuss the problem again, and in 1763 the London insurance offices formed a joint committee to campaign for further fire prevention legislation and to reinforce the regulations on party walls. The building acts of 1764-74 were part of a wider movement which embraced street widening, paving and lighting in London and Westminster, bridge building and the rebuilding or repair of public buildings.[18] The act of 1764 regulated the thickness and projection of party walls and the use of wood near hearths and chimneys, and introduced compulsory inspection for all new buildings. Builders who failed to comply faced a £50 fine or imprisonment. This act was amended two years later to extend penalties to the employees of master builders and to grant justices the right to issue warrants of entry to adjacent houses where a party wall needed repair or demolition.[19]

The 1774 act, described by Summerson as 'a milestone in the history of London improvement', was more adventurous than anything previously attempted by Parliament.[20] Seven classes of building were sanctioned, categorised by value, floor area, height or number of storeys, distance from public roads or other buildings, and type of use. Tallow shops, distilleries, breweries, iron foundries, sugar refineries, glass factories, warehouses, churches, chapels and stables, as well as dwelling houses, were included in the act. Within the first four classes the thickness of external and party walls and of foundations was specified. Almost all woodwork was to be banished from exteriors. Front walls were to be aligned with streets, and projections prohibited. District surveyors of buildings were appointed to enforce the legislation. Smaller detached industrial and commercial buildings and windmills and cranes on wharves or quays were left unregulated. The intention was to standardise most residential and commercial building in inner London to the best possible practice. Some changes did follow, such as the increasing use of artificial materials such as stucco and Coade stone for exterior ornamentation in fashionable west end houses.[21] On the whole, however, the act of 1774 effected only a gradual improvement, and parts of central London, the riverside and the east continued to have high proportions of timber-built structures.[22]

Evidence of the persistence of timber buildings can be found in the records of the three London mutual fire offices. These kept an account of sums insured on brick and timber properties, because the amounts levied on their members to meet the costs of claims varied according to whether the member's insurance was on a brick or timber building. Under regulations of 1743, those Hand-in-Hand members who insured timber properties paid twice the rate of levy - a percentage on the sum insured - of those insuring brick-built properties. Timber properties were defined as those with two or more exterior walls made from timber, or with a party wall built of timber. Buildings with just one side, front or back wall of timber were deemed part-brick, part-timber, and were rated separately. Far from declining, the proportion of timber properties insured increased during the century. In the case of the Hand-in-Hand it rose from 12 per cent during the 1720s to over 20 per cent during the last two decades of the century. The Union Fire Office's policies on goods held in timber buildings increased rapidly during the 1720s, from under ten per cent to over 30 per cent of sums insured, then more slowly to a peak of 39 per cent by 1755. Thereafter the proportion settled around 36 per cent until 1783 when the data series came to an end. Even the Westminster Fire Office, whose business was largely confined to the stone- and brick-built west end, saw timber insurances among its traditional seven year policies increase from five to nine per cent between 1760 and 1794. Among its annual policies, a product first launched by the office in 1782, timber property accounted for 15 per cent of sums insured in the mid 1790s.

Technical factors may have affected these trends. The Hand-in-Hand, concerned about the accuracy of its risk classification, surveyed nearly 20000 London houses between 1780 and 1800 with the object of reclassifying as many of them as possible from brick- to timber-built. Such reclassifications, however, amounted on average to less than half of one per cent of the total sums insured by the office, not enough to explain the rise by some five percentage points in its timber insurances during this period. Nor can the search by the mutual offices to maintain market share provide a full explanation. Although the willingness to underwrite less desirable properties may have increased during the second half of the century, the upward trend in timber insurances began long before the onset of the crises which blighted these offices after 1780.

The insurance evidence, therefore, points to the increasing use of timber in London buildings before the 1780s, and to the persistence of structures which were wholly or largely timber-built - comprising between one-fifth and one-third of insured property - until at least the end of the century. London's improvement measures may have provided a model for provincial towns between 1660 and 1780, and there was undoubtedly a greater use of brick and stone by the capital's builders, especially in the more public streets of the west end and the City. The diffusion of brick, however, was far from complete by 1780. Many new properties continued to be constructed partly of timber, and it is not clear that over the whole metropolitan area the proportion of timber buildings did not rise even after the 1774 Building Act.

Despite the best efforts of the state at regulation, London's residential building process resulted in a huge range of property types which made fire underwriting difficult enough. The increasing volume and diversity of London's manufacturing, commercial and service activities multiplied these difficulties. Over 750 different trades and occupations were recorded in the policy registers of the Sun and the REA in 1776, and nearly 500 were listed in the London directory of 1791.[23] Throughout the period London remained a major manufacturing centre. Industry employed perhaps 40 per cent of the city's workforce in the 1700s, and still one-third as late as 1851.[24] In most industries the trend was towards an increasing scale of operation and the accumulation of capital in the hands of a few, though the small artisan workshop continued to be the most common mode of production organisation. Space was a major fixed cost in high-rent London, and several industries, such as shipbuilding, ropemaking, saw milling and coachbuilding, used a great deal of space. The cost of equipment in glassmaking, brewing, sugar refining, soap boiling, vinegar making, printing, dyeing and malt distilling, and of silk looms, horse-powered saw mills, cutting and polishing machines for mirrors and shredding machines for tobacco, also added to capital values which were potentially insurable.

The stocks of manufacturers, merchants and shopkeepers, and the warehouses and storerooms of shops, created a further complicated market for insurance. As well as the more perishable foodstuffs, the metropolis drew in enormous quantities of wool, corn, malt and coal from the inland and coastal trades, and tea, coffee, sugar, molasses, wine, spices, silk, tobacco, oils, china, dyes, timber, iron and pitch from overseas. The largest accumulations of business wealth in London were to be found among the wholesale merchants who owned the huge warehouses dotted along the riverside from Upper Thames Street to London Bridge and down to Shadwell and Wapping. Large retailers with the smartest west end shops were not far behind.[25] The biggest drapers, mercers, hosiers and glovers had shops solely for the sale of goods, while other retailers might have manufacturing rooms at the back of their premises. The common retail shop was a general store with a stock of mixed goods, where small packets and parcels were stacked high on shelves and laid across counters and floors, adding to the fire hazard. Some shops were subdivided between different types of retailer, making assessment for insurance purposes even more difficult.[26] Catering was another large diverse market for insurers. In 1739 Maitland estimated there were 16000 victualling establishments in London ranging from around 200 coaching inns to thousands of back alley dram shops. Many of the latter, often chandler's shops selling provisions as well as gin to the poor, were untouchable for underwriters.[27] Inns, taverns, alehouses and coffee houses were often eminently insurable, though they could prove to be complicated risks. The great inns on the routes out of London provided lodging, stabling, warehousing, coachhouses, farriers', smiths' and ironmongers' shops as well as hosting markets in their coachyards. Finally, there were also the professional groups whose chambers and offices were highly likely to be insured. By the 1780s as many as one-third of all lawyers in England and Wales were located in the capital.[28] Altogether, the metropolitan economy offered a huge but often potentially hazardous extension to the residential property insurance market for those underwriters willing to explore the opportunities.

The London fire insurance offices

During the 1630s and again after the Restoration and the Great Fire a number of schemes were proposed for permanent insurance organisations in London to replace the old system of relieving victims of fire through charitable subscriptions to 'briefs'.[29] The first fire insurance offices, however, did not appear until the early 1680s. By 1720 ten had been established, excluding the speculative projects generated by the South Sea Bubble.[30] Three features of these early ventures stand out; first, that so many were successful, at least initially; second, that their business was confined to London; and third, that over half were established on a mutual basis, although this was not to become the dominant mode of insurance company organisation in the future. The second and third features help explain the first. By restricting business to London, some overview of risks was preserved and the costs associated with an agency network were avoided. By choosing the mutual form, company promoters could avoid having to calculate the cost of insurance in advance, and could bind their members together for the term of their assurances, usually seven years, thus guaranteeing some stability. In most mutuals members paid a deposit in proportion to the sum insured. Members also agreed to pay a levy or 'call', proportionate to the size of the insurance up to a specified limit, towards each claim made against the office during the period of membership. Members might also pay an annual 'premium', again proportionate to the size of the policy, which was intended to cover administrative costs rather than to reflect the fire hazard of the property insured. Some mutuals distributed an annual dividend derived from the interest earned on invested deposits. The intention was that these dividends, together with profits made from underwriting, would cover some of the premiums and all of the levies paid by members, and ensure that their full deposits were returned when their policies expired. Apart from the purported advantages of mutuality, close links with the London building industry also offered a basis for early success. The Hand-in-Hand office, which was established in 1696 and issued over 7300 policies during its first eight years, was 'chiefly carried on and supported by workmen and those concerned in building'.[31]

Supple rightly points to the narrow base of the industry before 1720.[32] Only one insurer, the Sun, underwrote goods and buildings in the same policy. Another, the Union, insured only goods while the rest insured only buildings. Insurance remained almost entirely confined to London despite a few attempts by the Sun to appoint country agents.[33] Moreover, three offices were closely connected with each other, further narrowing the entrepreneurial base. The Union, established in 1714, was the sister office of the Hand-in-Hand, underwriting goods in many of the buildings insured by the latter, while the Westminster Fire Office was formed in 1717 by some members of the Hand-in-Hand who were disgruntled at its move from Westminster to the City.[34] For the industry to expand further, the capital base needed to expand, the tight geographical and policy limits imposed on insurances had to be extended, and the organisation, underwriting and accounting procedures of all offices had to be placed on a more efficient and scientific footing. Only six London offices - three mutuals (the Hand-in-Hand, the Union, the Westminster) and three stock companies (the Sun Fire Office, the London Assurance, the Royal Exchange Assurance) - survived beyond 1720 to face these challenges. These offices alone ruled the capital's insurance markets for the next 60 years.

Two factors helped ensure their survival: first, the support of distinct constituencies in London, and, second, the adaptability of their organisational structures and underwriting practices. The three stock companies had connections with the great trading corporations and banking houses of the City, and with government, parliament and the landed aristocracy. From 1720 the Sun became controlled by a group with close links to the Duke of Chandos, the Scotch Mines, Royal African and East India companies, the Bank of England, the navy and parliament. During the course of the century several powerful family dynasties emerged within the self-electing board. The Sun's shareholders, about 130 in total, also formed a closed circle of military men, clergy, lawyers, merchants and lesser gentry, 80 per cent of whom resided in London and the home counties.[35] Similar social and dynastic features can be found in the two insurance corporations chartered in 1720. The London Assurance's court of directors comprised Turkey merchants, navy men and bankers. Most of the REA's directors and governors were overseas merchants, navy men, Blackwell hall factors, bankers and politicians. Like the Sun, both corporations located their head offices around the Bank and the Royal Exchange. All three companies drew deeply on the 'archetypal high-bourgeoisie of Hanoverian London', with their business orbits fixed around the City and parliamentary Westminster.[36]

Beneath these offices in rank were the mutuals, more modest in their social composition, but no less distinctive. After the Hand-in-Hand moved its main office from Westminster to Snow Hill, Holborn in 1711, it became increasingly identified with the City trades. The secession of its Westminster members in 1717 sealed its City-oriented character. Indeed the Westminster secessionists regarded the decision to move as a kind of palace coup carried out by the less wealthy (in terms of amounts insured) but more numerous City members.[37] One result was that the Hand-in-Hand won much of the lucrative business of insuring the properties of the City livery companies. The same is true of the Union, whose founders had close links with the City guilds.[38] An analysis of both offices in 1761 indicates that their directors were drawn from a wide range of trades located within the City and on its margins, particularly in the area from Cheapside to Holborn and Smithfield. Wholesale and retail dealers predominated, while only a few directors were drawn from the professions and finance.[39] The Westminster Fire Office had a higher social tone. It included many of the west end's leading developers and some of London's most notable architects, including James Gibbs, Sir William Chambers and Henry Holland.[40] This office also had the support of the Westminster gentry, tradesmen and manufacturers.[41] Its first office was located in a room above Tom's Coffee House in St Martin's Lane, until it moved into a purpose built office in Bedford Street in 1751. Its constitution prevented the office from being moved out of Westminster.[42] Each of the early fire offices thus had their own social and geographical identities within the rapidly expanding metropolis, helping to give them a foothold in their respective markets.

The business practices of the London offices varied, but only in a limited way. There were many opportunities for imitation which helped reduce set-up costs and competition, at least in the early years. The deposit and levy system was used by all three mutuals, and before the late eighteenth century all three offices issued policies only for terms of seven years.[43] The Union and the Westminster closely followed the Hand-in-Hand in many respects, modelling their constitutions on the older office, tracking changes in its policy conditions, declining to insure categories of risk which the latter had rejected. There were also organisational similarities within the two groups of mutual and stock offices. The REA and the London Assurance created nearly identical management structures, which were based on those of other large chartered companies, notably the East India Company. A court of directors was elected every three years by the proprietors voting in proportion to size of their individual shareholdings. The court met weekly to oversee the five or six standing committees and sub-committees which carried out the detailed business - treasury, accounts, fire, marine, and a 'committee of waiting' to examine proposals for insurance. In both corporations this structure remained largely unchanged throughout the eighteenth century.[44] The Sun Fire Office was organised slightly differently. There was no provision for consulting shareholders in a general meeting nor for shareholders to elect new managers. The managers met in their own 'general meeting' every quarter, while a 'committee of management' of seven met weekly, this being the real controlling body of the office. During the 1720s the Sun also established four sub-committees for accounts, Westminster, City and country insurances.[45] The organisation of the mutuals was less complex than that of the stock companies. Their supreme body was the general court of members, usually meeting twice a year. The boards of directors were accountable to and elected by these courts. The full boards of between 12 and 24 directors met weekly or fortnightly. The Hand-in-Hand and the Union also had a sub-'board' of five which met weekly with powers to make 'by-laws'. This may have doubled up as a committee for hazardous insurances which appears to have been the only type of standing committee created by mutual offices during the eighteenth century, although this is hardly surprising given their narrower scope of business - no marine, life or country agency business to manage. Other committees were usually temporary and specific, though all offices made considerable use of them - to examine 'the state of the office', to explore schemes for reorganisation, to draft constitutional amendments, to regulate the duties and conduct of staff, to devise new accounting methods, to draw up new rates, or to investigate the fire hazards of particular industries.

In general, the mutual offices had a flatter management structure, in which directors were actively involved in viewing risks proposed for insurance and in adjusting claims on damaged property. Less decision-making was devolved to senior salaried staff than was the case in the stock companies. In particular there was no equivalent to the position held by the secretary in the latter. The Sun's secretary was a salaried manager whose annual pay rose to £200 by 1778, excluding the gratuities and annuities bestowed upon him. Nominally the job required attending and taking the minutes of each of the sub-committees, and acting as an *ex officio* member of the committee of management. In practice the secretary operated as a managing director and had considerable scope for innovation. The post was a less powerful one in the corporations but still reasonably remunerative.[46] The chief officer in the mutuals was the principal clerk, whose responsibilities remained limited in scope before the early nineteenth century. At the Westminster the head clerk did not even have access to the office chest - the keys were kept by the treasurers - and the starting salary, at £30, was only based on a part-time appointment.[47] The weaker position of the senior officer in the mutuals may, in part, be explained by the smaller number of staff they had to supervise. Each mutual began with just three part-time office staff - a clerk, a surveyor and a messenger - compared with the London Assurance which had 15 employees by the end of 1721. Numbers grew as business expanded and the proportion of part-time and temporary staff fell in all offices. The Sun had a staff of over 30 by 1782 while the REA had about 20. The mutuals remained smaller, although the numbers employed by the Hand-in-Hand rose to 14 towards the end of the century.[48]

In the long run these different structures proved capable of responding to changing market conditions, but not necessarily in the most efficient way. Most offices faced two problems - staff discipline and adjusting rates to risks - which persisted throughout the century but were particularly acute in the early years. Three of the first five clerks employed by the Westminster office absconded with considerable amounts of cash. The London Assurance had to cope with persistent absenteeism and the Hand-in-Hand had repeated problems with its surveyors.[49] Price adjustment took up much time, inevitably for young companies still uncertain of the relationship between premium rate and risk. The Hand-in-Hand and the Union also faced other problems. Early in 1722 it was discovered that the Union's directors had neglected to fix the rates for members' levies, provoking vociferous protests from those asked to foot the bill. In 1729 the Hand-in-Hand's members appointed their own committee to examine the way the office had been run. They found that balloting for board seats had been held in a 'private manner'. Much worse, 'almost the whole management of the affairs of the contributionship'

Table 2.1 London fire insurance market shares, 1725-95

I = market share estimated by sums insured; P = market share estimated by premium income. *Italics* indicate where the underlying data is based upon estimates. All data are five year centred moving averages.

	Hand-in-Hand		Union		West-minster		Sun		REA		London		Phoenix		Total £ London premiums	Total £m London sums Insured
	I	P	I	P	I	P	I	P	I	P	I	P	I	P		
1725	29	*37*	5	5	3	3	*41*	*36*	*12*	*11*	*11*	9			33482	29.45
1730	26	*34*	5	6	3	3	*36*	*32*	*17*	*15*	*13*	11			42896	37.25
1735	28	*38*	5	8	5	4	*36*	*29*	*13*	*11*	*14*	11			44414	34.84
1740	29	*39*	6	9	6	4	*34*	*28*	*11*	*9*	*14*	11			47050	35.55
1745	29	*39*	7	9	8	5	*34*	*28*	*10*	*8*	*13*	10			47486	35.26
1750	28	*39*	8	11	9	6	*34*	*27*	*9*	*9*	*12*	9			55354	38.15
1755	26	*36*	9	12	9	6	*33*	*27*	*12*	*10*	*11*	9			64860	44.02
1760	25	*34*	9	12	*10*	7	*33*	*28*	*12*	*11*	*10*	8			74009	50.44
1765	22	*29*	10	14	10	7	*39*	*34*	*11*	*10*	*9*	7			94029	62.78
1770	19	*26*	9	12	10	6	*43*	*40*	*11*	*11*	*7*	6			110805	75.93
1775	17	*21*	9	11	11	7	*45*	*43*	*12*	*12*	*7*	6			122191	83.93
1780	16	*20*	8	10	12	7	*47*	*46*	*12*	*13*	*6*	5			125434	85.92
1785	15	*14*	7	6	13	7	*41*	*44*	*11*	*12*	*5*	5	9	12	116732	81.54
1790	12	*11*	4	4	12	6	*38*	*38*	*12*	*12*	*4*	4	19	25	139093	91.00
1795	10	*8*	3	2	9	4	*38*	*37*	13	14	4	4	23	30	165718	99.03

Sources: For full details of sources and methods of estimating each office's total premiums and sums insured, see appendices A and B. London shares were calculated as follows: *Hand-in-Hand, Union and London*: total sums insured and premiums minus ten per cent; *Westminster*: no country business was assumed; *Sun*: 1783-1800 London share of sums insured calculated from gross duty in GL Ms 15045, Sun, Duty Papers and Licences, 1782-1871, and from Ms 11933A, Sun, Annual Accounts. Before 1783 London share of sums insured estimated from London proportion of total annual premium income; *REA*: 1768-1800, London premiums given in GRE, Ms RED305, REA, Report of Home (London) Premiums 1768-1907. Before 1768 London premiums = total premiums minus estimated country premiums. London share of sums insured estimated from London proportion of total annual premium income; *Phoenix*: London premiums as given in Phoenix Annual Summary Sheets, a copy of which was kindly supplied to me by Clive Trebilcock. London sums insured estimated from London proportion of total annual premium income.

had been left to the direction of the head clerk, who had made a complete mess of the accounts, and had failed to keep the policy registers up to date. The head clerk was dismissed, the bookkeeping system was reformed, and managerial decisions were made more transparent.[50] By contrast, the Sun's new managers of the 1720s, who were less subject to external monitoring, demonstrated greater competence in coping with organisational change. Besides drafting major adjustments of rates and establishing a network of provincial agencies, they restructured and expanded the shareownership and created a new committee structure which served the company well for over a century. An administrative structure was also put into place with three departments, the secretary's, the accomptant's and the delivery (or policy) department. Further office and bookkeeping improvements were made in the following decade. [51]

The different qualities and structures of management may have been reflected in the market performance of each of the London offices. Estimating market shares is made difficult, first, by a lack of compatibility between the underwriting data of different offices, and, second, by a lack of data on London insurances. We have annual sums insured for the mutuals but not for the stock companies before 1782. We have annual premiums for the latter but no direct equivalent for the former. Furthermore, the London proportion of total business can only be accurately established for three offices.[52] Nevertheless, by applying notional average rates (of premiums earned per £100 insured) to the available data, and by making appropriate allowances for country insurances, annual estimates can be constructed of the metropolitan business of the London offices before 1800. From these estimates London market shares for each office have been calculated in table 2.1. Market shares based on both sums insured and premiums are presented in order to indicate the likely range of values for each office. The estimates in table 2.1 disagree about which insurer was the largest in the capital before 1760, the Hand-in-Hand by underwriting income, or the Sun by sums insured. However they do agree about trends. They suggest that all the mutual offices, despite their managerial problems, were able to preserve or improve their market positions until the 1760s or beyond. The early performance of the stock companies was less impressive. The Sun's share of the London market slipped during the 1730s, then stabilised. The REA also faced a shrinking market share during the second quarter of the century before recovering during the 1750s. The London Assurance had a similar experience, but its decline continued for the rest of the century. In general, mutual offices were powerful players in London for the first two-thirds of the eighteenth century, accounting for over half of all income earned from fire underwriting.

It is difficult to explain the inability of the stock companies to sustain expansion in the capital during the first half of the eighteenth century. The Sun certainly put more energy into extending its country business. Metropolitan premiums fell as a proportion of the Sun's total premium income from 90 per cent in 1730 to just 50 per cent by the 1750s, while total income doubled to £30000 during the same period. The two corporations were also developing their country sales, though fire insurance remained secondary to marine underwriting for both.[53] During the second half of the century, while the London Assurance's fire business continued to languish, the REA recovered its position in the capital and the Sun acquired nearly half the market. The sea-change occurred during the 1760s. The Sun took greatest advantage of the capital's building boom, its London premiums more than doubling in a decade. Extra clerical staff were appointed to cope with the 'great increase of business', particularly in Westminster where the local fire office was also flourishing.[54] By contrast, the Hand-in-Hand was barely touched by the rocketing demand for insurance. From the mid 1770s the office went into a steep decline which saw its market share fall by three-quarters. The Union followed, its insurances collapsing from £8m to £3m during the course of two decades. Of the mutuals only the Westminster Fire held up, though it too stumbled in the 1790s as competition in London became tougher. From the 1780s the rise of the Phoenix Assurance cut back the market share of all the older offices, and the collusion which soon emerged between the Sun, the Phoenix and the REA squeezed the other offices still further.

The reasons for the differing fortunes of the mutual and stock offices towards the end of the century are explored below. It remains here to consider the nature of their relationship before the 1780s. At the outset, with the exception of the friendly ties between the Hand-in-Hand and the Union, the London insurers regarded themselves as exclusive of each other. Most prohibited their directors from belonging to another fire office, and most banned their policyholders from co-insuring their property elsewhere.[55] In all offices there was a share- or policyholding qualification for directors or managers, and there seems to have been little inter-company mobility of executive personnel. Competition, however, generally remained muted. One reflection of limited ambition was the cautious expansion of the mutuals from their original limits of insuring only within a ten mile radius of their head offices to the whole of England and Wales by the 1780s. Within the capital there was a certain, mostly unwritten and therefore immeasurable, demarcation of insurances by district, and to an extent by type, between the offices. At an early date the Union and the Hand-in-Hand resolved not to diversify into each other's markets for goods and buildings. The Westminster also resolved, at least initially, to restrict its underwriting to west of Grays Inn Lane and not to compete with the Hand-in-Hand, either by meddling in areas where that office was the dominant insurer or by raising the maximum sum it would accept on policies to divert its business.[56] The Hand-in-Hand itself enjoyed the patronage of the City livery companies and the big London hospitals. The Sun, in turn, built up a powerful, if often hazardous, presence in the riverside district below London Bridge. The borough of Westminster, by contrast, was an arena where all offices crossed swords. Most of the City insurers established secondary offices in Charing Cross during the 1720s and some of these flourished. The Sun's house at Craig's Court issued over 1600 new policies generating more than £8500 in premiums during its first six years.[57]

A further area of competition centred upon the maxima insurers were prepared to underwrite in one policy. In 1720 the Sun noted 'several complaints made at the office (by policyholders) of the smalness of their policys as not insuring larger sums, especially on goods'. This had lost the office business. The Sun promptly increased its £500 ceiling to £1000, and then to £3000 in 1727. The two corporations were more generous, thus putting pressure on the Sun, but the mutuals hesitated to go so far.[58] The Westminster raised its limit to £2000 in 1724, but this remained the maximum in 1769. As late as 1743 the Hand-in-Hand would only insure up to £1000 on residential houses and double this on public buildings. Rising property values appear to have increasingly pressed hard upon the limits of insurance cover. During the 1750s, when the Union twice raised its ceiling, that office was receiving requests every week from members wishing to 'make up their accounts' and renew their policies for larger sums.

There was little overt price warfare between London offices during the eighteenth century. By 1727 insurable property everywhere was divided into three categories; common (brick buildings, non-hazardous goods), hazardous (timber buildings, hazardous goods and trades in brick buildings, non-hazardous goods in timber buildings), and double hazardous (thatched buildings, hazardous goods and trades in timber buildings). Within these general categories most insurers continued to modify their prices. All offices revised their premium rate schedules between 1727 and 1743. After mid-century there were some minor adjustments but no major revisions before the 1780s. Nevertheless price differentials existed which anyone could take advantage of. A comparison of rates suggests that the Sun was the cheapest of the stock offices, at least before the middle of the century. A policyholder insuring £2500 in the 1730s on a brick building paid £4.4 in premiums to the Sun, £5 to the REA and £7.5 to the London Assurance. Adding the premium and gross deposit for a seven year insurance and dividing by seven gives an approximate annual rate for the mutual offices.[59] This calculation suggests that they were often, but not always, cheaper than the stock companies. In the 1730s, for instance, the lowest rate on common brick buildings charged by the Hand-in-Hand was 1.7s% (shillings per £100 insured), while the stock companies charged 2.0s%. Stock offices were not slow to remind policyholders of the uncertainties of the mutual system, where the insured were always subject to calls on their deposits.[60] For their part, the mutuals claimed that they offered the cheapest insurance. In 1786 the directors of the Union, faced with a crisis of confidence after heavy losses, rather implausibly announced to their members, that, allowing for a return on deposits of 10s in the pound, they were insuring at 'more than 40 per cent lower than the rates of a common insurance in other offices'.[61]

Cooperation was as limited as overt competition. Coinsurance was initially banned by most offices but low policy ceilings and rising demand soon changed underwriters' views. The Sun approved coinsurance with the appropriate policy endorsement from 1723. The Union opened a 'book of double insurances' in the same year. The two corporations also accepted coinsurances from 1723, although later they both tried to restrict the practice. Coinsurance never formed a large part of any office's business but it did become a regular feature of the London market. There were nearly 300 coinsurances listed in the Union's board minutes between 1735 and 1760, insuring about £700000 in other offices. The average amount coinsured annually rose from £18000 to £37000 between the late 1730s and the 1750s, suggesting an increasing use of this device to get around the limits imposed by offices on the sum they would insure in one policy.

Coinsurance could be a minor source of competition. Policyholders might be persuaded to remove their coinsurances from a rival office if policy ceilings were raised or transfer charges abolished. Coinsurance, however, also brought fire offices together where losses had to be jointly adjusted and the task of repairing fire-damaged property had to be shared. After 1760 other forms of collaboration emerged. In 1765 all six London offices shared the costs of prosecuting arsonists at Wapping and Limehouse. In 1770 the London Assurance and the Hand-in-Hand responded to a request from the parish of St Clement Danes to contribute towards the costs of prosecuting an incendiarist there, although the Union rejected the same request. In 1779, at the instigation of the Hand-in-Hand, the fire offices established a joint committee to apply to parliament to tighten the laws against arson.[62] There were also moves to support improvements in London building regulations. In 1763, under the sponsorship of Lord Warkworth, a committee of the six fire offices drafted a bill for enforcing the use by builders of party walls to prevent the spread of fires. This bill received a speedy passage into law.[63] The major building act of 1774 does not seem to have attracted the same level of direct support. The Sun claimed to be the only insurance office which contributed to its costs though the London Assurance had also made a donation to the builders' committee. Meetings were also held between the offices in 1777 to discuss the increase of stamp duty imposed by the government, an additional 5s on all insurance policies over £1000. The insurers agreed to pass the whole of this cost onto their policyholders.[64]

It was not until the mid 1780s that the first great era of collusion began but these earlier examples of joint action paved the way. A new atmosphere was created in which expectations of cooperation rose. This is well demonstrated by the attempt, albeit abortive, by the Westminster Fire Office in 1773 to get other insurers interested in a chartered venture to bring a water supply to Marylebone. The Sun and the Hand-in-Hand did not wish to become involved in the costs of another bill but they did offer passive support. The Hand-in-Hand replied warmly that once the bill was in the Commons 'they will give it all the assistance in their power by speaking to their friends'.[65]

The size and diversity of London's insurance markets

Table 2.1 shows that insurances in London rose from £29m in 1725 to £99m by 1795. Comparing these figures with table 1.2 suggests that the capital accounted

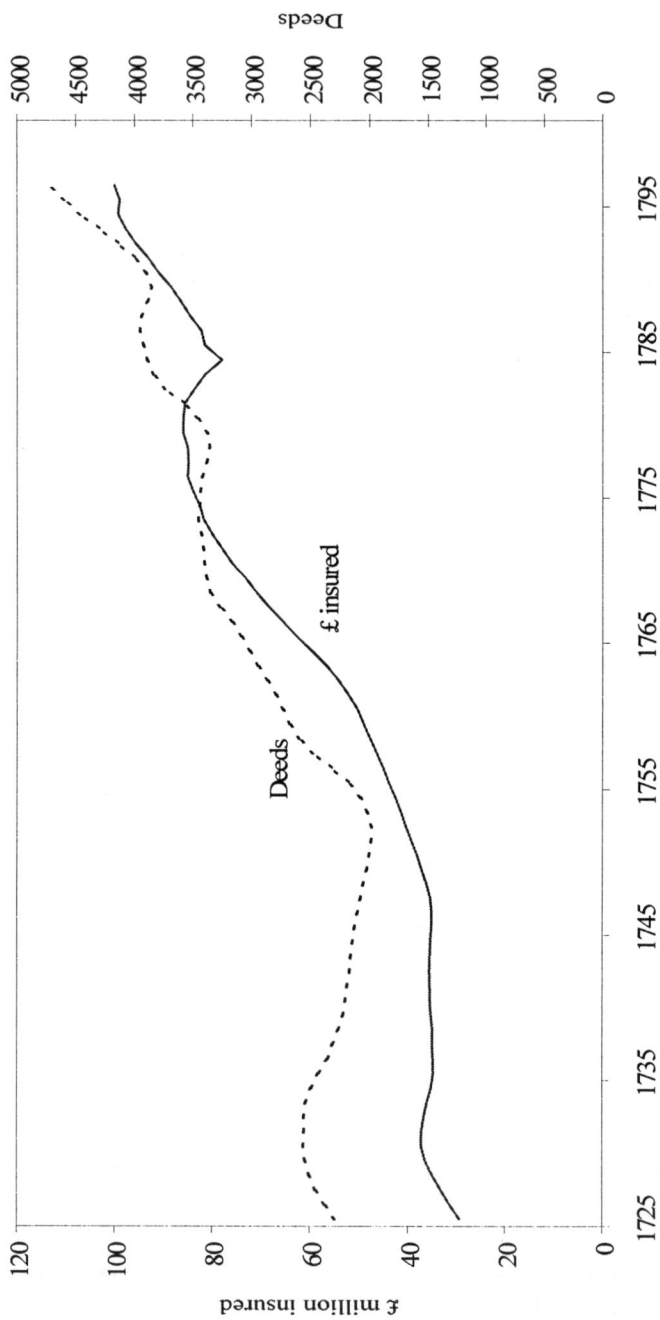

Figure 2.1 London insurances and Middlesex building deeds, 1725-96
Sources: see text.

for over 90 per cent of sums insured against fire in Britain in 1730, just over 70 per cent by 1750, and 55 per cent by the end of the century. The growth of London insurances may be plotted against the volume of construction in London, as represented by building deeds registered for Middlesex (figure 2.1).[66] The data are highly correlated at 0.95, suggesting a close relationship which appears to have lasted until the late 1770s. Until then building and property insurance grew in tandem, in one great roller-coaster of upswing, downswing and recovery. Both series initially rose to peaks around 1730. This period marked a surge in construction in west London and piecemeal development in the east end.[67] Speculative building and fire insurance then slowed down during the 1730s and 1740s. The so-called 'great depression' of the second quarter of the century has been often remarked upon and sometimes exaggerated.[68] London's coal imports, beer production and overseas trade all stagnated and imports did not fully recover until the end of the Seven Years War, although exports rose rather earlier.[69] It is generally held that economic slow-down was accompanied by zero growth or even a decline in the capital's population. The 1740s saw war, rebellion, tightening credit, rising rent arrears, the gin mania at its height, an abnormally high death rate, an agricultural depression and building activity at a low ebb. Recovery began, tentatively, during the 1750s, when Summerson noted a housing shortage.[70] Construction and fire insurance both expanded rapidly during this period. Insurance continued to grow until the late 1770s but building in London suffered a downturn as the war with America intensified. The short period between 1777 and 1782 marked a break in the parallel movement. From the early 1780s insurance declined sharply, while building expanded again. The best explanation for this break is likely to be found in the exogenous shock of taxation. First, the five shillings additional duty levied from 1777 raised the cost of every policy exceeding £1000 by nearly 60 per cent.[71] Second, the introduction in 1782 of the percentage duty on sums insured increased the cost of the cheapest categories of 'common' insurance by 75 per cent. Total sums insured in London, in current values, fell from £86m to £78m between 1780 and 1784, and did not recover their former level until 1788. A depression of demand for property insurance under the higher tax burden seems to have severed the link between the building cycle and insurance, as the latter moved into an era of high costs and slower real growth.

Because no record has survived of the number of properties insured, it is impossible to obtain accurate statistics for the proportion of property insured in the capital. Several contemporary estimates indicate a very fully insured metropolis. Hatton, writing in the early 1700s, gave a combined total of 41000 members and policyholders for the three largest fire offices.[72] Earle has estimated that there were between 23000 and 30000 middle-class and gentry households in London at this time. This suggests that a very high proportion of the households with the greatest propensity to purchase insurance were already protected by the end of Queen Anne's reign, and that the insurance habit had also begun to penetrate groups below the middle class.[73] Maitland stated in 1739 that the total number of houses within the bills was 95068, and that the Hand-in-Hand and the Westminster alone insured

50500 houses.[74] A more complete estimate of current insurance policies on London buildings in 1740 would be around 130000.[75] For comparison, there were about 155000 policies issued on metropolitan property by the six offices insuring buildings in 1795 (including Phoenix), while in 1801 there were 141000 inhabited houses in the whole conurbation.[76] It is impossible to derive accurate figures for houses from policy totals. Some policies will have covered only goods, some houses will have had more than one policy in the same or different offices, some policies will have insured more than one 'house', and some will have covered buildings other than houses. Nevertheless, the estimates suggest that it is likely that no more than a small part of residential London remained uninsured in both 1740 and 1795. It is safe to say that by the middle of the eighteenth century fire insurance in the capital reached well beyond the homes of the upper and middling classes.

Most houses probably were insured, although not for their total value, and the total value of property in London was certainly not covered by insurance. There is plenty evidence of underinsurance, both as a policy on the part of insurers and because of rising property values, so that replacement costs were nearly always greater than insured values.[77] Insurers' attitudes to what and how much they would insure greatly depended on their relationship to particular sectors of the London market. A major characteristic of the capital's huge insurance business was its fragmentation into many individual markets according to location or trade, reflecting the 'composite' metropolitan economy.[78] Insurance markets defined by location included the buildings on London bridge, waterside and dockland risks, and the gentry houses of Westminster. Even insurances in Leadenhall market were given a specific rating by the Union Fire Office in 1751.[79] The district by the river below London bridge provides a good example of how underwriters discriminated by location as well as by industry or trade. This area was exempt from early eighteenth-century building regulations, as it was believed that brick houses could not be built upon timber staves driven into the Thames mud. From the 1760s, as London's seaborne trade expanded vigorously, insurers became seriously concerned about risks in the area. Dwellings, workshops and warehouses were thrown up rapidly, with little regard to the quality or materials of construction or the goods and manufacturing processes they contained. They were squeezed between wharves, rope walks, tar and pitch boilers, sail cloth and turpentine factories, timber yards, cooperages and small docks along the lanes and alleys of St Katherine's, Wapping, Shadwell, Ratcliffe and Limehouse on the north bank of the Thames, and Shad Thames and Rotherhithe to the south. This became notorious to underwriters as the 'waterside district', as distinct from the docklands which were more of a concern after the opening of the West India Dock in 1800. These places had the reputation of being noxious, crowded, drunken and violent, inhabited by river workers, coal heavers and Irish labourers. As a young apprentice in the 1780s, Francis Place and his friends 'went frequently among' the prostitutes and the 'dirty' public houses of St Katherine's. Archenholtz wrote that 'the east end, especially along the shores of the Thames, consists of old houses, the streets there are narrow, dark and ill-paved; inhabited by sailors and other workmen who are employed in the construction of ships and by a great part of the Jews'. Schwarz, who compared income levels and distribution in the area between 1770 and 1813, suggested that the society there was becoming even poorer during this period.[80]

The Hand-in-Hand established a standing committee in 1762 to consider insurances in this district. Following several large fires in 1765, the office suspended insuring houses in any streets within 100 yards of the river on both banks between the Tower and Limehouse dock to the north, and between Battle bridge (just north of Tooley Street) and Cuckolds Point (opposite Limehouse) to the south. A rate was fixed of 6s% premium and 30s% deposit on all brick buildings in this district, with a higher rate for timber buildings. This seems to have been intended as a punitive additional charge for 'situation'. Fires continued to break out. The waterside rate was raised to 8s% and 40s% in 1781 after the three stock companies had raised their prices. The other mutuals restricted themselves to brick buildings in the district or repeatedly reclassified riverside property into higher rate categories.[81] The Sun ordered a second floating fire engine in 1767 to cope with fires by the Thames, but, although it recognised the district as 'very dangerous', little else was done until 1775 when, following further 'very great fires', a survey was carried out of its insurances there. Rates were increased by 50 per cent, but these were soon found to be too low and they were raised again by a further 50 per cent in 1781.[82]

Premium rates for waterside risks reached a peak in the early 1780s. Thereafter, exceptions w ere in creasingly m ade w here p roperty w as de emed t o b e safe, and rates began to fall. The downward trend in waterside premiums may have reflected insurers' willingness to compensate policyholders for the new tax burden on their policies. However, it also seems to have been the product of a real improvement in risk. Fire itself played a part in clearing some of the worst hazards, well before the commencement of the great era of dock building and slum clearance. There may have also been some increase in the replacement of timber by brick constructions, particularly in commercial property. Visiting the area in 1824, Francis Place observed that 'the old wooden houses in most of these places have either been pulled down or burnt down, and others of brick built in their place at different times commencing about 40 years ago'.[83] The insurance records support Place's dating of this improvement of the Thames waterfront to the 1780s.

The trades associated with the riverside or adjoining areas were among the most hazardous in London. Sugar bakeries, distilleries, breweries, gunpowder mills, glass-houses, soap and tallow manufactories, timber yards, ropemakers' yards, oil refineries and warehouses, biscuit bakeries, vinegar factories, turpentine houses, water and wind mills multiplied. London sugar refining firms increased from 80 in 1753 to over 140 by 1776, before the American War brought supply shortages, rising prices and bankruptcies. The number of common brewers in London fluctuated between 140 and 180, but their output grew from 0.9m to 1.3m barrels between 1748 and 1780 while production became concentrated in the hands of the largest firms. Over 430 wax and tallow chandlers already worked in London by 1710. The national output of candles, much of which was located in the capital, rose by 40 per cent between the late 1740s and the early 1780s.[84]

For many of these trades premium rates rose between the 1740s and 1780s. Some also faced outright exclusion by certain insurers. Between 1730 and 1756, at the height of the gin craze, the Union refused to insure compound distillers. In the latter year this ban was lifted and the risks were classified as double hazardous risks to be insured only after a survey. Reports on at least 44 distilleries were considered by the Union between 1758 and 1782. At first as many were rejected as were accepted, although from the mid 1760s, as premium rates rose, the readiness to insure such risks increased.[85] The Sun and the London Assurance refused to insure gunpowder while the Union had a limit on how much gunpowder it would insure per property. Owners of powder mills had to turn to the Hand-in-Hand as the only office which would insure their buildings.[86] The Sun refused to insure turpentine factories from 1721 although the mutual offices were prepared to consider them. In 1762 the Union resolved to insure chemist's shops only if they were inspected first. By 1787 at least 25 had been viewed and 18 accepted, suggesting that Union's directors believed that they could successfully select these risks.[87] Even pawnbrokers could face exclusion from insurance, although this had less to do with any latent fire risk in their premises than with the moral hazard perceived to reside in persons who apparently found it difficult to keep their account books safe for salvage in the event of a conflagration.

By far the greatest concern were the premises of sugar bakers. The largest of these - up to seven storeys tall with up to six giant boiling pans and a capital value of as much as £20000 in buildings and equipment - were quite distinctive among London's manufactories. Most sugar refineries were clustered in three locations around Upper Thames Street, Whitechapel and Wellclose Square.[88] Initially these were charged at modest rates, but underwriters' attitudes quickly changed and prices rose rapidly to a top rate of 30s% by 1734.[89] From the later 1730s fire offices moved in two opposite directions. The Union, the Westminster and the London Assurance abandoned the sugar industry altogether. By contrast, the Hand-in-Hand continued to insure at existing rates. By 1739 it had £50000 of sugar house insurances on its books which must have represented over 30 different sugar firms or perhaps one-half of the industry in London.[90] The Sun, facing complaints from sugar bakers about the cost of insurance, opted to reduce rates, so that it charged just 18s% for a £3000 policy by the late 1740s.[91] After mid-century both offices became more involved with the industry though claims increased in frequency. From 1761 the Sun began to keep a separate monthly account of premiums and losses on sugar houses. They were also reclassified by type of construction and by type of stove, a classification which remained largely unchanged until the late 1780s and was also adopted by the REA. The Hand-in-Hand kept its rates low but suffered repeated fires. Between 1721 and 1738 the office paid claims totalling nearly £5000 on just four sugar house fires. From 1751 to 1800 the office paid out over £14000 on 22 London sugar houses, 17 of which had burnt to the ground. As the average loss fell by half between these two periods this suggests that the Hand-in-Hand was insuring a greater number of smaller, possibly more hazardous, sugar houses after 1750 than before. If the sugar industry, particularly in the good years between the Seven Years War and the American War of Independence, expanded principally through an increase in the number of production units rather than through economies of scale, then the Hand-in-Hand seem to have tracked this expansion closely, though at some cost.

Other metropolitan markets proved more attractive. Aristocratic and gentry properties were eminently insurable. By the 1750s most English, Welsh and Scottish peers and members of parliament owned or rented a property in London.[92] All the London fire offices enjoyed some patronage. The Sun was insuring the town houses of several peers by the 1750s. The Hand-in-Hand insured Carlton House in Pall Mall, Apsley House, Bedford House, Ranelagh House, the houses of Lord Harvey and the Duchess of Kent in St James's Square, and those of the Duke of Buccleuch, the Earl of Hertford and Lord Carlisle in or near Grosvenor Square, for sums ranging up to £30000.[93] London's mansions were not immune from catching fire - Devonshire House burnt to the ground in 1733 and Northumberland House was damaged by fire in 1780 - but, in general, this was a lucrative market for underwriters to work.[94]

There were also institutional properties, sufficiently numerous in London to constitute several insurance markets of their own. Many of the city livery companies not only had their own halls to insure but also a great quantity of property in and around the capital, and their rental incomes were rising. The Haberdashers, for instance, had estates in Shoreditch and Camberwell, as well as several outside London.[95] With its connections to the guilds the Hand-in-Hand was favourably positioned for this business. During the century it insured the property of at least fourteen livery companies, with the REA, the Sun and the Phoenix participating in some of the risks as coinsurers. Between 1771 and 1794 at least seven guilds which insured with the Hand-in-Hand owned buildings which caught fire, including the halls of the Cooks and the Drapers. The former, rather inauspiciously for the craft it represented, burnt down twice, in 1764 and 1771.[96]

Hospitals also drew the attention of London insurers. Altogether there were nearly 40 hospitals, infirmaries and dispensaries in London by 1810, and this total excludes female refuges and orphan asylums such as Magdalen (1758) and Lambeth (1759).[97] The largest hospitals were expensive affairs. The three extensions to London Hospital carried out between 1758 and 1781 cost £60000.[98] Several institutions also owned other insurable property. Foundling Hospital, for example, possessed a sizeable block of land east of Southampton Row, on which nearly 600 houses had been built by 1802.[99] The Hand-in-Hand also insured a considerable portion of this market. Between the 1730s and early 1750s the office accumulated at least eight major London hospitals in its registers. In one year alone, 1746, six hospitals renewed 29 policies with the Hand-in-Hand worth £41700.[100] A close relationship to the medical world is further suggested by the fact that the Hand-in-Hand rented its main premises in Angel Court from Christ's Hospital.[101] Hospitals seem to have been relatively safe from fire. They often stood alone in open fields. The grandest were faced with stone and most others were of brick. Greenwich did burn down in 1779 and Bridewell and Immanuel Hospital in

Kentish Town suffered arson attacks, but generally hospital property, often cautiously managed by governing bodies, was good business for insurers. At times competition could be keen. In 1794, for instance, the Hand-in-Hand offered free policies to entice St Bartholomew's to transfer the insurances on 'several houses' from the Sun.[102]

London theatres and other places of entertainment attracted insurers because of their size and value which could rank with the large buildings in the capital. They proved hazardous to insure. The cost of rebuilding Haymarket Theatre after the fire of 1789 was said to be over £85000, plus a further £50000 for the cost of the furniture, wardrobe and scenery. Covent Garden cost £300000 to rebuild after the fire of 1808.[103] The number of playhouses in London remained low due to the monopoly on stage drama enjoyed by the two 'patent' theatres, Drury Lane and Covent Garden, under the Licensing Act of 1737. As opposition to this monopoly grew during the second half of the century, lesser ventures such as Astley's Amphitheatre or Sadler's Wells thrived, legitimately, on the popularity of spectacles, musical entertainments and pantomimes. This trend increased the fire hazards. As the patent theatres were enlarged to accommodate more customers, they led the way in replacing oil lamps with candles, adopting coloured silks and gauzes for dramatic lighting, designing illuminated transparencies and huge painted backdrops, and introducing traps, flying engines and machinery for scene shifting.[104] As early as 1758 the Sun introduced a clause on playhouse insurances exempting the office from liability for fire damage occurring during performances or rehearsals. The Hand-in-Hand inspected the Royal Circus and the Lyceum in 1795 and rejected both, being 'confirmed in this opinion from the frequency of fires happening to public theatres and the practice of other Offices - some of which increase the premium to a very considerable degree, and others who totally reject them'. Other buildings rejected included the Opera House and the Panorama in Leicester Fields, the latter due to the hazard of internal stoves. The Hand-in-Hand, however, did insure Sadler's Wells, Astley's, and the Pantheon in Oxford Road, the latter jointly with the Sun, the Phoenix and the REA for a total of £15000.[105] Concern was such that theatres were among the first risks to be considered by the Phoenix, the Sun and the REA when they began to cooperate in the late 1780s. In the year the King's Theatre in Haymarket burnt down, the REA invited its two partners to discuss premium rates for theatres, as 'the practice of exhibiting artificial fireworks in public theatres, and of using an extraordinary number of lights during the performance of pantomimes, and also for decorations on the holding of masquerades and other entertainments have much increased the danger of fire in such buildings'. Theatre rates continued to be revised upwards during the early 1790s, causing some theatre owners to underinsure. The Theatre Royal in Drury lane, for instance, was built by subscription in 1793 at a cost of £300000, but insured for only £35600, 'owing to the high terms demanded by the Insurance Offices'. This was a blessing for the latter as the hazards remained terrible. The Theatre Royal burnt down in 1809. Astley's Amphitheatre was gutted by fire in

1794, and again in 1803 when the conflagration, predictably, was caused by exploding fireworks.[106]

The fires of Georgian London

The multiplication of trades, industries and property types, together with the survival of timber structures and the limited impact of building legislation, made the task of underwriting in the capital increasingly complex. As figure 1.5 illustrates, losses by fire increased from the 1740s in four surges, with peaks in 1748, 1764, 1783 and 1793, each one higher than before. The majority of these losses were on property in the capital where contemporaries were well aware of the problem. 'I have heard it confidently asserted by persons well acquainted with London and Amsterdam', wrote Samuel Marshall in 1805, 'that after making all fair allowances, there is, upon average, more property destroyed by fire in the former in one year, than in the latter in seven'.[107] As to be expected from the geographical concentration of industries and building types, fires were very unevenly distributed throughout the capital. This can be seen from an analysis of 481 fires which occurred in London between 1735 and 1800 and destroyed over 1400 properties (see table 2.2).[108] The mean number of properties destroyed by each fire suggests the intensity of fires in the south and east, especially in the riverside districts of Southwark, Rotherhithe, Wapping, Shadwell and Ratcliffe, as well as the density of housing there. As argued above, the level of fire damage was due to the prevalence of timber structures and hazardous materials, and also to the inadequacy of fire-fighting facilities in these areas. The average cost of fires (excluding buildings only partially damaged) was also high in the east and the south, reflecting the volume of commercial property there, and in the City where property values were high. The rate of destruction, as measured by the ratio of houses burnt down (excluding other non-residential properties) to the total housing stock in 1801, was greatest in the crowded central London parishes, covering the area from Holborn to Soho and Covent Garden, as well as the City itself and the east. By contrast it was up to seven times safer to live in the north or west of the capital during the second half of the eighteenth century. This suggests that a timber/brick division persisted in Hanoverian London, running along east/west and south/north axes.

The insurance offices devoted considerable energy and resources to preventing and fighting fires in the capital. Each office had its own brigade of firemen, supplied with coats, badges, helmets and boots, a continually replenished stock of buckets, axes and hooks (known as preventers) for salvage work, and several engines of various sizes for pumping water. Brigades, at full complement, usually numbered 30, which was the maximum number of exemptions from naval impressment allowed by the Admiralty for the firemen of each office under a law of 1707.[109] Most insurance offices also kept an auxiliary force of some 20 'porters' or

Table 2.2   Fires and fire damage in London, 1735-1800

	Fires in sample	Replacement cost of property totally destroyed (£)	Houses totally destroyed	All properties destroyed
City	137	174318	257	349
East	128	154149	380	500
South	77	93822	187	291
Central	70	55870	117	150
West	38	22314	50	63
North	31	14568	31	58
Totals	481	515041	1022	1411

	Mean no. properties destroyed per fire	Mean no. houses destroyed per fire	Mean replacement cost per fire (£)	Per caput replacement cost 1801 (£)	Inhabited houses in 1801, per destroyed house
City	2.5	1.9	1272	1.39	61
East	3.9	3.0	1204	0.69	73
South	3.8	2.4	1218	0.90	126
Central	2.1	1.7	798	0.65	82
West	1.7	1.3	587	0.11	451
North	1.9	1.0	470	0.18	363

Notes and Sources: 1. Fires are those recorded by the Hand-in-Hand as having totally destroyed one or more insured properties. Compiled from GL Ms 8666/12-28, Hand-in-Hand, DM, 1735-1800 *passim*. 2. 'Houses' as counted by the Hand-in-Hand surveyors. All are assumed to be residential. Other properties were counted separately and cover a wide range of domestic and commercial property from sheds to sugar refineries. There was no weighting of any sort given to the size or type of property in the sample. 3. Locations traced using J. Wisdom's index to Richard Horwood's map of London 1792-9, in Laxton, *A to Z of Regency L ondon*. 3. Population and housing totals for 1801 from George, London *Life*, appendix B. 4. Districts comprised the following parishes, hamlets and liberties; City: City within and without the walls. East: St Botolph Aldgate without, Limehouse, Mile End, Old Ford, Ratcliff, Shadwell, Shoreditch, Spitalfields, St George in the East, St Katherine, Stepney, Tower, Wapping, Whitechapel. South: Bermondsey, Lambeth, Newington, Nine Elms, Rotherhithe, Southwark (six parishes). Central: Rolls, Saffron Hill, St Andrew Holborn, St Anne Soho, St Clement Danes, St Giles, St Mary le Strand, St Paul Covent Garden, Temple. West: St George Hanover Sq., St George Bloomsbury, St James Piccadilly, St Martin in the Fields, St Marylebone, Westminster (2 parishes). North: St Luke Old Street, St Pancras, Clerkenwell. All other locations, including the outer villages such as Chelsea, Stratford, Islington, Hammersmith, were treated as 'outside London'. There were 58 fires 'outside London' in the dataset, burning down 96 properties at a replacement cost of £42355. The locations of 12 fires could not be traced.

'supernumeraries' to assist with salvage, so that by 1780 there were about 300 firemen employed regularly in London by the insurance offices. Given the generous emoluments there was no shortage of recruits. A scale of fees was paid by most offices for every attendance at a fire or an alarm, which usually ranged from 6d to 2s 6d according to the seriousness of the incident.

Most firemen were recruited from the ranks of the Thames watermen. Despite the rewards, they proved a difficult lot to manage. Historians have pointed to the watermen's reputation as a rough, reckless and heavy drinking crew, although they have also highlighted the long service and loyalty of some firemen against what has been described as 'occasional' incidents of bad behaviour.[110] In fact company records reveal that such incidents were frequent and that the average turnover of firemen due to dismissals, resignations and deaths was between five and ten per cent a year during the last quarter of the eighteenth century. Between 1770 and 1799 the Hand-in-Hand and the Sun together dismissed, suspended or reprimanded at least 53 firemen, while the London Assurance sacked 27 firemen between 1761 and 1802. Disciplinary action was usually taken for drunkenness, abusive language or 'misbehaviour' at fires, for absenteeism, for falsely claiming attendance at fire alarms or for pawning their office badges which provided protection from the press gangs. Setting up as a publican or spirits retailer could also result in dismissal.

Occasionally firemen were sacked on suspicion of theft, and at least one Hand-in-Hand fireman went to the gallows for burglary before the office had the chance to show him the door.[111] In periods when fires and fire alarms were increasing, some insurers introduced a system of registration and certification of attendance for firemen and limited the number who could be paid for turning out. This was done in order to reduce costs and stamp out fraudulent invoices being made out on behalf of firemen and porters, as well as to reduce the moral hazard of false alarms. The Union first implemented such a system in 1734, making each man sign or mark a sheet upon arrival at a fire. The Hand-in-Hand acted in 1753, 1767 and 1785 to limit the number of firemen paid for turning out at alarms, and the Sun did the same in 1741 and 1767.

If insurers made strenuous efforts to discipline their brigades, they also recognised the bravery of their firemen and offered small amounts of compensation for their injuries. Such injuries were usually serious and sometimes fatal. Eyes and hands were burnt, arms, legs and ribs were broken, feet and hands were crushed by falling chimneys or walls. One of the London Assurance's firemen had a nail driven 'almost right through his foot' at a fire in 1750, while in 1758 the back of a Sun fireman was broken by a beam falling on him, so that he had to be carried home from the fire in a chair. Some firemen were buried alive in the ruins of collapsed houses. Others caught influenza from working in icy water and mud without adequate protection. The firemen of the Westminster office petitioned in 1763 to be provided with strong boots, 'as they are frequently obliged to stand in water in working the engines and their lives were in danger last winter from the extreme cold'. The Union and the London Assurance had already agreed to supply their firemen with new boots every few years.[112] Most offices offered a few guineas in relief payments to injured firemen or their bereaved relatives. The seriousness of the injury, length of convalescence and amount of surgeon's fees, as well as family size and the material condition of surviving relatives, determined the level of compensation. The modest sums thus combined elements of accident, medical and loss of earnings insurance with, on occasion, funeral and death benefits, although there was little consistency and no uniform scale of relief applied by the offices. The frequency of these payments reflected the dangers. Between 1736 and 1790 the Sun paid out over £230 in relief to 73 firemen or their widows, the equivalent of more than two brigades disabled by accidents. At least 20 of these firemen died of their injuries.

The number involved in firefighting was much larger than the size of the insurance brigades suggest, not only because of the high rate of attrition but also because of the many helping hands attracted by the excitement, and by the beer freely distributed to encourage efforts against a blaze. Spectators, if they pitched in to help, could expect some pecuniary reward for their efforts. In 1758, for instance, the Sun distributed £29 to those who had assisted at a large fire in Gun Dock, Wapping.[113] On such occasions whole neighbourhoods would turn out, with local innkeepers and employers ensuring that pubs and workshops spilled their occupants onto the streets to help. These events, and the noisy race to a fire by the different insurance brigades in their colourful liveries, became part of London street theatre. The miserly sculptor Nollekens, whose chimneys were rarely cleaned, was frequently annoyed by 'fire engines and their regular attendents, the mob'.[114] A large fire provided an opportunity for different social ranks to rub shoulders. Horace Walpole was not alone in being fascinated. 'You know I cannot resist going to a fire', he wrote to a correspondent in 1755, 'for it is certainly the only horrid sight that is fine'. At a fire in Downing Street he stood in the crowd for an hour 'to hear their discourse'. 'One man was relating at how many fires he had happened to be present, and did not think himself at all unlucky in passing by, just at this.'[115] At a fire in Old Street in 1771 a wall fell down under the weight of spectators, killing one and injuring several others.[116] The early Hanoverians carried on the royal tradition established at the Great Fire by turning out personally to supervise these battles, and the Lord Mayor and Aldermen were often present at fires in the City to encourage the firemen. On occasion, directors of insurance offices would arrive and pay firefighters out of their own pocket. In some offices the directors were obliged by regulation to attend fires and direct the firemen.[117] Insurers made great efforts to encourage property owners and others to salvage goods, by offering sums to cover the cost of removal to a secure warehouse and by reassuring policyholders that any damage caused to their goods whilst they were being removed from a fire would be reimbursed by the office.[118]

As less reliance was placed upon parishes to deal with fires, the insurance fire brigades became quasi-'public' institutions, a process more or less complete by the mid eighteenth century. By then firemen were regarded as holding a kind of public office. In 1751 the London Assurance posted 500 sheets for public consumption showing the instructions to and addresses of the office's porters and firemen. Most brigades marched with music on the days of their companies' general meetings. The offices recognised the publicity value of this. In 1789 the Union required its firemen on their march to distribute copies of 'an account of the design and state of the Office' as part of an effort to stem declining membership. The brigades were also used as a special constabulary at other public ceremonies such as the Lord Mayor's procession or George III's review of the City volunteers in 1799.[119]

There were several other private fire brigades in Georgian London such as those belonging to the 12 principal livery companies or the brigade of Lincoln's Inn. The main alternative to the insurance brigades, however, was the system of parish engines and equipment set up in the aftermath of the Great Fire and reinforced by legislation during Queen Anne's reign. Churchwardens were made legally responsible for the maintenance of buckets, ladders, axes, shovels, hoses, water squirts and an engine, and for installing stop-cocks on the water pipes in their parishes and ensuring that these matched the sockets on the engines. There were penalties imposed for default and rewards for those engine keepers who were first to arrive at a fire.[120] Defoe praised the 'great number of admirable engines, of which almost every parish has one...so that no sooner does a fire break out, but the house is surrounded with engines, and a flood of water poured upon it...'. In fact the efficiency of the parish brigades was questionable. As early as 1716 the Hand-in-Hand and the Union were warning churchwardens of their readiness to prosecute those who neglected their fire brigades. The Hand-in-Hand repeatedly tried to bully the parishes into improving their services. In 1730 it sent two officers 'to make inquiry into the fire plugs and stopcocks within the Bills...and report...all defaulters and the deficiencies they shall find anywhere'.[121] Such efforts were mostly in vain. Parish fire-fighting equipment often fell into disrepair and the brigades declined to the state later caricatured by Dickens, with his perspiring beadle and enthusiastic team of boys harnessed to a fire engine which they did not know how to operate.[122]

Another concern was the supply of water. Here too Defoe's optimistic account did not tally with the experience of the insurance offices.[123] London's firefighters had repeated problems finding enough water, or sometimes any water at all. Walpole, tempted out to view a fire in Sackville Street in 1761, reported that 'four houses were in flames before they could find a drop of water'. Even houses by the river could not depend on their vicinity to water. At a fire in Wapping in 1758, a sailmaker's, a biscuit baker's and 15 houses either side burnt down 'before water could be had to supply the engines, it being then ebb tide'.[124] Well into the last quarter of the century there were frequent accounts of fires raging uncontrollably for an hour or more while a source of water was sought. Sometimes, as at a fire in Limehouse in 1775, firemen could not find the plugs on water pipes and nobody present could help them. Often when the pipes were opened they were dry or did not contain enough water for all the waiting engines. At Limehouse the flames spread rapidly from the quantity of pitch, tar, resin and old junk in the buildings so that the firemen could not get close. The tide was out so that no water could be obtained from the river and the fire was only prevented from spreading by a firebreak caused by the slipway down to the horse ferry. When water was eventually obtained, it took 17 engines seven hours to bring it under control.[125] The consequence of chronic water shortages was that fires were allowed to take hold and burn longer and more intensely, causing greater damage than would otherwise have been the case.

It was viewed by some as an irony that a city which, it was argued, was so well furnished with piped water, especially by comparison with Paris, should have this problem. Numerous remedies were suggested, some of which presumed investment by the insurance offices. These included further extensions to pipes to bring water up to individual houses, regular inspection of stop cocks, and the construction of new reservoirs dedicated to the use of the insurance brigades.[126] The insurers themselves were slow to respond, wary of the costs, but during the 1780s several did contribute towards the construction of new reservoirs and pumps, at least where these were located near their head offices.[127] By this period many believed that an improvement was already visible, at least in Westminster and parts of the City. Streets were cleaner and in better repair, rainwater was properly caught in gutters and pipes, sewers and drains were deeper and better constructed, and 'by the addition of several new works', wrote a master at Christ's Hospital in 1781, 'water is become much more plentiful than it was heretofore'.[128]

As well as supporting fire-fighting facilities, the insurance offices also backed efforts to prevent fires in London. Some encouragement, though little cash, was given to the inventors of fire-prevention devices who appeared in numbers during the third quarter of the century. There was also support for the building legislation of 1764 and 1774. Although there was a residual scepticism among the insurance boardrooms about the efforts of the authorities, regulations were nevertheless invoked where it was thought they might help tackle a problem. One concern was the carelessness of domestic servants with candles. Under an act of Queen Anne, servants found guilty of negligently causing a fire could be heavily fined or face 18 months hard labour. In 1761 a coachmen was fined £130 under the act, as 'a warning...to other servants', for leaving a burning candle in a stable near Saville Row. The candle fell over and caused a fire which destroyed several houses. Four years later the Union printed one thousand copies of the act and distributed one with every policy, asking its members to display it 'in a conspicuous place in your kitchen'.[129] Another worry was the popularity of fireworks. Francis Place recalled that in his youth fireworks were freely sold in London 'at many oil shops and at most chandler's shops'. As part of the coronation preparations in 1761 all fireworks were banned from Whitehall to Millbank until seven days after the ceremony. In 1748 the Union offered a reward for information on those 'making, giving, selling or vending any squibs, serpents or other such fireworks', with a view to prosecuting those responsible for a fire at a 'squib or serpent seller's' house in Blackfriars, 'where many hundreds of these fireworks were carelessly discharged, bursting through the shop windows to the great danger of passengers, and also setting fire to the goods of the fire and shop'.[130]

It was arson which drove the insurers to have most recourse to the law. The Phoenix Fire Office filed lawsuits against at least 17 arsonists between 1782 and

1800, compared with just six between 1800 and 1830. Most of these individuals were policyholders attempting to defraud the office. The national trend in arson of all kinds, fraudulent, criminal, malicious and rebellious, was rising during the second half of the eighteenth century and the capital shared fully in this. At least 25 cases of metropolitan arson can be identified in the records of four insurance offices between 1760 and 1791. Insurers devoted considerable resources and energy to combating incendiaries. Rewards of £50 or £100 were commonly offered for information leading to convictions. Between 1765 and 1791 the Sun spent nearly £1400 supporting the detection and prosecution of 15 individuals. The office also used Bow Street Runners to catch arsonists outside London or those who had fled the capital, even contributing 12 guineas to the Runners' Christmas box in 1790.[131] The struggle brought insurers together in mutual interest as they shared the costs of prosecuting arsonists and supporting new legislation. Insurers also used the law to pursue looting at fires, often employing their own firemen and porters as witnesses to help catch and convict looters.[132]

Underwriting performance

The proportion of timber in London's buildings did not decline before 1800. The burden of fire damage on insured property was rising to new levels. Risk assessment was becoming more difficult with the diversification of the economy and the geographical concentration of fires within the capital. Dependence on the insurance fire brigades was growing with the deterioration of parish facilities. Arson, fraud and looting were on the increase. So how profitable was fire insurance in eighteenth-century London?

Contemporaries measured the profitability of underwriting by the proportion of premium income left after claims and management expenses had been deducted. Incomplete record survival means that this can only be partially reconstructed. We have annual premiums and losses (the amount paid out on claims) for the London Assurance from 1721, for the REA from 1732, and for the Sun from 1743. 'Loss ratios' (claims paid expressed as a percentage of premiums, gross of expenses) for these offices include differing amounts of provincial insurance. For the mutual offices there was no exact premium equivalent with which to calculate a 'loss ratio'.[133] Instead there are annual data for losses and sums insured by the mutuals (only from 1760 in the case of the Westminster), and this allows us at least to examine the relative burden of fire damage on their business.

Figure 2.2 presents the annual loss ratios of the three stock companies as five year moving averages. Figure 2.3 shows the losses of the London mutuals expressed as a percentage of their sums insured, also as five year moving averages. Both graphs reveal the 1730s and 1740s, the mid 1770s and the late 1790s to be the periods of greatest underwriting profitability. Several points might be made. First,

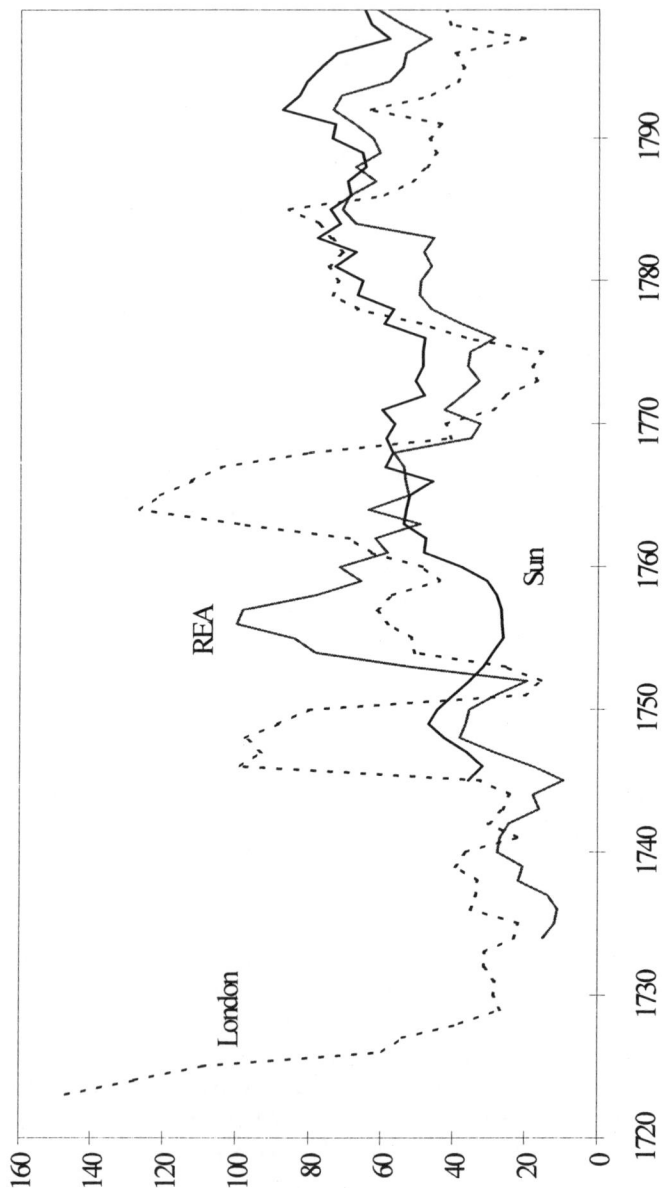

Figure 2.2 Loss ratios of three London proprietary offices, 1723-1800
Sources: see text.

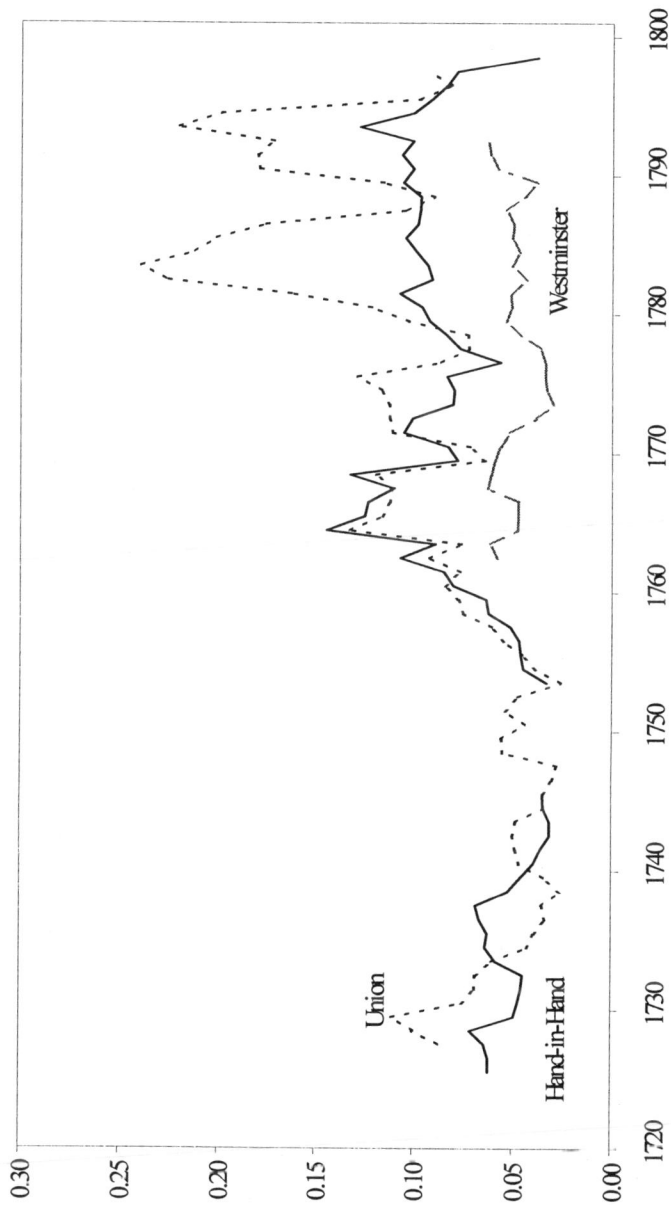

Figure 2.3 Loss ratios of three London mutual offices, 1723–1800
Sources: see text.

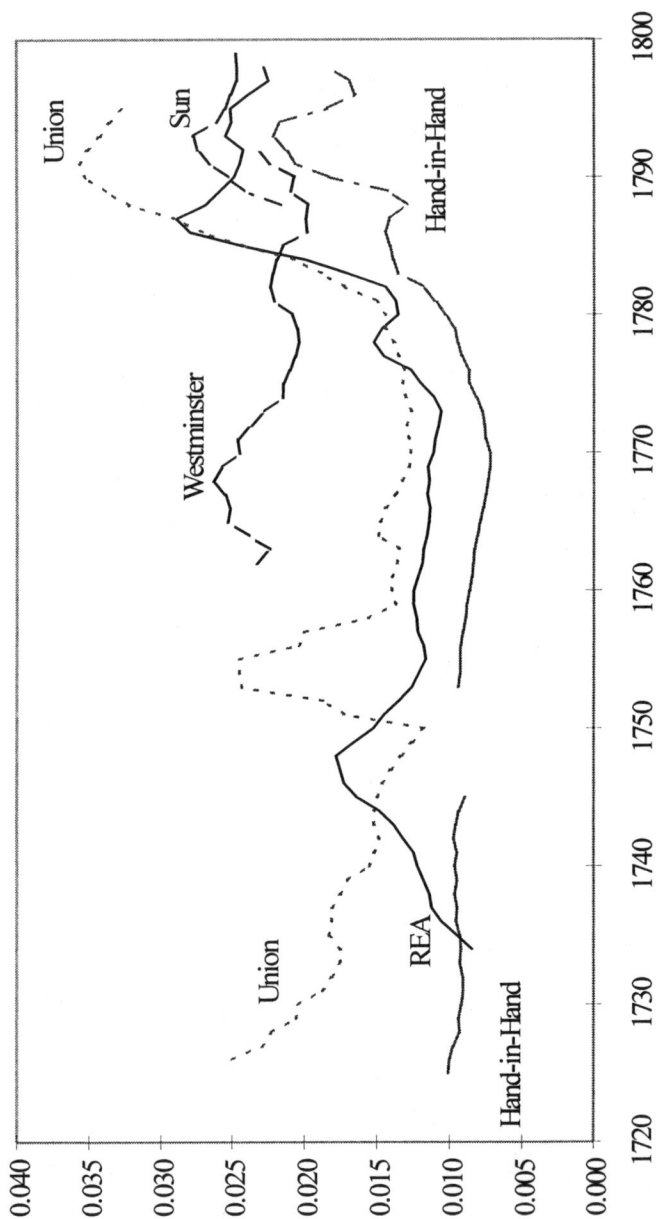

Figure 2.4 Operating costs of five London fire offices, 1723-1800
Sources: see text.

there was no correlation between the performance of the mutual offices, with one striking exception, the relationship between the Hand-in-Hand and the Union during the period 1753-70, when the claims experience of these offices moved nearly in tandem (r = 0.96). These sibling insurers, the one covering buildings and the other goods, were expanding into the same markets and suffering similar fluctuations in claims. By contrast, figure 2.3 demonstrates how comparatively free of fire damage the Westminster office remained during the second half of the century, probably reflecting the brick-built solidity of its west end insurances. Second, figure 2.2 shows that the two corporations, especially before 1770, experienced more volatile loss ratios than the Sun, with its larger fire business and greater geographical spread of risks. By 1770 the Sun had a premium income of £80000, compared with the REA's £16000 and the London Assurance's £7000.

Third, from the early 1770s there was some convergence between the claims experience of the three stock companies. The correlation coefficients rise substantially after 1771. The loss ratios of the REA and the Sun were correlated at 0.78 for the period 1771-99. It was argued above that the close association between the output (sums insured) of the London fire offices and the output of the London building industry did not survive the 1770s. Figure 2.2 suggests that a shared underwriting cycle was emerging among the London insurers about the same time, perhaps as a result of greater collusion between the offices and a common response to trends in fire hazards.

The extent to which loss ratios translated into underwriting profits depended upon the burden of operating costs, including management expenses, rent, salaries and commission. Here too haphazard record survival creates problems. We have unspecified annual expense data for the REA from 1732, but none for the London Assurance. Data for the Sun exist only from 1786. Figures for 'salaries and other disbursements' have survived for the Hand-in-Hand and the Union from 1723 and for the Westminster from 1760. These can be expressed as a percentage of sums insured in order to provide a comparison with the stock companies. Figure 2.4 reveals the relative stability of operating costs in both types of office between 1750 and the late 1770s, after higher levels experienced earlier in the century. The jump in the Union's costs during the early 1750s is explained by major expenditure on new purpose-built offices. Before 1780 the Westminster proved more costly to run than other offices, probably due to higher salaries and office rents. Expenses rose sharply in all offices during the 1780s and early 1790s before turning down again at the end of the century. The stock companies spent to extend their provincial agency networks, while clerical costs at both the Union and the Hand-in-Hand rose as their insurances collapsed. Salary inflation caused some of the increase in the early 1790s, and all offices were paying out more for surveying and risk inspection than before. Overall, figure 2.4 suggests that the mutual insurers, with no agencies and their business concentrated in the metropolitan area, had no obvious cost advantages over their joint-stock competitors, nor, indeed, does it indicate that there were any major economies of scale in the industry.

The London Assurance and the REA had difficult beginnings in the early 1720s with heavy losses which would have undermined their stability had fire underwriting been of much importance to them.[134] They survived because of their large marine insurance business and because of their high levels of capitalisation. As figure 2.2 shows, the London Assurance suffered terrible losses during the later 1740s, in particular from the huge fire in Cornhill which destroyed the company's head office and many of its records as well as 100 other houses.[135] In 1755-6 fires in Billingsgate and Wapping gave the REA its worst underwriting result of the century. During the 1760s the London Assurance again suffered badly, paying out nearly £9000 after one fire at Shadwell in 1763.[136] At these times fire underwriting certainly did not make money. For all three stock companies rising loss ratios from the late 1770s threatened to wipe out underwriting surpluses, once operating costs of 15 to 20 per cent were accounted for.

Generally, however, for most of the eighteenth century fire insurance was a profitable business for the stock companies. Certainly in none of these offices during the second half of the century did fire underwriting profits normally cover the annual dividends paid to shareholders, but this did not matter so long as they could rely on an expanding investment income. Dependency upon investments increased rapidly. During the 1760s the Sun was distributing an average of £19000 annually to its shareholders, while the average underwriting surplus was less than £16000. By the 1790s, the shortfall was six times larger than this, with the average dividend amounting to £31000 and the average underwriting surplus running at £12000 a year. Investment practices are examined in chapter nine below and it is sufficient to note here that the Sun's penchant for mortgage lending helped its shareholders enjoy annual returns which leapt from 13 per cent in the early 1740s to 65 per cent by the mid 1780s, while the market value of their shares also soared.[137]

For the two corporations, with their focus on marine insurance, fire underwriting profits were not critical to dividends, particularly as investment income also grew in importance. Nevertheless, the satisfactory nature of fire insurance profitability over the long term can also be seen in the way the REA's 'fire fund' grew after mid-century and gave the corporation the financial strength to deal with the losses of the 1780s and early 1790s.[138] By the end of the century the London Assurance was the weakest fire insurer among the stock companies, with market share declining and premiums stagnating.[139] Despite this, the corporation's loss ratios on fire insurance were improving in the mid 1790s, the overall profit rate doubled between 1784 and 1798, and the corporation managed to raise the dividend to over six per cent, only slightly below the return offered by the REA to its shareholders.[140]

The mutuals fared less well. Of these the Westminster had the best record. Although expensive to run, the office did not suffer from the fires which hit the City-based insurers. Sums insured doubled between 1760 and 1790 and its share of the metropolitan market continued to rise long after the decline of the two other mutual offices had begun. Nevertheless, 'neat profits', when expressed as a proportion of total income from underwriting and investments, fell from 12 per cent during the 1770s to six per cent in the early 1790s.[141] In 1782 the office launched annual policies, 'merely as a trade'. Annual policyholders were not regarded as members and were not entitled to any distribution of profits. This annual business proved profitable and it accounted for 24 per cent of total sums insured by 1805.

When losses were heavy, all mutual offices met them by selling stocks as well as through levies on members. Raiding investments in this way helped reduce the burden on members' deposits thereby encouraging loyalty and goodwill. If abused, however, this remedy could be fatal, especially in a period when the price of gilts was falling. Both the Union and the Hand-in-Hand dug deeply into members' deposits in order to meet claims from huge fires in the City and the waterside district during the 1760s. In an effort to protect its members, the Hand-in-Hand raided its investments even more frequently, so that by the end of 1794, after paying claims from a huge fire at Ratcliffe Highway, total net assets (stock, cash and property minus unpaid losses) were at their lowest level for over half a century. Other indicators were also in free-fall. There were 39000 members of the Hand-in-Hand in 1770, but just 16000 by the end of the century. In the same period sums insured by the office fell by 35 per cent to £10.6m, and its market share collapsed. The situation at the Union was even worse. The amount it paid out annually in claims, which was never above £5000 before 1760, fell below this level only six times between 1770 and 1792. The office's assets shrank from £84000 in the late 1760s to just £10300 by 1795. Many of the stocks sold were traded in at a loss on their book value in the bear markets of the 1780s. Sums insured, which had grown to £8m by the early 1770s, plunged to £3m by the late 1790s. Furthermore, while the insurance and investment base of the office was rapidly vanishing, operating costs rose steeply. By the 1790s, relative to size, the Union was by far the most expensively managed of all the London insurers.

Both mutuals engaged in an increasingly desperate search for solutions. The Hand-in-Hand rejected the answer found by the Westminster, the introduction of a separate class of lower rated but non-profit sharing annual policies. It did extend its business to the whole of England and Wales in 1789, and it also attempted to reclassify as many insurances as possible from brick to timber in order to increase premiums and deposits. By 1800 some 20000 houses had been surveyed for this purpose. This brought in several hundred pounds of additional income each year but at some cost to customer relations. The Union attempted a much wider range of measures. It stepped up its investigations into categories of hazardous insurances. In 1773 it ceased paying dividends on terminating policies, which had been introduced in 1759. It made two hefty deductions from members' deposits of 25 per cent and 50 per cent respectively in 1777 and 1781. A new bookkeeping system was introduced in 1782, and seven years later an emergency fund for 'extraordinary losses' was established. In 1785 the business was extended to all of England and Wales, and this was accompanied by various publicity drives. During the 1780s and 1790s, under continual pressure from a committee of members, there was a series of administrative reforms which included revising office procedures, cancelling customary perquisites enjoyed by clerks, and cutting directors' fees. Business, nevertheless, continued to decline to a low point in 1803-4, when sums insured amounted to just £2.3m. The office was then turned around by three innovations. Annual and short-term insurances were introduced. An agency network was established for the first time outside London and the Union embarked on a share issue, probably the first case of demutualisation in British business history.[142] The capital, £300000 in 1500 shares, helped refloat the office funds, while country agencies and the new types of policies restored sums insured to £6.1m by 1813.

The mutuals survived but the experience had been traumatic. In 1725 the Hand-in-Hand had been the biggest fire office in the world, insuring over one-third of the world's largest market. In 1760 the three London mutual offices remained highly competitive against their joint-stock rivals, accounting for about half of all income generated by fire underwriting in Britain. By the end of the century that aggregate share had slumped to less than ten per cent. The story of the mutuals belies the idea that fire insurance in eighteenth-century London was anything other than turbulent. The markets beyond the capital, which are the subject of the next chapter, proved no less difficult to master.

Notes

[1]   From 'London Sparrows' (1836), in Ashfield, *Romantic Women Poets*, p.250.

[2]   Corfield, *Impact of English Towns*, p.15. London population estimates from Woods, 'Population Growth', p.137.

[3]   Williams, *The Country and the City*, p.188.

[4]   George, *London Life*, p.319 and appendix IIIB.

[5]   Defoe, *Tour*, pp.286-7; Burke, *Correspondence*, vol.VII, p.85, letter to Reverend Robert Dodge, 29 Feb. 1792.

[6]   George, *London Life*, p.319.

[7]   Cobbett, *Rural Rides*, p.31. Cf. 'The Cit's Country Box' by Robert Lloyd (1756), in Lonsdale, *Eighteenth-Century Verse*, pp.470-72.

[8]   Cited in Rude, *Hanoverian London*, p.4.

[9]   For prominent examples see Sykes, *Private Palaces*.

[10] On the building process in London, see George, *London Life*, pp.89-90; Summerson, *Georgian London*, pp.76-9; Clarke, *Building Capitalism*, pp.106-14. See also Ayres, *Building the Georgian City*.

[11] GL Ms 8666/17, Hand-in-Hand, DM, 20 Sept. 1757.

[12] *AR*, (1765), p.113.

[13] Such bricks were often called 'Spanish'. See Clarke, *Building Capitalism*, p.95; Ayres, *Building the Georgian City*, p.104.

[14] Johnson cited in George, *London Life*, p.83. Cf. also Walpole, *Correspondence*, vol.24, p.228, letter to Sir Horace Mann, 16 July 1776; Defoe, *Tour*, p.578.

[15] Calculated from references in *London Magazine* and *Annual Register*. These were doubtless only fractions of the actual totals. They also exclude fatalities from houses and walls collapsing after fires.

[16] *LM*, 37 (1768), p.557; 36 (1767), p. 651; *AR*, (1767), p.156.

[17] 12 Geo. I c. 35. This act was amended in 1739 by 3 Geo. II c. 22, but to no great effect. George, *London Life*, p.84; Summerson, *Georgian London*, p.80; GL Ms 8666/18, Hand-in-Hand, DM, 10 Nov. 1758.

[18] Summerson, *Georgian London*, pp.123-5; Jones and Falkus, 'Urban Improvement'.

[19] 4 Geo. III c. 14; 6 Geo. III c. 37.

[20] 14 Geo. III c. 78.; Summerson, *Georgian London*, p.125.

[21] Coade stone was a type of frost-resistant terracotta. George Coade's factory at Lambeth opened in 1769. Ayres, *Building the Georgian City*, p.109.

[22] Summerson, *Georgian London*, pp.129-32; George, *London Life*, pp.90-94. Ayres has noted in passing the persistence of timber-framed construction 'for some humble dwellings', Ayres, *Building the Georgian City*, p.262 n67.

[23] Barnett, *London, Hub of the Industrial Revolution*, p.28; Rude, *Hanoverian London*, p.25. Cf also Harvey, Green and Corfield, 'Continuity, Change, and Specialization', p.482.

[24] Earle, *Making of the English Middle Class*, p.19; Schwarz, *London in the Age of Industrialisation*, p.14.

[25] Earle, *Making of the English Middle Class*, p.35; Schwarz, *London in the Age of Industrialisation*, p.65.

26   Westerfield, *Middlemen in English Business*, pp.343-4; Earle, *Making of the English Middle Class*, pp.45-6.

27   Earle, *Making of the English Middle Class*, p.50 n; George, *London Life*, pp.41-55.

28   By rental value victuallers, solicitors and surgeons were among the wealthiest groups in the Westminster electorate in 1784. Harvey, Green and Corfield, 'Continuity, Change, and Specialization', pp.480, 486-7.

29   On briefs, see Raynes, *British Insurance*, pp.76-8, and for a debate about their costs and abuses, see *GM*, (1748), p.125, (1749), pp.212-14, 258-9. Briefs were not abolished until 1828 by 9 Geo. IV c. 42.

30   The seventeenth-century origins of fire insurance are discussed in R aynes, *B ritish Insurance*, pp.76-96; Dickson, *Sun I nsurance*, pp.1-16; Supple, *Royal Ex change*, pp.8-11.

31   Hatton, *New View of London*, 2, pp.787-8.

32   Supple, *Royal Exchange*, p.11.

33   There was provision in the Sun's Deed of Settlement of 1710 for insuring throughout Britain and Ireland. On the foundation of the office, see Dickson, *Sun Insurance*, pp.17-31, 39.

34   Davies, *Westminster Fire*, pp.15-25.

35   Dickson, *Sun Insurance*, pp.287-91.

36   Drew, *London Assurance*, pp.6-33; Supple, *Royal Exchange*, pp.12-51; Trebilcock, *Phoenix Assurance*, vol.I, pp.30-36.

37   Cf. the preamble to the 'Agreement for the Establishment of the Westminster Fire Office', 1 June 1717, reproduced in Davies, *Westminster Fire*, appendix I.

38   Among the Union's founders was the clerk to the Blacksmiths' Company, while its first purpose built office was leased from the Goldsmith's Company. Union Assurance, *Bicentenary History*; GL Ms 14022/4, 9, Union, DM, 10 Jan. 1728, 27 June 1750.

39   Occupations and addresses were located for 15 of 24 Hand-in-Hand directors, and for the same proportion of Union directors, using *Kent's Directory* of 1761. Board members are listed in GL Ms 8666/18, Hand-in-Hand, DM, 12 Nov. 1761; Ms 14022/12, Union, DM, 30 Sept. 1761. A study of the annual general meetings of the Union in 1761, 1763 and 1771 revealed similar patterns. Occupations and addresses were located for members attending these meetings using *Kent's Directory* at each date. Members are listed in Ms 14022/12,15, Union, DM, 29 Sept. 1761, 27 Sept. 1763, 24 Sept. 1771.

40   Davies, *Westminster Fire*, pp.23, 35, appendix VII.

41   A conclusion based upon those signing the foundation agreement of 1717, given in Davies, *Westminster Fire*, appendix II. Fifty-nine of the 150 signatures gave occupations or status titles.

42   Davies, *Westminster Fire*, pp.26-7; Raynes, *British Insurance*, pp.93-4.

43   The principal variation was that the Westminster charged no annual premium, but instead built this into the original deposit for their members, which was 2s higher (at 12s%, twelve shillings per £100 insured) than the other mutuals.

44   Supple, *Royal Exchange*, pp.44-5, 69, 200, 354-9; Drew, *London Assurance*, pp.114-15. In both corporations life underwriting was conducted by the marine committees until the early nineteenth century.

45 GL Ms 11931/4, Sun, GCM, 9 Apr. 1730; Dickson, *Sun Insurance*, pp.48-51.
46 Dickson, *Sun Insurance*, pp.52-5; Drew, *London Assurance*, pp.171-4.
47 Davies, *Westminster Fire*, pp.36-7.
48 Staff numbers from Davies, *Westminster Fire*, pp.37-8; Drew, *London Assurance*, pp.106, 120; GL Ms 18833, London Assurance, Miscellaneous letters..., staff salary list, 1751; Supple, *Royal Exchange*, pp.51, 70; Dickson, *Sun Insurance*, pp.58, 61; GL Ms 8666/23-8, Hand-in-Hand, DM, quarterly staff salary lists, 1784-1800.
49 Davies, *Westminster Fire*, p.39; Drew, *London Assurance*, p.142; GL Ms 8666/12-13, Hand-in-Hand, DM, 24 July 1733, 16 Jan. 1739.
50 GL Ms 14022/3, 5, Union, DM, 16 Mar., 28 Mar. 1722, 10 June, 8 Sept. 1724, 22 Sept. 1730, 22 Mar. 1732; Ms 8666/10, 13, 14, Hand-in-Hand, DM, 8 May-4 Aug. 1730, 1 Nov. 1737, 30 Nov. 1742, 10 Nov. 1743; *GM*, III (1733), p.660.
51 GL Ms 11932/2, CMM, 4 Apr. 1734; Dickson, *Sun Insurance*, pp.46-52, 56.
52 The Sun from 1730, the REA from 1769 and the Phoenix from 1782, in each case by premium income. For three offices, the Hand-in-Hand, the London Assurance and the Union, where an accurate breakdown of total business is not possible, totals have been reduced by a constant ten per cent. It has been assumed that the Westminster underwrote no country property. Details of the sources and methods of estimation can be found in appendices A and B.
53 The REA's marine premiums were over three times as large as its fire premiums in the early 1760s. The London Assurance's ratio was over four to one in the same decade. Trebilcock, *Phoenix Assurance*, vol.I, pp.721-3; Supple, *Royal Exchange*, pp.61-2.
54 GL Ms 11932/7, 9, Sun, CMM, 25 July 1765, 29 Oct. 1772; WCA, Ms 343/75, Westminster, GCM, 16 Oct. 1760, 23 Oct. 1766.
55 The 1720 charters of the London and the REA forbade anyone from holding shares or offices in both corporations at same time. The Hand-in-Hand did not allow its directors to hold seats on other insurance boards, although from 1735 it did allow them to insure in other offices, reversing a earlier ban. The Sun prohibited boardroom pluralism from 1725. Drew, *London Assurance*, pp.226-7; GL Ms 8666/12, Hand-in-Hand, DM, 8 May 1735, 8 Nov. 1733; Dickson, *Sun Insurance*, p.265.
56 WCA, Ms 343/112/54, Westminster, Secretary's Address to the Board, 13 Dec. 1866; Davies, *Westminster Fire*, p.34.
57 GL Ms 11931/4, Sun, GCM, 9 Jan. 1733.
58 GL Ms 8735/1, London Assurance, FCM, 20 Jan. 1727; Supple, *Royal Exchange*, pp.49, 85.
59 The chief assumption here is that sums contributed to losses amount exactly to the value of deposits. This was seldom the case as mutual members usually either received back a part of their deposit when their policies expired, or else, as in the case of Union Assurance's members from the late 1770s, contributions exceeded the value of deposits. Nevertheless, the procedure adopted remains the simplest means of arriving at a premium rate equivalent, although it will overstate the cost of mutual insurance in the earlier period and understate it from the 1770s.
60 GL Ms 11931/4, Sun, GCM, 5 Apr. 1737.
61 GL Ms 14022/18, Union, DM, 12 Apr. 1786.
62 GL Ms 8666/19, 21, 23, Hand-in-Hand, DM, 5 Feb. 1765, 18 Sept. 1770, 18 May, 28 Sept. 1779; Ms 8728/8-9, London Assurance, DM, 17 Apr. 1765, 8 Aug. 1770; Ms

8735/3, London Assurance, FCM, 10 Aug. 1770; Ms 14022/14, 17, Union, DM, 15 Aug. 1770, 9 June, 29 Sept., 24 Nov. 1779.

[63] 4 Geo. III c. 14 (1764). GL Ms 8666/19, Hand-in-Hand, DM, 29 Nov. 1763, 20 Dec. 1763; Ms 8670, Hand-in-Hand, General Letter Book, to Lord Warkworth, 20 Dec. 1763; Ms 14022/12, Union, DM, 21 Dec. 1763, 21 Mar. 1764; Ms 11932/7, Sun, CMM, 8 Dec. 1763; Ms 11931/5, Sun, GCM, 5 Jan. 1764.

[64] GL Ms 11932/10, Sun, CMM, 3 Nov. 1774, 3 July 1777; M s 8728/ 9, L ondon Assurance, DM, 1 July, 22 July 1772.

[65] GL Ms 11932/10, Sun, CMM, 14 Jan., 28 Jan. 1773; Ms 8666/21, Hand-in-Hand, DM, 2 Feb. 1773. This may have been connected with the Marylebone Improvement bill of 1773, and the petition of the New River Company against it, *House of Commons Journal*, 34 (1772-4), pp.100, 262.

[66] Sheppard et.al., 'Middlesex and Yorkshire Deeds', pp.209-16.

[67] The following discussion of London economic fluctuations and building cycles is based upon Schwarz, *London in the Age of Industrialisation*, pp.79-85; Sheppard et.al., 'Middlesex and Yorkshire Deeds', pp.181-93; Parry-Lewis, *Building Cycles*, pp.16-23; Ashton, *Economic Fluctuations*, ch.4; Summerson, *Georgian London*, pp.111-12, 164-5.

[68] Cf. Little, *Deceleration*.

[69] French, 'London's Overseas Trade'.

[70] Most commentators suggest that building did not recommence on any significant scale until after the Peace of Paris in 1763, and the onset of more favourable credit and importing conditions, but this is belied by both series in figure 2.1.

[71] Fire offices raised their total charge for a policy, mark and policy stamp from 8s 6d to 13s 6d.

[72] At the time these were Barbon's Phenix Fire Office with 'about 10000' members, the Friendly Society Office of 1684, 'about 18000', and the Amicable Contributors (Hand-in-Hand), 'upward of 13000'. Hatton, *New View of London*, 2, pp.787-8.

[73] Earle, *M aking of the English Middle Class*, p p.78, 80-81. See also Supple, *Royal Exchange*, p.11.

[74] Raynes, *History of British Insurance*, p.207.

[75] This estimate is based on the average policy values of the Westminster Fire and the Hand-in-Hand in 1739 applied to my estimates of the total sum insured on London property, minus sums insured in the Union Fire Office, which covered only goods. Maitland's figure for the Hand-in-Hand seems rather low, but it purports to relate to 'insured houses within the bills' (42676), not to 'policies issued on London property'. The Hand-in-Hand's current policies were nearly 45000 at this time.

[76] The 1801 total covers London, Westminster, Middlesex, the borough of Southwark and the parish of Brixton. It is calculated from Abstract of Answers and Returns, 1801 Census of Great Britain, *PP* (1801-2) VI, 112. Schwarz calculated that there were some 32600 upper- and middle-class London households in 1798, Schwarz, *London in the Age of Industrialisation*, p.54.

[77] Underinsurance is discussed in Chapter 8 below.

[78] Harvey, Green and Corfield, 'Continuity, Change and Specialization', p.490.

[79] GL Ms 14022/9, Union, DM, 2 Oct. 1751.

80   Place, *Autobiography*, p.77; A rchenholtz, *Vie w of the British Constitution* (1794), cited by Rude, *Hanoverian London*, p.10; Schwarz, 'Occupations and Incomes', p.99.

81   GL Ms 8666/18, 19, 24, Hand-in-Hand, DM, 5 Jan. 1762, 25 June, 13 Aug., 22 Aug. 1765, 17-31 July 1781; WCA, Ms 343/75, Westminster, GCM, 24 Oct. 1765; GL Ms 14022/12, 17,18, Union, DM, 14 Sept. 1763, 14 Mar. 1764, 18 July 1781, 9 Mar. 1785.

82   GL Ms 11931/6, Sun, GCM, 9 Apr., 2 July 1767, 13 Apr., 1 June 1775, 6 Apr. 1781; Ms 11932/8, 10, Sun, CMM 7 May 1767, 4 May 1775. On waterside risks see Supple, *Royal Exchange*, pp.88-9; Dickson, *Sun Insurance*, pp.86-8.

83   Cited in George, *London Life*, p.345 n.

84   Sugar refineries from Deerr, *History of Sugar*, p.458; Trebilcock, *Phoenix Assurance*, vol.I, pp.21-2. London's supply of sugar nearly doubled between 1740 and 1769, Pares, 'London Sugar Market', p.254. Tallow firms from Earle, *Making of the English Middle Class*, p.344 n36, p.345 n38. Candle output calculated from Mitchell, *Abstract*, p.262. See also Deane and Cole, *British Economic Growth*, pp.57-8, 72. Breweries from Mathias, *Brewing Industry*, pp.21-7, 544, appendix table38.

85   Calculated from GL Ms 14022/10-17, Union, DM, 1758-82 *passim*.

86   GL M s 11931/ 3-4, S un, G CM, 31 M ay 1721, 5 A pr. 1737; Ms 8755/2, London Assurance, Out Letter Book, to Thomas Slack 1 Jan. 1771; Ms 14022/12, Union, DM, 17 Sept. 1760. For an example of an insurance of a gunpowder warehouse at Woolwich, see Ms 8666/24, Hand-in-Hand, DM, 26 June 1781.

87   GL Ms 14022/12, Union, DM, 12 May , 9 June 1762. Chemists' insurances counted from Ms 14022/12-18, Union, DM, 1762-87 *passim*.

88   66 of the 83 sugar refiners mapped by Trebilcock had addresses in these districts. This accounts for about two-thirds of all sugar refiners in London at this time. Trebilcock, *Phoenix Assurance*, vol.I, pp.59, 336.

89   GL Ms 11932/2, Sun, CMM, 14 Feb., 18 Apr. 1734; Ms 11931/4, Sun, GCM, 9 Apr. 1734.

90   GL Ms 8666/13, Hand-in-Hand, DM, 10 May, 2 Oct., 6 Nov. 1739. Earle reports about 80 sugar houses in London in 1750, with start-up costs ranging from £1000 to £5000. He also reports an average value on stock and utensils on 14 sugar houses insured by the Sun in 1730 of £3000. We do not know the ceiling operated by the Hand-in-Hand on single sugar house policies, and the office insured buildings only, not stock. If we assume an average of £1500 per insurance, the Hand-in-Hand would have insured 33 sugar houses in 1739. Earle, *Making of the English Middle Class*, pp.107, 345 n.

91   GL Ms 11931/4, Sun, GCM, 8 Apr. 1738; Ms 11932/5, Sun, CMM, 20 Dec. 1750.

92   Colley, *Britons*, p.68.

93   Supple, *Royal Exchange*, pp.83, 85; Dickson, *Sun Insurance*, p.76; GL Ms 8666/14-27, Hand-in-Hand, DM, 1740-96 *passim*.

94   *GM*, III (1733), p.548, 50 (1780), p.151; *LM*, 2 (1733), p.528; Sykes, *Private Palaces*, p.98.

95   Archer, *History of the Haberdashers*, pp.104, 108-12, 116-19. Cf. also the extensive properties of the Carpenters, Alford and Barker, *History of the Carpenters*.

[96] GL Ms 14022/13, Union, DM, 25 Mar. 1767; Ms 8666/10-27, Hand-in-Hand, DM, 1728-94 *passim*; Ms 8670, Hand-in-Hand, Letter Book, to the Goldsmiths Company, 16 July 1794.

[97] 40 is an estimate. There seems to be no definitive count of London medical establishments. Rivett lists 15 hospitals by 1809, but his list does not include, for instance, the hospitals at Greenwich and Kentish Town. Rudé refers to 'a score' of dispensaries opened between 1769 and 1810. Woodward's total of 10 new hospitals as 'the limit of hospital development in London until after the turn of the 19th century' appears unduly conservative. Rivett, *London Hospital System*, p.364; Rudé, *Hanoverian London*, p.232; Woodward, *To Do the Sick no Harm*, p.36. On London hospitals and dispensaries, see George, *London Life*, pp.60-63. On female refuges, see Lloyd, '"Pleasure's Golden Bait"'.

[98] Rudé, *Hanoverian London*, p.85; Summerson, *Georgian London*, pp.118-20.

[99] Summerson, *Georgian London*, pp.167-70. On the development of London Hospital's estate, see Clark-Kennedy, *The London*, pp.190-94.

[100] The Hand-in-Hand's hospitals were Guys, St Bartholomew, St Thomas, Bridewell, Bethlehem, Christ's, Foundling and London. To this list might be added the 'new hospital for lunaticks at Windmill Hill' (probably St Luke's), insured in 1751, and Imanuel Hospital in Kentish Town, insured in 1779. GL Ms 8666/13-27, Hand-in-Hand, DM, 1737-94 *passim*.

[101] GL Ms 8670, Hand-in-Hand, Letter Book, to the Governors of Christ's Hospital, 18 Jan. 1775.

[102] GL Ms 8666/27, Hand-in-Hand, DM, 11 Mar. 1794. On the Greenwich hospital fire, see *GM*, 49 (1779), p.45; *AR*, (1779) p.194. On the arson attacks, see GL Ms 8666/19, 23, Hand-in-Hand, DM, 5 Feb. 1765, 6 Apr. 1779.

[103] George, Prince of Wales, *Correspondence*, vol.VI, pp.51-2, memorandum of William Taylor, 10 Nov. 1806; Baer, *Theatre and Disorder*, p.21.

[104] Thomas and Arnold, *Theatre in Europe*, pp.307-8, 311, 336-7; Baer, *Theatre and Disorder*, p.47.

[105] GL Ms 11932/6, Sun, CMM, 13 July 1758; Ms 8670, Hand-in-Hand, Letter Book, to Mr Lingham, 11 Mar. 1795; Ms 8666/27, Hand-in-Hand, DM, 23 June 1795. The Pantheon had been built in 1772 at a cost of £60000, Langford, *Polite and Commercial People*, p.575.

[106] GL Ms 11931/7, Sun, GCM, 9 July 1789; Trebilcock, *Phoenix Assurance*, vol.I, p.131; 'Petition of the Proprietors of the late Theatre Royal, Drury Lane', 6 Sept. 1810, in Sheridan, *Letters*, pp.336-7.

[107] Marshall, *Treatise on the Law of Insurance*, p.682.

[108] These data were extracted from the minute books of the Hand-in-Hand which give details of all property totally destroyed by fire, including location and surveyors' estimates of replacement cost.

[109] 6 Anne c. 58. The text of the exemption clause is given in Davies, *Westminster Fire*, p.47. An further ten exemptions were granted to each office by the Admiralty in the aftermath of the Gordon riots of 1780, cf. GL Ms 11931/6, Sun, GCM, 6 July 1780. On insurance fire brigades, see Trebilcock, *Phoenix Assurance*, vol.I, pp.124-41; Blackstone, *History of the British Fire Service*, pp.65-77; Dickson, *Sun Insurance*, pp.62-5; Supple, *Royal Exchange*, pp.95-8.

110   Dickson, *Sun Insurance*, p.63.

111   GL Ms 8666/26, Hand-in-Hand, DM, 19 Aug. 1789. Numbers of firemen disciplined calculated from Ms 8666/21-28, Hand-in-Hand, DM, 1770-99 *passim*; Ms 11932/9-15, Sun, CMM, 1770-99 *passim*; Ms 8735/2-6, London Assurance, FCM, 1761-1802 *passim*.

112   GL Ms 8735/2, London Assurance, FCM, 28 Sept., 19 Oct. 1750; Ms 11932/6, Sun, CMM, 2 Nov. 1758; WCA, Ms 343/76, Westminster, GCM 14 Apr. 1763.

113   GL Ms 11932/6, Sun, CMM, 21 Sept.-12 Oct. 1758.

114   Smith, *Nollekens and his Times*, p.196.

115   Walpole, *Correspondence*, vol.35, pp.210-11, to Richard Bentley, 23 Feb. 1755, vol.17, p.496, to Sir Horace Mann, 14 July 1742. Cf. Southey's comment that 'the traveller who is at London without seeing a fire...is out of luck', Southey, *Letters from England*, p.457.

116   *GM*, 41 (1771), p.469.

117   Davies, *Westminster Fire*, p.35. For examples of George II and the Prince of Wales attending fires, see *LM*, 2 (1733) pp.214, 528, 6 (1737), p.50, 13 (1744), p.515. The latter also had his fire-fighting efforts captured in paint, Colley, *Britons*, p.221.

118   GL Ms 11932/3, Sun, CMM, 28 Oct. 1736, 12 Oct. 1738.

119   Drew, *London Assurance*, pp.49-52; GL Ms 8735/2, 6, London Assurance, FCM, 13 Dec. 1751, 17 June 1796; Ms 8666/27-28, Hand-in-Hand, DM, 17 Nov. 1795, 2 July, 3 Dec. 1799; Ms 14022/18, Union, DM, 17 June 1789.

120   Trebilcock, *Phoenix Assurance*, vol.l, p.124; Blackstone, *History of the British Fire Service*, pp.61-2

121   Blackstone, *History of the British Fire Service*, p.70; GL Ms 8666/10, Hand-in-Hand, DM, 27 Jan., 10 Feb. 1730.

122   Dickens, *Sketches by Boz*, ch.1.

123   Defoe, *Tour*, p.318.

124   Walpole, *Correspondence*, vol.9, pp.362-3, to Sir George Montague, 28 Apr. 1761; *GM*, 28 (1758), pp.447-8.

125   *AR*, (1775), p.102.

126   *LM*, 24 (1755), p.185; *London Chronicle*, 13-15 Jan. 1757; *AR*, (1765), p.144.

127   GL Ms 8728/11, 15, London Assurance, DM, 11 July 1781, 10 Apr. 1799; Ms 8666/24, Hand-in-Hand, DM, 4 Sept. 1781.

128   Cited by George, *London Life*, p.108. The Westminster paving act of 1762 was given some of the credit.

129   *AR*, (1761), p.103, act of 6 Anne c. 31; *GM*, 31 (1761), p.233; GL Ms 14022/13, Union, DM, 27 Feb. 1765.

130   Place, *Autobiography*, p.67; *GM*, 31 (1761), p.414; GL Ms 14022/9, Union, DM, 14 Dec. 1748. The sale or use of fireworks was eventually banned by an act of parliament in 1824.

131   GL Ms 11932/14, Sun, CMM, 14 Jan. 1790.

132   GL Ms 8735/3, London Assurance, FCM, 20 Dec. 1765, 11 July 1766; Ms 11932/8, 14, Sun, CMM, 29 Jan. 1767, 29 Apr. 1790. For an example of organised looting following arson, see *GM*, 35 (1765) p.342.

133   The 'premium' estimates for the mutual offices calculated for table 2.1 serve the purpose of examining the relative size and growth of these businesses in comparison

to the proprietary insurers, but are too crude to use as a basis for estimating margins of profitability.

[134] Supple, *Royal Exchange*, p.72. REA's average loss ratio for 1721-4 was 66 per cent with an expense ratio of 20 per cent. Calculated from GRE archives, REA, Doomsday Book.

[135] *LM*, 17 (1748), p.139.

[136] Calculated from GL Ms 8735/3, London, FCM, 22 July-25 Nov. 1763. This fire, at New Crane Stairs, destroyed over 110 houses and warehouses, a dock and a ship. Several lives were also lost, *AR*, (1763), p.88.

[137] Dividend rates from GL Ms 11931/4-7, Sun, GCM, 1741-97 *passim*. Dividend totals from Dickson, *Sun Insurance*, p.288. Underwriting surpluses calculated as premiums minus (losses plus expenses). Premiums and losses from *ibid.*, appendix I. Expenses for 1760-69 estimated as 20 per cent of premiums. Expenses for 1791-9 from GL Ms 11933A, Sun, Annual Accounts, 1791-1887.

[138] GRE archives, REA, Doomsday Book, 1721-99.

[139] GL Ms 18822, London Assurance, Notes and memoranda concerning the need to improve and increase the fire insurance business of the Corporation, 1794-1830, Memorandum of the Committee of Fire, 27 Feb. 1794.

[140] The London Assurance's overall profit rate is taken from the annual data in Mirowski, *Birth of the Business Cycle*, ch.9, and recalculated as five year moving averages. Dividend rates from GL Ms 8728/7-15, London Assurance, DM, 1760-98 *passim*. Returns are dividends expressed as percentages of the paid-up value of each share. For the latter see Drew, *London Assurance*, p.216.

[141] These data are derived from WCA, Ms 343/83-6, Westminster, General Account Books, 1759-94 *passim*.

[142] GL Ms 14022/23, Union, DM, 1805-6 *passim*; Union Assurance, *Bicentenary History*.

Chapter 3

Provincial Fire Insurance in the Eighteenth Century

Before the second quarter of the eighteenth century the market for fire insurance outside London was tiny. It then grew so rapidly that by 1800 it accounted for 45 per cent of all sums insured in Britain. The greatest part of this business was transacted by the London stock companies. Nationally, provincial insurers were of little importance. In 1800 there were 12 English fire offices based outside London. These accounted for just eight per cent of sums insured by all English offices.

This chapter explores the many regional, urban and rural markets for insurance which emerged in eighteenth-century Britain. It examines the business of the London mutuals in the home counties, the expanding agencies of the three stock companies, the emergence of provincial insurers and the growing competition with their metropolitan rivals. The markets developed in a very uneven way during the course of the century. Although fire insurance remained largely a metropolitan export, several country offices proved to be powerful competitors in their own locales.

Regions and the diffusion of fire insurance in eighteenth-century Britain

It is well recognised that the region formed a critical unit in the process of industrial transformation in the western world. Factors of production, markets, credit networks, transport systems, wage and price structures were all organised primarily with a regional focus. The regional specialisation of functions in agriculture and manufacturing was one of the most visible features of the industrial revolution, a process which accompanied, and probably depended upon, the increasing integration of the national economy.[1] This chapter presents the first attempt to measure the rate of diffusion outside London of an important financial service and to speculate on the relationship between its geography and the process of regional industrialisation. Without preempting the discussion below, it is clear from the data presented below that the early distribution of fire insurance was skewed towards the south of England. What is more remarkable is that fire insurance remained heavily concentrated in the south-east after a century of growth, and that it responded in such a limited way to geographical shifts in the distribution of population or income. Moreover, as the analysis below reveals, during the third quarter of the eighteenth century the diffusion of fire insurance stalled as the great London building boom of the 1760s and 1770s intensified the focus of insurers on property in the capital.

Most of the usual factor endowment explanations of one region's comparative advantage over another do not apply to a homogenous product such as insurance. It seems likely that the skewed distribution of insurance depended largely upon supply-side factors, the preferences of the metropolitan offices in choosing where to sell, the energy of agents and the presence of local offices. London undoubtedly played the key role in determining the rate at which the industry grew in different places for much of the period, not least because the metropolis provided such a large and expanding market on the very doorstep of the fire offices. It is possible that London's growth and wealth stifled or 'crowded out' the diffusion of insurance further afield. Thirty-nine per cent of all income tax paid in 1806 derived from the capital. London property values were also higher than elsewhere, making it an attractive market for insurers interested in volume growth. Fire insurance data suggest that the differential between property values in London and the home counties was in the order of 20-30 per cent. The average replacement cost of property insured by the Hand-in-Hand between 1735 and 1800 was £1071 in London (481 fires), but just £730 outside the capital (58 fires). The average sum insured by the London Assurance in 1166 metropolitan policies in 1760-61 was £993, compared with an average of £774 in 174 country policies.[2]

On the other hand, regional factors may have exercised an influence on the decision of the London offices about where to locate their agencies. Distance from London may have been one such factor. The rate of urbanisation in a region, the level of average incomes, and the concentration of wealth may have been others. There were possibly even regional differentials in attitudes towards fire hazards and business risk - contingent, for instance, upon variations in building types and the degrees of cyclical fluctuations in different trades and industries - which exerted a force of attraction or repulsion for insurers. Several of these factors are explored below.

The provincial insurances of the London offices

Table 3.1 estimates how quickly non-metropolitan insurance grew and its changing importance to individual London fire offices. Provincial property accounted for about ten per cent of all sums insured in 1730, rising to 30 per cent by 1760 (table 3.1, column 3). For the following 15 years 'country' insurances only kept pace with the growth of insurance in the capital. From the late 1770s they rose again to reach 45 per cent of the total. Virtually all of the increase in the provincial share of insurance before 1760 occurred via the operations of metropolitan offices outside the capital. During the last decades of the century new country offices contributed to growth as their share of total sums insured rose from two per cent in 1770 to eight per cent by 1800. By this date country business furnished 56 per cent of the REA's premium income, 50 per cent of the Sun's and about 40 per cent of the domestic underwriting income of the Phoenix.[3]

The six London fire offices which dominated the market between 1720 and 1780 sold insurance outside the City and Westminster, but only the three stock companies appointed country agents. The three mutuals cautiously extended their geographical limits up to 30 miles from the City by the second half of the century, but not until the 1780s did they insure throughout England and Wales, without, however, appointing any agents.[4] These offices were wary about straying far from their original market. Between 1760 and 1794 96 per cent of new sums insured by the Westminster Fire Office on its standard seven year policies covered property located within ten miles of the company's head office in Charing Cross. There was little attempt to sell insurance beyond this boundary, even though the office had established a 25 mile limit in 1748.[5]

The attractions of underwriting outside London were clear. The country houses and villas of the squirarchy, clergy and merchants were detached, well built, and often required several thousand pounds worth of insurance. The mansions of the aristocracy became larger and more numerous during the eighteenth century. In Northamptonshire and Hertfordshire 40 per cent of aristocratic owners carried out some modernisation or rebuilding of their houses in this period. Their values mostly ranged from £15000 to £80000, though there were also gigantic projects such as Blenheim on which £300000 was spent between 1705 and 1715. Wilson and Mackley have recently estimated that expenditure on country house building and alterations in the period 1770-1800 amounted to £3.8m, excluding the cost of houses built on estates of less than 3000 acres.[6]

The Hand-in-Hand insured a wide range of such properties, from the Jacobean Hatfield House, covered for £15000 in 1781 for Lord Salisbury, to giant stone and stucco palaces such as Woburn and more modest Georgian red brick mansions such as Kelvedon Hall in Essex or Lord Hyde's Grove Place near Watford.[7] From the 1750s landowners became increasingly concerned about fire hazards and many invested in fire-fighting equipment for their estates. Their country mansions, however, were probably less vulnerable than their town houses. In fires affecting provincial property insured by the Hand-in-Hand between 1735 and 1800, the average number of buildings destroyed was 1.7 compared to an average of 2.9 in London fires (see table 2.3). Nevertheless mansions did burn down. It has been estimated that fire destroyed at least ten per cent of all country houses in Hertfordshire every 100 years.[8]

More substantial difficulties were faced by underwriters outside the capital. If an office attempted to extend its 'country' market it encountered an ever greater proportion of timber buildings being proposed for insurance. Between 1760 and 1794 timber buildings accounted for 18 per cent of new sums insured by Westminster Fire Office on 'common' - mostly residential - property located between 10 and 25 miles of the company's office, compared with just seven per

Table 3.1 Country insurances as a proportion of business: English fire offices, 1725-95

	(1) Total country pre-miums £	(2) Col.1 as % of total pre-miums	(3) Country as % of total £ insured	(4) Sun country pre-miums as % of office total	(5) REA country pre-miums as % of office total	(6) Phoenix country pre-miums as % of office total
1725	2427	6.8	6.3	n/a	n/a	
1730	4275	9.1	9.9	n/a	n/a	
1735	8325	15.8	17.0	27.5	n/a	
1740	11998	20.3	22.4	39.7	n/a	
1745	14786	23.7	26.1	43.8	n/a	
1750	17871	24.4	27.4	45.4	n/a	
1755	23483	26.6	29.6	49.6	n/a	
1760	28146	27.6	30.1	49.4	n/a	
1765	36770	28.1	30.5	46.1	n/a	
1770	46815	29.7	31.2	44.4	26.4	
1775	56972	31.8	32.7	44.8	30.3	
1780	70933	36.1	36.6	47.4	38.9	
1785	71936	38.4	43.9	48.0	41.2	19.9
1790	94650	40.7	37.9	48.8	51.9	32.7
1795	137426	45.4	44.8	49.7	55.9	39.6

Note: premiums and percentages are calculated as five year centred averages, except for REA, 1770 (a three year centred average).

Sources: for columns 1-3, see table 2.1 and appendices A & B. Columns 4-6 calculated from CUL, PAA, Phoenix, Annual Summary, 1783-1877; GL Ms 11935, Sun, CCM, weekly agents' remittances; Dickson, *Sun Insurance*, appendix 1; GRE, Ms RED305, REA, Doomsday Book. I am most grateful to Clive Trebilcock for providing me with a copy of the Phoenix results.

cent of all new sums insured. Timber structures, though still a minority of properties insured, were thus over twice as likely to be underwritten outside London than within. Furthermore, any insurer wishing to expand beyond London also faced demands to underwrite a larger volume of non-residential structures, often timber-built, such as barns, stabling and other out-buildings. In the Hand-in-Hand dataset of fires properties other than those described as 'houses' accounted for 28 per cent of all insured property burnt down in London, but 68 per cent of property destroyed elsewhere.[9]

For the mutuals other problems included the costs of surveying and monitoring country risks as business expanded without a network of local agents. By contrast the stock companies opted for the latter. Before the establishment of the Phoenix in 1782, the Sun was the most adventurous of the London offices in this respect. Between 1730 and 1760 its agents operated in over 70 locations across England, Wales and Scotland, and this figure more than doubled by 1800. In many places the Sun was the only insurer for most of the period. Its agency system was so extensive that it warrants separate examination below, particularly as it can be comprehensively reconstructed from the surviving records. The same is not true of the two corporations. The REA's archives burnt down in 1838, leaving few records for the eighteenth century. The London Assurance also suffered losses when its head office was destroyed by fire in 1748, and there is no breakdown of its agency business before 1815.

We do know that the London Assurance appointed at least 14 agencies during its early years. Only two of these were in the north of England and there were none in Scotland, Wales or the Midlands. It is likely that the corporation began to wind down its agency system before mid-century, although some country agents continued to operate in a small way.[10] The only agencies which clearly survived were those in Ireland. Analysis of the one extant register, for 1760-61, reveals that country insurances - not all of which would have been sold by agents - accounted for just 12 per cent of the 1411 policies listed.[11] One-half of all sums insured outside London covered property in just four counties, Essex, Middlesex, Kent and Surrey.

During the second half of the century the directors of the London Assurance were very reluctant to extend their limited provincial business. Only two English agency appointments, in Newcastle (1769) and Whitby (1780), are recorded for this period, and various proposals to establish agencies elsewhere were turned down. The corporation's agencies in Ireland proved more durable, although they too eventually fell victim to a policy of retrenchment during the last quarter of the century. A loss-making agency in Waterford was closed down in 1728, but by mid-century it was reported that the agencies in Cork and Dublin had 'for some years been successful'. Premiums from both places slowly increased during the 1760s and 1770s. At their peak they accounted for nearly five per cent of the corporation's fire insurance income.

To an extent the London Assurance benefited from the great commercial and industrial expansion of these cities. As well as covering workers' tenements in Cork and houses in the fashionable streets of Dublin, other insurances ranged from printing shops, slaughterhouses, bakeries, malting houses, distilleries, corn mills and warehouses. Insurance, though, was limited by several factors. First, the premium rates charged by the London Assurance on Irish insurances were 50 to 80 per cent higher than in England, while high urban rents in Ireland only made the burden of insurance premiums still greater.[12] Second, the ceiling on the amount insured in any one policy also made insurance relatively expensive for Irish policyholders. Where a Cork merchant wished to insure £6000 on his goods, he was required to take out three policies (of £2000 each) and to pay several shillings more in charges than his counterpart in London. Furthermore, the London Assurance tried to insist upon including an average clause, especially in large mercantile policies covering goods in several warehouses, and to make commission merchants carry one-quarter of the cost of any loss as a pre-condition of insurance.[13]

Another obstacle to expansion was the order restricting the insurances sold by Irish agents to those 'in cities and considerable trading towns'. Many common dwellings in the Irish countryside were little more than hovels, regarded as simply uninsurable by London underwriters. Pressured by its Cork agents, the London Assurance allowed them to accept country insurances from 'people of known good character on good buildings', but this type of business does not seem to have been large.[14] There was also some competition. The REA's agent in Dublin was taking business from the London Assurance's Cork agency in the 1750s, and there were also three Irish offices operating by 1783 which may have acquired a sizeable share of the market.[15]

As with its agencies in the north of England, the Irish agencies of the London Assurance collapsed in the 1780s. The Dublin agent, James Vareilles, died in 1783, by which time 'very few assurances' were in force, and nothing is heard of the agency after 1786. The Cork agency was still operating in 1800 but remitting only a few pounds each year. Thus the agency network established by the London Assurance at its foundation had disintegrated. Increasing competition and the difficulty of finding suitable replacements for agents may have contributed to this decline. An act of the Irish parliament in 1785 requiring the licensing of the agents of English insurance offices was a further disincentive, for in England the London Assurance enjoyed an exemption from annual licences under its charter.[16] The chief factor, however, was the indifference of the directors towards fire underwriting outside London. Only in 1804, with new offices being formed every year and with its share of the metropolitan market evaporating, did the corporation change tack. A committee recommended a system of country agencies. By January 1806, 85 years after launching its first sales network, the London Assurance had appointed 26 agents in an attempt to re-establish itself in provincial England.

We know less about the agency system of the other corporation. The REA's historian refers to the only scraps of information available, namely the number of agents who appear in the few surviving balance sheets. There were four in 1734, 15 in 1758, 44 in 1775, 195 in 1788, and 319 (including three in Ireland) in 1805. By 1770 country agents accounted for 26 per cent, over £4200, of the corporation's total fire premium income, although this was a modest achievement compared to the £35000 remitted by the Sun's salesforce. The REA expanded outside London most rapidly during the last quarter of the century. Country premiums rose to over £30000, 56 per cent of the REA's total fire premiums by 1795. They continued to increase even in the early 1780s when total premium income temporarily declined. In this way the REA began to catch up with the Sun as a national insurer. The REA's agencies generated the equivalent of 12 per cent of the Sun's country income in 1770, but 49 per cent by 1795. Only the Phoenix had a sales network which grew faster. All three offices contributed to the great increase in the availability of fire insurance outside London in the last decades of the eighteenth century. For the previous 60 years, however, the Sun alone dominated English provincial insurance and its huge agency system merits particular attention.

The Sun's agency system

In 1710 the Sun became the first office to resolve to sell fire insurance outside London through a network of agents. Few were appointed before the office was restructured in 1720, but in the following decade sales outlets quickly became established in the provinces. By 1730 over 60 country agents had been appointed. Although only about half of these were active, this was probably enough to make the Sun's sales network larger than those of the REA and the London Assurance at this date.[17]

The development of the Sun's agency network can be reconstructed in detail. Agents' remittances, recorded weekly from 1730 in the minutes of the country committee, enable us to calculate continuous series of premium earnings for most agencies.[18] Because the Sun enjoyed a near monopoly in many areas before the 1780s, this data may be used to examine the growth of local insurance markets. After 1780, because of the rise of rival offices, this becomes a much more precarious exercise. The Sun's share of total premiums from outside London fell from 75 per cent in the mid 1770s to 44 per cent by the mid 1790s. Even where we know the premium income of local fire offices, we do not know individual agency earnings for the REA and the Phoenix, both of whom expanded rapidly in the last two decades of the century. Because of this difficulty, the analysis of the Sun's agencies was terminated in 1801 though the record of agents' remittances continued into the nineteenth century.

Table 3.2 shows the number of the Sun's active agents at decennial intervals between 1730 and 1800, grouped by region, together with an estimate of the total number of agents on the company's books.[19] During the 1730s, thanks to vigorous monitoring and selective dismissals and appointments, the proportion of active agents rose to over 90 per cent, a level maintained for the rest of the century. The number of remitting agents grew most rapidly during the 1760s and 1780s, though the Sun's closest rivals more than kept pace. The Phoenix had appointed 170 agents by 1785, some 50 more than the Sun. The REA had 195 agents by 1788.[20] Furthermore, while the average amount remitted by the Sun's agents in current values rose more than ten fold between 1730 and 1780, it fell by some 20 per cent during the 1780s before recovering. The expansion of the Sun's agencies during the era of greater competition and higher taxation after 1780, therefore, was not accompanied by a sustained growth in their productivity.

From the outset the distribution of the Sun's agency network was heavily skewed. Fourteen of the 27 remitting agents in 1730 were located in southern

Table 3.2   Sun's country agents: numbers remitting by region and average remittance, 1730-1800

	1730	1740	1750	1760	1770	1780	1790	1800
S.East II	5	7	7	7	13	16	21	27
S.East III	3	14	15	17	20	22	25	28
E.Anglia	4	7	7	8	11	11	12	13
S.West	6	13	14	14	16	18	27	28
W.Mids	3	5	7	11	12	13	14	14
E.Mids	3	7	7	8	11	13	14	16
N.West	1	5	4	6	6	6	5	8
Yorkshire	1	4	4	5	5	5	8	10
North	1	2	2	2	5	5	8	7
Wales						1	1	1
Scotland		2	2	2	5	5	6	4
Active agents	27	66	69	80	104	115	141	156
Agents on books	62	71	74	84	110	119	143	171
Average £ remitted per agent	40	120	180	256	337	449	361	421

Notes: The table shows the number of 'active' agents, defined as those remitting in the given year, or in adjacent years. Average sums remitted per agent are calculated from five year averages of total premiums remitted by all agents, centred on the given year, divided by the number of active agents. Regions modified from Lee, *British Economy*, table 7.1, p.127, as follows; South-East II = Middlesex, Kent, Surrey, Hertford, Essex. South-East III = Bedford, Berkshire, Buckingham, Hampshire, Oxford, Sussex. East Anglia = Cambridge, Huntingdon, Norfolk, Suffolk. South-West = Cornwall, Devon, Dorset, Gloucester, Somerset, Wiltshire. West Midlands: Hereford, Shropshire, Stafford, Warwick, Worcester. East Midlands = Derby, Leicester, Lincoln, Northampton, Nottingham, Rutland. North-West = Cheshire, Lancashire. North = Cumberland, Durham, Northumberland, Westmoreland. Yorkshire = West, East and North Ridings.

Sources: see text.

England. Seventy years later this level of concentration had scarcely changed, despite major shifts in the population. In 1800 53 per cent of the Sun's active agents were located in southern English counties containing 29 per cent of the British population. The Sun paved the way for others to follow. Fifty-two per cent of the Phoenix's salesmen appointed by 1785 were found in southern England and their degree of regional dispersal was virtually identical to the Sun's.[21] Measured by the number of agents appointed, neither the infant insurer nor the elderly market leader paid undue attention to the fastest growing region in England, the north-

Table 3.3   Sun's country business: regions ranked by premium income

Regions ranked by five year centred annual averages of premium income.

	1740	1750	1760	1770	1780	1790	1799
1	SE III	SE III	SW	SW	SE III	SE II	SE II
	£1902	£2787	£5021	£7912	£10996	£9944	£11735
2	SW	SW	SE III	SE III	SW	SE III	NW
	£1689	£2756	£3990	£7149	£10076	£9804	£10922
3	EA	EA	EA	SE II	SE II	SW	SE III
	£1407	£2019	£2803	£4826	£8690	£8492	£10308
4	SE II	SE II	SE II	EA	EA	EA	SW
	£915	£1486	£2496	£4346	£6689	£5540	£9084
5	EM	EM	EM	EM	Scotld	Scotld	Scotld
	£677	£1087	£1551	£2591	£3854	£4413	£8215
6	Yorks	NW	NW	NW	EM	NW	EA
	£344	£781	£1397	£2241	£3388	£4239	£4897
7	WM	Yorks	Scotld	Scotld	WM	EM	EM
	£320	£507	£1134	£1944	£2717	£3505	£3903
8	NW	WM	Yorks	WM	NW	WM	Yorks
	£295	£454	£849	£1780	£2343	£2201	£3127
9	Scotld	Scotld	WM	Yorks	Yorks	Yorks	WM
	£197	£319	£804	£1544	£1916	£2149	£2460
10	North	North	North	North	North	North	North
	£165	£246	£430	£746	£902	£564	£950
11					Wales	Wales	Wales
					£47	£31	£34
Total	£7911	£12442	£20475	£35079	£51618	£50882	£65635

Note: regions as given in table 3.2. EA = East Anglia, WM = West Midlands; EM = East Midlands.

Sources: see text.

west. Each office had only four agents active in Lancashire during the 1780s.

A small number of agents, however, could generate impressive earnings in a developing region. Table 3.3 shows the distribution of the Sun's agency earnings by region. The south remained important throughout the eighteenth century, but the table also illustrates the rise of Scotland and north-west England, the relative decline of East Anglia, and the relatively unimpressive performance of Yorkshire. The Sun's earnings in Scotland grew above the average throughout the period. North-west England also expanded rapidly, although this came to a temporary halt

Table 3.4 Regional distribution of population and fire insurance, 1730-99

(Percentage distribution by region of Sun's premium income, population and houses)

	1720/30		1751		1758		1781		1799/1801	
	Popn	Prems	Popn	Prems	Houses	Prems	Popn	Prems	Popn	Prems
SE	28.8	94.9	23.8	66.4	25.0	64.5	23.9	69.3	24.9	67.8
East	16.8	1.9	14.4	12.8	15.2	12.5	13.9	11.3	12.6	8.0
SW	14.5	1.3	14.9	10.0	13.1	11.3	13.1	8.9	12.5	6.7
Midlands	20.2	1.8	20.8	5.2	22.7	5.6	21.7	6.0	21.3	5.3
North	17.0	0.3	19.3	5.7	20.1	6.1	20.7	4.6	22.6	12.2
Wales	5.1	0.0	6.9	0.0	5.7	0.0	6.6	0.04	6.1	0.03
Coefficients	0.76		0.63		0.59		0.57		0.64	

Notes and Sources: For 1720/30, population refers to the former, premiums to the latter year. For 1799/1801, the reverse is true. Regions, population and houses from Langford, *Polite and Commercial People*, table 7, p.673. SE = Middlesex, Kent, Sussex, Surrey, Berks., Hants., Essex, Herts.. East = Norfolk, Suffolk, Hunts., Cambs., Beds., Northants., Lincs., Bucks. Midlands = Warwick, Worcs., Leics., Notts., Staffs., Salop., Oxon., Ches., Derby., Glos., Hereford. North = Westmoreland, Cumberland, Northumberland, Durham, Lancs., Yorks.. For premiums, see text.

in the 1770s, probably as a result of the fire offices newly established in Manchester and Liverpool. Other rapidly growing regions were south-west England before 1750 and the home counties between 1760 and 1790.

The Sun's premium income, therefore, remained heavily skewed. In table 3.4 it is correlated with the distribution of population in the six regions of England and Wales adopted by Langford. For most of the eighteenth century the correlation became weaker not stronger. Only after 1780 was this trend reversed as the Sun's country business at last began to follow the regional shifts in population. The decline in East Anglia and the south-west and the rise of the north-west mirrored demographic change, but the office continued to earn a disproportionate amount of its income from the south-east. In 1799 still over two-thirds of the Sun's (English and Welsh) premiums came from south-eastern counties containing one-quarter of the population, while only 18 per cent of premiums were earned in the midlands and north of England where 44 per cent of the population lived. The Sun clearly had difficulty in overcoming the geographical bias established in its earliest years.

Table 3.5 utilises Deane and Cole's estimates to show the Sun's premium income per 1000 inhabitants for each English county at three dates, 1751, 1781 and 1799. The counties are listed left to right in descending order of per caput premiums in 1799. This table vividly illustrates the greater income yields in London, Middlesex and in much of the south-east than elsewhere. At all three dates, six or seven of the top ten counties for insurance were located in the south-east, with most of the rest in eastern England. The only northern county included was Lancashire, which had climbed into ninth place by 1799. It is also noticeable that of the top 20 counties in 1781 only five had generated agency earnings that outstripped population growth by 1799. Four of the five, Berkshire, Cambridge, Bedford and Essex, were near London.

The overall picture lends support to the thesis put forward by Lee, Rubinstein and others that the regional specialisation of services, so visible in the Victorian censuses, was already well established by the eighteenth century.[22] In 1751 the Sun received ten times more premiums from every Londoner than from every Lancastrian. This ratio rose to 18 in 1781 and then fell to five in 1799 as the agencies in Manchester and Liverpool prospered. Given the affluence of London and the home counties, their continued predominance as a source of fire insurance is not surprising. Thirty-eight per cent of all income tax paid in 1801 came from London where only about ten per cent of the population lived.[23]

Table 3.6 explores this relationship further by calculating per caput taxable income and per caput premiums in the south-east as ratios of other regions c.1800. As a comparison between regional levels of affluence and the regional density of fire insurance, it is flawed, to the extent that the income tax data may suffer from incomplete or missing returns, or from tax evasion, and by the fact that the premium data derive from only one insurance office. Despite these problems the exercise may still be useful. First, regional aggregation largely dispenses with the

Table 3.5   Sun's per capita premium income by county, 1751-99

Average premium income £ per 1000 inhabitants
Counties ranked by order of premium density in 1799/1801

	1751	1781	1799/1801
Middlesex	26.07	84.62	72.83
Berkshire	6.15	22.16	25.47
Hertfordshire	4.66	25.18	22.78
Cambridgshire	3.92	18.21	21.55
Kent	6.59	19.10	17.96
Dorset	6.66	25.22	17.13
Huntingdonshire		19.11	15.27
Hampshire	7.98	20.12	15.24
Lancashire	2.50	4.73	14.91
Northamptonshire	5.96	13.32	12.92
Buckinghamshire	3.06	21.68	10.16
Bedfordshire	7.47	8.31	9.52
Essex	0.65	6.00	9.03
Devon	4.03	12.88	8.91
Wiltshire	4.33	11.65	8.35
Sussex	1.76	10.63	8.10
Oxfordshire	4.81	13.93	7.97
Nottinghamshire	2.52	4.71	5.56
Suffolk	2.58	6.77	5.40
Lincolnshire	0.96	4.26	4.61
Gloucestershire	0.83	4.35	4.34
Worcestershire	2.02	6.99	4.20
Norfolk	6.46	12.49	4.06
Westmoreland		1.71	3.98
Somerset	1.47	2.31	3.77
Warwickshire	1.79	4.70	3.58
Yorkshire	1.12	2.77	3.53
Surrey		2.70	3.41
Cheshire	0.62	2.28	2.88
Staffordshire	0.17	2.34	2.74
Durham	0.11	1.09	2.55
Herefordshire	0.55	1.42	2.38
Cumberland		0.89	1.96

	1751	1781	1799/1801
Leicestershire	1.05	2.44	1.55
Shropshire		2.32	1.10
Derbyshire			0.85
Northumberland	1.88	3.79	0.74
Cornwall		1.47	0.55
Wales		0.08	0.06

Sources: County populations are from Deane and Cole, *British Economic Growth*, table 24, p.103. The data for 1781 is taken from column b in this table, and the data for 1799 utilises the population figures for 1801.

principal problem encountered in the county totals, of the underestimation of metropolitan incomes by London businessmen living and paying taxes outside the capital.[24] Second, while the efficiency of tax collection did improve during the Napoleonic wars, historians have agreed that evasion 'was not sustained or widespread enough to make the statistics ineffective for the purposes of historical analysis'.[25] Third, the Sun remained the largest fire insurer in the country at the end of the eighteenth century, accounting for over one-third of all premium income, thus the regional concentration of its business was a major factor shaping the distribution of fire insurance across the country as a whole. Moreover, the second largest office, the Phoenix, distributed its agencies in a similar way to the Sun, and these two offices together accounted for two-thirds of all premiums generated by fire insurance agents outside London in the late 1790s. The other major office to operate on a national scale before 1800 was the REA for which we have no comparative data. This conservative office was unlikely to have had a regional pattern of income very different from that of its old rival. In sum, it can be argued that table 3.6 provides a good indication of the lead held by the south-east over other regions by levels of per caput income and density of fire insurance coverage at the beginning of the nineteenth century. Most of provincial England had an average taxable income three to four times below that of London and the south-east, while Scotland and Wales were poorer still. In terms of fire insurance the regional differentials were even greater. The south-east generated three times more premiums per caput than the north-west, between nine and eleven times more than Yorkshire and the midlands, and 17 times more than the north. With the exception of north-west England, where the insurance habit had spread rapidly during the 1790s and where the cotton industry generated high premium yields per sum insured, the lead of the south-east over other regions was everywhere greater in terms of property insurance than it was in terms of personal income. The geographical concentration of this financial service in Britain *circa* 1800 was thus greater than the concentration of taxable, largely middle-class wealth, suggesting that the supply of insurance across the country at this date still lagged

Table 3.6   Regional distribution of wealth and fire insurance, c.1800

Ratio of South-east to:	Per caput income 1800-1	Per caput premiums 1799/1801
South-west	2.8	5.0
East Anglia	3.0	4.2
East Midlands	3.1	8.5
Yorkshire	3.4	9.1
North-west	3.5	2.6
West Midlands	3.7	11.4
North	3.9	16.7
Scotland	5.7	6.3
Wales	7.5	530.4
Correlation coefficient	0.84	

Notes: for regions see table 3.2. Per caput premiums in 1799 are calculated from five year annual average premiums centred in 1799, divided through by the respective regional population totals from 1801. Taxable income is the *gross* assessment upon income for the year ending 5 April 1801.

Sources: Taxable income from 'Accounts respecting the Income Duty', *PP* (1801-2), IV, 155. Population of England and Wales in 1801 from Deane and Cole, *British Economic Growth*, table 24, p.103; for Scotland in 1801 from Mitchell, *British Historical Statistics*, p.9. For premiums, see text.

behind the regional dispersion of wealth. What is also striking is that fire insurance, even after a century of growth, was far more closely correlated to the distribution of middle-class wealth than to the distribution of the population as a whole.

Table 3.7 shows the top ten premium earning agencies at decennial intervals from 1740. For most of this period the Sun's biggest stream of income came from Exeter, where the agency profited from the continuity of management under Thomas Gearing and his son, from a buoyant, diversifying economy and modest urban growth, from a rich hinterland of gentry properties, and from the terrible record of fire damage in the cob, thatch and timber towns of east Devon which induced a high demand for insurance. Until 1790 the only northern agencies to rank in the Sun's top ten were Liverpool and Edinburgh. These were then joined by Manchester, Glasgow and Leeds, so that by 1800 Britain's biggest cities, with the interesting exception of Birmingham, were also the Sun's largest sources of income. For most of the eighteenth century, however, the Sun's major agencies were found in the south-east, in East Anglia and the west country. The hierarchy of the company's sales network experienced relatively little change between 1740 and

Table 3.7 Sun's agencies: the top ten by premium income, 1740-99

(5 year centred annual average premiums)

	1740	1750	1760	1770	1780	1790	1799
1	Exeter £594	Exeter £1050	Exeter £1760	Exeter £2625	Exeter £3191	Edinburgh £2705	Manchester £6743
2	Poole £406	Norwich £548	Edinburgh £989	Edinburgh £1352	Edinburgh £2426	Manchester £2674	Edinburgh £4495
3	Andover £395	Liverpool £547	Norwich £791	Liverpool £1254	Norwich £1600	Exeter £2241	Glasgow £3046
4	Lynn Regis £374	Lynn Regis £492	Liverpool £775	Norwich £1186	Poole £1560	Portsmouth £1399	Liverpool £2292
5	Norwich £325	Poole £492	Lynn Regis £696	Poole £897	Ware £1419	Glasgow £1206	Exeter £2134
6	Oxford £279	Leighton Buzzard £394	Canterbury £553	Chatham £841	Portsmouth £1335	Canterbury £1188	Portsmouth £1911
7	Canterbury £274	Portsmouth £362	Chatham £515	Canterbury £822	Canterbury £1266	Chatham £1152	Leeds £1740
8	Maidstone £263	Buntingford £351	Portsmouth £481	Marlborough £786	Chatham £1150	Cambridge £1128	Canterbury £1521
9	Winchester £251	Oxford £350	Bath £479	Oxford £737	Oxford £1141	Norwich £1070	Chatham £1206
10	Portsmouth £230	Blandford £320	Leighton Buzzard £474	Salisbury £709	Liverpool £1111	Liverpool £1058	Cambridge £1162

Sources: Agents' remittances from GL Ms 11935/1-9, Sun, Country Committee Minutes, 1730-1801.

Table 3.8   Sun's agencies: the top twenty by per capita premiums

(Premiums are five year centred annual averages).

	Agency	Premiums (1799)	Population (1801)	Premiums £ per 1000 inhabitants
1	Potton, Beds	352	1103	319
2	Huntingdon	592	2035	291
3	Maidenhead, Berks	638	2403	266
4	Hertford	1040	4226	246
5	Chelmsford, Essex	918	3755	244
6	Portsmouth, Hants	1911	7839	244
7	Epping, Essex	414	1729	239
8	Blandford, Dorset	538	2326	231
9	Gravesend, Kent	477	2483	192
10	Marlborough, Wilts	420	2367	177
11	Uxbridge, Middlesex	685	3894	176
12	Daventry, Nthants	446	2582	173
13	Canterbury, Kent	1521	9097	167
14	Wallingford, Berks	291	1744	167
15	Newbury, Berks	685	4293	160
16	Weymouth, Dorset	565	3617	156
17	Kettering, Nthants	454	3011	151
18	Lewes, Sussex	723	4909	147
19	Windsor, Berks	585	4105	143
20	Ely, Cambs	547	3948	139

Sources: Premiums as table 3.7. Populations calculated from *PP* (1831) XVIII, 'Comparative Account of the Population of Great Britain in 1801, 1811, 1821 and 1831'.

1780. It was only towards the end of the century that this *stasis* began slowly to move.[26]

By 1800, however, several major cities generated nowhere near the insurance income the Sun was entitled to expect from them given their size. Birmingham, the third largest provincial city in England by this time, ranked only 42 among the company's agencies and yielded the same amount of annual premiums (£440) as Chichester in Sussex, which had a population 16 times smaller. Sheffield, the eighth largest conurbation in Britain, had a population 19 times larger than Dorchester, but earned Sun about the same premiums (£210). In relative terms the richer pickings for insurers were to be found in the smaller country towns rather than in the big cities. The Sun's agencies in 1799 have been ranked by the level of per caput premium yield in their localities. The top 20 agencies by this measurement are shown in table 3.8. All of them were located in the south of England. Only two were in towns with populations over 5000.[27] Market towns in the home counties, quiet cathedral towns, the ports and docks of the south coast, and declining west country textile centres dominate the ranking. Potton in Bedfordshire, the Sun's most productive agency thanks partly to the patronage of the Whitbread family, generated over six shillings of premiums for every inhabitant, or roughly £1200 of insurance per household, ostensibly a huge sum for the tiny market town.[28] In the cities insurance was spread much more thinly. Manchester and Liverpool were ranked 54th and 93rd respectively, with £61 and £30 in premiums earned per 1000 inhabitants. In Manchester, the Sun's largest agency in 1799, this translated into an annual average of just over one shilling per inhabitant, which in turn represented perhaps £160 of fire insurance per household.[29] The manufacturing towns of the midlands were also relatively unproductive. Birmingham, Sheffield, Wolverhampton, Coventry, Walsall, Leicester and Nottingham, all with populations over 10000 in 1801, each yielded £20 or less per 1000 inhabitants and were ranked in the bottom third of the table.

How can this pattern be explained? First, population growth and house-building in the cities was many times more rapid than it was in the smaller urban centres. Between 1775 and 1801 most of the places ranked amongst the Sun's top agencies by per caput premiums expanded by only a few houses each year. Larger towns, such as Cambridge, Reading or Maidstone, added between 15 and 40 new buildings a year. By contrast, several hundred new houses were, on average, built each year in Manchester, Liverpool, Birmingham and Leeds during the same period.[30] While the middle-class property market in such cities also grew, a great deal of housing development was the wrong sort for insurers - in-filling in central areas creating the densely populated courts and warrens which rapidly became slums, cellar dwellings excavated from the foundations of existing structures, new terraces of back-to-backs erected quickly by speculative builders.[31] Much low value, overcrowded inner-city tenement, cottage and workshop property was insured, but it generated a poor rate of per caput premium income in comparison to the richer and more thinly populated property markets of the south. Moreover, the increasing number of industrial and commercial buildings insured at higher premium rates did not offset the low per caput premiums earned on the mass of tenement and cottage insurances in the big northern cities.

Because of the limited size of their local urban markets, the Sun's agents in the smaller southern towns had to cast their net wide. Some of the earliest agencies, such as Buckingham and Cambridge, aimed to serve an entire county. Occasionally, vacant agencies were taken over by other agents residing elsewhere, thus increasing the geographical dispersal of business, sometimes across counties. The use of town populations to calculate the rankings in table 3.8 thus exaggerates the per caput premiums earned by small town agents, for they served extensive and shifting rural areas as well. Nevertheless, even if it was possible to recalculate table 3.8 to account for the rural populations covered by small town agents, the rank order would probably not alter greatly, for two reasons. First, it is likely that average property values in the south of England were higher than in the midlands, the north or Scotland. Little work has been carried out on eighteenth-century urban property markets, so we cannot be sure of our ground. As noted above, however, average insured property values were up to 30 per cent greater in London than elsewhere, and, though suffering distance decay, one might expect London's higher values to affect property in much of the home counties as well. Second, many of the towns listed in table 3.8 and their hinterlands were wealthy. Those providing professional and financial services enjoyed the patronage of local gentry and clergy as well as the custom of tradesmen and merchants. It was the region, not the city alone, which made Exeter the Sun's biggest agency for most of the eighteenth century (see table 3.7). Devon was full of modest country houses. Donn mapped 656 'gentlemen's seats' in 1765, many of which had been built or rebuilt in fashionable brick since 1700.[32] Across east and south Devon, and in the vicinity of Exeter itself, there were also a number of larger mansions which were partly remodelled in the palladian style during the course of the century. Together with the growing volume of middle-class terraced property in Southernhay and other suburbs, these helped sustain insurance income from Exeter even as the region's woollen industry declined.[33]

Many of the southern counties prospered from the continuous diffusion of the capital's wealth. When in 1729 the Sun sent one of its early 'riding officers' to tout for business in East Anglia and the home counties, he was instructed to 'go through the several countys as well as into the villages as Great Towns and engage as much as possible the insurances of gentlemen's seats and single houses'.[34] The Medway valley, flanked by high yielding insurance agencies at Chatham, Maidstone, Canterbury and Sevenoaks, was 'everywhere spangled with populous villages and delicious seats of the nobility and gentry'. The same was said about other major river systems in the south. In the early 1800s Southey noted the 'many fine seats...situated on the left bank [of the Thames], amid hanging woods', upstream of Maidenhead (ranked 3). Visiting the Avon valley in the early 1820s, Cobbett claimed that half a century earlier there had been 50 mansion houses standing within 30 miles of Salisbury (ranked 28). Where a town captured through traffic by water or road, commerce might compound the insurer's prospects. Defoe found Chelmsford (ranked 5), for example, to be 'a large thoroughfare town, full of good inns, and chiefly maintained by the excessive multitude of carriers and passengers which are constantly passing their way to London'.[35] Such towns were invariably well-built and improved, and thus offered attractive terrain for fire insurers.

The devastation of farms, villages and small towns by fire often stimulated the replacement of timber and thatch by brick, stone and slate, while the fear of fire - when heightened by a close encounter with the hazard - also encouraged sales of insurance. The fires which swept repeatedly through east Devon helped make Exeter the Sun's biggest earning agency. Eight of the 19 provincial towns most often visited by large fires were located in this region.[36] The effect of fire damage on insurance demand was also noticeable elsewhere in southern England. The 'great fire' of Gravesend in 1727 destroyed over 100 buildings at a cost of £44000, and made over 500 people, nearly half the town's population, homeless.[37] The Sun's income from Gravesend had ranged between £30 and £50 before the fire.

After the town was rebuilt, which took about six years, annual remittances climbed to over £130.

Jones and Falkus have demonstrated how urban improvement during the later eighteenth century was concentrated in market towns and non-industrial ports, especially in the south.[38] As well as rebuilding in brick or stone, im provement encompassed paving, lighting, street cleaning and widening which also helped prevent the spread of fires. Several of the towns in which the Sun earned the greatest volume of per caput premiums obtained improvement acts during the century, including Canterbury (1727), Salisbury (1737), Poole (1756), Exeter (1760), Portsmouth (1768), Windsor (1769) and Weymouth (1776). The 'improved' towns benefited from the public involvement of a resident middle-class as well as the patronage of a well-heeled local gentry. The insurer consciously sought out such locations. We may gain some measure of this by comparing the Sun's agency income in 1757 with Langford's list of 132 'polite towns', ranked by the number of residents paying duty on plate that year.[39] All but four of the top 34 towns in Langford's list had Sun agents in 1757. Two-thirds of all 'polite towns' (90) had agents appointed by the Sun at some date before 1800, while most of the rest were covered by nearby agencies. This, together with the evidence presented in table 3.6, underlines the close link between eighteenth-century fire insurance and the distribution of middle- and upper-class wealth.

The census figures for town populations in 1801 and the taxation data from 1757 provide only snapshots of the relationship between the Sun's agency income and urban growth. It is more difficult to say how successfully the office kept pace with the growth of insurable, improved property outside London over the course of the century. Before 1801 for most towns there are almost no figures on house numbers and very limited data on population. Table 3.9 brings together the available evidence for 25 places to illustrate changes in per caput premiums from 1740 to 1800. In two of the biggest agencies the performance w as im pressive. Premium income rose three times faster than Manchester's population and four times faster than Edinburgh's during the second half of the century. In other large cities of the north and midlands the Sun's per caput premium income was lower in 1799 than it had been earlier in the century, suggesting a failure to keep pace with urban growth. In several places, the Sun's income was badly affected by competition from local offices. This was true in Liverpool and Leeds from the 1770s, as well as in several market and residential towns further south - Bath after 1770, and Norwich, Cirencester, Worcester and Evesham from 1790. In Birmingham, Hull, Sheffield, Derby, Nottingham and Leicester, however, local offices were not a threat. Although there was competition from the REA and after 1782 from the Phoenix, it is probable that the rate of population increase in these large industrial towns made it difficult for the Sun's agencies to expand as quickly as their markets. The data for Hull and Nottingham suggest that the 1770s marked a turning point where rapid growth in per caput premiums gave way to a long secular decline.

By contrast, the per caput income of the Sun's agencies in southern England,

Table 3.9 Per caput premium income - selected Sun agencies, 1740-99

(current £ per 1000 inhabitants; agencies ranked by population size in 1801)

	1740	1750	1760	1770	1775	1780	1790	1799	Population in 1801
Manchester					21		46	61	110938
Glasgow						22	21	32	95822
Edinburgh		12						52	86436
Liverpool					36		20	30	77653
Birmingham		6		13		9	5	6	73760
Leeds	2	6		28	26		40	33	53162
Sheffield							8	5	45755
Norwich		18						14	36832
Hull	18			37		34	22	18	29508
Nottingham	15	18	17	28	30	27	22	20	28861
Bath	20			24		8	7	8	27686
Leicester						9		7	16953
Worcester						48		44	11182
Derby							18	13	10832
Lancaster						8		37	9030
Maidstone						141		88	8027
Southampton			43					67	7913
Kendal						14	22	25	6892
Poole					213			126	4761
Chichester	14		61	80				93	4744

Newbury			106		160	4293
Cirencester	4	13		49	38	4130
Evesham			97		40	2837
Dorchester		120			85	2402
Blandford			409		231	2326

Notes: Where appropriate, the population of the greater urban area is taken, e.g. Manchester includes Salford, Glasgow includes Govan. Per caput premiums are calculated by dividing the five year moving average premium by the nearest population estimate falling within five years either side of the date shown. Thus, the figure for Bath in the column labelled 1740 is actually the average premium in 1743 divided through by the population total for 1743.

Sources: Premiums as in table 3.7. Populations from 'Comparative Account', *PP* (1831) XVIII, 1.; Clark and Hosking, *Population Estimates*; Chalklin, *Provincial Towns*, appendix VI; Corfield, *Impact of English Towns*, pp.129, 183; Chambers, 'Three Essays', p.351, for Nottingham; Morgan, 'Demographic Change', for Leeds; Jackson, *Hull in the Eighteenth Century*, p.2; Neale, *Bath*, p.44; Smout, *History of the Scottish People*, p.243, for Edinburgh; Gibb, *Glasgow*, p.105.

where no local fire offices emerged as rivals, continued to increase to the end of the century. There were exceptions to this north-south division. The yield from the Dorset towns and from Maidstone declined, while premiums from Lancaster and Kendal outstripped the growth of those towns. Obviously the circumstances of individual agencies and the efficiency and zeal of agents were factors. Generally, though, the available data indicate that the country's biggest fire insurer had difficulty in coping with the great wave of urbanisation which transformed parts of Britain during the last quarter of the eighteenth century. Insurance offices were not the only institutions to suffer from this problem. One thinks, for example, of the failure of the Church of England to build new churches in urban-industrial areas during the same period. The London fire offices with agency systems, however, were the only business organisations of the time to have to deal with urban growth on a national, rather than a local, level. The experience of the Sun suggests that the problem of reorienting the geographical focus of a large sales network away from the south of England and towards the industrial conurbations of the midlands and north had not yet been overcome by 1800.

Provincial fire offices before 1800

In an increasing number of locations the Sun's agents coexisted with those of the REA, but there is little evidence of competition between them. In most places a working accommodation was probably reached which required no comment by the Sun's managers. In towns where a local fire office was established the situation was very different.

In Scotland no fire insurance office was established between the foundation of the 'friendly societies' of Glasgow and Edinburgh in 1720, and the offices which opened in Dundee and Aberdeen in 1798 and 1800. The Edinburgh society was the largest in Scotland with £2.4m insured in 1805. This produced annual premiums of around £3500, which was £1000 less than the Sun's earnings from its Edinburgh agency. The Glasgow office earned around £3100 in 1805, similar to the Sun's income from that city.[40] At the beginning of the nineteenth century, therefore, the Sun was the largest insurer in Scotland.[41] Indeed, before 1800 none of the Scottish companies appear to have provided the London office with any competition worth the comment. By the middle of the eighteenth century the Sun was already firmly established in Scotland with agencies in Edinburgh and Aberdeen. In 1756 the office set up its own fire brigade in the capital, 'upon the representation of the Lord Provost and Town Council of Edinburgh, and in consideration of the number of insurances in that City and in hopes of extending the business of the Office in that part of the Kingdom'.[42] These hopes were realised as the agency's income nearly doubled to £1100 during the following five years. This was only the prelude to the greater expansion of business which accompanied the building of Edinburgh's first new town. The Sun's earnings soared to £4500 by the end of the century, by which time the city was 'increasing and improving with rapid strives and likely to become one of the most elegant and flourishing capitals that Europe can boast of'.[43] For much of the eighteenth century fire insurance in Scotland depended heavily upon English imports, while the development of the native insurance industry lagged far behind that of other financial services such as banking.[44]

The first English insurance office established outside London was the Bristol Crown Fire Office founded in 1718. Half a century later, a further two offices were opened in the city, the Bristol Fire Office in 1769 and the Bristol Universal in 1774. The latter expired in 1778 but the others survived until the 1830s. Unlike the local insurers in Glasgow and Edinburgh, the Bristol offices did leave an impression on the Sun's business. As a co-partnership of some 80 individuals with a capital of £40000, the Bristol Crown was powerful enough to draw an early response from the Sun, which refused to accept any proposals from the city. This ban was only lifted in 1730 under pressure from local residents.[45] An agency was eventually set up in 1738 but it foundered for the next fifteen years, barely earning £100 a year. In 1752 the managers noted that it had been 'long observed that the business done by this Office in the City of Bristol was very inconsiderable, excepting two or three sugar houses...'. The agent was dismissed for having failed to advertise sufficiently.[46] From this point the Sun's business in Bristol picked up. Premiums rose rapidly to a peak of £750 by the mid 1760s and the drive for business was reinforced by investing in a fire brigade in 1763. Accommodation was sought with the local fire office too, with the Sun following the lead of the Bristol Crown in matters such as the rating of part-brick houses in 1753 and the allowances paid to firemen in 1767.[47] The establishment of two new offices brought the Sun's expansion in the city to a sudden end. Premiums collapsed by 38 per cent between 1765 and 1773. As can be seen in figure 3.1, which charts the Sun's income from Bristol with the annual tonnage of shipping using the City's port, the agency enjoyed none of the fruits of the high-water years of Bristol's trade between the end of the Seven Years War and the outbreak of war with the American colonies.[48] Recovery was slow, though it was sustained through the depression in trade which accompanied the American war. As late as 1801 the Sun's position in Bristol remained weak. Bristol ranked only 136 out of 167 Sun agencies by per caput earnings, and the income from the agency amounted to only about 11 per cent of the aggregate business of the two local offices.[49]

In nearby Bath, the Sun also found that local offices could prove calamitous for business. Here, however, the situation was different in that the Sun enjoyed four decades building up a presence before the first Bath Fire Office was established in 1767. During these decades agency income increased two and a half times faster than Bath's population and housing. The Sun found itself in a very advantageous position at the onset of the resort's first building boom from 1726. Its first two agents there were Chandos men. The second agent, Richard Marchant, Quaker banker and merchant tailor, was one of several 'creditmen' responsible for financing the Chandos buildings in the town. Marchant occupied the Bath agency

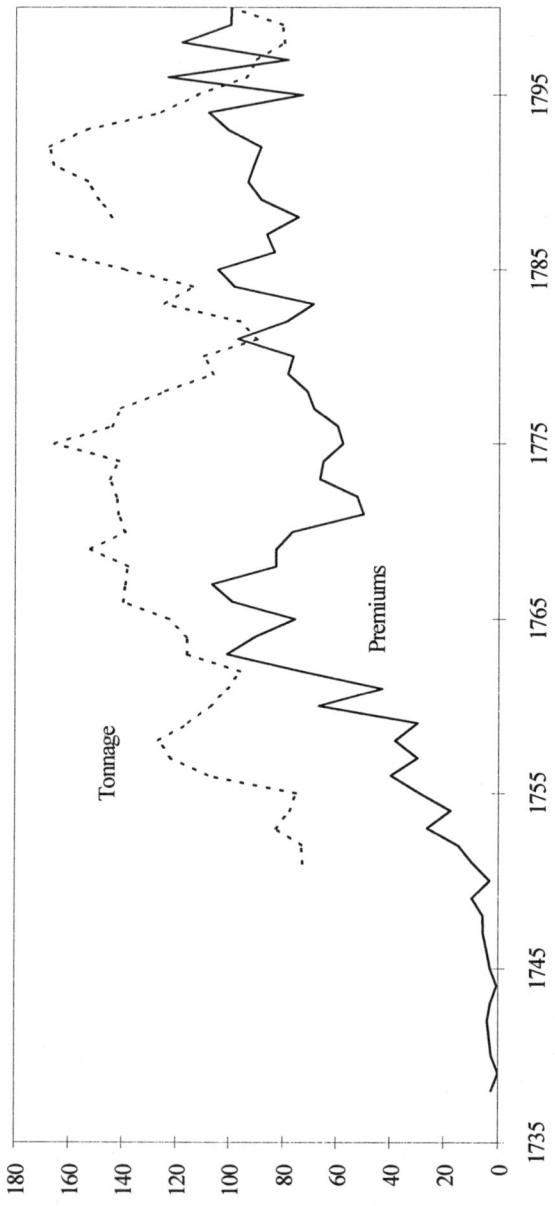

(Annual premiums from Sun's Bristol agency, annual shipping tonnage, indexed 1800 = 100)

Figure 3.1 Insurance and trade in Georgian Bristol
Source: see text.

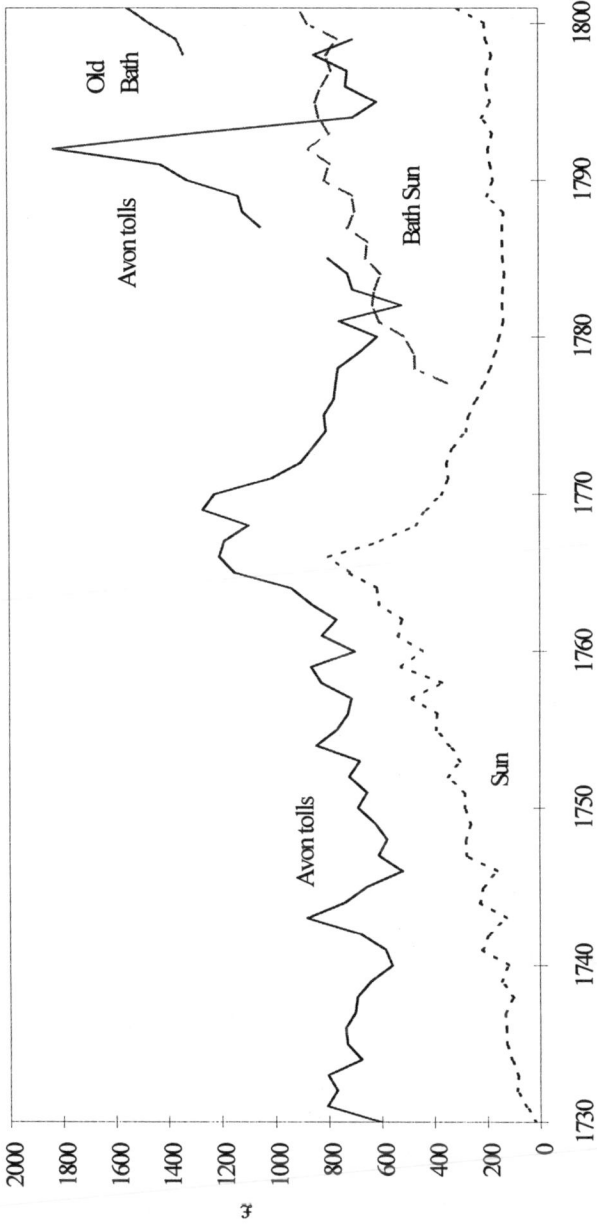

(Premiums of three fire offices; Avon tolls, all annual)

Figure 3.2   Fire insurance and the economy of Bath
Source: see text.

for 25 years, retiring in 1752 by which time annual income had risen to over £300. Chandos himself was a major shareholder (until 1729) with close connections to the Sun's boardroom and exercising patronage which extended to nominating several candidates for agencies.[50] Chandos's builder in Bath, John Wood, together with his son, went on to build nearly 350 houses between 1728 and 1787 for some £334000. The cost of these and other houses built by leading developers, often exceeding £1000, were largely beyond the means of small building tradesmen, but were just the type of properties an insurer would seek. The new stone-built town created a lucrative market for property insurance.[51]

The Sun's interest in Bath can be measured in part by the effort it made to support the parish fire brigades. Some 300 buckets had been sent to the town by 1764, representing over seven per cent of the Sun's total donations by this date, while the agency accounted for less than three per cent of the office's provincial income.[52] By the mid 1760s the Sun's premiums from Bath had reached nearly £800, and per caput earnings had more than doubled since 1743. Its business had expanded through three successive building booms in the town between 1726 and 1760, but the insurer was not to benefit much from the later upswings in construction, those peaking in 1771 and 1792.[53] As Bath reached the height of its Georgian prosperity in the later 1760s, the Sun's agency began to decline. Figure 3.3 reveals the impact of the first local office in 1767. Premiums crashed to £235 in 1776, at which point a second local office, the Bath Sun, was opened.[54] The London office's premiums continued to fall to £127 in 1784, making an 84 per cent decline since 1766. By contrast both Bath offices grew rapidly. The Bath Sun's premiums in its first full year of business were already 40 per cent greater than those earned by the Sun agent. Figure 3.2, which presents the insurance data together with the annual tolls on shipping tonnage using the River Avon, shows how the local office participated in the local economic upswing of the later 1780s and early 1790s.[55] By the 1790s the Bath Sun's income was regularly over £800. The Bath Fire office, by now known as the 'Old Bath', was larger still, earning over £1400 by the end of the century.[56] By this date the Sun's premiums from Bath amounted to less than ten per cent of the aggregate income of the two local insurers, similar to the position it faced in Bristol. The Sun's per caput income stagnated below half the level of 1743 while the town's population continued to grow to nearly 28000. Overall the impact of the local offices was to help spread the insurance habit through Bath and its region. While the Sun's premiums had amounted to £49 per 1000 inhabitants in 1766, the aggregate income of the Sun's agency and the local offices reached £89 per 1000 by 1801.

As well as the four insurance offices founded in Bath and Bristol between 1767 and 1776, a further four offices opened in the north of England during the twelve years to 1783. The impact of these on the Sun varied by locality. Late in 1771 an insurance service was established by Manchester's first private bank, which styled itself the Manchester Bank and Insurance Office.[57] Its policies and its advertised rates were almost identical to those of the Sun, although its charges for new policies, stamps and firemarks were higher.[58] The Manchester office seems to have done considerable business. At least 2600 firemarks were issued by the office during its 16 year lifespan, possibly many more.[59] When the bank foundered in 1788, the insurance business was offered to the Phoenix who snapped it up, although, when losses on cotton insurances began to rise, reservations were expressed about the quality of the business acquired.[60]

Around the time of the foundation of the Manchester office, the Sun's business there was affected by the deaths of successive agents in 1770 and 1772 and premiums fell. Between the end of the 1770s and 1800, however, the agency's income grew nearly ten fold. Any sign of the Manchester Bank and Insurance Office is invisible in the graph of Sun's soaring business (see figure 3.3). The Sun's premium income closely tracked the rise of Manchester's staple trade, although it is noticeable that its agency earnings did not suffer the disruption which the cotton industry suffered following the outbreak of war with France in 1793. Over the whole period 1730-1801 there was a correlation of 0.91 between annual insurance earnings and the cotton trade.

Across the Pennines an insurance office was opened by Beckett's bank in Leeds in 1777.[61] The new venture followed its predecessors in Bath, Manchester and Liverpool by offering free policies to those who transferred their insurances from other offices. It also dispensed with the three per cent deduction upon claims which the London insurers charged, and it set the same premium rates as the Liverpool office established the year before. Agencies were opened in nine Yorkshire towns and in Kendal and Lancaster.[62] In 1782, however, it was reported that the office 'intended to decline insuring any longer, on account of the intended duty on property insured from fire'. It is not clear why Beckett's bank felt compelled to withdraw from fire insurance on account of the new stamp tax. It was the only institution in the country to do so. The bank offered to recommend that its policyholders transfer to the Sun, provided the Sun would agree to issue free policies to all those who did so. Although averse to the notion of free policies, the London office concurred.[63]

Before 1777 the Sun had enjoyed a near monopoly as the sole insurer represented in Leeds. The average number of policies issued annually rose from eight in the 1750s to 23 during the following decade, and income increased from £6 per 1000 inhabitants in 1754 to £28 in 1771. Business then stagnated. From 1777, under an energetic new agent, the agency commenced an upward surge which was little affected by the local rival nor by the arrival of several other fire offices from 1783. The annual number of policies doubled and premium income per 1000 inhabitants rose to £40 by 1790. The Sun's earnings from Leeds advanced hand in hand with the development of the region's economy (see figure 3.4). The correlation between insurance premiums and building deeds registered in the West Riding was close, at 0.88, and even closer with Yorkshire broad cloth production, at 0.97. Beresford, who used the surviving policy registers to analyse the Sun's business at Leeds, found a trend during this period towards larger

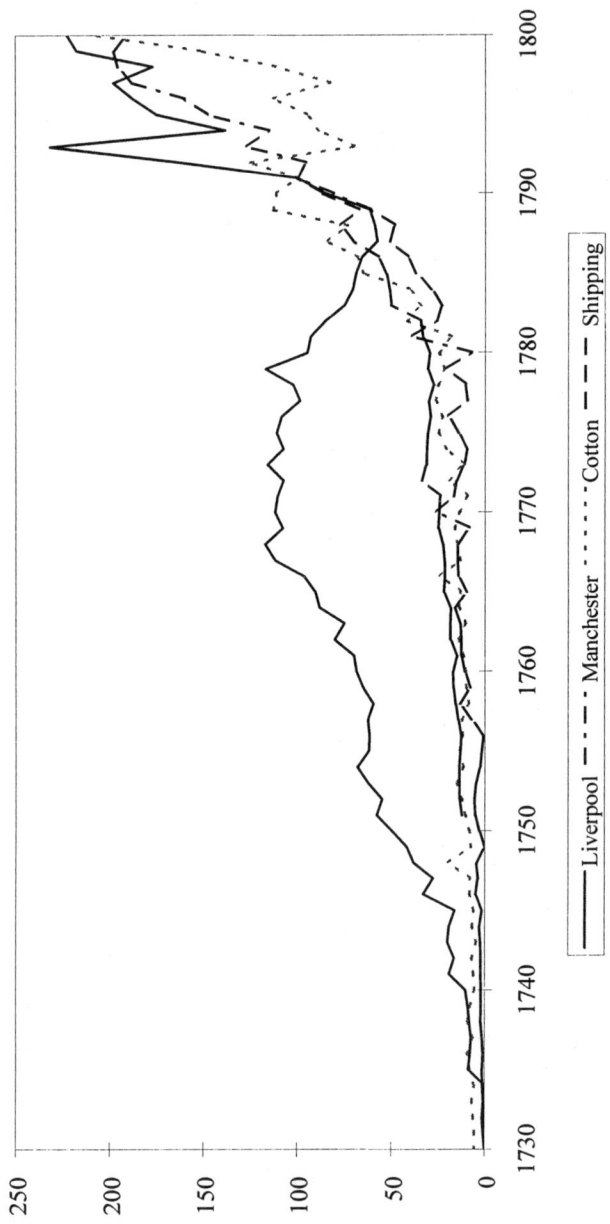

(Sun's premiums, Liverpool and Manchester agencies; cotton imports and exports, lbs; shipping tonnage, Liverpool outbound. All annual, indexed 1791 =100)

Figure 3.3 Fire insurance and economic growth in Lancashire
Source: see text.

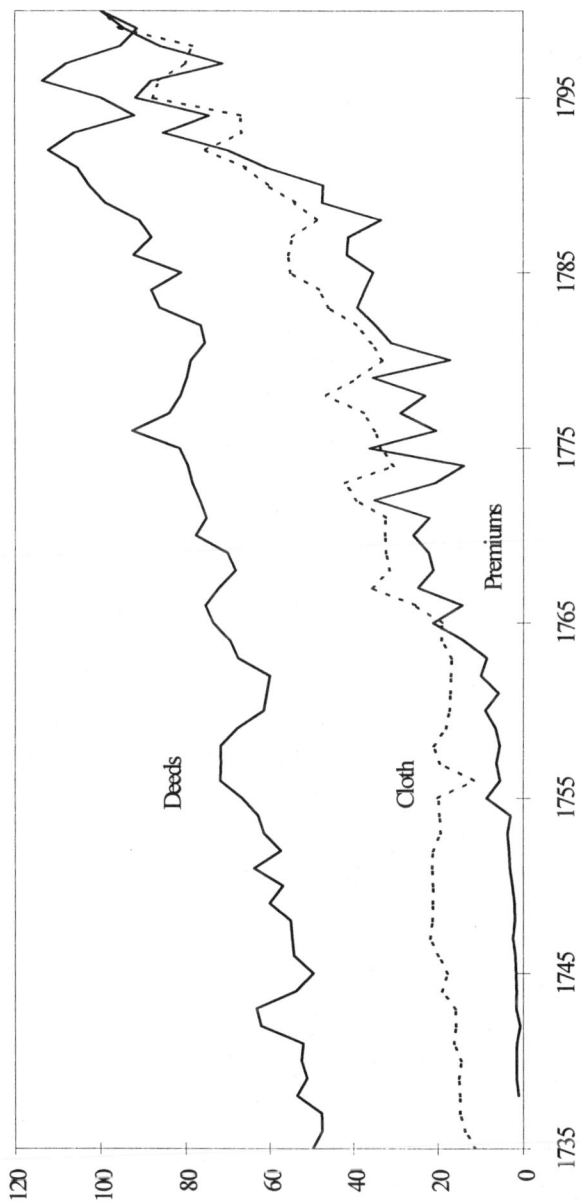

(Sun's premiums, Leeds agency; building deeds registered in the West Riding; broad cloth milled. All annual, indexed 1800= 100)

Figure 3.4 Fire insurance and the West Riding economy
Source: see text.

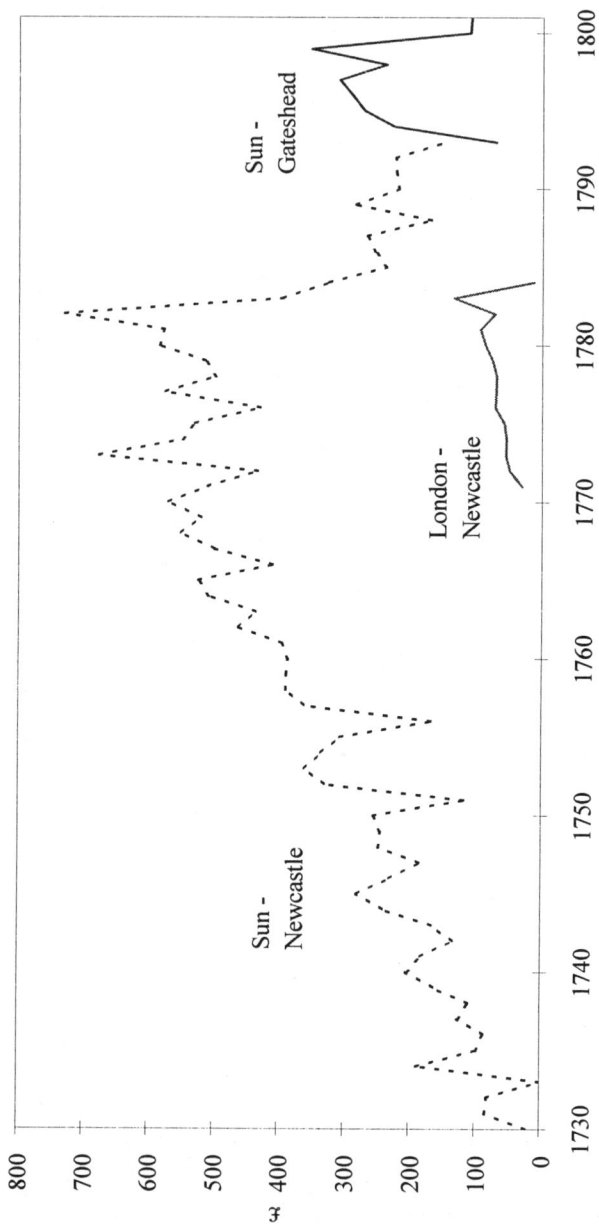

(Annual premiums of Sun and London Assurance agencies)

Figure 3.5 Insurance in the north-east, 1730-1801
Source: see text.

insurances, particularly with the growing number of bigger industrial properties, and towards multiple properties combined in one insurance.[64]

In Liverpool and Newcastle, by contrast, the Sun's income was seriously affected by local competition. The Sun had long enjoyed a monopoly in the Lancashire port. In 1766 only the Sun's agent and five brokers sold insurance there.[65] Towards the end of 1776 eight prominent merchants founded the Liverpool Fire Office (LFO) to insure 'houses and other buildings, goods, wares and merchandise in any part of Great Britain'. Within a decade LFO agents were to be found in 'most of the principal towns' in Cheshire, Lancashire, Derbyshire, Staffordshire, Leicestershire, Yorkshire and in Edinburgh. A nominal capital of £80000 was subscribed to, policies were issued free of administrative charges to those who moved their insurances from other offices, and the London insurers' practice of deducting three per cent on the adjusted value of claims was also abandoned. During the 1780s the office benefited from the powerful business and political connections of its partners, particularly in capturing the insurances of public buildings in Liverpool. In 1788 it competed vigorously for the business of the Manchester office as the latter was being transferred to the Phoenix.[66] By 1790, however, the LFO's proprietorship had declined from 14 to ten, and in the winter of 1794-5, when many of the partners' trading activities were struggling, the LFO also fell into the hands of the Phoenix. The acquisition brought the Phoenix at least £1.2m of insurances, considerably strengthening its position in the local market.[67]

The arrival of the LFO was followed by a halving of the Sun's income from over £1200 in 1775 to £650 by the mid 1780s (figure 3.3). If we correlate cotton imports and tonnage of outbound shipping from Liverpool with the Sun's agency premiums from Manchester and Liverpool for the sub-period 1751-91, the years for which we have annual shipping data, the contrast between the Sun's experience in both towns is highlighted. While the correlations between Manchester premiums and both sets of trade data were high (>0.9), there was no correlation between commerce, shipping and the Sun's insurance income from Liverpool during this period.[68] Figure 3.3 shows that the Sun's agency in Liverpool expanded during the third quarter of the eighteenth century when it still enjoyed a monopoly position, but declined during the economic boom of the 1780s when competition from the local fire office was keenest. It seems that the Liverpool market for property insurance was not yet expanding quickly enough to allow the two most prominent offices to participate equally in that expansion. As in Manchester, premiums did recover. The boom in the cotton industry and the commercial and urban expansion which accompanied it ensured rapid growth for the Sun's agency during the 1790s. By 1791, four years before the demise of the LFO, the Sun's premiums from Liverpool had almost returned to their level of 1775, and in the following decade they doubled. The main effect of local competition was to delay the take-off of the Sun's insurances in the port, so that the Liverpool agency lagged behind its counterpart in Manchester in profiting from the cotton boom. Consequently the long-run association between the cotton trade and the Sun's earnings from Liverpool over the period 1730-1801, at 0.71, was weaker than it was at Manchester.

For the Sun the greatest impact of a local office was felt in Newcastle. The Newcastle Fire Office was established in 1783 as a co-partnership with over 20 proprietors and a fund of £105000.[69] The town's business elite filled the new boardroom, with bankers at the heart of the venture. Several promoters were connected to Newcastle's common council, several were investors in local turnpikes and most had backgrounds in manufacturing, lead and coal mining, and trade.[70] The office thus posed a formidable threat to London insurers operating in the region. It offered free policies for transfers, made no deductions from adjusted claims, conducted a vigorous advertising campaign in the Newcastle press, and appointed 16 agents during its first nine months of business. As was the case with the Liverpool Fire Office, the Newcastle office's close connection with the town corporation immediately gave it the kind of quasi public status which the Sun was often able to acquire elsewhere in the absence of local competitors.

Between 1740 and 1777 the Sun's income from Newcastle had expanded at nearly three times the rate of the town's population growth, despite some competition from the agencies of the REA and the London Assurance.[71] With the foundation of Newcastle Fire Office in 1783, the Sun's business, and the much smaller income of the London Assurance, collapsed (figure 3.5). In part this may have been due to the new stamp duty which depressed demand in many places. Unlike elsewhere, however, no recovery followed. The London Assurance closed down its Newcastle agency in 1784. The Sun's agency was wound up in 1793 and most of the policies were transferred to a new agency established across the Tyne in Gateshead which enjoyed only temporary success. Thus the Sun failed to derive advantage from the improvements to Newcastle which were gathering pace from the 1780s - the construction of Dean and Mosley streets, broad thoroughfares driven through the heart of the old town, the clearing away of old buildings which blocked the middle of Newgate and congested the head of Cowgate, the building of new squares within the walls and the development of new residential streets beyond the walls.[72] The Sun's other rivals among the London offices remained in the district and may have succeeded in competing for the new properties coming onto the market. The REA's agent, the bookseller and stationer Edward Humble, was very active in advertising his post as agent and receiver not only for the town, but also for 'the counties of Durham, Cumberland, Northumberland, and the town of Berwick and parts adjacent'. By 1784 Humble's agency, and his counterpart at Darlington, were supplemented by a string of nine further REA agencies across the north-east. The Phoenix's sales network was similar, with nine agencies situated by 1785 in a line running southwards from Berwick to the North Riding, while the Sun had only three agents in this area.[73] The Newcastle office also proved a formidable opponent. By 1805 it was the second largest of the country offices with over £3m insured.[74] Its annual premium income over the period 1783-1809 averaged £2856, nearly four times greater than the Sun's aggregate income from the four northern counties and the north Riding of Yorkshire.[75]

Whatever the limitations of particular markets, many of the new offices of the 1760s-1780s posed a considerable challenge in their own towns and regions to the

Sun and the REA. Overt competition by price or product was uncommon. Instead it was conducted through the personal connections and business reputations of the promoters of local offices, which to an extent seem to have compensated for the greater security offered by the big London insurers. Competitiveness was also achieved through non-price entry mechanisms such as free policies and abolition of the three per cent drawback on claims, as well as through the more concentrated agency networks which local insurers were able to establish in a region. In 1778 the Leeds Fire Office sold insurance out of 11 Yorkshire towns, compared to the Sun which had five Yorkshire agencies, and the Liverpool Fire Office which had three. In 1784 the Liverpool office was represented in at least eight Lancashire towns, while the Sun and the Phoenix had just four agencies each in the county. The Salop Fire Office, founded in Shrewsbury in 1780, had opened seven agencies by 1788 in Shropshire, north Staffordshire and north Wales, while the Phoenix, the Sun and the REA had only two or three agencies each in this area. The Newcastle Fire Office had appointed eight agents between Stockton and Berwick by the end of 1783 compared to the three agencies each operated by the Sun and the Phoenix. There was some attempt made by London insurers to increase the density of their sales networks in regions where a local office emerged to do business. The REA was advertising 11 agencies in the north-east by 1784 in response to the threat posed by the Newcastle office, and by 1796 the REA could also advertise seven agents in the Shrewsbury newspapers, the same number as the Salop Fire. Without the relevant underwriting data we cannot say whether this amounted to a genuine challenge by the REA to the local offices. These may just be examples to support the dismissive view of the secretary of the Phoenix, who declared in 1795 that the REA 'stuff the Country papers with a pompous list of Agents but they do very little business in the fire branch'.[76]

With their more intimate knowledge of local risks, the country offices should have been able to assess risks more efficiently and underwrite more profitably, and in this way offset the advantages of risk spreading which the major London offices, with their national sales, possessed. Unfortunately almost no figures have survived which would enable us to test this. The Bath Sun, the smaller of the two Bath offices, is the only local insurer to have left a complete series of annual premiums and losses from its foundation (in 1776). Its results demonstrate how profitable it was. Claims absorbed just 15 per cent of premiums over the period 1777-1801.[77] The Newcastle Fire was also successful. Its average annual profit over the period 1783-1807 amounted to £1356, or an impressive 47 per cent of annual premium income.[78] A note in the accounts of the Salop Fire Office from 1787 states that the 'increase in capital in seven years after defraying all expences' amounted to £3714. This represented a handsome return of nearly two and a half times the founders' original investment, or an annual compound rate of 13.8 per cent.[79]

It is impossible to measure precisely the Sun's underwriting performance in individual locations for most of the eighteenth century as no loss data have survived for agencies. For some districts minute book references offer a glimpse of underwriting at the local or regional level. In Lancashire the number of claims suffered by the Sun had grown to a steady stream by the late 1780s. Between 1786 and 1791 payments for fire damage to the county's cotton industry amounted to nearly £19000, or 97 per cent of the aggregate income of the Sun's three Lancashire agencies operating during that period. This staggering rate of attrition underscored the concern of London insurers to create an adequate tariff for the cotton industry, a concern which increased during the following decades. In the West Riding wool textile district too, as early as 1781 the Sun voiced its alarm about the 'great number of losses by fire for some years past'.[80]

Given the limited evidence of large urban fire disasters in the big northern cities during the second half of the eighteenth century, it is tempting to speculate that two general types of underwriting loss in the north and south of the country emerged before 1800.[81] In the market towns of the south huge fires could wipe out dozens of houses at once, but these were interspersed with many years of profitable insurance. In the north, if we take the example of the Sun's losses through its Manchester agency, claims were more numerous and more frequent than in southern towns, but fires seldom involved more than a few properties together. Instead the steady flow of small and medium sized claims were intermittently, but much too frequently, accompanied by large claims from fires which destroyed a mill or a warehouse.

What may have emerged, therefore, is a kind of insurance subsidy by the prosperous south for key industrial districts in the north. This subsidy could have operated in at least two ways. First, there were direct money transfers from southern premiums to help London offices pay for northern claims, especially on industrial and commercial risks. Second, the large London fire offices could support the insurance of northern industrial properties by cross subsidies from other more profitable regions and categories of insurance, reducing the need to withdraw from the riskier markets in the event of a sudden upturn in claims, and keeping premium rates lower than the claims experience may have warranted. Because of their capital assets and the greater spread of their liabilities geographically and by category of risk, London insurers helped to expand underwriting capacity beyond the scope of local offices with their more limited funds and narrower spread of risks. There was nothing easy about this process and the London offices soon found themselves steering between the rocks of rising taxation, stagnating demand, increasing competition and the difficulty of assessing the new risks associated with the factory system as it spread through particular regions of the country.

Notes

1   The most explicit statement about the conjunction of these processes can be found in Daunton, *Progress and Poverty*, p.279-80. See also Hudson, 'Regional Perspective'; Pollard, *Peaceful Conquest*, pp.4-41; Langton, 'Industrial Revolution'.

2   Rubinstein, ' Wealth a nd t he Wealthy', map 20.4. Average policy and replacement values calculated from GL Ms 8666/12-28, Hand-in-Hand, DM, 1735-1800 *passim*; Ms 8747/2, London Assurance, Fire Policy Register, 1760-61.

3   The Phoenix had a rapidly growing overseas business. Its figures in table 3.1 are net of premiums remitted by foreign agents, but gross of premiums collected on foreign insurances is sued b y t he company's London head office (so-called 'home foreign' premiums). Consequently table 3.1 understates the proportion of the Phoenix's domestic insurances outside London, but probably not by a large amount. Foreign agents accounted for an average of 14 per cent of all premiums in the period 1796-1800. 'Home foreign' business was probably much less than this. Calculated from Trebilcock, *Phoenix Assurance*, vol.I, table 5.1, p.165.

4   The Union began appointing country agents in 1805 and the Westminster in 1853. Davies, *Westminster Fire*, pp.63-4.

5   The percentage of new sums insured on septennial policies beyond the 10 mile radius rose between 1760 and 1794 from 2.8 per cent to 3.8 per cent (trend values). Calculated from WCA, Ms 343/83-6, Westminster, General Account Books, 1759-94. From 1782 Westminster commenced selling annual insurances on a non-mutual basis. These increased to 24 per cent of all sums insured by 1805. A proportion of these would have insured property between ten and 25 miles from London.

6   Wilson and Mackley, 'How Much Did the English Country House Cost to Build?'; Stone and Stone, *An Open Elite?*, pp.349-94; Beckett, *Aristocracy in England*, pp.326-7.

7   GL Ms 8666/19, 21, Hand-in-Hand, DM, 16 Apr. 1765, 25 Aug. 1772; Pevsner, *Essex*, p.229; Pevsner, *Bedfordshire*, pp.166-70; Pevsner, *Hertfordshire*, p.268.

8   Stone and Stone, *An Open Elite?*, pp. 368-9.

9   65 of 96 properties insured by Hand-in-Hand and destroyed by fire outside London, compared to 389 of the 1411 London properties analysed in table 2.3.

10   There is a reference, but no details, to a set of 'Instructions to Country Agents' in 1762. G L M s 8735/ 2, L ondon A ssurance, FCM, 14 May 1762. A previous set of instructions had been issued in 1728.

11   GL Ms 8747/2, London Assurance, Fire Policy Register, 1760-61.

12   For higher rents in Irish towns compared to England, see O'Brien, *Economic History of Ireland*, p.370.

13   GL Ms 8735/2, London Assurance, FCM, 12 June 1752, 2 Nov., 9 Nov. 1753, 8 Mar. 1754.

14   GL Ms 8735/2, London Assurance, FCM, 7 Sept., 14 Sept. 1753, 14 Apr. 1755.

15   These offices were the Hibernian (1771), the General (1779) and the Dublin (1782). Harrison, *Irish Insurance*, pp.3-4.

16   GL Ms 8755/2, London Assurance, Out Letter Book, to Piersy & Waggett, 2 May, 16 May 1785.

17   Dickson, *Sun Insurance*, pp.39, 67; Supple, *Royal Exchange*, p.99.

[18] GL Ms 11935/1-9, Sun, CCM, 1730-1805. Other relevant minute books are Ms 11931/2-8, Sun, GCM, 1715-1808, and Ms 11932/1-15, Sun, CMM, 1725-1800. The lists for 1786 are found in Ms 18856, Sun, Agents' Accounts, 1786, and Ms 14386, Agents' Bond Book, 1786. Contrary to Beresford's assumption in his study of the Sun's agency in Leeds, agents' remittances of cash and bills were almost certainly net of the various taxes on fire insurance policies collected by the agents on behalf of the Stamp Commissioners, even after the introduction of the new duty on sums insured in 1782. Agents' remittances, however, did probably include payments to the office for firemarks and policies. Beresford, 'Prometheus Insured', p.377.

[19] The estimates are based on all recorded references to agencies in the committee books listed in the previous footnote.

[20] Trebilcock, *Phoenix Assurance*, vol.I, pp.82-4; Supple, *Royal Exchange*, p.99.

[21] Calculated from Trebilcock, *Phoenix Assurance*, vol.I, table 3.2, p.84. The coefficient of variation measures the relative dispersion of the numbers of agencies per region around the mean. This coefficient was 0.63 for Phoenix in 1785 and the same for Sun in 1790. There are no records upon which to base a comparable calculation for REA.

[22] Lee, *British Economy since 1700*, p.135; Rubinstein, *Capitalism, Culture and Decline*, pp.25-35; Cain and Hopkins, *British Imperialism*, pp.19-22.

[23] Calculated from the gross assessment totals in 'Accounts respecting the Income Duty', *PP* (1801-2) IV, 155. Rubinstein and Lee each found a similar proportion, 39 per cent, as London's share of the total taxable income, for the tax years 1806 and 1812. Rubinstein, 'Wealth and the Wealthy', p.158; Lee, *British Economy*, p.130.

[24] Rubinstein, 'Victorian Middle Classes', p.616.

[25] O'Brien, 'British Incomes', p.257. I am grateful to Michael Turner for this reference. There is also no suggestion in the literature that administrative inefficiencies or fraud skewed the 1801 tax data geographically in any particular direction, although Hope-Jones does conclude that tradesmen and merchants were more successful in avoiding Pitt's first income tax than landowners or big farmers. Hope-Jones, *Income Tax*, p.20.

[26] Successive columns in table 3.7 are highly correlated at > 0.9 until the 1780s, when the coefficient falls to 0.82 (for 1780/90).

[27] Canterbury and Portsmouth.

[28] The average household sum insured in Potton is estimated by multiplying the per caput premium by an average premium rate of 2.5s% (per £100 insured), and dividing through by 4.6 persons per household (average household size in 1801). The average premium rate is a guess, based upon the assumption that most property covered by this agency was insured at the rate for common residential dwellings.

[29] Calculation as in footnote 28, but employing an average rate of 5s%, to reflect the greater proportion of higher-rated industrial and commercial property in the Manchester agency, and an average household size in 1801 of 6.7.

[30] The annual averages were 303 new houses in Manchester, 272 in Birmingham, 227 in Liverpool and 122 in Leeds (township). House building rates were calculated from data in Corfield, *Impact of Towns*, p.183; Law, 'Some Notes'; Clarke and Hosking, *Population Estimates*; Beresford, 'Face of Leeds', p.73; 1801 Census of Population.

[31] Beresford, 'Back to Back House in Leeds'; *idem.*, 'Making of a Townscape'; Chapman, 'Working Class Housing in Nottingham'; Treble, 'Liverpool Working Class Housing'; Butt, 'Housing'.

[32] Minchinton, 'Economic History', p.177.

[33] Pevsner and Cherry, *Devon*, p.363; Hoskins, *Industry, Trade and People*, p.149.

[34] GL Ms 11932/1, Sun Fire, CMM, 17 July 1729.

[35] Defoe, *Tour*, pp.57, 108, 119, 132, 144, 277, 347-8; Southey, *Letters from England*, pp.169-70; Cobbett, *Rural Rides*, p.313.

[36] Jones et al., *Gazetteer*. The authors define a large fire as one which destroyed ten 'houses' (as defined by contemporaries) or more.

[37] Porter, 'Great Fire of Gravesend', pp.24-5.

[38] Jones and Falkus, 'Urban Improvement', table 3.

[39] Langford, *Polite and Commercial People*, pp.402-3. There are a few surprising omissions from Langford's list as candidates for 'politeness', including Cambridge, Norwich, Lynn, and Salisbury, all of which had substantial Sun agencies in 1757. On the gentility, 'good manners' and wealth of these places, see Defoe, *Tour*, pp.96-7, 194, 426; Borsay, *Urban Renaissance*, pp.35, 123, 140, 153.

[40] Raynes, *History of British Insurance*, pp.90-91; Dickson, *Sun Insurance*, appendix 4; Walford, *Insurance Cyclopedia*, vol.V, p.421. Premiums estimated by dividing sums insured through by average rates of 3s% for Edinburgh, and by 4s% for Glasgow, reflecting the latter's greater volume of commercial and industrial property.

[41] Assuming, as seems likely, that the Scottish agencies of the REA and the Phoenix were not larger than those of the Sun. The Phoenix earned just £326 from Edinburgh in 1812 while it was 'lamentably weak' in Glasgow before 1811. Trebilcock, *Phoenix Assurance*, vol.I, pp.468-9.

[42] GL Ms 11935/4, Sun Fire, CCM, 4 June 1756; Ms 11931/5, Sun Fire, GCM, 8 Apr. 1756. The Sun had previously supported municipal fire brigades in Edinburgh and Leith through donations.

[43] Sinclair, *History of the Public Revenue*, vol.III, p.205. On the building of new town, see Youngson, *Classical Edinburgh*, pp.70-110.

[44] In 1801 the Sun alone insured about £5.5m through its four Scottish agencies, compared with a total of £3.8m insured by Scottish offices at this date.

[45] Raynes, *History of British Insurance*, p.90; GL Ms 11935/1, Sun Fire, CCM, 24 July 1730; Ms 11932/2, Sun Fire, CMM, 3 Dec. 1730.

[46] GL Ms 11932/2-3, Sun Fire, CCM, 10 Feb. 1738, 24 Nov. 1752.

[47] GL Ms 11931/5, Sun Fire, GCM, 5 Apr. 1753; Ms 11932/8, Sun Fire, CMM, 21 May 1767.

[48] The shipping data in figure 3.1 is taken from Minchinton, *Trade of Bristol*, appendices C and D. Over the whole period, however, there was a positive correlation between the volume of trade, measured by coastal and foreign shipping tonnage, and the Sun's premiums from Bristol, at 0.55.

[49] Eleven per cent is an estimate based upon the Sun's sum insured in Bristol in 1801 (annual remittance in 1801 multiplied by an estimated average rate of 4s%), and the total insured by both Bristol offices in 1805, calculated from the duty returns given in Walford, *Insurance Cyclopedia*, vol.V, p.421.

[50] On Marchant and Chandos in Bath, see Neale, *Bath*, pp.131-50. On Chandos and Sun, see Dickson, *Sun Insurance*, pp.69, 244-5, 271-4.

51   Neale, *Bath*, pp.151-7. Cf., however, the more jaundiced view of Smollett's Matthew
      Bramble about the 'slightness' of new housing in Bath, 'contrived without judgement,
      executed without solidity...'. Smollett, *Humphrey Clinker*, p.36.

52   Calculated from GL Ms 11935/1-5, Sun Fire, CCM, 1730-64 *passim*.

53   Building booms from Neale, *Bath*, appendix B, p.396.

54   Trebilcock, *Phoenix Assurance*, vol.I, table 8.4, p.495 lists three offices, the Old Bath
      of 1760 (merged with the Sun in 1827), the Bath Fire of 1767 (merged with the Sun
      in 1782), and the Bath Sun of 1776 (merged with the Sun in 1838). There is no
      supporting evidence of any fire office founded in Bath in 1760 nor of a Bath office
      acquired by the Sun in 1782. The Bath Fire Office of 1767 was almost certainly that
      which later became known as the Old Bath and was acquired by the Sun in 1827.

55   Avon tolls from Neale, *Bath*, appendix A , pp. 384-90.

56   Bath Sun premiums from GL Ms 11935E , Sun Fire, Take over Papers. Old Bath Fire
      Office premiums from Ms 14116, Sun Fire, Simplified Profit and Loss Accounts. The
      latter are only available from 1798.

57   *Manchester Mercury*, 3 Dec. 1771, 31 Mar. 1772. On the foundation of the bank, see
      Grindon, *Manchester Banks*, pp.23-31.

58   9s 6d for an insurance of <£1000 and 14s 6d for insurances >£1000, compared with
      8s 6d charged by the Sun and the London Assurance. CUL, PAA, PX1766,
      Manchester Fire, Proposal Form, 26 Dec. 1771; Relton, *Account of the Fire
      Insurance Companies*, p.211.

59   This assumes consecutive numbering of firemarks. Relton, *Account of the Fire
      Insurance Companies*, p.210. A firemark numbered 2618 of the Manchester office is
      referred to in *The Policyholder*, 2 Mar. 1973.

60   Trebilcock, *Phoenix Assurance*, vol.I, pp.361-2. On the collapse of the Manchester
      bank and the 1788 crisis, see Pressnell, *Country Banking*, pp.111, 292, 452-5;
      Grindon, *Manchester Banks*, pp.45-6.

61   On Beckett's bank, see Pemberton, *Banking in Leeds*, pp.56-8.

62   *Leeds Mercury*, 18 Mar., 2 Dec., 9 Dec. 1777.

63   GL Ms 11931/6, Sun Fire, GCM, 11 June 1782; Ms 11932/12, Sun Fire, CMM, 17
      Oct. 1782.

64   Average policy values at Leeds rose from £1162 in 1782 to over £2000 in 1796.
      Beresford, 'Prometheus Insured', p.383.

65   Brown, 'Fire Insurance in Liverpool', p.5.

66   *Prescott's Manchester Journal*, 8 Feb. 1777; *Leeds Mercury*, 1 Apr. 1777;
      Manchester Mercury, 24 June, 1 July, 8 July 1788.

67   *Lewis's Liverpool Directory*, 1790, p.85; *Billinge's Liverpool Advertiser*, 12 Jan.
      1795; Brown, 'Fire Insurance in Liverpool', p.16; Peet, *Liverpool Vestry Books*,
      vol.1, p.340; Trebilcock, *Phoenix Assurance*, vol.I, pp.361-2, table 8.4, p.495.

68   The coefficients were -0.02 for shipping tonnage, and -0.19 for cotton imports. Cotton
      imports and re-exports in figure 3.3 are from Mitchell, *British Historical Statistics*.
      Shipping tonnage (outward only, excluding coastal shipping for which there are few
      data) from LRO, Ms 942 Hol 10, Holt & Gregson Papers, pp.361, 363, 415-17.
      Coastal shipping tonnage has been deducted from the totals for 1785-6, and the
      average proportion of coastal tonnage to total tonnage for these years has been used to
      estimate total tonnage, net of coastal shipping, for 1788. All other years appear to be

net of coastal shipping. I am grateful to David Richardson for a transcript of this data, and for his advice on these points.

[69] *Newcastle Courant*, 1 Feb. 1783.

[70] The business activities of the promoters and directors of Newcastle Fire Office are examined in Chapter 6 below.

[71] From £8 per thousand inhabitants in 1740 to £21 in 1777. Population estimates from Middlebrook, *Newcastle upon Tyne*, p.321.

[72] Middlebrook, *Newcastle upon Tyne*, pp.144-50.

[73] *Newcastle Courant*, 6 Nov. 1784; Trebilcock, *Phoenix Assurance*, vol.I, p.87, map 3.2.

[74] Walford, *Insurance Cyclopaedia*, vol.V, p.421.

[75] The Sun's income is calculated for the nearest comparable period for which we have data, 1783-1801. Gateshead Central Library, Cotesworth Mss, CM/4/17, Newcastle Fire, Accounts.

[76] *Leeds Mercury*, 1.Apr. 1777, 6 Jan. 1778; Trebilcock, *Phoenix Assurance*, vol.I, table 3.2, p.84; *Newcastle Chronicle*, 6 Nov. 1784; *Salopian Journal*, 1 Apr. 1795, 28 Sept. 1796; CUL, PX1010, Phoenix Assurance, Agents Extra Letter Book, letter of March 1795.

[77] GL Ms 11935E , Sun Fire, Take over Papers, Bath Sun.

[78] Gateshead Library, Ms CM/4/2,17, Newcastle Fire, Accounts.

[79] SRO, Ms 30081/2/10, Salop Fire, Accounts 1780-1822, note of 1 May 1787.

[80] *Leeds Mercury*, 25 Sept. 1781.

[81] In Jones's *Gazetteer* of urban fire disasters, Liverpool appears three times, Garstang, Wigan and Chorley appear just once in the period 1760-1800. No other Lancashire towns, nor most of the largest Yorkshire towns, are listed, nor do the newspapers of these towns record any major urban fires, although they do not ignore fire hazards and, on occasion, the benefits of insurance.

Chapter 4

Insurance in Wartime, 1782-1815

Their town was large, and seldom pass'd a day
But some had fail'd, and others gone astray;
...Quarrels and fires arose; and it was plain
The times were bad; the saints had ceased to reign.

George Crabbe.[1]

During the first two decades of the reign of George III fire insurance enjoyed a surge of growth. Where there had been about nine fire offices in Britain and Ireland in 1760, there were over twenty by the end of the American War of Independence. The value of property insured expanded faster than the economy, and even faster than industrial output, while the proportion of assets covered by insurance also rose. Progress between the end of the American war and the defeat of Napoleon was less sure-footed. On the one hand, this period saw increasing competition with innovative, well-funded metropolitan firms emerging to challenge the older market leaders, while new provincial insurers seized valuable portions of country business. A few offices also began to extend their business overseas during this period, charting paths followed by major British insurers later in the nineteenth century. On the other hand, relative to the growth of the economy and the population, the insurance industry slowed down and stalled from the early 1780s. As figure 1.2 and table 1.4 show, real per caput sums insured stagnated and the proportion of assets insured declined. Demand for insurance suffered under an ever heavier tax burden, while high premium rates, kept up by an oligopoly of the three largest London firms, added to the deterrent for consumers. Despite high prices, the profit margins of the big insurers were threatened by competition and by persistent losses on industrial and commercial insurances. These losses reflected a failure of the fire offices to adjust their risk categories sufficiently, and to improve assessment procedures quickly enough to keep up with technical change and the new types of property associated with the industrial revolution. In several senses fire insurance did not serve the British economy well during these years.

Taxation and insurance

The problems which faced the insurance offices were not all of their own making. With the stamp duty on insurances introduced in Lord North's budget of 1782, the fiscal burden on policyholders suddenly became heavier. A stamp on fire insurance policies had been first introduced in 1694 at a flat rate of 6d. This rate was raised several times, with additional duties on engrossed or printed paper, until in 1776 it reached 3s 2d for policies issued within the bills of mortality and 5s 6d for policies issued elsewhere.[2] One year later these rates were raised again, by five shillings for policies insuring over £1000. The effect of the fixed rate duty before 1777 was regressive, penalising those insuring only a small amount of property. A duty of 5s 6d represented, for instance, nearly three times the annual premium for a policyholder insuring a dwelling house for £100 at the common rate (two shillings per cent) in the London offices, but only about one-quarter of the premium paid by someone with a policy for £1000.

The huge increase in the duty on large insurances in 1777 worried the London fire offices, who collectively agreed to pass all the extra cost of the tax onto their new policyholders. The Treasury, however, was less concerned about the impact of the duty than by the fact that it failed to contribute much to state revenue in a time of war. Between 1774 and 1782 the annual average net yield was only £9000, which represented a tiny proportion of the total revenue from stamps in this period.[3] North pointed out in his budget speech that this duty had not produced the sum at which it had been calculated because the fire offices had fallen into the habit of renewing annual and septennial insurances without issuing new policies. The Westminster Fire Office, for example, introduced 'perpetual' insurances to this effect in 1777, and, as North consulted this office when drafting his bill, he may well have had the Westminster's practice in mind.[4] Certainly the number of policies taxed by this duty was only a fraction of the total. Only about 59000 policies paid the stamp in 1775, largely accounting for the new policies issued that year, whereas there were probably about 420000 policies then in force.[5] North's complaint was not that that the stamp duty on policies was being evaded, but that, because new policies accounted for such a small proportion of the total number of current insurances at any one time, the impost was too light and the duty was simply not raising enough revenue.[6]

The new duty of 1s 6d on every £100 insured against fire, which took effect from 24 June 1782, formed part of a bundle of tax increases by which North aimed to raise nearly £800000. North thought that this was 'not an immoderate tax: and (that) it would be a productive one'. Basing his calculations upon figures probably supplied to him by George Browne, secretary to the Westminster office, North estimated that the proposed duty would raise £112500 on £150m insured, 'but he would take the tax only at £100000'. Only the proposed taxes on soap, tobacco and carriage of goods were projected to raise more towards the chancellor's target. In the Commons the opposition to the new duty was muted. Fox denounced it as 'very unwise and highly impolitic', and 'a very foolish tax'. Far greater concern was expressed by members over the proposed taxes on the carriage of goods, on soap and on theatre admissions, than over the massive new burden on fire insurance.[7] This suggests, to employ O'Brien's terms, that parliament continued to perceive insurance as a 'superfluity', rather than as a 'decency', still less a 'necessity'.[8]

Outside parliament the response of the fire offices was vigorous. On 19 March 1782, eight days after the budget debate, the Sun appointed a committee of managers to wait upon North and to 'endeavour to render the said bill as little prejudicial to the interest of the Society as possible'. The beleaguered North, who had only days left in office, did not reply. The Union passed a motion condemning the bill as 'a tax very prejudicial to the public and a peculiar burden on trade in particular...we conceive (it) will tend to the ruin of this Office'.[9] Early in April, the Sun wrote to the new Prime Minister, Rockingham, pointing out the drawbacks of the proposed duty. Most of the other London offices followed the Sun's lead, and they undoubtedly cooperated as the texts of the various petitions were so similar.[10] The Sun claimed that 'great numbers of people' across the country had signalled their intention to stop insuring if the tax was introduced. The Sun's fear was not that insurances would decline, but that the best properties, those least at risk from fire, would be lost. It argued that the proposed duty was a tax on the prudent, not on those who neglected to insure, and that trade, as well as the insurance offices, would suffer. From the frequency and magnitude of fires in town and country in the previous four or five years, 'the Offices in general have sustained losses to a degree beyond what was known to them before', while the duty would prevent them from being able to raise premiums in proportion to the increased risk.[11] Given the growing losses in places such as Manchester, there was substance to the Sun's argument.

The insurers proved far less successful as a lobby than other special interest groups such as the West India merchants or the Scotch whisky distillers.[12] Despite further submissions, the new chancellor, Lord John Cavendish, proceeded with North's tax.[13] Insurers were thrown into a frenzy of activity. The proprietors of the Leeds Fire Office announced that they would cease insuring 'on account of the intended duty on property insured from fire' and offered their business to the Sun. The Salop inquired of the Bath and Bristol offices 'what steps they take in consequence of the tax' and revised its proposal forms in line with the alterations made by the Bristol Fire Office to take account of the new duty.[14] The London offices set about appointing extra clerical staff to deal with the expected increase in workload as the duty payments came in.[15]

Supple has stated that there were economies of scale in duty collection which worked to the advantage of the larger offices, in addition to the poundage allowance paid to the fire offices for their labour in collecting the duty, and the interest they could earn on the unremitted balances held between the quarterly returns of the duty to the stamp commissioners.[16] Initially, though, the set-up costs of administering the new tax were considerable, especially for the biggest offices. The Sun established a new committee to supervise the returns, which were kept separately in a series of duty books. After ten months the members complained that the allowance they received was 'not adequate to the very great trouble and frequent and long attendance which the business of the committee necessarily requires'.[17] The new act also required the insurers to deposit a bond with the stamp office in proportion to the amount of duty which they anticipated would be generated by their insurances. In turn, fire offices also required their agents, who were charged with collecting the duty from country policyholders, to deposit a bond and the names of two guarantors. Here was another expense, for the fire offices had to employ their solicitors to draft new contracts of appointment and bonds. The amount of bond was fixed according to the level of premium income earned by the agency, which may have been one reason why there was a flurry of agents' resignations in the summer of 1782.[18] Another new requirement, at least for the unincorporated fire offices, was an annual licence to insure. The licence was issued in the names of two nominated directors, while a further four directors were required to enter into the bond with the two licencees. In consequence, some offices released their directors from any personal liability for losses or expenses arising from the bond or licence.[19] Insurers also faced the problem of collecting the duty from existing policyholders. The Union wrote to all its members asking them to bring in their policies to the office to pay the duty, on pain of their insurances being declared void. The Sun's agents advertised in the press for policyholders to bring in their policies in order to ascertain the exact sum to be paid for duty - yet another expense.[20]

Generally the tax collection was efficiently managed but the fear that the new duty would become a disincentive to insure was soon realised. Sums insured tumbled from £171m in 1782-3 to £133m three years later, a fall of 22 per cent.[21] The response to this varied. The Westminster office introduced annual insurances for the first time in July 1782, advertising them by 'posting 1000 large bills...in red and white' throughout London. The Sun, the REA and the Phoenix abolished the customary three per cent deduction from claims payments. The Union reduced premiums on a few hazardous insurances such as brewers, dyers, maltsters and chemists. The Phoenix and the Sun raised their limits on the amount they would insure on sugar refineries. The Sun also relaxed its rates on Thamesside insurances. However, no price war broke out, nor, contrary to predictions, did any insurance office other than the Leeds cease business. Moreover, as with other taxes on consumption during the late eighteenth century, the downturn in demand was not sustained. Together with their rising profits, dividends and share values, this tended to weaken the insurers' case against the government at the time of future tax increases.

In its first year of operation the yield from the duty, at £130000, was considerably greater than expected. The contribution of fire insurance to the total revenue from stamp duties soared from under two per cent to 16 per cent in 1783, before falling back to eight per cent, the level at which it remained until the end of the Napoleonic wars. There were three further hikes in the percentage duty during this period. In his budget of 1797 Pitt raised the duty by sixpence, 'a small addition' which he thought would bring in £35000.[22] In fact the additional yield amounted to nearly £49000. Another sixpence was added in 1804, although at the same time the stamp on policies was reduced to a flat rate of one shilling. The only other concession came in 1786 when the percentage duty on insurances issued

Table 4.1 Insurance taxation and public revenue

Annual averages

	1	2	3			
	Duty on insurance £	Total stamp duties £m	Total public revenue £m	col.1/ col. 2 %	col.2/ col.3 %	Col.1/ col.3 %
1774-82	9018	0.47	11.81	1.9	4.0	0.1
1783-5	116211	1.02	13.81	11.4	7.4	0.8
1786-90	104635	1.28	16.43	8.2	7.8	0.6
1791-5	129240	1.44	18.61	9.0	7.8	0.7
1796-1800	175285	2.22	26.22	7.9	8.5	0.7
1801-3	231446	3.20	37.47	7.2	8.5	0.6
1804-10	380432	5.14	62.93	7.4	8.2	0.6
1811-15	526735	6.30	74.60	8.4	8.4	0.7
1816-20	626969	7.02	60.86	8.9	11.5	1.0
1821-5	673392	7.22	59.48	9.3	12.1	1.1
1826-30	777840	7.24	55.24	10.7	13.1	1.4
1831-5	831108	7.18	50.46	11.6	14.2	1.6
1836-40	934053	7.26	51.54	12.9	14.1	1.8
1841-5	1043452	7.36	55.14	14.2	13.3	1.9
1846-50	1129872	7.18	57.26	15.7	12.5	2.0

Notes: Column 1: stamps on policies, England & Wales, 1774-82; percentage fire duty, GB 1783-1803, UK 1804-50. Column 2: total revenue from stamp duties, GB net 1774-1800, GB gross 1801-3, UK gross 1804-50. Column 3: total public revenue, GB net 1774-1800, GB gross 1801-3, UK gross 1804-50.

Sources: Lambert, *Sessional Papers*, vol.38, pp.161-6; Coode, 'Revised Report', table of duty; Mitchell, *British Historical Statistics*, pp.388-93.

abroad was abolished. This was largely the result of a campaign by the Phoenix which had begun to build up a valuable overseas business.[23] In 1794 Irish insurances became subject to the percentage duty and in 1810 policies issued in London on property in the colonies were also subjected to the same charge as UK insurances. Finally in 1815 chancellor Vansittart added another sixpence to the duty on domestic insurances, pushing it up to three shillings per cent, while colonial duties were also raised. Despite repeated complaints from the fire offices, the domestic stamp duty remained at this level until the 1860s when it was finally abolished. The only further major concession came in 1833 with the exemption granted to farming stock insurances.[24]

Despite the rate increases between 1782 and 1815, tax revenue from insurance did not quite keep pace with the growth in income generated from all stamp duties

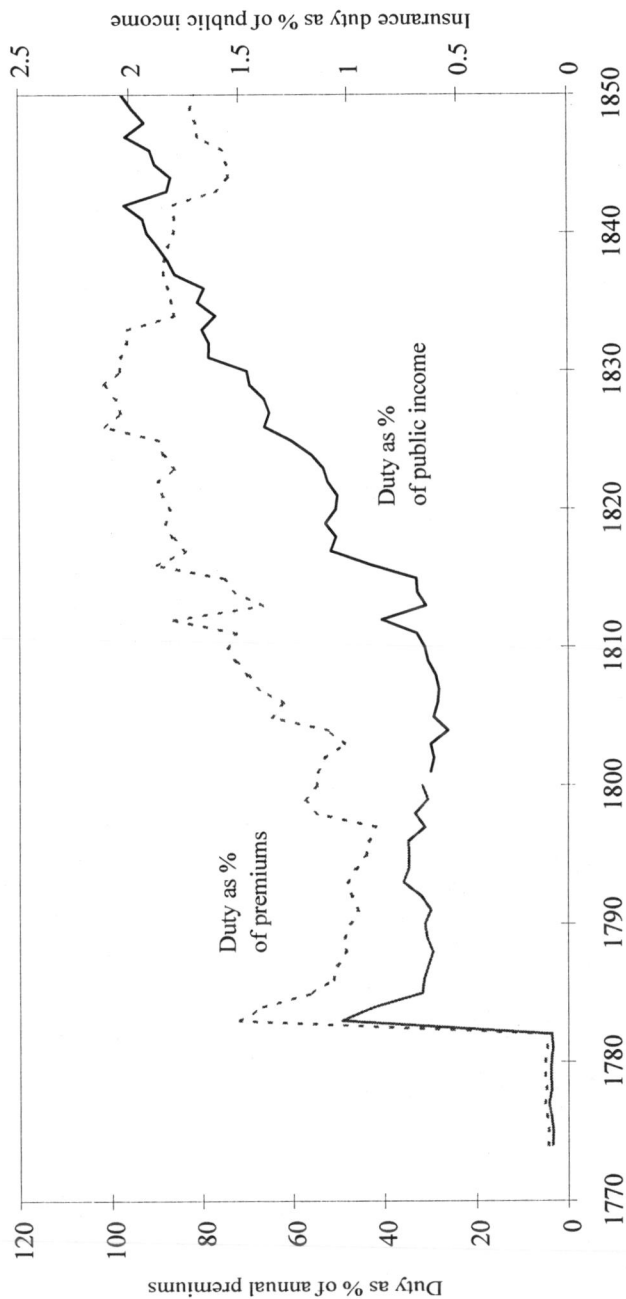

Stamps on policies 1774-82, percentage duty 1783-1850: (i) as % of net income, GB 1774-82, as % of gross income, GB 1801-3, UK 1804-50; (ii) as % of total annual premiums, English fire offices

Figure 4.1 Fire insurance and taxation, 1774-1850

Sources: see text.

Table 4.2 Stamp duty as a percentage of total premiums

Annual averages, selected offices

	Sun	London	Kent	County	Bath Sun	MFLAC	Sheffield
1782-5	43.7	54.2					
1786-90	49.6	51.3					
1791-5		49.2					
1796-1800		58.6					
1801-5	*81.0	65.3	*71.6		*107.2		
1806-10	*87.6	87.6	83.4	*109.9	*97.3		
1811-15		94.7	*83.3	131.5			
1816-20		107.4		109.6			
1821-5	*102.1	110.7	*100.8	100.4	*118.8		*126.6
1826-30	113.6	126.2	114.5	100.0	144.9	65.2	154.3
1831-5	104.1	97.5	94.8	93.7	138.2	61.0	140.0
1836-40	99.5	92.1	93.4	84.4		64.7	128.6
1841-5	93.4	81.9	94.6	82.8		*59.8	122.7
1846-50	93.3	76.2	92.4				123.5

Notes: data marked * are as follows; 1801-5 = 1805 for Sun, Bath Sun, average of 1802-5 for Kent. 1806-10 = 1810 for Sun, 1809 for Bath Sun, average of 1807-10 for County. 1811-15 = average of 1811-13 for Kent. 1821-5 = average of 1822-5 for Sun, Kent, Bath Sun, Sheffield. 1841-5 = average of 1841-3 for Manchester. For all offices the average of 1836-40 excludes the year 1837 when the printed duty returns are deficient. Premiums are 'net' of commission for Sun and County, gross for other offices. Dickson estimates gross to be about 10 per cent greater than net premiums. Dickson, *Sun Insurance*, appendix I. This implies that where the duty is in the range of 80-100% of gross premiums, it would be about seven to nine points lower as a percentage of net premiums.

Sources: GL Ms 15045, Sun, Duty Papers and Licences; GL Ms 8746A, London Assurance, Fire Assurance - Annual Account; CKS, U2593/B15, B43, Kent, Financial Summary 1802-14, Pencil Copy of List of Statistics 1815-90; County, Annual Accounts 1807-29; GL Ms 11935E, Sun, Take over Papers, Bath Sun; Ms 16223, MFLAC, GCM, 1825-44; Ms 15032/8, Sun, Take over Papers, Sheffield Fire Office; Accounts relating to Stamp Duty paid on Insurance from Fire, *PP* (1823-51), *passim.*; GL Ms 16206/1, Essex & Suffolk, DM, no.1, Account of Fire Duty, 1809; Walford, *Insurance Cyclopaedia*, vol.V, pp.420-21; Dickson, *Sun Insurance*, appendix I.

during this period. After 1815, while other sources of tax revenue declined or stagnated, the percentage duty on fire insurance nearly doubled in yield and rose three fold as a proportion of public revenue. (See table 4.1 and figure 4.1). By mid-century over £1.1m in duty was being paid to the Treasury by policyholders each year. Fire insurance thus made a not inconsiderable contribution to the revenue of the British state. As early as 1788-92, at an average of 47 per cent of total premiums, the insurance duty was among the highest of 18 *ad valorem* taxes listed by O'Brien. Only the excise on salt, the customs duties on rum and tobacco, and the stamp on newspapers were more punitive. By 1810 stamp duty amounted to 72 per cent of total domestic expenditure on fire insurance premiums, far greater than the burden of direct taxes on agrarian incomes (20 per cent), customs duties on retained imports (36 per cent), or the excise on industrial goods (18 per cent).[25]

As figure 4.1 shows, the weight of taxation on insurance continued to grow until by the late 1820s the average policyholder was paying as much in duty to the government as he or she was paying in premiums to the insurer. Like other stamp duties, the duty on fire insurance, as a tax on property, was generally progressive in character. As contemporaries pointed out, however, within the body of policyholders the burden of the percentage duty was very unevenly distributed. It was greatest for those insuring ordinary brick-built dwelling houses at the common premium rate. After 1826 the duty amounted to 200 per cent of the annual premiums paid by such policyholders. By contrast, those insuring industrial or commercial properties at any of the higher rates had less reason to grumble. For a cotton mill insured in the 1820s at the basic rate of 14s%, the stamp duty amounted to only one-fifth of the premiums. To an extent the differential impact of the duty can be seen in the figures for individual fire offices. Table 4.2 reveals the differences between an insurer in a manufacturing district, such as the Manchester Fire & Life Assurance Company (hereafter MFLAC), with its accumulation of industrial policies, and a small insurer in a centre such as Bath or a conservative office such as the London Assurance, with their preponderance of residential insurances. While the tax amounted to 65 per cent of the premiums paid by the average policyholder insuring with the Manchester company in the late 1820s, it represented 145 per cent of premiums paid by the policyholders of the Bath Sun. It is too simple, however, to suggest this was another subsidy from the residential south to the industrial north, for, as table 4.2 shows, the tax burden on the customers of the Sheffield Fire Office was highest of all at 154 per cent. The business of this office was described as 'confined to Sheffield generally', and, given that many of the town's metal-working industries - with their open furnaces - were uninsurable, this small local office probably restricted itself mostly to common residential properties insured at the lowest rates.[26]

The cross-subsidisation effect created by the percentage duty therefore operated between those insuring dwellings, wherever they were situated, and those who insured hazardous buildings and their contents. State taxation of ordinary householders thus eased the cost of providing the industrialist with this financial service. For the first three decades of the nineteenth century the tax burden on common domestic policies rose substantially and thereafter it remained at a very high level. The majority of such policyholders, it is true, were located in the south, so the stamp duty may also have helped reduce the regional disparities in fire insurance to the advantage of the industrial districts of the north and midlands. These disparities, as noted in the previous chapter, persisted until at least 1800 on a scale far greater than the geographical inequality in the distribution of taxable wealth. We cannot be sure, however, that the duty had such a redistributive effect. What is certain is that one of the most lightly regulated services during the British industrial revolution was one of the most heavily taxed.

The emergence of oligopoly

In January 1782 a new insurer opened its doors for business in London, the first new fire office in the capital for 60 years. It was an initiative of the London sugar refiners who had become tired of the expense and difficulty in obtaining adequate insurance cover from the existing offices. Of about 100 sugar refiners in the capital, no fewer than 84 subscribed to the new venture from a total of 89 original shareholders. So concentrated was the Phoenix's proprietorship in 1782 that a circle of one mile radius centred upon its head office in Lombard Street encompassed the addresses of all but six of its first shareholders.[27]

The early strength of the Phoenix lay in this homogeneity, in its connections to the sugar industry, and in its adventurous approach to marketing. What commenced as a 'captive' insurer soon became an ambitious competitor, cutting premiums on London dockside insurances, moved swiftly into the markets for mills, distilleries and breweries, and, unsurprisingly, acquiring the lion's share of London's sugar insurances.[28] This powerful new office fuelled the competition which had already begun to emerge with the provincial foundations of the late 1760s and 1770s. One issue was quickly resolved, namely the long cherished practice of deducting three per cent from the value of all adjusted claims before they were paid. The Bristol Fire Office was the first to dispense with this in 1769. Other provincial offices followed, but it was only in 1782, when the Phoenix announced that it would not impose the drawback, that the REA and the Sun at last abandoned the practice.[29]

Competition largely centred on two other areas. First, sales rivalry increased between agents in particular districts. In the north-west all three major London insurers were kept busy reorganising and adding to their agency networks throughout the period 1788 to 1795. Agents were occasionally poached by one office from another and a keen eye was kept on the activities of competitors. Second, there was the practice of offering free policies, that is with the cost of the stamp duty and firemark discounted, to those who transferred their insurances from other offices. This had been used intermittently since the 1730s, but by the early 1780s virtually every new office in England had resorted to the device. In 1784 the REA began to give free policies to all its new policyholders. The Sun resisted and, after several false starts, an agreement was reached with the REA and the Phoenix in 1788 that all advertising of free policies was to cease and no more were to be issued by the three offices anywhere in England and Wales. Parallel agreements were reached between the three London offices and the local offices in Bristol and Bath not to poach each other's business by this device.[30]

Containment proved difficult as insurers manoeuvred for competitive advantage. A new office established at Worcester in 1790 offered free policies. The following year the agreement at Bath was broken by one of the local offices, and in 1792 a new office at Norwich issuing free policies compelled the London insurers to consider a limited use of the device. Finally in 1795 the agreement to resist free policies collapsed when all three London offices began to offer them to former customers of the Liverpool Fire Office upon its acquisition by the Phoenix, and when the REA broke the agreement not to compete with free policies in Bristol.[31] In their indignation about their rivals' actions each London insurer loudly protested about 'honour' and 'sacred engagements'. They were all at it, however, driven to use this simple competitive tool by the growing ferocity of the struggle for market share in different places. In 1799 the Sun was still denouncing free policies as 'improper', yet by this date they had ceased to be a major issue. Two years earlier Pitt had reduced the duty on policies.[32] In 1804 the advantage provided by the free policy was all but removed by the introduction of a new flat rate of one shilling on all policies.

The issue of free policies revealed the fragility of relations between the big three London insurers, as well as the difficulty of shoring up collective defences against provincial newcomers. Despite this relations were characterised by the remarkable level of cooperation which developed during these years. After an initial round of manoeuvring, the Sun, the REA and the Phoenix together constructed one of the most elaborate and ambitious cartels to be found in the contemporary economy. This should be seen in its wider context. Since the early seventeenth century manufacturers and merchants had come together to regulate prices and output, to influence fiscal policy and to lobby for protection. Formal collusion became an increasing feature of British business during the late eighteenth century. From the 1760s price-fixing combinations emerged in the north-east coal industry, in the paper, glass, tobacco, sugar and brewing industries, in iron and silver plate manufacturing and in copper mining. Chambers of commerce could be found at London, Exeter, Bristol, Birmingham, Halifax, Leeds, Manchester, Liverpool, Glasgow and Edinburgh during the 1780s. In the early nineteenth century price and output regulation emerged in the salt trade, and among pinmakers, shipbuilders, silk manufacturers, nailmakers and cutlers.[33] Mathias has argued that such collaboration was largely driven by state interference through the taxation, bounty and licensing systems. The level and type of collaboration, however, depended upon the structure of the industry concerned. The incentive to cooperate was greatest where firms were few in number, producing largely for one market, with high fixed costs.[34]

Among financial services, fire insurance was unique in generating collusion among big firms. This was not found among the fragmented banking, marine insurance and stockbroking sectors, and contemporary life assurance was too weakly developed and dominated by one large company to require such collaboration. Cooperation between the fire offices was also distinguishable from many of the associations of merchants and manufacturers in being almost exclusively a question of business. There were few extraneous dimensions in the form of social, political, cultural or familial networks to the regular conferences of the Sun, the REA and the Phoenix during the late 1780s and 1790s. Their strategies were largely developed by correspondence and by small meetings between the principal executive of each firm, usually Samuel Fenning of the REA, Hugh Watts of the Sun, and George Stonestreet of the Phoenix. Although doubtless accompanied by a good bottle of port, the meetings were tightly focused on particular issues and entirely functional in their nature. There was nothing anachronistic about their collusion as has been suggested.[35] Rather here, as in other areas, the large insurance offices were at the cutting edge of business development in industrialising Britain.

Mathias is doubtful of the economic effect of price associations in manufacturing, arguing that they were 'mainly regional affairs, operative in just depression years, and had no control over national outputs - indeed very often their existence was really evidence of effective competition'.[36] This may understate the importance of business collusion during the industrial revolution. Certainly it does not hold true for fire insurance. Despite continuing market entry, the big three fire offices succeeded in deflecting pressure on prices, raising profit margins and increasing their aggregate market share. It is likely that collusion had an inhibiting impact on the national output of insurance and on its distribution. The Sun, the Phoenix and the REA together accounted for 74 per cent of all sums insured by London offices in 1786, but 86 per cent by 1795 after ten years of collaboration. The principal losers were the London mutuals, whose market share fell from 24 per cent in 1785 to nine per cent in 1800.[37]

In 1786 the first of the meetings were held which developed into a regular and structured system during the next decade. This was no 'limited cooperation'. Rather it ranged over an extraordinary number of areas. The thorny issue of free policies was on the first agenda, but joint measures to deter fraud through arson, premium rates on waterside insurances in London and farming insurances were also discussed.[38] As table 4.3 shows, collaboration quickly extended to other areas of underwriting. A tariff for cotton mills in June 1790 provided the platform for a more ambitious scheme to cover most hazardous and non-hazardous risks. For this purpose 'several conferences' were held in which the London Assurance also participated. The first 'book of rates' was printed in October 1790. An amended version, the first of many, was drafted in December. This reduced the premium rates on waterside risks and on 19 other categories of property, and increased the rates on 18 further types of risk, from cabinetmakers' shops to 'engines for draining fens'. The book of rates became still more comprehensive and complex as

Table 4.3   Cooperation between the Sun, the REA and the Phoenix, 1786-1806

Subjects refer to premium rates and risk classification, unless otherwise stated

Year in which the subject is first raised	Subjects discussed at meetings between the three offices
1786	Free policies; Arson and fraudulent claims; Farming stock; Thameside property
1787	Ships in dock; Short-term insurances; Valuation of non-contiguous buildings and stock therein
1788	Sugar houses; Cotton mills; Drying stoves; Velvet & fustian dyers and dressers; Windmills
1789	Theatres
1790	Common insurances in London; Worcester Fire Office, joint response; Book of rates - over 40 types of risks rated; London fire patrol; Joint survey of cotton mills
1791	Policy endorsements
1793	Joint reward re. arson
1794	Goods in trust/commission; Policy renewals - 15 days grace; Joint survey of London waterside insurances; Office hours; Fire-fighting fund for outside London
1795	Joint agents' instructions
1796	Mill losses
1798	Minerva Assurance Office - no coinsurances
1799	British Fire Office - joint response; Globe Insurance Company - joint response
1800	West India produce
1802	Joint survey of West India docks; Joint lobby of the Treasury v. proposed new fire office 'for the protection of the poorer class of persons'
1803	Average clause
1806	Liverpool warehouse insurances

Sources: GL Ms 11931/7-8, Sun, GCM, 1786-1806 *passim*; Ms 11932/13-16, Sun, CMM, 1786-1806 *passim*; Trebilcock, *Phoenix Assurance*, vol.I, pp.445-7.

cooperation intensified. Fifty-one types of risk were listed in the edition of November 1792, at a time when Fenning, Watts and Stonestreet were meeting 'for the most part three times a week'. By December 1794 the book regulated rates for 100 specified risks. At every revision of rates the new edition was deposited simultaneously at each office to ensure no competitive advantage was gained by any party. The book was still being updated in this way as late as June 1803, although by this time tensions between the three offices in some areas were approaching breaking point.[39]

Table 4.3 also shows the extent to which cooperation ranged well beyond problems of rating. On several occasions the three offices united against a threat from market entrants such as the Worcester Fire Office in 1790 and new metropolitan offices, the Minerva, the British and the Globe in 1798-9. In 1791, with the blessing of the City authorities, they commenced a joint fire patrol for London which operated for nearly 15 years, a forerunner of the London Fire Engine Establishment of 1833. In 1794 a joint fund was set up to defray expenses incurred in fighting fires outside London. The Sun, the REA and the Phoenix also jointly commissioned surveys of particular hazards such as cotton mills and London waterside and dockside insurances, jointly lobbied the government on several occasions, agreed on common wording for agents' instructions, and even resolved to fix common public opening hours for their head offices.[40] The winter of 1794-5 marked the peak of this intimacy. In the spring of 1795 the agreement not to issue free policies collapsed. Thereafter meetings between the offices were less frequent, but this may just have been a reflection of their success in adjusting tariff rates to risks and in enforcing compliance. It probably also helped that the average loss ratio was tumbling downwards during the late 1790s from its historic peak (see figure 1.5).

The greatest test for the cartel was rating the cotton industry. After years of adjustment in the face of rising losses, a tariff for cotton mills was once again agreed upon at the end of 1796. These rates remained more or less intact for five years, despite repeated calls for amendments from the new British Fire Office. At the end of 1801 Watts, Fenning and Stonestreet met in response to the 'heavy losses' which had been sustained on cotton, flax and woollen mills since 1796. It was agreed to suspend all renewals pending a revision of the rates, but this proved difficult and acrimonious. The Phoenix claimed that the Sun was pushing through new price schedules which were 'wild, extravagant and impractical', while at the same time trying to suggest that the Phoenix itself was behind the increase. Eventually, new rates were agreed upon by all three offices and published in March 1802.[41] In November, faced with continued losses, the REA pressed for another rate increase on cotton, flax and lint mills where buildings were less than six feet apart. The Sun's managers consulted their agent in Manchester, Robert Duck, who conveyed his doubts about this. Replying to the REA, the Sun accepted that physical contiguity posed an extra hazard, 'but as very few claims have been made for losses occasioned by fire from an adjoining mill' there was no immediate need for a change in the premiums. Claiming that the Phoenix had already agreed to an increase, Fenning pleaded with the Sun; 'we have hitherto gone very smoothly on together and I have no doubt of your concurrence'. However, the Sun, influenced by Duck, raised a further objection to the REA's failure to take building size into account. In any case, the Sun argued, the establishment of several new offices made it an unpropitious time to raise rates.[42]

Both the REA and the Phoenix still believed that cotton mill rates were 'alarmingly low' and pressed for a conference which took place in January 1803. The Sun presented a new plan drawn up by Duck which rated mills by volume of floor space and number of storeys. This became the source of lasting disagreement. The Phoenix had already resolved to rate mills by floor area only, while the REA set rates for all mills according to the traditional categories, defined largely by construction materials and physical hazards such as open stoves. The Sun was willing to amend Duck's plan but refused to give way on the principal of dual-rating by height and floor space. After a fortnight of discussions, and 'seeing there was no prospect of the three offices acting in concert on these special insurances', the Sun went ahead and issued its own revised rates.[43] The result was that a gap opened up between the premiums of the three offices. The insurer of a large six-storey cotton mill, occupying over 3000 square yards, for instance, paid 42s% with the Sun but just 27s% with the REA - a difference of 36 per cent. Recognising that this 'might tend to injure the credit of this Office', the Sun quickly reduced its rates on 'first class' mills to levels approaching those of the REA, but a gap remained.[44] In 1804 the Sun revised its mill rates again, this time without consulting the other offices. The new price schedule was more elaborate than ever, fixing a basic premium for 80 categories of cotton, flax and lint mills, rating them by class, height, floor space and number of occupants. The effect was a substantial reduction, especially for the largest mills, but by this time the Sun was already beginning to lose mill insurances to the Phoenix and to new interlopers such as the Imperial and the Norwich Union.[45]

The convoluted problem of rating cotton mills, at its most intractable during 1803-4, lay at the nub of discord. Initially this problem does not seem to have soured relations unduly. As late as September 1803 the three offices combined to undercut the British Fire Office's premiums on farm insurances.[46] The habit of disagreement, however, soon spread beyond cotton mills to other areas. The Phoenix refused to accept a rate increase on sugar refineries proposed by the Sun and the REA, while the Sun rejected a rate proposed by the Phoenix and the REA on property in the West India warehouses. In 1804 the Phoenix unilaterally reduced its rates on warehouse merchandise on the Isle of Dogs. In turn, the Sun carried out its own survey of the West India and London docks and raised its policy ceiling on brick-built warehouses there. During 1805 the Phoenix complained about the cost of the joint fire patrol in London and questioned the continuing validity of the plan for sharing expenses at fires. In 1806 it circulated a tariff for the insurance of goods in warehouses at Liverpool, claiming that the 'principal London fire offices' supported it. The Sun, however, did not concur, even though its agent at Liverpool pointed out that the company's prices for warehouse insurances were being undercut by the Phoenix and the Imperial, and that this branch of business was 'very fast declining'.[47]

A nadir was reached by 1807-8 as cooperation over almost any rating proposal evaporated. It is difficult to explain why the cartel unravelled in this torturous manner. Disagreements certainly sharpened after the death of the Phoenix's charismatic secretary, George Stonestreet, in 1802, dissolving what had probably been a personal chemistry with his colleagues from the REA and the Sun. The arrival of the Phoenix's new negotiator, Colonel Matthew Wilson, perhaps introduced a more brusque manner to their meetings - this is suggested by the tone of his letters to the Sun - although Trebilcock concludes that 'he cannot be proved to have possessed any strong characteristics of any kind'.[48] Other factors probably played a greater role in the break-up of the cartel - rising loss ratios during the early 1800s, the increasing technical difficulty of rating ever more complex industrial and commercial risks, usually at a distance, and the pressure of increasing competition from new offices.

In spite of their eventual difficulties, the REA, the Sun and the Phoenix stuck together for a remarkably long time under rapidly changing circumstances. Collusion had three direct outcomes. First, the combined market share of the cartel members rose to a peak of 85 per cent in the period 1796-1800. By 1807-8, when cooperation was a thing of the past, the aggregate market share of the three offices was in free fall, reaching 43 per cent in the period 1811-14 and 31 per cent in 1826-30.[49] Second, a more sophisticated and risk sensitive pricing regime was developed as the result of the exchange of good practice. At the outset of their cooperation the three offices agreed to classify cotton risks by type of stove located in the premises. Twelve years later, however, the classification of cotton mills had become more rigorous, taking into account size, location and construction. Although elements in the classification remained objects of contention, the dispute between underwriters itself indicated a more engaged and complex approach to risk measurement.

The third outcome of collusion was a series of major shifts in the price structure of fire insurance. Collusion commenced in a period when rates were being reduced on several types of hazardous risk such as sugar and cotton mills. This phase of falling prices soon came to an end. During the three years to 1796 the three London offices were losing an average of £1000 a week on cotton mill insurances.[50] Their response was firm. Cotton mill owners found that their basic premiums more than quadrupled. This eased the burden of claims on insurers. For the seven years ending 1802 the offices estimated that the average loss ratio on mill insurances was 75 per cent.[51] The margin, though, remained too narrow once expenses had been deducted. At the end of 1802 the REA proposed a further increase to 25s% on this class of risk. At this point the dispute over the method of rating mills broke out, resulting in differences in classification and making the price trend more difficult to follow. It seems, however, that the fierce upward ratcheting of the premium rate for textile mills reached a ceiling by the mid 1800s. Thereafter, improved fireproofing in the best mills and increasing competition from new offices brought about a gradual decline in the price. By the early 1820s 14s% had become the standard rate for cotton mills. This price reduction was encouraged by better profits in those areas which had experienced the worst losses during the 1790s and early 1800s. The Phoenix's agency at Manchester enjoyed average annual premiums of £6400 during the first two decades of the nineteenth century, while incurring average losses of only £1100.[52] There is some irony in the fact that those categories of insurance which had caused the greatest disagreement among the three London fire offices became profitable just as their cartel was breaking up.

The new offices of Regency London and the rise of bilateralism

The collapse of oligopoly was in part due to the emergence of several new metropolitan offices during the 1800s. Just 14 fire offices had been founded in the 30 years to 1797. Between 1797 and 1809 no fewer than 25 offices were established. Only ten of these were located in London, but they included five of the biggest and most successful enterprises of the period - the British, the Globe, the Imperial, the County and the Atlas.[53] These five had certain features in common. They were all unchartered joint-stock companies with large capitals and, by comparison with the cartel offices, large numbers of shareholders. They all sought a distinctive identity within the industry, primarily by establishing strong positions in particular areas using traditional marketing methods, although towards this goal there was some resort to strategy and product innovation. The early histories of these offices illustrate central themes in the development of fire insurance during the Napoleonic wars - the emergence of a new generation of entrepreneurs with imaginative and ambitious plans for the industry, the expansion of share ownership and the rising scale of investment in new companies, the changing forms of cooperation which evolved within a context of more intense competition and increasing market fragmentation.

The British Fire Office counted among its first directors one peer, one baronet and three members of parliament, boasted agencies 'in every considerable town in the United Kingdom', and also aspired to sell insurance overseas. It made repeated efforts to entice the cartel into a dialogue about rates and other aspects of underwriting, but met only with rebuff.[54] Nevertheless, after barely two years it had overhauled the three London mutual offices and the London Assurance by market share. Cold-shouldered by the cartel, the British tried a different tactic towards the end of 1804 by moving into an 'association' with the newly founded Imperial Insurance Company. This marked the beginning of a trend towards bilateral arrangements between offices which replaced the multilateral collaboration of the REA, the Sun and the Phoenix. Cooperation began with a coinsurance arrangement. Then a standing committee was set up by the two offices in which

> measures of general utility would be discussed....where the rates of insurance could be proposed to be fixed so as to prevent the ruinous competition which the want of some plan is fraught with; where means might be devised to lessen the expenses so justly complained of, and where by a communication of suspicious claims, frauds that may now be practised might be detected.[55]

The committee wrote to the Phoenix, the Globe, the Sun, the REA and the London Assurance suggesting that they join together for these ends. Reaction remained frosty. The Phoenix was the only office to respond positively, temporarily joining the two newcomers for a meeting at which it was agreed to 'assimilate' their general regulations. The call to agree rates and for a 'settled plan of general meetings' between all offices, however, found no resonance elsewhere.[56]

The cartel's reaction to the foundation of the Globe Insurance Company was even more hostile. Its founder, Sir Frederick Eden, already well known for his research into the condition of the poor, drafted a plan in 1798 for a multi-functional financial institution which would provide fire, life and endowment insurance, grant annuities, provide death benefits for widows and children, manage the savings of friendly societies and act as a deposit bank for the working class.[57] An application for a charter foundered on the opposition of the other London insurance offices, the Attorney General, the Chancellor and the Bank of England, and eventually in 1803 the Globe opened for business as an ordinary unchartered stock company selling fire and life insurance, with a huge capital of £1m.[58] Two hundred and fifty-three agencies were established by the end of 1805 and the older offices soon felt the Globe's presence in several markets. Despite heavy losses in 1807 and 1813, the company managed to remain profitable during the war years and maintained a market share of six per cent.[59]

As Eden was approaching the end of his marathon effort to launch the Globe, the directors of the West India Dock Company, angered by new limits imposed on dock insurances by the cartel, founded an insurance venture of their own. The office was entitled the Imperial, seven of its 21 directors were appointed directly by the Dock Company, and rooms were provided in Dock House for their meetings. £1.2m was issued in £500 shares which were soon fully subscribed. By the end of 1807 the Imperial had established 80 domestic agencies, some in places in the industrial north which had seldom seen an insurance agent, such as Ellesmere, Ormskirk, Colne and Rotherham. It extended its operations to Ireland and Scotland, and began to compete with the Phoenix in the Caribbean. In 1804 it opened agencies in Europe, insuring mercantile property in Memel, St Petersburg, Gothenburg, Gibraltar, Italy, and recent British conquests such as Heligoland.[60] Considering the limitations imposed by wartime, the international scope of the Imperial's early business was impressive and went some way to justify its title. It also used coinsurance to spread risks. As early as 1804 it was negotiating with the Sun about 'reciprocal insurances' and insurances were exchanged with the British Fire and foreign insurances shared with the Phoenix. In 1805 the Imperial purchased a Liverpool office, the St George, founded just a few years earlier by a group of local merchants.[61] The £3.5m of insurances acquired amounted to about 20 per cent of the Imperial's total business at the time and gave it 'great weight and influence' in the town. Moreover, the Imperial enjoyed an edge with its low rates, and demonstrated sensitivity to mercantile needs by not insisting on the warranty against hazardous trades required by the Sun before that office would insure warehouses in multiple occupation.[62]

Two other important new London offices, the County and the Atlas, were established after the final collapse of the cartel. In April 1807 the County Fire Office was launched at the house of John Thomas Barber in Covent Garden. Barber, later known as Barber Beaumont, was one of most colourful characters in the history of insurance.[63] In his early career he had specialised in miniature portraiture. He exhibited regularly at the Royal Academy and moved freely in aristocratic, theatrical and radical whig circles. After the turn of the century he became interested in social, economic and political questions, writing a series of pamphlets on public house licensing, parish savings banks, criminal jurisprudence and parliamentary reform, and establishing the Provident Institution for Life Insurances in 1806. During the Napoleonic wars he also founded a company of volunteer riflemen, the Duke of Cumberland's Sharpshooters. Alongside such sound credentials as a patriot, his radicalism brought him notoriety, particularly when he backed the cause of George IV's estranged wife, Queen Caroline, by decking out the County Fire Office's new building in Regent Street with coloured lamps in the shape of 'CR' to celebrate the withdrawal of the royal divorce bill in 1820.

Barber's f ire o ffice was as singular as its promoter. It began with a modest capital of £350000 in £100 shares, and in this respect it resembled its provincial counterparts rather than the large metropolitan offices established between 1803 and 1808. The proprietorship was organised as an 'association' by residence in 12 rural counties north of the Thames. Each annual county meeting of shareholders elected five representatives to an unwieldy court of 60 directors which was supposed to meet weekly in London. Barber was appointed managing director on a salary of £500 a year, with the same powers as directors but responsible to their court. Another unusual feature was the distribution of a share in the profits to all policyholders holding their policies for seven consecutive years. The County thus became the first fire office in Britain to introduce the 'bonus' or 'with profits' policy, a product which became widely imitated and a major focus of competition during the following decades.[64]

Unsurprisingly, given its founder's connections, the County's directors and trustees comprised a formidable combination of gentry and bankers with a rich topping of peers. By the end of 1807 90 agents had been appointed in 18 English counties and a fire brigade established for the west end of London, where County's metropolitan business was 'almost exclusively' located. Insurances rose to over £20m by 1814 and the company's market share grew relentlessly.[65] Losses remained low, never rising above 39 per cent of premium income in any one year. For the duration of the war the focus of its business remained in its original 12 counties, which accounted for 88 per cent of all sums insured. When Henry Desborough of the Atlas visited Nottingham and Leicester in 1811, he remarked on County's 'commanding influence...in all the Midlands counties, independent of the long established agencies of other offices'.[66]

Despite its success, the County had less impact on the older London offices than the Imperial and the Globe, probably because it expanded in markets which were less contested and which experienced less building and troublesome technological change than confronted insurers in London docks, Liverpool, Leeds, Glasgow or Manchester. Given its cumbersome structure, the County only worked because managerial power was so concentrated in the hands of one very capable individual. Much of the company's success may be attributed to Barber Beaumont himself, his elevated social and business connections, tireless energy and attention to detail, for which his early training as a miniaturist must have stood him in good stead. The weekly directors' meetings were usually attended only by three men, Beaumont and the bankers Scrope Bernard and William Praed, but it was Beaumont who pulled the County's loose federalist structure into a tightly centralised organisation. Success was also due to careful risk selection in markets of relatively low hazard. The extensive agency network, monitored daily by Beaumont, secured these markets while the promise of profit sharing to long-term policyholders was consistently advocated to the County's salesmen as a powerful weapon in their armoury.[67]

In the week before Christmas 1807, six businessmen met in Will's coffee house in Cornhill to found an office for fire and life assurance. They called their enterprise the Atlas to reflect their global ambition. A huge capital of £2m was issued in 40000 shares. Against the background of a speculative boom in stock company foundations, over 2000 shares were subscribed to within a week, and the promoters' committee grew to 70 members by May 1808.[68] Analysis of the latter indicates that the Atlas was dominated by City merchants, with clusters specialising in overseas trades, especially in the import of wine and spirits, and a contingent of Spanish and Jewish brokers and traders.[69] The key to early success was the large share issue specifically targeted at lawyers, bankers and property-owners resident in counties without a local insurance office. One-quarter of the shares were set aside for sale in the 'principal provincial towns' in order to avoid a proprietorship dominated by Londoners and the difficulty of expanding in the crowded metropolitan market. Shares were linked to the sale of insurance policies. Atlas proprietors, who did not insure to the value of their shares, were required to procure insurances from non-subscribers for an amount double the value of their shares, or else face a fine.[70] Thus an extensive proprietorship guaranteed an large and well-distributed volume of business from the outset. 114 agencies were established within the first year. Over one-third were in the home counties and the south-east, but there were also clusters in the north-west, along the Staffordshire-Cheshire-Welsh borders, in the west country and in Ireland.

Through its expanding sales network and generous levels of commission, the Atlas's country business grew more rapidly than its metropolitan insurances. Agents accounted for 45 per cent of sums insured by 1813-16 and sums insured rose to £9.0m.[71] Mill insurances, in particular, became important to the Atlas, and they probably generated a larger proportion of its income than for any other contemporary fire office. Cotton mills alone may have accounted for up to one-third of the total income from fire underwriting during the company's first three years.[72] By 1811 the Atlas had earned over £9000 on cotton mills, but paid out only £92 in claims. This early favourable experience encouraged the company to remain with mill insurances when trade conditions rapidly deteriorated during 1812. Locked into this market, the Atlas tried to seek out the best risks even while losses mounted. A vain attempt was made to win the agreement of other London offices for a cotton mill tariff. The wave of Luddite attacks on textile property in the midlands and the north during the winter of 1811-12 raised a further problem. In Leeds the Atlas temporarily suspended all underwriting of woollen mills, while in Manchester, where a number of millowners had received threatening letters, the company arranged for watchmen to guard the mills it insured. However, an attempt by the Atlas to secure the cooperation of other offices for a scheme to combat Luddism did not succeed.[73]

Despite the burning mills, rates continued to fall, albeit more slowly. By this stage the long-running war of attrition was nearing exhaustion. The decline in rates had been precipitous since the break up of the cartel. Everywhere bigger mills than before were being insured at lower prices. Overall premium rates on cotton mills fell by between 20 and 40 per cent from their peak around 1803 to the trough of 1811-14. Prices on the best classes of mills bottomed out at 12-14s%, and thereafter were held at this level into the 1820s. Amidst this furious competition, attempts to cooperate continued. The trend towards ever bigger commercial and industrial insurances, stretching far beyond the resources or willingness of any single insurer to underwrite, ensured that coinsurances increasingly involved two or more offices from outside the former cartel. By itself coinsurance was unlikely to reintroduce peace and stability to the industry. The last decade of the war, however, witnessed a new form of cooperation, the bilateral agreement, which replaced the older idea of multilateral tariffs for different categories of risk. Bilateralism was prompted by the low acceptance limits which the smaller country offices persisted with in the face of decisions by London insurers to underwrite ever larger amounts on single risks. By this period demand was outstripping supply in many markets. Country offices, flooded with requests for cover which they could not or would not accept, either resorted to the new device of reinsurance or, more commonly, they 'transferred surpluses' as coinsurances to other fire offices given a 'most favoured partner' status. Thus they hoped to retain customer goodwill while dividing up or entirely off-loading large or unwanted risks.

The earliest bilateral schemes of the Imperial and the British were noted above. In 1808 the Atlas told its Manchester agent

> that it would prove beneficial to him if he could have an understanding with the agent of some other office, to give him a portion of risks - where motives of prudence deter this office from taking the whole, on his allowing him to participate on the like occasion.[74]

Similar moves were made by other offices. The Kent Fire Office proposed giving the Atlas 'the preference in all cases of risk offered to them exceeding the amount that that Office may be inclined to take...'. The Atlas agreed that

> the whole assurances of the Kent...be transferred to this Office for Deptford, Greenwich and Woolwich, which towns are out of their immediate inspection, and such sums as may exceed in other parts of the County etc. the amount they may be inclined to take...

The Atlas also yielded to the demand to pay the Kent 20 per cent commission on fire insurance premiums and five per cent on life insurances.[75] A similar proposal was received from a new Edinburgh office, the Hercules, which promised the Atlas a preference

> in cases of risks offered to them exceeding the amount they have limited themselves to, and particularly for sugar houses, cotton mills and other risks deemed special, which they do not for the present intend assuring, provided a satisfactory allowance be made on the premium upon such sums as this Office may be inclined to take.

The Atlas accepted the proposal, but offered the Scots a miserly ten per cent on all fire premiums.[76] Other arrangements, several on an *ad hoc* basis, were made. The Wiltshire & Western proposed £10000 on wool in two warehouses at Bristol, which the Atlas accepted on the basis of a transfer of a direct insurance. The REA's agent in Dublin proposed

> a mutual cooperation between his office, the Imperial and Atlas offices in the fire business and to give each other a mutual preference in the division of such risks as may be beyond the limits of each office to accept.[77]

On his northern tour of 1811, the secretary of the Atlas, Henry Desborough, proposed to the Sheffield Fire Office an agreement to take that office's surplus proposals - 'for the Assurance of any sums above what your office may be disposed to take.' A commission of 15 or 20 per cent was to be allowed, and the accounts were to be settled quarterly. Desborough also proposed that the Sheffield office act as a life assurance agency for Atlas for a commission of five per cent. Desborough made similar proposals to the local offices in Shrewsbury and Worcester, while 'the Birmingham office had an understanding with the Imperial office for their surplus risks'.[78] Together with the Phoenix, the Atlas was involved in a similar agreement with the Norwich Union. When an agent asked whether the office would accept an insurance of £20000, the secretary of the Norwich Union, Samuel Bignold, replied that

> We would go as far as £5000 tho' the Directors normally restrict themselves to £3000...But we can procure policies...from the Phoenix and Atlas...for the difference, say £15000. And those offices have, by an arrangement which we have made with them agreed to allow our agents commission.[79]

Thus by the spring of 1811 a network of alliances had emerged between several London offices and their provincial counterparts. Furthermore, some simple transfers of 'surplus' insurances were transmuted into reinsurances proper, presaging the more formal reinsurance treaties of the 1820s between British and European offices. In 1815, for instance, the Kent accepted £7000 on a paper mill, but resolved 'that £2000 of the insurance be reassured in the Imperial Office'.[80] It is a curious feature of the rapidly developing regional insurance markets in this period that the extremities of competition, inexorably driving down prices on a wide range of hazards, were accompanied by the diffusion of an innovation which worked to push firms together, to spread risk and bring supply and demand nearer to equilibrium.

The new provincial offices, 1790-1815

By 1790 there were still just 14 fire offices situated outside London, and seven in the capital. During the following quarter century 30 offices were established in Scotland, Ireland and the English counties, while a further ten were founded in London. In 1810 there were 51 fire insurance companies operating in the Kingdom. Those areas which remained void of local offices were so for two reasons which made entry difficult - the intensity of competition and the increasing technical difficulty of underwriting in complex markets. South Lancashire is the most obvious example. By 1810 15 fire offices were competing in Liverpool, all based outside the region, while three local offices had come and gone. Other rapidly industrialising regions such as the West Riding and the west of Scotland were also unable to sustain a local office for any time. Between 1784 and 1815 only four offices were opened in the midlands and the north of England. Of the remaining 16 new enterprises in the English provinces, seven were located in East Anglia, four in the west of England, and five in Essex, Kent, Sussex and Hampshire. Southern England thus proved a more congenial territory for local fire offices. In terms of the distribution of new companies, British insurance failed to mimic the migration of labour and capital into the industrial regions during this period.

The new provincial ventures were predominantly joint-stock partnerships, although at least nine mutual fire offices were also founded between 1784 and 1809.[81] These were mostly small affairs, but they prospered on the basis of a highly selective membership and great attention to minimising risks. The mutual office established in Devizes in 1784 is a good example. Its founders comprised 15 gentlemen who initially came together to insure each other's property, mostly country houses in Wiltshire. The society only intended to operate for seven years, at the end of which term any surplus was to be divided up among the members. In the event a new office with 30 members emerged out of the old in 1791. This also flourished. The connections enjoyed through the presence of some of its members as office holders in Devizes corporation probably ensured that it underwrote only the best town properties. Most claims were on insurances outside Devizes. Net profits were recorded each year between 1784 and 1810. Success attracted new entrants and in 1799 it was resolved to limit membership to 150. This indicates its exclusivity when compared with its contemporary, the Norwich Union, whose membership approached 6000 within eight years of its foundation.[82]

For reasons not entirely clear, East Anglia became the home of mutual fire insurance. By 1809 six mutual societies in Essex, Suffolk and Norfolk together insured £11.8m.[83] Almost all mutuals restricted underwriting to their own areas. Even societies such as the Essex Equitable with 24 agencies confined their business to county boundaries.[84] Trans-regional organisation was particularly difficult for mutual offices in an era when communications and banking services were still developing. It was especially cumbersome to organise levies on members if they were scattered nationwide. The older London mutuals continued to focus on the metropolis until the turn of the century. The Norwich Union was the first mutual to attempt a national coverage but its early business was based at home. Seventy-three per cent of its new premium income between 1797 and 1804 came from Norfolk and Suffolk.[85]

The Norwich Union was the creation of a wine and spirits dealer, Thomas Bignold, another of the extraordinary insurance entrepreneurs who emerged in this period.[86] In 1797 he quit his post as secretary to the Norwich General Assurance, having fallen out with its directors over his plans for expansion. The Norwich General had been founded as a partnership seven years earlier and was dominated by the town's brewing and banking families, a boardroom fusion of Whig Quakers and Tory Anglicans. Bignold turned to Norwich radicals, mostly wealthy tradesmen, to form his new company. Twenty-eight founding members each paid £1000 into a guarantee fund and underwriting was begun from Bignold's wine shop.

The company historian suggests several reasons for the adoption of the mutual system by Bignold and his new colleagues. The office was launched in the week that the Bank of England suspended cash payments, and because of the limited resources of the traders backing Bignold, mutuality may have been regarded as a less risky option than trying to float shares to an anxious public. For political reasons too, the radicals may have been more sympathetic to a cooperative type of arrangement rather than the joint-stock organisation typical of the big London offices, who were widely believed to be exploiting country policyholders in order to subsidise their loss-making metropolitan insurances. Security was also afforded by the issue of seven year policies - an idea borrowed from the London mutuals - which gave the new office some time to determine its average losses before distributing a bonus to its members.

Bignold initially adopted a conservative approach. No industrial risks were accepted, a £3000 limit was placed on each policy, and all London property was excluded. Forty-five of the 70 agents appointed by 1804 were located in East Anglia. Caution reaped dividends. A bonus of 75 per cent was declared in 1804 with which the directors were well satisfied. Bignold, however, was ambitious to expand the business further which quickly brought him into conflict with his directors. At a meeting in 1805, called to secure Bignold's dismissal, he overcame his critics by winning a huge majority of the members' votes. The old directors were dismissed and a new closed board was filled by local Tories, including many farmers. Together with his sons, Bignold was left to run the society with almost a free hand. The Norwich Union began to expand rapidly outside East Anglia. The number of agents increased to over 400 by 1815 while the proportion of new premiums originating in Norfolk and Suffolk fell to 17 per cent. In Lancashire, Yorkshire and Gloucestershire, the office embarked on an aggressive strategy of securing textile mill insurances. Expansion was helped by the creation of nearly 50 local members' committees in 22 English counties, which provided a link between head office and the agencies by scrutinising accounts, investigating claims and occasionally securing new business. Premiums rose to £49000, membership increased to 60000, and underwriting was extended to Scotland, Ireland and London. In the space of ten years the Norwich Union had outgrown the largest provincial offices and most of the new London offices. Soon it became Britain's third biggest fire insurer.[87]

At the time of the Norwich Union's foundation, the idea that any provincial office could challenge the market leaders at a national level was inconceivable. Nevertheless, there was already an awareness at the Sun, the Phoenix and the REA that country offices could make serious inroads into their share of local markets. This is evident from the frank assessment of the distribution of fire insurance which the Sun's secretary Hugh Watts presented to William Pitt in the summer of 1797.[88] Table 4.4 shows Watts's figures, which can be compared with the sums insured by country offices where surviving records allowed this to be calculated. In Wiltshire, Watts estimated that the Sun accounted for only 35 per cent of the sums insured in the county, while the Wiltshire & Western, founded only six years previously, had about 40 per cent. In Worcester and Gloucestershire the Sun's share was estimated at 31 per cent and 23 per cent respectively. In Scotland it was 44 per cent. In Somerset, where Watts thought the Sun had just 16 per cent of fire insurances, the two Bath offices together accounted for 41 per cent of the total insured, while the remaining 43 per cent was shared between the REA and the Phoenix. In Shropshire, the Salop Fire held about 58 per cent of sums insured, while the Sun had 17 per cent and the other London offices 25 per cent. These figures may tend to exaggerate the market share of local offices, in as far as they sometimes insured beyond county boundaries. The Salop sold insurance as far north as Lancashire and across north and central Wales, while the Bristol Fire Office had agencies as far east as Norfolk in the 1790s.[89] Nevertheless, even where one can take account of extra-county insurances, the picture of local offices with a powerful presence in their own markets remains largely intact. The business of the Newcastle Fire Office, for instance, extended across northern England from Darlington to Carlisle, but summing Watts's totals for Northumberland, Durham, Westmoreland and Cumberland would still give the Newcastle office 72 per cent of insurances in

Table 4.4 Geographical distribution of sums insured: Watts's estimates for 1796

Counties	Sun £m	% of County	Other Offices £m	% of County	Total £m	% GB Total
Middlesex	38.000	38.0	62.000	62.0	100.000	53.4
10 Home Counties	17.370	60.0	11.549	40.0	28.919	15.4
Norfolk*	1.212	27.8	3.141	72.2	4.353	
Cambridgeshire	1.377	60.0	0.918	40.0	2.295	
Suffolk	0.855	62.6	0.511	37.3	1.366	
Somerset*	0.739	16.0	3.877	84.0	4.616	
Wiltshire*	1.141	34.5	2.189	65.5	3.330	
Gloucestershire*	0.741	22.9	2.494	77.1	3.235	
Dorset	1.546	60.0	1.030	40.0	2.576	
Devon	1.170	60.0	0.780	40.0	1.950	
Cornwall	0.220	60.1	0.146	39.9	0.366	
Northamptonshire	1.141	60.0	0.760	40.0	1.901	
Lincolnshire	0.943	60.0	0.629	40.0	1.572	
Warwickshire	0.800	60.0	0.533	40.0	1.333	
Staffordshire	0.542	60.0	0.361	40.0	0.903	
Nottinghamshire	0.479	60.3	0.315	39.7	0.794	
Leicestershire	0.190	58.8	0.133	41.2	0.323	
Derbyshire	0.136	59.9	0.091	40.1	0.227	
Worcestershire*	0.537	31.2	1.182	68.8	1.719	
Salop*	0.167	16.8	0.729	83.2	0.996	
Herefordshire	0.184	59.9	0.123	40.1	0.307	
Lancashire	3.378	60.0	2.252	40.0	5.630	
Yorkshire	2.170	60.0	1.447	40.0	3.617	
Cheshire	0.273	60.0	0.182	40.0	0.455	
Northumberland*	0.279	12.5	1.950	87.5	2.229	
Westmoreland	0.117	60.0	0.078	40.0	0.195	
Cumberland	0.085	59.9	0.057	40.1	0.142	
Durham	0.036	60.0	0.024	40.0	0.060	
Wales	0.037	59.7	0.035	40.3	0.062	
Scotland*	5.202	44.2	6.565	55.8	11.767	6.3
UK Total	81.067	43.3	106.171	56.7	187.238	

Notes: Counties ordered by regions. * = counties with local fire offices. Watts's figures reproduced here with the exception of Norfolk, where £2.333m insured by the Norwich General has been added to Watts's total for 'other offices'. This estimate is calculated from the premium income of £3500 for 1797, given by Ryan, 'Norwich Union and the British Fire Insurance Market', p.40, and an average rate of 3.03s% , the midpoint of the range for 1796-1805 given in Ryan, 'History of the Norwich Union', table 12, p.966.

Source: PRO 30/8/187/ 230-40, Chatham Papers.

these counties compared with the Sun's 20 per cent. In Norfolk Watts neglected to allow for the Norwich General. The latter insured about £2.3m at this time, which when added to Watts's total, would give that office 54 per cent of the county's insurances and the Sun just 28 per cent.

By the late 1790s, therefore, provincial offices had secured strongholds from where they were able partly to roll back the advance of the big metropolitan insurers. Positions had been already established by the earliest country fire offices in the period 1767-84. In the 1790s and 1800s a wave of new offices joined the battle. The majority of these were stock companies, mostly launched with nominal capitals of over £100000 and wealthy, if not in every case numerous, proprietorships. Three offices were floated between 1790 and 1792, the last years of peace. The Wiltshire & Western was established by 60 co-partners each holding one £2000 share.[90] They were drawn largely from the woollen industry of Wiltshire and Somerset, and included representatives of some of its oldest clothier families. To ensure a regional coverage, the new company established four co-equal administrative offices at Warminster, Bradford, Trowbridge and Frome. This device of underwriting from several centres was subsequently imitated by several other country offices.[91] By 1805 the Wiltshire & Western had become the fifth largest English provincial fire office, insuring £2.26m.[92] A fire office was also opened in Worcester by 27 members of the civic elite, with Lord Sandys and the Dean of Worcester at their head. It too had ambitions across county boundaries. By 1814 it possessed 29 agencies in Worcestershire and as far south and east as Gloucester, Cheltenham, Birmingham and Coventry. It issued some 7500 policies before being sold to the Phoenix in 1817.[93] The Norwich General began as a 30 year partnership with a nominal capital of £160000 to insure in 'Norwich and elsewhere', with the exception of London where the level of fire hazard was deemed too high. Within five years the number of shareholders, all local residents, had risen to nearly 290. The office followed the rates of the London insurers, kept individual policy ceilings limited to £3000, and avoided almost all industrial property. Premiums grew to about £5000 by the end of the century.[94]

In the difficult early years of the war against France there were no further company foundations. In 1797, however, a wave of new promotions commenced which continued unabated until 1809. As well as the Norwich Union, fire offices were founded in Brighton, Maidstone, Colchester, Ipswich, Exeter, Liverpool, Birmingham and Sheffield, while one was established for the counties of Hampshire, Sussex and Dorset. Four offices were also established in Ireland and seven in Scotland. Three of the latter were based in Edinburgh, the others were in Dundee, Aberdeen, Glasgow and Fife. The Glasgow Fire Office drew its shareholders from the town's tobacco and cotton mercantile firms, but a huge fire in the town in 1807 undermined confidence in the office. Thereafter, suffering repeated losses from mill insurances, business stagnated until the company was sold to the Phoenix in 1811. Thus by the end of the first decade of the nineteenth century, Edinburgh had emerged as the country's leading insurance centre, to complement its role as the centre of Scottish banking.

The experience of Manchester, Leeds, Liverpool and Glasgow suggests that, on the whole, the best chance of survival for local offices during this period lay in the market towns and rural districts of southern England, where underwriting could be conducted at a more leisurely pace than in the great cities, where there were fewer industrial and technological hazards of the modern sort, and where substantial patronage and capital could be accumulated for a new insurance venture through an alliance of local landed and urban wealth. The Kent Fire Office is a good example. Thanks to the energy of its promoters, a surveyor and a solicitor from Maidstone and a gentleman from Rochester, investment was attracted from numerous peers and members of parliament, the county gentry and members of several corporations. A capital of £100000 was raised, and, after failing to obtain a charter, the office was established by deed of settlement at the end of 1802.[95] Underwriting was initially confined to Kent and Sussex or to property outside the county owned by Kent residents.

The Kent office grew quickly not only because of the patronage it enjoyed, but also because it could undercut the prices of the big London insurers once it realised that the local risk of fire was lower than in the capital, especially among the country mansions of the type which it sought to insure. By 1805 it was already the largest provincial fire office in the Kingdom, although it was soon overtaken by the Norwich Union. Before 1818 its business remained confined to Kent and Sussex, but here it proved a powerful competitor.[96] Although country residences were its preferred diet, it also underwrote an assortment of farming, commercial and industrial property. Inns, hop oasts, paper mills, distilleries, windmills, limekilns, oil mills and tanneries were all insured before 1815, although, as for other insurers, some of the industrial properties were eventually to cause problems.

Underwriting performance and profitability

How profitable was fire insurance underwriting during the quarter century 1790-1815? Tables 4.5 to 4.8 bring together data from individual company accounts for this period. Several points can be made. First, the ratio of losses to premiums were generally higher throughout this period for London offices than for country offices (table 4.5). The worst results for the older offices were experienced in the early 1790s and early 1800s, while the newer offices, the Globe, the Imperial and the Atlas, suffered badly in the years 1812-14. According to incomplete figures collected by the Phoenix, the underwriting results of the Hope (1807) and the Albion (1805), two of the new London offices about whom little is known, were worse still.[97] The exception to this awful record of metropolitan underwriting was Barber Beaumont's County, whose claims ratio resembled that of a typical provincial insurer, which, given the orientation of its business, was not surprising. Of the local offices, those with the worst claims records tended to be located in industrial districts or large towns. The Glasgow Fire Office, for instance, had an

Table 4.5 Average premiums and loss ratios, 1791-1815

P = Average annual premiums £ (UK business only)
L = Losses (claims paid) as a percentage of premiums, annual averages

Offices	1791-5 P	1791-5 L	1796-1800[a] P	1796-1800[a] L	1801-5[b] P	1801-5[b] L	1806-10[c] P	1806-10[c] L	1811-15[d] P	1811-15[d] L
LONDON										
Sun	115090	82.9	126215	63.3	121845	69.2	107611	61.5	113985	64.1
Phoenix[e]	71210	91.9	98742	51.3	120099	59.9	88555	55.5	85273	52.5
REA	45769	71.5	63997	54.8	79820	63.8	72949	66.1	71274	64.6
London	6539	46.2	7963	41.2	8470	53.7	8455	52.4	8801	43.3
Globe					32683	45.1	36527	62.2	37257	74.2
Imperial							59131	70.1	58749	76.3
County					35035	39.3	11648	17.7	22103	26.8
Atlas									19903	81.9
COUNTRY										
Wiltshire	996	31.5	2432	39.2	3661	60.8	4161	33.9	4485	43.1
Bath Sun	823	40.3	807	4.4	960	24.9	1265	9.7	1405	47.5
Old Bath			1388	155.9	1551	13.3	1554	18.9	1577	16.1
Norwich Union			403	1.4	3276	13.3	13693	20.4	35861	36.2
Kent					3759	21.7	7368	45.4	7975	20.1
Newcastle							4811	53.4	4220	47.4
Sheffield							958	11.0	1116	0.0
Glasgow							3429	66.7		
Essex & Suffolk									3939	25.9

Notes: [a] Old Bath, 1798-1800, Norwich Union, 1797-1800; [b] Globe, 1804-5, Imperial, 1803-5, Kent, premiums, 1802-7; Imperial, 1803-5, Kent, premiums, 1802-5, loss ratios, 1802-7; County, 1807-10, Newcastle, 1808-10, Sheffield, 1809-10, Glasgow, 1804-12, Kent, loss ratios, 1808-10; [d] Atlas, 1812-14, Kent, 1811-13 and 1815, Essex & Suffolk, 1813-15; [e] The premium totals differ slightly from those given in Trebilcock, *Phoenix Assurance*, vol.1, table 5.1, p.165. I do not know why. I believe the same sources have been used.

Sources: Dickson, *Sun Insurance*, appendix 1; Supple, *Royal Exchange*, p.149; Trebilcock, *Phoenix Assurance*, vol.I, table 13.1, p.710; GRE Archives, REA, Doomsday Book; Phoenix, Annual Summary Sheets; GL Ms 8746A, London Assurance, Fire Assurance Annual Accounts, 1721-1854; Ms 11674/1-3, Globe, Ledgers, 1803-50; Ms 18274, Imperial, Tabular Statements, 1803-1901; County, Annual Accounts 1807-29; GL Ms 16170/1-2, Atlas, DM, 1807-16; Ms 11935E, Sun, Take over Papers, Salamander (1835), Bath Sun (1838), Old Bath (1827); SRO, Ms 30081/2/10, Salop, Income and Capital Account Book, 1780-1822; CKS, U2593/B15, B16/1, Kent, Financial Summary, 1802-14, Secretary's Statements, 1806-7; GL Ms 15032/8, Sun, Take over Papers, Sheffield (1858); Ryan, 'History of Norwich Union', table 12, p.966, table 26, pp.998-9; GL Ms 14116, Sun, Simplified Profits and Loss Accounts (for Glasgow, 1804-11); GPL, Cotesworth Mss, CM4/1-21, Newcastle, Accounts 1808-22; GL Ms 16203/1, Essex & Suffolk, DM, 1802-21.

Table 4.6   Expense ratios, 1791-1815

Management expenses as a percentage of premiums, annual averages

Offices	1791-5	1796-1800[a]	1801-5[b]	1806-10[c]	1811-15[d]
LONDON					
Sun	18.0	15.2			
Phoenix	11.3	13.1	12.6	12.3	17.9
REA	14.8	11.6	13.5	13.6	13.1
Imperial			29.9	21.9	21.2
County				27.4	20.9
Atlas					38.8
COUNTRY					
Old Bath		19.5	23.7	29.0	24.9
Kent				43.1	
Newcastle				21.1	20.7
Glasgow				20.8	
Essex & Suffolk					29.4

Notes: [a] Old Bath, 1798-99. [b] Imperial, 1803-5. [c] County, 1807-10; Kent, 1806-9, Newcastle, 1808-10, Glasgow, 1804-12. [d] Atlas, 1814; Essex & Suffolk, 1813-15.

Sources: as table 4.5.

average loss ratio of 67 per cent for the seven years it existed (1804-11). Second, while the underwriting results of the older London offices were worse, their 'expense' ratios of management costs to premium income were lower than those of the provincials (table 4.6). Expenses, that is salaries, directors' remuneration, fees for various services and the fixed costs of a head office, plus commissions and allowances paid to agents, accounted generally for 20 to 30 per cent of premium income among the country offices, compared to less than 18 per cent for the cartel offices. On the other hand, the new London offices of the 1800s, with their large, rapidly constructed sales networks, were more costly ventures. The most expensive of these was the Atlas, which incurred huge legal bills from contested claims. Overall the fragmentary evidence presented in table 4.6 does not suggest that there were general economies of scale to be tapped in the fire insurance industry.

Table 4.5 also shows how average premium incomes for several offices stagnated or fell during the 1800s and early 1810s. The exceptions were the Norwich Union and the County, both of whom were partly competing in the same markets. To some extent this was the result of a falling price trend, so that premium income might decline even though sums insured remained stable or even increased. Above all it was falling rates on industrial and commercial risks which caused the overall price decline, for premium rates on common residential properties remained largely stable throughout this period.

Table 4.7 Average rates, 1791-1815

Annual average premium in shillings per £100 insured

Offices	1791-5[a]	1796-1800	1801-5[b]	1806-10[c]	1811-15[d]
LONDON					
Sun	3.08	3.26	3.07	2.84	2.77
Phoenix	4.20	4.47			3.58
REA	3.44	3.93	4.29	4.21	4.11
London	3.05	3.17	3.24	2.85	2.66
Globe			5.81	4.04	3.57
Imperial			4.84	4.47	4.00
County				2.27	1.92
Atlas					4.69
COUNTRY					
Salop	2.77	2.78	2.73	2.62	2.59
Wiltshire			3.53	4.51	
Norwich General			3.03		2.92
Norwich Union			5.58	4.03	3.77
Newcastle				3.03	
Coefficient of Var.	0.149	0.171	0.273	0.229	0.234

Notes: [a] Salop, 1792-5. [b] Globe, 1804-5; Imperial, 1803-5; Wiltshire, 1805; Norwich General, 1796-1805. [c] County, 1807-10; Wiltshire, Newcastle, 1809. [d] Atlas, 1812-14; Norwich General, 1806-14.

Sources: as table 4.5.

We are able to calculate average premium rates for eight London offices and five country offices for this period (table 4.7). In all cases where a comparison across time is possible, the average rate fell substantially between 1801-5 to 1811-15. This fits in with the story of market entry, growing competition, the break up of oligopoly and market fragmentation. The average rate, however, is not a straightforward measure of price, for its level was determined not just by an office's premium rates, but also by the proportion of high-priced hazardous risks among its insurances. The low average rate for the County accords with what we know of its concentration of business in the rural counties, while the higher average rates of other offices indicates their focus on industrial and commercial risks. The decline of the Sun's average rate from 1796-1800 reflects not only the fall in premium rates, but also the loss of mill and warehouse insurances to its rivals in Manchester, Liverpool and Glasgow during this period, a shedding of dangerous risks which as table 4.5 shows, brought modest benefits in the way of improved claims ratios.

The price differentials between the offices, measured by the coefficients of variation of the average rates given in table 4.7, were lowest, as might be expected, during the era of the London cartel. The collapse of the cartel was accompanied by an increase in the variation of average rates, which suggests the extent of market disintegration. The differential narrowed a little before the end of the Napoleonic wars, and then fell sharply, so that by the early 1820s the variation in rates was nearly one-third lower than it had been in 1811. The preponderance of bilateral agreements between provincial and London offices, and the intermittent attempts to establish tariffs for particular categories of risk, may have helped reduce price differentials. The consolidation of offices such as the Atlas, the Imperial and the Globe in industrial and commercial markets, and the Sun's retreat from underwriting cotton mills and warehouses, probably also resulted in a wider dispersal of these high-priced risks across the insurance industry and helped lower differentials in average premium rates.

We have few figures for net profits, returns on shares or premiums, or any other direct or indirect measure of overall profitability, but the available evidence supports the picture of a generally prosperous time for country offices. After a difficult period in the later 1790s, as table 4.8 shows, the Old Bath Fire Office recorded large surpluses on its underwriting. The Norwich Union paid its members a bonus of 75 per cent on their deposits at the first septennial declaration in 1804, and followed this with a 50 per cent bonus in subsequent years. The Essex & Suffolk paid a 50 per cent dividend at its first septennial division of profits in 1810. In the following years, this office paid out to insurers bonuses averaging 23 per cent of its premium income. The average annual 'net gains' of the Newcastle Fire Office increased from 25 to 31 per cent of average premiums between 1808-10 and 1811-15, with 1808 being the only year in which a net loss was recorded.[98]

The cartel offices consistently made impressive surpluses on their UK underwriting after 1795. The REA paid an average dividend of 17 per cent in the period 1806-15, although in the same period the Phoenix's dividends were reduced to six per cent by heavy losses overseas. The County was the most successful of the new metropolitan insurers. Barber Beaumont declared a 25 per cent dividend to shareholders at the first septennial distribution of profits in 1815, and followed this with 20 per cent dividends in subsequent years. Other offices were less fortunate. The Imperial's surpluses were paltry, and the company paid just six per cent in dividends between 1806 and 1815.[99] The Atlas also returned five or six per cent from 1809 to 1812 when the office was declared to be in a 'flourishing state'. In 1812, however, high legal costs were incurred in resisting the claims, not always successfully, 'of a description of assurers who it is to be hoped will not in future appear in the company's books'. Liquidity problems began to emerge as the office frequently ran short of cash to pay mounting claims. No dividends were declared for 1814 and 1815, provoking protests from shareholders.[100] Fires in Ireland were

Table 4.8   Underwriting surpluses, 1791-1815

Premiums minus losses plus expenses, expressed as percentage of premiums

Offices	1791-5	1796-1800	1801-5	1806-10	1811-15
LONDON					
Sun	- 0.9	21.5			
Phoenix	- 3.2	35.6	27.5	32.3	29.6
REA	39.0	33.6	22.7	20.3	22.3
Imperial			30.8	8.0	2.5
County				54.9	52.3
Atlas					- 20.7
COUNTRY					
Old Bath		- 75.4	63.0	52.1	59.0
Kent				11.5	
Newcastle				25.5	31.9
Glasgow				12.5	
Essex & Suffolk					44.7

Sources: as table 4.5.

blamed for most of the losses in these years. The Atlas experience demonstrates that the sources of hazard for those offices which aspired to a national business were not only found in London and the northern manufacturing cities. It also indicates that the need for insurance companies to maintain shareholders' confidence was greater than ever in an age of intensifying competition, when everyone - agents, policyholders and shareholders alike - might be bought by a rival firm. Market conditions became no easier in the years which followed the end of the long war against France.

Notes

[1] From Tale VI, 'The Frank Courtship' (1812), in Crabbe, *Complete Poetical Works*, II, p.87.

[2] A separate rate for London and country insurances was introduced in 1765. Some of the rates given by Coode in his 'Revised Report', p.2, were incorrect and were amended by Walford, who consulted the original statutes. Walford, *Insurance Cyclopaedia*, vol.III, pp.483-4, 553. Walford himself also made errors in calculating the aggregated rates for 1757 and 1765. The correct rates were 3s 10d per policy, 1713-44; 1s 6d, 1744-6; 1s, 1746-57; 2s, 1757-65; 2s 2d (London), 4s 6d (rest of Great Britain), 1765-76; 3s 2d (London), 5s 6d (rest of Great Britain), 1776-7; 8s 2d (London), 10s 6d (rest of Great Britain) for policies insuring £1000 or more, as before for policies <£1000, 1777-97. In 1797 common rates were reintroduced for both London and elsewhere of 3s for policies <£1000, and 6s for £1000 and upwards. In 1804 these rates were replaced by a 1s duty on all policies.

[3] Calculated from Mitchell, *British Historical Statistics*, p.388, and 'An Account of the Net Produce of all the Taxes from Michaelmas 1773 to Michaelmas 1782', in Lambert, *Sessional Papers*, vol.38, pp.161-6. I am grateful to Michael Turner for directing me to this source.

[4] Cobbet, *Parliamentary History*, vol.22 (1781-2), pp.1155-6; WCA, Ms 343/17, Westminster, DM, 1 July 1784; Walford, *Insurance Cyclopaedia*, vol.III , p.485.

[5] These figures are estimates, based upon the net yield from stamps on policies in each of the years ending Michaelmas 1774-6, the estimated share of London insurances in total sums insured, from the five year averages centred on 1775 given in table 2.1 above and Appendix A below, and the proportion (14 per cent) of new policies among the Hand-in-Hand's total current policies in 1775. Yield from stamps from Lambert, *Sessional Papers*, vol.38, pp.161-66. The Hand-in-Hand's policies from GL Ms 8666/22, Hand-in-Hand, DM, 1773-6.

[6] There are no references to tax evasion by policyholders or insurance offices in the three reports of the parliamentary committee which examined revenue fraud in 1783-4. Lambert, *Sessional Papers*, vol.38, pp.215-389.

[7] Cobbet, *Parliamentary History*, vol.22 (1781-2), pp.1162-8.

[8] O'Brien, 'Political Economy of British Taxation', pp.13, 27.

[9] GL Ms 11931/6, Sun, GCM, 19 Mar., 21 Mar. 1782; Ms 14022/17, Union, DM, 20 Mar. 1782.

[10] GL Ms 11931/6, Sun, GCM, 2 Apr. 1782; Ms 8755/2, London Assurance, Out Letter Book, 5 Apr. 1782; Ms 8666/24, Hand-in-Hand, DM, 16 Apr. 1782; Ms 14022/17, Union, DM, 10 Apr. 1782.

[11] GL Ms 11931/6, Sun, GCM, 2 Apr. 1782.

[12] O'Shaugnessy, 'Formation of a Commercial Lobby'; Dietz, 'Politics of Whisky'.

[13] The bill became 22 Geo. III c. 48.

[14] GL Ms 11931/6, Sun, GCM, 11 June 1782; SRO, Ms 3008/1/2/1, Salop, DM, 25 June, 28 Nov. 1782.

[15] GL Ms 8666/24, Hand-in-Hand, DM, 18 June, 15 Oct. 1782.

[16] Supple, *Royal Exchange*, p.124.

[17] GL Ms 11931/6, Sun, GCM, 29 May 1783.

18 Sun agents resigned at Blandford, Newcastle under Lyme, Peterborough, York, Durham, Leicester, Brecon, Bath and Lancaster.

19 GL Ms 14022/17, Union, DM 21 June 1782. The annual licence remained a requirement until 1842, when it was repealed by 5&6 Vict. c. 79, which made the licence perpetual unless the office defaulted on its duty payments or went out of business. Walford, *Insurance Cyclopaedia*, vol.III, p.420.

20 GL Ms 14022/17, Union, DM, 11 July 1782; *Leeds Mercury*, 2 July 1782.

21 These are the annual figures from Coode, 'Revised Report', rather than the five year averages reported in appendix A below.

22 Cobbet, *Parliamentary History*, vol.33 (1797-8), p.433.

23 Trebilcock, *Phoenix Assurance*, vol.I, p.153.

24 Exemption was also granted in 1860 to insurances on workmen's tools, if insured for no more than £20. The duty was halved to 1s 6d% in 1864, and abolished in 1869. For recurring opposition to the tax, see Anon, 'Observations on the Duties on Insurance'; Association for the Abolition of the Duty, *The Fire Insurance Duty*; Trebilcock, *Phoenix Assurance*, vol.I, pp.151-61.

25 O'Brien, 'Political Economy of British Taxation', tables 5 and 6.

26 GL Ms 15032/8, Sun, Take over Papers, Sheffield Fire Office.

27 Trebilcock, *Phoenix Assurance*, vol.I, pp.28-9, 61.

28 Trebilcock, *Phoenix Assurance*, vol.I, pp.341-53, 444.

29 GL Ms 11932/12, Sun, CMM, 10 Oct. 1782.

30 GL Ms 11931/7, Sun, GCM, 7 Apr. 1786, 11 Jan.- 1 Mar., 3 May 1787, 10 Jan.-7 Feb. 1788; Ms 11932/12-13, Sun, CMM, 27 May 1784, 4 Oct. 1787, 28 Feb. 1788; Dickson, *Sun Insurance*, p.95; Supple, *Royal Exchange*, p.93; Trebilcock, *Phoenix Assurance*, vol.I, pp.449-50.

31 GL Ms 11931/7, Sun, GCM, 7 Jan., 11 Mar. 1790, 14 July 1791; Ms 11932/14, Sun, CMM, 11 Aug. 1791, 29 Nov., 20 Dec. 1792, 1 Jan. 1795; Dickson, *Sun Insurance*, p.95; Trebilcock, *Phoenix Assurance*, vol.I, pp.451-2; CUL, PAA, PX1010, Phoenix, Agents' Extra Letter Book A, March 1795.

32 GL Ms 11931/8, Sun, GCM, 9 Apr. 1799. The duty was lowered from 8s 2d for London policies and 10s 6d for country policies insuring £1000 and upwards to a common rate of 6s, and from 3s 2d (London) and 5s 6d (country) on policies less than £1000 to a common rate of 3s.

33 Ashton, *Iron and Steel*, pp.162-85; Sweezy, *Monopoly and Competition*, pp.32-6; Levy, *Monopolies, Cartels and Trusts*, pp.106-56; Redford, *Manchester Merchants*, pp.1-14; Beresford, *Leeds Chambers of Commerce*, pp.12-22; Barker, *Pilkington Brothers*, p.70; Coleman, *British Paper Industry*, pp.131-2, 155, 270-77; Mathias, *Brewing Industry*, pp.218-28; Iredale, 'John and Thomas Marshall'; Alford, *W.D. & H.O. Wills*, pp.27-31; Devine, *Tobacco Lords*, p.61; Harris, *British Iron Industry*, pp.73-4; Harris and Roberts, 'Eighteenth Century Monopoly'; Jones, 'Price Associations'; Trebilcock, *Phoenix Assurance*, vol.I, pp.17-22; Smail, 'Sources of Innovation', footnote 41.

34 Mathias, *Brewing Industry*, pp.214-18.

35 Trebilcock, *Phoenix Assurance*, vol.I, p.455.

36 Mathias, *First Industrial Nation*, pp.386-7.

37 Calculated from Trebilcock, *Phoenix Assurance*, vol.I, table 8.1, p.443.

38   Trebilcock, *Phoenix Assurance*, vol.I, pp.445-6, 450; GL Ms 11931/7, Sun, GCM, 11
      Jan. 1787.
39   GL Ms 11932/14, Sun, CMM, 24 Jan. 1793; Ms 11931/7-8, Sun, GCM, 21 Nov.
      1792, 18 Dec. 1794, 23 June 1803.
40   GL Ms 11932/14, 15, Sun, CMM, 23 Dec. 1790, 13 Oct., 27 Oct., 10 Nov. 1791, 16
      Oct. 1794; Trebilcock, *Phoenix Assurance*, vol.I, p.132; Dickson, *Sun Insurance*,
      pp.60, 65.
41   CUL, PAA, Agents Extra Letter Book A, 21 Jan. 1802; GL Ms 11932/16, Sun, CMM,
      31 Dec. 1801, 11 Mar. 1802.
42   GL Ms 11931/8, Sun, GCM, 11 Nov. 1802.
43   GL Ms 11931/8, Sun, GCM, 13-27 Jan. 1803. Duck had drafted his plan in the last
      week of December, probably moved to do so by the REA's initiative.
44   GL Ms 11931/8, Sun, GCM, 3 Mar., 12 May 1803.
45   GL Ms 11931/8, Sun, GCM, 9 Feb., 22 Mar., 19 Apr. 1804; Dickson, *Sun Insurance*,
      pp.93, 144-5; Trebilcock, *Phoenix Assurance*, vol.I, p.364. The Sun's premium
      income from Manchester fell from over £9000 in 1803 to less than £4400 by 1811.
      Policies on cotton mills issued by the Sun at Manchester collapsed from 123 to just
      14. GL Ms 11935A/1, Sun, Report Books, vol.1, Bewicke's Report, 8 Oct. 1812.
46   GL Ms 11932/16, CMM, 14 Oct. 1802, 8 Sept. 1803.
47   GL Ms 11932/16, CMM, 21 June, 11 Oct. 1804, 21 Feb. 1805, 6 Mar. 1806;
      Trebilcock, *Phoenix Assurance*, vol.I, p.455.
48   Trebilcock, *Phoenix Assurance*, vol.I, p.114. For examples of Wilson's letters,
      transmitted only in summary form by the Sun's clerks, see GL Ms 11932/16, CMM,
      21 June 1804, and 6 Mar. 1806.
49   Calculated from Trebilcock, *Phoenix Assurance*, vol.I, table 8.2, p.461.
50   Trebilcock, *Phoenix Assurance*, vol.I, pp.356, 363.
51   GL Ms 11931/8, Sun, GCM, 20 Jan., 3 Mar. 1803.
52   Calculated from Trebilcock, *Phoenix Assurance*, vol.I, p.363.
53   Two London offices, the Minerva and the Palladium (established, probably, in 1797),
      were very short-lived. The other new offices were the Albion (established for fire and
      life insurance in 1805, with a capital of £1m in 2000 shares - it gave up the fire business
      in 1827), the Hope and the Eagle (both established 1807, also for fire and life). The
      Eagle had a capital of £2m in 40000 shares. It sold its fire business to the Protector in
      1826. Raynes, *History of British Insurance*, pp.231-2.
54   Trebilcock, *Phoenix Assurance*, vol.I, p.35; Raynes, *History of British Insurance*,
      p.213; GL Ms 11931/8, Sun, GCM, 9 Apr. 1799, 7 Oct., 28 Oct. 1802; Ms 11932/16,
      Sun, CMM, 26 Feb. 1801, 8 Sept. 1803; Dickson, *Sun Insurance*, p.96.
55   GL Ms 12160A/2, Imperial, DM, 27 Feb. 1805. See the reference to a number of
      insurances passed to the Imperial by the British in 1804-5, in Ms 12160A/5, Imperial,
      DM, 25 Oct. 1812.
56   GL Ms 12160A/2, Imperial, DM, 13 Mar. 1805; Dickson, *Sun Insurance*, p.97;
      Trebilcock, *Phoenix Assurance*, vol.I, pp.459-60; GL Ms 8735/6, London Assurance,
      FCM, 22 Mar. 1805.
57   Eden's *The State of the Poor* was published in 1797. See his entry in *Dictionary of
      National Biography*, vol.VI, pp.356-7. Details of Eden's first plan for the Globe are
      taken from the prospectus, *The Globe or General Insurance Office*, 15 May 1799. An

annotated copy can be found in LRO, LL&G Mss., Globe, Committee Minutes, 25 May 1799. See also Eden's *Observations on Friendly Societies* (1801) for an elaboration of his ideas.

[58] Eden's struggle for a charter continued with two further applications in 1806 and 1810, this time with a provision to sell marine insurance, which directly challenged the monopoly of the two London corporations. These applications generated counter-petitions from other insurance offices and a lengthy debate about monopolies which culminated in a parliamentary investigation into marine Insurance in 1810. See Raynes, *History of British Insurance*, pp.190-99. Eden died at the Globe office in November 1809.

[59] The Globe's concerns were such in 1807-8 that it approached the Sun and the Phoenix for rate agreements, both in vain. Trebilcock, *Phoenix Assurance*, vol.I, p.462.

[60] GL Ms 12160A/1, Imperial, DM, 18 Apr., 25 May 1803, 4 Jan., 15 Feb. 1804; Trebilcock, *Phoenix Assurance*, vol.I, pp.216-18. Heligoland, 28 miles off the German coast, was seized from Denmark in 1807, and formally ceded to Britain in 1814. Imperial sold their first insurance there in November 1808.

[61] The Liverpool St George had run into trouble when a fire in 1802 destroyed the Goree warehouse district in Liverpool, nearly bankrupting the new company with claims.

[62] GL Ms 11935A/1, Sun, Report Books, fols.22-9, report of Philip Bewicke on his late journey to Liverpool, Oct. 1806. The Imperial's commanding position in Liverpool was also noted by Henry Desborough, the secretary of the Atlas Assurance, when he visited the town in 1809. Ms 16170/1, Atlas, DM, 30 Mar. 1809.

[63] 'Beaumont' was added as a surname in 1812, for unknown reasons. Biographical details are based on Pearson, 'Beaumont'; Noakes, *County Fire Office*, pp.5-14, 20-26; *GM*, XVI (July 1841), pp.96-8, obit.; Walford, *Insurance Cyclopaedia*, vol.I, pp.261-2; Keeson, 'Barber Beaumont'; Beaumont, *Barber Beaumont*.

[64] GL Ms 18574, County, Deed of Constitution, 25 Feb. 1808. Chronologically, County was probably the first to introduce bonus policies. However the West of England Fire and Life Insurance Company, also founded in 1807, divided profits among policyholders too, on a five yearly basis. See Raynes, *History of British Insurance*, p.235. On the 'reversionary bonus', see Trebilcock, *Phoenix Assurance*, vol.I, pp.476-80.

[65] County, DM, 17 Nov. 1808; County, Minutes of County Meetings 1807-25, Northampton, 23 July 1814. Most of the records of County Fire Office were still held privately by Sun Alliance plc and were uncatalogued when the author consulted them. These records have subsequently been transferred to the Guildhall Library, London.

[66] GL Ms 16170A/1, Atlas, DM, 9 May 1811.

[67] County, Agents' Circular from J.T. Barber, 25 June 1809.

[68] GL Ms 16170A/1, Atlas, DM, 19 Dec., 23 Dec. 1807, and Prospectus dated 6 Apr. 1808. There were 42 new joint-stock promotions during 1807 across a wide range of sectors. Harris, *Industrialising English Law*, p.216.

[69] Calculated from the lists of new members of the committee given in GL Ms 16170A/1, Atlas, DM, 19 Dec. 1807 to 2 May 1808. Occupations from *Post Office Directory of London* (1807), *Holden's Triennial Directory of London* (1808).

[70] GL Ms 16170A/1, Atlas, DM, Prospectus, 6 Apr. 1808, article V, 3 Aug. 1808.

71 Calculated from quarterly accounts of duty paid, recorded in GL Ms 16170A/1-2, Atlas, DM, 1810-16.

72 This estimate is based on cumulative cotton mill premiums of £9121 by May 1811 and total current premiums in 1812 of £18436. Calculated from GL Ms 16170A/1-2, Atlas, DM, 9 May 1811, 30 June 1814. No totals are available before 1812. The estimate assumes that the growth of total premiums was in the order of £6000 in year one, £9000 in year two, £12000 in year three.

73 GL Ms 16170A/2, Atlas, DM, 23 Jan., 27 Feb., 12 Mar. 1812. On Luddism, see Hammond, *The Skilled Labourer*, chs.9-11; Thompson, *Making of the English Working Class*, ch.14.

74 GL Ms 16170A/1, Atlas, DM, 1 Dec. 1808.

75 GL Ms 16170A/1, Atlas, DM, 1 Dec .1808, 2 Feb.- 27 Apr. 1809; CKS, U2593/B6/5, Kent, DM, 28 Dec. 1808.

76 Five per cent commission was agreed on life premiums. GL Ms 16170A/1, Atlas, DM, 20 Apr., 27 Apr. 1809.

77 GL Ms 16170A/1, Atlas, DM, 21 Dec. 1809, 25 Oct. 1810; CKS, U2593/B6/6, Kent Fire, DM, 30 May, 27 June 1810.

78 GL Ms 16170A/1, Atlas, DM, 9 May 1811.

79 Cited by Ryan, 'Norwich Union and the British Fire Insurance Market', p.62.

80 CKS, U2593/B6/8, Kent, DM, 14 June 1815.

81 This figure includes Suffolk & General Fire Office, founded as a partnership in 1802, which turned mutual as the Suffolk Amicable in 1809. The others were Devizes (1784), Norwich Mutual (1785), Norwich Union (1797), Essex Equitable (1802), Finchingfield (1804), Wooler (Northumberland, 1805), Norwich Equitable (1807), Anchor (Norwich, 1808).

82 Ryan, 'History of the Norwich Union', p.177. Details of the Devizes Mutual are taken from Cunnington, *Annals of the Borough of Devizes*, appendix L, pp.235-9.

83 Calculated from duty returns in GL Ms 16206/1, Essex & Suffolk, DM, 'Accounts of Fire Duty by Country Offices, Christmas 1808 - Christmas 1809'.

84 GL Ms 16206/1, Essex & Suffolk, DM, see the list of agents at the back of this volume.

85 Calculated from Ryan, 'Norwich Union and the British Fire Insurance Market', table 5, p.60.

86 The following draws on Ryan, 'Norwich Union and the British Fire Insurance Market'; Ryan, 'History of the Norwich Union'.

87 Trebilcock, *Phoenix Assurance*, vol.I, table 8.2, p.461.

88 This was furnished in response to a request for data upon which the Treasury could estimate the likely yield from an increase in stamp duty on insurances. PRO 30/8/187/ 230-40, Chatham Papers, Watts to Pitt, 10 June, 22 June 1797.

89 Ryan, 'History of the Norwich Union', p.125.

90 GL Ms 11935E, Sun, Take over Papers, Salamander, Deed of Settlement, 8 Jan. 1823, preamble.

91 For example, Kent Fire Office alternated its directors' meetings between Maidstone and Sittingbourne, while Suffolk & General had two 'divisions' based at Bury St Edmunds and Ipswich. CKS, U2593/B6/1, Kent, DM, 1802-3; Ryan, 'History of the Norwich Union', p.76.

92 Calculated from the duty return given in Raynes, *History of British Insurance*, p.210.

93   *Berrow's Worcester Journal*, 7 Jan. 1790; CUL, PAA, PX1773, Phoenix, Take over
      Papers, Worcester Fire Office.
94   Ryan, 'History of the Norwich Union', pp.112-47; Raynes, *History of British
      Insurance*, p.210.
95   CKS, U2593/B6/1, Kent, DM, 5 Apr., 19 Oct. 1802; Dickson, *Sun Insurance*, p.96.
96   Agents were appointed in the rest of England from 1818, Reed, *Kent Insurance
      Company*.
97   CUL, PX509, Phoenix, Statistical Analysis, fol.118.
98   GL Ms 16206/2, Essex & Suffolk, DM, 26 Mar. 1810; Ryan, 'Norwich Union and the
      British Fire Insurance Market', p.53; GPL, Cotesworth Mss, CM 4/1-21, Newcastle
      Fire, Accounts, 1808-22.
99   County, DM, 1 June 1815; GL Ms 18274, Imperial, Tabular Statements, 1803-91;
      Trebilcock, *Phoenix Assurance*, vol.I, table 13.4, p.715.
100   GL Ms 16170/2, Atlas, DM, 17 June 1812, 16 Sept. 1813, 30 June 1814, 27 June
      1815.

Chapter 5

Insurance in and out of Crisis, 1815-50

It was a town of red brick, or of brick that would have been red if the smoke and ashes had allowed it; but as matters stood it was a town of unnatural red and black like the painted face of a savage.

Charles Dickens.[1]

The pace of urban and industrial change accelerated in the decades following the end of the long war against France, creating a larger and more complex set of markets for property insurance. Whereas urban dwellers in 1801 comprised about one-third of the population, by 1851 England was officially an urban nation with 54 per cent of its citizens living in towns.[2] The big conglomerations dominated this growth. By mid-century 31 per cent of the population of England and Wales lived in places with more than 50000 inhabitants. London more than doubled its size from 1m in 1811 to 2.4m by 1851.[3] Liverpool, Glasgow and Manchester had populations over 300000 while Dublin, Birmingham and Edinburgh had over 200000.

Urban growth was closely related to the expansion of industry and commerce. The proportion of the workforce in manufacturing rose from 30 per cent in 1811 to 43 per cent in 1851. In the same period capital investment grew by a factor of 2.5 in real terms.[4] Textile factories multiplied. Many were converted from former warehouses, let out to several tenants, and filled with new types of machinery, products of the expanding engineering and iron industries. Larger scale production also spread to workshop-based economies such as that of Birmingham. The cost of freight fell and trade increased with the development of railways and shipping. New docks were constructed and existing port facilities extended in London, Liverpool and Hull. Nine of the ten most rapidly growing big towns in the Kingdom were centres of manufacturing and trade.[5]

For the most part these urban populations were not self-sustaining, but depended upon migration, largely from adjacent rural areas. House-building generally kept pace with population growth, but the cyclical nature of construction often led to shortages, especially of the cheaper types of housing. When poorer migrants moved to towns they frequently found little, if any, improvement in comfort from the rural squalor which many of them had left. Typical features of the larger towns were ring and ribbon development, increasing residential segregation by class, and the emergence of the 'classic' east-end/west-end division which had characterised London for some time.[6] While rows of new suburban houses and cottages were built for the better-off artisans and clerks in steady employment, housing for the poorer working class took the form of 'filling in' existing east-end, dockside and inner suburban sites. Overcrowding was the result, as offices, warehouses and railway sidings replaced residential areas and squeezed labourers' families into courts and alleys, into single-storey lean-to's, multi-storey tenements, uniform terraces of back-to-backs, or damp and insanitary cellars. In Liverpool 39000 people inhabited 8000 cellars in 1840. In Glasgow the wynds were full of 'ill-ventilated, high-piled, waterless and dilapidated houses'. The town's chief of police described lower-class housing there in 1842 as 'unfit even for sties'.[7]

Slums were unattractive to insurers as well as to middle-class observers. Although urban conglomerations were increasing in size and their physical fabric was becoming more dense, the centrifugal force, by which areas of big cities were being separated by function, wealth and social class, helped insurance offices to differentiate residential property markets. The suburban villas appearing in Headingley, Edgbaston, Ardwick and Highgate were of great interest to underwriters. Thomas Gradgrind's Stone Lodge, on the edge of Coketown and 'fire-proof from top to bottom', was eminently insurable. In southern England too the emergence of new classes of property owner encouraged insurers. Cobbett may have disliked Margate because it had become 'so thickly settled with stock-jobbing cuckolds', but these were exactly the people most likely to insure their lives and property.[8]

Sums insured by English fire offices grew from £378m in 1815 to £731m by 1850. Urban and industrial development not only stimulated this growth but also created new types of hazard such as railway accidents and steam boiler explosions. Almost none of these risks were underwritten by the existing fire offices. Instead they tempted a small number of pioneering specialist insurers to try their hand. The fire offices, however, were concerned with the dangers of conflagration posed by new, larger and faster types of machinery, by the storage of novel mixes of combustible materials and goods, by the sub-letting of factories and workshops to several tenants often manufacturing entirely unrelated products, and by the steadily increasing value of goods and property in Britain's industrial centres and commercial entrepôts.

Sources of competition in the post-war years

After a few quiet post-war years, fire insurance was rocked was by the first of two waves of company foundations. Twenty-two English offices were established between 1821 and 1826, together with six in Scotland and seven in Ireland. Many of these were small and short-lived. Others, such as the Guardian and the Alliance, quickly attained national and international importance. The Guardian Assurance, founded in 1821, sold over half of its 20000 shares to investors living outside London. It constructed a huge sales network of more than 300 agents in the UK

Table 5.1 Market share and sums insured of leading British fire offices, 1816-50

	Market shares %				Sums insured (£m)						
	1816-20	1826-30	1836-40	1846-50	1822	1825	1830	1835	1840	1845	1850
Sun	19.7	15.9	16.9	15.7	76.1	72.5	80.4	89.9	114.8	132.0	128.9
Phoenix	12.2	8.8	13.8	10.5	43.9	41.0	45.9	51.7	93.6	89.8	85.1
REA	8.6	6.6	7.4	6.5	34.3	31.1	34.6	41.8	51.4	54.2	54.7
Norwich	7.6	8.6	7.3	7.1	42.1	42.7	41.6	49.3	54.9	57.0	58.6
Imperial	6.2	3.9	3.2	3.8	22.1	20.6	18.1	18.5	21.1	32.3	30.9
County	5.1	6.1	5.0	5.0	26.0	28.0	29.4	33.4	36.8	40.3	41.9
Globe	5.0	3.5	3.5	2.8	18.4	16.8	17.6	19.5	22.6	23.6	22.9
British	2.8	2.2	2.0	-	9.0	9.9	10.5	11.9	12.9	-	-
Atlas	2.2	2.8	2.7	2.8	10.1	12.2	13.8	15.3	18.0	21.9	24.3
Protector	-	6.0	1.5	-	-	9.9	37.4	37.8	-	-	-
Guardian	-	4.1	3.7	2.6	9.6	18.2	20.7	22.3	22.8	21.4	21.8
Alliance	-	2.6	2.8	3.1	-	10.0	13.5	15.5	18.0	19.3	32.1

West of England	?	3.2	3.5	3.7	10.3	13.5	16.8	19.2	23.4	28.6	32.0
Manchester	-	2.2	2.2	1.5	-	9.9	11.2	12.6	14.3	12.3	13.2
Scottish Union*	-	2.3	2.2	1.8	-	?	?	13.7	14.6	12.7	15.5

Notes: Sums insured include British farming stock, but exclude Irish and foreign business. Scottish Union* - figures relate to calendar years 1836, 1840, 1846, 1850.

Sources: Market shares from Trebilcock, *Phoenix Assurance*, vol.I, table 8.2, p.461. Sums insured calculated from stamp duty returns, 1822-50.

and Europe and was soon insuring risks as far away as Russia and India. The Alliance was backed by some of the biggest names in the City - Nathan Rothschild, Samuel Gurney, Moses Montefiore, Francis Baring - and began with a huge capital of £500000. By the early 1830s some 45 per cent of the company's fire insurance premiums came from overseas.[9] Among the many new country offices two ventures at Manchester and Leeds stood out. Both were founded in 1824 by groups of textile merchants and manufacturers. The Manchester office spread quickly beyond the north-west, establishing 116 agencies by 1829.[10] By then it was the third largest English fire office outside London. The Leeds office grew more slowly, but became the fifth largest country office in England by the early 1830s.

The wave of new foundations, together with the growth of a few of the offices established before 1810, helped reduce the market share of the three largest insurers from 41 per cent in 1816-20 to 33 per cent by 1826-30 (see table 5.1). The business of other older offices such as the Globe, the London Assurance, the Imperial and the Hand-in-Hand, also declined. Increasing competition led to price cuts and a squeeze on margins which drove many smaller firms to the wall. Between 1824 and 1831 at least 17 companies ceased fire underwriting, and the net increase in the number of English offices over the period 1822-32 was just three. A second wave of promotions from 1834 generated a further 18 new offices, but the net gain by 1843 was nil. Mergers, bankruptcies and w ithdrawals r esulted in a rising level of concentration. The decline in the position of the three leading London firms was reversed, so that their market share reached 38 per cent by 1836-40. This improvement in the market power of the largest firms led to a revival in oligopolistic behaviour during the early 1840s, manifested in greater cooperation and the establishment of a comprehensive tariff system which in turn increased premium rates and improved underwriting margins.

Competition in the post-war decade took the form of price cutting, product innovation - hitherto a rare phenomenon in fire insurance - and more aggressive marketing. While prices for ordinary residential insurances remained stable, premium rates for 'special risks', industrial and commercial insurances, drifted downward, before falling precipitously during and after the company boom of 1824-5. Rates which fell included those on wool textile, flax and silk mills, sugar refineries, Scottish distilleries and floating insurances in Liverpool docks. Even the premiums charged for insuring London pawnbrokers' pledges were reduced in 1823.[11] Not surprisingly, given the earlier anguish caused by the problem of rating cotton mills, the greatest efforts were made after the war to stem the downward slide in these prices. The Phoenix took the lead, twice proposing a tariff in vain. The basic premium of 15s% on cotton mills 'of the safest kind', suggested by the Phoenix in 1817, was soon undercut by other offices insuring mills for as little as 10s%. It is hard to disentangle the sometimes conflicting evidence about price cutting from the accounts of different offices. In one place an office is portrayed as a price maker, while elsewhere it followed or even resisted the market trend. Weak or inattentive boards could be bullied or beguiled into reducing rates by local agents desperate for a competitive advantage. Where price cutting was deliberately employed before 1825, it was usually a short-term expedient in particular markets, often in response to consumer demand, rather than a long-term strategy to increase total market share. This is true of other competitive devices, such as raising the maximum limit on any one risk or offering blanket discounts to a locality. Other non-price forms of competition, notably the reversionary bonus, revealed a greater sense of strategy. The reversionary bonus enabled some offices to attract policyholders by offering them, in return for slightly higher premium payments, a share in the underwriting profits at regular intervals, usually every five or seven years.[12] This sharpened the edge of competition. In 1821 the Newcastle Fire Office blamed a decline in its country premiums on the bonus 'temptations' held out by the Norwich Union and the County.[13] The reversionary bonus was loathed by the non-bonus paying offices who tended to regard the 'with-profits' policy - the first new product in fire insurance since the early eighteenth century - as financially unsound and a betrayal of shareholders' interests.

Alongside the reversionary bonus, the development of territorial strongholds gave the established insurers most cause for alarm. Large, often regionally concentrated shareholdings gave some of the new stock companies an immediate foothold in particular markets, especially when the purchase of a policy was made a prerequisite for the purchase of a share. This was the case, for example, with the MFLAC which had over 2000 shareholders, three-quarters of whom lived in the north-west. Shareholders were commonly expected to promote the business of a new office and to enhance its public image. Several companies employed local boards of prominent shareholders to monitor agents, to help with risk assessment and loss adjustment, and to supply market intelligence. As competition increasingly shifted toward marketing, it found expression through posters, pamphlets, circulars and newspaper advertisements. The best example was the publicity war between Thomas Bignold and Barber Beaumont, which is said to have cost the Norwich Union several thousand pounds in advertising and legal expenses between 1816 and 1818.[14] Disputes between companies quickly became personalised in the heated atmosphere of the post-war insurance markets, especially where the individuals involved were strong-willed characters. Public attacks on rivals were also encouraged by agents, though managers generally reacted cautiously. When the Norwich Union was asked by its Hertford agent in 1824 to respond to the new fire office there w ith a p oster ' exposing the unsoundness of the scheme', the board modestly replied that they 'never attack any other office or allow their agents to do so'.[15]

The expansion of sales networks multiplied such sources of conflict. The Norwich Union employed up to 700 agents and the Protector and the Guardian over 300 each by the end of the 1820s. The Imperial was typical in establishing a committee to appoint agents for towns where none had yet been appointed.[16] The task of finding and retaining suitable agents became tougher than ever. In 1821 the County found that it was losing agents to the Norwich Union, where, as Barber Beaumont admitted, the commission was 'in some respects' better. In the following year the Phoenix complained that the Guardian had 'seduced' its agents at

Guildford. The latter found it increasingly difficult to appoint and in 1824 it devolved the task of recruiting new salesmen onto some of its existing agents, a move that reflected the level of despair at head office.[17]

Niche markets and underwriting losses

The concentration of business in market niches, aided by committees of local shareholders, a greater density of sales outlets, bonus policies, price cuts and vociferous advertising, eased the entry of new offices and offered the prospect of expansion for existing insurers. In some regions, provincial offices were able to establish a presence far out of proportion to their national ranking. In 1824 the Birmingham Fire Office insured over three times the value of property covered by the Birmingham agency of the largest provincial fire office, the Norwich Union.[18] In the same year the three Bristol fire offices together received premiums of about £7400, compared with the Norwich Union which earned about £1800 from Bristol, the Phoenix which earned less than £500, and the REA which had a local income of just £84.[19]

Tables 5.2 to 5.9 present data on a range of markets defined by location and type of risk. From 1815 the 'poundage' allowed to the fire offices for collecting stamp duty was paid at two different rates, 4s% on the duty returned for policies issued on London property, and 5s% on duty collected from country insurances. From 1831 these poundage allowances were differentiated in the printed returns of stamp duty, making it possible to calculate the amount each office insured in London and elsewhere. Unfortunately it is not possible to distinguish sums insured by English offices in Scotland, so although we have duty returns for Scottish offices from 1824, we cannot reconstruct a complete picture of the fire insurance market in Scotland.[20]

Tables 5.2 and 5.3 show that the Sun had a greater share of fire insurance in the capital than elsewhere, which helps explain why London was the most concentrated of all markets in the 1840s. The share of top five offices rose between 1831 and 1840, largely through mergers, but during the following decade the Phoenix lost some of the £6m additional business it had acquired in this way, so that the aggregate share of the leading firms fell back by 1850. The number of offices operating in London increased rapidly and the average sum insured per office fell by 30 per cent, making conditions more difficult for new entrants. No company founded after 1824 made any inroads into the aggregate share of the leading fire insurers in the capital before mid-century, and those larger offices which managed to expand in the 1840s, such as the Union and the Westminster, were among the very oldest. By contrast, the market outside the capital expanded more rapidly than the number of offices, so that there was a 27 per cent rise in the average sum insured per office. Here too there was a notable stability in the hierarchy. The Sun, the Phoenix, the REA and the Guardian featured in the top ten at all three dates in table 5.3. Other large London offices such as the Globe, the Alliance and

Table 5.2 London insurances: the ten largest offices by £ insured, 1831-50

	1831			1840			1850	
		£m	Market share		£m	Market share		£m	Market share
1	Sun	42.8	23.5	Sun	48.4	24.1	Sun	51.0	23.1
2	Protector	22.4	12.3	Phoenix	33.3	16.5	Phoenix	27.1	12.2
3	Phoenix	16.6	9.1	REA	18.1	9.0	REA	19.9	9.0
4	Imperial	13.1	7.2	Imperial	13.0	6.5	Imperial	15.9	7.2
5	REA	12.1	6.6	Westminster	12.5	6.2	Westminster	14.9	6.7
6	Westminster	10.1	5.5	Globe	10.9	5.4	Union	10.2	4.6
7	Globe	9.7	5.3	Alliance	10.5	5.2	Guardian	10.0	4.5
8	Guardian	9.3	5.1	Guardian	9.5	4.7	Globe	9.8	4.4
9	Alliance	9.2	5.0	Union	9.1	4.5	Alliance	9.7	4.4
10	Hand-in-Hand	7.7	4.2	Hand-in-Hand	7.3	3.6	London	9.6	4.4
	Top 5 firms		58.7	Top 5 firms		62.3	Top 5 firms		58.2
	Total £m	182.3		Total £m	201.3		Total £m	221.3	
	No. of offices	15		No. of offices	21		No. of offices	26	
	Avg £ per office	12.2		Avg £ per office	9.6		Avg £ per office	8.5	

Sources: see text.

Table 5.3 English provincial insurances: the ten largest offices by £ insured, 1831-50

	1831			1840			1850		
		£m	Market share		£m	Market share		£m	Market share
1	Norwich Union	45.6	14.3	Sun	59.6	15.0	Sun	69.8	14.5
2	Sun	39.9	12.5	Phoenix	55.6	14.0	Phoenix	53.2	11.1
3	Phoenix	29.7	9.3	Norwich Union	45.1	11.4	Norwich Union	48.9	10.2
4	County	26.7	8.3	REA	28.6	7.2	West of England	30.9	6.4
5	REA	24.3	7.6	County	24.7	6.2	REA	30.3	6.3
6	Protector	17.4	5.5	West of England	22.5	5.7	County	28.3	5.9
7	West of England	17.1	5.4	MFLAC	13.9	3.5	Alliance	20.0	4.2
8	Guardian	11.9	3.7	Guardian	12.7	3.2	Atlas	15.5	3.2
9	MFLAC	11.6	3.6	Atlas	10.7	2.7	Imperial	14.3	3.0
10	Atlas	8.3	2.6	Globe	10.7	2.7	MFLAC	12.8	2.7
	Top 5 firms		52.0	Top 5 firms		53.8	Top 5 firms		48.5
	Total £m	319.3		Total £m	396.6		Total £m	480.6	
	No. of offices	39		No. of offices	43		No. of offices	46	
	Avg £ per office	8.2		Avg £ per office	9.2		Avg £ per office	10.4	

Sources: see text.

Table 5.4 Farm insurances, Great Britain: the ten largest offices by £ insured, 1836-50

	1836			1840			1850		
		£m	Market share		£m	Market share		£m	Market share
1	Norwich Union	8.8	19.2	Norwich Union	9.6	17.7	Norwich Union	9.4	15.3
2	Sun	6.0	13.1	Sun	6.8	12.5	Sun	7.8	12.7
3	County	5.8	12.6	County	6.6	12.2	County	7.1	11.6
4	Phoenix	4.1	8.9	Phoenix	5.0	9.2	Royal Farmers	5.1	8.3
5	REA	4.1	8.9	REA	4.6	8.5	REA	4.5	7.3
6	Suffolk	2.0	4.4	Yorkshire	2.5	4.6	Phoenix	4.3	7.0
7	Yorkshire	1.9	4.1	Suffolk	2.1	3.9	Yorkshire	3.1	5.1
8	Kent	1.1	2.4	Essex & Suffolk	1.1	2.0	Scottish Union	1.3	2.1
9	Essex & Suffolk	1.0	2.2	York & London	1.1	2.0	Essex & Suffolk	1.2	2.0
10	West of England	0.9	2.0	Globe	1.1	2.0	Globe	1.1	1.8
	Top 5 firms		62.7	Top 5 firms		60.1	Top 5 firms		55.2
	Total £m	45.9		Total £m	54.3		Total £m	61.3	
	No. of offices	51		No. of offices	52		No. of offices	54	
	Avg £ per office	0.9		Avg £ per office	1.0		Avg £ per office	1.1	

Note: This table includes farming stock insured by Scottish offices. The figures for the East Suffolk & the West Suffolk have been combined for 1831. These offices joined to become the Suffolk Amicable in 1837.

Sources: see text.

Table 5.5   Ireland: the ten largest offices by £ insured, 1836-50

	1836			1840			1850		
		£m	Market share		£m	Market share		£m	Market share
1	REA	3.2	12.6	REA	3.8	12.6	Sun	5.2	14.7
2	National	3.1	12.3	National	3.7	12.2	West of England	4.1	11.6
3	Atlas	2.8	11.1	Sun	3.3	11.1	National	3.9	11.2
4	Sun	1.7	6.7	Atlas	2.9	9.7	REA	3.5	10.1
5	Patriotic	1.6	6.3	West of England	2.3	7.6	Atlas	3.0	8.5
6	Globe	1.5	5.9	Patriotic	2.0	6.8	Alliance	2.6	7.4
7	West of England	1.4	5.5	Alliance	1.7	5.8	Patriotic	2.6	7.3
8	Phoenix	1.3	5.1	Globe	1.6	5.2	Globe	1.6	4.5
9	Alliance	1.3	5.1	British & Irish	1.3	4.2	Imperial	1.5	4.4
10	British & Irish	1.2	4.7	Phoenix	1.2	4.0	County	1.1	3.1
	Top 5 firms		49.0	Top 5 firms		53.2	Top 5 firms		56.1
	Total £m	25.3		Total £m	29.9		Total £m	35.2	
	No. of offices	28		No. of offices	28		No. of offices	30	
	Avg £ per office	0.9		Avg £ per office	1.1		Avg £ per office	1.2	

Note: This table includes sums insured on farming stock in Ireland.

Sources: see text.

the Imperial were generally less significant outside the capital than they were within it.

As tables 5.4 and 5.5 demonstrate, other rapidly growing markets were structured differently from the metropolis. The insurance of British farming was highly concentrated with the Norwich Union dominant. Ireland was the least concentrated market in the 1830s and was the only one where the share of the five leading firms rose. The REA was the market leader until the 1840s, when it was overtaken by the Sun. Two Dublin companies, the National and the Patriotic, were also important. Tables 5.2 to 5.5 suggest that divergent trends in different insurance markets have been hidden by the national aggregates hitherto presented by historians.[21] Fire offices which were of only modest significance nationally could occupy dominant positions in local or niche markets. The success of the older London offices and the trend to gigantism has tended to give the impression of a relatively integrated national market. Instead the disaggregated data suggests that there were many specialist insurance markets, each with different trajectories and competitive conditions. It is hard to demonstrate this conclusively, for, given the gaps in record survival, it is impossible to reconstruct any particular market in its entirety. Tables 5.6 to 5.9 present the available data for Manchester, Leeds and cotton and wool textile mills.

Manchester was the largest domestic agency for several fire offices. Its head office receipts, about £8900, made the MFLAC the largest fire underwriter there within a few years of its foundation.[22] The MFLAC provides a good example of the position which a provincial office could attain in its own market. The north-west produced 19 per cent of the Phoenix's domestic premiums in 1824, but 80 per cent of the MFLAC's fire insurance premiums as late as 1843. The Manchester office also earned more than the biggest London insurers in Lancashire cotton towns such as Preston and Blackburn. The contrast was greatest with regard to cotton mill insurances. Between 1815 and the early 1830s cotton mills provided the Sun with just two per cent of its premiums, the REA with six per cent, and the Phoenix and the Guardian each with about 13 per cent. The MFLAC, however, earned almost 34 per cent of its fire premiums from cotton mills, making it the second largest mill insurer in the country (table 5.7). The company insured 65 out of 67 cotton mills in Stockport and also acquired one-third of the market in Oldham and one-half in Ashton. Twenty-five of the 44 cotton mills in Blackburn in 1838 possessed a MFLAC policy, while only six were insured by the Sun. The Manchester firm also captured one-quarter of the warehouse insurances in its home town worth £6000 per annum.[23] In Leeds the Sun had long been the dominant insurer. Philip Bewicke noted on his journey there in 1806 that 'no office does much compared with Sun'.[24] In the late 1820s the Sun was underwriting nearly half the wool textile and flax mills in the town for about £250000. Its position was weakened by the foundation in 1824 of the Leeds & Yorkshire Assurance Office, for which we have no data. By this date, as tables 5.8 and 5.9 indicate, the Norwich Union and the Guardian were also substantial competitors. The Norwich office was probably Britain's leading

Table 5.6   Fire insurance in Manchester: selected offices

	Average annual premiums (£)		Average annual premiums (£)	
MFLAC	(1826-30)	8873	(1842-3)	*11992*
Phoenix	(1824)	6530		
Sun	(1825-9)	5209	(1835-9)	7388
Guardian	(1826-8)	*3500*		
Norwich Union	(1826-9)	3054		
REA	(1820-29)	2660		

Notes: Estimates in italics. MFLAC estimates based upon the head office remittances for 1842-3 (38%), calculated from GL Ms 16222/8, MFLAC, DM, 4 Oct. 1843, 1 Feb. 1844, 'Statement of fire premiums and duty'. Guardian estimates based upon agency losses calculated from GL Ms 14281/2, Guardian, GCM, 1826-8.

Sources: Supple, *Royal Exchange,* p.154; Dickson, *Sun Insurance*, pp.145, 302; Ryan, 'History of Norwich Union', p.522; GL Ms 11935A/1, Sun, CCM (calculated from agency remittances); CUL, PAA, PX508, Phoenix, Annual Analysis; PX509, Phoenix, Statistical Analysis; GL Ms 14281/2, Guardian, GCM, 1826-8; Ms 16222/2-8, MFLAC, DM, 1824-46, auditors' accounts.

Table 5.7   Fire insurance on cotton mills: selected offices

	Average £ insured p.a.		Average annual premiums (£)	
Phoenix	(1821-30)	1308660	(1821-30)	9672
MFLAC	(1824-32)	995286	(1824-32)	7838
Guardian	(1823-8)	540850	(1821-30)	4106
REA	(1822-8)	407314	(1826-35)	3202
Sun	(1819-28)	300000	(1814-29)	1878
Protector	(1825-8)	75650	(1825-8)	*530*

Note: Protector's cotton mill premiums estimated from sum insured at a premium rate of 14s%.

Sources: Supple, *Royal Exchange*, p.154; Dickson, *Sun Insurance*, pp.145, 302; CUL, PAA, PX508, Phoenix, Annual Analysis; PX509, Phoenix, Statistical Analysis; GL Ms 14281/2, Guardian, GCM, 1826-8; Ms 16222/2-8, MFLAC, DM, 1824-46, auditors' accounts

insurer of woollen mills at the time, although the bulk of its business was in the west country.[25]

The prominence of certain offices in different markets was to an extent predicated on the acquisition of technical expertise in particular fields of underwriting. The Norwich Union's leadership in agricultural insurance rested upon a core of business among the farmers and landowners of Norfolk and Suffolk.

Table 5.8   Fire insurance in Leeds: selected offices

	Average annual premiums (£)		Average annual premiums (£)	
Sun	(1825-9)	3077	(1835-9)	3522
Guardian	(1826-8)	*2000*		
Norwich Union	(1821-30)	1639		
REA	(1820-9)	510		
Phoenix	(1824)	< 500		
MFLAC			(1842-3)	183

Notes: Estimates in italics. MFLAC estimates based upon the head office remittances for 1842-3 (38%), calculated from GL Ms 16222/8, MFLAC, DM, 4 Oct. 1843, 1 Feb. 1844, 'Statement of fire premiums and duty'. Guardian estimates based upon agency losses calculated from Ms 14281/2, Guardian, GCM, 1826-8.

Sources: as table 5.6.

Table 5.9   Fire insurance on wool textile mills: selected offices

	Average £ insured p.a.		Average annual premiums (£)	
Norwich Union	(1823)	1080000	(1823)	*5760*
Sun	(1815-30)	247953	(1818-24)	768
MFLAC	(1824-32)	*144563*	(1824-32)	*655*
REA	(1815-30)	100100	(1815-24)	679
Phoenix	(1815-30)	90573	(1816-30)	474

Notes: The MFLAC's wool textiles sum insured estimated from premiums given in GL Ms 16222/5, MFLAC, DM, 29 Feb. 1832, using the Phoenix's average premium rate on woollen mills of 10s 8d% for 1824-32. The Norwich Union's premium figure for wool textile insurances also estimated from sum insured in 1823 using the Phoenix's average rate.

Sources: Supple, *Royal Ex change*, p.154; Dickson, *Sun Insurance*, pp.145, 302; Ryan, 'History of Norwich Union', p.522; CUL, PAA, PX508, Phoenix, Annual Analysis; PX509, Phoenix, Statistical Analysis; G L M s 14281/ 2, G uardian, G CM, 1826- 8; M s 16222/ 2-8, MFLAC, DM, 1824-46, auditors' accounts.

Similarly the County and the Kent offices cultivated landed interests to build up their rural insurances. The Norwich Union also benefited from the influx of worsted merchants and manufacturers as directors following its merger with the Norwich General and conversion to a stock company in 1821. The MFLAC brought with it business expertise in the cotton industry. Two-thirds of its shareholders were textile merchants or manufacturers, mostly resident in the north-west. The MFLAC's founders expressed confidence that their knowledge of local risks would enable them to underwrite more profitably than London offices working at a distance through agents.[26]

Specialisation in regional or niche markets could bring competitive advantages, but it also risked accumulating dangerous concentrations of liabilities. Scotland and Ireland, for example, caused increasing concern to several English offices. The Imperial's agency in Glasgow revealed a 'considerable loss' over the period 1803-22, while the Newcastle Fire Office withdrew from insuring in Scotland altogether in 1819. Claims paid out by the Atlas on Irish fire insurances - partly due to incendiarism and losses occasioned 'from acts of turbulent and malicious people' accounted for 183 per cent of the office's premium income from Ireland between 1816 and 1824.[27] Farm insurances were also a worry, especially given the increasing incidence of arson and labour unrest in rural districts. In 1818 Thomas Bignold claimed that two-thirds of the Norwich Union's losses had arisen from fraudulent or incendiary fires.[28] Other loss-making insurances included woollen, flax and corn mills and sugar houses.

The crucible of fire underwriters' difficulties remained the north-west of England and its cotton industry. The REA suffered a net loss on cotton mills between 1815 and 1824, while the Sun's loss ratio was 75 per cent between 1814 and 1829. Several smaller offices pulled out of insuring cotton mills altogether.[29] At Liverpool the Imperial lost £34199 between 1803 and 1832, while the Norwich Union lost £22000 on dockside insurances there between 1818 and 1821. There were a number of reasons for such appalling losses. Apart from the continuing problems of fraud by arson and incendiarism sometimes linked to labour disputes, the risk of accidental fires was greatly increased by the slipshod manner and frenetic pace of mill and warehouse construction and operation during economic upswings. In Liverpool private warehouse owners fiercely resisted plans to enclose docks so that development remained chaotic, with warehouses and depots pressed along narrow wharves and notorious for a rapid turnover of tenants. Hazardous and non-hazardous goods were stacked together 'indiscriminately', while sources of combustion were found in open fireplaces, cockles and stoves. 'Common moveable pitch kettles are in use with no sort of regard to the danger they make', reported the Sun's surveyor in 1805, who found Liverpool warehouses 'risques of great hazard'. Liverpool's warehouse district continued to lack an adequate water supply and fire prevention facilities until the mid 1830s, and the dockside police, responsible for fighting fires as well as combating petty pilfering, were notoriously corrupt and inefficient. It is not surprising, therefore, that between 1816 and 1825 the four major insurers in Liverpool together paid out in claims more than twice the sum they earned in premiums.[30]

For some offices, other difficulties stemmed from their refusal to insure premises with more than one tenant, and their maintenance of high premium rates and low ceilings on the amount which could be insured in single policies, while the largest millowners were improving safety. Where discounts for enclosing naked lights, safeguarding shafts and machinery, improving ventilation and cleanliness, and 'fireproofing' mills and warehouses were not given, manufacturers and merchants looked elsewhere for insurance. The Sun's insistence that policyholders should guarantee that no hazardous trades were carried on anywhere in their warehouses alienated many merchants who occupied just one or two floors of a building.[31] In the early 1820s the situation intensified. As cotton merchants diversified into manufacturing, pressure grew on commercial and industrial space in urban centres. Parts of warehouses were converted into reeling, spinning and weaving rooms and sublet to several tenants, thus increasing the fire hazard and the complexity of risk assessment.[32] Factory owners and occupiers were able to turn for cheaper policies and bonus payments to new offices who were not discouraged by the earlier losses of the market leaders. By the mid 1820s there were 28 fire insurance companies operating in Manchester and 22 in Liverpool. While the largest London insurers attempted to maintain high premiums based on their awful underwriting experience, their income was continually squeezed by rate-cutting and a declining market share.

Given this situation, why did companies persist in these markets? First, the largest insurers, operating on a national or international scale, could sustain such liabilities because they represented only a small proportion of their total business. During the post-war decade the combined losses on cotton mills, woollen mills and sugar refineries absorbed just eight per cent of the REA's premiums, seven per cent of the Sun's, and ten per cent of total premiums earned by the Phoenix.[33] Such figures were achieved by retaining a high proportion of liabilities, generally over 90 per cent of sums insured, in 'ordinary' domestic risks, such as private dwellings, household goods and retailers' stock.[34] The profits made on these safer residential insurances usually more than covered the losses from underwriting factories and warehouses. Second, insurers believed they needed to retain some industrial risks because of the importance of 'goodwill' and tied business. Such policies, particularly when sold among the close-knit networks of urban merchants and manufacturers, could bring with them more profitable commercial and domestic insurances, such as tied workmen's cottages, or the property of relatives, friends and business partners of the insured. The Phoenix was regarded as particularly competitive in Manchester because of its practice of offering discounts on mill rates in return for tied business.[35] While tied business persuaded older companies to remain in the market for industrial insurances, it also encouraged new insurers to enter. Although most millowners and merchants were primarily interested in short-term protection for their buildings, machinery and stock, if insuring their private dwellings they could also be tempted by the return of profits offered by the newer companies. One response of the non-bonus companies was to cut premium rates. Although it was the safer 'ordinary' insurances which could bear such reductions, it was the most hazardous 'special risks', with their rapidly changing technologies and complex range of rates, which provided the greatest scope for imaginative and competitive discounting. Industrial and commercial insurances, therefore, formed the main arena of conflict between old and new fire offices in the provinces.

Responses to competition: the dual strategy of 1825-6

The initial reaction of the established offices to the numerous company foundations in 1824-5 was uncertain. Some responded with the usual mischief-making. The County, for instance, circulated an erroneous report announcing that the new Manchester office 'had been broken up'.[36] Others appeared too stunned to react. The Guardian was rocked by a wave of defections in 1824, losing several members of its shareholders' committees in Manchester and Leeds to the new offices in those towns, losing its auditor to the Alliance, and, most painfully, discovering that the superintendent of its fire department was secretly negotiating a transfer to the MFLAC with the apparent connivance of a Guardian director. Pressed by their local agents, second rank metropolitan insurers like the Guardian and the Imperial considered cooperating with the new provincial offices. Ultimately, though, their response was determined by the attitude of the Sun and the Phoenix who were dismissive of the newcomers.[37]

By the beginning of 1825 this view had changed. With some urgency the Phoenix formulated a dual strategy and submitted it to the Sun and the REA for their consideration. First, the Phoenix proposed a general reduction in the rates for 'common' insurances. In London the reduction was to be confined to private dwellings. Large country houses, 'very hazardous manufactories', and 'the more confined parts of the great northern manufacturing towns' were to be excluded. Rate cutting was to be achieved by cross-subsidising domestic underwriting from profits on foreign insurances, a tactic which suited the Phoenix with its huge overseas income. Second, premiums on mercantile insurances in Liverpool and London docks were to be raised. These risks were to be more carefully assessed, paying particular attention to 'the subject of locality' and ensuring that 'no very large sum should be taken on any one risk, so that no risk should be overloaded'.[38] This scheme became the subject of 'frequent meetings' between the Phoenix, the Sun and the REA during the spring of 1825. Early in the summer four other non-bonus London offices were invited to join the discussions. By June they had agreed to a 6d% reduction on all classes of ordinary risks, twice the discount the Phoenix had originally proposed. 'Boundary lines' were mapped out in Liverpool, Manchester and Stockport within which the discount was not to apply. Agents were instructed to 'exercise discretion outside the boundary and reduce upon as few trading risks as possible', and not at all on 'public warehouses and manufactories'. The Phoenix's agent in Manchester was warned that 'the new era as applicable to fire insurance does require attention to every shade of risk' and that agents must 'exercise great discrimination and sound discretion'.[39]

The dual strategy contained a contradiction. On the one hand the old cartel offices wanted to reduce residential premiums in order to squeeze out those offering bonus schemes. On the other hand they wished to increase rates on mercantile and industrial insurances to restore their profitability, which required the agreement of a much wider circle of offices. The non-bonus insurers were torn between cutting domestic rates to drive out the bonus offices, or cooperating with some of them in order to raise commercial premiums to profitable levels. Despite misgivings, the former tactic prevailed. At no point in the discussions were country offices brought into the charmed circle. To eliminate provincial competitors and the 'with-profits' policy remained the primary object.

Mercantile rates were raised in the summer of 1826. Discussions were held between the four major metropolitan insurers operating in Liverpool - the Sun, the Phoenix, the REA and the Imperial. It was estimated that a rate increase of 150 per cent w as r equired. T his proposal was circulated among some 20 offices, nearly three times the number involved in the price reduction of the previous year. The correspondents included the three largest provincial offices, the Norwich Union, the West of England and the MFLAC.[40] The MFLAC's directors wanted to carry rate revision 'much further', especially for mill insurances, but they also rebuked the major London offices for exacerbating competition by their recent reduction of rates on residential insurances. The Manchester insurers were concerned that indiscriminate discounting by agents was reducing premiums to 'a matter of special bargain'. The Sun's manager, Charles Ford, responded by defending the cuts of 1825, claiming that the reversionary bonus compelled the non-bonus offices to fight back with discounts.[41] The Phoenix's secretary, Jenkin Jones, justified the reduction as a defensive move against attack by 'a triple plan of competition' - new offices, price cuts and bonus policies. The only expedient was to lower ordinary premium rates to unprofitable levels in order to check 'the disposition to form insurance companies at every point'. Jones suggested that the MFLAC abandon the 'with-profits' policy, as it stood 'on the threshold of every question connected with the general improvement of the premiums'.[42] The battle lines were thus drawn and they remained so for some time. In 1829, for example, when Samuel Bignold of the Norwich Union proposed 'a general return to the old rates of insurance' on ordinary business, he was rebuffed by Ford with the usual refrain - that this was impossible 'unless the return system was abolished'.[43]

The reduction of ordinary rates in 1825 set off a spiral of indiscriminate discounting on all types of risks. Much of this was due to the London offices themselves, who failed to stand by their own hard-won agreement. Only one week after announcing the reduction Ford unilaterally extended it to a variety of non-residential property in London. In November the Sun reduced rates on London dock warehouses, again breaching the agreement reached only months earlier. The pace of discounting became infectious. The Guardian invested its 'sitting director' with a 'discretionary power' to reduce rates if necessary.[44] For smaller offices a flexible response was the only means of survival. The competition was such that not only agents but also policyholders came to expect both lower premiums and higher limits on the sums which could be insured on individual risks.

Competition became still more cut-throat towards the end of the decade. In 1827 the Leeds & Yorkshire was discovered to be undercutting the Liverpool warehouse tariff by as much as 17 per cent and the tariff itself led to demands from local merchants for cheaper fire insurance.[45] London offices believed that they were locked in mortal combat with upstarts who threatened their share of niche markets.

In a frank letter to the West of England Office, Jenkin Jones claimed that it was the 'monopolising' tendency of provincial offices which drove the Londoners to erect their 'system of defence'. His language was replete with military metaphors. He believed that the struggle might be protracted, but that eventual victory would lie with the old cartel offices able to draw on their experience in risk assessment and to tap economies of scale.[46]

The price reductions of 1825 were predatory, short- or medium-term devices for eliminating rivals, financed by the cross-subsidisation only possible within large and diverse insurance portfolios. Although this discounting was intended as a means of controlling markets, in the hands of eager country agents it became more indiscriminate. According to one observer in 1832, the strategy of the previous seven years had pushed things too far.

> In consequence of the reduction…in 1825, many offices which had previously been on an amicable footing with those taking the lead in this measure, became their rivals; and thus a reduction, greater than ever was contemplated, followed. Many risks were drawn into this vortex, which it was intended to except; and eventually insurance premiums have become mere matters of bargain, and are now, in the majority of cases, fixed far below remunerating rates.[47]

Other responses: retrenchment and unilateralism

The dual strategy backfired by increasing rather than reducing uncontrolled discounting and by souring market relations. There were other tactics which avoided fuelling the downward spiral of rates and profits. Among these were retrenchment, sometimes leading to the abandonment of loss-making markets altogether, and unilateralism, raising premiums on particular types of risk without the agreement of competitors. Wool textile mills were abandoned by several insurers in the late 1820s. The Norwich Union ceased underwriting woollen mills at the end of 1827. Two years later it had only one such mill on the books of its Leeds agency and even this caught fire in 1829.[48] Given the importance of tied business and the higher premium rates on mills, to abandon such insurances could have serious consequences for the income of agencies in industrial towns. Premiums earned by the Norwich Union at Leeds fell by 57 per cent during the 1820s. Other examples of retrenchment can be found in Stockport where the Imperial began rejecting cotton mills in 1827, in Belfast where at least four firms had given up cotton mills by the end of 1828, and in Glasgow where the Norwich Union ceased underwriting cotton mills in 1839 and where the MFLAC closed down its agency in 1841.[49]

Competition also propelled some offices to take unilateral action to improve results. Between 1829 and 1832 several firms conducted investigations of their performance in categories of special insurances. Policy conditions were revised, ceilings were lowered on single risks and rates were raised. In 1828 the MFLAC proceeded with its own classification of Manchester warehouse insurances, having failed to get its scheme accepted by the London offices. Also without their cooperation, the MFLAC introduced an extra charge for cotton mills working through the night, reduced its policy ceilings on Liverpool warehouses and on calico print shops, and increased its rates on joiners' and carpenters' shops. In 1832 the Phoenix unilaterally raised its woollen mill rates by 50 per cent. Jenkin Jones explained to the Phoenix's agent at Leeds that this increase effectively meant withdrawal from woollen mill insurances and related business. By this date there was a sense of frustration among the Phoenix management with the continued depression of industrial insurances, with the lack of agreement among offices, and with the high level of customer expectation which was a product of the competition.[50]

Another response: the merger and acquisition

A further response to competition was to purchase the business of others. Takeovers offered the most direct means to increase market share and to snuff out competition. If economies of scale could be tapped as well as the conflict over rates reduced, acquisitions might also improve profitability. This tactic was employed by a range of London and Scottish offices as well as by a few provincial offices in England, though before 1850 the latter were usually unsuccessful in their bids.[51]

The corporate merger has been commonly regarded as a modern feature in British economic history, closely linked to limited liability and the transition of the joint-stock company from a proprietorial to a managerial form of enterprise during the second half of the nineteenth century. Stock companies, protected by legislative recognition and with large amounts of outside (non-directorial as well as non-familial) traded capital, have been seen as essential preconditions for the development of the modern merger.[52] In insurance, banking and transport, however, the corporate takeover was already common before 1850. The amalgamation of turnpike trusts gathered pace from the 1820s and some 30 canal firms were acquired by railway companies before mid-century. The 1840s also saw the beginnings of mergers between railway companies, with 29 taking place at the peak of railway mania in 1846-7. Banks were even more precocious in pursuing consolidation through mergers. At least 122 amalgamations occurred between 1826 and 1843. The great majority consisted of private houses purchased by joint-stock banks enjoying their new freedom to expand under the bank acts of 1826 and 1833. Over 20 per cent of the private banks in existence in 1825 had been acquired by other banks by 1843.[53]

In fire insurance around 50 mergers and acquisitions took place between 1782 and 1850. Forty of these occurred after 1825 and are listed in table 5.10.[54] Fourteen firms, accounting for £46m of insurances and nine per cent of the UK market, were swallowed up between 1825 and 1831. Merger activity commenced again in the mid 1830s and continued, with a brief pause in 1845-6, into the 1850s. Between

Table 5.10 Corporate mergers and acquisitions in UK fire insurance, 1825-50

(a) Companies absorbed	(b) Date established	(c) Year of merger	(d) Purchasing company	(e) Last full year of trading	(f) £m insured at date (e)	(g) Market share at date (e)
British Commercial	1820	1825	Protector	1824	1.99	0.42
Sussex County	1824	1826	Guardian	?	?	?
Hope	1807	1827	Protector	1825	9.06	1.85
Beacon	1821	1827	Protector	1826	4.90	0.97
Royal Irish	1823	1827	Phoenix	1824	1.20	0.25
Old Bath	1767	1827	Sun	1826	1.06	0.21
Eagle	1807	1828	Protector	1826	8.93	1.76
Albion	1805	1828	Protector	1827	8.58	1.71
East Kent	1824	1828	Phoenix	1827	1.28	0.26
Finchingfield	1804	1829	Sun	1828	0.03	0.01
Commercial (Dublin)	1799	1829	Guardian	?	?	?
Palladium	1824	1830	Phoenix	1829	3.59	0.68
Hertford, Cambridge	1824	1831	Phoenix	1830	3.62	0.67
Berkshire, Gloucestershire	1824	1831	Protector	1830	1.74	0.32
Salamander	1790	1835	Sun	1835	3.96	0.65
North & South Shields	1826	1836	Sun	1835	0.49	0.08
Protector	1825	1837	Phoenix	1835	37.01	6.03
Bristol Crown	1718	1837	Sun	1836	1.19	0.19
Bath Sun	1776	1838	Sun	1836	1.11	0.17
Newcastle & North of England	1835	1838	Leeds & Yorkshire	1837	0.79	0.15
Metellus	1823	1839	Phoenix	1838	3.03	0.44
Coventry & Warwickshire	1836	1839	Sun	1838	0.32	0.05
Hibernian	1824	1839	Sun	1838	0.89	0.13

Bristol	1769	1840	Imperial	1839	2.28	0.32
Reading	1823	1841	Phoenix	1840	0.16	0.02
Glasgow	1803	1841	Sun	1841	1.83	0.25
York & London	1834	1842	Imperial	1841	8.15	1.10
Leicestershire	1834	1843	Sun	1843	1.31	0.17
British	1799	1843	Sun	1842	12.78	1.71
Bristol Union	1818	1844	Imperial	1843	2.12	0.28
English & Scottish Law	1840	1844	Phoenix	1842	0.88	0.12
County & City (Perth)	1824	1844	Scottish National	1843	0.69	0.09
Insurance Co. of Scotland	1821	1847	Alliance	1846	4.94	0.61
Western	1844	1847	Northern	1846	1.31	0.16
Friendly Society of Edinburgh	1720	1847	Sun	1846	6.16	0.77
Winchester & South of England	1841	1847	Sun	1846	0.55	0.07
Preston & North Lancashire	1845	1848	Sun	1847	0.46	0.06
Bon Accord	1845	1849	Northern	1848	0.58	0.07
Hercules	1809	1849	Scottish Union	1848	4.41	0.54
Suffolk Amicable	1802	1850	Alliance	1848	10.03	1.24

Notes and Sources: £ insured and market share are calculated from the quarterly duty returns, plus the separate returns of sums insured on farming stock in England, Ireland and Scotland. There are no returns of the latter for Scottish offices before 1836 and from 1842 to 1845 inclusive, nor for Ireland before 1835 and from 1841 to 1845 inclusive. Where no quarterly duty returns are available, I have used the annual totals given by Inland Revenue Commissioners, *PP* (1870) XX, 193, Report of the Commissioners of Inland Revenue. In sum, market share above is calculated as a percentage of: 1825-33, 1835-50 = All UK insurances; 1834 = UK insurances excluding Irish and Scottish farming stock insurances. This procedure will slightly underestimate the share of two offices - York & London in 1841, and English & Scottish Law Fire in 1842 - which may have had some Irish farm insurances not included in their total sum insured. The sum insured by County & City (Perth) is calculated from the duty return for 1843 as given by Walford, *Insurance Cyclopedia*, vol.II, p.137, added to the sum insured on Scottish farming stock in 1841, the nearest year available.

1835 and 1850 26 firms were purchased. These accounted for £107m of insurances or 15 per cent of the market. In all, acquisitions accounted for more than three-quarters of the firms ceasing to underwrite during the second quarter of the nineteenth century. These figures, together with those from banking, press the claim of financial services to be *the* sector of the British economy which pioneered the modern merger. The largest number of acquisitions fell to a small group of offices. The Phoenix acquired eight offices worth £51m of insurances between 1825 and 1850. The Protector took over the fire business of at least six offices insuring £35m, while the Sun acquired 14 offices insuring £32m.[55] Behind these came seven other fire offices which acquired businesses before 1850. At least another six were unsuccessful in take over bids.[56] Thus, while the net effect was to boost the income of only a few offices, a larger number of insurers were involved in take over activity.

As several large London insurers concerned themselves with extending their country sales in the mid 1820s, they became eager to snap up business from ailing companies.[57] By the spring of 1827 the movement was in full swing, driven by the prospect of picking up business from five offices - the Eagle, the Surrey, the British Commercial, the Hope and the Beacon - which were abandoning fire underwriting.[58] Four of these were quickly acquired by the Protector despite competition from the Guardian and the Sun. The Phoenix acquired the fire insurances of four offices between 1827 and 1831. It pursued in vain at least three other provincial insurers, including the second largest country office, the West of England, and rejected an invitation to buy the local fire office in Dundee. The Sun acquired two offices during this first merger cycle, the Old Bath and the tiny mutual society at Finchingfield in Essex.[59] It also tried to coax the shareholders and directors of the Bath Sun and the Bristol Crown to sell up in the wake of heavy losses. The Sun's lobbying, its cultivation of inside contacts at both offices, and its collection of vital underwriting data in anticipation of making a bid, eventually bore fruit when it acquired these offices in the later 1830s.[60]

Between 1832 and 1834 there were no further takeovers, although the large London offices continued to keep an eye open for likely purchases. An approach from the Phoenix to the Protector led in 1836 to the biggest insurance merger of the first half of the century.[61] With £39m insured by the early 1830s, the Protector had grown to become the fourth largest fire office in the country. The Phoenix's stated objectives were to increase volume, boost market share and gain economies of scale. Its expense ratio subsequently fell from 23 to 19 per cent during the 1830s, while its underwriting surplus rose from 20 to 29 per cent. Having added nearly £80000 to its annual income, the Phoenix's market share also climbed from 10 to 14 per cent.[62]

The Phoenix-Protector merger was the highlight of the second merger wave which commenced in the mid 1830s. Between 1835 and 1848, the Sun, the Phoenix, the Alliance and the Imperial together acquired 21 offices accounting for 15 per cent of the British fire insurance market. The total market share of the three leading offices rose from 33 per cent in 1826-30 to 38 per cent by 1836-40.

Furthermore, the acquisition of a provincial office could enhance a London insurer's share of a local market far more than its increased share of the national market would imply. So while its rivals never hooked the size of the fish caught by the Phoenix in 1836, smaller catches were also significant. West country insurers, in particular, were swept up. Between 1827 and 1844 all three Bristol offices and both Bath offices disappeared, together with the Wiltshire-based Salamander. The fire office in Worcester had been bought by the Phoenix in 1818, and the one new office in this region, the Gloucestershire, Herefordshire & Cheltenham, ceased underwriting in 1828. Only the Exeter-based West of England survived. Several Scottish and Irish offices also disappeared. At least nine of the 21 Scottish fire offices founded before 1850 were taken over before mid-century, four of these being purchased by other Scottish insurers.

At times the competition to acquire insurance offices was so intense that relations between the major offices deteriorated sharply. Manoeuvring was particularly adroit in the battle for the west country offices. The Salamander contest of 1835 brought out the worst in all parties concerned.[63] The Wiltshire office, recognising its attractiveness to suitors, tried to gain the maximum advantage by changing the bidding rules at the eleventh hour. The rival negotiators, John Richards for the Sun, Jenkin Jones and Thomas Richter for the Phoenix, and Frederick Lewis for the West of England, met in Warminster and agreed to withdraw from the process unless the Salamander board consented to a 'fair' contest of sealed tenders with the highest bid winning. Following a negative response, the Phoenix and the West of England representatives promptly left to return home. Richards, however, stayed on in Warminster, and within 24 hours, assisted by an inside contact among the Salamander proprietors, he had concluded a deal for his office, effectively behind the backs of the others, and contrary to what they had understood to be a gentleman's agreement not to negotiate. The reaction of Richards' manager, Charles Ford, was to shrug his shoulders at the 'misunderstanding', but the fury of Jenkin Jones could be heard down Lombard Street. He made the Phoenix's intentions clear in a frosty exchange with Ford:

> With respect to the other points in which you express a hope that we shall not resort to any extraordinary means of competition, I must beg you to be under no mistake upon the subject - we shall attack the Salamander policies by every means in our power...[64]

With the dispute over Richards' behaviour at Warminster rumbling on, the Sun and the Phoenix threw themselves into a dog fight over the Salamander's profitable agency business. After several weeks of frantic canvassing of agents and policyholders, Ford drew up a balance sheet in which he estimated that the Sun had collected nearly £5000 in premiums for insurances removed from the Salamander. This suggests that the fierce and very public contest surrounding the takeover resulted in the Sun losing up to 20 per cent of the Salamander's business.

The Salamander affair marked a watershed in the development of the 'rules of the game' about how take over contests were to be conducted. Thereafter no bidding offices would accept anything other than a procedure of sealed tenders. Duplicity continued, of course, and the degree of trust, both between rival bidders and between vendors and purchasers, remained low. As a direct result of the Sun's cunning at Warminster the monitoring between rival offices rose to a new level. During the difficult negotiations with the Bristol Crown in 1837, the Sun empoyed one or more informants within the Phoenix's head office to keep track of the movements of Richter and Jones, as well as lookouts posted in Bristol to keep a watch in case the Phoenix men, or Lewis of the West of England, should arrive there.[65]

As the decade advanced the take over war was increasingly conducted on several fronts at once. Each year the appetite for acquisitions sharpened as the underwriting results of the Michaelmas quarter became known. Having lost a contest in 1837 for the Newcastle & North of England, and having beaten off the Phoenix and the West of England for the business of the Bath Sun, Charles Ford cast an eye around the country for further victims. During 1838 a speculative letter was sent to the Essex Economic Fire Office in a vain attempt to persuade its directors to sell up. An approach to the new Liverpool office, which had suffered heavy losses, was also unsuccessful. The Phoenix opened negotiations with the Glasgow-based Metellus Fire Office which concluded with a purchase in January 1839. That month the Sun bought the Hibernia of Dublin and followed this with the acquisition of the Coventry & Warwickshire and with approaches, both rebuffed, to the large Edinburgh offices, the Caledonian and the North British.[66]

The feeding frenzy peaked in 1837-9. Merger activity continued during the 1840s but at a slower pace. During the winter of 1839-40 several offices competed for the Bristol Fire, one of the two remaining local insurers in the city. The Imperial emerged triumphant and acquired 13 former Bristol agents in the south-west, which helped to plug a gap identified in its sales network. The Imperial proceeded to purchase the fire business of the York & London in 1842, and returned to Bristol in 1844 to snap up the last native office there, the Bristol Union, in the teeth of opposition from the Sun. These three acquisitions helped increase the Imperial's insurances from £34m in 1840 to £44m by 1844 and its premium income from £50000 to over £90000. The Imperial's business in Bristol expanded so rapidly that in 1845 it bought the premises adjacent to the former Bristol Union Office in order to provide its agency there with more space.[67] The biggest acquisition of this period was the British Fire Office, bought by the Sun in 1843 for £12000 after some tough bargaining over the price and compensation for British Fire staff. As a result the Sun's domestic premium income rose from £175000 to £198000 during the two years following the merger. What made the big insurers expend so much time, effort and nervous energy in buying up what were, for the most part, very small businesses? And what were the reasons for selling?

There is little evidence of speculative motives, even on the part of the directors of those new offices which sold out within a few years of foundation, although there were individuals, such as the Bristol Crown's avaricious secretary, Thomas Camplin, who sought to profit as much as possible by acting as agents in the sale of their office to a rival. More usually, a sudden rush of claims which overwhelmed a modest premium income was the principal reason for country fire offices to consider selling up. Unease in the boardroom about future prospects, discontent among shareholders about suspected mismanagement, poor underwriting performance, falling share values and declining dividends could be enough to create a momentum for closure. Shares in the Eagle office had fallen five per cent below their par value by the time its fire business was sold to the Protector, while another London office bought by the Protector had reported net losses of £40000.[68] Recent heavy losses were also critical in the sale of the Bristol Union, the Bristol Crown, the Bath Sun, the Hibernia and the Salamander. Losses and rumours of losses not only created unease in boardrooms, they also alerted predators to potential targets. Thus the unsuccessful attempts of the Sun to buy the Caledonian, the Liverpool, the Newcastle, and the Birmingham District offices in 1837-9 were sparked by reports of underwriting losses, as was the approach made by the Phoenix to the West of England in 1827.

Sellers sometimes approached buyers, and business could also be acquired by renegade agents or by managers deserting their companies and taking lists of policyholders with them. In several cases, existing reinsurance arrangements between purchaser and vendor may have smoothed the path of negotiations and given the former some inside knowledge of the latter's business. There were prior reinsurances between the East Kent and the Phoenix, and between the Guardian and the Commercial (Dublin), when these merged in 1828-9. For the most part, however, the initial approach to purchase an office was made 'cold'. It was followed by lengthy and careful preparations for a bid, which by the mid 1830s had come to follow a recognised pattern. Most negotiations lasted several months, some took much longer. From a close analysis of the Sun's take over attempts between the 1820s and the 1850s - it is unlikely other purchasers operated very differently - five tactics can be identified in the construction of a bid.[69] The first was to find an insider (preferably more than one) in the targeted office who could supply critical information. Phelps, a director of the Salamander, provided this service to the Sun in 1835, while Wilmer Harris, the secretary of the Protector, and Thomas Harvey, the secretary of the Bath Sun, filled the same role for the Phoenix and the Sun respectively in 1836 and 1838. Ideally, an informant would be in a position to provide not only the financial data required for an accurate estimate of the office's value - details of underwriting performance, capital structure and investments, composition of insurances - but also personal details about his firm - information about divisions in the boardroom or among shareholders, about the character, opinions and influence, and even the salaries, pensions, personal and family circumstances of individual directors, shareholders and office staff. More than one informant was desirable in order to check information for reliability. After the Sun had been abandoned in 1837 by Thomas Camplin, the treacherous secretary of the Bristol Crown, it acquired the services of a Mr Ward, one of the Bristol directors. Ward's information was compared against that supplied by Griffiths, the head clerk in the Bristol Crown office, who was also employed by the Sun to spy on his immediate superior, Camplin.

Second, it was important to have individuals promoting the cause of the purchasing office both internally and externally. In his efforts to acquire the Bath Sun in 1838, Charles Ford employed the services of his eldest sister, who lived in the town, her friends, the family apothecary who attended Ford's widowed mother, and several other business contacts he had previously met through his father. To have too many confidants, of course, was risky. During early discussions with potential vendors and the initial preparation of a tender, secrecy was essential. The object at this stage was to steal a first mover advantage over any rivals who might enter the field, by working on the agents, directors, shareholders and officers of the targeted firm in the weeks prior to bidding. The aim was to create a pool of loyalty from which the purchasing office could then draw prior to the takeover, and immediately after the dissolution of the purchased company, when it became open season for rival offices to poach as many of the latter's former agents and policyholders as possible. The relative importance of secrecy, however, changed for the purchaser and vendor as the date fixed for the sale of an office approached. At first, the purchasing office was the party keenest to keep its interest quiet, for the entry of rivals into a bidding process would only drive up the price. Later, if no rival offices had emerged as prospective bidders, and if information then leaked out about the proposed sale and poaching commenced prematurely, the value of the business would rapidly decline, and the vendors might suffer from a reduction in the price they could negotiate.

The third tactic was to avoid any bidding if possible by a *fait accompli* before other offices arrived to make offers. If several insurers were in the fray, the object was above all to avoid a public tender or a Dutch auction. Sealed bids, with a supposed guarantee of victory to the highest bidder, became the accepted rule after the Salamander affair. Everything possible was done, however, to undermine a rival's negotiating position. In the case of the Salamander, the Sun's negotiator, John Richards - by the most malign interpretation of his actions - carried out a double bluff on his protagonists from the Phoenix and the West of England. The reaction against the Sun's behaviour in this incident was so hostile, and left such lingering feelings of resentment, that Richards and Ford never tried this particular trick again. This did not prevent later take over battles from being accompanied by much moral posturing and self-justified duplicity. There were clearly parallels to be drawn with the contemporary political debate over the need for the secret ballot to reduce corruption and bribery at elections. Despite the acceptance of the sealed tender as normal procedure, offices were still sold to those who had not always bid the highest price, as the Sun's acquisition of the Bath Sun in 1838 demonstrated. The bid price was important, but what also counted was the financial inducement held out to those insiders who proved their loyalty to the purchasing office both before and after the takeover, and the degree of influence they were able to exert on their fellow shareholders and directors. The groundwork in the weeks or months before a takeover was critical to success.

Two further tactics were applied immediately following an acquisition. First, it was crucial to prevent the list of insurances held by the purchased firm being sold or passed on to rivals, either by agents or discontented officers. Treachery was a real danger for the Sun in the Bristol Crown takeover of 1837 when the Bristol secretary Camplin tried to sell the register of policyholders to the highest bidder for his own pocket. To counter this was only possible through repeated exhortation to an individual's 'honour', through bribes and the promise of rewards for loyalty, and through a careful monitoring of those suspected of imminent betrayal. Second, the purchasing office attempted to prevent the leakage of the business just acquired to rivals. This was achieved by giving attention to individual agents and policyholders, not only through circulars and letters, but also through personal visits to secure their loyalty. It was also important to ensure that directors' pledges made at the time of the contract were kept. These pledges were normally three fold: first, to ensure that all existing books and ledgers were delivered up to the purchasing office; second, to transfer one's own insurances to the purchaser and to recommend that others do the same; third, not to establish a new fire office in the locality in the future, nor to work for any other office. The average loss of business to purchasers in the wake of takeovers is difficult to measure. Generally managers such as Charles Ford were satisfied if they captured four-fifths of the insurances of an office they had purchased, which was the outcome of the Sun's takeover of the Salamander in 1835. The proportion lost, however, could be much higher. Following the Sun's purchase of the small Preston & North Lancashire Office in 1848, an account was kept of the destination of its 347 current policies. Just 51 per cent of these were recorded as transferred or 'expected/promised' to the Sun. Five other offices between them acquired 16 policies worth eight per cent of the total insured. The fate of the remaining 153 policies, accounting for 39 per cent of the sum insured, was unclear. The Sun's clerks recorded these as either 'uncertain', 'written to...doubtful', 'not known', or 'property sold'.[70]

Given their great cost and trouble, and the uncertainty about how much of a business might actually end up with the purchaser, why did mergers take place at all? Hannah has noted a positive correlation between share prices and the 'intensity of merger' activity for British manufacturing industry in the period 1880-1918, which lends support to the hypothesis that financial factors played an important part in stimulating the industrial mergers of that period.[71] There is little evidence to suggest that adding value to shares was ever a motive for insurance mergers before 1850. Even the financial assets of the target company were only occasionally the object of discussion. The share value of the vendor office was a factor. Underwriting losses could hit the price of shares and quickly weaken a small insurer, as was the case with the Bristol Crown in 1829. Share value was also an important factor in the Protector-Phoenix merger of 1836, where the Phoenix's willingness to guarantee the par value of their shares seems to have been critical in winning over the majority of Protector shareholders. The price of the purchasing office's shares, however, did not play a part in most takeovers.

The desire to achieve economies of scale was a motive in some cases such as the acquisition of the Protector. A more important factor was the volume and quality of the insurances being purchased. In all takeovers purchasers were keen to check the medium- and even long-term underwriting record of the vendor. The total insured appears to have been of less interest than the annual volume of premium income, although, of course, data on sums insured was widely available through the printed duty returns. Loss ratios were calculated by prospective buyers, and detailed analyses were made of the extent and composition of special risks and large insurances. As well as underwriting results and the structure of the insurances, purchasers were also interested in expense ratios and net profits, in staff salaries, agency commissions and pensions. It seems that this was usually treated as supplementary information in the decision about where to fix the price of a tender. Offices were usually valued by their annual premium income, the price bid being usually expressed as a proportion of the latter.[72] In several negotiations the Sun commenced with a bid which was lower than the annual premiums, but then adopted a higher price as a fall-back position. Writing in the 1870s, Walford stated that the 'goodwill' paid for a fire office normally amounted to one year's premium (three years for a life assurance office).[73] How often this was the case before 1850 can be seen in table 5.11, which presents data from 20 different takeovers and attempted purchases. Overall, the bid or purchase prices in table 5.11 offer limited support for Walford's contention, although one year's premium income does seem to have been the benchmark around which negotiators haggled. Of 18 cases where we can calculate the bid price as a percentage of average annual premiums, only five fell between 80 and 120 per cent of annual premiums. Ten bid prices were well below this range, three were higher.

Several further conclusions are suggested by table 5.11. First, it indicates that bid prices rose as the pace of take over activity quickened. Five out of six tenders in the period 1827-35 were below 2s%, while just seven out of 18 bids in the years 1836-48 fell below this price. Other evidence also points to an inflationary tendency in the cost of takeovers during this period. When approaching the directors of the Newcastle Fire Office in 1836 about a possible sale, the Sun's officials expressed the fear that these would 'be exorbitant in their demands...in consequence of the large amount given for the purchase of the [Shields] office...'.[74] As the table shows, the £1000 paid by the Sun for the North & South Shields Office in 1836, relative to the volume of insurances it bought, was indeed one of the more expensive purchases of the period. Word could get around about negotiations and the outcome of previous mergers. Thomas Camplin, the Bristol Crown's secretary, used his knowledge about the bad blood between the Sun and the Phoenix resulting from the Salamander affair, to try to play off the two offices for his own benefit in the run up to the sale of the Bristol Crown in 1837.

Second, there is evidence that large offices cost more. The correlation between the bid price per £100 insured and the average annual premium income of the office purchased was 0.82. Purchasers were therefore paying a premium for a solid stream of income, while the smaller offices could be had relatively cheaply.[75] Third, there was also a correlation, 0.68, between the average premium rate and the bid price per £ insured, which suggests that high yielding insurances - industrial properties and the like - if carefully selected and managed, were a ttractive t o t he b uyers. Charles Ford and John Richards carefully scrutinised the insurance portfolios of target offices, not in order to exclude all risky and large insurances, but to determine their quality. Fourth, there was a negative correlation between average loss ratios and bid prices, which also seems logical. Heavy losses could reduce the price obtained for a business in spite of the competition between rival bidders, but ultimately it was expected future income stream which mattered.

Of course such calculations suggest a degree of precision which was not really characteristic of the bidding process, for all the careful scrutiny of the businesses to be purchased. Prices tendered, though carefully adjusted to take into account underwriting volume and profitability, retained something of the character of a 'ball park' figure. The quality of the surviving records is not good enough always to be certain of what it was the purchaser was buying with the price tendered. There were also extra costs borne by purchasing companies, which are excluded wherever possible from the estimates in table 5.11 for comparability, but which were nevertheless real enough. There were emoluments to those who helped in a takeover, especially to the officials of the acquired firm, as well as one's own. The Phoenix gave £50 in 1833 to the widow of the former secretary of the Hertford & Cambridge, 'in consideration of his exertions in procuring for Phoenix the business', and £100 to the former secretary of Palladium 'for his assistance' in the acquisition of that office in 1830.[76] Such rewards became known and encouraged some of those in a position to profit from the sale of the office for which they worked. Purchasers were also frequently obliged to buy the fire engines, engine houses, premises and furniture of the business they acquired. Above all purchasing offices had an eye on market share. This motive was pronounced where agencies came with the business acquired. Agents often brought sales skills and established connections to their new employer, and with country offices these were usually concentrated geographically. Behind the series of fierce contests for the purchase of the Salamander, the Bristol Crown and the Bath Sun between 1835 and 1838, lay an explicit objective, namely the Sun's determination to contain the upstart Exeter-based West of England office and to prevent it expanding further out of Devon.[77] This territorial imperative echoed that underlying the great railway amalgamations of the 1840s and 1850s, namely to create regional monopolies and remove competitors, in what has been described as a 'species of imperialism'.[78] The insurance mergers of the 1820s and 1830s were the product of an aggressive 'policy of aggrandisement' by several leading offices, a process of removing competitors in preparation for the price-fixing tariffs of the 1840s and beyond. When in 1860 a Sun manager looked back over the past 30 years of acquisitions, he declared that they had been the means 'by which much dangerous competition has been put a stop to, and many valuable connections strengthened and confirmed'.[79]

Table 5.11   Tender prices for selected fire insurance offices, 1827-48

1 Year of bid	2 Purchased office	3 Bid or purchase price £	4 Average insured p.a. £m	5 Average premium p.a. £	6 Loss ratio	7 Expense ratio	8 Average premium rate s%	9 Price per £100 insured s%	10 Price as % of average premium
1827	Old Bath to Sun	500	1.12	1291	45.4	26.0	2.31	0.89	38.7
1828	East Kent to Phoenix	800	1.04	1563	58.6	24.0	3.01	1.54	51.2
1829	Bristol Crown Sun's inquiry	1600	1.28	1546	83.4	42.5	2.42	2.51	103.5
1833	Bristol Crown Sun's inquiry	1200	1.24	1397	36.3	43.4	2.26	1.94	85.9
1835	Salamander to Sun	2000	4.06	5408	65.1	29.7	2.66	0.99	37.0
	West of Eng.'s bid	3000						1.48	55.5
1836	Protector to Phoenix	150000	39.56	142914	81.5		7.22	7.58	105.0
1836	Nth & Sth Shields to Sun	1000	0.49	?	?	?	?	4.04	?
1836	Newcastle Sun's inquiry	2000	3.71	4471	39.0	?	2.41	1.08	44.7
1837	Birmingham District Sun's inquiry	5000	1.92	?	?	?	?	5.22	?
1837	Bristol Crown to Sun	1300	1.21	1360	35.0	41.5	2.26	2.83	95.6

Year	Company									
1838	Bath Sun to Sun	1680	1.10	1157	23.7	?	2.11	3.06	145.2
1838	Newcastle & North of England to Leeds & Yorks	460	0.79	1158	55.0	44.5	2.91	1.16	39.7
1839	Sun's bid	350						0.88	30.2
	Metellus to Phoenix	8000	2.88	?	?	?	?	5.56	?
1839	Hibernia to Sun	400	1.06	1310	25.1	?	2.47	0.75	30.5
1839	Coventry & Warks to Sun	600	0.32	1376	73.9		8.73	3.81	43.6
1843	British Fire to Sun	12000	12.34	13517	59.7	37.0	2.19	1.94	88.8
1844	Bristol Union to Imperial	3760	2.07	2587	38.2	?	2.49	3.63	145.3
	Sun's bid	3500						3.38	135.3
1845	Shropshire Salop's bid	1000	1.17	1427	45.7	46.7	2.43	1.70	70.1
1847	Insurance Co. of Scotland to Alliance	22916	4.94	?	?	?	?	9.27	?
	Alliance's 1st bid	19896						8.05	
1848	Hercules to Scottish Union	4000	4.19	?	?	?	?	1.91	?

Notes: 1) £ insured includes English, Scottish and Irish farming insurances from 1834 and all Irish insurances from 1836. Before 1836 £ insured excludes all Irish non-farming insurances, and excludes all Irish insurances before 1834. 2) As far as it is possible to determine, bid and purchase prices represent the cost of the 'goodwill' of the acquired office, and are net of other costs to the purchaser, such as fire engines, office rentals, staff pensions, emoluments etc. 3) The bid price shown (in italics) for Birmingham District is the amount demanded by the vendor office, but rejected by Sun. 4) The annual averages shown in columns 4 and 5 relate to the following periods: Old Bath, 1822-6; East Kent, 1825-7; Bristol Crown, 1827-9, 1830-33, 1832-6 respectively; Protector, 1831-5 for £ insured, 1831-4 for premiums; Salamander, 1831-5, excepting expense ratios, 1835 only; North & South Shields, 1831-5; Newcastle, 1832-6; Birmingham District, 1836 only; Bath Sun, 1832-6; Newcastle & North of England, 1837 only; Metellus, 1836-8; Hibernia, 1836-8; Coventry, 1838 only; British, 1833-42; Bristol Union, 1839-43; Shropshire, 1841-3 and 1845; Insurance Company of Scotland, 1846 only; Hercules, 1846-8. 5) For Protector and Coventry it is not possible to separate losses from expenses when calculating these as percentages of premium income. 6) The purchase price shown for Protector is the £250000 cited by Trebilcock, *Phoenix Assurance*, vol.I, p.502, 'defrayed by £100000 in consols' acquired by Phoenix with Protector's assets. This may or may not be comparable with the other tender prices shown, and must be treated with caution. It is also unclear whether the premium figure for Protector includes life business or not, which again renders comparison difficult. 7) Column 8 shows the average premium income per £100 insured (column 5/(column 4/100), expressed as shillings %. 8) Column 9 shows the bid price expressed as shillings per £100 insured (column 3/(column 4/100). 9) Column 10 shows the bid price expressed as a percentage of average premium income (column 3/(column 5*100).

Sources: Fire Insurance Duty Returns 1822-50; GL Ms 11935E, 15032, 15033, Sun, Take over Papers; Ms 14116, Sun, Simplified Profits and Losses (for Old Bath's underwriting results); PAA Ms 1761, 1765, Phoenix, Take over Papers; GL Ms 12160A/15, Imperial, DM, 17 July 1844; Ms 12162A/4, Alliance, DM, 12 May, 2 June, 30 June, 11 Aug. 1847; Trebilcock, *Phoenix Assurance*, vol.I, pp.499-502.

Towards collusion

None of the tactical responses to the competition of the late 1820s and early 1830s secured victory over the bonus offices. Eventually the major London insurers came to see cooperation as inevitable, even desirable. This proved a slow and difficult process, requiring a change of attitude among leaders of the industry which was not readily forthcoming.

Cooperation had never entirely disappeared even during the troublesome post-war decade. There were joint campaigns against the stamp duty in 1815, and again in 1825 when a petition to the Treasury was signed by 16 London fire offices.[80] After the first Liverpool tariff there were hopes for further cooperation. The Phoenix, the REA, the Sun, the Atlas and the Union agreed to pool their fire-fighting equipment for use in London and to work their brigades under one superintendent. Proposals circulated for united action over stamp duty in Ireland and for a scheme to 'facilitate the discovery of fraudulent insurances by an annual subscription'. In the summer of 1826 the Sun agreed with the Atlas and the Norwich Union to increase premiums on silk mills by 40 per cent. In 1829 the Atlas succeeded in persuading the majority of fire offices in Belfast to raise their premiums on local cotton mills, and a year later the Phoenix and the Imperial had some success in orchestrating a rate increase for sugar refineries.[81]

Nevertheless, the atmosphere of habitual price cutting and predatory takeovers limited the extent of trust. Provincial offices initiated many of the moves to cooperate. In 1829 the Kent Fire Office proposed a system for sharing fire-fighting expenses which was summarily dismissed by the Phoenix, the Sun and the REA. The Leeds & Yorkshire circulated a classification of textile mills but received little response.[82] The two most complex tariffs of the time owed their success, at least in part, to the efforts of non-metropolitan insurers. In the summer of 1829 the Scottish offices, led by the Scottish Union, opened negotiations with nine London offices. Agreement was reached by December on rates for textile mills, sugar refineries, distilleries and drying stoves in Scotland.[83] The Scottish tariff prepared the ground for the first national tariff agreement of any kind in Britain, that for drying stoves in the textile industries. Jenkin Jones orchestrated negotiations between London, provincial and Scottish offices by travelling between London, Manchester, Leeds and Glasgow in September 1830. A coordinating committee of Scottish offices was then established, while Jones liaised with the major English offices. After nine months of negotiations, 14 English and nearly a dozen Scottish insurers accepted a classification with rates extending from 10s 6d% for the best class of stoves heated by outside steam boilers, to a prohibitive 84s% charged for drying stoves used by sizers. This tariff was a major achievement given the variety of stoves used in different textile process and the 'diversity of opinions upon this branch of business'. In the wake of this success, however, Jones remained oddly pessimistic about further progress. When the Glasgow agents of several offices suggested a common tariff for the town, Jones 'conceived so extensive a measure at that time to be impracticable', and the proposal was shelved. Exhausted, and with his spirits drained after months of mediation, the 50-year-old Phoenix secretary was highly sceptical about the prospect of unanimity amongst offices even on the most pressing matters.[84]

Nevertheless by the early 1830s cooperation had progressed further than some had dared to believe possible. New mercantile rates were agreed for Liverpool in 1832 and ten offices met in the following summer to discuss farming stock insurances.[85] Most progress was made in the area of firefighting. A proposal circulated by the Sun, the Phoenix and the REA for a joint fire brigade for the capital, building upon the existing service operated by five offices, resulted in the establishment in 1833 of the London Fire Engine Establishment, with a managing committee consisting of delegates from each contributing office. The Sun's Charles Ford was given the credit for bringing together 11 London fire offices, representing two-thirds of the fire insurances in the capital, to support this venture. The LFEE cost £8000 annually, a sum borne by each office in proportion to the amount of its insurances. It operated successfully, tackling over 35000 fires in the capital, until it passed to the Metropolitan Board of Works in 1866.[86]

Following its failure in 1828 to obtain a tariff for cotton mills, the MFLAC made two further attempts in 1832-3. On the second occasion, the Manchester insurer was invited by several London offices to submit a table of rates, but after weeks of preparation, surveying mills and meeting with local agents, the MFLAC's scheme again foundered on the opposition of the Sun and the REA.[87] Instead of price regulation, price competition persisted into the 1830s. To a considerable extent, however, the efforts of the Manchester office paved the way for metropolitan acceptance of the need to cooperate with country insurers. In autumn 1842 the first of a series of meetings were held between provincial and London offices which quickly culminated in tariffs for warehouses at Liverpool and Manchester and for English cotton mills. The new Liverpool tariff divided the town into two districts and raised warehouse rates by 83 per cent. The cotton mill tariff distinguished between grades of cotton spinning and raised premiums on fireproof mills by one-third.[88] Policyholders reacted strongly. Manchester fine cotton spinners demanded and obtained an increase in premium differentials between coarse and fine spinning. Pressure from Liverpool warehouse owners, as well as concern about disagreements between fire offices over their respective liabilities in shared losses, led to three revisions of the Liverpool tariff during 1843. The Manchester warehouse tariff was revised twice in 1844 and extended. Price regulation spread rapidly to other areas such as woollen and flax mills, warehouses in Hull, Glasgow and London, and textile mills in Ireland. By the end of 1843 some 24 insurance offices were meeting regularly to discuss issues such as gas lamps and blowing rooms in cotton mills, waste storage in Manchester railway warehouses, and warehouse construction in Liverpool. A central fund was established to pay for a surveyor for Liverpool docks.[89]

After years of sustained competition and intermittent efforts at cooperation, insurers had come together with remarkable speed to establish a set of wide-ranging agreements which helped reduce price competition in industrial and commercial insurances, and restored profitability to these markets for the first time in decades.[90] Several reasons may be suggested for this sudden turnaround. The economic recession and labour unrest of 1842 may have persuaded insurance offices to combine to raise premium rates at a time when policyholders would be most concerned to protect their assets, especially from incendiarists. Legislative efforts to improve warehouses in Liverpool may also have played a part. Although the Liverpool Fire Prevention Act of 1842 came too late to prevent the warehouse fires which swept through the town in 1842 and 1843, the legislation did convince the Liverpool Fire Office 'to make another effort to obtain the cooperation of all companies doing business in the town...', in order to raise rates and to force policyholders to improve warehouse construction, safety and management. By 1846 its directors were able to report success in these areas, while the tariff offices had established the Liverpool Fire Salvage Association,

> for the purpose not only of salving goods but also of securing improvements in warehouse construction and equipment, and of helping forward, by periodical inspection, fire prevention methods....[91]

Liverpool proved to be the cockpit of change, although not quite in the way anticipated by the London offices in 1826. The increased tariff imposed on Liverpool warehouses in 1833 had reflected insurers' concerns about the town's inadequate water supply and fire-fighting services after the huge fire of that year. The tariff helped return mercantile insurances there to profitability while encouraging the municipal authorities to do something about fire prevention.[92] Similarly in 1838 the threat of a tariff imposed on Glasgow risks by the fire offices successfully forced Glasgow magistrates to maintain the city's fire service when it was about to be disbanded.[93]

Accompanying these successes was a declining level of competition, a rising market share for the three leading offices, higher levels of growth and larger profit margins. It is notable that the two periods most productive of cooperation, the early 1830s and 1842-4, coincided with brief periods of stability in the total number of insurance companies.[94] By the early 1840s price regulation was conducted by the major firms from positions of relative strength. Moreover, as relations between London and provincial insurers grew warmer, the specialist expertise of the latter was increasingly valued. The divisive issue of the bonus policy never entirely disappeared before mid-century, but cooperation came to be accepted as an alternative response to the destructive tactics which had emerged after 1825. Thus the 1840s witnessed the reemergence, on a much larger scale than before, of the cooperative practices pioneered by the London cartel of the late eighteenth century. It might be argued that, after several false starts, collusion had finally asserted itself as the 'natural' state in British fire insurance. The series of meetings which began in September 1842 were to culminate, eighteen years later, in the creation of a formal tariff organisation, the Fire Offices Committee. In turn, the FOC was to dominate the industry for over one hundred years until the decline of tariff control in the 1970s.[95]

Underwriting performance, 1815-50

Between 1815 and 1850 the sums insured by English fire offices increased by more than three fold in real terms. Incomes from this rapidly expanding volume of business ebbed and flowed. Table 5.12 presents the annual average premium incomes from the UK fire underwriting of 22 English offices. As the price of insurance fell steeply after 1815, the premium incomes of most established London offices declined. The older provincial offices with modest volumes of business were generally less affected. Their premium incomes either remained stable, or, as with the Kent and Essex offices, rose a little. Around 1830 prices began to climb again for the first time in nearly three decades. This, together with the corporate acquisitions of the 1820s and 1830s, ensured that the incomes of the larger offices quickly recovered, while those of medium-sized and smaller provincial offices also grew.

Table 5.13 illustrates how most offices followed the downward trend in insurance prices to the early 1830s, and thereafter enjoyed an increase in average rates. Two other points emerge from this table. First, the price differential - measured by the coefficients of variation of average rates - rose by 16 per cent during the period of low prices, fierce competition and the first wave of predatory takeovers in the later 1820s. During the following decade the differential fell, and, although it rose again in the early 1840s, by mid-century the variation in the average premium rates of fire insurance offices was lower than at any time since the 1790s. This suggests the effect of reduced levels of competition and an increasing degree of tariff cooperation on market integration. It may also indicate that insurance portfolios across the industry were becoming more similar, though this cannot be proven without a detailed analysis of the type of property insured by each office. Second, table 5.13 shows a division between the majority of metropolitan offices with high average rates, and the majority of country insurers with low premium rates. In each of the sub-periods over half the London offices listed had average rates greater than 3s% - which amounted to twice the basic premium for a common residential insurance after 1825 - while fewer than half of the provincial offices had rates above this level. Some provincials, the MFLAC, the Norwich Union and the Essex & Suffolk, were in the high rate group. The Manchester office enjoyed a high premium yield from its many industrial and commercial insurances. The East Anglian offices may have been especially affected by higher rates on farming insurances due to persistent agrarian unrest in the region, although this does not appear to hold for the Kent, which was also located in a Swing county.[96]

How well did underwriters perform after 1815? Table 5.14 shows a mixed picture for the London offices. The County, the Guardian and the London Assurance enjoyed loss ratios at or below the 55 per cent deemed by the oldest firms to be an acceptable margin of profitability, while the Sun and the Imperial suffered losses above this level for all or most of the period.[97] On the whole, country offices performed better than their metropolitan counterparts. With the exceptions of the MFLAC and the Norwich Union, and disregarding the sudden catastrophic losses which forced several provincial offices to sell up, most of the country insurers in table 5.14 had remarkable success, with claims which absorbed far less than 55 per cent of their premium incomes. The results for the Wiltshire, Sheffield and Leeds offices also demonstrate that insurers located in industrial regions w ere n ot necessarily fated to suffer high loss ratios, provided their risk selection was careful enough. Thus, with some exceptions, the broad dichotomy between high-loss London offices and low-loss country offices, which was evident before 1815, persisted through the first half of the nineteenth century.

During the war the better underwriting performance of the provincial offices had been largely offset by their higher management costs. After 1815 the differential between the expense ratios of provincial and London insurers became less marked, as a common trend emerged towards lower management costs (see table 5.15). This trend was associated in many offices with wholesale investigations into underwriting and managerial performance, which were aimed at expanding sales networks and improving agency monitoring, reducing head office costs, abolishing 'traditional' employee perquisites and increasing organisational efficiency. The result of these investigations was often a greater volume of business processed by only slightly larger numbers of clerical staff. At several metropolitan offices the expansion in the numbers of agents, especially in the greater London area during the 1830s and 1840s, more than paid for itself through increased revenue.

Underwriting surpluses - premiums minus claims plus expenses, net of investment income - are shown for 10 firms in table 5.16. Some offices specialising in country insurances, such as the Essex and the County, as well as those with a small volume of good quality residential business in a genteel location, such as the Old Bath, made underwriting profits in the range of 30 to 65 per cent of premium income. Surpluses were more modest among the bigger London offices, although they were still usually over ten per cent and frequently much higher. Many offices, however, experienced falling margins during the 1820s, in some cases due to heavy losses in Liverpool, and some had to postpone the payment of bonuses to their 'with-profits' policyholders.[98] From the early 1830s there was some diminution in the severity of underwriting fluctuations and surpluses stabilised or improved. The early 1840s, marked once again by large fires at Liverpool, witnessed another sharp deterioration in underwriting profits for several offices. Surveying the entire period from 1816 to 1850, it can be said that net losses on underwriting were relatively rare, and that handsome surpluses were made at different times by different offices. Of the 51 data observations in table 5.16, however, only 23 (45 per cent) were at or above the 25 per cent surplus regarded as a satisfactory return.[99] This is a lower proportion than that for the period 1791-1815, namely 56 per cent, or 15 of the 27

Table 5.12 UK premium income of London and country offices, 1816-50

(gross income, annual averages, fire insurance only)
* denotes missing data

Offices	1816-20	1821-5[a]	1826-30[b]	1831-5[c]	1836-40[d]	1841-5[e]	1846-50
LONDON							
Sun[f]	127662	120873	110802	133003	167969	204551	195257
Phoenix	82676	75703	70782	89479	147154	166378	166722
REA	63951	60991	51346	61661	84475	101621	103995
Imperial	52155	43614	41036	44730	50437	76961	97288
Globe	33227	28605	24123	28897	34458	46202	51693
County	31096	41406	41894	47806	53388	59567	*
London	8383	7303	5905	9074	13980	20008	26865
Guardian		24419	30407	31416	30042	31074	*
Alliance		15525	18873	25058	29656	39362	52003
Atlas	*	*	*	*	*	47906	*
COUNTRY							
Norwich Union	68932	66064	61140	66979	75637	82586	93504
Kent	7774	7856	8058	10972	11926	12690	13625
Essex & Suffolk	5568	6220	6784	7177	7889	8354	*
Wiltshire	4258	4170	4367	5408			
Newcastle	3867	3814	3958	4472	*	*	*
Salop	1988	2023	1857	2162	2501	3015	
Old Bath	1494	1364					
Bath Sun	1259	1299	1090	1134	1165		

Sheffield					*
MFLAC	14530	23349	28569	30984	32639
Bristol Crown		1517	1372	1335	*
Leeds & Yorks	*	*	*	*	22258	*

Notes: [a] Guardian, 1822-5; Alliance, MFLAC, 1824-5; Newcastle, 1821-2. [b] Newcastle, midsummers 1826-31; Bristol Crown, 1827-30. [c] Newcastle, midsummers 1831-6. [d] Bath Sun, Bristol Crown, 1836-7. [e] MFLAC, Essex & Suffolk, 1841-4; Leeds & Yorkshire, 1843-5. [f] 'net' UK premiums, plus ten per cent commission.

Sources: as for table 4.5, plus Trebilcock, *Phoenix Assurance*, vol.I, table 9.1, p.515, table 13.3, p.713; Ryan, 'History of Norwich Union', table 43(i); GL Ms 18102/1, Guardian, Annual Account Book, 1822-45; GL Ms 18106, Guardian, Fire ledger, 1821-67; Ms 16222/2-8, MFLAC, DM, 1825-45, Auditors' annual accounts; Royal Insurance plc, Leeds & Yorkshire, DM, vol.2, 1843-55; GL Ms 14075/1-2, Alliance, Ledgers, 1824-55; Fire Duty Returns, 1822-50.

Table 5.13 Average rates, 1816-50

(Annual average premium in shillings per £100 insured)
* denotes missing data

Offices	1816-20	1821-5	1826-30	1831-5	1836-40	1841-5	1846-50
LONDON							
Sun	2.83	2.83	2.52	2.63	2.63	2.76	2.76
Phoenix	3.61	3.55	3.28	3.45	3.34	3.68	*
REA	3.82	3.71	3.25	3.20	3.38	3.68	3.67
Imperial	3.91	3.82	3.54	3.54	3.18	3.75	4.06
Globe	3.42	3.23	2.83	3.11	2.91	3.72	4.28
County	2.74	2.98	2.86	2.98	2.92	2.95	*
London	2.79	2.71	2.38	3.06	3.12	3.47	3.69
Guardian		3.35	3.07	2.91	2.65	2.84	*
Alliance		3.81	3.05	3.54	3.13	3.77	3.88
Atlas	*	*	*	*	*	4.81	*
COUNTRY							
Norwich Union	4.73	3.56	2.96	2.93	2.88	2.96	3.23
Kent	*	2.98	2.62	2.99	2.83	2.83	2.90
Essex & Suffolk	*	3.02	3.21	3.31	3.28	3.27	*
Wiltshire	*	3.13	2.81	2.91		*	
Newcastle	*	2.74	2.40	2.98	*	*	*

Salop	2.58	2.59	2.13	2.21	2.21	2.17	*
Old Bath	*	2.40					
Bath Sun	*	2.53	2.07	2.13	2.19	2.94	2.92
Sheffield	*	2.37	2.42	2.59	2.78		*
MFLAC		3.96	4.28	4.55	4.19	4.57	
Bristol Crown	*	*	2.38	2.26	2.26		
Leeds & Yorks						4.70	
N =	9	19	19	19	17	17	9
Coeff.Variation	0.198	0.158	0.184	0.180	0.164	0.206	0.150

Note: Years as given in table 5.12 unless otherwise stated.

Sources: as table 5.12.

Table 5.14 Loss ratios, 1816-50

(Claims paid as a percentage of gross premiums, annual averages)
* denotes missing data

Offices	1816-20	1821-5	1826-30	1831-5	1836-40	1841-5	1846-50
LONDON							
Sun	66.6	70.8	60.5	69.2	60.7	68.3	60.3
Phoenix	54.0	62.7	62.8	63.1	49.6	55.6	*
REA	55.2	57.1	57.3	53.1	70.7	84.7	57.5
Imperial	68.5	63.2	86.4	66.7	48.0	48.7	47.5
Globe	56.0	56.7	61.2	45.4	65.9	70.2	58.9
County	35.9	50.5	43.4	55.8	37.2	46.0	*
London	56.9	43.2	45.8	37.2	46.9	45.8	35.4
Guardian		30.3	56.0	53.9	52.5	38.4	*
Alliance		39.5	75.3	68.0	54.6	65.2	52.6
Atlas	*	*	*	*	*	63.2	*
COUNTRY							
Norwich Union	71.5	55.6	62.0	54.2	50.9	60.4	68.5
Kent	41.4	36.8	45.9	34.7	38.5	28.7	55.2
Essex & Suffolk	29.0	24.4	25.4	44.1	33.1	52.5	*
Wiltshire	38.8	33.0	33.6	65.1			
Newcastle	58.9	75.4	22.2	39.0	*	*	*
Salop	*	*	*	16.1	31.6	*	*
Old Bath	9.8	41.3					

Bath Sun	11.0	7.5	42.1	20.8	72.9		
Sheffield	7.1	12.4	17.9	18.3	26.7	36.9	55.4
MFLAC	*	*	79.1	67.4	61.0	72.8	*
Bristol Crown			63.8	34.6	70.2		
Leeds & Yorks			*	*	*	46.6	*

Note: Years as given in table 5.12, unless otherwise stated.

Sources: as table 5.12.

Table 5.15 Expense ratios, 1816-50

(Management expenses as a percentage of premiums, annual averages)

* denotes missing data

Offices	1816-20	1821-5[a]	1826-30	1831-5	1836-40[b]	1841-5[c]	1846-50
LONDON[d]							
Phoenix	21.6	22.4	24.5	22.5	19.0	19.6	20.8
REA[e]	20.8	22.8	24.4	19.0	14.9[f]	16.9	19.3
Imperial	23.2	27.2	31.6	28.5	29.4	26.0	26.6
County[g]	20.4	21.6	21.9	20.6	19.1	20.3	*
Guardian		40.7	33.2	32.8	33.6	33.6	*
Alliance[h]			20.1	15.4	12.6		
COUNTRY							
Norwich Union	*	30.0	31.5	29.4	30.0	28.2	26.3
Essex & Suffolk	28.8	15.3	14.8	15.6	16.7	16.4	*
Old Bath	24.8	23.9					
MFLAC			17.8	16.0	15.3	14.9	*
Leeds & Yorks			*	*	*	18.6	*

Notes and Sources: Years and sources as table 5.12 unless otherwise stated. [a] Norwich Union, 1822-5. [b] Alliance, 1836-7, 1839. [c] County, 1841, 1843, 1845. [d] Phoenix, Guardian: expense ratios are for UK *and* foreign business. [e] Trebilcock's allowance for commission has been added to Supple's figures to give the ratio for total expenses. Trebilcock, *Phoenix Assurance*, vol.I, table 13.2, p.712; Supple, *Royal Exchange*, table 7.1, p.149. [f] Supple gives 14.5%, which appears to be an error. [g] Expenses *exclude* stationery, postage, printing, property tax, marks, legal, carriage, furniture, boards and bills, and, from 1830, advertising and travel expenses. From 1828 directors' and auditors' allowances are *included*. [h] Expense ratios on all business, UK and foreign, fire and life.

Table 5.16 Underwriting surpluses, 1816-50

Offices	1816-20	1821-5	1826-30	1831-5	1836-40	1841-5	1846-50
LONDON[a]							
Phoenix	25.2	17.3	12.8	19.5	29.4	10.1	13.9
REA	24.0	20.1	18.3	27.9	14.4	- 1.6	23.2
Imperial	8.3	9.6	- 18.0	4.8	22.6	25.3	25.9
County	43.7	27.9	34.7	23.6	43.7	33.7	*
Guardian		21.2	12.6	14.2	14.4	28.3	*
COUNTRY							
Norwich Union	*	14.4	6.5	16.4	19.1	11.4	5.2
Essex & Suffolk	42.2	60.3	59.8	40.3	50.2	31.1	*
Old Bath	65.4	34.8					
MFLAC			3.1	16.6	23.7	12.3	*
Leeds & Yorks			*	*	*	34.8	*

Note: [a] Phoenix, Guardian: surpluses are on UK *and* foreign business.

Sources: as table 5.12.

data observations in table 4.8. Fire insurance, therefore, could still prove to be a lucrative business, but by the middle of the nineteenth century the really big profits were becoming increasingly difficult to obtain.

Notes

[1] Dickens, *Hard Times*, p.65.

[2] 'Towns' as defined by the census, i.e. most, but not all, settlements of >2000 inhabitants, see Waller, *Town, City and Nation*, pp.1-2.

[3] Lawton, 'Population Mobility', p.151; Waller, *Town, City and Nation*, p.8; Schwarz, *London in the Age of Industrialisation*, p.126.

[4] Fisher, *Industrial Revolution*, pp.44, 55.

[5] Bradford, Salford, Preston, Liverpool, Glasgow, Manchester, Wolverhampton, Leicester and Oldham. My definition of a 'rapidly growing big town' is one with over 50000 population in 1851 that had grown by over 200 per cent since 1811. The exception was Brighton, which grew from 12000 to 66000 in this period. Calculated from Mitchell, *British Historical Statistics*, pp.24-6; Census of Ireland for 1841, *PP* (1843) XXLV, appendix, p.lxvi; Census of Ireland for 1851, *PP* (1852-3), XCI, 44; *PP* (1856) XXXI, 620.

[6] Gauldie, *Cruel Habitations*, chs.2-3; Engels, *Condition of the Working Class*, p.79; Beresford, 'East End, West End'.

[7] Ashworth, *Genesis of Town Planning*, pp.17, 49; Rodger, 'Victorian Building Industry', p.152.

[8] Dickens, *Hard Times*, p.55; Cobbett, *Rural Rides*, p.205.

[9] GL Ms 14281/1-3, Guardian, GCM, 1821-30 *passim*; Ms 18111, Guardian, Agents' List; Schooling, *Alliance Assurance*, pp.1-12; Ms 14075/1, Alliance, Ledger 1824-37; Ms 12162A/1, Alliance, DM, 1824-34 *passim*.

[10] Pearson, 'Collective Diversification', table 2, p.405.

[11] Ryan, 'History of Norwich Union', table 19; County, Letter Book M, letter to J. Muff, 10 Dec. 1821; GL Ms 14116, Sun, Simplified Profit and Loss Accounts; Ms 16222/2, MFLAC, DM, 20-24 Jan. 1825; Ms 12160A/7-9, Imperial, DM, 13 Jan., 30 June 1819, 19 Mar., 2 Apr. 1823, 22 Dec. 1824, 23 Mar. 1825; Ms 14281/2, Guardian, GCM, 5 Sept. 1823;

[12] Bonuses are discussed in Trebilcock, *Phoenix Assurance*, vol.I, pp.476-83, and Ryan, 'Norwich Union and the British Fire Insurance Market'.

[13] GPL, Cotesworth Mss, CM/4/17, Newcastle, Accounts, Note to C.E. (Cuthbert Ellison).

[14] Ryan, 'Norwich Union and the British Fire Insurance Market', p.57.

[15] Ryan, 'History of Norwich Union', pp.336-7.

[16] Ryan, 'History of Norwich Union', p.338; Trebilcock, *Phoenix Assurance*, vol.I, p.499; GL Ms 12160A/7, Imperial, DM, 12 Apr. 1820; Pearson, 'Collective Diversification', table 2, p.405.

[17] County, Letter book M, letter to W. Banton, 7 July 1821; GL Ms 14281/1-2, Guardian, GCM, 14 June, 5 July 1822, 5 Nov. 1824.

[18] Calculated from CUL, PAA, PX509, Phoenix, Statistical Analysis.

[19] Bristol premiums calculated from the duty returns of 1824, using an estimated average rate of 3s%. The latter is based upon the average rate of the Bristol Crown Office for 1827-9 which was 2.4s%. Premium yields fell during the 1820s as a result of the 25% cut in the rates on common insurances imposed by the big London offices in 1825. The Phoenix's Bristol agency was not among the 13 (out of 386) which earned >£500 in premiums in 1824. CUL, PAA, PX509, Phoenix, Statistical Analysis, fol.50. The REA's figure is for 1825, see Supple, *Royal Exchange*, p.154. The Norwich Union's premiums are estimated from £1.26m insured in Bristol in 1822 at an average rate of 2s 11d%, see Ryan, 'Norwich Union and the British Fire Insurance Market', table 6, p.61.

[20] Nor is it possible to distinguish the sum insured by the Norwich Union in the capital from the duty returns. This office sold insurances in London worth £1.2m in 1822 but received no poundage allowance at the £4% rate for duty collected on London insurances. Table 5.3, therefore, probably exaggerates the size of the Norwich Union's provincial business.

[21] Cf. Trebilcock, *Phoenix Assurance*, table 8.2, p.461; Ryan, 'Norwich Union and the British Fire Insurance Market', table 2, p.49.

[22] The MFLAC quickly established an extensive agency system, so one can assume that most proposals taken to its office in King Street were Mancunian in origin.

[23] Pearson, 'Taking Risks', table 3, p.51; Blackburn Central Library, B368, MFLAC, Blackburn Agency Policy and Endorsement Book 1830-43; Returns of Mills and Factories, *PP* (1839) XLII, p.1; GL Ms 16222/8, MFLAC, DM, 4 Apr. 1844.

[24] GL Ms 11935A/1, Sun, Report Books, Report of Philip Bewicke on his late journey to Liverpool, Oct. 1806.

[25] Ryan, 'History of Norwich Union', pp.486-7, p.518 n. Details of Norwich Union's woollen mill insurances in 1823 given in CUL, PAA, PX509, Phoenix, Statistical Analysis.

[26] Ryan, 'History of Norwich Union', pp.166-72, table 13, p.968; Norwich Union, DM, 11 Oct. 1824, 25 Apr. 1825; GL Ms 16223/1, MFLAC, GCM, 4 May 1825. I am grateful to Dr D.T. Jenkins for providing me with a copy of his notes from the Norwich Union minute books.

[27] GL Ms 12160A/8, Imperial, DM, 18 June 1823; Ryan, 'History of Norwich Union', p.182; GL Ms 16170/2, 4, Atlas, DM, 6 Oct. 1814, 16 May, 25 July 1816, 22 Nov. 1825.

[28] Ryan, 'Norwich Union and the British Fire Insurance Market', p.63. On rural disturbances, see Hobsbawm and Rudé, *Captain Swing*; Hammond, *Village Labourer*; Archer, *By a Flash and a Scare*.

[29] Trebilcock, *Phoenix Assurance*, vol.I, pp.363, 387; Dickson, *Sun Insurance*, p.145; GL Ms 12160A/12, Imperial, DM, 17 Oct. 1838; Ryan, 'History of the Norwich Union', pp.487, 522, 201 n, 223, 182.

[30] GL Ms 11935A/1, Sun, Report Book, Report of James Hall on the Liverpool docks, 17 Jan. 1805; Anderson, 'Financial Institutions and the Capital Market on Merseyside', Hyde, *Liverpool and the Mersey*, p.80; Trebilcock, *Phoenix Assurance*, vol.I, p.387; Mulhearn, 'Police and Pilferers at the Port of Liverpool'; GL Ms 14281/2, Guardian, GCM, 20 June 1826, letter to C.B. Ford.

[31] GL Ms 11935A/1, Sun, Report Book, Bewicke's Reports of 1806, 1812.

32   Lloyd-Jones and Lewis, *Manchester and the Age of the Factory*, ch.7; Gatrell, 'Labor,
     Power, and the Size of Firms'.
33   Calculated from data in GL Ms 14116, Sun, Simplified Profit and Loss Accounts,
     fols.3-4; Trebilcock, *Phoenix Assurance*, vol.I, table 7.1, p.333; Phoenix, Annual
     summary sheets; CUL, PAA, PX508, Phoenix, Annual Analysis; Dickson, *Sun
     Insurance*, appendix I, p.302.
34   Dickson, *Sun Insurance*, p.77 n; Ryan, 'History of the Norwich Union', p.41 n.
35   GL Ms 11935A/1, Sun, Report Book, Bewicke's reports, 1806, 1812, Green's report,
     1816. For further evidence of the importance of tied business, see Ms 14281/4,
     Guardian, GCM, 1 Oct. 1830, 4 Mar. 1831, Report of the Fire Committee on Special
     Risks.
36   GL Ms 16222/2, MFLAC, DM, 6 Oct., 17 Oct. 1825.
37   GL Ms 14281/2, Guardian, GCM, 27 Feb., 5 Mar., 19 Mar., 2-20 Apr., 24 Sept., 1
     Oct. 1824; Ms 12160A/9, Imperial, DM, 4 Jan. 1825; CUL, PAA, PX1010, Phoenix,
     Agents' Extra Letter Book A, fol.253-4, Jones to Tate, 2 Oct. 1824; Trebilcock,
     Phoenix Assurance, vol.I, p.400.
38   GL Ms 14116, Sun, Simplified Profit and Loss Accounts, Memorandum, Feb. 1825.
     The Phoenix had already imposed a £10000 ceiling on Liverpool warehouses in
     October 1824, see CUL, PAA, PX1010, Phoenix, Agents' Extra Letter Book A, Jones
     to Liverpool Agent, 9 Oct. 1824. On subsidised price cutting as a competitive
     strategy, see Utton, *Diversification and Competition*, ch.5.
39   GL Ms 14116, Sun, Simplified Profit and Loss Accounts, Circular to Agents, 20 Sept.
     1825; Ms 11935A/1, Sun, Special Report Book, Report of the Special Committee, 1
     June 1825; CUL, PAA, PX1010, Phoenix, Agents' Letter Book A, Jones to Green, 24
     Sept. 1825, Wilson to Tate, 29 Sept. 1825.
40   By early August 1826 over 20 firms, including all but three London offices, had
     joined the Liverpool tariff. GL Ms 14281/2, Guardian, GCM, 4 Aug. 1826.
41   GL Ms 16222/2, MFLAC, DM, 1 June, 12 June 1826.
42   CUL, PAA, PX1010, Phoenix, Agents' Extra Letter Book A, Jones to Morton, 22
     July 1826.
43   Cited by Ryan, 'History of Norwich Union', p.491.
44   GL Ms 14116, Sun, Simplified Profit and Loss Accounts, Ford to Town Dept., 29
     Sept. 1825; Ms 14281/2, Guardian, GCM, 6 Jan. 1826.
45   GL Ms 16222/3, 6, MFLAC, DM, 22 Mar., 12 July 1827.
46   CUL, PAA, PX1010, Phoenix, Agents' Extra Letter Book A, Jones to Lewis, 9 July
     1827.
47   Smith, *Practical Remarks*, p.2.
48   Norwich Union, DM, 24 Dec. 1827, 7 Dec. 1829. The mill was Calverley mill, near
     Leeds. Norwich Union did not resume insuring woollen mills until 1875. Ryan,
     'History of the Norwich Union', p.519.
49   Ryan, 'History of the Norwich Union', pp.201 n, 518-25, table 23, p.993; GL Ms
     12160A/10, Imperial, DM, 26 Sept. 1827; Ms 16222/4, 7, MFLAC, DM, 31 Dec.
     1828, 15 Jan. 1829, 14 Dec., 30 Dec. 1841.
50   GL Ms 16222/3-5, MFLAC, DM, 3 Apr. 1828, 2 July 1831, 23 Apr. 1829, 29 Dec.
     1831, 29 Feb., 1 Mar. 1832; CUL, PAA, PX1010, Phoenix, Agents' Extra Letter Book
     A, Circular 'To Leeds Only', 6 Dec. 1832, Jones to Tate, 29 Dec. 1832.

51 Of the 49 recorded takeovers and mergers which took place between 1782 and 1849, only three involved an English provincial insurer as the acquiring company. These were the acquisition of the business of the Anchor, a small Norwich mutual, by the Norwich General in 1810, the merger of the latter with the Norwich Union in 1821, and the purchase of the Newcastle & North of England by the Leeds & Yorkshire in 1838.

52 Pollard, 'Entrepreneurship 1870-1914', p.70.

53 Bagwell, *Transport Revolution*, pp.147-8; Jackman, *Development of Transportation*, pp.371-3, pp.644, 730-31, appendix 9; Ward, *Finance of Canal Building*, pp.56-64; Dyos and Aldcroft, *British Transport*, pp.131-2; Sykes, *Amalgamation Movement in English Banking*, pp.1-4. According to Sykes, there were 554 private banks in 1825, and 116 had disappeared by amalgamation by 1843.

54 The number of takeovers (involving fire insurance only) in 1782-1800 = 3; 1800-15 = 4; 1815-25 = 5; 1826-30 = 11; 1831-5 = 3; 1836-40 = 9; 1841-5 = 8; 1846-50 = 8. In addition, Walford refers to a merger between the Friendly Insurance Society and the Union at some point between 1781 and 1790, although I have found no corroboration of this elsewhere, Walford, *Insurance Cyclopedia*, vol.IV, p.376.

55 Trebilcock, *Phoenix Assurance*, vol.I, pp.493, 497. Trebilcock has understated the Sun's position by overlooking two of its acquisitions, the Coventry & Warwickshire (1839) and the British Fire (1843). As table 5.10 shows, the latter was the second largest takeover of the period.

56 In addition to the purchasing offices listed in table 5.10, other offices involved in bidding included the Atlas, the West of England, the REA, the Bristol Fire, the York & London, and the Salop. This list is probably not exhaustive.

57 Some fire and life composite offices were also interested in enhancing their life insurance portfolios in this way. In 1822 the Guardian took over the Star Life Insurance Office and negotiated for the fire and life business of the Sussex County & General in 1826. The Atlas acquired the Gloucestershire, Herefordshire & Cheltenham Life Assurance Company in 1826 but not the fire office of the same name when it folded two years later. The Atlas also acquired two agencies of the South Devon Fire & Life when it folded in 1827 and the life business of the Berkshire, Gloucestershire & Provincial in 1828. GL Ms 16170/4, Atlas, DM, 25 Aug., 3 Nov. 1826, 13 Feb., 10 July, 11 Dec. 1827, 13 May, 18 July, 23 Dec. 1828; Ms 14281/1-3, Guardian, GCM, 5 July 1822, 17 Mar., 7 Apr. 1826.

58 GL Ms 14281/2, Guardian, GCM, 6 Apr. 1827.

59 Trebilcock, *Phoenix Assurance*, vol.I, pp.493-7; CUL, PAA, PX1010, Agents' Extra Letter Book A, Jones to Lewis, 9 July 1827; GL Ms 11935E, Sun, Take over Papers, Old Bath, Agreement of 1 Mar. 1827. There is no evidence to support the idea that an earlier Bath office had been acquired by the Sun in 1782, as Trebilcock suggests. See Dickson, *Sun Insurance*, appendix 4.

60 For correspondence and accounts relating to these approaches, see GL Ms 11935E, Sun, Take over Papers, Bristol Crown.

61 For a full account of the merger negotiations, see Trebilcock, *Phoenix Assurance*, vol.I, pp.499-507.

62   CUL, PAA, Phoenix, Sundries File, Protector merger, draft agreement attached to the letter, Harris to Jones, 30 June 1835; Trebilcock, *Phoenix Assurance*, vol.I, table 13.1, p.710.

63   The following account is based on GL Ms 11935E, Sun, Take over Papers, Salamander.

64   GL Ms 11935E, Sun, Take over Papers, Salamander, Jones to Ford, 2 Nov. 1835.

65   GL Ms 11935E, Sun, Take over Papers, Bristol Crown, Ford to Richards, 26 Oct. 1837, Memoranda by Richards, 31 Oct., 1 Nov. 1837.

66   GL Ms 15032/4, 7, Sun, Take over Papers, Essex Economic, Ford to Parker, 29 Aug.1838, Liverpool, Ford to Bunnell, 8 Oct. 1838; CUL, PAA, PX1765, Phoenix, Take over Papers, Metellus; GL Ms 11935E, Sun, Take over Papers, Hibernia, Coventry & Warwickshire; Ms 15032/3,5, Sun, Take over Papers, Caledonian, Ford to Allen, 8 Feb. 1839, Richards to Morinet, 23 Mar. 1839.

67   GL Ms 12160A/14, 15, Imperial, DM, 18 Sept., 6 Nov. 1839, 29 Jan., 12 Feb. 1840, 14 Dec. 1842, 17 July 1844, 9 Apr. 1845; Ms 15032/1, Sun, Take over Papers, Bristol Fire, draft tender by Sun, 8 Jan. 1840; Ms 12162A/3, Alliance, DM, 27 Nov. 1839; Ms 15032/2, Sun, Take over Papers, Bristol Union, Memoranda on Premiums and Losses, Carlisle to Richards 22 Apr. 1844, Richards to Carlisle, 22 Apr. 1844.

68   Walford, *Insurance Cyclopedia*, vol.I, p.260, II, p.431.

69   The following is based upon a detailed reading of GL Mss 11935E, 15032, 15033, Sun, Take over Papers, supplemented by CUL, PAA, PX1759, 1763, 1765, 1769, 1771, Phoenix, Take over Papers, and related records of other offices.

70   GL Ms 11935E, Sun, Take over Papers, Preston & North Lancashire, calculated from 'List of Policies uncancelled'.

71   Hannah, 'Mergers in British Manufacturing Industry'.

72   Less commonly, an office might be valued by an average of its underwriting profits, net of interest on invested capital. Sun's bid price for the Salamander in 1835 was expressed as a multiple of average annual profits, given as 'years purchase', obviously a form of price derived from the property markets. See GL Ms 11935E, Sun, Take over Papers, Salamander, Ford to Richards, 19 Oct. 1835, Pole to Ford, 23 Oct. 1835.

73   Walford, *Insurance Cyclopedia*, vol.V, p.465.

74   GL Ms 15032/8, Sun, Take over Papers, Newcastle, Ford to Richards, 24 Oct. 1836.

75   The correlation with the average sum insured was 0.46. This and the following coefficients are of the Pearson's product moment variety.

76   Trebilcock, *Phoenix Assurance*, vol.I, pp.496-8.

77   GL Ms 11935E, Sun, Take over Papers, Bath Sun, Ford to Richards, 16 Aug. 1838.

78   Dyos and Aldcroft, *British Transport*, p.129; Bagwell, *Transport Revolution*, p.176.

79   Dickson, *Sun Insurance*, p.160.

80   Trebilcock, *Phoenix Assurance*, vol.I, p.228; GL Ms 12160A/9, Imperial, DM, 12 Jan. 1825; Ms 14281/2, Guardian, GCM, 25 Feb. 1825.

81   GL Ms 16222/3-4, MFLAC, DM, 7 Sept. 1826, 31 Dec. 1828, 15 Jan., 30 Apr., 11 June 1829, 22 Apr., 3 June 1830; Ms 14281/2, Guardian, GCM, 6 Oct. 1826; Ms 16170/4, Atlas, DM, 20 June 1826; Trebilcock, *Phoenix Assurance*, vol.I, pp.132, 393, 397.

82   CUL, PAA, Phoenix, Agent's Extra Letter Book A, Jones to Kent Fire Office, 5 Dec. 1828, 5 Jan., 7 Jan. 1829; GL Ms 14281/3, Guardian, GCM, 3 Apr. 1828.

[83] For details of the tariff negotiations, see Smith, *Practical Remarks*, pp.60-62; GL Ms 16222/4, MFLAC, DM, 3 Dec. 1829.

[84] GL Ms 16222/4, MFLAC, DM, 10 Mar.1831; Smith, *Practical Remarks*, pp.119-21; CUL, PAA, Phoenix, Agents' Extra Letter Book A, Jones to Green, 26 Sept. 1831.

[85] GL Ms 12160A/11-12, Imperial, DM, 6 Feb., 26 June 1833.

[86] Trebilcock, *Phoenix Assurance*, vol.I, pp.132-3; Supple, *Royal Exchange*, pp.165-6; Walford, *Insurance Cyclopedia*, vol.III, p.321; GL Ms 12162A/2, Alliance, DM, 4 July 1832; Ms 12160A/11, Imperial, DM, 2 Jan. 1833; Blackstone, *History of the British Fire Service*, ch.8.

[87] GL Ms 16222/5, MFLAC, DM, 2 Feb. 1832, 14 Feb.- 3 Apr., 27 June 1833.

[88] GL Ms 16222/7-8, MFLAC, DM, 29 Sept., 13-20 Oct. 1842.

[89] GL Ms 16222/8, MFLAC, DM, 24 Nov., 1 Dec., 15 Dec. 1842, 2 Mar., 4 May, 25 May, 15 June, 13 July, 7 Sept., 14 Sept., 26 Oct., 14 Dec., 21 Dec. 1843, 25 Jan., 14-23 Mar., 4 Apr., 18 Apr., 30 Oct., 1 Nov. 1844; Raynes, *History of British Insurance*, pp.339-40.

[90] Phoenix loss ratios on industrial risks, for instance, fell from 76 per cent to 59 per cent between 1821/30 and 1841/50. Trebilcock, *Phoenix Assurance*, vol.I, table 7.1, p.333.

[91] Dyer Simpson, *1936 Our Centenary Year*, pp.23-5; Raynes, *History of British Insurance*, p.339.

[92] Under 7 Geo. IV c. 57 (1826), Liverpool's Watch, Lamps and Scavengers' Committee were empowered to establish a fire police. The insurers' complaint in 1833 was that nothing had been done. GL Ms 16222/5, MFLAC, DM, 31 Jan. 1833. In 1836 the corporation abolished the dock police and merged it with the more efficient town police force. Mulhearn, 'Police and Pilferers'.

[93] GL Ms 16222/6, MFLAC, DM, 8-15 Mar. 1838.

[94] Pearson, 'Taking Risks', table 1, p.44.

[95] The FOC was finally wound up in 1985. On its history, see Westall, 'Marketing Strategy'.

[96] On rural unrest, see the references in note 28 above.

[97] Trebilcock, *Phoenix Assurance*, vol.I, p.711

[98] GL Ms 16223/1, MFLAC, GCM, 4 May 1826, 10 May 1827, 7 May 1829.

[99] Trebilcock, *Phoenix Assurance*, vol.I, p.711.

Part II

Chapter 6

Company Foundation

The art of association...becomes...the mother of action.

Alexis de Tocqueville.[1]

With the exception of the earliest decades of fire insurance, when mutual societies were important, the unincorporated joint-stock partnership was the most common form of organisation among the 170 fire insurance enterprises founded before 1850. Such partnerships were commonly formed under the law of trusts, based on a ruling of 1673 which stipulated that assets held on trust could not be claimed by the trustees' creditors. The court of chancery permitted unincorporated companies to vest their assets in trustees through a deed of settlement, thus allowing the liability of individual shareholders to be limited to their share in the company. The legality of such a limitation was always in doubt after the passage of the Bubble Act in 1720. Trust law also did not cover the question of transferable shares, which were prohibited by the Act unless a company obtained a specific royal or parliamentary charter.[2] Nevertheless, the lack of formal incorporation did not prevent hundreds of joint-stock partnerships forming satisfactorily under the law of trusts, raising capital and even inserting clauses into their constitutions which purported to protect the liability of their investors.[3]

Beyond the official histories of the big three London offices, we know relatively little about the internal workings of such partnerships, or about the relations between shareholders, directors, managers and their staff, and between the firms and their customers.[4] The first four sections of this chapter examine the process of company formation, the key relationships between directors, salaried managers and shareholders, and the legal and extra-legal elements upon which those relationships were based. The final section examines those who promoted and directed the new provincial offices of the late eighteenth and early nineteenth centuries, and the social, political and business networks within which they operated.

Flotation and legitimisation

The establishment of an insurance office was essentially about creating a 'public' interest in the venture and constructing a proprietorship, and in this it differed little from the process by which contemporary gas or canal companies were formed.[5] A few individuals would meet to discuss their project and to form a promotion committee, which would then call by newspaper advertisement, poster and private letter for a public meeting of potential investors. Promoters would also personally canvas the support of key patrons, the prominent merchants and professionals of a town, the leading gentry of a county.

At this stage, even before the public meeting had taken place, a minute book was opened and a secretary or clerk to the committee was appointed. The task of the committee was to decide the purpose of the venture and the structure of the capital to be raised, with these decisions to be put to the meeting for ratification or amendment. The first board of directors was generally selected from the membership of the committee. Four or five trustees were also appointed, usually from the ranks of the wealthiest promoters. A bank account and subscription book were then opened and written pledges to subscribe were sought from those attending the first meeting and from others who had expressed an interest. Share certificates were printed and distributed to those who paid up their subscriptions. At the same time, with legal counsel, a deed of settlement would be drafted, setting out the constitution and the regulations prescribing the share capital, the forms of underwriting and investment, and the structure of the office funds. During the late eighteenth century it was common for deeds of existing companies to be used as models for new offices. Thus the Salop Fire Office consulted the deed of the Bath Fire Office, while the London sugar refiners, who founded the Phoenix Fire Office in 1782, borrowed from the deed of the office already established by their fellow sugar refiners in Bristol.[6] Once a version was finalised, the deed was ready to receive the signatures of subscribers. If necessary, the deed was also taken around the region where the office was located to enable those subscribers living at a distance to sign it without undue delay. The whole process of company foundation could take from just a few months to several years before all capital was subscribed and all shareholders had signed the deed.

From this process one can identify several common elements which underpinned director-shareholder relations in the insurance industry. First, the quasi-public nature of most provincial insurance companies was reflected in their close ties to local corporations and guilds, to the magistracy, and to the senior county officeholders. This profile was typical of most insurance companies founded outside London between the 1760s and the 1840s. The overlapping of business, social, political and cultural networks was characteristic of those who promoted and directed these companies. Insurance promoters explicitly identified their interests with those of their neighbours. Worcester's new fire office of 1790 was declared to be

> peculiarly appropriate to the safety, interests, convenience, and welfare of the city and its inhabitants, and not less to those without the city who insure property in it...its firm composes principally of residents within the city, the interests of the insured and the insurers are thence so intimately blended, that they become mutual guarantees of each

other's property, and ultimately the most effectual safeguard of the city at large that could be provided to its general or particular service.[7]

The Reading Fire Insurance Company invited the inhabitants of the town

to consider the advantages this Institution promises, connected as it is solely with the Town, and enabling the Insurers to reap a profit not only by the distribution of the premiums, but from the money they actually pay being again circulated among themselves.[8]

By contrast with insurance companies based in large cities, which could draw upon deep pools of urban middle class patronage, many offices in market towns also reached out to the landed estates, rural parishes and smaller towns for support. The 30 individuals who founded the Salop Fire Office in 1780 included prominent members of the county gentry, as well as a cluster of Anglican clergy and the cream of the town's merchants and shopkeepers.[9] The Salop promoters announced that they hoped for,

the same encouragement from the inhabitants of Shrewsbury, the county at large and neighbouring counties, which is customarily manifested towards undertakings of public utility...and which similar Institutions at Bath, Bristol, Manchester, Liverpool etc. have all experienced.

The founders devised a badge and firemark based on the Shrewsbury town arms, ordered a copper engraving of Shrewsbury as a header for the office's policies, and incorporated the town arms into the seal of the new office. General meetings of proprietors were held in the town hall, where the deed of settlement was signed and subscribers paid the deposits on their shares. The office's first fire engine was borrowed from the wardens of the mercers company, the most important guild in Shrewsbury.[10] All these activities manifested a fusion of corporate and urban identity, of private and public interests, and were designed to encourage local investors to support the new venture.

This notion of the public utility of a private enterprise was also expressed in other ways, such as the prominent head office in the high street offering residents easy access to services and reinforcing the impression of solidity and respectability. The ubiquitous brightly painted metal firemarks fastened to the wall of every insured building further announced the presence of the local fire office as a public institution. Their fire brigades were commonly perceived as 'public' facilities for the benefit of all residents of the town, and in some places, such as Liverpool in the 1780s and Canterbury in the 1800s, municipal councils paid the insurance company to maintain and operate the parish engines alongside those of its own, even housing the engines under one roof.[11] Public buildings were generally insured with the local office, and in some cases, it also functioned as a pivotal investor by which capital was moved easily from one 'public' institution to another. This concept of the 'public utility' of stock companies blurred the boundaries between the public and private sphere, and contrasted sharply with the view of contemporary commentators, such as Adam Smith, that stock companies were usually poorly managed and 'scarce ever fail to do more harm than good'.[12] Many local worthies believed that such companies were in fact no bad thing. They could provide a variety of services to local and regional economies, and generally in a more accountable way than if those services were bought from offices based in London.[13]

A second aspect of insurance company foundation related to the impact of the Bubble Act on the legality of partnerships. The insurance industry benefited both from benign neglect and from several positive developments during the second half of the eighteenth century. In 1786 the lawyer James Park noted with regard to insurance company deeds, by-laws and policy conditions that 'the construction to be put upon those regulations has but seldom become the subject of judicial enquiry'.[14] When in 1757 the promoters of the Equitable Assurance Society applied for a charter, the application was rejected by the Attorney General. However, he did suggest that,

> if the petitioners...are so sure of success there is an easy method of making the experiment by entering into a voluntary partnership of which there are several instances now subsisting in the business of insuring.

A modicum of official sanction was thus accorded to this unofficial form of company organisation. The Equitable proceeded without a charter, within a few years becoming Britain's largest life assurer. In 1783 the Attorney General told the promoters of the Phoenix Fire Office, who had also applied for a charter, that the public would be better served by the voluntary association of respectable individuals than by incorporated societies. Furthermore, the percentage stamp duty on fire insurance introduced in 1782 required the annual licensing of unincorporated insurance offices. Under the new statute, the fire offices were obliged to act as the tax collecting agencies of the Stamp Commissioners, thus cementing another brick in the edifice of legal recognition.[15]

Nevertheless, even in insurance the legal status of unincorporated partnerships remained precarious. Towards the end of the eighteenth century the number of insurers' petitions for incorporation mounted, and the number of rejections increased, partly as the result of lobbying by established offices opposed to new foundations. In 1807, in the wake of a wave of company promotions, the Attorney General indicated that he was prepared to activate the Bubble Act against those who presumed to act as a corporate body, who raised a transferable stock, or who ventured to limit the liability of their partners by deed of trust. The publisher of the prospectuses of two stock companies, the London Paper Manufacturing Company and the London Distillery Company, was prosecuted before the King's Bench, and a stern warning was issued against similar promotions in the future. During the following decade further cases were brought before the courts. On the other hand, there were also contrary and more favourable developments. Between 1807 and

1815 some 20 companies, mostly insurance offices, successfully applied to Parliament for private acts enabling them to sue and be sued in the name of an executive officer.[16]

The legal position was thus very confused, with different signals being sent from different quarters.[17] None of this hindered the foundation of new partnerships, but investors continued to worry. In 1809 shareholders in the County Fire Office expressed their concern 'that insurances effected at this Office are illegal on account of the office not having any Charter or Act of Parliament, and that many persons are deterred from insuring on that account'. Sometimes, following legal counsel, companies who lacked charters preferred to call themselves 'societies' and refer to their capital as 'subscription capital', indicating a nervousness about the bubble connotations of joint-stock companies.[18]

One response to this legal uncertainty was the attempt to restrict partners' liability for the debts of their firm to the value of each partner's investment. Such a restriction had no legal foundation under the statute of 1720, but this did not prevent most unincorporated partnerships from writing it into their constitutions. In order to underpin this indemnity, most insurance offices also specified in their deeds the ceilings to be placed on dividends and the type of investments which could be purchased, rules which aimed to provide some security to shareholders. By the 1800s company promoters were becoming more assertive in limiting the liability of their subscribers.

Company constitutions also aimed to protect trustees and to protect offices from defaulting trustees. Most new insurance offices selected four or five individuals, usually the wealthiest and most prominent subscribers, as trustees. In their names stock would be transferred, all actions brought against the company would be contested, and all contracts and engagements relating to the company, including investments, would be entered into. The deed of the Birmingham Fire Office stipulated that 'the Capital of the Company, and all the real and personal estate of the Company shall be held in the names of the Trustees'.[19] A clause also gave the directors power to call upon the trustees if the capital fell below £20000. Thus the personal wealth of the trustees was intended as the copper-bottomed security for the survival of the firm. It was logical therefore to include a further clause stating that, if any trustee's financial circumstances became suspect, he was obliged either to give a security or to sell his shares. If he had not done so within 60 days of a notice being given, he would forfeit those shares.[20]

Deeds usually limited the liability of both trustees and directors for any losses or debts incurred by the company to the amount of their shares or to the amount of their own personal debts.[21] Shareholders were also commonly indemnified beyond their share of the capital against all claims which might be made upon them by policyholders. Some insurance offices wrote such indemnities into every policy they issued.[22] The unincorporated gas companies which began to appear in numbers after 1810 also seem to have resorted to limiting the liability of investors to the amount they spent on shares.[23] The clauses restricting the liability of gas company shareholders were almost identical to those found in insurance, which suggests that by the early nineteenth century limited liability had become a convention in company deeds of settlement, and that such deeds were regarded as providing adequate legal protection for most purposes.

As well as banning limited liability without a charter, the Bubble Act was also supposed to have outlawed the issue of tradable shares by unincorporated partnerships. The deeds of most insurance offices, however, implicitly recognised that shares could be sold or assigned by proprietors. In some cases shares were explicitly declared transferable as the personal estate of their owners, and 'convertible into money by sale'.[24] Because of the widely accepted principle of share transferability, insurance shares became traded commodities, the demand for which usually outstripped the supply. When the West India Dock Company floated the Imperial Insurance Office in 1803, it issued £1.2m in shares of £500 each, with ten per cent paid up. Within a couple of months this huge issue was fully subscribed to and the directors of the new company discovered to their alarm that the Imperial's shares were being sold by 'public auction and otherwise', threatening the control of the proprietorship which most boards liked to retain. A warning was issued against 'all gaming and speculation in the shares of the Company's capital', and it was reiterated that no share could be sold without the board's consent. Similarly at the end of 1824 the directors of the Leeds & Yorkshire found that the market value of their shares had doubled within the first 12 months of business, and that the shares were being 'eagerly bought up' at a premium.[25] Such shares were all too tempting for some. In 1808 the Bedford agent of the County Fire Office was sacked for fraudulently selling 63 shares at a premium of ten shillings per share (five per cent) and absconding with the proceeds, £600 in total.[26]

Most new companies fixed the amount to be paid up on shares at a modest level - usually in the range from £10 to £100 - in order to attract the widest interest among the comfortable middle classes. The line between the respectable and less respectable shareholder was finely and quite deliberately drawn. This is evident from a comment made in 1838 by the Sun's deputy manager, John Richards, about the Newcastle & North of England Office, whose business the Sun eventually declined to buy. 'The sum paid was £2 per share', noted Richards in a letter to Charles Ford, 'so that you may imagine the description of persons the shareholders are composed of'.[27] Rather like the Whigs' extension of the parliamentary franchise in 1832 to include £10 householders, the aim of company promoters was to define an entry threshold which would attract sufficient investors, without opening up the proprietorship to any 'who might not safely and wisely be enfranchised'.[28] Some were particularly cautious. The founders of the North British Fire Office in 1809 explained in their first prospectus that the reason they had divided the company's capital into £200 and not £100 shares (with ten per cent paid up), was 'to prevent in so far as is practicable the admission of doubtful or improper names among the subscribers'.[29]

The maximum number of shares permitted to be held by an individual was often kept low, especially during the first year of business, in order to avoid a concentration of shares in too few hands. Where the share capital was modest, under

£50000, and was drawn from a small group of proprietors, the shares could become a goldmine for their owners. The 30 shares in the Salop Fire Office rose from their original par value of £50 in 1780 to reach £800 by 1800 and £1400 by 1820.[30] This was largely due to the tight control exercised by the board over access to shares, a solid underwriting performance, a steady accumulation of capital based on careful investments in gilts and mortgages, and the ploughing back of almost all profits during the company's first 20 years. The shares became so valuable that on occasions they were subdivided for the purposes of raising money, although there was no provision in the deed for doing this. Thus a share owned by one of the original co-partners, Thomas Eyton, a banker from Wellington, was assigned in 1783 to a Shrewsbury tanner, Nathaniel Betton, for £70. This was then sold by Betton's widow in 1804 for £1000 to Joshua Peele, a Shrewsbury wine merchant. Peele, in turn, sold half his interest in the share to a Shrewsbury architect, John Hiram Haycock, and the other half to a local surgeon, Edward Humphreys. Haycock bought the second half of Peele's share from Humphreys for £525 in 1808, thus reuniting Eyton's original share. It would appear that these were purely private arrangements, for they were not separately listed in the Salop's share transfer and assignment registers. Nevertheless, it seems that the Salop board allowed such subdivision and private transfer of shares where it approved of the individuals involved. Salop shares were also occasionally used in part payment of a debt, such as in 1816 when Lord Berwick sold Thomas Pemberton of Milnthorpe Park a share for £385. The agreed price was £1200, but Berwick owed Pemberton £800 from a loan dating back to 1808, which, together with the £15 interest accrued, was accounted for in the sale price.[31]

The rise in the value of shares in existing offices could help to entice investors to join new ventures. What went up, however, could also come down. Trebilcock has shown how the fluctuating value of Phoenix shares between 1783 and 1840 was closely related to the size and profitability of that company's overseas business.[32] During the 1820s insurance shares rose and fell with the rest of the market. In 1829, for instance, shares in the Leeds & Yorkshire were selling at 'much below their real value' despite the office's early success.[33] We have little evidence on the turnover of insurance shares. Phoenix shares were traded in every year except one during the period 1783-1840. There were 330 transfers of Kent Fire Office shares between 1805 and 1811, an average of 47 a year, which may be compared with an annual average of 30 shares traded each year in the Sun between 1803 and 1823. These figures are quite high relative to the number of shareholders in each office. The Sun had 224 shareholders in 1830 while the Kent had about two hundred proprietors. By contrast, the Salop, with 30 proprietors, recorded just 43 share transactions between 1780 and 1820.[34]

Almost none of this trade, nor the prices which resulted from it, ever appeared in the printed lists of stocks which served the main London market. Traces can only be found in the few surviving share transfer books of the insurance offices, or, still more rarely, in the private papers of individual proprietors. Such transactions were partially visible to some contemporaries, though few had a good overview of these markets. Eighteenth-century observers of the stock exchange, such as Thomas Mortimer and Adam Anderson, were aware that there were companies whose shares were seldom seen in Change Alley.[35] The few quotations for insurance shares in the printed share lists, however, did not signify inactivity and price stability. Share transactions in unincorporated insurance companies were becoming increasingly commonplace towards the end of the century, and this must also have been the case in other industries where joint-stock organisation predominated. The capitals of many of these companies, especially the non-metropolitan firms, may have been small relative to the size of government issues, but cumulatively the activity in their shares was more significant than historians, with their gaze fixed upon the published price lists, have allowed.[36] As well as the growing number of canal incorporations, unincorporated companies in insurance, utilities and other sectors of the economy multiplied. It was estimated in chapter one that £1.5m had been paid up on the shares of fire insurance offices alone by 1800, rising to £10.6m by 1850. By 1800 some £9m had been raised on canals and rivers, while a further £4m had been invested in the gas industry by 1826.[37]

Share ownership and the active proprietor

A *de facto* legitimacy and the functional operation of limited liability and share transferability were the factors which enabled shareholding in unincorporated partnerships to expand from the mid eighteenth century. The central principle underlying transferable shares was strict boardroom control over entry to the proprietorship. It was common practice for directors to retain a veto over transfers, assignments or sales of shares in the company. This included determining who could own shares, operating a ceiling on the number of shares which could be held by any individual, making the votes of shareholders proportionate to the number of shares held, monitoring the liquidity of shareholders, and charging fees for share dealings. Some offices were meticulous in monitoring the process by which the deed of settlement was signed by shareholders. All signatures had to be witnessed by someone who was not a shareholder. Illegible signatures were rejected. Trustees and assignees, who received shares belonging to a bankrupt or deceased shareholder, were required to sign a deed of covenant declaring that they held the shares on the same terms as other shareholders, thus binding them to the constitution of the office. Dividend payments were held back until this condition was fulfilled. Whilst some executors did sign deeds without first signing a covenant, this was not considered 'strictly proper'. As it was explained to one Leeds & Yorkshire agent, as long as the shares were not fully paid up, and as long as the office remained unincorporated by act of Parliament,

> which Act could not be obtained without the whole of the shares being paid up, which it would be manifest impolitic (sic) to require - so long these formalities must be attended to.[38]

Many offices exercised strict control over the acquisition of shares by females and minors. The Salop did not allow them to become directors or vote in any ballot to elect board members. Women and minors inheriting shares were required to appoint an attorney or a deputy to act in their stead, which deputy had to be approved by a general meeting of the proprietors.[39] The Leeds & Yorkshire initially permitted each female shareholder to hold up to five shares during its first year of business (ten for men), but it soon decided that women proprietors were not wanted. When a Miss Piercy from Hull applied for two shares, her application was rejected by the board who declared that 'they are generally unwilling to admit female shareholders deeming them but unprofitable partners in business'. Presumably women did not come under the board's definition of 'individuals of influence...in good towns such as Hull' to whom it gave priority in the distribution of shares.[40] In an overwhelmingly male-dominated business world, and in the face of a rapidly shrinking 'public' sphere for middle-class females, it was assumed that women, even if in business for themselves, could bring little in the way of extensive insurances through colleagues and friends without a male intercessor. The Salamander's deed stated that male and female legatees could administer shares, but the latter could not buy them. The constitution of the Manchester office required that female shareholders give the company notice of marriage, and, upon producing the marriage certificate, their husband's name and address would be entered into the share register book in the same way as the names of the executors or assignees of deceased or bankrupt proprietors were recorded. The marriage certificate thus equated to a letter of administration and pronounced the legal death of the woman concerned.[41]

Unsurprisingly, given the legal fragility of their declarations of limited liability, boards of insurance companies endeavoured to monitor the personal liquidity of shareholders as closely as possible. The Birmingham Fire Office made each proprietor sign a declaration that they were *bona fide* worth the value of their shares before any were transferred to them. The Salop's constitution of 1780 allowed that if any partner was suspected of being 'reduced in his or her circumstances', then a general meeting could demand a security from him, to be approved of by the majority of partners. Failing this, he would have to sell or assign his share within 60 days.[42] Another form of control was to make share transfers expensive. Anyone coming into possession of Salop shares had to pay a ten shillings 'enrollment fee'. The Birmingham office charged a fee to the person selling the shares, 'not exceeding ten shillings per cent on the amount of shares so transferred', and a 'further fee of ten shillings, in addition to the stamp duty' for the 'deed of assignment' which was charged to the purchaser. The Salamander charged a share transfer fee of one guinea.[43]

Several offices attempted to manipulate the distribution of shares in order to create the kind of proprietorship which the promoters envisaged. The Phoenix did not permit share transfers to take place until the board had decided whether or not shares might be passed on to individuals who were not London sugar refiners. The Atlas reserved 10000 shares - one quarter of the total issued - 'as an inducement for persons residing in the country to unite in this undertaking...'. The object was to create a national office to rival the other great London insurers operating on a nationwide basis. Similarly the Guardian resolved in 1821 that nobody resident within a ten mile radius of London was to be permitted to hold shares without being recommended by five directors in writing - and no more than five shares each were to be given to residents of London. This had the desired effect. By 1823, of the 20000 shares issued, over half were placed outside London. The Guardian's prescription even extended to regulating the number of shares sold by individual agencies.[44]

Many offices, either deliberately or as the result of an incomplete share issue, retained a number of unsold shares which were at the disposal of the board. This provided directors with another means of influencing the composition of the proprietorship, and, if share values were rising, of exploiting the demand. During take over negotiations in Bath in 1838, Charles Ford proposed that a handful of the Sun's shares be offered, at a price of £200 per share, to any 'influential' proprietors of the Bath Sun Fire Office who might wish to invest in the London office, subject to the takeover going ahead. Although the price does not seem to have been discounted, this was still an attractive offer for the Sun's shares rarely came on the open market.[45] The Alliance also deployed its shares to entice those who might bring a large number of insurances to the office. In 1825, for example, it offered the builder of Kemptown, near Brighton, 50 shares at par if he agreed to insure his new properties there with the company. The Alliance's constitution stipulated that five per cent of annual net profits were to be retained to buy or redeem shares, provided they could be bought at, or below, a certain price. In this way the board retained a pool of shares under its control, over and above those owned by individual directors.[46]

Some offices reserved blocs of shares for different agencies, which contributed to a shortfall in supply in some places and to a rising price. Shares increasing in value were regarded as a means of acquiring business - but sometimes there existed a tension between this aim and the desire of existing proprietors and directors to maximise their holdings in order to profit from the rising values. The board of the Leeds & Yorkshire, for instance, allocated 100 shares to Glasgow, but it also told the chairman of its shareholders' committee there not to offer a single share,

> to any but willing purchasers, and they such as have themselves good insurances to offer in the fire or life department, and likewise possess sufficient influence by their station in life, to promote the interests of the Company in your town and district.

The Glasgow agent was informed that many of the directors had recently increased their holdings by buying additional shares at a premium of 30s per share, and that 'the price would be higher were so many shares not kept in reserve for distant towns'.

They (the shares) were offered solely in the hope of creating a considerable interest for the Company and by that means facilitating the acquisition of business....If you think the business can be obtained without any assistance from shareholders, it would be much more agreeable to the Directors not to part with a single share.[47]

To others who sought shares, the directors pointed out that they were doing a favour by selling the shares at original cost, and that 'some exertion' by the shareholder on behalf of the office would be expected in return. By February 1825 Leeds & Yorkshire shares had reached £10 per share, double their original value. At this point the board resolved to cease selling shares at par, and to take advantage of the market premium. The list of 'shareholders at original cost' was then closed for good.[48]

Other offices exercised more caution. When in 1803 the directors of the Kent Fire Office discovered that some 27 shares remained unsold, they decided that first option be given to existing proprietors holding shares not proportionate to the amount they insured. Control preceded any temptation to sell shares on the open market. The deed of the MFLAC limited to 100 the number of shares which could be held by the board, in forfeiture or unsold, at any one time, explicitly to prevent speculation by directors in the company's shares. The deed of the County permitted its directors to issue up to 250 shares above the original issue of 35000, and to 'extinguish' shares from time to time, but they were not permitted to extinguish more shares than existed above the original capital sum.[49] In 1810 the office decided to write down 'the reasons which govern the Court of Directors in authorizing the transfer of shares...'. The statement agreed upon was one of the most explicit produced by any insurance company on the subject of controlling entry to a proprietorship.

That it appears...(the) present success of the County Fire office is due to original measures to produce a copartnery of the leading persons throughout the associated counties and to diffuse the shares extensively and in equal proportions among those counties. That to perpetuate this success three principles have to be borne in mind when admitting new partners by transfer, viz. (1) It is expedient that no transfer from the present proprietors to others of less rank or influence should take place for more than one share. (2) It is expedient to prevent as much as possible the shares converging into a less number of holders than they are in at present. (3) It is expedient to prevent the transfer of shares from one county or district to another, excepting in such particular cases as it shall appear that in a general view the proper quota is preserved. [50]

Although aspects of this were peculiar to the County, in particular the quota system of allocating shares across the office's 12 'associated counties', the general principles were common to most unincorporated joint-stock partnerships. Transfers were to be carefully scrutinised by the board, with the objectives of preventing any dilution of the status, 'social respectability', and, implicitly, the liquidity of the proprietorship, and of preventing any concentration of shares. Both objectives had sound financial risk spreading motives underpinning them. What all boards of insurance offices also sought, however, was the right kind of shareholder, one whose wealth and influence would be exercised for the benefit of the company.

Central here was the ideal of the active proprietor. Many new companies aimed to create a critical mass of business by requiring shareholders to take out a policy, often for a sum fixed in proportion to the number of shares held. In this way stock companies tapped the same source of business which mutual offices enjoyed, where all members were policyholders and *vice versa*. Fines, sometimes deducted directly from dividend payments, could be levied to enforce this regulation. The Bristol Union imposed an obligation on each proprietor to insure a property or a life to the nominal amount of his or her shares, 'or be annually debited with two shillings for each share held by him or her so long as such proprietor shall not make an insurance to that amount'.[51] Other offices had variants of this requirement, but the object was the same, to create a proprietorship which had a vested interest in the underwriting performance of the office, not just in the level of dividends being paid each year.

Some offices refused to countenance obligatory insurance. Their promoters' expectations, however, remained the same. The Leeds & Yorkshire board anticipated that shareholders would insure with their office, and complained bitterly when they did not. In 1825 the company secretary told the agent at Halifax:

> It is but a sorry return we have from your principal shareholders in Halifax after granting so large a proportion of our shares to them. It would have been an easy matter to introduce a compulsory clause respecting insurance as the Manchester has done, but we consider such a step as degrading to the company. If, however, the shareholders in your district, whom you know to have insurances to give, do not come forward to support us as they ought to do, I shall request you to give me their names and address that I may bring their conduct before the Directors.[52]

This was the language of schoolmasterly reproof and moral rectitude. Compulsion was 'degrading' to the office, but the shareholders ought to have felt morally obliged to support their own institution. Continuing complaints about the lack of business received from shareholders led to the dismissal of agents in Sheffield and Doncaster, further admonitions for the agent in Halifax, and a flurry of circulars sent directly to proprietors in Bradford, Wakefield, Dewsbury, Pontefract and Barnsley reminding them of the expectations of the office. The function of such circulars was explained to the Barnsley agent.

> To those who have already given insurance to the office it may bring to mind other property requiring insurance - To those who have hitherto done no business with us it will I hope have the effect of reminding them that some exertion on their part is expected by the Directors and that their shares were granted under the implied condition that they would support and recommend the Institution as much as lay in their power.[53]

This was a clear statement that shareholding was a 'privilege', 'granted' in return for some reciprocal service - the use of influence to extend the company's business, or the giving up of one's time to sit as a member of the local committee of shareholders. Moral pressure was sometimes supplemented by more practical methods of awakening proprietors to their duties. Non-insuring shareholders, for instance, were forced to pay for the postage of the circulars sent to them. Another device used to 'punish' recalcitrant shareholders was to refuse to send the deed of settlement to their locality for signing. When a Leeds & Yorkshire shareholder in Skipton complained, anonymously, that the deed was not being sent there for signing, the company secretary retorted by referring to the 'disinterest' in the affairs of the office which had been shown by all but one shareholder in Skipton. 'I think the directors will scarcely deem it necessary to accommodate those who from some cause or other give their insurance business to other offices.' Similarly it was thought unnecessary to send the deed to York, 'where the shareholders have done no one single act for the advantage of the Company in any way'. The directors perceived their new venture as 'a cause in which we are embarked', and they expected all proprietors to be fully on board.[54]

In the light of this attitude in the boardroom, the proportion of Leeds & Yorkshire shareholders who insured with their own office may give some indication of the level of their 'active' commitment. By the summer of 1825 this ranged from 60 out of 110 shareholders in Halifax to 26 out of 30 shareholders in Dewsbury. Thus, while in most places there were some non-insuring shareholders, generally the majority - between 50 and 90 per cent - did insure with the office in which they invested.[55] How representative in this respect the Leeds office was of other provincial offices, that did not have compulsory insurance, is impossible to say.

Another manifestation of the concept of the active proprietor was the increasing use of local committees. Several offices used committees of shareholders to extend business. These represented local concentrations of expertise and commercial contacts on which companies could anchor their promotional efforts. The Norwich Union had established nearly 50 shareholders' committees by 1817, the Guardian had 19 by 1823 and the MFLAC had nine by the early 1830s.[56] By contrast, the older London offices continued to rely on their long-established agency networks. The principal tasks allotted to shareholders' committees were to recruit agents, to superintend agency business, including the operation of fire brigades, to appoint medical referees for life insurance proposals, to help the agent assess properties proposed for insurance and vet the proposers, to advise on limits to risks, to adjust losses, and to provide intelligence on the local market. They were usually regarded as executive extensions of the board of directors and were sometimes given considerable autonomy. In 1826, for instance, the Guardian's committee in Brighton was charged with the task of negotiating the takeover of the local fire office.[57]

Shareholder rights

In all joint-stock insurance offices the power of the proprietors was enshrined in the company's constitution. Shareholders' rights commonly included the power to elect and sack directors, to determine the level of remuneration for the leading officers of the firm, to declare dividends, to inspect the books, to amend the constitution and, ultimately, to terminate the partnership. The deed of the Bristol Union provided for the minutes of all meetings of both directors and proprietors to be 'open to the inspection of any proprietor at all seasonable times'. The Salamander's deed permitted proprietors who were not directors to attend board meetings and 'take part in any proceedings', although they were not eligible to vote at such meetings.[58] The MFLAC's deed entitled 30 or more proprietors to nominate someone to assist in the calculation of the bonuses on life assurance policies. The board was also empowered to nominate someone and the two nominees would together select a third person to assist in the calculations. The aim was to ensure transparency in an area which might, and indeed did, lead to conflict between directors and shareholders. It was also in keeping with the 'liberal principles and equitable policies of the management', trumpeted by the company chairman at the first annual general meeting. In the same spirit, provision was made for policyholders who were not proprietors to inspect the accounts and to nominate someone to assist the actuary in calculating bonuses. 'Thus the assured have a certain method of ascertaining and enforcing their rights'. The contrast was drawn with other offices where no such provision existed.[59]

The chief vehicle for shareholder power was the general meeting. At these meetings proprietors had the opportunity to question management decisions as well as the performance of the office. Between 1819 and 1824 the County's directors were quizzed about investment policy, underwriting losses, the annual accounts, salary costs and the wisdom of insuring property in London.[60] The most important power possessed by shareholders was the ability to change the constitution of their office. The conditions surrounding the exercise of this power, however, were often restrictive. Constitutions normally could only be altered by two successive quorate shareholders' meetings. The Bristol Union required 30 proprietors to approve alterations to its deed. Special general meetings could be called by a group holding at least 100 shares of the 2500 issued. Two-thirds of proprietors at two successive meetings was enough for a vote to dissolve the Bristol company, provided the meetings were announced in the local newspapers and by general circular.[61] Any number of MFLAC proprietors, each holding at least five shares for six months or longer, with an aggregate of 480 of the 20000 shares issued, could call an 'extraordinary general court'. A general court was quorate with 48 shareholders. Two successive courts could amend any regulation, except to pass any ruling which limited the individual liability of a shareholder. The voting at the MFLAC's meetings was, as in most offices, weighted by the number of shares each individual held. Thus five shares or less bought one vote, up to 29 shares bought two votes, and 30 or more shares bought three.[62]

Other offices had more stringent requirements. The Salop required the signatures of ten partners out of 30 for an extraordinary general meeting to be called. Each partner was permitted to hold one share only, so there was no weighted voting system. The Salamander required a minimum of 20 shareholders out of 110 to call a meeting. Each was allowed one vote, with no votes for minors or for female shareholders. The votes of four-fifths of those attending were needed to dissolve the company and these had to represent over half the proprietorship. The Birmingham Fire Office required the votes of three-fourths of its subscribers to alter the constitution or rescind any appointments. For a general meeting to be quorate, at least 25 had to be present, each of whom had to own at least £1000 of the company's £300000 capital stock. Proprietors wishing to amend the rules had to get at least five others to sign their proposal and to give the directors ten days notice.[63]

The power of the general meeting, therefore, was circumscribed in several ways. As the legal bedrock of an unincorporated company, it is hardly surprising that company founders endeavoured to make their deeds of settlement as legally watertight and as difficult to change as possible. At the outset of a share issue, promoters never knew quite what kind of proprietorship they would get, and there were always the Crown law officers to worry about, as well as the hostile view in some circles that all unchartered stock companies were bubbles. As many offices discovered, however, the solidity and rigidity of their constitutions had costs, especially when they wished to expand from fire into life or marine insurance, or when they wanted to diversify their investments into annuities or mortgage lending.

It was at times of crisis brought about by heavy losses and falling dividends, financial mismanagement, or the discovery of fraud, that relations between directors and shareholders were most likely to break down and proprietorial power was most likely to be tested. The Kent Fire Office, for example, was burdened by internal conflict for more than a decade after its foundation in 1802.[64] There was a concerted attempt by a 'cabal' of auditors, who were also directors, to undermine the position of the company secretary, Thomas Lediard, and to take over complete control of the office, even to the extent of dispensing with the annual meeting of proprietors. Lediard himself was accused of receiving hundreds of pounds for which no satisfactory account had been given and he was forced to resign. In 1814 a proprietors' committee was finally set up to examine the accounts. I ts r eport recommended granting executive authority to the general meeting, with the power to overturn resolutions of the board. At this point the directors stood their ground. They rejected the proprietors' recommendations, but agreed to put the relationship between the secretary and the board on the same footing as in other insurance offices, and to present a standardised and more detailed set of annual accounts to the general meeting. With these reforms, and a new company secretary, the shareholders appeared mollified and the turbulence came to an end.

The central dispute in the Kent office was about the right of shareholders to have an overview of the company's affairs, to monitor the management and to scrutinise the accounts. Similar issues arose in other offices during the early nineteenth century. In the Atlas disquiet about rising losses in Ireland, high costs and the suspension of dividends led to protests from shareholders in London, Cork and Macclesfield in 1816.[65] Concern was also expressed about the bonus policy scheme which the board intended to adopt as a remedy for its troubled fire insurance business. A meeting to question the board's decision was called by a London shareholder, but attendance was poor and nothing came of it. The Atlas board survived and bonus policies proved successful. The board's tactic had been to address the discontented as individuals, rather than treat them as representative of any large body of proprietorial opinion. This tactic may have been helped by the size of the proprietorship. Some 1100 Atlas shareholders were scattered across the British Isles, and they were clearly more difficult to organize into an effective lobby than, for example, the 200 shareholders of the Kent Fire office, who were mostly resident within the county. The proprietors of other large insurance offices, such as the MFLAC which had over 1000 shareholders, faced similar difficulties. Many shareholders did attempt to take an active part in the business of their companies, to an extent reciprocating the expectations of promoters and directors. At critical times in the history of several firms, shareholders took matters into their own hands, calling extraordinary general meetings and establishing their own investigative committees. On the whole, however, for all their constitutional powers, proprietors were generally out-manoeuvred by executive officers. Ultimately the key to shareholders' rights was transparency and access to information. For the most part, decisions were taken behind closed doors, usually by the company secretary and a small inner group of directors. Some offices, such as the Phoenix, even held a series of 'private' directors' meetings, with their minutes written up roughly in a set of books which were locked and kept parallel to the 'public', and more formal, meetings of the board. The development of more elaborate committee structures within the large firms, with strategic as well as technical issues being devolved to sub-groups of directors, also contributed to the opacity of decision making, to the disadvantage of both contemporary shareholders and business historians.

Officers

The typical responsibilities of directors in most insurance offices were neatly summarised by the promoters of the Bristol Union in 1819. They were to manage the finances and 'pecuniary transactions' of the office, to appoint and dismiss the secretary and 'all inferior servants', to require security from them and grant allowances as they think fit, to rent premises for the business, to sign policies, cheques, annuity and share certificates, to decide the terms and rates of insurances and annuities, to accept or reject proposals for insurance, to approve or reject applications for shares, to make calls on the subscription capital, to enforce payments of share instalments, to declare shares forfeit and to sell them when appropriate.[66]

To help directors carry out these tasks, all offices appointed a secretary, the chief officer, whose tasks were to supervise the daily work of the clerical and other waged staff, to oversee the provincial agents, to check their remittances were accurate and up to date, to consider proposals for insurance and make recommendations to the board, to communicate with agents regarding losses on insurances sold through their agencies, and to arrange for the adjustment of losses and the inspection of property proposed for insurance. The secretary was also usually the first line of communication with shareholders and policyholders. Thus most of the daily operations of the company were devolved upon his office.

All secretaries were answerable to their board of directors, and an important part of their duties was to attend upon and report to the several sub-committees of the board. Some were trusted with considerable autonomy, but most continued to work within a clear line of command. This was especially true in the oldest and largest offices. Charles Ford is a good example. Ford joined the Sun as secretary in 1814 and went on to become the leading insurance figure of his era. Yet for most of his career he was entirely subordinate to the directors who appointed him. During the 1820s he turned the Sun's fortunes around by leading the price war which helped stem the inflow of new entrants to the market. He negotiated 17 successful takeovers of other offices which reversed the downward trend in the Sun's market share. In 1836 he took the Sun abroad for the first time in its 130 year history, and in the 1840s he was at the forefront of efforts to construct tariff agreements across a range of markets. The frequent generous bonuses awarded to him marked the high regard in which the Sun held his managerial skills. It was only gradually, however, that this most elevated of company servants became accepted as a near equal by the members of the board to whom he reported. After more than 30 years in post, and following a reorganisation of the office, Ford was appointed 'deputy chairman and secretary' in 1846. The purpose of this was to relieve Ford, who by then was over 60 years old, from the 'too great pressure of hourly and constant business'. His duties were confined to the general direction of the business, taking decisions on special risks, and communicating with other offices. Ford retired on a pension of £1000 in 1856 and he died four years later.[67] Over the course of his career Ford transformed the post of Sun secretary, the servant of the board, into a role more akin to that of the modern managing director, but the line of accountability - agents and office staff to the secretary, secretary to the directors, and, in theory, directors to shareholders - still remained intact.

When that line was threatened or broken, boards of directors were usually quick to reassert their authority. Most directors expected, as a minimum, appropriate and 'respectful', if not deferent, behaviour on the part of company officers. They did not always get it. John Chalk, *pro tempore* secretary to the Atlas, was not amused at being replaced in June 1808 by a new appointment, Henry Desborough, after having worked for six months with the promoters of the new office. Chalk declared to the board that he would keep the books and vouchers belonging to the Company 'until he shall have been satisfied for his services'. In an interview with the board, with Desborough present, Chalk, under the influence of disappointment in not having succeeded to the Secretaryship, conducted himself with much intemperance manifesting a want of respect to the Board and a disregard for his own character as a gentleman.

Notwithstanding this, a compromise was reached. Chalk was paid a guinea a day for his services from his first day of work to the day of Desborough's appointment, plus one guinea for each occasion his room and the assistance of his servants were used by the Atlas. The result was that Chalk received £427, a handsome sum for half a year's work.[68]

A new secretary sweeping into an office could also upset directors. When Herbert Spring took over as secretary to the MFLAC in 1844, he instigated a series of changes to the accounting system and office organisation, and drew the reins of control tightly into his hands. One consequence was a more perfunctory relationship between the secretary and the board, a change which led to the resignation of one director from the MFLAC's managing committee in 1845.[69] Such clashes were not uncommon where the line between the social rank of directors and the principal officer was thinly drawn, or where the secretary was also a promoter and founding shareholder. Some individuals so dominated their companies that they achieved, or claimed to achieve, preferential proprietorial rights over the institution. One prominent example was Thomas Bignold, the wine and spirits dealer who founded the Norwich Union in 1797. Bignold held an unusually powerful position for a secretary of an insurance office. Extraordinarily he was not paid a fixed salary but instead received ten per cent of annual premiums. By 1815 he was earning £5000 a year, plus a similar sum from the Norwich Union's sister life office founded by him in 1808. This was far more than his counterparts in even the largest London offices were receiving at the time. In recognition of his role as founder, it was written into the society's constitution that he could only be dismissed by a majority vote at a general meeting of members. Thus when he fell out with his fellow directors in 1805 over his plans for expansion, Bignold succeeded in defeating his opponents by winning a vote of confidence at a general meeting. The old board was dismissed, a new board full of Bignold's supporters was elected, and the society's constitution was amended to cement his position as managing director still further. When, in the wake of rising losses, declining bonuses and delays in the payment of claims, members finally rebelled in 1818, Bignold refused to resign. He was eventually dismissed, but he continued to cling on to the apprehension that he was the Norwich Union, and used his premises to carry on selling insurance under that name. The experience of the Norwich Union demonstrates how difficult it could be for a company to loosen the grip of a founder after years of autocratic control.

A similar, less painful, example was Bignold's great rival at the County, John Thomas Barber Beaumont. Like Bignold, Barber Beaumont was widely recognised as the principal promoter of his office. His position as managing director, with the same 'privileges as the directors', was written into the County's constitution. This also stipulated that the managing director could appoint further staff as necessary, and it gave him the power to set salaries. He could only be sacked by two successive general meetings of proprietors held at least three months apart.[70] With the same boundless energy he applied to all his diverse interests, Barber Beaumont immersed himself in the daily affairs of the company - corresponding with agents, policyholders and other offices, attending the county meetings of proprietors, scrutinising proposals for insurance, fixing rates, monitoring the accounts, appointing and supervising the clerical and ancillary staff. In 1823, to acknowledge his achievements, a joint court of the directors of the County and its sister office, the Provident Life, ordered a portrait and a marble bust to decorate each office.[71] The inscription on the base of the bust was to describe him as the 'Projector and Founder' of both offices. One of the original trustees, however, Sir Scrope Bernard, banker, MP for St Mawes, objected to the inscription and proposed instead the phrase 'active promoter'. Barber Beaumont was indignant. He declared that none of the trustees 'had furnished a single idea upon the subject, nor had he any conversation with them on it previous to the publication of the Prospectus'. The joint court then adjourned to reconsider its resolution. When it reconvened some days later, Barber Beaumont emerged triumphant. Bernard's objections were overruled, and his proposed inscription was erased from the minutes of the meeting and replaced with the original phrase.

Unlike other managing directors of an autocratic disposition, Barber Beaumont always succeeded in carrying his directors and shareholders with him, and so in the County the principal agent problem was never tested. Elsewhere other managers could delude themselves into blurring proprietorial boundaries. A good example is Thomas Camplin, the managing director of the Bristol Crown, who in 1829 was approached by the Sun's representative, Eden Harwood, with a view to buying the office. Camplin was keen to effect a sale, as he held out for himself the prospect of a considerable gain. Harwood reported to his superiors that Camplin claimed to have the entire management of the Bristol Crown and to be able to carry out a dissolution of the office 'at his pleasure...He said as much in strictest confidence...'. Camplin's father had been the managing director of the office 'for many years' before him, and the premises used by the Bristol Crown belonged to him, so that 'he appears to consider it quite his own concern'. Harwood suggested that the Sun might be able to buy the Bristol office for a sum equivalent to one year's premiums, but it would not be able to keep the business together 'unless we also bought Mr Camplin who places a very high value upon his influence and services'.[72] This particular approach by Sun came to nothing. Two further attempts were made to buy the Bristol Crown, in 1833 and, finally with success, in 1837. On each occasion the Sun's negotiators distanced themselves from Camplin as it became clear that he was playing several potential bidders off against each other with a view to maximising his own personal gain. In the end Charles Ford bluntly told Camplin to his face that 'his influence was not so great as he seemed to think it', and that Camplin's demand for a sum of £500 in return for delivering up the office to the Sun 'was a thing out of the question'. The Sun eventually won enough support among the other directors and shareholders of the Bristol Crown for its tender to be accepted without further resort to Camplin. The latter continued to make trouble after the takeover, threatening to sell off lists of Bristol Crown policyholders to the highest bidder and to open up a rival office. Neither of these threats materialised, but in his delusion of proprietorial rights Camplin had lost all sense of accountability and obligation to his fellow directors and the Bristol Crown shareholders.

These examples indicate that there were real principal agent problems in some insurance offices by the early nineteenth century, with secretaries such as Camplin and promoter-managers such as Bignold overtly claiming proprietorial rights over their firms. Even those company secretaries who laboured under no such delusions, such as Charles Ford and Jenkin Jones, came as close to the position of the modern chief executive officer as any manager to be found in British business before 1850. It is hard to estimate the scale of the principal agent problem as it related to managers, directors and shareholders in the insurance industry. The shock expressed by the Sun's officials at the brash claims of Thomas Camplin suggests that it was not, in fact, commonly encountered. On the whole this study of the role of insurance company managers reinforces the conclusion that effective power lay with boardrooms throughout this period.

Founders, directors and their networks

Many insurance company boards were powerful because their members were drawn from close-knit networks of business elites which dominated the life of the districts where their offices were based. Economic networking - the regularisation of relations between individuals and groups within the marketplace - could alleviate the pernicious effects of mistrust and deliver efficiency gains through reductions in transaction costs, as commercial information, and sometimes also capital resources, were shared across a web of acquaintances. Non-economic forms of association - familial, social, religious, political and cultural - assisted networking, as did the transparency of urban middle-class public life in the late eighteenth and early nineteenth centuries. In towns, publicity, diffused by the gossip of the clubs and coffee houses and by the increasing number of provincial newspapers, helped to ensure a degree of moral behaviour, to underpin reputations and to engender trust. The public and civic aspects of middle-class behaviour also helped reduce the free rider problem created by the very networks of which they were a part. As Fukuyama has pointed out, 'a moral system was needed to supply the personal loyalties necessary to the development of firms outside the family...'. This 'moral system', and the social solidarity which necessarily accompanied it, allowed the 'radius of trust' to expand, while at the same time minimising the likelihood that a network member would 'fail to contribute his or her share to the common effort'.[73]

The pooling of knowledge and capital was an essential precondition of the spreading of risk when a number of associates resolved to diversify collectively into new forms of business activity. My earlier study of the directors of the insurance office founded in Manchester in 1824 suggested that networking underpinned collective diversification, and that this was a major vehicle by which textile merchants and manufacturers moved into other sectors of their local economies.[74] Similar processes were underway in Leeds, Liverpool, Bristol, London and Wiltshire from the late eighteenth century.[75] The following case study of the founders of the Newcastle Fire Office (hereafter NFO) will suffice here to reinforce these points.

The NFO was established in 1783 by 20 businessmen with a capital of £105000.[76] The group consisted of some of the region's leading industrialists and bankers. James Liddell, William Ord and Charles Brandling were members of three of the families which made up the 'Grand Alliance' in the Tyneside coal industry, while Sir Thomas Clavering, Sir Matthew White Ridley and John Simpson were descendants of colliery owning families which had been rivals to the Grand Allies earlier in the century. The great coal magnates were also substantial landowners. The Ridleys owned 30000 acres in Northumberland as well as several hundred acres of urban property in Newcastle, Elswick and Heaton. The Liddells became the Lords Ravensworth, and like other coalowners, diverted themselves by building Gothic castles on their estates.[77]

All three Newcastle banks were represented on the board. The partners of the Tyne Bank (founded in 1777) and the Exchange Bank (1768) were corporate shareholders in the NFO, while Ridley, who was an individual NFO shareholder, became a full partner in the Old Bank in 1791.[78] Two other NFO proprietors, William Surtees and Rowland Burdon junior, were sons of the founding partners of the Exchange Bank. This web of mining, banking and landed interests continued into the nineteenth century, partly because NFO shares were passed down within families. Sir Matthew White Ridley's son - who inherited both his father's name and title - succeeded him as a shareholder in the insurance office and the Old Bank upon Ridley's death in 1813. The nephew and heir of Sir Thomas Clavering, Thomas John Clavering, inherited his uncle's baronetcy as well as his NFO share when the seventh baronet died in 1794. NFO proprietors in 1831 included Ridley and Clavering, as well as bankers such as Thomas Gibson and Isaac Cookson, a partner and former partner respectively with Ridley in the Old Bank, and Thomas Fenwick, a partner in another Newcastle bank, Davison-Bland & Co, founded in 1788. The proprietors of 1831 also included several coal, glass and iron manufacturers such as Thomas Cookson, William Clark, and William Cuthbert of Benwell.[79]

As elsewhere, the Newcastle insurers were amongst the wealthiest men in their region, but the connection with land was stronger here than among the mercantile-manufacturing networks of Manchester, Liverpool and Leeds. William Surtees, for example, left his grandson and heir enough to purchase the estate of Dinsdale on the bank of the Tees, the early home of his ancestors, for £42000 in the early 1830s.[80] Several NFO proprietors were involved in politics and local government. The Ridley family represented Newcastle in parliament for the Whig interest continuously between 1747 and 1836, while the Brandlings established a similar monopoly over the town's second seat between 1784 and 1812. In the latter year another NFO proprietor, Cuthbert Ellison, took over Brandling's seat, probably with the support of the family. Sir Thomas Clavering of Axwell Park was returned four times for county Durham between 1768 and 1784, and William Ord, brother of the secretary to the Lord Lieutenant of Ireland, chaired meetings of Newcastle burgesses in the early 1780s in the Association movement's reform campaign.[81] Sir Matthew White Ridley was mayor of Newcastle in the year the fire office was established, and during the 1780s NFO proprietors usually occupied about half a dozen places among the town's common councilmen and electors, while the solicitor to the insurance office, Nathaniel Clayton, was also town clerk.[82]

The insurers were also prominent in other public positions. For example, nine NFO proprietors, almost half the office, were members of the committee for Newcastle Infirmary in 1783-4.[83] As elsewhere, interlocking business and political interests could facilitate the flow of credit and increase the velocity of infrastructural investment. Numerous small loans of a few hundred pounds each were made by the banks owned by NFO proprietors to turnpike trusts in the north-east between the 1770s and the 1810s. As in the west country, there were also connections between the local insurance office and county finances. In 1793 and again in 1811 Ridley's bank advanced three loans of £500 to the county of Northumberland, whose treasurer was Christopher Blackett, the long-serving secretary of the fire office. This was one insurer, in his role as banker, lending to another insurer, in his role as chief financial officer for the county.[84] The insurance men also helped shore up confidence in local banking institutions during the recurrent crises. Eight future NFO proprietors signed the declaration of support for the notes of the two Newcastle banks in 1772. In 1793 seven NFO proprietors were among those who announced their intention to give 'every possible support to public Credit, and to the Commercial Engagements of this part of the Country', by accepting the notes issued by the Newcastle banks and doing 'our utmost Endeavours to induce others to do the same'. Three insurers, Brandling, Ord and Clayton, sat on the liquidating committee for the failed bank of Surtees & Brandon in 1803, and five NFO names appear among the 25 signatures guaranteeing the debts of the Tyne bank in 1816.[85]

The proprietors of the insurance office also intervened in a more direct way to bolster local economic development. In 1797 the NFO purchased the company of Ralph Lodge and partners, which had possessed a lease to supply the town with water since 1769. No details of the purchase have survived, but Newcastle corporation had long been dissatisfied with the performance of Lodge's company, and the insurers, being well represented among the aldermen and common councilmen, were advantageously placed to take over as the monopoly supplier.[86] The NFO, together with the other insurance offices operating in Newcastle, were the sole providers of fire-fighting facilities in the town, and thus had a direct interest in maintaining a sufficient supply of water. Despite efforts in this direction elsewhere, no other insurance office in this period took over and operated a water company as a corporate concern.

Following the purchase, the insurers sought to augment the existing water supply. They bought a field to the east of the town moor, drove down a shaft to some abandoned colliery workings, and erected a windmill there to pump the water to a reservoir at the foot of the moor. The supply, however, was only enough to provide a few streets with water at certain times of the week. During the following decades the insurance office attempted to find additional sources of water, and on occasion it was driven to extract water from the Tyne by steam engine. Following criticism of the lack of water provision during the cholera epidemic of 1832, a new water company was established in Newcastle by the political opponents of the traditional elite represented by the NFO proprietors. After a few years of bitter competition between the two water companies, the NFO sold up to its rival in 1837.

The insurance office also established Newcastle's first gas works in 1817.[87] As with its water venture, the NFO initially enjoyed a monopoly in Newcastle but apparently failed to make the most of it. A second gasworks was built near NFO's engine house at the Manors in 1823 and by 1827 the company was supplying gas to the corporation for nearly 400 street lamps. Large areas of the town and suburbs, however, remained lit by oil lamps. There were frequent complaints about the price, quality and regularity of the gas supplied, and about the high-handedness of the company in dealing with its customers. A contemporary remarked caustically that,

> the proprietors of this concern are understood to be the same *gentlemen* that belong to the water works and the Newcastle Insurance firm, and are therefore incapable of taking advantage of a virtual monopoly, or of knowingly harassing the public with vexatious or unreasonable demands.[88]

The political opposition, led by the radical *Tyne Mercury* and its editor, Henry Mitchell, seized the opportunity and established a rival gas company in 1829, which raised a capital of £30000 from 245 proprietors. Within a year the new company had purchased the gasworks and plant of the insurance office.

By the early 1830s, therefore, the network, of which the NFO formed an important part, was being seriously challenged. The apogee came in 1835 when the same opposition group, which had torn the gas and water concerns away from the NFO, set up a rival insurance office, the 'New Newcastle and North of England Fire Insurance Company'. This proved less successful and it was sold to the Leeds & Yorkshire in 1838, while the NFO survived for another two decades as an independent company.

The insurance office in Newcastle, like those in Liverpool, Manchester, Leeds and Wiltshire, was positioned at the centre of a network dominated by an urban-based mercantile and manufacturing group, with varying degrees of involvement from landed and professional capital. In other fire insurance offices landed and professional capital was predominant and merchants and manufacturers played a lesser role. These included the 'county fire offices' established in towns such as Maidstone, Shrewsbury, Worcester and Colchester. These offices saw themselves primarily as providing a public service for their counties, rather than harbouring ambitions to expand into a national concern. They established close links to both borough and county administrations, and were patronised by the cream of county gentry and the occasional peer. Their active managers and proprietors were often tradesmen in the county town, together with clergy and professional people, especially attorneys, land agents and bankers. By contrast, the insurance offices in Manchester, Leeds, Liverpool, Birmingham and Wiltshire had roots in mercantile and manufacturing capital, and their proprietors and directors played out their public life largely in the urban arena. The local prominence of many investors in insurance offices facilitated their promotion as a public good, as well as a private gain. Although insurers generally represented those whom Cobbett disparaged as 'snugglers' in classic, unreformed and closed corporations, it is noticeable that evangelical, reforming and improving spirits could also be found among them.[89] Several insurance offices boasted a well-known social reformer in their midst. The Salop had its secretary Isaac Wood, enthusiastic promoter of Shrewsbury's House of Industry, the County had Barber Beaumont, the Globe had Sir Frederick Eden, and the MFLAC had Benjamin Braidley.

As Pressnell has observed, banking capital was important.[90] Each insurance enterprise had representatives of a 'family bank' or two amongst the original proprietors. For the Liverpool Fire Office of 1776 it was Heywood's, for the Salop it was Eyton's bank in Shrewsbury. The Newcastle office was supported by all three town banks, while the Kent office had several bankers among its directors, and bankers were prominent in the foundation of the East Anglian offices around the turn of the century.[91] The majority of the provincial directors of the County Fire Office were also bankers. Nevertheless, throughout this period only two early and short-lived insurance offices were direct offshoots of banks - the Manchester office of 1771, founded by Byrom, Sedgwick & Allen, and the Leeds office of 1777, founded by Beckett's. In most insurance offices banking capital played a supplementary role to the capital invested by merchants, manufacturers, tradesmen, gentry and professionals. The relationship of insurance to banking was therefore not that of a subordinate or peripheral financial service to its centre. Instead a new insurance venture was far more likely to arise out of manufacturing, mercantile or gentry capital than it was out of banking.

The analyses of proprietors and directors demonstrates that insurance was regarded as an important activity for collective diversification alongside other moves into transport, gas and water services and commercial property. This form of diversification gave a great impetus to the economic development of towns and regions during the classic period of the British industrial revolution. Economic historians have recognised the great range of business interests held by individual merchants in the eighteenth and early nineteenth centuries, but when they have turned to examining groups of businessmen, most of their work has been circumscribed by decisions to focus on a few criteria, rather than the whole array of economic, social, religious, political, cultural and familial linkages which made up a network.[92] The presence of networking is clearly indicated in the multiple associations of those who promoted and owned the insurance offices, but we are only beginning to explore the significance of this phenomenon to economic growth in industrialising Britain.[93]

Notes

[1] Tocqueville, *Democracy in America*, p.206.

[2] Daunton, *Progress and Poverty*, pp.238-40. The law of trusts was developing rapidly towards the end of the seventeenth century, and there were several judgements relating to the rights, duties and liabilities of trustees dating from the 1670s and 1680s. Holdsworth, *History of English Law*, vol.VI, p.642. For a recent survey of the development of company law before and after the Bubble Act, see Harris, *Industrializing English Law*.

[3] 'Without benefit of Parliament or Crown and in the face of denial of incorporation, company organization in the form of numerous partnerships grew especially in insurance, as well as here and there in manufacturing'. Hunt, *Development of the Business Corporation*, p.11. Dubois drew the same conclusion, Dubois, *The English Business Company after the Bubble Act*, p.39.

[4] The histories of the Sun, the Royal Exchange and the Phoenix provide analyses of shareholdings, of their founders' commercial and social backgrounds and interconnections, and of the offices' relationship to the state as tax collecting agencies. The role played by shareholders in these offices, however, appears to have been generally an 'acquiescent' one, cf. Dickson, *Sun Insurance*, pp.267, 292.

[5] Hadfield, *British Canals*, p.34; Wilson, *Lighting the Town*, p.68.

[6] SRO, Ms 3008/1/2/1, Salop, DM, 18 May 1780; Trebilcock, *Phoenix Assurance*, vol.I, pp.69-70. In the early stages of a new company's existence, such imitation could extend further. Thus the Salop also sought advice from the Bath about how to transfer shares; and both the Bath and Bristol offices were consulted in June 1782 about what steps they were taking with regard to the new stamp duty. A few months later the Salop adopted for its own prospectus a clause in the proposals of the Bristol Fire Office relating to the requirement to pay duty. SRO, Ms 3008/1/2/1, Salop, DM, 18 May 1780, 25 June, 28 Nov. 1782; Ms 3008/1/158, Salop, General Meeting Book, 12 Nov. 1782.

[7] Green, *History of Worcester*, vol.2. I am most grateful to Julia Lane for bringing this reference to my attention.

[8] *Reading Chronicle*, 3 July 1841.

[9] *Shrewsbury Chronicle*, 13 May 1780. Such networks are examined more closely below.

[10] *Shrewsbury Chronicle*, 24 June 1780; SRO, Ms 3008/1/2/1, Salop, DM, 26 Apr., 17 June 1780, 11 Jan. 1781.

[11] Peet, *Liverpool Vestry Books*, pp.264-5, entry for 17 Apr. 1781; CKS, U2593/B6/3, Kent, DM, 26 June 1805.

[12] Smith, *Wealth of Nations*, vol.II, p.758. Cf. also Anderson, *Origin of Commerce*, vol.1, p.lxiii.

13   Cf. the claim by the promoters of the Kent Insurance Company that Kentish people
      were less likely to trust London insurance offices, however respectable, than a local
      office. PRO, Chatham Papers, 30/8/277, fols.96-109, Prospectus of the Kent
      Insurance Company: Propositions made in 1 Jan. 1802.

14   Park, *Law of Marine Insurances*, p.441.

15   Raynes, *History of British Insurance*, pp.130-31, p.212; Dubois, *The English
      Business Company*, p.30; Trebilcock, *Phoenix Assurance*, vol.I, p.72; Hunt,
      Development of the Business Corporation, p.12.

16   Hunt, *Development of the Business Corporation*, p.23; Harris, *Industrializing English
      Law*, pp.236-41.

17   Hay has recently argued that judicial attitudes towards economic issues around 1800
      were considerably influenced by the preferences of individual attorney generals. Hay,
      'The State and the Market in 1800'. Harris adds other variables such as the lobbying
      of interest groups and contemporary concerns over blockages in the Court of
      Chancery. Harris, *Industrializing English Law*, pp.236-49.

18   County, Minutes of County Meetings, 31 July 1809; GL Ms 12160A/1, Imperial, DM,
      12 Jan. 1803.

19   Birmingham Fire Office, *Deed*, p.19. cf. also GL Ms 16170/1, Atlas, DM, Prospectus,
      6 Apr. 1808, clause IX.

20   *Aris's Birmingham Gazette*, 4 Feb. 1805.

21   Birmingham Fire Office, *Deed*, p.29. For other examples of such indemnities, see
      Trebilcock, *Phoenix Assurance*, vol.I, pp.75-6; GL Ms 16217, MFLAC, Deed of
      Settlement, 1 May 1824, clause 145.

22   For example, GL Ms 12160A/1, Imperial, DM, 12 Jan. 1803.

23   Wilson, *Lighting the Town*, pp.73-5.

24   GL Ms 15032/2, Sun, Take over Papers, Bristol Union, Deed, 25 Mar. 1819, clause
      51.

25   GL M s 12160A/1, Imperial, DM, 7 Mar. 1803; LCA, acc.3393, box 41, Leeds &
      Yorkshire, Secretary's Letterbook, Wilks to Hewitt, 11 Dec. 1824.

26   County, DM, 15 Sept. 1808.

27   GL Ms 15032/8, Sun, Take over Papers, New Newcastle Office, Richards to Ford, 7
      Feb. 1838.

28   Thompson, *Making of the English Working Class*, pp.899-900.

29   GCA, TD446/5/18/1, North British, DM, Preamble to the List of Subscribers, 9 Mar.
      1809.

30   Indeed in the summer of 1820 the Salop's directors demanded a price of £1500 for
      one share which came into their possession, but this price was rejected by the
      prospective purchaser. SRO, Ms 3008/1/1/58, Salop, General Meeting Book, 2 June
      1820.

31   SRO, Ms 3008/1/4/16, Salop, Share Assignments, 1783-1864; Ms 3008/1/4/17,
      Salop, Share Transfers.

32   Trebilcock, *Phoenix Assurance*, vol.I, table5.10, p.240.

33   LCA, acc.3393, box 41, Leeds & Yorkshire, Secretary's Letterbook, to T.J. Parker, 24
      June 1829, to James Turnbull, 15 July 1829; Harris, *Industrializing English Law*, p.268.

34 Trebilcock, *Phoenix Assurance*, vol.I, pp.717-19; CKS, U2593/B37, Kent, Waste Transfers 1805-11; Dickson, *Sun Insurance*, p.290 n; SRO, Ms 3008/1/4/16, Salop, Share Assignments 1783-1864; Ms 3008/1/4/17, Salop, Share Transfers.

35 Mortimer, *Everyman his own Broker*, pp.36-7; Anderson, *Origin of Commerce*, vol.3, p.105.

36 Mirowski, 'Rise (and Retreat) of a Market'. Cf. the fuller discussion in Mirowski, *Birth of the Business Cycle*, pp.271-6.

37 See p.21 above. Harris has estimated that the capital in all English stock companies rose from £19m in 1740, to £90m in 1810, and to £210m by 1844. Harris, *Industrializing English Law*, pp.193, 223.

38 LCA, acc.3393, box 41, Leeds & Yorkshire, Secretary's Letterbook. to S. Baines, 10 July 1829.

39 SRO, Ms 3008/1/1/1, Salop, Articles of Agreement, 22 June 1780, clauses 39, 40, 43.

40 LCA, acc.3393, Box 41, Leeds &Yorkshire, Secretary's Letterbook, to T. Hewitt jr., 3 Jan., 22 Jan. 1825.

41 GL Ms 11935E, Sun, Take over Papers, Salamander, Deed of Settlement, 8 Jan. 1823, p.61; Ms 16217, MFLAC, Deed of Settlement, 1 May 1824, clause 94.

42 SRO, Ms 3008/1/1/1, Salop, Articles of Agreement, 22 June 1780, clauses 39, 40, 43; Ms 3008/1/1/58, Salop, General Meeting Book, 10 Aug. 1792.

43 SRO, Ms 3008/1/1/58, Salop, General Meeting Book, 10 Aug. 1792; GL Ms 11935E, Sun, Take over Papers, Salamander, Deed of Settlement, 8 Jan. 1823, p.50; *Aris's Birmingham Gazette*, 4 Feb. 1805; Birmingham Fire Office, *Deed*, pp.23-4, 26.

44 Trebilcock, *Phoenix Assurance*, vol.I, pp.46, 351, 391; GL Ms 16170/1, Atlas, DM, 13 May 1808; Ms 14281/1, Guardian, GCM, 19 Nov., 27 Nov. 1821, 7 Feb. 1823.

45 GL Ms 11935E, Sun, Take over Papers, Bath Sun, Ford to Richards, 25 July 1838.

46 GL Ms 12160A/1, Alliance, DM, 23 Feb., 2 Mar. 1825; Schooling, *Alliance Assurance*, p.7.

47 LCA, acc.3393, box 41, Leeds & Yorkshire, Secretary's Letterbook, Wilks to Gilmour, 31 Dec. 1824.

48 LCA, acc.3393, box 41, Leeds & Yorkshire, Secretary's Letterbook, Wilks to Hewitt, 11 Dec. 1824, Wilks to H. Stott, 11 Feb. 1825.

49 CKS, U2593/B6/1, Kent, DM, 4 Apr. 1803; GL Ms 16217, MFLAC, Deed of Settlement, 1 May 1824, clause 89; Ms 18574, County, 'Deed of Constitution, 25 Feb. 1808, clauses 64-5.

50 County, DM, 21 June 1810.

51 GL Ms 15032/2, Sun, Take over Papers, Bristol Union, Deed, 25 Mar. 1819. For a similar example, see Ms 16170/1-2, Atlas, DM, Prospectus, 6 Apr. 1808, clause V, 8 Aug. 1811.

52 LCA, acc.3393, box 41, Leeds & Yorkshire, Secretary's Letterbook, to S. Baines, 4 Jan. 1825.

53 LCA, acc.3393, box 41, Leeds & Yorkshire, Secretary's Letterbook, to W. Shepherd, 17 Mar. 1825.

54 LCA, acc.3393, box 41, Leeds & Yorkshire, Secretary's Letterbook, to W. Sedgewick, to A. Thorpe, both 25 July 1825, to S. Baines, 21 Mar. 1825.

55 Calculated from data in LCA, acc.3393, box 41, Leeds & Yorkshire, Secretary's Letterbook, to T. Taylor., S. Baines, R. Thornton, M. Hale, all 18 June 1825.

56   Ryan, 'Norwich Union and the British Fire Insurance Market', p.59; Pearson, 'Collective Diversification', p.403.

57   GL Ms 16222/3, MFLAC, DM, 15 Mar. 1827; Ms 14281/2, Guardian, GCM, 7 Apr. 1826.

58   GL Ms 15032/2, Sun, Take over Papers, Bristol Union, Deed, 25 Mar. 1819, clause 18; Ms 11935E, Sun, Take over Papers, Salamander, Deed of Settlement, 8 Jan. 1823, p.58.

59   GL Ms 16217, MFLAC, Deed of Settlement, 1 May 1824, clause 74; Ms 16223/1, MFLAC, GCM, 4 May 1825.

60   County, Minutes of County Meetings, 17 Mar. 1819, 18 Mar. 1820, 5 Mar., 15 Mar. 1822, 18 Mar., 8 Apr. 1823, 1 Mar., 15 Mar. 1824.

61   GL Ms 15032/2, Sun, Take over Papers, Bristol Union, Deed, 25 Mar. 1819, clauses 46, 48, 55.

62   GL Ms 16217, MFLAC, Deed of Settlement, 1 May 1824, clauses 9, 16, 28, 30, 119.

63   GL Ms 11935E, Sun, Take over Papers, Salamander, Deed of Settlement, 8 Jan. 1823, p.24; SRO, Ms 3008/1/1/1, Salop, Articles of Agreement, 22 June 1780, clauses 4, 39; Birmingham Fire Office, *Deed*, pp.11-12, 14.

64   The following account is based upon CKS, U2593/B6/2-8, Kent, DM, 1805-15 *passim*; CKS, U2593/B15, Kent, Financial Summary for the Seven Year Period to Dec. 1809 (including Lediard's note dated 7 Sept. 1810); Reed, *Early History of the Kent Insurance Company*, p.33.

65   The following is based upon GL Ms 16170/2-3, Atlas, DM, 1816-17 *passim*.

66   GL Ms 15032/2 Sun, Take over Papers, Bristol Union, Deed, 25 Mar. 1819.

67   Pearson, 'Charles Bell Ford'; Dickson, *Sun Insurance*, pp.117-19.

68   GL Ms 16170/1, Atlas, DM, 22-3 June, 2 Aug. 1808.

69   GL Ms 16222/8, MFLAC, DM, 30 Jan. 1845.

70   County, Deed of Constitution, 25 Feb. 1808, clauses 19, 20, 25, 52.

71   The following story is recounted by Noakes, *County Fire Office*, pp.28-9. For further details of Barber Beaumont's career, see Pearson, 'Barber Beaumont'; Keeson, 'Barber Beaumont'. The portrait was displayed in Sun Alliance's office in Shaftesbury Avenue, London, in 1994.

72   GL Ms 11935E, Sun, Take over Papers, Bristol Crown, Harwood to Richards, 26 Mar. 1829.

73   Fukuyama, *Trust*, pp.154-7, 204-5.

74   Pearson, 'Collective Diversification'.

75   On Leeds, Liverpool and Wiltshire, see Pearson and Richardson, 'Business Networking'. On Bristol and London, see Trebilcock, *Phoenix Assurance*, vol.I, pp.15-66.

76   The original Deed of Partnership of the Newcastle Fire Office has not survived, but a list of the first proprietors is given in *Newcastle Courant*, 29 Mar. 1783.

77   Cromar, 'The Coal Industry on Tyneside'; Brett, 'Newcastle Election of 1830', p.105; Flinn, *British Coal Industry*, p.327.

78   Phillips, *Banks, Bankers and Banking in Northumberland*, p.180.

79   Phillips, *Banks, Bankers and Banking in Northumberland*, p.244. This list of proprietors is given in GL Ms 15032/8, Sun Fire Office, Take over Papers, Newcastle, Policy Schedule, 25 Dec. 1831.

80   Hedley, *Northumberland Families*, vol.I, p.70.

81   Brett, 'Newcastle Election of 1830', pp.101-5; Hedley, *Northumberland Families*, vol.I, pp.171-5; *Newcastle Courant*, 5 Mar. 1785.

82   Calculated from the lists published in *Newcastle Journal*, 11 Oct. 1783, 6 Oct. 1787, *Newcastle Courant*, 9 Oct. 1784, 8 Oct. 1785.

83   *Newcastle Courant*, 4 Oct. 1783.

84   Pressnell, *Country Banking*, pp.369, 382.

85   Phillips, *Banks, Bankers and Banking in Northumberland*, pp.29, 48, 158, 388.

86   Rennison, 'Supply of Water to Newcastle'.

87   Campbell, 'Gas Lighting in Newcastle'; Jackson, *Short History of the Newcastle Gas Company*.

88   E. Mackenzie, *Descriptive and Historical Account of Newcastle* (Newcastle, 1827), vol.II, p.725 n, cited by Campbell, 'Gas Lighting in Newcastle', p.198.

89   Cobbett, *Rural Rides*, p.39.

90   Pressnell, *Country Banking*, pp.55-6.

91   Bankers accounted for six of the 16 strong committee to establish the Norwich General in 1792, five of the 24 founding directors of the Essex Equitable in 1802, and eight of the founding directors of the Suffolk & General Counties in 1802, Ryan, 'History of the Norwich Union', pp.73-6, 120-21.

92   Cf. Devine, *Tobacco Lords*; Wilson, *Gentlemen Merchants*; Smith, *Conflict and Compromise*; Morris, *Class, Sect and Party*. Trainor is an exception, but, while recognising the pluralism of élites in Glasgow and the Black country, he too focuses upon the membership of only a small number of institutions and neglects the economic linkages. Trainor, *Black Country Élites*; *idem*, 'The Élite'.

93   Cf. the discussion in Pearson and Richardson, 'Business Networking', which expands upon some of the points made here.

Chapter 7

Marketing

Some miles further on, when they felt they were safe, they stopped. They confirmed that Mr Essanjee was indeed dead. His suit and jacket were soaking with blood, rendered all the more coruscating by the contrast it made to the patches of gleaming white. They rearranged his body in a more dignified position, so that it looked like he was dozing in the side-car, his head thrown back.

'Damn good shots, those fellows,' Wheech-Browning observed as he wedged his rifle between Mr Essanjee's plump knees. 'He was a plucky little chap for an insurance salesman. What did you say the name of his company was?'

'African Guarantee and Indemnity Co.'

'Must bear that in mind'.

William Boyd.[1]

Insurance has usually been interested in marketing its product. With the exception of the early London mutuals, every fire office in Britain between 1700 and 1850 appointed agents to sell beyond the place where the office was located. Notices in newspapers, handbills and circulars distributed by post, and an array of other advertising devices supplemented this effort. In this way insurance resembled the trade in commodities or other financial products such as lottery tickets, rather than the less bustling practice of private banking. As consumers became more familiar with insurance, they became more assertive in negotiating the terms of their policies. Yet by the early nineteenth century there remained much ignorance about the purpose and nature of insurance, not only among customers but also among agents of the offices. This chapter examines the size, distribution and occupational structure of insurance sales forces, and compares the regional networks of provincial offices with the national networks of the bigger metropolitan companies. The second and third sections of the chapter explore the process of establishing agencies and indicate some of the 'principal agent' problems which insurers faced in keeping control of them. The final section looks at the changing relationship between the insurance companies, their customers and the general public.

Agency networks

Table 7.1 presents agency data for 30 English fire insurance offices in the period 1730-1850. Two points stand out. First, the size distribution of agency networks

Table 7.1   Agency Numbers, 1730-1850

LONDON OFFICES

Sun		London		REA		Phoenix	
1730	27	1730	12				
1740	74						
1750	74			1766	26		
1760	89			1775	44		
1770	111			1780	60		
1780	118			1788	195	1783	121
1786	123	1786	0	1805	316		
1790	155			1816	320	1821	251
1799	167	1805	23	1830	430	1840	506
1846	677			1848	555	1850	755
Imperial		County		Atlas		Protector	
1803	35			1808	82		
1805	47	1807	90	1809	116		
1808	80	1811	151	1811	152		
		1827	*238	1812	168	1828	331

COUNTRY OFFICES

Norwich Union		Kent		Worcester		MFLAC	
1800	26			1791	18		
1804	70	1803	36	1802	24		
1805	99						
1808	200	1809	31	1807	25		
1810	261						
1811	300			1814	29		
1813	340						
1815	402					1825	92
1818	>500					1829	*120
1824	6-700					1842	121
Bath Sun		Salamander		N. & S. Shields		Bristol Fire	
1835	25	1835	83	1836	3		
1837	19					1839	13

Notes: * figures represent the number of agents appointed over a period up to the date given, viz. County, 1821-7, MFLAC, 1825-9. Other fire offices for which we have only one observation (dates in brackets) are as follows: *London*: Globe, 309* (1803-10), Guardian, 323* (1821-9). *Country*: Leeds 11 (1777), Newcastle 16 (1783), Liverpool 8 (1784), Salop *7 (1788), Old Bath 4 (1798), Essex & Suffolk *24 (1821), Leeds & Yorkshire *57 (1824-9), Berkshire & Gloucester 19 (1831), Bristol Union 3 (1840), Shropshire 36 (1844), Preston 10 (1848).

Sources: GL Ms 11935/1-9, Sun, CCM 1730-1801; Trebilcock, *Phoenix Assurance*, vol.I, pp.82, 499, table 10.3, p.541, table 12.3, p.694; Drew, *London Assurance*, p.48; GL Ms 8735/1-6, London, FCM; County, DM, 1807-27, Bedford agency register, 1811-13; GL Ms 16170/1-2, Atlas, DM, 1808-12 *passim*; *Williamson's Liverpool Advertiser*, 14 Oct. 1784; SRO, Ms 3008/1/2/1, Salop, DM, 1780-88 *passim*; GL Ms 11935E, Sun, Take over Papers, Bath Sun, Bristol Union, Bristol Fire, British Fire, Preston & North Lancs., Salamander, Shropshire, North & South Shields; Relton, *Account of the Fire Insurance Companies*, p.212; GL Ms 16206/1, Essex & Suffolk, DM, 1802-21 *passim*; *Bath Herald*, 13 Jan. 1798; Reed, *Kent Insurance Company*; CKS, U2593/B125, Kent, Rough List of Agents, 1809; CUL, PAA, PX1759, Phoenix, Take over Papers, Berkshire & Gloucestershire; GL Ms 11674/1, Globe Insurance, Ledger, nr.1; Ms 18111, Guardian, Agents' Lists, 1821-9; Ms 12160A/1-4, Imperial, DM, 1803-8 *passim*; *Leeds Mercury*, 1777 *passim*; LCA, acc.3393, box 41, Leeds & Yorkshire, Secretary's Letter Book, 1824-9 *passim*; GL Ms 16222/2-4, MFLAC, DM, 1825-9 *passim*; *Newcastle Chronicle*, 1783 *passim*; Ryan, 'History of Norwich Union'.

was polarised between the largest, amounting to hundreds of agents by the early nineteenth century, and the smallest, usually fewer than 40 agents, employed by most country offices. Some of the oldest provincial insurers, such as the Worcester, the Bath Sun and the Bristol offices, continued to have a modest number of agents well into the nineteenth century. This was often the result of limited horizons and ambitions. Many country offices restricted the geographical scope of their underwriting, p artly to emphasise their local roots, and they never subsequently expanded beyond their original boundaries. The new office established in Reading in 1822, for example, proclaimed in its deed that it would sell fire insurance only within the borough. Twenty years later it was still announcing itself as the 'Borough of Reading Fire Insurance Company...for the purpose of insuring such property as situated within the Borough only'.[2] Second, table 7.1 indicates that some sales forces could grow rapidly within just a few years. The number of agents employed by the REA more than trebled between 1780 and 1788. Those of the Atlas doubled between 1808 and 1812. Agencies established by the Norwich Union doubled between 1805 and 1808, then doubled again by 1815. Sometimes, as with the Atlas, such rapid growth was associated with the expansion of a new office. Sometimes it was the result of a recruitment drive by a mature office targeting particular regions where its sales force was weak. Occasionally a sales network became swollen with agents acquired following the takeover of another office. Thus the Sun acquired 55 former Salamander agents in 1835 and 149 British Fire agents in 1843. Often the agents of a purchased office were concentrated in one region. The Imperial took on 13 former Bristol Fire agents in the south-west when it purchased that office in 1840, and the number of Phoenix agents in Kent rose from ten to 33 following its acquisition of the East Kent & Canterbury office in 1828.[3]

An analysis of their geographical distribution illustrates how concentrated were the agency systems of the smaller offices, but it also reveals how their pretensions to extend beyond a single county or area were sometimes belied by the distribution of their agents. The Essex & Suffolk Fire Office, based in Colchester, largely focused its sales efforts on Essex. Just five of its 24 agents in 1821 were located in Suffolk. The Berkshire & Gloucestershire, although having administrative offices in both Reading and Cheltenham, did not have a single agent in Gloucestershire, and concentrated most of its 19 agents in 1831 in eastern Berkshire, south Oxfordshire and west Buckinghamshire.[4] A gravitational force, holding agencies in an orbit around a head office, also appears among other provincial insurers at different times. In its first eight years of business, the Salop Fire Office appointed just seven agents. Four of these were located in the county at Ludlow, Broseley, Market Drayton and Newport. The remainder were based across the county border at Newcastle and Stafford and at Aberystwyth.[5] By the end of its first full year of operations the Manchester Fire & Life Assurance Company had appointed nearly 100 agents in Scotland, Wales and England. Map 7.1 shows that its sales outlets were concentrated in the north-west and the office had virtually no presence at all in southern England. The Salamander had 83 agencies on its books in 1835. Map 7.2 illustrates how these stretched across 14 counties of England and Wales. Seventy of these, however, were located in five core counties, Somerset, Wiltshire, Dorset, Gloucestershire and Hampshire. There were no agents north of Worcester or east of Brighton. Even those new London offices, which aspired to national coverage, found themselves concentrating their sales efforts in some regions at the expense of others. Map 7.3 shows how thinly represented the Atlas was in its early days in eastern and central England. The Guardian, established in 1821, was much better represented in eastern England after its first year, than the Atlas had been 13 years earlier (see map 7.4). However, like the Atlas, the Guardian's salesforce was thinly stretched across the agricultural counties of central England. It appointed very few agents between Huntingdon in the east and Hereford in the west.

Were the blank spaces in the maps the result of recruiting problems faced by new metropolitan offices in these counties, or of their disinterest in insuring farm and small town property? The latter seems unlikely given the number of small town agencies established by London insurers in other areas. The Guardian, for example, had a chain of agents across east and north Yorkshire in market towns such as Malton, Pickering, Beverley, and Selby. In some places there may have been a lack of suitable candidates due to low numbers of lawyers, clerks and tradesmen. Competition among fire offices did exacerbate the shortage of recruits by the 1810s and 1820s.[6] Furthermore, the persistence of large numbers of shopkeepers and craftsmen as agents of the London offices suggests that these groups were still keenly sought after as salesmen as late as 1850. This would have done nothing to resolve recruitment shortfalls in the smaller towns and rural areas. Nevertheless some offices did succeed as rural specialists. The County concentrated its initial sales force in just 12 rural counties stretching through Hertfordshire, Buckinghamshire and the east midlands, as far north as Richmond and Whitby in the north riding of Yorkshire (see map 7.5). By 1813, despite an expansion in agencies from 120 to 149, this pattern had not changed.

Table 7.2 shows the regional distribution of agencies for eight fire offices at

Map 7.1   MFLAC agencies, 1825 (England and Wales only, n = 90)

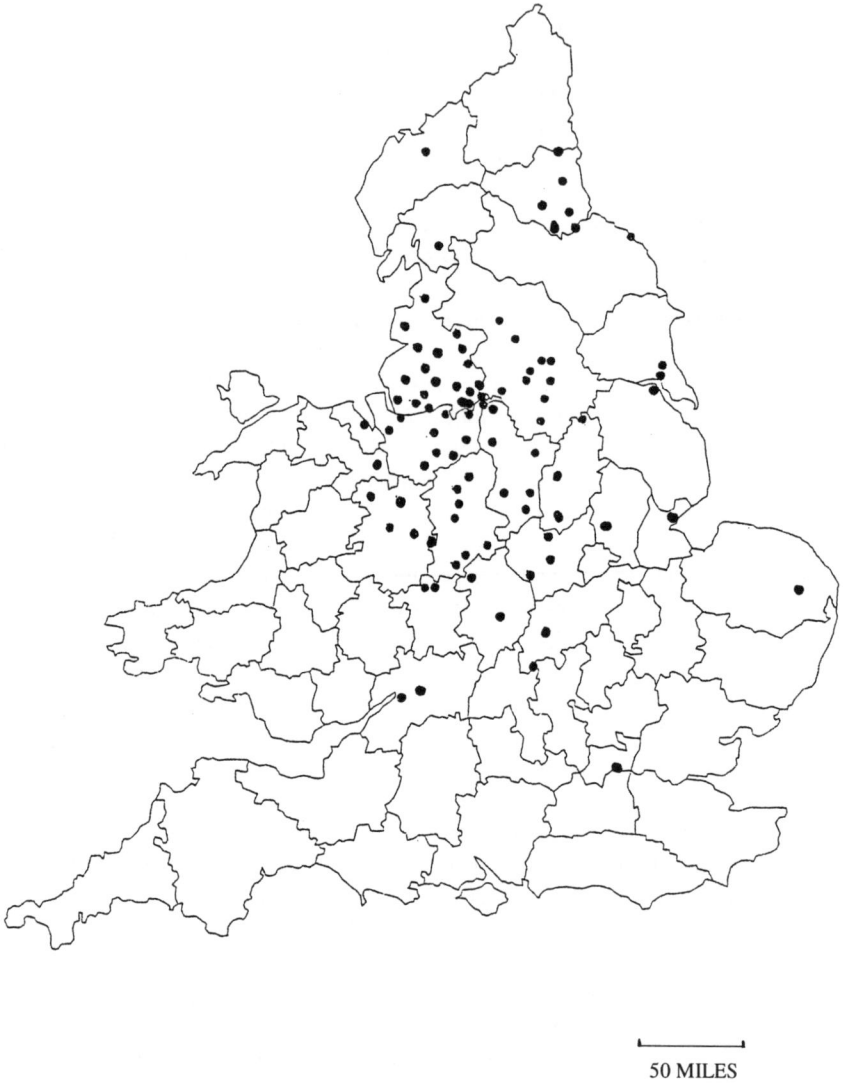

50 MILES

Map 7.2 Salamander agencies, 1835 (n = 79, excluding 4 second agencies)

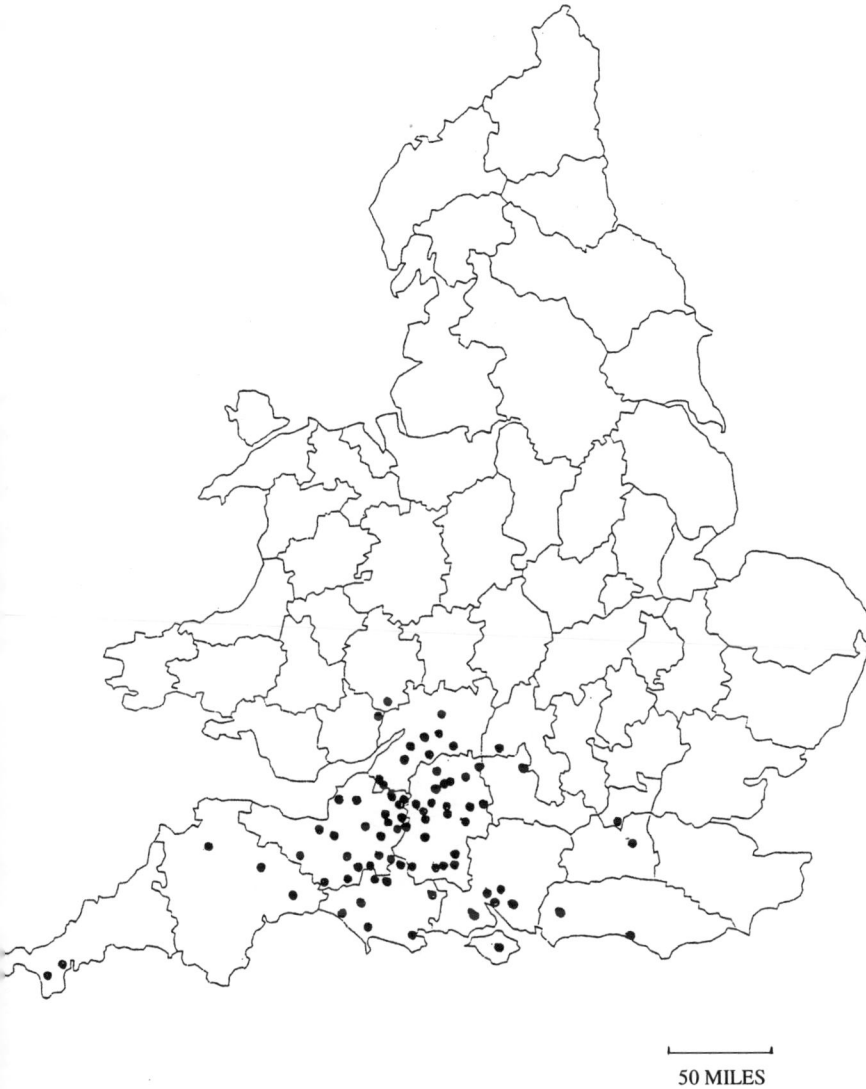

50 MILES

Map 7.3 Atlas agencies, 1809
(England and Wales only, n = 103, excluding 3 not located)

50 MILES

Map 7.4 Guardian agencies, 1822 (England and Wales only, n = 149)

50 MILES

Map 7.5   County agencies, 1809 (n = 120)

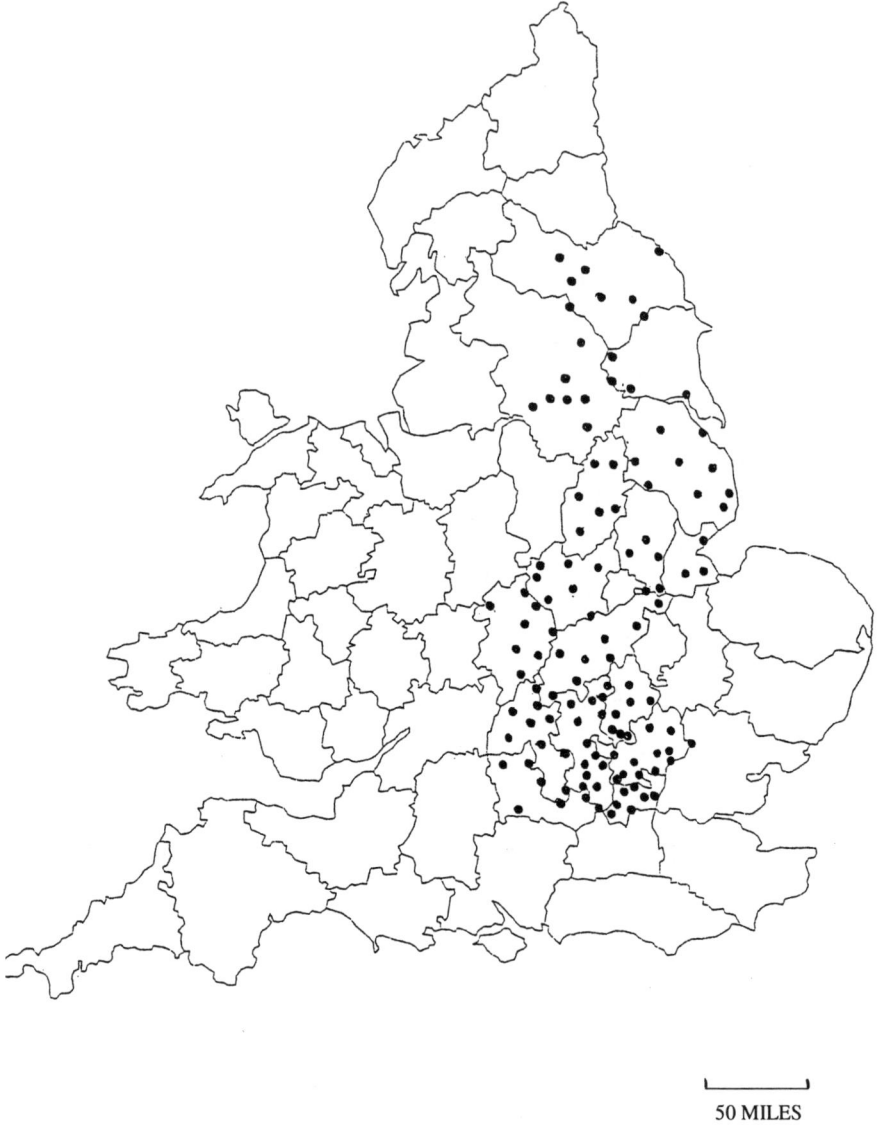

50 MILES

different dates between 1782 and 1843, together with the regional distribution of the population. Certain patterns emerge. Most striking is the continued over-representation of the metropolitan offices in the south-east of England. Across the period the south-east accounted for a persistent 24 per cent of the population of Britain, while the proportion of insurance agents located there ranged from 29 per cent to 47 per cent among the London offices. In 1843 the British Fire Office had over 100 agencies in London alone. The metropolitan offices were also well represented in the midlands and the south-west, with the exceptions of the Atlas in the former, and the County in the latter. By contrast, in East Anglia the rise of the Norwich Union during the 1800s appears to have dissuaded new London offices from opening many agencies there. Earlier, both the Sun and the Phoenix were well represented in this region.

At first glance this would appear to indicate common marketing strategies among London insurers. Yet when the agency patterns are examined more closely, idiosyncrasies emerge. For example, there were interesting differences between London-based offices. In 1809, after one year of business, the Atlas located proportionately more of its agents in the metropolitan area than the Phoenix had in 1785, after three years of business, and the Sun had in 1800. The same is true of the Guardian during the 1820s which had 23 per cent of its agents based in London, Middlesex and the four contiguous home counties, compared to just 11 per cent of Phoenix agents in 1821. This suggests that the new metropolitan offices of the early nineteenth century with national, even global ambitions, first dropped anchor in the market on their doorstep. Even the County, whose interest was not chiefly in London, had agents in Hampstead, Hackney, Stepney, Tottenham, Somers Town and Kentish Town by 1813, as well in several villages to the west of London. The evidence also suggests that once a new office had established the core of its sales force, its geographical focus did not fundamentally change, at least not within a decade or two of the company's foundation. This is true of the Phoenix during the period 1782-1821, as well as several of the new offices founded during the 1820s.[7]

Like their London counterparts, the biggest provincial insurers embedded their sales teams in their home regions before expanding further afield. The MFLAC located over 30 per cent of its earliest agencts in Lancashire and Cheshire. Subsequently, although the number of agents increased, and many of the early agencies were replaced by new outlets, the basic pattern did not change. In 1843 32 per cent of all MFLAC agents were still located in the north-west. Similar concentrations can be observed for the smaller provincial offices. The Preston & North Lancashire, for example, established just ten agencies in its short life-span, 1845-8. All of these were in south Lancashire, Kendal and Cockermouth.[8]

Table 7.2 also indicates the lack of marketing resources devoted by English offices to Scotland and Ireland even by the second quarter of the nineteenth century. During this period Ireland accounted for nearly one-third of the population of the United Kingdom, yet those English offices selling fire insurance there allocated it only between two and six per cent of their salesmen. The gap was

Table 7.2 Regional distribution of agencies: eight fire offices, 1782-1843

Percentages

	GB Population 1781	Phoenix 1782-5	GB Population 1801	UK Population 1801	Sun 1800	Atlas 1809	Globe 1810	County 1809	County 1813
South-east	23.5	35.3	23.9	16.3	35.2	34.6	29.3	45.8	45.6
East Anglia	6.4	9.4	5.9	4.0	8.3	1.8	4.9	-	-
South-west	13.9	15.9	13.1	8.9	17.9	22.1	17.9	-	-
Midlands	16.3	18.2	15.5	10.6	19.3	12.4	19.9	38.4	36.8
North-west	6.6	4.1	8.3	5.7	5.1	6.2	4.9	-	-
Yorkshire	8.0	7.1	8.3	5.6	6.4	8.0	8.1	15.8	17.7
North	4.9	4.1	4.6	3.1	4.5	3.5	4.6	-	-
Wales	5.6	2.9	5.2	3.6	0.6	4.4	2.3	-	-
Scotland	14.7	1.8	15.2	10.3	2.6	5.3	5.5	-	-
Ireland		-		31.8	-	1.8	2.0	-	-
Channel Isles		1.2				-	0.7	-	-
N =		170			156	113	307	120	147

	GB Population 1831	UK Population 1831	Phoenix 1821	Guardian 1822	Guardian 1830	MFLAC 1825	MFLAC 1843	British 1843
South-east	24.2	16.4	23.9	31.4	35.5	1.0	2.5	47.4
East Anglia	5.5	3.7	7.2	7.1	6.3	1.0	0.8	4.3
South-west	12.3	8.3	18.7	13.5	16.4	2.1	1.7	15.4
Midlands	15.3	10.3	19.2	18.4	16.2	33.4	25.8	15.0
North-west	10.4	7.0	8.4	7.7	4.8	30.2	31.7	5.1
Yorkshire	8.5	5.8	7.2	8.3	7.2	14.6	14.2	3.6
North	4.3	2.9	5.2	1.9	3.0	8.3	7.5	2.8
Wales	5.0	3.4	5.2	5.8	4.5	2.1	3.3	4.5
Scotland	14.5	9.9	5.2	3.2	4.5	5.2	6.7	1.8
Ireland		32.2	-	1.9	1.5	2.1	5.8	-
Channel Isles			-	0.6	0.3	-	-	0.2
N =			251	156	335	96	120	507

Note and Sources: Regions derived from table 3.2. South-east = south-east II and III. Midlands = east and west midlands. Population calculated for England and Wales, from Deane and Cole, *British Economic Growth*, table 24, p.103; for Scotland, from Daunton, *Progress and Poverty*, table 15.1, p.406; for Ireland, 1781, 1831, from Mitchell, *British Historical Statistics*, pp.8, 10; 1801 from Schofield, 'British Population Change', table 4.7, p.93. For Sun agents, see table 3.2 above. Other agents' numbers calculated from Trebilcock, *Phoenix Assurance*, vol.I, table 3.2, p.84; GL Ms 16170/1, Atlas, DM, 1807-9; County, DM, 1807-13; GL Ms 11674/1, Globe, Ledger, 1803-10; Ms 18111, Guardian, Agents' List; Ms 16222/2-4, MFLAC, DM, 1825-9; Ms 11935E, Sun, Take over Papers, British Fire, Agents' List.

narrower but still visible in Scotland. Scotland accounted for 15 per cent of the population of mainland Britain but no more than seven per cent of any office's agencies in this period. The largest sales force examined here, that of the British Fire Office, was especially poorly represented, with just nine Scottish agents out of 507 employed in 1843.[9] This left a large market vacant for native offices, an opportunity seized with alacrity by the Scots. In their prospectus of 1809 the founders of the North British Fire Office of Edinburgh remarked that there were about 20 English companies with agencies in Scotland who together accounted for about three-quarters of all fire insurance transacted there. The Edinburgh men noted, however, that 'it is generally calculated' that not more than one quarter of insurable property in Scotland was insured against fire.

> There seems no reason to doubt that a company established on a broad and national basis, which should merit the support of a great majority of the most wealthy individuals in the Country, would speedily attract a very large proportion of all the insurances in this part of Great Britain.[10]

This concept of a national Scottish office formed the basis of the North British marketing strategy. In its first two decades, the company appointed 70 agents across Scotland, from border towns such as Dumfries to Highland and Island locations such as Skye and Stornoway.[11] Many of these places had never seen the agent of an English insurance office. From 1823 the North British began to venture south of the border. 12 agencies were established in towns as far south as Derby, reflecting the rising ambitions of an office which was to become one of the great global insurers of the later nineteenth century. Other Scottish offices did the same. The West of Scotland and the Caledonian both advertised agents in Manchester in 1824 and eight Scottish firms were among the 30 fire and life insurance offices operating there by 1838.[12]

    Who were the agents? This question has attracted some attention from insurance historians. There is a general consensus that during the period 1780-1850 the major offices increasingly recruited their agents from the professions. In 1786, according to Dickson, the majority of the Sun's agents 'were still drawn from the ranks of small craftsmen and traders, with marginal additions from other classes'. By the 1840s, however, the practice of appointing solicitors had become 'increasingly common'.[13] Trebilcock's analysis of the Phoenix agents also shows the retreat of the retailers and a 'sweeping advance' by the lawyers, which marked the search by the Phoenix for increasing 'respectability, even increasing bourgeoisification...as the Victorian era approached'.[14] Exactly when this transformation began is difficult to say. Ryan claims that the Norwich Union agents appointed by Bignold in his drive to expand out of East Anglia after 1805 'were typical of most insurance offices, with attorneys figuring prominently, followed by local businessmen such as brewers, various kinds of merchants and shopkeepers'.[15] The trend towards appointing professionals as salesmen, therefore, may have commenced during the first two decades of the century. This is also suggested by the deliberations of the

London Assurance about reestablishing an agency network in 1806. Worried by the 'small figure' made by the office in country insurances - particularly in the home counties - 'when compared with the juvenile efforts of institutions possessing neither the antiquity nor advantages of this Corporation', its directors concluded that 'exertions proportionate to the competition and rivalry of the present day are absolutely necessary in order to preserve a respectable rank in the opinion of the public'.

> Much success has resulted with other offices...from the encouragement given to architects, surveyors and other professional gentlemen who have been the medium of making insurances, and viewing the continued increase of buildings round the metropolis, it may not yet be too late to resort to this mode for the improvement of business.[16]

Regrettably occupational information about agents is deficient, especially for the period before 1840. The high proportion of unknowns in the agency lists, or of those described unhelpfully as 'gentlemen', renders their analysis problematic.[17] Different occupational categories used by different authors also makes comparison difficult. Nevertheless, an examination of the agents of the British and the Guardian reveals similarities with those of the older London offices.[18] Five or six of their most numerous occupations can be also found among the top seven occupations for the REA and the Phoenix (see table 7.3). A comparison using Supple's more general categories also throws up similarities (see table 7.4). Like the other insurers, the British and the Guardian used considerable numbers of lawyers, auctioneers, builders, surveyors, grocers, drapers, booksellers, postmasters, schoolteachers and clerks to sell their policies.

Major differences can also be discerned. First, the proportion of solicitors and bankers among the agents of the British Fire Office was considerably lower than among its rivals, and professional men generally were less prominent. Although, as table 7.4 shows, a large proportion of the *new* agents recruited by the Phoenix in the 1820s were drawn from retailing and craft trades, these were additions to an agency system already heavily loaded with lawyers. Counting only those whose occupations are known, nearly half of the agents employed by the Norwich Union in 1813 and by the Phoenix in 1821, and 25 per cent of the Sun's agents in 1846 and 17 per cent of the agents of the Guardian in 1830 and the REA in 1848 were drawn from the legal profession.[19] Including those in the total for whom occupations are unknown, Trebilcock found 72 lawyers among 227 agents listed by the Phoenix in 1821 (32 per cent), while there were 44 lawyers among the 335 agents appointed by the Guardian between 1821 and 1830 (13 per cent). By comparison, the British had just 29 lawyers out of a total of 507 agents in 1843 (six per cent).

Second, although a high proportion of the Guardian's agents fell into the 'professional/official' category (see table 7.4), many of these were clerical

Table 7.3   The most common agents' occupations: four offices, 1821-48

Percentages of all agents with known occupations, absolute numbers in brackets

	Phoenix Agents employed 1821			Phoenix Agents appointed 1821-30			Guardian Agents appointed 1821-30		
1	Attorneys	(72)	48.6	Manufac- turers/ Other crafts	(17)	16.5	Attorneys	(44)	17.5
2	Other small retailers	(17)	11.5	Attorneys	(16)	15.5	Clerks	(28)	11.1
3	Bankers	(14)	9.5	Drapers	(10)	9.7	Grocers	(17)	6.7
4	Small craftsmen	(13)	8.8	Booksellers	(10)	9.7	Booksellers	(17)	6.7
5	Full time agents	(12)	8.1	Grocers	(9)	8.7	Builders	(14)	5.6
6	Grocers	(7)	4.7	Auctioneers	(7)	6.8	Drapers	(14)	5.6
7	Booksellers	(4)	2.7	Ironmongers	(6)	5.8	Auctioneers	(7)	2.8

	Phoenix Agents appointed 1841-50			British Agents employed 1843			REA Agents employed 1848		
1	Attorneys	(102)	15.8	Grocers	(44)	15.7	Attorneys	(95)	17.1
2	Auctioneers	(67)	10.4	Attorneys	(29)	10.3	Grocers	(39)	7.0
3	Bankers	(55)	8.5	Builders	(19)	6.8	Drapers	(34)	6.1
4	Other merchants	(55)	8.5	Auctioneers	(18)	6.4	Booksellers	(27)	4.9
5	Grocers	(42)	6.5	Booksellers	(17)	6.0	Auctioneers	(27)	4.9
6	Builders	(42)	6.5	Drapers	(13)	4.5	Bankers	(25)	4.5
7	Booksellers	(39)	6.0	Clerks	(13)	4.5	Builders	(20)	3.6

Notes: 1. Phoenix: 'other small retailers' (1821) exclude grocers, booksellers, drapers; 'other crafts' (1821-30) exclude builders and goldsmiths; 'other merchants' (1841-50) exclude wine and spirit merchants. All offices: attorneys include solicitors; booksellers include stationers; auctioneers include appraisers; drapers include mercers, haberdashers; builders include masons, joiners, carpenters, bricklayers. 2. In Guardian's list there were also seven wine and spirit merchants, ranking equal seventh with auctioneers.

Sources: Trebilcock, *Phoenix Assurance*, vol.I, tables 3.3b, p.89, 12.5, p.698; GL Ms 18111, Guardian, Agents' List; Ms 11935E, Sun, Take over Papers, British Fire, Agents' List; Supple, *Royal Exchange*, p.154.

workers. The REA and the Phoenix were more likely to appoint a solicitor or a banker than their clerks or cashiers (see table 7.3). By contrast there were proportionately more small dealers, manufacturers and builders among the ranks of the British agents than in the other offices examined. Grocers, for example,

Table 7.4 All agents' occupations: four offices, 1821-48

(Supple's categories, percentages, absolute numbers in brackets)

	Phoenix agents appointed 1821-30	Guardian agents appointed 1821-30	Phoenix agents appointed 1841-50	British agents employed 1843	REA agents employed 1848
Professional men, officials, agents and 'gentlemen'					
	(42) 40.0	(134) 52.8	(344) 52.1	(115) 40.8	(271) 48.8
Merchants, manufacturers and businessmen of various sorts					
	(47) 44.8	(52) 20.5	(159) 24.1	(76) 27.0	(112) 20.2
Shopkeepers					
	(16) 15.2	(68) 26.8	(157) 23.8	(91) 32.3	(172) 31.0
N =	105	254	660	282	555

Sources: as table 7.3.

comprised 16 per cent of the British agents in 1843, compared with between five and seven per cent of the REA in 1848, the Guardian in 1830 and the Phoenix in 1821. 'Small craftsmen' accounted for nine per cent of agents employed by the Phoenix and the Guardian but 17 per cent of those employed by the British. The latter group included a dozen watchmakers, recruited presumably because they brought the promise of selling insurance to customers of steady income and some property. Craftsmen in the building trades, with their obvious links to the housing market, were also recruited more frequently by the British Fire than by the other London offices.

Whether these patterns - more clerks among the Guardian's agents, more craftsmen among the agents of the British Fire - were the result of deliberate marketing strategies, a sign of the lower social aspirations of these offices, or merely a function of the shortage of recruits from the most desirable occupations, is impossible to say. What can be stated is that, despite these differences, the agents of the British and the Guardian in the second quarter of the nineteenth century more closely resembled their contemporaries in the REA and the Phoenix, than those employed by the Phoenix in the late eighteenth century. In the period 1783-1802 small retailers accounted for 59 per cent of all Phoenix agents, over twice the proportion employed by the Guardian and by the Phoenix itself in the 1820s, and almost twice the proportion employed by the British and the REA in the 1840s. The analysis of the British and the Guardian, therefore, while indicating intriguing differences between fire offices in the occupational distribution of agents, does nothing to contradict the thesis that the insurance industry was moving towards a greater reliance upon the professional classes, and 'white-collar' workers more generally, in order to sell its products.

Establishing agencies

Agencies became important to the business of most offices, including some of the smallest. The ten agents of the tiny Preston & North Lancashire contributed 39 per cent of its premium income in 1848. Sixty-nine per cent of the Salamander's total premiums in 1835 were earned by its agents. By the end of the eighteenth century agency income was already important to the older London offices. Fifty per cent of the Sun's premiums and 56 per cent of the REA's were remitted by agents in 1795. The Phoenix's agencies accounted for 56 to 61 per cent of its UK underwriting income during the period 1806-40. The agents of the British provided 48 per cent of its premiums in 1843.[20] Of all the national insurers the Norwich Union was the most heavily dependent on agency sales, which accounted for 95 per cent of its sums insured in 1816 and 1822.[21] This is not surprising given the limited size of the local insurance market. With a population of 36000 in 1801, Norwich was less than half the size of Manchester or Liverpool and 27 times smaller than London.[22]

Even with a huge market on their doorstep, the London stock companies made early attempts to sell further afield. The first task was often to identify those locations most likely to produce sales. The Sun's earliest provincial insurances were mostly sold by 'riding officers' on their regular tours of different regions, but during the 1730s the office began to expand its agencies. The small number of insurances sold in a town, the absence of any Sun agents nearby, or the guarantee that a new agency would not encroach on the business of an established outlet, were reasons given for nearly a dozen appointments during that decade. In some places, for example Dorchester, the agreement of the nearest local agent, in this case at Poole, was obtained before a new agency was opened.[23]

During the eighteenth century aristocratic and gentry patronage of agents was important, most notably that of the Duke of Chandos, who was a major shareholder in Sun until 1729 and who proposed candidates for at least seven Sun agencies. Other recommendations came from the Denbighshire MP, John Middleton, who proposed a candidate for a new agency at Ruthin in 1738, and from a variety of Sun policyholders and the 'principal inhabitants' at Dorchester in 1735 and 1781, at Newbury in 1735 and 1740, and at Epping in 1786. Urban corporations also lobbied to have a Sun agency situated in their town. At East Retford the corporation successfully applied in 1786 for an agent 'for the greater conveniency of the persons insured and as East Retford is upwards of 20 miles from Nottingham'.[24]

By the early nineteenth century the commercial and professional bourgeoisie had come to play the dominant role in recruitment. The Guardian's first agent in Blackburn, Thomas Rogerson, was recommended by Cunliffe's bank in 1821, with James Cunliffe standing as one of the sureties. Eleven years later, when Rogerson gave in his notice, it was noted that 'Mr R. Cunliffe wishes to be informed when the agency is vacant [so] that he and the proprietors at Blackburn may recommend Mr France, clerk in Cunliffe & Co's bank'.[25] It was not unusual for prominent shareholders, who were used to exerting influence in this way, to regard agency appointments as sinecures for their personal disposal. There was little resistance to this from insurance companies. It was in their interest to retain the goodwill of local worthies, and they saved much trouble and expense by appointing agents recommended by proprietors of some social standing.

Retiring agents also frequently recommended their own successors. Often such recommendations would fall upon family members and relatives, so that dynasties of agents developed over several generations. Joseph and Thomas Gearing, father and son, occupied the Sun's agency at Exeter between 1728 and 1776. Richard Boore and then his widow, Elizabeth, held the Sun's agency at Shrewsbury for 41 years. The Pole family supplied the Sun with several generations of agents at Liverpool between 1751 and 1831. Similarly, three generations of the Tate family represented the Phoenix at Manchester for nearly a century, 1785-1880.[26] Although such dynasties were a minority and the most durable were found in the largest agencies, kinship links remained a prominent feature of insurance sales forces. In the case of the Sun, sons succeeded retired or deceased fathers at least 25 times in 23 different agencies between 1747 and 1800. Nephews followed uncles at Leeds, Kettering, Chester and Hull. Brothers replaced brothers at York, Aberdeen and Colchester. A son succeeded his mother at Scarborough, a daughter replaced her mother at Aylesbury, and widows inherited agencies from their deceased husbands, for example at Shrewsbury in 1775 and Ware in 1784. Candidates might also submit their own applications without 'insider' recommendations. Character references, however, were usually required. Material assets, a reputation for moral rectitude, and extensive local connections of the right sort were ideal qualifications. Thus Thomas Ashbourne proposed himself to the Sun as agent in Kendal early in 1746, just weeks after the occupying Jacobite army, who had threatened to torch the town, had departed. The country committee made enquiries and appointed him, 'being as we are informed a person well-known and esteemed'.[27]

By the early nineteenth century it was increasingly common for committees of directors to be established with a brief to recruit in specific areas. This often involved recruiting journeys by managers which sometimes doubled up as inspection tours of existing agencies. One of the purposes of Philip Bewicke's travels in the north of England and Scotland in 1806, 1807 and 1812 was to select new agents for locations where the Sun was not yet represented, and in doing so, to counteract the competition from local offices. In 1826 and 1834 the Sun established special committees to consider ways of increasing the number of agents. The first of these managed to make 49 appointments although this was considered a disappointing result. On a more modest scale, eight agencies in Sussex were established by the Kent Fire Office following a tour by two directors in 1803, and Henry Desborough appointed eight agents for the Atlas when he visited the north-east in 1810.[28]

Offices could face considerable difficulties and costs when establishing agencies outside their home regions. Signboards and posters were common devices to get a new agency noticed. In 1738 the Sun sent its agents 'some large proposals with instructions to place them up in the most publick places and adjacent towns'. John Byng came across 'several broad wheel'd waggons with the *Phoenix*

Insurance fixed upon them' just outside Towcester in July 1789, probably the initiative of an enterprising local agent.[29] Some agents also advertised by letter to selected property owners, although before the middle of the nineteenth century most offices paid such expenses only on an *ad hoc* basis. The MFLAC, for instance, met the cost of circulars sent out by its agent at Liverpool in 1825, but the money had first to be paid by the agent out of his own pocket before he was reimbursed. In 1812 the Atlas paid their agent in Greenwich only five guineas towards the £10 cost of a 'shewboard' he had ordered, presumably because it advertised more than just the insurance agency.[30] On a trip to Liverpool, Barber Beaumont developed a characteristically precise marketing strategy for the County's local agency, which consisted of the mailing of households in streets selected from the town directory. Upon his return to London he was 'mortified' to find that the agent's clerk had failed to send letters to more than one-third of the households chosen, 'as when the pages which chanced to be allotted to a street were filled up, instead of opening a new page, all further inhabitants in such street were omitted'. This led the manager to question the Liverpool agent's commitment.

> Your avocations taking you so much from home must be a serious impediment to the success of your agency at best - but surely you ought to leave your directions and in such hands that we should not have to complain of neglect in mere manual operations.

Beaumont advised the agent to get 'an intelligent man to go round personally after the delivery of the letters and to add half your allowances to our guinea per week for the new orders he may procure - but this ought to have been arranged and in training before now'.[31]

Before 1850 few insurance agents received a permanent allowance over and above their commission and reimbursements. Such payments were considered where a large business was anticipated. In 1822, for instance, in response to a request from its local committee, the Guardian granted a salary to its Manchester agent of £150 a year for two years, to cover the rent of an office, bills and the wages of a servant. It was emphasised that this was an exception due to the 'influence and exertions' of the committee and the 'activity and zeal' of the agent, and that

> the business to be expected from the wealth and population contained in the Manchester agency and the high rate of premiums incidental to local circumstances of factories and other works not applicable in many other places...must be lucrative to the agent.

The implication was that the Manchester agent, by receiving the normal percentage of premiums as commission, but from a location which yielded a higher than average premium for every pound insured, would benefit disproportionately relative to his counterparts elsewhere. Any additional payment to him was therefore unfair, and 'cannot be made permanent or become a precedent for other agencies'.[32] It was not until the third quarter of the nineteenth century, as insurers focused on competition by marketing through branch offices, that fixed allowances to agents became common.[33]

The exact location of an agency was also important. In 1798 the Sun's agent at Manchester, Robert Duck, reported that the agents of the REA and the Phoenix had lately moved into 'advantageous situations...particularly the latter, who had fitted up a very elegant office for their agent'. Recognising the significance of Duck's agency, the Sun agreed to lend him £2000 to pay for new premises 'in a public and eligible part of the town'.[34] By the early nineteenth century, insurance offices were already clustered in particular streets in the larger towns - the core of future 'business districts'.[35] In 1821 Barber Beaumont wrote to a County shareholder in Edinburgh:

> We are quite sure that if we could get one of the shopkeepers or office-keepers in that conspicuous part of the New Town, viz. the South Bridge, to take our agency and to exert himself for a year or two in making known our advantages, a very leading business might be established there, for your far-sighted countrymen would not fail to appreciate the advantages which we exclusively yield, if they were duly offered to their attention and if the agent were conveniently accessible.

At Liverpool, where he was keen to have a more 'effective' agency, Beaumont urged his agent to relocate to 'a more public situation'. 'If you were in a more striking and imposing house I am sure we might stir up the Town this quarter'.[36]

It was also usual for agents to advertise in local newspapers, and those agents who had connections to a newspaper, or who were editors themselves, could prove extremely useful. Articles encouraging readers to insure could be 'planted' anonymously. A fire which destroyed 19 houses in a Staffordshire village in 1781 provided the occasion for 'Salopiensis' to point out the 'blessings' of fire insurance in the *Shrewsbury Chronicle*, just a year after the local fire office had opened, and to lament the numbers who did not make use of this, 'when such a method of securing their property is within everybody's reach'.[37] Soon local papers were full of agents' notices jostling with each other for column inches, especially just before the quarterly renewal dates for policies, and some offices came to regard this advertising medium as increasingly ineffective.[38]

Big fires also offered scope for advertising and gave insurers numerous opportunities to impress a local populace both with their benevolence and their fire-fighting expertise. The Sun, for example, paid ten guineas in expenses to 'above 100 men' who helped put out a haystack fire adjacent to a barn insured by the office at Farnham, Surrey, in 1765.[39] In addition to such minor cash payments to retain goodwill, the extensive distribution of fire engines, hoses, buckets and fire hooks by the Sun during the eighteenth century, often upon the express request of a local body of leading citizens, undoubtedly helped raise its public profile and secure business for its agents. Many local offices also enjoyed close connections with municipal corporations which included sharing, and sometimes replacing, public fire-fighting facilities. As well as display boards, posters, circular letters and a prominent office location, most agents of country insurers could count on the paraphernalia of firefighting to advertise their services. The Kent Fire Office were typical in sending buckets and firemarks, as well as showboards and printed proposal forms, to their new agents. Most country offices followed the Sun in supporting public fire brigades well into the second quarter of the nineteenth century, despite more competitive conditions. Provincial insurers also utilised their firemen as walking advertisements in the same way as the London offices organised a 'day of marching' by their firemen and watermen before shareholders' meetings and at public events.[40] The Leeds & Yorkshire, for example, sent a new fire engine to their agent in Halifax together with circulars for distribution,

> for which purpose we employ here [in Leeds] the foremen and deputy, who are clad in the firemen's uniform for the occasion - perhaps the same mode of distribution will be the best for you to adopt as it gives some little *éclat* to the business.[41]

Monitoring agents

It was one thing for an insurance office to identify a promising market, appoint an agent and advertise his or her services. It was quite another to ensure that the new agent delivered the expected business. The Imperial was quite ruthless in removing agents who generated no policies during the first two years of the office. The Kent Fire Office required a minimum of ten insurance proposals from their new agents in the first six months after appointment, though it was unusual to set targets in this way. In his annual circulars to the agents of the County, Barber Beaumont liked to name the twelve top salesmen of the previous year who received a vote of thanks for their 'eminent services'.[42] The most direct inducement to activity, however, was commission, which commonly took the form of a percentage of the annual premiums earned by the agent.

For most of the eighteenth century the standard commission rate was five per cent. An exception was the London Assurance, which was paying its few country agents ten per cent in the 1760s, and its agent in Dublin as much as 15 per cent in 1785.[43] From the middle of the century links were made between the commission, the average premium rate produced by an agency, and the level of an agent's income. Thus Irish commission rates were usually higher than in Britain because premium rates were higher in Ireland. The growth in the number of offices after 1780 and the subsequent fluctuations in average premium rates pushed and pulled commission rates in different directions, so that there was an increasing variance offered across the industry but against a general trend towards more generous remuneration. Under conditions of wartime inflation at the end of the century, complaints began to be voiced about the low rates. The Sun's agent at Bath protested in 1805 that he had served the office for 23 years and greatly increased the business, but that his five per cent was 'not adequate to the labour and exertions of an active agent'. During the 1800s commission rates crept upwards to ten per cent, with several offices linking agents' fees for new policies to the sums insured.[44] The Atlas tied the level of commission paid to its Manchester agent for cotton mill insurances to the premium rate he achieved on those risks. Thus if the premium was 10s% or above, the commission would be 20 per cent, falling to 15 per cent if the premium rate was lower. This was an interesting way of trying to stop rate-cutting competition between local agents while maximising yield per sum insured.[45] It was also the practice at the Phoenix to pay important agents, such as William Tate at Manchester, a higher fee for new policies than that paid to its other agents.[46] This was fine for insurers when premium rates were rising, but commission rates proved sticky once premium rates began to tumble at the end of the Napoleonic Wars.

The ten per cent commission became the industry standard in Britain for several decades, though it crept still higher later in the nineteenth century.[47] In some quarters there was resistance to the upward pressure and a considerable deviation emerged around the standard rate. In 1825 the West of England and the Norwich Union were paying 15 to 20 per cent on annual premiums. The Sun and the Phoenix gave their Manchester agents ten per cent on premiums, plus generous travelling allowances when away on business. The Alliance allowed ten per cent on premiums plus a further five per cent on the company's annual profits. Other offices paid much less. The MFLAC paid just five per cent on premiums, plus three shillings for every new policy sold which insured over £300, except where the agent was also a shareholder. The Protector paid five per cent on premiums plus, unusually, a further ten per cent on premiums every three and a half years, less claims on policies insured through the agency during that period. In his annual circulars to the County's agents, Barber Beaumont scorned the appearance of new offices with 'trifling premiums...and preposterous rates of commission', and claimed that they must all be losing business. As late as 1828 the County continued to pay just five per cent. In that year, following increases in commissions elsewhere and pressure from the County's own agents, the office raised the rate to seven and a half per cent for those who submitted their premium receipts promptly. The British Fire Office also used this device to encourage efficiency, paying ten per cent to those remitting within 40 days and five per cent to others.[48]

In return for commissions, agents were expected to undertake a variety of duties which included canvassing for business, inspecting certain properties proposed for insurance, reporting on the character of those proposing an insurance, forwarding proposals to and issuing policies sent from head office, collecting premiums and duty and remitting bills, cheques and accounts to head office, supervising firefighting and salvage and the office's local brigade, arranging the survey and valuation of fire loss, and inquiring into arson, fraud and other suspicious circumstances.[49] Where competition was most fierce, many insurers allowed their agents considerable freedom of action. In 1812, for example, the Imperial told its agent at Liverpool, who wanted to follow the Sun in reducing the premium rate on floating policies there, that he was 'not to take any insurance under the terms of the Sun, to use such discretionary means as adviseable, but not to commit this Company by any form of printed notice'.[50]

Inducements to sell and a leeway to act on their own initiative were balanced by devices to monitor agents' performance. In Britain there existed no system of independent agency firms as emerged in the US from the 1830s. Distances were smaller so that there was less of a principal agent problem and no need for the 'general agents' which came to dominate American property insurance markets. For the most part, personal methods of control remained viable through the relationships between the company secretaries and agents, and between agents and local shareholders. Printed instructions for agents became increasingly elaborate, from the single sheet sent to agents by the London Assurance in 1762 and 1805, to the three pages sent by the Salamander in 1834, the 35 page booklet issued by the Globe in 1857, and the 122 pages of instructions circulated to the Sun's agents in 1865. No British insurer in this period, however, produced the type of voluminous and moralising guides published by the large US fire offices, most notably the 'Aetna Bible' of the 1860s.[51]

Nevertheless, the absence of extensive conduct guides did not mean that dealings with agents were trouble-free. Four problems continually surfaced throughout this period, namely fraud, incompetence, indiscipline and inactivity. Personal bonds and sureties were demanded by almost all insurers. Only ten per cent of the Sun's 118 agents in 1786 provided no security to the office.[52] The value of the Sun's agents' bonds was highly correlated at 0.86 with the estimated volume of their premium income. Of the 11 Sun agents earning £1000 or more, seven provided security of £1000 or more. Agents earning £100 or less were all bonded for £300 or less. Similarly in 1843 the correlation of the MFLAC's bonds to the volume of its agents' remittances (fire and life premiums plus duty) was 0.75. In the two largest MFLAC agencies, Liverpool and Dublin, the agents were bonded for £1000. In the other 11 agencies remitting over £1000 the agents were bonded for sums between £200 (Carlisle and Cork) and £750 (Rochdale).[53]

Sometimes personal agreements were made in which the agent guaranteed the company a particular sum in case of default. Such sums were usually small. Most of the personal agreements made by the MFLAC with its agents were for £50. Some agents were allowed to offer shares in the company as their surety. A few carried on business without any formal agreement or bond. The great majority, however, had to provide the signatures of two other persons as guarantors, and the names, addresses and occupations of the latter were duly recorded in the lists kept by offices. Being a guarantor could be risky. When the MFLAC sacked their agent at Rochdale in 1828 for falling into arrears with his quarterly remittances, the board immediately applied to the agent's two unfortunate sureties, a widow and a 'yeoman', for payment of the sum due. The office also raised the bond required of the replacement agent from £500 to £750.[54] The level of bonds might also be revised when they were found no longer to relate to the volume of business done by the agency concerned. The MFLAC carried out a survey in 1843 which resulted in the bonds being increased in 26 agencies.

In contrast to the populous ranks of light-fingered clerks who troubled insurance offices throughout the period, few examples of theft or fraud can be found among insurance agents. An agent's incompetence, however, was sometimes difficult to distinguish from fraudulent intent. This was a frequent occurrence and it could be costly. The Norwich Union lost £17000 through insolvent agents between 1822 and 1871, an average of £350 a year. The Phoenix faced persistent arrears from its large agencies in Bristol, Manchester and Edinburgh between 1815 and 1835.[55] The Sun frequently dismissed agents who became insolvent and owed the office money. Sometimes it retained even heavily indebted agents once new personal securities had been found, though only if those securities were deemed adequate. For example, the agent at Leighton Buzzard was dismissed in 1805 for failing to clear his outstanding balance of £1800, despite having managed to find security for over half of the sum.[56]

The trouble which could be caused by a recalcitrant and incompetent agent is well illustrated by Thomas Slack, who represented the London Assurance in Newcastle from 1769 to 1784. Slack was printer and founder of the *Newcastle Chronicle* and successfully established in the town at the time of his appointment. Notwithstanding his business skills in the printing trade, he was hopeless as an insurance agent. Nearly 100 letters were sent by the London Assurance to Slack over the course of his agency, an average of a letter every six or seven weeks.[57] Many of these complained about errors and an inattentiveness to detail which did not improve with the passage of time. Slack frequently charged the wrong premiums for risks. He had a particular difficulty with malthouses that exasperated the corporation. In 1778, for instance, Slack charged 2s% for goods in a maltster's house, which, being in a hazardous building, should have been rated at 10s%, 'as I think the experience you have had in assurances ought to have dictated to you'.[58] He also repeatedly failed to fix separate values on each item within an insurance and failed to describe such items properly. The corporation's secretary wrote to Slack in 1773 about 'jumbling together' houses and outhouses in one policy.

> You must excuse my telling you that you never observe your instructions, nor do I suppose you ever pay any attention to my letters to you, as you have been told, both by Mr Harrison and myself, of blending houses and outhouses together numberless times.[59]

Slack also repeatedly neglected to describe the employment of those occupying properties proposed for insurance, the goods stored in such properties, and the materials with which the buildings were constructed. Other problems included his acceptance of proposals to insure categories of risk which the corporation did not insure, such as gunpowder, corn and hay stacks, windmills, paper and other mills, bridges, flax dressers and pawnbrokers, his issue of free policies, his failure to keep copies of his own letters, and one case of an exaggerated expenses claim.[60] The obvious question is why did the London Assurance persist with him? The answer probably lies in their hope of a large volume of good business from the agency. Slack was a man of considerable local connections and some property. At his death in 1784 he left five houses and two shops in Newcastle, a small family estate at Wreay near Carlisle, and stock, stationery and books in his printing office.[61] His average premium remittances, however, only amounted to £61, about one-eighth of the amount earned by the Sun's agency in Newcastle during the same period. Slack's average income from his agency came to just £8 a year, which was probably either the cause or effect of him giving no priority to this business. The London Assurance probably also persevered because Slack's agency was profitable in a small way and because his balances were usually remitted without abnormal delays, although like many of his contemporaries his accounts were seldom in order for long. He almost never remitted his entire balances in one sum, and sometimes he sent the corporation too much money, which it also disliked. Thomas Slack died owing £13 for the last quarter of 1783, which was soon recovered. All offers to replace him were declined and his policyholders were instructed to pay their premiums direct to London or to a new agent appointed at Whitby.[62]

The problem of incompetence converged with that of indiscipline. All offices had agents who persistently accepted insurance proposals, or gave some guarantee to customers about the terms of a policy without reference to their managers or directors. There was a fine line between the discretion accorded an agent to negotiate with policyholders, and his responsibility to act within the limits of company regulations and underwriting practice. The accountability and obligations of an agent could be sorely tested by increasingly fierce competition with local rivals. On occasion, competition between neighbouring agents of the same office could lead to problems. In 1805 the Sun's agent at Leeds, James Kitchingman, complained that the office's new agent at Skipton had 'engrossed many of his customers' and had spoken 'not very favourably of his character and conduct during the time he was in the employ of Mr Kitchingman'. The Sun noted that the Skipton agent was punctual with his accounts and saw no reason to act on Kitchingman's complaint.[63] The company manager's distrust of too much zeal was typically expressed by Barber Beaumont in a letter to a County policyholder in 1821, when he wrote that 'we cannot be guided [on setting premium rates] by the opinion of the agent to the Royal Exchange. Agents are frequently misleading their offices with their opinion of risks.'[64]

Inactivity, the converse of zeal, also caused headaches for managers. Barber Beaumont's letters to his agents are full of advice, admonishing and goading them to do better. His annual circulars were used to express Beaumont's own views about the County's market position in relation to its rivals. These views were informed by the observations made on personal visits to agencies. Typical in tone, substance and attention to detail, was his letter to a Yorkshire agent in 1821.

> In passing through Halifax and its neighbourhood last week, I did not observe any of our marks up - which considering the extent of your business I wondered at. Pray employ a man to fix them on all places insured by us for which fixing we will allow 2d each. Always fix them in this way. If you deliver them to the parties they are wasted. They cost us nearly 1s 6d each.[65]

More formal tours by office managers and directors were commonly employed from the beginning of the nineteenth century as a means of monitoring and reforming agencies. George Stonestreet and John Hawes carried out a 'fierce' inspection of the Phoenix agents in more than a dozen counties and 30 towns in 1800. Other examples include several tours on behalf of the Sun by Philip and Calverley Bewicke and by Green, the head of the Sun's country department, between 1805 and 1816, the visit to south-west England by Thomas Richter for the Phoenix in 1811, the tours of Henry Desborough for the Atlas in 1809 and 1811, and the series of inspections launched by the Norwich Union in the 1820s.[66] For the most part agents appear to have accepted this form of monitoring with good grace. However, where an agent was faced with a visit from an official lower in rank than a company secretary or director, quarrels could arise and deference might wear thin. When the Guardian sent its surveyor, Mr Sumner, to Manchester in 1827, he clashed with the agent there, Thomas Langston, over the assessment of warehouses and mills proposed for insurance. This resulted in a series of allegations and counter allegations which the office was compelled to investigate, and which led to a general court of directors being called to hear the arguments. A couple of extracts give a flavour of the contest.

> The case of Gardner & Atkinson: Mr Langston states that there were only four stoves, the fifth being merely temporary as intimated to Mr Sumner. He attributed the omission to notice this to Mr Sumner's defective hearing....
> Excess of limits etc.: Mr Langston is of opinion the Manchester risks are considerably improved since the establishment of this Office in consequence of the use of stoves instead of fire grates, the introduction of gas lights and improvement in the construction of buildings. Thinks Mr Sumner's inspections were not sufficiently numerous to enable him to form a correct judgement on the Manchester risks in general...Mr Sumner does not consider the warehouse risks in Manchester improved by the use of pipe stoves instead of fire grates, and the improvements in buildings are not very general, being mostly in Market Street....States that his inspections were as various and extensive as the short period of his visit would admit.[67]

This dispute illustrates some of the serious information problems which London insurers continued to face on the eve of the railway age when operating in provincial markets. Whom was the Guardian to believe when the details of individual risks and the impact of technical change were so hotly disputed by its two representatives on the spot? More generally this case typified the difficulty insurance offices had in consolidating the interests of agents with their own. Agents often tended to adopt an inclusive approach, driven by the need to keep the goodwill of their customers and to keep ahead of their rivals. The offices, on the other hand, keen to ensure accurate and careful risk selection, often preferred a more exclusive underwriting strategy. These problems were only more fully addressed with the creation of branch offices during the second half of the nineteenth century.

Customer relations

Why did insurance companies go to the effort to establish agencies in the first place? Despite the concentration of insurance sales in London, there was some demand at an early date for a convenient service outside the capital. The London livery companies often required their tenants outside London to insure their properties as part of their leasehold agreements.[68] Among the minor gentry, businessmen and educated classes in the home counties before 1750 there was already an appreciation of insurance. Upon the death of Sir John Lade in 1739, the trustee of his estate, John Fuller of Brightling Park, Sussex, urged Lade's steward to purchase insurance for Lade's London houses, in addition to carrying out a check on his tenants.[69] Without a agent nearby, however, those living in the provinces could find it difficult to obtain cover, even when they wanted to insure property in London. If he was out of town at the quarter days when his insurances were due for renewal, the poet Thomas Gray had to ask his friends to pay the annual premiums for policies on his houses at Wanstead and Cornhill to the London Assurance office in Birchin Lane.[70] Henry Purefoy of Shalstone, Buckinghamshire, described the bother he had experienced in a letter to his London attorney in 1743.

> You proffered your service to take out Policies of Insurance for my mother's house in Cursitor's Alley, but when wee sent them to Buckingham you was gone to Town. I have sent them by the Carrier and hope they will come time enough. I will have the insurance for six years from Midsummer, but if they won't insure under seven years it must be so.[71]

In 1732 the Sun discovered that of the 45 policyholders at Huntingdon, where the company had no agent, 28 of them paid their premiums directly to the Sun's head office in London. These payments were probably sent first by carrier to the policyholder's agent or attorney. The remainder paid their premiums to the agent at Lynn, John Scott, who occasionally rode over to Huntingdon to collect the money, and who, not unreasonably, requested that his expenses be covered for doing so. After checking the Huntingdon insurances in Scott's accounts, and finding that many were 'old and at old premiums', it was decided that Scott should have some gratuity for costs already incurred,

> but that it be signified to him he need not go thither on purpose, but if he happens to be there occasionally, and do receive any premiums or gett any new policies, he will have the common allowance.[72]

Thus, at this early date the Sun scarcely went out of its way to market itself in places where the premium flow was modest but steady. The Sun's managers may have continued to harbour doubts about the effectiveness of agency selling. The convenience of policyholders was certainly balanced against the costs of collection, with the former not always given the priority. When the London Assurance decided to close its agency in Newcastle in 1784, its advice to several dozen policyholders was 'to get some friend' to pay their premiums at its head office, or else to the nearest agent who was located in Whitby. In Peterborough in 1734, where the Sun's agent had been suspended for falling into arrears, the office's auditor found that 'most of the insured in and about Peterborough have desisted paying for want of an agent there'.[73]

Once insurance was obtained, a policyholder's problems did not necessarily cease. In 1751 the Sun's policyholders in Newcastle 'took offence' at letters giving them notice of premium arrears, after they had already paid their premiums to the local agent, a mistake which the Sun was quick to rectify by stopping any further notices being sent directly to customers. Instead, agents would receive a list of arrears each quarter for their district with directions for them to give notice.[74] Difficulties with agents also drew protests. In 1736 Josiah Perry of Worcester wrote to the Sun to complain of 'several neglects and bad treatment' from the agent there, who was promptly replaced. In 1782 'several noblemen and gentlemen, meeting in a committee for assisting the poor sufferers by fire at Great Horwood in Buckinghamshire', complained about the behaviour of the Sun's agent at Buckingham in settling the losses and paying the victims. The Sun called the agent to London in order to 'minutely investigate' the affair, but the agent was able to 'exculpate himself from the charges' to the office's satisfaction.[75] Shareholders could frequently be relied upon to keep an eye on the local agent. In 1825, for example, a Birmingham shareholder complained to the MFLAC 'that the agent there did not obtain as much business for the company as might be reasonably expected'. The agent was promptly invited to resign. Similarly the Rochdale committee of MFLAC shareholders demanded and obtained the dismissal of the local agent when he fell into arrears.[76]

Customers also pressed their insurance offices for competitive premium rates and policy conditions, and may often have been encouraged to do so by local agents. In 1785 several Sun agents claimed that

> some of the other offices have withdrawn the exception relating to hay and corn being stacked too wet or green, and that farmers and others would withdraw their insurances in this office if the said exception should be continued.[77]

The office yielded to this pressure. Collective action by consumers was not uncommon and often successful. The London sugar bakers objected to the Sun's new rates for their properties in 1738. Brandy and tobacco factors in Dublin in 1754 forced the London Assurance to give up their attempt to introduce an average clause into their policies. In 1832 the Imperial reduced its sugar house rates under great pressure from refiners in London and Liverpool.[78] In 1753, following 'a long debate', the Union resolved to reclassify metropolitan breweries from 'half-hazardous' to 'whole hazardous', thus increasing the premiums charged. The trade reacted by convening a general meeting of insured brewers in Cornhill. One week later, despite dissenting voices on its board, the Union reversed its decision, having accepted the brewers' arguments that

> the brewing trade does not appear...so dangerous as to be deemed whole hazardous, because they generally keep engines to assist themselves and neighbours at fires; and that a great part of their goods are portable and moveable.[79]

Public ignorance of the principles of underwriting also led to discontent. At Bristol in 1805 a policyholder with the London Assurance complained that he had to pay a higher premium because of hazardous goods in his warehouse which were owned by others. In fact it was common practice to set the premium rate for a building in multiple occupation by the most hazardous trade or goods present there.[80] For most of the eighteenth century insurers made allowances for the public's lack of understanding. There were numerous examples where the payment of renewal premiums had been forgotten, or where policies were omitted to be endorsed for changes of circumstance and where the wrong rate of premium had consequently been paid. Policyholders frequently blamed such errors on their own ignorance and appealed, often successfully, to the insurer's generosity, although usually payments were made only after the office had checked the veracity of their stories. On occasion, victims of fires would receive a partial payment of their claim in advance of the final settlement when they needed the money to keep them in business.[81] The often hostile attitude of the courts towards insurance offices who contested claims undoubtedly encouraged this spirit of compromise.[82] Claims litigation could result in adverse publicity. The Imperial, for example, received a letter in 1822 from a London resident who declined to renew his insurance 'in consequence of his unfavorable opinion against this Office from Messrs Severn, King and Co's trial'.[83]

As insurance became better known outside London, the plead of ignorance by policyholders and claimants wore thin. Instead customers increasingly bargained or played off one office against another to obtain advantageous terms. In 1814 the Kent Fire Office rejected a threat from a policyholder at Hythe to remove his insurance to the Norwich Union if the Kent did not offer the same terms as that office.[84] A Bingley cotton mill owner and Leeds & Yorkshire shareholder, J.G. Horsfall, had no compunction about trying to extract a discount from his own office in 1824 by threatening to accept a better offer from elsewhere. The Leeds insurers stood firm, but found it uncomfortable when details of a letter, which suggested that the office was not interested in insuring Horsfall's mill, were leaked to Horsfall by their agent at Bradford. In their response, whilst trying not to antagonise an important proprietor, the company secretary asserted a position of moral authority.

> I had indeed a wish to take your insurance as coming from a shareholder and being situated on ground particularly well known to me, but I conceive that I should not fulfil my duty to the shareholders generally if I were to run a race of low premiums with offices and agents who have but little knowledge or discretion to guide them...Our

terms are made in perfect fairness and openness, without any captious regulations which leave a hole to creep out of in case of accident, and as all our business will be transacted with perfect liberality, we conceive we are entitled to an equitable premium on all the risks we take, and are unwilling to be beaten from our high station.[85]

There were also occasions when customers demanded, usually via their agents, that companies diversify the range of cover offered. In 1752 the Sun finally agreed to insure corn and hay ricks after nearly twenty years of pressure from its rural agents.[86] In the early nineteenth century efforts were made to get the Atlas to extend its insurance cover to house rent and legal expenses. These were only partially successful. In 1811 the company passed a resolution that 'rent (not specifically assured) is only intended to be allowed when the building of the house is assured'. In 1815 Richard Ashley of London asked the Atlas to insure 'a sum to cover the rent which by his lease he is bound to pay in case of fire; and also such legal expenses as he may be subject to in compelling his landlord to reinstate his dwelling house'. The office agreed to insure the rent, but not the legal costs incurred in the event of a fire. A further example was the Liverpool & Manchester Railway Company which in 1835 failed to persuade the MFLAC to insure goods in transit, despite the business interest of several MFLAC directors in the railway.[87]

As already noted, conflicting interests could emerge among local agents, torn between loyalty to their customers and their obligations to their offices, and over premium rates when a shareholder was also a policyholder. The Leeds & Yorkshire expressed the attitude of many insurers when they told James Ackroyd & Sons of Halifax that 'being shareholders they ought not to force us upon fixing too low premiums on mills risks'.[88] The potential for such conflict was always greatest where an insurance office had been established by a group of merchants or manufacturers. Merchants turned insurers felt compelled to follow the logic of their new business, which not infrequently raised tensions with the mercantile community of which they remained a part. The greatest complications occurred when the interests of agents, shareholders and policyholders became intertwined, and then stacked against the insurer. This is illustrated by an account of the MFLAC's experience in dealing with all three groups in Liverpool between 1825 and 1827.[89]

From the outset the MFLAC's agent in Liverpool, Richard Dawson, demonstrated an excessive propensity to act independently of his board of directors, and, indeed, to adopt a 'rather too dictatorial' tone in his letters to them. He was frequently admonished for endorsing policies without the company's permission, and for pressing for rate reductions in the face of competition from other agents. He also fell into arrears and the MFLAC's secretary had to be dispatched to Liverpool in 1826 to recover an outstanding balance of £2700. The MFLAC had its committee of local shareholders, chaired by Robert Gladstone, to monitor Dawson's performance, but Dawson appeared to enjoy an unduly close relationship to them. Nevertheless, relations with the Liverpool shareholders remained smooth until a fire on the night of 16 October 1825 destroyed a large amount of cotton in the Gradwell Street warehouse of Cropper & Benson, one of Liverpool's premier merchant firms. Quaker cotton importers and speculators in corn, one of the firm, James Cropper - 'canting Jemmy' according to Cobbett - was a major political figure in the town.[90] Another partner, Robert Benson, was a MFLAC shareholder and a member of Gladstone's committee. Cropper & Benson were insured for £235000 in several fire offices, including two policies with the MFLAC for a total of £30000.[91] Doubts arose in Manchester over the validity of one of these policies. In response, Gladstone wrote on behalf of his committee to support the claim, even though the policy had expired, for the fire had occurred within what they asserted was the customary 15-day period of grace for policyholders to renew their insurances. The MFLAC rejected this argument, suggesting that Cropper & Benson at the time had no intention of renewing the policy, thereby rendering the office no longer liable once the policy had expired.

Dawson was accused by the MFLAC board of failing to pass on information pertinent to the validity of the claim. This consisted of the declaration by one partner that the firm did not intend to renew the policy, the 'substance of a conversation with one of the partners on the morning after the fire' that the company did not consider the MFLAC liable, the failure to pass on the name of this partner, and the failure to inform the board of a change in the opinion of the Liverpool committee about the validity of the claim. The board rejected Dawson's assertion that such information was given to him privately. 'Any communication made to their agent affecting the justice of a claim upon the company ought not and cannot be considered "private conversations"'. Had the MFLAC directors themselves not inquired into the merit of Cropper & Benson's claim, 'they would not have been made acquainted with the principal of these facts and they might consequently have been subjected to the payment of upwards of £2000 more than there was any equitable claim upon them for'.

For their part, the Liverpool committee restated their opinion that the Cropper & Benson policy was in full force for a year and 15 days, and threatened to resign. The MFLAC directors stood their ground. They regretted that the Liverpool shareholders disapproved of their decision, but 'it is quite impossible for them to delegate to a Committee the power of deciding upon claims'. The company was in some difficulty here, for the power of adjustment had in practice been devolved to the Liverpool committee on several previous occasions. All the Manchester board could do was to hope that the Liverpool shareholders would not carry out their threat. Early in 1827 Cropper & Benson called for arbitration for their unsettled claim, but this was rejected. Although the other insurance offices had paid up, the Manchester insurers did not give way and became very irritated when Dawson wrote to express his disappointment that the board had not come to a different conclusion. The Liverpool agent received a tart reply that '...after the repeated decisions come to by the Board on Messrs Cropper, Benson & Co's claim, they consider his interference therein improper and offensive.' Dawson's response was a somewhat affected indignation that he had only made suggestions for the good of the company, that every such suggestion 'has originated from my personal feeling of the effects likely to be produced on the minds of the public'. Henceforth, he would 'most studiously avoid making any remarks that may in the slightest degree be termed either improper or offensive'.

In fact Dawson, under enormous competitive pressure from other offices, continued to make suggestions about cutting rates on commercial risks in Liverpool and to give his views on the local property market, which he saw as indispensable functions of his agency. And he continued to be rebuffed. Dawson was still the MFLAC's agent when Liverpool suffered a huge fire in the warehouse district in 1833 that was followed by a substantial increase in rates. He was still agent ten years later when his annual remittances came to over £8000, the largest income from any of the MFLAC's agencies by a considerable margin.[92] The history of the MFLAC's Liverpool agency suggests that the company succeeded in picking its way through a minefield which might have destroyed a large portion of its business at an early date. The story illustrates the importance to contemporary insurers of maintaining goodwill in a close-knit mercantile community, where the confluence of interests of agents, shareholders and policyholders could prove an explosive mix.

Notes

[1]   Boyd, *An Ice-Cream War*, p.129.
[2]   CUL, PAA, PX1771, Reading Insurance Company, Deed of Settlement, 25 Nov. 1822; *Reading Chronicle*, 3 July 1841.
[3]   Dickson, *Sun Insurance*, p.133 n1; Trebilcock, *Phoenix Assurance*, vol.I, p.499, table 12.4, p.695; GL Ms 12160A/14, Imperial, DM, 29 Jan. 1840; *Kentish Gazette*, 26 Sept. 1828.
[4]   GL Ms 16206/1, Essex & Suffolk, DM, 1802-21; CUL, PAA, PX1759, Phoenix, Take over Papers, Berkshire & Gloucestershire.
[5]   SRO, Ms 3008/1/2/1, Salop, DM, 1780-88.
[6]   GL Ms 16170/1, Atlas, DM, 9 May 1811.
[7]   Trebilcock, *Phoenix Assurance*, vol.I, pp.695-6.
[8]   GL Ms 16222/8, MFLAC, DM, 4 Oct. 1843; Ms 11935E, Sun, Take over Papers, Preston & North Lancashire, 1848.
[9]   Calculated from GL Ms11935E, Sun, Take over Papers, British Fire, 1843.
[10]   GCA, TD446/5/18/1, North British, Minute Book no.1, Preamble to List of Subscribers, 9 Mar. 1809.
[11]   Agencies counted from entries in GCA, TD446/4/3/1, North British, Ledger no.2, 1822-9.
[12]   Baines, *History of Lancaster*; *Wheeler's Manchester Chronicle*, 10 Jan., 27 Mar. 1824; *Cowdray's Manchester Gazette and Weekly Advertiser*, 27 Mar., 20 Nov. 1824. Fire insurance agents counted from *Pigot's Directory of Manchester and Salford*.
[13]   Dickson, *Sun Insurance*, pp. 70-71, 133-4.
[14]   Trebilcock, *Phoenix Assurance*, vol.I, pp.87-8. Cf. also Supple, *Royal Exchange*, pp.99, 154.
[15]   Ryan, 'Norwich Union and the British Fire Insurance Market', p.57.

[16] GL M s 18822, London Assurance, Memorandum of the Fire Committee, 26 Sept. 1806. The London Assurance did indeed appoint eight lawyers among its first 19 agents, but a comprehensive list of its agents has not survived from this period. Calculated from Ms 8755/2, London Assurance, Out Letter Book, Circular letter to agents, March-July 1805 *passim*.

[17] Ryan, for example, traced occupations for just 65 out of the 340 agents (19 per cent) of the Norwich Union in 1813, while subtracting the unknowns, and the non-specific 'gentlemen, widows' categories from Trebilcock's data leaves 130 known occupations for 222 agents (59 per cent) appointed by the Phoenix between 1783 and 1802, and 148 occupations for 227 Phoenix agents (65 per cent) in 1821. Ryan, 'History of Norwich Union', pp.192-3; Trebilcock, *Phoenix Assurance*, vol.I, table 3.3, p.89.

[18] Agencies counted from GL Ms 18111, Guardian, Agents' List; Ms 11935E, Sun, Take over Papers, British Fire, Agents' List. The Guardian appointed 335 agents between 1821 and 1830. The occupations of 252 (75 per cent) of these are known. The British listed 507 agents in 1843. Occupations are given for 281 of these (55 per cent).

[19] Except where indicated in the text, all the percentages given in the following paragraphs are calculated from totals of agents whose occupations are specified, rather than all agents.

[20] Calculated from data in GL Ms11935E, Sun, Take over Papers, Salamander, Preston & North Lancashire, British Fire and table 5.4 above. Sun and REA figures from table 3.1 above. Phoenix percentages calculated from Trebilcock, *Phoenix Assurance*, vol.I, table 3.1, p.82.

[21] Calculated from Ryan, 'Norwich Union and the British Fire Insurance Market', table 6, p.69.

[22] Schofield, 'British Population Change', table 4.5, p.88.

[23] GL Ms 11935/1,2, 7, Sun, CCM, 21 Jan. 1732, 22 Mar., 23 Aug. 1734, 7 Nov. 1735, 25 June, 10 Dec. 1736, 15 Dec. 1738, 13 Apr. 1744, 28 Sept. 1781.

[24] GL Ms 11935/1, 2, 7, 8, Sun, CCM, 24 Feb., 26 May, 1 Dec. 1726, 30 Mar. 1727, 6 Nov. 1730, 21 Mar., 6 June 1735, 10 Feb. 1738, 28 Nov. 1740, 28 Sept. 1781, 23 Aug., 24 Nov. 1786; Dickson, *Sun Insurance*, p.69.

[25] GL Ms 18111, Guardian, Agents' List, fol.22. Rogerson was at the time the publisher of the *Blackburn Gazette*.

[26] Dickson, *Sun Insurance*, p.277; Hurren, *Phoenix Renascent*, p.170.

[27] GL Ms 11935/3, Sun, CCM, 24 Jan. 1746; McLynn, *Jacobite Army in England*.

[28] GL Ms 11935A/1, Sun, Report Books, vol.1, Reports of Philip Bewicke, Oct. 1806, 7 Oct. 1807, 8 Oct. 1812, First report of the special committee to increase the number of country agents, 2 Jan. 1827, Second report, 2 July 1827, First report of the special committee to inquire into the state of the agencies, 3 Apr. 1834; Dickson, *Sun Insurance*, p.132; CKS, U2593/B6/2, Kent, DM, 30 Aug. 1803; GL Ms 16170/1, Atlas, DM, 30 Aug. 1810.

[29] GL Ms 11935/1, Sun, CCM, 17 Feb. 1738; Torrington, *Diaries*, vol.II, p.120.

[30] GL Ms 16222/2, MFLAC, DM, 28 Apr., 9 May 1825; Ms 16170/2, Atlas, DM, 20 Aug. 1812.

[31] County, Letter Book 'M', to W. Reynolds, 17 Sept. 1821.

[32] GL Ms 14281/1, Guardian, GCM, 3 Jan. 1823.

[33] Westall, 'Marketing Strategy'.

34 GL Ms 11937/7, Sun, GCM, 4 Jan. 1798.
35 GL Ms 11935/8, Sun, CCM, 5 Jan. 1787. Cf. King Street, Manchester, and, of course, Lombard Street and Cornhill in London. Pearson, 'Collective Diversification', p.400; Trebilcock, *Phoenix Assurance*, vol.I, map 2.2, pp.64-5.
36 County, Letter Book 'M', to D. Muir, 7 July 1821, W. Reynolds jr, 21 Aug. 1821. See also the support given to the rent of a 'conspicuous' house by the agent at Newington Butts, County, DM, 17 Dec. 1818.
37 *Shrewsbury Chronicle*, 14 July 1781. Cf. also the *Chelmsford Chronicle*, described as 'praising the benefits of insurance at every opportunity'. King, 'Prosecution Associations', p.203 n115.
38 LCA, acc.3393, box 41, Leeds & Yorkshire, Secretary's Letterbook, 1824-9, to W. Edwards, 16 June 1825.
39 GL Ms 11932/7,11, Sun, CMM, 10 Oct. 1765.
40 Supple, *Royal Exchange*, p.97; Trebilcock, *Phoenix Assurance*, vol.I, pp.91-3; Noakes, *County Fire Office*, pp.12-13; Dickson, *Sun Insurance*, p.63.
41 LCA, acc.3393, box 41, Leeds & Yorkshire, Secretary's Letterbook 1824-9, fol.283-4.
42 GL Ms 12160A/1, Imperial, DM, 20 Nov. 1805; Reed, *Kent Insurance Company*; County, Circular to Agents, 12 July 1810, 10 June 1811.
43 GL Ms 8728/8, London Assurance, DM, 26 May 1762, Instructions to Agents; Ms 8755/2, London Assurance, Out Letter Book, to W. Allen, 8 June 1785.
44 GL Ms 11935/9, Sun, CCM, 1 Feb. 1805; Reed, *Kent Insurance Company*; CKS, U2593/B6/3, Kent, DM, 28.Aug. 1805; Trebilcock, *Phoenix Assurance*, vol.I, p.464; Ryan, 'Norwich Union and the British Fire Insurance Market', p.57.
45 GL Ms 16170/1, Atlas, DM, 28 June, 19 July 1808, 26 Apr., 21 June 1810. The Atlas agent at Bristol, however, had less luck in 1812 when he requested a commission of 20 per cent on premiums of London insurances effected through his agency. Atlas would give him only the standard ten per cent. Ms 16170/2, Atlas, DM, 7 May 1812.
46 Trebilcock, *Phoenix Assurance*, vol.I, p.362.
47 Supple, *Royal Exchange* p.134; Dickson, *Sun Insurance*, p.133.
48 County, Circular to Agents, 12 July 1810; County, Letter Book 'M', to W. Banton, 7 July 1821; County, DM, 11 Sept. 1828; GL Ms 11935E, Sun, Take over Papers, British Fire, 1843.
49 Cf. Jenkins, 'The Practice of Insurance', p.25.
50 GL Ms 12160A/5, Imperial, DM, 16 Sept. 1812.
51 GL Ms 8728/8, London Assurance, DM, 26 May 1762; Ms 8735/6, London Assurance, FCM, 8 Feb. 1805, General Instructions to Agents; Ms 11935E, Sun, Take over Papers, Salamander, Instructions for Agents, 1834; Ms 11657, Globe, Instructions to Agents (Private), 1857; Carter, *Order out of Chaos*, p.72; Baranoff, 'Principals, Agents and Control', pp.98-9. I am most grateful to Dr D.T. Jenkins for allowing me to consult his notes on the Globe. On the inadequacy of the instructions for Sun agents, see Dickson, *Sun Insurance*, p.71.
52 Calculated from GL Ms 18856, Sun, Agents' Accounts, 1786.
53 GL Ms 16222/8, MFLAC, DM, Statement of Premium and Duty received by each Agent, 25 Mar. 1842-24 Mar. 1843.
54 GL Ms 16222/4, MFLAC, DM, 27 Nov. 1828.

55 Ryan, 'History of Norwich Union', pp.446-8; Trebilcock, *Phoenix Assurance*, vol.I, pp.550-51.

56 GL Ms 11935/10, Sun, CCM, 27 Sept. 1805.

57 GL Ms 8755/2, London Assurance, Out Letter Book, 1751-1805.

58 GL Ms 8755/2, London Assurance, Out Letter Book, to T. Slack, 2 July 1778. For other malthouse examples, see letters of 12 Sept. 1776, 29 Mar., 16 June 1780.

59 GL Ms 8755/2, London Assurance, Out Letter Book, to T. Slack, 1 Feb., 17 Feb. 1773.

60 GL Ms 8755/2, London Assurance, Out Letter Book, to T. Slack, 9 June, 19 Sept. 1770, 1 Jan. 1771, 14 Apr., 19 June 1772, 1 Feb., 10 Dec. 1773, 5 Sept. 1774, 19 Apr., 4 June 1776, 22 Mar., 20 Aug., 21 Oct. 1777, 10 Sept. 1778, 29 June 1780, 20 Jan. 1782.

61 Hodgson, 'Thomas Slack of Newcastle', pp.149-50.

62 GL Ms 8755/2, London Assurance, Out Letter Book, to T. Slack, 20 Sept. 1782, 15 July 1783, to S. Hodgson, 15 Mar. 1784, to Brown & Thompson, 2 Apr. 1784. Slack's agency was continued at Whitby by John Monkman until its final closure in 1789, when a positive balance of £207 for the whole period 1771-89 was carried over to the profit and loss account. Calculated from Ms 8746/1, London Assurance, Fire Charter Ledger A.

63 GL Ms 11935/10, Sun, CCM, 8 Nov. 1805.

64 County, Letter Book 'M', to T. Vine, 13 Nov. 1821.

65 County, Letter Book 'M', to R. Swaine, 21 Sept. 1821.

66 Trebilcock, *Phoenix Assurance*, vol.I, p.88; Ryan, 'History of Norwich Union', p.448.

67 GL Ms 14281/3, Guardian, GCM, Committee for Fire Purposes Report, 31 Jan. 1828.

68 For an example, see Porter, 'Great Fire of Gravesend', p.26.

69 John Fuller sr. to Richard Allen, 22 Nov. 1740, in Crossley and Saville eds., *The Fuller Letters*, p.139.

70 Gray, *Letters*, vol.I, no.CXVIII, to Wharton, 9 Mar. 1755, vol.III, no.CCL, to Mason, 6 Mar. 1763.

71 Henry Purefoy to John Land, 25 June 1743, in Eland ed., *Purefoy Letters*, vol.I, p.196.

72 GL Ms 11935/1, Sun, CCM, 9 June 1732, 9 Feb. 1733.

73 GL Ms 8755/2, London Assurance, Out Letter Book, to S. Hodgson, 15 Mar. 1784; Ms 11935/1, Sun, CCM, 14 June 1734.

74 GL Ms 11935/3, Sun, CCM, 15 Nov. 1751.

75 GL Ms 11932/1,12, Sun, CMM, 27 Feb. 1736, 11 Apr., 25 Apr. 1782.

76 GL Ms 16222/1, 4, MFLAC, DM, 20 June 1825, 27 Nov. 1828.

77 GL Ms 11931/7, Sun, GCM, 8 Dec. 1785.

78 GL Ms 11931/4, Sun, GCM, 8 Apr. 1738; Ms 8735/1, London Assurance, FCM, 8 Mar. 1754; Ms 12160A/11, Imperial, DM, 4 Apr., 9 May 1832.

79 GL Ms 14022/10, Union, DM, 3 Jan., 14 Mar., 21 Mar. 1753

80 GL Ms 8755/2, London Assurance, Out Letter Book, to W. Tanner, 21 June 1805. The problem of rating property in multiple tenure is discussed in chapter 8 below.

81 For example, the case of Michael Lejeune, victim of a fire at Covent Garden in 1774, GL Ms 11932/10, Sun, CMM, 19 May 1774.

82   Cf., for example, the Sun's defeat in the Court of King's Bench over a £1700 claim by a Mr Butler, GL Ms 11932/6, Sun, CMM, 23 Mar. 1769.

83   GL Ms 12160A/8, Imperial, DM, 1 May 1822.

84   CKS, U2593/B6/8, Kent, DM, 25 May 1814.

85   LCA, acc.3393, box 41, Leeds & Yorkshire, Secretary's Letter Book, to R. Thornton, 23 Dec. 1824, to J.G. Horsfall, 27 Dec. 1824.

86   GL Ms 11935/3, Sun, CCM, 15 Sept. 1752.

87   GL Ms 16170/2, Atlas, DM, 24 Oct. 1811, 30 July 1812, 20 Apr. 1815; Ms 16222/6, MFLAC, DM, 6 Aug. 1835.

88   LCA, acc.3393, box 41, Leeds & Yorkshire, Secretary's Letter Book, to J. Ackroyd, 21 Mar. 1825.

89   The following is based upon GL Ms 16222/2-3, MFLAC, DM, 1825-7 *passim*.

90   Cobbett, *Rural Rides*, pp.157, 343. On Cropper, see Jarvis, 'James Cropper'. On Cropper & Benson, see Williams, 'Liverpool Merchants and the Cotton Trade', appendix, pp.203-5.

91   GL Ms 12160A/9, Imperial, DM, 19 Oct. 1825.

92   GL Ms 16222/5, 8, MFLAC, DM, 31 Jan.-14 Feb. 1833, Statement of Premium and Duty received by each Agent, year ending 24 Mar. 1843.

Chapter 8

Underwriting

And Accident & Chance were found hidden in Length Bredth & Highth

William Blake.[1]

This chapter considers the development of the practice of fire insurance underwriting in Britain over a period of 130 years. It did not evolve smoothly. Rather it staggered along, pushed by sporadic heavy losses in individual markets and by technological change in manufacturing, pulled by imitation of what other underwriters were doing, shaping and being shaped by demand for insurance cover on new types of risk, and, to a lesser extent, by the regulations to improve building in London and provincial towns.

As an example of technical change in a evolving financial service, the subject is interesting in its own right. Underwriting, however, is also one of the few areas of insurance history to have touched the wider historiography of the industrial revolution. Over the past thirty years the central policy registers of the Sun and the REA have attracted increasing interest from historians, particularly from those attempting to employ the property valuations in the registers to reconstruct capital formation.[2] The pioneers were Chapman and Jenkins working on the cotton and wool textile industries respectively.[3] They and other authors agreed that the policy values provided decent proxies for the replacement values of property, and, by extension, for current values of fixed capital. In turn, the capital estimates based on insurance valuations reinforced the view that the early phase of British industrialisation was not capital intensive. The distribution of the SSRC microfiche indexes of the Sun and the REA registers in the mid 1980s made these sources more accessible to a wider range of researchers who also accepted the consensus that policy values were 'essentially reliable' as indicators of property values.[4]

The registers were the final product of those underwriting procedures which are the subject of this chapter. Its findings, therefore, directly relate to the debate about the meaning and accuracy of insurance values. The first section below surveys the uses to which the registers have been put and summarises the debate. The second, third and fourth sections examine the changing procedures of risk assessment and the key issues of underinsurance and coinsurance. The fifth section explores the extent to which customer perceptions of risk were changed, and the safety of property improved, as a result of the experience of being assessed for insurance. It also looks at the way insurers utilised, or failed to utilise, underwriting data to make their own businesses safer and more profitable.

The debate about insurance valuations

Hitherto the policy registers of the Sun and the REA have been used in three ways. First, they have been used to illustrate the types of property within a locality or industry. Beresford, for example, examined property insured by the Sun in Leeds and Butt used the Sun's policies to examine the occupational distribution of investment in Glasgow tenements.[5] This kind of analysis has not fundamentally depended upon the accuracy of the insurance valuations. That is not true for two other uses of the registers, namely to estimate wealth distribution and capital formation.[6] Chapman used 'typical' policy values to create a classification of cotton mills for the period 1770-1800, which became the benchmark for other investigations of mill property. National estimates were produced for total fixed capital formation (TFCF) in cotton spinning, some of which were substantially based on insurance valuations.[7] Jenkins used policy values to estimate the average fixed capital in wool textile mills between 1800 and 1835, and he estimated TFCF from these average values. Butt, Donnachie and Orbell also used policy values to estimate TFCF, respectively in Scottish cotton and brewing and in the corn milling industry.[8]

The initial problem for these historians was to establish what the sums insured actually meant. It is generally agreed that policy values represented replacement cost and that they were unlikely to overstate property values. Fraud existed, but given the care with which insurance companies adjusted losses, there was little point in owners overvaluing their property. In claims disputes independent arbitrators were always likely to spot overinsurance. Most historians have agreed that underinsurance is a more probable source of error. First, there is the omission from insurance policies of non-hazardous items of fixed capital, such as dams and reservoirs, although these may have involved only small sums. Second, there is the question of stock and moveable utensils. Chapman noted that insured values for these 'cannot be realistic estimates', but he argued that the sums involved were small and he included them in his fixed capital totals, as did Orbell and Donnachie. Third, unintentional underinsurance may have occurred when a manufacturer did not know the accurate value of his property, for instance when renewing a policy in a period of rising prices. Jenkins dismissed this as a relatively improbable source of undervaluation. Mill policies were reviewed regularly and their values were therefore unlikely to lag behind replacement cost.[9]

There was also the possibility of intentional underinsurance. All fire offices imposed ceilings on the amount insured on any one risk. As a result, some properties were coinsured with several offices. Jenkins argued that this is not a major difficulty for historians. The average ceiling of £5000 would only have induced coinsurance on the largest properties, and, in any case, 'fire offices required sums insured in other offices to be declared, and these sums were normally recorded in the policy registers'. 'It seems likely', he claimed, 'that the information was rarely omitted'. Chapman agreed that unendorsed coinsurances amounted to 'minor omissions and discrepancies'.[10] There remained the question of sample bias.

Donnachie noted that some of the smaller Scottish breweries were missing from the Sun's registers, and Orbell terminated his study of corn mills in 1820, because, with the rise of provincial fire offices, the sample of properties insured by the Sun became less representative. Jenkins also found that the larger wool textile mills predominated among those insured by the Sun and attempted to adjust his TFCF estimates accordingly.[11]

Suspicions of underinsurance did raise early doubts about the policy values, but in general the consensus has been that they do provide reliable reflections of property values.[12] In his history of the Phoenix Assurance Trebilcock disputed this conclusion. First, he argued that it was common practice among insurers to promote underinsurance of industrial premises by establishing strict ceilings on the amount insured in any single risk, and by specifying ceilings for separate items within one risk. The Phoenix believed that full cover induced moral hazard. Where the insured had to carry some of his own risk, the temptation to neglect safety was reduced. Second, Trebilcock argued that it was also 'common practice' for a textile mill to be separately insured with several offices, in which case it becomes essential for historians interested in mill values to trace all policies relating to a single risk. When cross checking a sample of the Sun and the REA registers for the 1790s, Trebilcock found that several large coinsured cotton mill policies had been either inaccurately endorsed or not endorsed at all. Third, given the absence of the Phoenix's policy registers, the problem of missing coinsurances becomes insurmountable. Where the Phoenix coinsurances have not been accurately endorsed in the Sun and the REA registers, all record of them has been lost, as well as those risks insured only by the Phoenix. Trebilcock concluded that the systematic nature of underinsurance, the importance of the Phoenix as an industrial insurer and coinsurer, and the unreliability of endorsements in the surviving registers of the Sun and the REA means that accurate capital values cannot be obtained from these sources.[13]

Jenkins responded to these points in an unpublished but widely circulated and influential paper.[14] First, he argued that from the early 1780s fire offices, needing to maximise premium income, were increasingly willing to insure the full risk. Furthermore, Trebilcock's evidence of deliberate underinsurance as a policy against moral hazard relates specifically to large mill risks and may never have formed part of general underwriting practice. Second, 'only relatively few types and numbers of large and hazardous industrial property' would have been affected by insurers' ceilings on risks. The owner of a typical small mill or workshop would have been able to obtain full cover, if necessary through coinsurance, had he wished to. The existence of faulty and missing endorsements was also chiefly a problem of 'very large industrial property, and that of a particularly hazardous nature'. Despite the 'great uncertainties', 'Trebilcock's stricture that most industrial property is affected by this problem is too pessimistic'.[15] These central problems, underinsurance and coinsurance, are addressed in the following analysis of fire underwriting practice, which extends beyond industrial insurance to all types of property insured against fire between 1720 and 1850.

Assessing risk

Unlike life assurance, fire insurance did not produce a body of scientific or practical literature in the eighteenth century to help underwriters assess risk. Early fire underwriters learnt from experience and imitation although the latter was not pervasive enough to ensure complete uniformity of practice. From the early eighteenth century most offices employed surveyors, usually builders by trade, to inspect property proposed for insurance. For the three mutuals - the Hand-in-Hand, the Union and the Westminster - such surveys were a precondition of insurance, because the level of contributions paid by their members depended upon whether their property was rated as brick, timber, or part brick, part timber. These offices only insured buildings and/or goods in London and its environs. Generally their surveyors inspected the smaller domestic properties alone, while committees of directors, usually accompanied by the surveyor, would view risks deemed hazardous or especially large. Thus, at various times, the Union established committees on dangerous chimneys, soapmakers, breweries and chemists. As well as viewing industrial hazards in the capital, the Hand-in-Hand sent its directors to inspect larger country properties such Lord Portmore's house in Weybridge or Lord Hyde's house near Watford.[16] The London Assurance employed a surveyor only for the capital and before the 1780s relied on its few agents to provide descriptions of country property proposed for insurance. From the mid 1780s to 1805 'out of town' risks were accepted or rejected solely on the basis of a description from a third party nominated by the proposer.[17] The REA also used surveyors to inspect London risks only. Country property appears to have been left to its agents who may or may not have viewed proposals before sending them in to head office.[18] It is also unclear whether the Sun used its resident agents to inspect risks. In its early years the company's peripatetic agents, called riding officers, did assess properties proposed for insurance. Occasionally, the Sun's Inspector of London Risks, first appointed in 1733, was asked to view hazardous risks in the provinces, such as sugar mills in Liverpool. Generally, however, both this official and the office's surveyors concentrated on inspecting London buildings only, though they adjusted losses throughout the country. In 1773 the Sun appointed two permanent surveyors and later in the century sub-committees of directors were also set up to inspect particular risks.[19]

Whatever the differences between the fire offices in the scope of their surveys, and however inefficient surveying could be - the Hand-in-Hand had terrible problems disciplining its surveyors during the 1730s - there is no question that property in the capital was the most comprehensively inspected of any in the Kingdom. The London building act of 1764 required that all new buildings be surveyed upon completion, with the surveyor having to swear to the honesty of his surveys before a magistrate. The act of 1774 specified in great detail seven classes of property, each with regulations about dimensions, thickness of walls, and building materials.[20] Indeed it was not unusual, especially for the mutual offices, to order second surveys of property if the initial description was found to be inadequate or when septennial policies came up for renewal. The Hand-in-Hand resurveyed over 20000 houses in London between 1780 and 1800. Outside the capital, procedures remained less certain, particularly with regard to the newer forms of industry appearing towards the end of the century. London underwriters acquired most of their information on early textile mills from a plan and description of the premises submitted to the local agent by the person proposing the insurance. Mills were occasionally inspected by agents, and even more occasionally visited by officials from head offices in London. Few of the latter had direct experience of northern risks and they relied greatly on the expertise of their agents. Visiting Liverpool docks in 1806, Philip Bewicke, the Sun's secretary, commented that 'with the little local knowledge we possessed, it is really surprising how well the rates appear to meet the different degrees of risk'.[21]

In the years after the Napoleonic Wars, as losses on industrial insurances soared, risk assessment became more meticulous. By the early 1820s the Phoenix was determining premiums on Liverpool and Manchester warehouses according to storage conditions, the number of trades and processes carried out, and proximity to other risks. According to the Phoenix, the latter had been 'a point overlooked in the ordinary practice of fire insurance'.[22] Some recognised that such information could only be acquired by personal inspection and that this was crucial to competitiveness. Barber Beaumont wrote to the County's agent at Leeds in 1821:

> In respect to the gig cropping mill we should have liked to have had given the premium charged by the Sun, and your ideas of the risk and the premium that ought to be charged for it. So much depends upon the precautions used or neglected by the manufacturers in cases of this kind that without an ocular examination one is always in danger of charging too much or too little.[23]

During this decade the most careful underwriting of industrial risks was carried out by new provincial specialists. The fire offices in Manchester and Leeds, for example, relied not only on the skills of local agents but also on the commercial expertise of their directors, which was used to instruct agents in the technicalities of textile manufacturing and to inspect risks. From the late 1820s a committee of five MFLAC directors, all cotton merchants or spinners, frequently convened to classify risks and survey categories of insurances in particular localities. Although some of the London offices had a long history of establishing such committees for metropolitan hazards, none repeatedly sent board members on personal inspections of northern properties as the Leeds and Manchester insurers did. The quality of information required by both firms meant that a wide range of industrial property was inspected, not just the largest mills. Their insistence on agents submitting their own opinions on special risks also led many agents to view premises for themselves.[24]

Several points can be made about these developments which relate to the debate about insurance valuations. First, the great variety of underwriting practice must be taken into account. Factors such as the quality of risk inspection, the changing classifications of special risks and the range of risks and geographical areas excluded from cover, all determined the shape of an insurance portfolio. The range of cotton mills insured by the Sun after 1803, for instance, was particularly skewed by its low ceiling of £3000 per risk, and by its rejection of all but single tenure mills in a period when cotton mills were getting larger and multiple occupancy was increasingly common.[25] Second, the potential for an inaccurate assessment of a building was fairly limited in eighteenth-century London, though greater elsewhere. Towards the end of the century the quality of provincial risk assessment improved, and it reached new levels of refinement during the 1820s. Although early mills and machinery p osed p roblems for London-based underwriters, in the later period a much larger proportion of textile insurances was accounted for by new provincial offices with a superior technical knowledge of local industries. Third, it is misleading to state that underinsurance could not have occurred as a deliberate policy to protect insurers against moral hazard, because risks were not inspected 'as a matter of course'.[26] The practice of inspecting all types of property was widespread in London from the early eighteenth century. It became increasingly familiar outside the capital towards the end of the century and quite common after 1800.

Turning f rom the procedures to the objects of risk assessment, the evidence suggests that from an early date the primary concerns of underwriters were building materials and construction, sources of heat, hazardous trades and goods, and location. A tripartite classification of risks into common, hazardous and doubly hazardous had been adopted by the REA, the London and the Sun by 1727, and later a fourth class of 'special' risks, which included most large industrial properties, was created out of the double hazards. Sugar bakeries and distilleries were the first to be treated by the Sun as 'special' risks.[27] The brick-timber division was used by all fire offices, and, together with the location of property, was the basis of the rating system of the mutuals.

There were soon refinements to the basic categories. In 1739 the three London stock offices agreed to classify as hazardous all houses without a brick or stone front, back and party walls, although the Hand-in-Hand refused to follow suit. Thatched roofs were generally not insured and the Hand-in-Hand did not insure contiguous timber buildings more than ten miles from London. The Sun regarded 'no premiums...adequate to the risk' of wooden chimneys, while the Hand-in-Hand required its surveyors to inspect houses for wainscotting, chimneys, construction materials, number of storeys, and the dimensions and locations of rooms. In the 1730s the Hand-in-Hand's surveyors were also measuring the dimensions of warehouses thought likely to be enlarged, and identifying the location of ovens in malthouses.[28]

Sources of heat were naturally a concern. Fire was used in countless urban trades, from tallow melters and chemists dissolving drugs, to distillers' stills and sugar bakers' pans. The use of stoves, kilns and ovens drew the early attention of insurers. In 1735 the Union rated thread, linen, silk and wool dyers hazardous if they used stoves and rejected any maltster who kept a charcoal oven next to any part of his malthouse. In 1743 the Hand-in-Hand told their surveyors to value separately any kilns in malthouses, mills and similar buildings. When the Sun began to keep a regular account of its sugar refinery insurances in 1762, it also re-rated these risks principally according to the construction of the stove and chimney. The same method was applied to calico printers in 1767.[29] The Sun's underwriters wanted to be sure that fire was safely contained in brick surrounds and removed from combustible materials, that a distance was kept between hot metal pipes and timberwork, and that smoke and flames were safely conveyed out of the building. This remained true 21 years later when the Sun, the REA and the Phoenix agreed upon a premium tariff for sugar mills based upon the construction of stoves.[30] This approach was also adopted for the cotton industry, where there had been 'frequent losses occasioned by the stoving houses of fustian dyers, and other trades where drying stoves are used'.[31] Given their familiarity with this hazard from workshop, sugar mill and dockside insurances in the capital, it is not surprising that the London offices commenced rating the less familiar northern cotton risks by type of stove.

By the 1790s it had become the accepted practice to classify all manufacturing premises in London and elsewhere by the type of their stoves. In the early 1800s, however, a change occurred in the approach to underwriting textile mills. The central focus on stoves was replaced with a concern about the size of buildings. The Sun's agent in Manchester convinced his managers to rate mills by the number of storeys and by floor yardage. The REA and the Phoenix rejected this plan and determined premium rates either by floor space alone, or by contiguity with other hazards.[32] As with the earlier concern over stoves, the desire here was to identify one key criterion upon which a simplified rating system could be based. This was illusory, for industrial risks were becoming ever larger and more complex. The continued uncertainty of underwriters about how to deal with these demonstrated their dif ficulty in k eeping p ace with and mastering technological change. There remained no satisfactory approach to the insurance of technologically complex risks until the second quarter of the nineteenth century and the emergence of provincial offices with a specialist knowledge of textile manufacturing. By this stage insurers had come to accept that there was no single criterion, which could be elevated above others, for the safer underwriting of industrial risks.

Underinsurance

Although they became preoccupied with stoves and the size of properties, underwriters had always given consideration to other sources of hazard. The location and situation of buildings or goods proposed for insurance were particular concerns. For much of the eighteenth century property on London bridge and by the banks of the Thames was an especial worry because of its closeness, the presence of hazardous goods and the dangerous concentration of risks. In London and elsewhere, buildings in narrow streets, alleyways and yards - 'where two carts cannot pass' - were looked upon with suspicion.[33] This concern with situation increased with the proliferation of textile mills towards the end of the century. By the 1820s the Manchester and Leeds offices only rated buildings of different types and hazards separately if they deemed them far enough apart. The MFLAC invariably turned down proposals on premises which stood near to property they already insured, and where both insurances combined would exceed the firm's standard £5000 limit on special risks. Insurance might also be refused where the amount proposed on a building by its owner, when added to the sum insured by a tenant on stock or machinery, would exceed this ceiling. Where mills and warehouses were built close to other hazards, the MFLAC wanted to know the number of tenants and nature of trades in surrounding buildings, the precise distances involved, how buildings were joined and the materials used in the construction of such links. At this date metropolitan offices lagged behind in their attention to such dangers.[34]

The multiple occupation of mills and warehouses became an increasing concern during the early nineteenth century. The ubiquity of multiple tenure and the growing competition between fire offices drove most underwriters to accept premises occupied by up to four tenants, but premium supplements were charged, usually 1s% for each additional tenant in a warehouse, 2s 6d% in a woollen mill and 4s% in a cotton mill. Nevertheless, multiple tenure and sub-letting made insurers nervous about unidentified hazards and frequently led to insurance being refused.[35] This attitude towards property in multiple occupation could have important consequences for the accuracy of insurance valuations. First, sub-letting could create obvious difficulties for the accurate valuation of total capital in a mill, where each tenant took out his own insurance, and where the millowner, insuring the building, might have little idea of the quantity or value of his tenants' machinery and stock. Moreover, where a building was deemed 'fireproof', the building might be underinsured but the machinery and stock, especially if insured separately by tenants, might not.[36] Second, underwriting restrictions on multiple tenure undoubtedly led to the dispersal of insurance policies by tenants across several fire offices. Furthermore, it is unlikely that there was a direct relationship between the size of premises and the number of tenants. Indeed it was often the smaller mills in towns like Oldham which were the most partitioned and the most likely to be either coinsured across a large number of offices or underinsured. The belief that it was only the largest industrial properties which were likely to need coinsurance, and likely to be underinsured if their values exceeded insurers' ceilings on single risks, is therefore misplaced.[37]

Throughout the period all fire offices repeatedly adjusted the limits to the cover they were prepared to issue on single risks. Generally these limits rose over time. The Sun's maximum cover on a single policy rose from £3000 in 1727 to £10000 by 1785. The Union progressively raised its maximum from £1000 in 1714 to £8000 in 1776, before reducing it again to £6000 in 1783 after heavy losses.[38] Another means of limiting liability was the widespread practice of inserting a rebuilding clause into policies by which, in the event of a loss, the fire office would either pay the amount of the insured damage, as estimated by its surveyor, or pay for the repairs, whichever cost was found to be lower. This practice was given legal sanction by the London building act of 1764. As hazards became more complex but better understood, underwriters increasingly emphasised the importance of subdividing risks and imposing limits building by building, room by room, and item by item within single policies. This was applied to all types and sizes of property, not just the largest and most hazardous risks. The London Assurance took great care to specify the cover on buildings, out-houses, households goods, utensils, stock in trade, clothing, plate and pictures within single policies on residential property. The Hand-in-Hand's surveyors were asked to resurvey all houses insured for more than £1000 which had not been 'particularly described...nor the sections distinctly valued'.[39] Those most involved in insuring industrial property refined the principle further. Both the Manchester and Leeds offices repeatedly admonished agents who failed to insure different types of property in separate sums.

Limits on risks and their subdivision had a greater impact on insurance valuations than has been suggested. Just as there was no correlation between the size of a risk and the propensity to insist on its subdivision, there was none between the size of an office and its limits on single policies. This is clear from a list of ten insurers in Belfast in 1829 whose limits on cotton mills ranged from none, through £2000 to £5000, to those firms who rejected such risks entirely.[40] Policy limits were generally determined by the degree of hazard and the level of competition. The Guardian, referring to limits on Liverpool warehouses in 1823, noted that there were many instances when 'it would have been imprudent to have adhered strictly to them, as the doing so would have occasioned the loss of valuable connexions'.[41] Policy limits were therefore flexible at the margins, but downwards as well as upwards, especially given the increasing complexity of subdividing risks. Some underwriters also required the separate valuation of parts of a risk where the total sum insured was deemed to be less than the estimated replacement cost. If this had not been insisted upon, a building insured for less than its worth might partially burn down, and the policyholder could claim the whole of the sum insured.[42] Occasionally, as an alternative to rejecting a proposal outright, underwriters might accept only part of the total proposed for insurance, even when the total was below their limit on single risks. When a cotton firm renewed a MFLAC policy on their 'fireproof' mill in 1829, they not only found the premium increased but also the cover reduced from £7000 to £4600 after the insurers discovered the attic ceiling was not covered by sheet iron as originally described.[43] Many fire offices acknowledged the undervaluation of some risks. The Leeds & Yorkshire, for instance, complained to their agent at Settle that the description of a cotton mill proposed for insurance was incomplete. 'The sums given on the two mills bear no proportion to the value, being on no.2, £30, on no.3, £60. These two buildings and their contents, if employed in spinning cotton waste as in no.1, would be at 16/-'.[44] Here the concern was not with the undervaluation itself but with the nature of the hazard and the premium rate to cover it. This was also true of an Oldham mill where the sum proposed for insurance, '...if one may judge by the size of the mill will not be one-tenth of the real value, and therefore if a fire were to happen...we might suffer a loss equal to the whole amount (but) be receiving only one-tenth of the proper premium'. The underwriters' difficulty lay not with the underinsurance, as suggested by Jenkins, but with the fact that the premium proposed would not reflect the liability the insurers were being asked to accept. In other cases where undervaluation did present a problem, the usual remedy was not to insist on full cover, but either to insert an average clause into the policy or to place an exact figure on each item within it, a figure which did not have to represent the full value of the item concerned. Indeed the Leeds & Yorkshire were quite certain that the latter was 'rarely given' in a policy.[45]

Various forms of the average clause - by which the amount paid out in a claim was made dependent on the ratio of the sum insured to the full value of the property at the time of the loss - were widely used by the stock offices as early as the 1720s. The London Assurance applied it in 1725 to all policies on buildings and goods above £1000, to sugar bakers' insurances, and to all policies issued in Ireland where it was used to ensure systematic underinsurance. The average clause was also used by provincial insurers and it gained legal recognition in an act of 1828.[46] While its application did become more widespread between the early eighteenth and the early nineteenth centuries, the claims, either that it originated with the 'floating policies' on London dock insurances during the 1800s, or that it was little used before 1830, are highly misleading.[47] The existence of the average clause is a problem for anyone attempting to correlate property values with insured values. It weakened the relationship between the replacement value of property and the amount the policyholder wished to insure. By inserting the clause into a policy, insurers could accept a larger sum than they would otherwise have insured. For example, a firm of Dublin merchants, who in 1765 requested that the London Assurance underwrite £6000 on a house, a warehouse and its goods, were told that this could be taken at 8s% with an average clause, or else £3000 could be insured at 6s% without the clause.[48]

Maitland, describing London in 1739, claimed that '...the several fire offices, to prevent their being imposed upon, insure (at most) only three-fourths of the value of each house...'.[49] There is conclusive evidence that from their earliest days insurance offices systematically underinsured property to force the policyholder to bear a proportion of the risk. In 1718 and 1724 the Westminster insisted that houses be insured to a maximum of three-quarters of their value. The London Assurance resolved in 1727 that 'no more than two-thirds of the value be assured by this Corporation on any nobleman or gentleman's seat in the country', where the sum to be insured by the London, or together with any other office, came to more than £3000. The corporation also confirmed that the average clause was always to be inserted into the policies of sugar bakers, and that 'the assured do always run one fourth part of the risque'.[50] Advising Viscount Torrington on the insurance of a dwelling house and oasthouses in Yokes, the London Assurance argued that some policyholders were advantaged by underinsurance.

...if you are not particularly bound to maintain a house on the premises it will be more for to your advantage to under insure it, at least not to insure it for more than it is worth, as in case it should be burnt down the Corporation have a right to chuse whether they will pay the sum at which it is insured or rebuild it on the same plan.

The reasoning here was that, in the event of a fire, if Torrington wished to build something else on the Yokes site, or plough it up, he would be advised to underinsure in order to make certain he received his claim in full. For if the sum claimed came to more than the cost of replacing the original building, the insurers would rebuild it themselves rather than pay the claim.[51]

In their recent study of country house building, Wilson and Mackley examined insurance policies for 36 houses in eighteenth-century Suffolk, Norfolk and Yorkshire. All the insurance valuations were considerably lower than the historic cost of building and the replacement cost. In London some building contracts, such as the agreement of 1788 between Jacob Leroux and Lord Somers to develop Somers Town, carried a stipulation that the developer was responsible for insuring all buildings to three-quarters of their value.[52] The clearest evidence of the extent of underinsurance comes from the Hand-in-Hand. From the 1730s every valuation of damage to buildings insured by the office was recorded in the board minutes, in most cases together with a note of the sum for which the property was insured and coinsured. For properties described by the surveyor as 'demolished' or 'destroyed' the estimated cost of rebuilding is also given. During the year ending March 1735, for instance, 34 houses and one pub, all in London, were recorded as burnt to the ground. None of them were fully insured to their estimated replacement value. An analysis of over 1100 properties insured by the Hand-in-Hand and destroyed by fire between 1760 and 1800 reveals that the aggregate sum insured represented only 70 per cent of their estimated replacement value.[53] These properties mostly comprised residential houses in London of all sizes, but they also included workshops, barns, sheds, stables, washhouses, coachhouses, cooperages, inns, mills, warehouses and sugar houses. Thirteen country houses which burnt down in this period were also underinsured by about one-quarter of their estimated value. The Hand-in-Hand consistently encouraged underinsurance although it is nowhere stated explicitly that this was company policy. Compulsory underinsurance was certainly applied by other fire offices well into the nineteenth century, making policyholders carry the risk for between one quarter to one half of the value of their property.[54]

The practice of sub-dividing all types of risks and imposing insurance limits on those sub-divisions, and the concern with multiple tenure and contiguity, increased the propensity of policy values not to reflect the full cost of property. It is also evident that underwriters readily accepted underinsurance. They were able to do this because of risk specification and sub-division and because of the widespread use of the average clause. In the process of risk assessment, the measurement of hazard, not the valuation of property, was uppermost in the underwriter's mind. The primary function of property plans and descriptions was to identify risk and to adjust supplementary charges accordingly. Such charges, particularly in industrial and commercial insurances, were highly lucrative and an important source of income for fire offices. Fifty warehouse policies current with the MFLAC in 1844, for example, realised £164 of premiums at the normal rate, but an additional £652 was charged for multiple tenure, contiguity, timber walls, well holes, wooden cornices, wood linings, pipe stoves, and hazardous goods and trades.[55] Historians have widely assumed that 'companies needed maximum available premiums and thus preferred...to insure to their full value'.[56] The evidence demonstrates, however, that, where fire offices did not wish to exceed their own policy limits and overstretch their liabilities in hazardous categories of insurance, there were other, safer ways to maximise premium income - by refining assessment, by subdividing risk and by increasing special charges.

It was not property at the point of assessment, but losses which w ere m ost rigorously valued by insurers. Statements of loss, sworn by the claimant, were required by the earliest mutual fire offices who also employed 'some skilful or able builder or workman' to estimate and report on the damage incurred. This followed on from the practice established in the seventeenth century whereby, in the wake of a fire, justices of the peace appointed assessors of the claims made by those who requested assistance from the charitable funds raised by voluntary subscription.[57] The first insurance offices also required the builder's certificate of loss to be 'affixed at the gates' of London and Westminster or published in the *Gazette* to ensure transparency and to reduce fraud. In 1710 the Sun introduced the requirement, which became the industry standard for 130 years, that any loss must be sworn to before the mayor or chief magistrate of the town and in the presence of the agent, and that it must be accompanied by an affadavit certified by the minister or churchwarden of the parish. From the 1780s this requirement was relaxed by some offices, but this caused problems whenever an uncertificated claim was disputed by the insurer. The 'churchwardens' clause was not finally dispensed with by the major offices until 1844.[58]

Thus detailed valuations of fire damage were carried out by insurers as a matter of course from the earliest days of the industry. They were conducted by a range of persons - local builders, tradesmen and especially auctioneers and valuers, as well as insurance agents, clerks and other officials sent from head office, and, increasingly, 'surveyors', often builders, kept on a retainer fee by the fire offices. There was not enough loss adjustment work, however, available to keep anyone in regular occupation. Malachy Postlethwaite, writing in 1774, was of the view that appraising or valuing was 'not a business of itself', and full-time professional non-marine loss adjusters remained unknown before the middle of the nineteenth century.[59] Nevertheless the insurer's valuation of fire damage was important, not least because differing estimates often emerged in cases where the claimant had his own valuation carried out with a view to challenging the accuracy of the former.[60] The bundles of individual fire claims covering the period 1771 to 1787, which, unusually, have survived in the Sun's archive, reveal pages and pages of detailed estimates of losses, damage and salvage, listed item by item - inventories which were far more comprehensive than those contained in the Sun's policy registers for the same period.[61] The question of salvage lay at the centre of loss adjustment. Regardless of the type of insured property, most offices encouraged salvage by paying towards the costs of removing goods during fires. For the insured salvage could result in a full replacement of the value of goods lost or damaged without incurring the maximum premium charges to cover this value, for it could always be insisted that any salvage related to the uninsured part of the property.[62] Salvage had become so valuable by the 1840s, partly in consequence of a higher proportion of buildings being only partially destroyed in fires, that the fire offices cooperated to establish salvage corps in Manchester, Liverpool and Glasgow.[63]

In sum, the practice of risk assessment varied between offices and became increasingly refined over the period 1720-1850, and the propensity of almost all aspects of risk assessment was to produce underinsurance. For several reasons to do with underwriting practice, values insured on all types of property by individual fire offices were unlikely to reflect replacement cost accurately. The values given to lost, damaged and salvaged property by loss adjusters were more likely to be accurate. Newspaper reports of the values of damaged buildings were likely to relate to those properties most fully insured and most completely destroyed, as fire offices preferred, for obvious reasons, to publicise their fullest claims payments, rather than the partial claims paid on property only partially insured.[64]

Coinsurance

Coinsurance was another aspect of underwriting with consequences for historians interested in the accuracy of insurance valuations. This was a risk-spreading practice widely adopted in London from the early eighteenth century. The Sun and the Union offices permitted their policyholders to insure in other fire offices from 1723. The London Assurance initially allowed coinsurance in 1726, but in turn restricted and then extended its scope during the following years, indicating uncertainty about its impact on the corporation's business. The Hand-in-Hand accepted numerous buildings coinsured with other London offices. These included many small properties such as the 15 houses insured by John James in 1773 for sums ranging from £150 to £550 in the Hand-in-Hand and £50 to £350 in the REA.[65]

With the increasing prevalence of multiple tenure in industrial and commercial properties, and the growing sophistication of the classification and sub-division of special risks, coinsurance had become important by the early nineteenth century. Almost one in four of the Sun's policies issued on textile mills in Leeds, and more than one in six of its policies in Blackburn between 1824 and 1830, were on property insured with other offices.[66] Forty-one per cent of the insured value of flax mills and 23 per cent of the insured value of wool textile mills covered by the Sun at Leeds, and 50 per cent of the insured value of textile risks covered by the MFLAC at Blackburn, were accounted for by coinsurance. Coinsurance could multiply the sum insured on a single property by a factor of eight. Nova Scotia mills in Blackburn were insured by the MFLAC in 1840 for £4475 but they were coinsured with seven other offices for £31325. The propensity to coinsure may have increased during this period. The number of coinsured policies issued by the MFLAC in Blackburn increased between 1830-34 and 1840-43, while the sum coinsured rose from 18 per cent to 154 per cent of the total amount insured. Coinsurance might also be encouraged by competition. The decline of new business coming to the Sun at Manchester during the 1820s was accompanied by a rapid increase in sums coinsured across its renewal policies.[67]

The importance of coinsurance, however, has been doubted. Jenkins argued that the number of risks affected by policy limits and therefore requiring coinsurance was 'very small' and limited to 'very large industrial property'.[68] In fact the average sum insured by the MFLAC on coinsured property in Blackburn between 1830 and 1843 was £3138, well below its £5000 limit on single risks. Of 38 coinsured policies, 17 were insured for sums less than £3000, including several for just a few hundred pounds. Similar results emerge from an examination of the 157 policies issued by the Sun at Manchester between 1824 and 1830 on property which was coinsured. Seventy per cent of policies on coinsured mills and 63 per cent of policies on coinsured warehouses were for sums below £5000, while 38 per cent of both types of policy were under £3000. Moreover the range of property coinsured was wide. As well as large mills and calico works, a variety of smaller property was also coinsured, including weaving shops, silk winding rooms, drapers' and grocers' shops, the warehouses and stock of oil merchants, drysalters and bleachers, brewhouses and even residential housing. To suggest that 'only relatively few types and numbers of large and hazardous industrial property' required coinsurance conflates 'large' with 'hazardous' too readily.[69] In fact the motive behind coinsurance derived less from the valuation of a property than from the assessment of its risk. If industrial property was propelled towards coinsurance by policy limits, it was mostly due to the sub-division of risk, not to the pressure of very large properties on the standard £5000 limit on single risks.

If coinsurance was not just limited to a few very large industrial risks, it is more significant to the debate about insurance valuations than hitherto believed. It has been generally argued that all or most coinsured sums were endorsed in the central policy registers of the Sun and the REA.[70] In response to Trebilcock's evidence of faulty endorsements among large cotton mills in the 1790s, Jenkins accepted that there was 'a real risk that for larger property details of joint insurances are incomplete in the policy registers'.[71] In fact the problem could affect a wide range of coinsured property. Over a dozen Sun policies issued by its Manchester agency during the 1820s had omissions or inaccurately endorsed coinsurances. A systematic cross check of available records doubtless would reveal many more. There were no instances in the Sun's registers between 1824 and 1830 where a Leeds woollen mill was endorsed with a MFLAC coinsurance, yet we know of at least four such mills insured by the Sun in this period which were simultaneously insured by the Manchester office. Other examples of unrecorded coinsurances can be found in Ashton, Stockport, Manchester and Blackburn, so the problem is not confined to only one Sun agency. Even where a coinsurance is indicated, the information may be incomplete. On three occasions where the Sun recorded coinsurances with other offices, their clerk omitted, or was unaware of, other sums insured by the MFLAC. In three other entries where the register states that the Sun had accepted a proposal based on a mill plan deposited with the REA, the relevant endorsement of a coinsurance is absent.

The best explanation for incomplete and inaccurate endorsements lies with clerical error and administrative inefficiency. Fire offices certainly insisted that details of coinsurances be supplied to them with a proposal as a measure against fraud. Claims could be invalidated where it was discovered that the liability of another insurer had not been declared. The usual practice of noting endorsements on policies, however, has not produced a very accurate record from which to reconstruct total insurance valuations. From the second half of the eighteenth century property owners outside London generally submitted proposals for insurance via their local agent. If accepted, the fire office would issue a policy which was sent, via the agent, to the policyholder, and which had to be produced in the event of a claim. Often the details of coinsurances would be sought by the agent after the policy had been returned to him. For the purpose of assessing the risk, it was apparently sufficient for the underwriters to know approximately for how much a property was coinsured. The agent was then instructed to ascertain the details of insurances with other offices and endorse them on the policy itself. The agent was also to copy these details into his own agency register and then pass them on by letter to head office, so that they could be entered into the central policy register. In this procedure, therefore, the central register, as the least 'active' record of the insurance, was usually last to be endorsed. Indeed, where a policyholder was negotiating insurances with several offices simultaneously, the process of information retrieval and copying up could take months. Where an insurance was being transferred from another fire office, confusion could arise about whether all the insurance was brought over or whether a sum remained coinsured with the policyholder's original insurer. Some agents were more diligent than others in copying endorsements into their own books. The scope for missing or inaccurate endorsements in the central registers was even greater.

The central policy registers of the Sun and the REA, therefore, cannot be regarded as a dependable guide to the insured values of premises of all sizes listed within them, not just the largest mills. Coinsurances, which might multiply the insured value of a property by a factor of eight, cannot be regarded as not existing if not recorded. From the 1760s the absence of records for many provincial and London fire offices presents a serious problem. As fire insurance markets fragmented under increasing competition after 1800, the problem of missing registers and the difficulty of keeping track of all endorsed coinsurances on individual premises becomes worse. Yet any comprehensive survey of the insured values of particular categories of property must take these problems into account.[72] Furthermore, the limited scope of Sun's business outside London means that its central registers are far from comprehensive for a variety of markets. Orbell, for example, has calculated that 'insured corn mills', that is mills insured with the Sun, amounted to only six per cent of all corn mills in the home counties and the west of England in the early 1750s and less elsewhere.[73] The existence of several fire offices operating in the south-west from the mid eighteenth century also casts doubt on Chapman's claim that 60 per cent of capital in the Devon cloth industry was insured by the Sun in the 1790s, and that the proportion was even higher in earlier decades.[74] Finally, underinsurance was common throughout the eighteenth century, adding to the problem of using policy values as a proxy for property values.

The impact of underwriting practice

If historians have found it difficult to come to terms with the complexities of this evolving financial service, how did contemporaries react to the vagaries of underwriting? Did insurance raise awareness of risk, change attitudes towards fire, make lives and property safer, make industry more efficient and productive? The surviving records of insurance companies generally make unpromising material with which to answer such questions. In references to policies on residential property it is difficult to find evidence of any greater sense of fire hazard emerging during the eighteenth century, still less one which was fostered by the presence of insurance. Indeed some contemporaries continued to believe that the security provided by insurance 'naturally' gave rise to 'carelessness and inattention' as well as more sinister features of moral hazard.[75] Nor is the public record very forthcoming about the impact of insurance on attitudes to risk. In newspaper accounts of fires, for instance, uncovered candles remained as much a concern at the end of the century as they had been at the beginning. Their careless handling by domestic servants, children and the elderly continued to result in death and maiming by fire, and continued to draw warnings from the insurance offices. The Act of 1707, to punish 'any menial or other servant' convicted of causing a fire in any house or out-building through 'negligence and carelessness', was reprinted many times during the eighteenth century and was circulated as handbills by several insurance offices.[76] Such publicity certainly had an effect on those of a nervous disposition, such as the poet Thomas Gray, who, upon reading about several London fires in 1759, became worried.

'Tis strange that we all of us (here in town) lay ourselves down every night on our funeral pile, ready made, and compose ourselves to rest, while every drunken footman and drowsy old woman has a candle ready to light it before the morning.[77]

Where life was cheap and expectations low, the consequences of mishandling fire were not given undue attention. Even in a world where man's relationship to God was increasingly seen in terms of 'probation not retribution', and where measurable patterns were being found in nature, fires were regarded by most as the products of divine will, which could deliver moral lessons about prudence and conduct but not data upon which to base probabilistic estimates of risk.[78] The failure of even the wealthy to learn from experience was remarked by Walpole in 1763 in response to the incineration of Lady Molesworth and her family in their London home. Fire, opined Southey 40 years later, was 'a tremendous calamity which is every day occurring in England, and against which daily and dreadful experience has not yet taught them to adopt any general means of prevention'.[79] Such impressions are supported by the evidence scattered in insurance records and newspapers of a persistent carelessness in the handling of dangerous materials, in the near ubiquitous proximity of gunpowder, oil and open fires in workshops and shipyards, in the presence of children increasing the hazard of fire in the workplace, and in a devil-may-care attitude towards danger shared by all social classes, which can be associated with the general rumbustiousness for which eighteenth-century England was renowned. Several of these elements came together in Plymouth in 1765 when a house fire was caused by a boy letting some linseed oil boil over. This kindled a barrel of gunpowder and the explosion blew up the house and extinguished the flames. In 1730 the Sun sued 'two young gentlemen' at Bury for firing their pistols among thatched houses and causing a fire.[80]

Insurance, therefore, did not change popular attitudes to physical risk quickly, if at all. Fire prevention and control were not the products of the insurance industry. There had been frequent attempts to control and regulate new buildings in London since the fifteenth century, and many provincial towns had passed ordinances against thatched roofs, wooden chimneys and dangerous kilns, the careless stocking of combustible materials and the carriage of fire in uncovered containers between buildings. Fire-fighting equipment was commonly held in many early modern towns. At least 60 fire engines had been built by 1662.[81] However, the rapid rebuilding of many towns substantially destroyed by fire, such as Warwick in 1694, Gravesend in 1727 and Wareham in 1762, ensured that timber construction continued to be widespread, especially for the cheaper properties. Even in the capital, timber buildings still accounted for one-third of all insured buildings at the end of the eighteenth century. The deterioration of parish fire-fighting equipment and the persistent problem of water supplies in many places also suggest that lessons about fire hazards were not fully taken on board.[82]

Nevertheless, there is some evidence that insurance helped increase awareness among educated and propertied classes of the need for better protection. Lobbying by insurance companies obtained a clause in the London building act of 1764 empowering the offices to rebuild or repair houses damaged by fire rather than pay a claim, where the offices had a suspicion of fraud. This gave insurers direct control over at least some of the building in the capital. Insurance offices also supported the building act of 1772, which encouraged chimney sweeping by imposing fines for occupiers of properties whose chimneys caught fire.[83] Public awareness of fire hazards must also have been raised by the substantial amounts of money and fire-fighting equipment donated to towns throughout England by the Sun and other offices, by their investment in water supplies, and by the expense, time and effort they invested in prosecuting arsonists from the 1760s.

A greater awareness of insurance, the growing threat of arson, and the need to regulate construction and the storage of hazardous goods, were accompanied from the 1750s by increasing public attention given to fireproofing, water raising technologies and fire escapes. In 1755 Sir John Fielding called for more turncocks and an improved water supply for fire engines in London, and numerous articles were published during the 1760s and 1770s giving advice on precautions to take against fire and making suggestions for better fire escapes and fire-fighting facilities in the capital. In the early 1760s several engravers, most notably Hogarth in 'The Times', turned to fire-fighting motives to make political points.[84] The Great Fire was commemorated in articles in the *Gentleman's Magazine* and *London Magazine*, while these and other journals carried accounts of Ambrose Godfrey's fire-extinguishing experiments in 1760-61, the trials of the rival fire-proofing systems of David Hartley and Viscount Mahon in the 1770s, and several improved designs of the fire engine and water pump. These efforts to innovate were well received. Hartley's patented system, which consisted in covering the underside of wooden floors and timber parts in buildings with thin iron plates, was adopted in the royal naval stores at Portsmouth and Plymouth in 1777 following the arson attempts by John the Painter. Ten years later an Italian tourist was impressed by the column outside the house at Putney where Hartley's experiments had taken place, which had been erected 'with public ceremony in honour of him'.[85]

The reaction of insurance offices to large fires also put pressure on those looking for insurance to ensure that their properties complied with insurers' requirements. After the fire at Gravesend in 1727 which cost the Sun £9400, the office resolved to insure timber and thatch properties in future only where they did not adjoin a similar building. The Hand-in-Hand refused to insure any thatched buildings from 1743 while the Sun charged extra for such properties in Devon from 1767 and in Dorset from 1800.[86] Concern over stoves could also produce punitive action by insurers determined to reduce risk. In 1811, for instance, a Limerick firm, Creagh & Arthur, paid 3s% to insure their store with the Atlas for £10200, but subsequently erected 'a furnace for melting lard'. Upon discovering this monstrosity, the London office threatened to reduce the insurance to £3000 at a premium rate of 10s 6d% if the firm persisted in using the furnace.[87]

The measures taken to improve risk assessment of the biggest industrial properties encouraged policyholders to make them safer. These included sub-dividing risks and hiking up premium rates in response to unguarded machinery, timber and unsecured combustible materials in buildings, contiguity to fire hazards, dangerous stoves, pipes projecting through floors and roofs, candles instead of oil or gas lights, and dirt, grease and hazardous waste materials accumulating on floors, in candle-lit rooms and around flues and engines. All these factors resulted in higher premiums and lower limits on the amount which an insurer was willing to cover, or they could lead to cancellation or a refusal to renew policies. In 1830 the MFLAC notified policyholders at Glossop that they were required to remove waste, not including 'strippings, flyings or pickings', from their cotton mills daily. Two years earlier the office had cancelled the policies of 17 Glossop cotton firms who were deemed to have kept dirty, and therefore dangerous, workspaces. [88]

The lack of consistency among insurers about the terms, conditions and rating of industrial insurances meant that different messages were sent out about degrees of hazard, which probably weakened insurance as a force for physical change in manufacturing industry. Nevertheless there was clearly a greater awareness among al parties of the dangers of fire following the heavy losses of the 1790s. Some of the larger Yorkshire woollen and flax mills during the 1800s and 1810s began using iron roof frames and sheet iron covering on floors, while worsted mills were replacing stoves and grates with warm air heating systems. Across the Pennines the 'fireproofing' of mills came into vogue, which the Salford cotton spinner, George Lee, believed would render insurance unnecessary and deliver a saving 'equal to ten p(er) Cent upon the Extra Cost'.[89] The Sun's inspector found a 'spirit of improvement' among millowners, dyers and calico printers in Manchester in 1806, where 'several (mills) are heated by steam, several are preparing to be lighted by gas and several are covering their wooden floors with iron plates and changing their wooden machinery for cast iron'. Several millowners had also 'incurred considerable expense in fire and water apparatus'. Ten years later another Sun inspector at Manchester noted the extension of gas lighting, steam heating, stone staircasing and iron machinery, with more boilers being positioned outside buildings and gasometers erected at greater distances from mills.[90] The 1820s witnessed a second wave of improvements. The Guardian's agent at Manchester in 1827 believed that the town's cotton warehouses had 'considerably improved' since 1821 'in consequence of the use of stoves instead of fire grates, the introduction of gas lights and improvement in the construction of buildings'. Several 'fireproof' woollen mills were built at Leeds, notably Benjamin Gott's giant mill at Bean Ing with iron pillars, beams and roof trusses. Shafts, wheels, gears, spiked drums and carding rollers were boxed in, ventilators introduced to remove dust, and cleanliness and waste disposal improved.[91]

Although it is difficult to pinpoint motives, it seems that some of the improvements during wartime were the result of textile manufacturers attempting to reduce the amount of insurance cover they needed and escape the very high premium rates. In 1796 Gott was paying £82 a year for the £31000 he insured on Bean Ing and his houses in Leeds while the flax spinner John Marshall was paying £238 for the £25000 insured on his mills.[92] The additional cost of totally fireproofing a mill has been estimated at 25 per cent in the 1790s and much more by the 1830s.[93] It was tempting to offset some of this extra cost by reducing or dispensing with insurance, in the same way as merchants had long been accustomed to accepting a degree of self-insurance when marine insurance premiums were high.[94] Mills, such as Lee & Philips' cotton mill at Salford, which were regarded as safe or 'completely incombustible', were often under- or uninsured, particularly when the London offices were slow to reduce premiums in recognition of 'fireproofing'. Insurers were not entirely unhappy at this development. According to the Sun's inspector in Manchester, a degree of self-insurance could also improve safety.

Where the magnitude of the concern renders it difficult, or it is deemed too expensive to effect insurance on the whole, (the cotton spinner) will consequently be induced to use every precaution in his power to prevent fire, having himself so much at stake, beside the loss of four or five years trade, if his mill be destroyed.[95]

During the period 1780 to 1830, however, the financial burden of insurance on the textile industry was more than counterbalanced by the aggregate sums paid back to its policyholders in claims.[96] So the insurance premium was probably not the most important factor determining the pace of safety improvements. Indeed, during the 1820s, a period of low and falling premiums, it is more likely that some of the alterations in the interior of textile mills were the result of the greater stringency of risk assessment, the increasing sub-division of risks, and the implementation of supplementary charges on extra hazards. To be sure many of the later safety improvements which related specifically to mill accidents were the consequence of factory reform and factory inspection. Yet it is not unlikely that structural alterations and changes in internal organisation, including lighting, heating, ventilation, waste removal and the precise location of production processes within buildings, were, to an incalculable degree, the result of the pressure exerted by underwriting requirements, as millowners and their tenants searched for reliable insurance cover. By this period many manufacturers had come to accept fire insurance as a necessity. For the Dundee flax spinner, William Brown, writing in the early 1820s, fire insurance was an essential part of the business of mill management, 'a precaution so obviously proper that it is needless to say anything on the propriety of it'.[97]

If underwriting practice influenced customer choice about where and how to insure, what was the impact of underwriting on the insurance offices themselves? What use did insurers make of the huge amounts of information gathered in the processes of risk assessment and loss adjustment? As we have seen, from the early eighteenth century insurers categorised properties by degree of hazard and drew up lists of hazardous trades, processes, goods and materials which required higher premium rates or were to be insured by 'special agreement'. These lists became longer as the industrial economy developed. Just 16 hazardous trades were listed by the Sun in 1721 while 105 were listed in a guide to fire insurance published in 1822.[98] What was absent from all fire offices throughout the eighteenth century, however, was a comprehensive, systematic and ongoing approach to data collection on the most hazardous categories of risk. Instead, the tendency was for insurers to resort to sudden measures when they faced a flurry of claims on particular types of property such as sugar mills or chemists' shops. In such circumstances the directors of an office would order a rapid investigation of the outstanding liability on such risks. Extra clerks might be drafted in for the purpose and sometimes they were required to trace back the underwriting results on the category of risk for several years to give the board some idea of historical performance. Armed with this information, the directors determined whether any changes to pricing and underwriting policy were necessary. What seems never to have happened before the early nineteenth century, at least as far as we can tell from the surviving records, was for the analysis of historic underwriting performance to be instituted as a regular clerical procedure and extended across all classes of risk.

Fire insurers appeared to have been unable or unwilling to understand the need to maintain an ongoing analysis of the data contained in policy and claims registers in order to monitor the long-run underwriting performance of the company, or even to find out the industrial and geographical spread of its liabilities. For a business which fundamentally needed to spread risk, it is remarkable how limited was the overview which boards of directors possessed of the pattern of their insurances. The accounts of the three London mutual offices, for example, proved totally incapable of supplying the directors with the data they required to trace the sources of the heavy losses in the metropolitan area which nearly brought them to their knees during the last quarter of the eighteenth century. This deficiency was typical of most contemporary offices.

When special investigations were ordered in a hurry, the results were often alarming. The Union calculated in 1728 that it had accumulated over £17000 of insurances on London bridge, 'which is too great a sum for this office to risque in so dangerous a situation'.[99] Despite its early concerns about sugar houses, not until 1761 did the Sun begin to keep a monthly account of its premiums and losses on this type of risk. Such a step was unusual. Although an investigation into losses on a specific category of insurance, if thorough, could enhance the technical knowledge of underwriters and lead to a more careful risk selection, it seldom resulted in an improved and permanent method of monitoring current liabilities and underwriting performance. It was always tempting to leave caution behind and to increase the proportion of hazardous risks accepted once premium rates on such risks rose.

Typically the new offices of the early nineteenth century, in their eagerness for market share, repeated many of the mistakes made by their older rivals. Thus, during its first year of business the Imperial overloaded itself with liabilities in the West India docks, many of which were properties insured by the company's own directors, before it began to set limits on its insurances there.[100] During the second decade of the century, driven by high levels of losses, both London and provincial offices began to undertake more frequent and long-run surveys of their underwriting performance in particular markets. The Atlas carried out the first analysis of its fire business in Ireland in 1816 and discovered a horrendous loss record. In 1823 the Imperial discovered that its Glasgow agency had been operating 'at a considerable loss' since the company's foundation. In 1821 the Newcastle Fire Office found that its premium income from country insurances had been declining over the previous decade as a result of increasing competition. In the mid 1820s the big three London offices collected a wide, if disparate, array of data on the underwriting of industrial property over the previous three decades, with the aim of measuring the aggregate losses incurred on mills and warehouses, and in Manchester, Liverpool and Glasgow.[101]

Overall, such developments were belated, incomplete, and often confined to market segments regarded as especially hazardous. Even the Phoenix, the great industrial specialist, did not begin to keep annual records of its performance in the major categories of special risks until 1810, nearly 30 years after the foundation of the firm. The Imperial first commenced a 'book of risk classifications', to be 'constantly updated', in 1820, 17 years after the office opened. Others were still more tardy. The London Assurance apparently did not begin an annual 'classification of fire assurances' until 1832.[102] By the late 1820s, under intense competition, more offices began to review their whole approach to utilising the data in their books. The MFLAC was typical in establishing a committee of three directors in 1831 'to consider the best mode of classifying risks' with the aim of obtaining a more accurate overview of their underwriting. They drew up a list of 40 headings from 'bleach works' to 'confectioners with hot hearths or candy stoves', with a separate account to be taken of Liverpool insurances.[103] In 1837 the Imperial extended its risk classification to 33 headings, from 'corn mills' to 'ship chandlers and oil and colourmen'. All new policies and renewals coming under these headings were to be entered separately into a book kept for that purpose, which would show the 'names and occupations of parties insured, the amount insured, the premium received thereon and the losses...'. 'By this means the amount depending on each description of risk will soon be ascertained and in due time a general result produced as to the quality of risk and sufficiency or otherwise of premium'.[104]

It seems extraordinary that major insurance companies only came to instigate this type of analysis of its own underwriting record so late in the day. The explanation for this tardiness cannot lie in good results and fat margins, for few offices showed a profit on industrial and commercial insurances between the 1780s and 1830s. A more likely explanation is that for most insurers, even those most committed to dockside, sugar and textile mill insurances, industrial risks formed only a small, if disproportionately troublesome, part of their overall liabilities. Handsome profits made on ordinary residential insurances, described by the Phoenix as 'the quieter risks of town', were commonly used to cross subsidise more hazardous workshop, factory and warehouse insurances.[105] The latter yielded a high ratio of premiums to sum insured and in good years could generate big profits. In bad years losses were heavy but most insurers recognised that it was necessary to keep the goodwill of large commercial and industrial policyholders, often the most influential businessmen in their communities, in order to secure a stream of profitable residential insurances.

Labour costs may also have been a factor in delaying the acceptance of the need for an ongoing analysis of underwriting performance. Such time-consuming examination of the books was beyond the resources of the small and hard-pressed clerical staff employed by most offices. In 1838 the Imperial recognised that they would need one or two additional clerks, 'probably an expert accountant with the assistance of a younger man', in order to bring the work up to date. Subsequently a number of reports were produced over the following years; on cotton mill insurances and Liverpool business since 1803, on London insurances between 1831 and 1837, on sugar houses between 1838 and 1846, and on foreign insurances between 1841 and 1845.[106]

In the more complex underwriting world of the mid nineteenth century, where price competition was being replaced by tariff collusion and non-price forms of competition, a key factor determining company survival was the capacity to draw lessons from one's own underwriting experience and to tailor practice accordingly. In the process, risk measurement became more sophisticated than it had ever been, and the business of insuring the British economy became somewhat less of a gamble.

Notes

1   Jerusalem, ch.2, v.35-6, in Blake, *Complete Poetry and Prose*, p.178.

2   The registers are held in the Guildhall Library, London, GL Mss 11936 (Sun), 253 (REA).

3   Chapman, 'British Cotton Industry'; Jenkins, *West Riding Wool Textile Industry*.

4   Feinstein a nd P ollard, *Studies in Capital Formation*; Cockerell and Green, *British Insurance Business*; James, 'Personal Wealth Distribution'; Jackson, 'Personal Wealth'; Berg, 'Commerce and Creativity'.

5   Beresford, 'Prometheus Insured'; *idem.*, 'East End, West End'; Butt, 'Housing'. Cf. also Devine, 'Colonial Trades and Industrial Investment'; Berg, 'Commerce and Creativity'.

6   For analyses of wealth distribution using the policy registers, see Schwarz and Jones, 'Wealth, Occupations and Insurance'; Schwarz, *London in the Age of Industrialisation*, pp.57-73; Barnett, *London, Hub of the Industrial Revolution*; Pollard, 'Insurance Policies'; James, 'Personal Wealth Distribution'; Jackson, 'Personal Wealth'.

7   Chapman, 'British Cotton Manufacturing Industry'; Cullen, 'Eighteenth-Century Flour Milling'; Chaloner and Marshall, 'Major John Cartwright', p.286 n; Chapman and Butt, 'Cotton Industry'. The proportions of the cotton capital estimates derived from insurance valuations were 31 per cent, 58 per cent and 20 per cent for 1788, 1795 and 1811 respectively.

8   Policy values provided the basis of the fixed capital estimates of 63 per cent of wool textile mills counted by Jenkins for 1800, 23 per cent for 1810, and 11 per cent for 1820 and 1835. Jenkins, *West Riding Wool Textile Industry*, pp.xiv, 156; *idem.*, 'Wool Textile Industry'; Butt, 'Scottish Cotton Industry'; Donnachie, 'Sources of Capital'; Orbell, 'Corn Milling'.

9   Chapman, 'British Cotton Industry', pp.253-5; *idem.*, 'British Cotton Manufacturing Industry', p.89; *idem*, 'Devon Cloth Industry', pp.x-xi; Jenkins, *West Riding Wool Textile Industry*, pp.278-9, 282, 287-8; Orbell, 'Corn Milling', pp.153, 155-7; Chapman and Butt, 'Cotton Industry', p.110; Pollard, 'Insurance Policies', p.227; Donnachie, 'Sources of Capital', p.280.

10 Jenkins, *West Riding Wool Textile Industry*, pp.286-9; *idem.*, 'Practice of Insurance against Fire', p.30; Chapman, 'British Cotton Industry', p.255; Chapman and Chassagne, *European Textile Printers*, p.59.

[11] Donnachie, 'Sources of Capital', p.280; Orbell 'Corn Milling', pp.158, 163; Jenkins 'Wool Textile Industry', pp.127-30; *idem.*, *West Riding Wool Textile Industry*, pp.152-4.

[12] For doubts, see Butt, 'Scottish Cotton Industry', p.121, table 1; Donnachie, 'Sources of Capital', pp.279-80.

[13] Trebilcock, *Phoenix Assurance*, vol.I, pp.367-79.

[14] Jenkins, 'Indexes of the Fire Insurance Policies'. Cf. the discussions about the accuracy of insurance valuations in James, 'Personal Wealth Distribution', pp.547-8, in Cockerell and Green, *British Insurance Business*, pp.49-50, and in Barnett, *London, Hub of the Industrial Revolution*, pp.5-8.

[15] Jenkins, 'Indexes of the Fire Insurance Policies', pp.27-31.

[16] GL Ms 14022/4-12, Union, DM, 16 Aug. 1727, 15 Dec. 1731, 21 Mar. 1753, 12 May 1762; Ms 8666/18, Hand-in-Hand, DM, 31 Mar. 1761, 16 Apr. 1765.

[17] GL Ms 8755/2, London Assurance, Out Letter Book, to Lord Torrington, 1 July 1793, to Liverpool Fire Office, 31 July 1793. The London Assurance dismantled its agency network during the mid 1780s and reconstructed it from 1805.

[18] Supple, *Royal Exchange*, pp.89, 92, 99.

[19] Dickson, *Sun Insurance*, pp.68, 82, 88; GL Ms 11935/1, Sun, CCM, 11 Apr. 1735.

[20] 4 Geo. III c. 14 (1764); 14 Geo. III c. 78 (1774).

[21] GL Ms 11935A/1, Sun, Report Books, Bewicke's Report, 1806.

[22] Trebilcock, *Phoenix Assurance*, vol.I, pp.368, 387-8.

[23] County, Letter Book 'M', to J. Muff, 10 Dec. 1821.

[24] LCA, acc.393, box 41, Leeds & Yorkshire, Secretary's Letter Book, fol.271, 11 Oct. 1825, fol.46, 17 Dec. 1824, fol.41, 9 Dec. 1824, fol.71, 7 Jan. 1825; GL Ms 16222/2-8, MFLAC, DM, 1 Sept., 31 Jan., 3 May 1825, 3 Apr. 1828, 19 Feb. 1829, 30 June, 2 July 1831, 29 Feb. 1832, 25 Feb., 3 Apr. 1833.

[25] See the comments by the Sun's Manchester agent on the rise of multiple tenured cotton mills, CUL, PAA, PX1010, Phoenix, Agents' Extra Letter Book A, 12 Dec. 1801.

[26] Jenkins, 'Indexes of the Fire Insurance Policies', pp.23, 28.

[27] Supple, *Royal Exchange*, p.85; GL Ms 11931/4, Sun, GCM, 9 Apr. 1730.

[28] GL Ms 8666/13,14,16, Hand-in-Hand, DM, 22 Mar. 1732, 26 Mar. 1735, 13 Feb., 6 Nov. 1739, 2 Aug., 10 Nov. 1743, 12 Dec. 1751; Ms 11935/4, Sun, CCM, 21 Jan. 1757.

[29] GL Ms 14022/5, Union, DM, 12 Nov. 1735; Ms 8666/14, Hand in Hand, DM, 25 Jan. 1743; Ms 11932/7, Sun, CMM, 1 Apr., 22 Apr. 1762; Ms 11931/6, Sun, GCM, 8 Oct. 1767.

[30] For an extensive discussion of sugar mill insurances in this period, see Trebilcock, *Phoenix Assurance*, vol.I, pp.334-42.

[31] GL Ms 11931/7, Sun, GCM, 23 Oct. 1788.

[32] See Chapter 4, p.154.

[33] Dickson, *Sun Insurance*, p.87; GL Ms 14022/4, Union, DM, 31 Aug. 1726, 3 Jan.1727/8, 25 Sept. 1728; Ms 8666/19,22, Hand-in-Hand, DM, 25 June 1765, 10 Oct. 1775; WCA, Ms 343/75, Westminster, GCM, 24 Oct. 1765.

[34] GL Ms 16222/2-3, MFLAC, DM, 24 Nov. 1825, 26 July, 1 Nov. 1827, 23 Oct. 1828; LCA, acc.393, box 41, Leeds & Yorkshire, Secretary's Letter Book, fol.44, 6 Dec. 1824, fol.51, 23 Dec. 1824, fol.89, 21 Jan. 1825; CUL, PAA, PX1010, Phoenix,

Agents' Extra Letter Book A, 12 Mar. 1821; GL Ms 14281/1-4, Guardian, GCM, 28 Nov. 1828.

35   GL Ms 16222/4, MFLAC, DM, 13 May 1830; LCA, acc.393, box 41, Leeds & Yorkshire, Secretary's Letter Book, fol.57, 28 Dec. 1824, fol.68, 5 Jan. 1825, fol.83, 17 Jan. 1825, fol.130, 9 Mar. 1825, fol.217, 2 July 1825. On insurers' realisation of the dangers of the multiple occupancy of mills, see Trebilcock, *Phoenix Assurance*, vol.I, pp.358-60.

36   LCA, acc.393, box 41, Leeds & Yorkshire, Secretary's Letter Book, fol.35, 3 Dec. 1824.

37   Jenkins, 'Indexes of the Fire Insurance Policies', pp.30-31.

38   GL Ms 14022/17, Union, DM, 19 Nov. 1783.

39   GL Ms 8735/1, London Assurance, FCM, 12 Jan. 1728 (Irish Proposals); Ms 8666/13, Hand-in-Hand, DM, 9 Sept. 1740.

40   GL Ms 16222/4, MFLAC, DM, 15 Jan. 1829.

41   GL Ms 14281/2, Guardian, GCM, 5 Sept. 1823.

42   GL Ms 8670, Hand-in-Hand, General Letter Book, 1752-1842, letter of 16 July 1794.

43   GL Ms 16222/4, MFLAC, DM, 15 Oct. 1829. For another example, see Ms 16222/2, MFLAC, DM, 29 Aug., 1 Sept., 29 Sept. 1825. Cf. Jenkins, 'Indexes of the Fire Insurance Policies', p.28.

44   LCA, acc.393, box 41, Leeds & Yorkshire, Secretary's Letter Book, fol. 51, 23 Dec. 1824.

45   LCA, acc.393, box 41, Leeds & Yorkshire, Secretary's Letter Book, fol.340, 24 June 1829, cited by Jenkins, 'Practice of Insurance against Fire', p.32. For an example of this approach to undervaluation, see LCA, acc.393, box 41, Leeds & Yorkshire, Secretary's Letter Book, fol.72-3, 7 Jan. 1825.

46   9 Geo. IV c. 13. On the average clause, see Supple, *Royal Exchange*, pp.83-4; GL Ms 8735/1-6, London Assurance, FCM, 8 Dec. 1725, 16 Feb., 16 Mar. 1726, 20 Jan. 1727, 28 Feb. 1755, 14 Dec. 1804; Ms 8755/2, London Assurance, Out Letter Book, letter to G. Piersy, 2 May 1767; LCA, acc.393, box 41, Leeds & Yorkshire, Secretary's Letter Book, fol.98, 28 Jan. 1825, fol.106, 3 Feb. 1825; GL Ms 16222/2, MFLAC, DM, 28 Feb. 1825. The principle of average had long been used in marine insurance, cf. Stevens, *Essay on Average*.

47   Dickson, *Sun Insurance*, p.80; Jenkins, 'Practice of Insurance against Fire', pp.32-3. See also the comments in James, 'Personal Wealth Distribution', p.547, and the inaccurate account in Jenkins and Yoneyama, *History of Insurance*, vol.II, pp.1-2.

48   GL Ms 8755/2, London Assurance, Out Letter Book, to J. Vareilles, 28 Feb., 16 Mar. 1765. For a similar case, see the letter to G. Piersy, 2 May 1767.

49   Cited by Raynes, *History of British Insurance*, p.207.

50   WCA, Ms 343/75, Westminster, GCM, 24 Apr. 1718, 9 Apr. 1724, 19 Apr. 1759; GL Ms 8735/1, London Assurance, FCM, 20 Jan. 1727, 8 Mar. 1754.

51   GL Ms 8755/2, London Assurance, Out Letter Book, to Viscount Torrington, 26 June 1793.

52   Wilson and Mackley, 'How Much Did the English Country House Cost to Build'; Clarke, *Building Capitalism*, p.127.

53   I am grateful to Sarah Pearson for her work on the Hand-in-Hand valuations, from which these figures are derived.

54 For examples, see GL Ms 16170/1, Atlas, DM, 2 Nov., 30 Nov. 1809, on the insurance of drying stoves by a skin dyer in Manchester, and insurance in Kingston, Jamaica. See also Ms 14078/1, Alliance, Foreign Committee Minutes, no.2, 4 Feb. 1835, 7 Mar. 1838.

55 GL Ms 16222/8, MFLAC, DM, 30 Oct. 1844.

56 Jenkins, 'Indexes of the Fire Insurance Policies', p.27; Cockerell and Green, *British Insurance Business*, pp.49-50; Barnett, *London, Hub of the Industrial Revolution*, p.8.

57 Porter, 'Great Fire of Gravesend', p.24.

58 Carter, *Order out of Chaos*, pp.13-21, 36-58.

59 Malachy Postlethwaite, *Dictionary of Trade and Commerce* (1774), cited by Carter, *Order out of Chaos*, p.84. Carter counts just two surveyors listed in *Lowndes' London Directory* of 1779.

60 GL Ms 8735/4, London Assurance, FCM, 19 Jan. 1776; WCA, Ms 343/16, Westminster, DM, 27 Apr. 1780.

61 GL Ms 12019B, Sun, Accounts of Fire Claims, 1771-87. Some of these are examined in detail by Carter, *Order out of Chaos*, pp.23-32.

62 CUL, PAA, PX1010, Phoenix, Agents' Extra Letter Book A, 27 Oct. 1836. Cf. also letters of 14 July 1831 and Jan. 1795; GL Ms 16222/3, MFLAC, DM, 18 Jan., 22 Mar., 14 June 1827.

63 Dickson, *Sun Insurance*, pp.150-52.

64 Cf. LCA, acc.393, box 41, Leeds & Yorkshire, Secretary's Letter Book, 29 Oct. 1824, where the Leeds board resolved not to notify the press of a small claim at a Huddersfield mill only partially insured, because it was 'too trifling a character to become the object of a newspaper paragraph'. Cf. also the claim of 18 'country manufacturers' who lost their stock in a fire at a Saddleworth mill in 1829, where the threat of bad publicity drove the MFLAC to pay out £324 even though only the building had been insured by its owner. GL Ms 16222/4, MFLAC, DM, 29 Oct. 1829.

65 Dickson, *Sun Insurance*, p.84; GL Ms 4022/11, Union, DM, 20 Nov., 11 Dec. 1723; Ms 8735/1,5, London Assurance, FCM, 19 Jan. 1726, 20 Jan., 1 Dec. 1727, 12 Jan., 13 Sept. 1728, 11 July 1783; Ms 8755/2, London Assurance, Out Letter Book, to T. Slack, 2 Mar. 1771, to J. Monkman, 30 May 1781; Ms 8666/22-23, Hand-in-Hand, DM, 21 Sept. 1773, 13 Aug. 1776, 25 Nov. 1777.

66 These and the following data were calculated from GL Ms 11937/144-88, Sun, Fire Policy Registers, Country Series; Blackburn Central Library, B368, MFLAC, Blackburn Agency Policy and Endorsement Book, 1830-43.

67 Coinsurances rose from 33 per cent to 48 per cent of the total insured by the Sun's Manchester agency while sums insured in new policies fell by 53 per cent between 1823-5 and 1829-30 (£960595 to £453880). Calculated from GL Ms 11937/144-88, Sun, Fire Policy Registers, Country Series; Ms 11935/11-12, Sun, CCM, 1820-29 *passim*.

68 Jenkins, *West Riding Wool Textile Industry*, p.289; *idem.*, 'Indexes of the Fire Insurance Policies', p.31.

69 Jenkins, 'Indexes of the Fire Insurance Policies', p.31.

70 Jenkins, 'Practice of Insurance against Fire', p.30; Chapman, 'British Cotton Industry', p.256.

71 Jenkins, 'Indexes of the Fire Insurance Policies', p.30.

72   Cf. Schwarz and Jones, who dismissed country offices as 'insignificant'. Schwarz and Jones, 'Wealth, Occupations and Insurance', p.373. Cf. also Jackson, who uses the Sun's registers to analyse insured wealth in Warrington, but makes no reference to the presence of two other local insurers in the area. Jackson, 'Personal Wealth'.

73   Orbell, 'Corn milling', p.158.

74   Chapman, 'Devon Cloth Industry', pp.xi, xvii. Chapman's claim appears to rest on an estimate made by the Sun in 1797 of the distribution of fire insurance, which used a notional 60:40 division of insurances by county between the Sun and the Phoenix/REA. See Chapter 4, pp.164-6 and table 4.4.

75   Marshall, *Treatise on the Law of Insurance*, p.682.

76   6 Anne c. 31. This stated that servants would face 18 months hard labour in gaol or else a fine of £100, to be distributed among the victims of the fire. LRO, Liverpool, London & Globe archives, Globe 5, Handbill, 24 June 1803. An extract from this Act was attached to the agents' instructions circulated by the Sun in 1807. Sun Fire Office, 'Instructions', pp.292-3.

77   Gray, *Letters*, vol.II, letter CXVI, p.115.

78   Thomas, *Religion and the Decline of Magic*, pp.93, 98, 128-9.

79   Walpole, *Correspondence*, to Sir Horace Mann, 28 May 1763; Southey, *Letters from England*, p.37.

80   *GM*, 35 (1765), p.244; GL Ms 11932/2, Sun, CMM, 13 Aug. 1730, 17 Feb. 1732.

81   George, *London Life*, pp.78-82; Porter, 'Great Fire of Gravesend'; Blackstone, *History of the British Fire Service*, pp.15-34.

82   See Chapter 2, pp.83-4. Cf. also Porter, 'Great Fire of Gravesend', p.29.

83   Knowles and Pitt, *History of Building Regulation in London*, p.40; *AR*, (1772), pp.178-9.

84   Paulsen, *Hogarth*, vol.2, p.371; West, 'Wilkes's Squint'.

85   Angiolini, *Lettere sull' Inghilterra*, p.24; *Dictionary of National Biography*, 'David Hartley', p.68.

86   GL Ms 11932/1, 15, Sun, CMM, 31 Aug. 1727, 24 Apr. 1800; Ms 11931/6, 7, Sun, GCM, 9 Apr. 1767, 3 Jan. 1793; Ms 8666/14, 15, 16, Hand-in-Hand, DM, 10 Nov. 1743, 19 June 1744, 12 Dec. 1751; Porter, 'Great Fire of Gravesend', pp.28-9.

87   GL Ms 16170/1, Atlas, DM, 7 Mar. 1811.

88   GL Ms 16222/3, 4, MFLAC, DM, 3 Jan. 1828, 23 Dec. 1830, 6 Jan. 1831.

89   Boulton and Watt, Selected Papers, document 151, G. Lee to J. Watt jr., 16 July 1800.

90   Jenkins, *West Riding Wool Textile Industry*, pp.59-60; GL Ms 11935A/1, Sun, Report Books, Bewicke's Report, Oct. 1806, Green's Report, 10 May 1816.

91   GL Ms 14281/3, Guardian, GCM, 11 Jan. 1828; Jenkins, *West Riding Wool Textile Industry*, pp.60-61; RC on Employment of Children in Factories, Drinkwater's report, Leeds, evidence of Mark Best, C1, p.74, John Hannam, C1, p.89, John Sunderland, C1, p.45, various children, C1, p.97; *Ibid.*, Power's Report, Leeds, evidence of Benjamin Bradshaw, C2, p.35, John Dawson, C2, p.44; Factory Inspectors' Reports, Report of R.J. Saunders, p.442; Special Reports of the Inspectors of Factories, pp.240-66. For examples of Yorkshire firms employing ventilators by 1833, see RC on Employment of Children in Factories, Supplementary Report, pt.II, C1, pp.44, 51, 52, 57, 61, 75.

92   Beresford, 'Prometheus Insured', p.387.

93   Tann, *Development of the Factory*, p.147.

94   In 1759, for example, the British Linen Company calculated that the insurance of its goods from Scotland to London had cost a total of £1660 since 1747. The firm resolved 'for the future that the Company should run the risk to the amount of £300 for each bottom from Leith to London without insuring, when the ships shall happen to sail with convoy...', British Linen Company, DM, 1 Mar. 1759.

95   GL Ms 11935A/1, Sun, Report Books, Green's Report, 10 May 1816.

96   Pearson, 'Fire Insurance and the British Textile Industries', table 3.

97   Brown, *Early Days in a Dundee Mill*, pp.52-3.

98   Dickson, *Sun Insurance*, p.83; Anon, *Fire Insurance Guide*, pp.49-56.

99   GL Ms 14022/4, Union, DM, 25 Sept. 1728.

100   GL Ms 12160A/1, Imperial, DM, 3 Aug.-28 Sept. 1803.

101   GL Ms 16170/2, 4, Atlas, DM, 16 May, 25 July 1816, 22 Nov. 1825; Ms 12160A/8, Imperial, DM, 18 June 1823; GPL, Cotesworth Mss, CM/4/17, Newcastle, Accounts, Note to C.E. (Cuthbert Ellison); GL Ms 14116, Sun, Simplified Profit and Loss Accounts.

102   GL Ms 12160A/7, Imperial, DM, 8 Nov. 1820; Ms 8746A, London Assurance, Fire Assurance Annual Accounts. 'Apparently' is a necessary qualifier because the random nature of record survival makes such judgements about what contemporaries had at their disposal always uncertain.

103   GL Ms 16222/5, MFLAC, DM, 2 July, 7 July 1831.

104   GL Ms 12160A/13, Imperial, DM, 31 Jan. 1838.

105   Trebilcock, *Phoenix Assurance*, vol.I, ch.9.

106   GL Ms 12160A/12-15, Imperial, DM, 17 Oct., 28 Nov. 1838, 5 June 1839, 27 Oct. 1841, 5 June 1844, 11 June 1845, 16 Sept. 1846.

Chapter 9

Investments

'If you're in such a state of mind as that', he grumbled...'why don't you make over your property? Buy an annuity cheap, and make your life interesting to yourself and everybody else that watches the speculation'.

Charles Dickens.[1]

The finances of early insurance offices have interested historians for several reasons. First, insurance investment has a relevance to the debate about the role of institutional finance during the industrial revolution. Second, the rates charged by insurers for lending have been examined to illuminate the workings of the money market during the eighteenth and nineteenth centuries. Third, the share prices and dividends of insurance companies have formed part of the study of profits and the business cycle during this period.[2] In examining how a range of insurers deployed their capital funds this chapter touches upon all these areas of financial history. It also asks to what extent the investment behaviour of the three London offices, which are the subject of major company histories, was representative of the industry as a whole.

Insurance investment during the eighteenth century

Most eighteenth-century insurance offices placed the bulk of their funds in the national debt. This climbed upwards with every wartime surge of government borrowing, from £17m at the end of the Nine Years War to a peak of £844m after the war against Napoleon.[3] The debt has been regarded as one of the strengths of Hanoverian Britain. Together with a remarkably efficient revenue collection, an extensive public ownership of the 'funds' has been seen as a bulwark of the military-fiscal state. The debt was largely funded by the stocks, bonds and notes issued by the Bank of England, the South Sea Company and the East India Company, which together provided the volume of interest-bearing securities required for a stock market to function effectively. After the joint-stock bubble of 1720 had burst, the range of these securities remained narrow - newspapers usually quoted no more than 25 prices of stock before the end of the eighteenth century. Nevertheless, several hundred dealers in these stocks were concentrated in the City of London by 1800 and the number of investors across the country increased from some 10000 in the reign of Queen Anne to 530000 by 1815.[4]

The London insurance offices were among the largest holders of public debt and are regarded as having contributed significantly to the development of the City's money and capital markets.[5] Table 9.1 presents new estimates of the total assets of fire insurance offices between 1720 and 1845. These include the life funds of those offices which underwrote both fire and life insurance, as well as the marine insurance funds of the chartered corporations and the current deposits of the three London mutual fire offices. The estimates are based upon total capital funds given in the ledgers or accounts of a number of companies, ranging from four offices in 1730 to 16 in 1824. The funds are sometimes described as 'capital plus accumulation', and usually recorded at cost or purchase price rather than current market value, but a uniform definition was not possible even across this limited number of companies.[6] Before 1780 some guesses had to be made about the assets of a few offices, most notably the London Assurance in 1720 and 1730, where it was assumed they were roughly of the same order as those of the REA as both offices commenced with the same volume of capital. From 1780, when the number of offices began to increase rapidly, the procedure was to multiply the total known funds by the market share of the offices concerned, given by the duty returns or by premium income. As the period progressed and a rising proportion of insurance offices sold both life and fire insurance, this procedure will understate the capital assets of such composite companies. Life funds usually accumulated much faster than fire funds in new offices as they were seldom required to cover large and unpredictable fluctuations in underwriting losses. By 1845 this has become such a problem that only a minimum approximation of funds can be given in table 9.1.

The estimates suggest that the sums invested by fire insurers rose particularly rapidly between 1800 and 1825, buoyed by high wartime yields on government securities and the capital of dozens of new stock companies entering the industry. During the first half of the nineteenth century insurance funds doubled relative to the national debt, although an increasing proportion was being diverted into other forms of investment. Even if all insurance capital had been placed in gilts, however, over the whole period it would never have accounted for more than a tiny fraction of the national debt.

During the eighteenth century the significance of insurance investment lay not in its aggregate amount, but in the fact that a small number of companies held much larger volumes of government stock than the average investor and were particularly active in trading them. In 1760 there were 2399 owners of three per cent annuities, each with an average holding of £854, while the Hand-in-Hand and the Union together held nearly £60000 of the same stock.[7] For most of the century the three London mutual offices invested their members' deposits almost exclusively in the public funds. The funds also accounted for 49 per cent of the REA's assets in 1734 and 73 per cent by 1760. The Sun was the major mortgage lender among the fire insurance offices but in 1786 it also held 34 per cent of its investments in the funds. Even the Phoenix, the most adventurous of contemporary underwriters, made no investments outside the funds before 1816.[8]

Table 9.1   Total funds of English fire insurance offices, 1720-1845

	Estimated Funds £m	Funds as % of National Debt
1720	0.32	0.6
1730	0.84	1.6
1760	1.64	1.6
1780	2.18	1.3
1800	2.82	0.6
1810	5.40	0.9
1824	8.66	1.0
1845	>11.00	>1.4

Notes: Hand-in-Hand, 1720-1800, deposits; Union, 1720-1800, funds, book value; Westminster, 1720-1800, stocks held, nominal value; Bristol Crown, 1720, paid up capital, assuming this was ten per cent of nominal capital of 1718; REA, 1720, paid-up capital less price of the charter, thereafter fire and marine funds; London Assurance, 1760-1800, fire and marine balances including capital stock; Sun, 1720-30, paid-up capital, thereafter funds; Salop, 1780-1845, Essex & Suffolk, 1810-45, Imperial, 1810-45, Newcastle, 1810-24, Guardian 1824, 'capital'; Kent, 1810-45, 'capital + accumulation'; Norwich Union, 1800, 1824-45, 'assets'; Atlas, 1810, Phoenix, 1800-45, total investments; County, 1810-45, investments (book value) plus agents' balances; Alliance, Protector, Beacon, Palladium, 1824, current value of share capital calculated by English; MFLAC, 1824-45, total funds.

Sources: National debt from Mitchell and Deane, *Abstract of British Historical Statistics*, pp.401-3; Insurance funds from GL Ms 8666, Hand-in-Hand, DM, 1723-1800 *passim*; Ms 14022, Union, DM, 1723-1800 *passim*; WCA, Ms 343/83-6, Westminster, General Account Books; Ms 343/89, Westminster, Stock Books; GL Ms 8749A/2, London Assurance, Fire-Marine Accounts; Supple, *Royal Exchange*, pp.45, 71, tables 3.2, p.74, 13.1, p.315, 13.2, p.322, p.325; Dickson, *Sun Insurance*, p.47; Raynes, *History of British Insurance*, p.154; GL Ms 11931, Sun, GCM, 1715-1808 *passim*; Ms 15042/1, Sun, Quarterly Accounts, 1786-1812; Ms 11932/4, Sun, CMM, 5 July 1750; Trebilcock, *Phoenix Assurance*, vol.I, p.622, tables 11.3, p.626, 13.7, pp.728-9; GL Ms 15042, Sun, Take over Papers, for Bristol Union, Newcastle & North of England; Ms 16206/3, Essex & Suffolk, DM, Report for 1835; CKS, U2593/B43, Kent, List of Statistics, 1815-90; GL Ms 16170/1, Atlas, DM, 2 July 1810; Ms 14281/1, Guardian, DM, 7 Feb. 1823; Ms 16223, MFLAC, GCM, 1825-46 *passim*; GPL, CM/4/1-21, Newcastle, Accounts, 1809-22; GCA, TD446/4/2/1, North British, Journal no.1; Ryan, 'History of Norwich Union', table 81, pp.1159; SRO, Ms 3008/1/2/10-11, Salop Fire, Income & Capital Account Books; GL Ms 18274, Imperial, Tabular Statements; County, Annual Accounts, 1807-46; English, *A Complete View*.

Contrary to John's assertion that exclusive investment in the public funds can be equated with a certain 'passivity' on the part of the mutuals, the turnover of such stock by both mutual and stock insurers was considerable.[9] In the first instance this was because most offices sold stock directly to meet cash needs and to pay claims. Such sales, often involuntary, were complemented by the practice of switching between securities, albeit within a narrow range, in response to relative changes in prices and yields. As indicated in chapter 2, the London mutuals were particularly badly hit in the second half of the eighteenth century by the need to sell stock to pay recurrent heavy insurance claims. As the price of the funds drifted downwards, the urgency of such sales frequently compelled them to sell at a loss. One consequence was that the assets of the mutuals became concentrated in an ever narrower range of gilts, exposing them to the fluctuations of just a handful of prices. The Hand-in-Hand held eight categories of stocks in 1768 but just four by the late 1790s. The Union held eight different stocks in 1764 but just one by 1781.

Although they were not always able to avoid selling near the bottom of a bear market, especially when faced with a clamour from claimants, or with members complaining about repeated calls on their deposits, there is ample evidence that insurance offices kept a keen eye on the movement of the public funds. In October 1797, following the suspension of convertability, Thomas Watts reported that he had postponed selling any of the Sun's £22000 consols, as directed by the board, on account of the 'great fall in the price of stocks and the few losses outstanding'.[10] Some insurers valued their stocks at cost price in their ledgers while keeping a mental note of the current market valuation. The securities held by the Hand-in-Hand were initially listed at par, but, commencing in 1731, at each biannual account the office noted that the market price of these would fetch several £1000 above the book value. At some point after 1736 a decision was taken to record the market values. Revaluations of stock could also go the other way, especially in the second half of the century. In 1787 the Sun's managers noticed large discrepancies between the book values of the office's securities and the current market values, and they marked down seven categories of stock by a total of 14 per cent.[11]

The historian A.H. John pointed out two conditions fundamental to insurance investment. These were, first, the need for liquidity, which placed an emphasis on investing in easily realisable assets. Second, there was the need for capital and income security, which meant avoiding the more speculative securities, especially the unfunded debt and new loan issues.[12] The first of these conditions was more relevant for fire insurance than for life assurance.[13] Liquidity was frequently a pressing requirement, even for the largest offices. Most of the major funds could be sold quite quickly in times of heavy losses, but, despite this, some offices had to resort to borrowing from their own directors. The greatest liquidity was offered by cash, but cash balances fluctuated enormously. Several London offices began by acting as their own cashiers, but most eventually opened a bank account.[14] The cash deposits of the insurance companies thus provided an irregular but potentially lucrative business for their bankers.

Another means of increasing liquidity was to invest in short-term securities. The mutuals were cautious about these, preferring to maintain the bulk of their gilts in the bigger and less volatile funds. Between 1751 and 1800, for instance, the Hand-in-Hand held no bonds or East India stock or short-term paper such as Navy bills and Exchequer bills. The stock offices traded more actively in such securities, but the requirements of liquidity and security did not lead them to concentrate exclusively on the public funds. The Sun began making short-term loans in the

1730s and 1740s, especially to its own managers and shareholders, on a wide range of securities, including the company's own shares, various stock and shares in other ventures, diamonds, lottery tickets, clothing assignments for the army, and navy and victualling bills. With the rise in the value of its assets and shares, the Sun increased the amount directors could lend on each share from £50 in 1767 to £100 in 1778.[15] The total lent by London Assurance on personal and other securities rose from £44000 in 1726 to £356000 by 1761. Such loans were usually for sums between £5000 and £20000 for periods up to 12 months, and were mostly made to City merchants and brokers, especially in periods when other sources of credit were tight.[16]

Following the financial crisis of 1763, the funding operation to clear the market of miscellaneous government paper and the subsequent expansion of the banking system, the demand for short-term loans from insurance companies appears to have declined. Insurance offices increasingly invested in government securities, whose average yields were rising.[17] The Sun also greatly expanded its mortgage business. Its mortgage loans increased from £98000 in 1750 to £345000 in 1780. Thereafter the total remained fairly constant until it began to decline after 1815.[18] For most of the period 1740-1815, mortgages represented between one-half and two-thirds of the Sun's investments, a concentration not found anywhere else in the industry at this time with the exception of some small provincial fire offices such as the Salop, where one or two big loans could account for a large proportion of total assets.

The Sun first resolved to lend on landed security in 1731 when the managers were empowered to lend up to £20000. The first loan was made in the following year for £7000 to the Duke of Powis on his Hendon estate.[19] The Sun soon found itself tapping into an expanding mortgage market. Several reasons have been put forward for this expansion. It has been argued that the establishment of entail for landed estates and the reduced likelihood of foreclosure made borrowing on mortgage more attractive by the end of the seventeenth century than it had been previously. Mortgaging for consumption purposes has been regarded by Allen as 'an indispensable tool of prudent estate management' in the eighteenth century, the principal way of consuming capital gains without selling land. Others agree that mortgaging was primarily for consumption or liquidity rather than for productive purposes.[20] A.H. John, however, observed a concurrence between mortgage lending by insurance offices and the rate of enclosures. More recently, Clark has been sceptical of the economic gains from enclosure, which, in turn, casts doubt on the propensity to borrow for land improvements. The mortgage market clearly expanded both in times of falling and rising land prices, and there are indications that in different places during the 1730s and 1740s some mortgaging was associated with falling agrarian incomes and distress. A.H. John also believed that mortgage lending increased in response to low peacetime interest rates, although Dickson noted that the volume of the Sun's mortgages rose during some wartime years.[21] Some historians have argued that land was sold close to economic value during the eighteenth century, and if this was so, the mortgage rate should have reflected movements in the capital markets. Contemporaries generally agreed that the mortgage rate was determined by the state of the money markets. Indeed, Homer found that the Sun's average mortgage rate tended to move in the same direction as the yield on funds, although the differential between the two rates was highly variable over time.[22]

Unfortunately, insurance records shed little light on the reasons for borrowing, or on the demand factors which helped to determine what rate the mortgage market could bear. What is certain is that the burden of landed debt was growing and that it was becoming easier to gain access to funds as lawyers, of whom there were several thousand by 1760, routinised the practice of mortgages.[23] Once in this market, the Sun remained an enthusiastic player, not least because lending to landowners and property developers also brought goodwill and the prospect of additional insurances. The number of its mortgagors varied between six in 1750 and 26 in 1800, mostly drawn from the landed elite. Some loans were related to the industrial exploitation of estates or infrastructural improvements, most notably the £35000 lent in 1769 to the Duke of Bridgewater for his canal.[24] Most insurance offices strove to keep their rates as close as possible to the five per cent ceiling imposed by the Usury Laws. The Sun's mortgagors were normally covenanted to pay a fixed rate for a term of years, but it was unusual to fix a redemption term - the average mortgage was repaid in about 20 years, although some could continue for much longer.[25] The Sun usually lent up to 70 per cent of the value of estates mortgaged to it, although occasionally this limit was exceeded. Mortgages were always accompanied by an inspection and valuation of the property concerned, and the estimated rental incomes, if invested at the market rate, were usually sufficient to pay off the capital of the loan within ten years.[26] The Sun always familiarised itself with the type of leases and tenants and with the methods of collecting rent. Guarantors of the interest payments were also usually required, or else an affadavit of the value of the rental income might suffice.[27] In this respect the Sun set the standard which other insurance offices were to follow in the mortgage and annuity markets of the nineteenth century.

In these and other ways the Sun attempted to exercise quality controls over its rapidly expanding loan business. On several occasions the office resolved not to lend on securities outside England and Wales. Problems of insolvency and foreclosure, however, did arise, and were compounded during the American War of Independence as stock and land values fell and rental and mortgage arrears rose. By the end of 1781 the Sun had eight mortgagors over a year in arrears, together owing £166000. In 1789 the office wrote to all its mortgagors that the maximum five per cent would be charged unless the interest was paid regularly on their loans. At this time consols were yielding 4.3 per cent and the Sun was charging 4.5 per cent on regular mortgages. After the French wars commenced in 1793, land prices steadied, rising yields on public funds made these more attractive, the proportion held by the Sun in mortgages fell and the problem of arrears declined.[28]

Investment during the French wars 1793-1815

A.H. John described the 1770s as 'a watershed' in insurance investment, marking a shift towards government paper which accelerated during the French wars. By 1800, he claimed, some 80 per cent of assets of all insurance companies were placed in the funds.[29] Government securities became more attractive to investors, not just because of their liquidity, homogeneity and certainty of payment, but also because the differential between average mortgage rates and the yield on consols fell from over 20 per cent in the 1770s to less than five per cent during the 1780s and 1790s.[30] For long periods during the war, consol yields rose well above the five per cent which was the legal maximum which could be charged for loans on real security. The mortgage market shrank rapidly as lenders shifted their attention to the funds. The Sun reduced the proportion of its assets held in mortgages from 63 per cent in the early 1790s to 44 per cent by 1806-10, while gilts increased from one-third to one-half of its total investments. The Phoenix, too, joined the rush to buy government stock at falling prices. Most new insurance offices also placed their capital in the public funds. The County used £30000 of its £35000 subscription capital to buy exchequer bills in 1807, then diversified into four per cent annuities and five per cents in 1810. The Atlas also invested its original share capital in exchequer bills, but then sold some of them during 1808 to buy three per cents on a rising market. This pattern of buying exchequer bills with initial share capital, followed by a rapid move into the larger central funds, exemplified the elements of liquidity and solidity which new insurance offices required.

Despite the claim of some contemporaries, the market for mortgages and other types of lending did not entirely collapse at the end of the eighteenth century.[31] In his study of freehold land, Clay argued that land prices moved in the same direction as the funds, not least because the sale of government securities was the usual way of financing a land purchase. Thus, *ceteris paribus*, low wartime prices for securities would have been accompanied by a shrinkage in the land market, and, in turn, a decline in the mortgage market. Low land values gave potential mortgagors less capacity to borrow, while high yields on funds gave institutional lenders a greater incentive to invest in government paper. Rents, however, rose rapidly in the final decades of the century and Allen has argued that they accounted for most of the gap between the mortgage rate and the average return on the purchase of land. While interest rates rose after 1772 and land prices fell, the latter did not fall as much as the rise in interest rates would have predicted. This was due to the anticipation of rising rentals, particularly as landowners exercised considerable control over the enclosure process, and enclosures in many instances were intended to result in the renegotiation of tenants' contracts at higher rents.[32] This, in turn, helps explain why insurance mortgage lending did not dry up during the American war. The demand for mortgages, based on a capacity to borrow against the value of land, remained more buoyant than would have been predicted by the relative movements in interest rates. Moreover, while one component in land values - agricultural output - remained unpredictable, two other components - rental income and the 'positional' premium for holding land - lay, at least partly, within the ability of landowners to forecast. This information gave landowners some bargaining power in the mortgage market. By contrast, while the promise of repayment on government securities may have been 'gilt-edged', consol values were highly unpredictable, being often the product of political and fiscal decisions, the fortunes of war and the vagaries of the City's money markets. During the French wars, the prices of the funds fluctuated violently around a low mean. To estate owners, their land agents and attorneys, the money markets were more uncertain and obscure than they had ever been. Land values also fluctuated from year to year, but, on average, they increased modestly while the number of enclosures rose steeply.[33] According to recent estimates, capital gains, coupled with sharply rising rent rolls, raised the realised returns on land above the equivalent returns on consols whose prices remained very low.[34] This provided some incentive to retain unencumbered land, and to mortgage it rather than sell it if funds for increased consumption were required.

While many insurance offices reduced their mortgage liabilities or avoided such lending altogether, others entered the wartime market with varying degrees of caution. Some of the continuing mortgage demand derived from urban construction and public bodies seeking cash for infrastructural improvements. The REA made one very large loan for £300000 to finance the construction of Regent Street in 1814, insisting on compulsory insurance with the corporation for tenants in the new street. Shortly after its foundation in 1808 the Atlas received loan requests from Worthing council, the parish of Hampreston, Dorset, and from 'an eminent surveyor' to borrow £4000 on the mortgage of houses.[35] What is interesting is the expectation by builders and local authorities in southern England that sums might be lent by insurance offices for the purposes of urban development, a trickle which anticipated the deluge of such requests to hit the larger offices some 25 to 30 years later.

Between 1811 and 1815 several insurance offices succeeded in obtaining private acts of parliament to enable them 'to sue and make investments in the name of an individual on their part'. Mortgage lending subsequently increased. Even before this several provincial insurers had begun to diversify their investments. During the 1780s the Bristol Fire Office bought shares in a local venture, the Bristol Brass Company, and the Newcastle Fire Office invested over £10000 in the town's waterworks, which it had purchased in 1797, a sum which accounted for 15 per cent of the company's assets in 1813.[36] The Salop Fire Office made one large £10000 mortgage loan in 1792 to a shareholder and former director, the Reverend Edward Powys of Marton. During the war it also made a loans of a few hundred pounds each to the Capel Cerig Turnpike and to the trustees of St Alkmond's in Shrewsbury, the latter to help towards the cost of rebuilding the church.[37] Other types of investment outside mortgages and the public funds were also undertaken. The Newcastle office had purchased over £16000 on annuities by 1809, apparently under the government scheme introduced the year before. Notoriously this was based on the Northampton tables of mortality, which exaggerated the mortality of annuitants and cost the state some £2m before it was replaced in 1828. The Newcastle's annuities increased to 51 per cent of its total assets by 1822.[38]

It can be concluded that insurance investment during wartime was far more varied than the picture provided by the company histories of the REA, the Phoenix and the Sun. Some, though certainly not all, new metropolitan and country offices were already spreading their assets out beyond the public funds, not just into local landed estates, but also into various types of urban and commercial mortgages. There was, it is true, still little direct lending to industry.[39] Indeed, well into the nineteenth century net capital movements generally continued to be in the reverse direction, from industry and commerce into insurance as merchants and manufacturers subscribed to new fire offices. As noted in chapter 8, however, the substantial levels of claims payments received often offset the premiums paid by sections of British industry, while the profits and dividends and capital gains on their insurance shares usually more than compensated those businessmen who diversified in this way. Moreover, the evidence shows that during the 1790s and 1800s credit from insurance offices was already beginning to flow towards local infrastructural and urban development as well as into land, increasingly complementing the personal investments of individual partners in insurance concerns. This trend towards the diversification of corporate investment was to gather pace after 1815.

The diversification of insurance investments, 1815-50

Upon the end of the war, the price of government securities rose rapidly and their yields plummeted. In one year, 1816-17, consols climbed from 54 to 84. After fluctuations, the price rose again to reach 97 by 1824, an increase of 80 per cent in eight years. This provided a windfall for the majority of insurance offices which had bought heavily in the funds during the war. These proved to be capital gains which were not soon repeated. Consol prices remained high, usually above 80, for the rest of the century and yields remained low. By the 1840s the return on consols hovered around three per cent, occasionally dipping below this. Low yields and high prices made the funds increasingly unattractive to insurance investors.[40] It is true that the prices of government securities became more stable after 1830 and that their liquidity remained attractive to fire offices needing to retain a 'live reserve' for use in case of sudden underwriting losses.[41] These considerations, however, were less important for the increasing number of new companies who combined life and fire insurance under one roof and who were able to transfer monies internally from one account to another. Other fire offices had separate but closely related life insurance organisations, usually with overlapping directorates, which could be tapped for short-term loans when cash flow was tight. This new life assurance dimension gave most early nineteenth-century insurers an investment flexibility which many of their predecessors had lacked. In addition, as noted above, several fire offices obtained private acts of parliament, partly to give them greater legal security when investing outside the public funds.

This capacity to diversify out of government paper was not always fully utilised. After 1815 insurance companies of all types continued to retain a large proportion of their assets in gilts. The Imperial invested only in the funds before 1838. The Atlas held 75 per cent of its assets in gilts in 1825, and the REA 77 per cent in 1838. As late as 1855 the Phoenix still placed 63 per cent of its assets in this way.[42] Many small country offices also continued to rely on the safety of the funds. The Salamander held all of its assets in three types of government stock in 1835 and the Newcastle & North of England placed 92 per cent of its capital in the three per cents in 1837.

For several fire offices, however, the flight out of UK gilts began well before the watershed of *circa* 1840 identified by insurance historians.[43] The new government annuity scheme of 1828-9, for instance, whose rates were still very favourable to investors at older ages, attracted insurance money. The Alliance purchased nine annuities between 1828 and 1830, the Guardian bought a 20 year annuity in 1830, and the Phoenix and the Atlas purchased such annuities from 1834.[44] For a few offices, foreign government securities also became attractive. French *rentes* and Colombian and Indian bonds averaged over eight per cent of the County's investments in the early 1820s, while Russian, Portugese, Austrian and French government securities accounted for 19 per cent of the assets of Rothschild's Alliance by the end of 1824. Other means of diversifying assets were to open interest-bearing bank accounts and to make personal loans against a range of securities, including government stock, life insurance policies, and reversionary interests in estates and trust funds, or to provide short-term credit against bills. The Sun commenced the latter business in the 1830s, lending usually only for a few weeks at a time on the security of commercial bills of exchange, and carefully selecting the firms it lent to. The banker George Carr Glyn reported large sums of money being lent by insurance companies against bills when interest rates were high during the winter of 1839-40.[45] Some offices lent to their own directors, usually on terms favourable to the borrower. By 1832, for instance, Nathan Rothschild had borrowed £40000 in several loans from the Alliance, secured on stock, at just two and a half per cent.[46] Loans secured against reversionary interests were also occasionally agreed, but these were not common among fire insurance offices. The Alliance made very few of these loans after 1829 when its lawyers advised against buying into reversions, partly owing to the potential problems and expense of sorting out any contested claims by other parties interested in the reversion, and partly due to the 'improvident' character of many borrowers.[47]

Far more important to insurance offices in the two decades after 1815 was the business of lending on private annuities. Such loans were secured on a policy taken out on life of the borrower or a third party, often the survivor of three nominees with policies taken out on all three lives. Annuity loans were usually further secured against real security, often rent rolls of estates, so that such loans were made predominantly to the landed classes.[48] On average, private annuities were repaid within ten years, so they provided a much more rapid means of circulating investment capital than did mortgages.

Annuity loans had a long history stretching back to at least the sixteenth
century. They grew rapidly in popularity as a form of gambling during the 1760s
and 1770s. In part this was because they generated interest of up to 15 per cent, and
because they contained a *bona fide* hazard - the life of the seller - thereby
circumventing the usury laws, being not counted as true loans. They were seldom
purchased by eighteenth-century insurance offices, however, even after the
introduction of an (incomplete) registration procedure in 1777.[49] During the
Napoleonic wars fire insurance offices began to buy private annuities, beginning a
trend which reached its peak in the early 1830s. This trend was in part determined
by the rapid shrinkage of the mortgage market during the war which drove many
estate owners, increasingly desperate to raise money, to grant annuities at punitive
rates. After the war, this became a matter of sufficient concern to warrant a
parliamentary investigation into the effect of the usury laws on landed
indebtedness. A second factor behind the shift in insurance investment was the
Annuity Act of 1813. This repealed the old act of 1777 and helped put a stop to the
voluminous litigation which had accompanied much annuity business in the
previous century. A clause inserted into the act by the House of Lords gave explicit
recognition to companies with more than ten partners, by permitting them to
register their purchases in Chancery using their corporate name, provided they were
empowered by their own deeds to buy annuities. Several insurance companies had
already sought by private bill to amend their constitutions in this way and there was
a further rush to do so after the act became law.[50]

Some new insurance offices, such as the Albion, began purchasing annuities as
early as 1807, claiming to be taking the 'annuity traffic' out of the hands of less
reputable moneylenders, to the benefit of landed borrowers.[51] Most commenced
shortly after the passage of the Annuity Act. The Sun's first annuity loan was made
in 1814. By 1835 £167000 was tied up in annuity loans, amounting to 31 per cent
of its total investments. The Phoenix made its first annuity loan in 1815 and by
1835 annuity lending accounted for 27 per cent of its investments.[52] The Atlas and
the County offices also eagerly embraced annuity lending. For other offices annuity
loans remained peripheral. They accounted for only one per cent of the REA's
investments. The Alliance made just three annuity loans at the height of the trade in
the early 1830s, while rejecting 17 proposals worth £260000. Outside London,
none of the smaller country offices examined purchased private annuities, although
in one of the larger offices, the MFLAC, they amounted to eight per cent of total
funds by 1829.[53]

For many fire and life offices, a combination of elements - the high interest rate
and the prospect of fire and life assurance accompanying the annuity - were
considerable attractions. While the payments were coming in, annuity loans were
lucrative. They helped push up the average yield on the Phoenix's investments to
over eight per cent during the 1820s, whereas at other times it was usually close to
the three or four per cent earned from the public funds.[54] The high rates charged,
however, soon led many borrowers into difficulties. Not only did they find
themselves unable to keep up with the annuity charges and the life insurance

premiums, the demand of some lenders that the loan capital be redeemed in stock proved to be an additional cost in a rising market. Where estates were entailed, or where the annuity was based upon a life interest, insurance offices were not always able to turn the annuities into mortgage loans, and they became increasingly exasperated with defaulting and evasive aristocrats. By the early 1830s mounting arrears drove many offices to reduce the rate on annuities to around six per cent, excluding the cost of insurance.[55] They also began to wind down this business. The Guardian commenced restricting its annuity lending in 1828. Annuity lending by the Phoenix fell by 35 per cent between 1829 and 1833 and by 71 per cent between 1834 and 1851. The MFLAC reduced its annuity loans to below one per cent of its investments by 1846.[56]

Dickson noted that those borrowing on annuity from the Sun were from the same class of landed gentlemen as the office's mortgagors. Trebilcock, however, has suggested a 'two-tier' system of insurance lending to the aristocracy, namely mortgages for the better risks and annuity loans for those most in debt and least likely to pay.[57] Whether the stiffer terms of the annuity loan induced this division in the character of borrowers, rather than reflected it, is open to question. The dichotomy itself may be overdrawn. Most of those who granted annuities were holders of life estates which could not be mortgaged, while some estate holders borrowed both on mortgage and annuity against a range of property and life securities. In 1818 the London attorney James Gibbs thought that those who borrowed on annuity were

> persons in all situations in life; almost all persons in a situation to give good security for money; many in very opulent situations, and many in the very reverse, but still in a situation to give security for money.[58]

Indeed many aristocrats, who borrowed heavily on mortgages after the war, also fell into arrears when confronted by rising debt charges and falling rent rolls. Whatever the status of annuity borrowers, there is no doubt that the blame for much post-war aristocratic indebtedness was placed upon the annuity loan by those who wished to see an end to the restrictions imposed on the money markets by the usury laws.

The low reputation of the annuity loan, having been partially restored by the entry of respectable insurance offices into the market, was blackened again by arrears, defaults and the mounting legal costs for lenders. With this experience, and against the background of low and falling yields on the funds, various forms of mortgage lending grew in popularity as the differential between the mortgage rate and the yield on consols climbed to reach 40 per cent during the 1830s and 1840s.[59] Mortgages expanded from 13 per cent of the Phoenix's total investments in 1835 to 49 per cent by 1860. During the 1830s they accounted for about one-third of the County's investments and just under 30 per cent of the Sun's. At different times between the 1820s and 1840s they also accounted for nearly half the investments of the REA, the Norwich Union and the Salop, nearly 60 per cent at the Shropshire & North Wales office and 85 per cent at the MFLAC.[60]

Mortgages on freehold estates continued in demand. However, against a background of aristocrats defaulting on annuity loans, most insurers remained cautious about how much, where and to whom they lent money. Limits on the amount to be lent were generally lower than those permitted by the Sun during the previous century. The County had an 'office rule' not to lend more than two-thirds of the value of the mortgaged property, while the MFLAC's rule was to lend no more than one-half.[61] The volume and distribution of loans were also monitored. Irish securities were generally not well regarded due to sporadic rural unrest and the difficulty of enforcing writs for debt. With the legal interest rate in Ireland at one per cent above that of England, Irish landowners pressed hard for mortgages and many insurance offices rejected a disproportionate number of loan applications from Ireland during this period.

Other types of mortgage became increasingly attractive, including loans to urban developers, local authorities, parish and county institutions, railway companies and other commercial firms. House construction surged ahead and required huge amounts of finance. Some 2.2m houses were built in Britain between 1811 and 1850, and the gross stock of dwellings in constant prices doubled.[62] By 1854 the REA had lent £888000 to builders, mostly to a small number of contractors in the west end of London. These built houses ahead of demand rather than to order, and thus required large amounts of capital. The REA lent from one-half to two-thirds of the value of the completed property and anticipated that fire insurances would follow.[63] The 1840s witnessed a marketing drive by fire and life offices in the capital - agencies in the metropolitan area multiplied - and the dozen or so insurers, who were involved in lending to developers, viewed their mortgage activities in part as a competitive device. Although urban property could represent a useful diversification of investment, caution had to be exercised. Falling house prices, or the failure of new houses to reach their sale price, could undermine the value of the security and the ability of the borrower to meet his payments. The REA's biggest debtor of the period was the builder George Wyatt, who went bankrupt owing £139000 to the corporation in 1846. In the volatile housing market many insurance investors trod carefully. Not even the promise of considerable insurances could persuade the Alliance to lend to developers in Brighton in 1826-7.[64]

Stronger guarantees were offered by local government bodies, such as poor law unions, parish vestries, county justices, town councils, improvement commissions, burial boards and boards of health, seeking to borrow against rates over long periods, often 20 to 30 years. The larger insurance offices were best placed to tie up some of their capital in this way, and, where the loan took the form of an annuity purchase, to find outlets for the annual income. Because small investors were less able to compete in this market, the interest charged by insurance offices tended to be higher than with other forms of loan, even though the security was better.

Furthermore, as with urban property developers, local authority borrowers might also purchase fire insurance for their public buildings.[65]

Supple has explained the rise of local authority borrowing by the impact of the new poor law of 1834, and by the entry into the capital markets of improvement commissions, burial boards, boards of health and county justices during the 1840s and 1850s. Section 24 of the Poor Law Amendment Act, for instance, allowed the commissioners, subject to the consent of a majority of local poor guardians, to borrow sums up to the average annual poor rate of the previous three years in order to build workhouses.[66] By the middle of the century over 400 of the 647 poor law unions in England and Wales had new workhouses built or under construction. These institutions were usually substantial, some four times larger than the parish workhouses which they replaced. By this date the authorised expenditure on workhouse construction and alteration under the new poor law already totalled £3.7m. The proportion of this raised by loans was probably high.[67]

By 1838 the REA had lent £202000 to several poor law unions, giving support to Supple's thesis. As noted above, however, well before the late 1830s local authorities had begun to regard insurance offices as potential creditors. Some provincial insurers responded vigorously to local demand for infrastructural capital. During the 1820s and 1830s the MFLAC lent £20000 to the commissioners of Market street, Manchester, £800 to the police commissioners of Ardwick and £9000 to Manchester Poor Law Union, all secured against local rates. Other authorities in the north-west who approached the MFLAC included the police commissioners of Ashton and Chorlton and Medlock and the poor law guardians of Stockport. Provincial insurance offices were also willing to lend to commercial firms. Most investment in this area was concentrated on the utility and transport sectors where the demand for capital was huge. Between 1810 and 1850 the combined net stock of fixed assets of gas and waterworks, railways, canals, docks, harbours, highways and bridges rose by 360 per cent in constant prices, from £58m to £267m.[68] Much of this was financed through loans and issues of debentures, bonds and promissory notes.[69] Another feature was its local and regional orientation. The MFLAC lent thousands of pounds to various turnpike roads in the north-west, and to the Manchester & Salford Water Works, the Macclesfield Canal Company, the Manchester Botanic Gardens, the Manchester-Leeds Railway and the Birmingham & Gloucester Railway.[70] It had also paid out £34500 by 1846 in a series of loans to Manchester corporation on security of the gas rates, confirming the MFLAC as the town's major creditor.

This pattern of investment can only partly be explained by the higher yields generated by mortgages.[71] It is clear that one of the objectives of the office was to help allied public and private ventures of the MFLAC directors. Thus, the loans to the Market street commissioners, the Botanic Gardens, the Gas Works, and the Macclesfield Canal Company were all made to bodies whose management shared an overlapping membership with the board of the insurance office. Insurance capital thus helped develop the infrastructure of the town and region, while at the same time bolstering the collective economic and political power of the cotton merchants who ran the insurance office.[72] Over 60 per cent of the MFLAC's mortgagors had connections with the north-west, while just 30 per cent of those refused a loan came from the north-west, making the acceptance rate for local loan applications much higher than from those from further afield. This suggests a greater capacity or willingness on the part of the insurers to evaluate local risks compared with those further afield. Given the interlocking directorships characterising the members of the insurance board, the higher local acceptances may have been a way of creating internal capital flows, so that investment risk was reduced as money was retained within the network. This sort of 'collective self-lending' suggests a system sustained, at least for a time, by the rising velocity of circulation of a comparatively fixed total. Certainly the MFLAC soon came to be regarded by businesses in the region and further afield as an institution which could provide credit as well as insurance. In addition to its mortgagors, those who applied unsuccessfully to the MFLAC between 1825 and 1838 included Liverpool merchants, textile mill owners in Blackburn, Macclesfield, Fife and Dundee, the Blackburn-Preston and Preston-Garstang turnpikes, the Rochdale canal company, gas companies at Derby, Ashton and Birmingham, the Liver steam corn mill in Liverpool, the owners of a public house in Macclesfield, and Ibstock Colliery in Leicestershire.

Other provincial insurers also invested in local enterprises. The Newcastle Fire Office purchased a water company in 1797 and established the town's first gas works in 1817. The Salop Fire Office invested in Shrewsbury's new water works in 1827 and the Liverpool Fire and Life Office bought shares in the bank of its chief promoter, George Holt, in 1836. By comparison with their country cousins, most London insurance offices were slower to invest in commercial ventures. The County bought £5300 Grand Junction canal debentures in 1813 but this was only a short-term investment. Between 1819 and 1821 the same office declined mortgages on a wharf company at Wapping, the Waterloo Bridge company and the Kilburn turnpike. The London Dock company managed to borrow £300000 from the Globe in 1826 and £100000 from the Guardian in 1829 in order to finance a new dock at Shadwell.[73] The Alliance included among its mortgagors between 1825 and 1837 two steam navigation companies, the Metropolitan Road Trust North of the Thames and the Stanhope & Tyne railway.[74] The Phoenix made small loans to two clubs and two hotels, while the REA lent to a hotel company, Liverpool Docks, St Katherine Docks, the Royal Mail Steam Packet company, the Pacific Steam company, two colliery companies and Calvert's brewery.[75] The burgeoning demand for capital from railway companies also met by insurers, although ordinary railway shares were usually deemed to be too risky, and bonds, or loans secured on tolls, real estate, or debentures were preferred. By 1842 the REA had lent £216000 to seven railways on such securities. The Sun first purchased railway bonds in 1844 and held £240000 by the mid 1850s, accounting for 30 per cent of its investments. The Phoenix was more reticent, making only one railway loan before 1863.[76] But this was unusual. More typical was the response of the Imperial, who, upon discovering in 1840 that its deed did not permit it to invest in 'rail road bonds or debentures or debentures on mineral estates', quickly obtained an act of parliament to remove the offending clause.[77]

In sum, the principal trend between the eighteenth and nineteenth centuries was towards the diversification of insurance investments, as capital was transferred from the public funds to private outlets, and from mortgages on landed estates and a limited range of government securities towards a wider range of annuity, mortgage and debenture loans, loans to local authorities and commercial enterprises, and colonial and foreign government bonds. There were, however, many different trajectories for individual offices, particularly after 1800. The investment watershed around 1840, identified by the historians of the Sun, the REA and the Phoenix, was typical of only one section of the insurance industry. Even within this leading group, there were important differences, the REA and the Sun moving more rapidly into non-landed forms of mortgage than the Phoenix.[78] Other insurers were quicker still, and in some cases investment outside landed estates and the public funds occurred during the last decades of the eighteenth century. Several provincial offices, such as the Salop, the Newcastle, the Liverpool and the MFLAC, invested early in local ventures and to a degree which would have appeared ambitious, even foolhardy, to the most venerable London offices. Among the ranks of the new metropolitan offices after 1800 there were also those who did not conform to the orthodox investment pattern, notably the Alliance and the County, who during the 1820s anticipated the general outflow of British insurance capital abroad by several decades.

Supple has pointed out that there were relatively few financial intermediaries during the nineteenth century, and that in this respect insurance companies stood alongside banks, friendly societies and building societies in providing an essential channel for savings to flow into investments. He argues that the insurance companies' 'relative size and rapid growth, the absence of great variety in the capital market, and their long-run outlook, gave them a special place in the history of savings and investment'.[79] This point is underlined by the investment activities of several provincial offices, who played an important, perhaps pivotal, role in facilitating capital flows across their town or region. It was less the total amount of funds that these offices could make available for the local infrastructure, but rather the strategic character of insurance investment which was significant. Moreover, the loan applications flooding into offices such as the MFLAC, the Alliance or the County from the 1820s clearly indicate that by this date there was an expectation among businessmen and the managers of public institutions that an insurance company was an important port of call for those in need of development capital.

Investment income, profits, dividends and shares

How important was their investment activity to the fire insurance companies of the industrial revolution? The short answer is, far less important than it has become since the end of the nineteenth century. It is common in the modern insurance industry for underwriting to be done at a loss and for insurers to rely upon interest earnings to cover the loss and deliver a profit. In the largest companies, huge reserves, accumulated from decades of investment income, often match or exceed the income from underwriting. For example, the reserve funds of 16 major UK general insurers in 1960 ranged from 64 per cent to 129 per cent of their premium incomes.[80] Modern reserves are normally divided into a fund from which shareholders' dividends were paid, a 'technical' reserve to accommodate unexpired risks and outstanding claims, and a contingency reserve to cover for the event of exceptional losses or a sudden collapse in premium income. Shareholders' and other funds are regarded as the last line of defence, to be drawn upon to meet exceptionally heavy underwriting losses. Since the beginning of the twentieth century insurance companies have largely paid their dividends out of interest earnings, with underwriting surpluses being put directly into contingency and 'general' reserves for the security of policyholders.[81]

Before the end of the nineteenth century the situation was different. Many companies recognised the need to separate capital from income and sometimes this resulted in the creation of separate funds. Thus, the Phoenix, after heavy losses, established a proprietors' fund in 1800 from which dividends were to be paid, and, two years later, a guarantee fund, which formed a contingency reserve for policyholders. The Imperial too operated separate premium and capital accounts with losses paid out of the former and dividends from the latter.[82] The separation of accounts also enabled several offices to operate clauses restricting or postponing the payment of dividends to shareholders from the capital fund before it had grown to a specified level. For example, the North British resolved to pay no dividends for six years after its foundation in 1809, for, as its first board of directors put it, the 'security of the public rested on the extent of the capital...framed on a principle of gradual increase'.[83]

Thus a variety of measures to guard shareholders' capital from encroachment were taken by early insurance offices. Their fund management techniques, however, did not provide a similar level of protection for policyholders. Capital and income accounts, premium and investment funds, may have been separated by some insurers, but they were seldom ring-fenced, still less hermetically sealed. While in some cases interest earned on invested capital was not expected to help cover losses on underwriting, the reverse was never true. Across the industry dividend payments were regularly met from underwriting profits, which, as Dickson observed, was 'a violation of a fundamental principle of modern British insurance practice'.[84] Insurers commonly placed some or all of their annual premiums into an account from which dividends were paid. During the later 1820s there were attempts by several offices to create additional contingency funds.[85] The Guardian set aside a tiny reserve of £3500 in 1829 for 'disputed and unsettled claims', and in the same year, the County drafted a 'mode of calculating [a] reserve for outstanding risks'. Other offices drifted more slowly in this direction. Not until 1883 did the Sun create a separate reserve fund dedicated to dividend payments, and not until

1889 did it establish a technical reserve of 40 per cent of premiums (which became the industry standard) to cover unexpired risks.[86]

A modern insurance company, according to Clayton and Osborne, 'is apt to be judged by its dividend record and by the margin between investment income and the cost of dividend payments'.[87] Insurance commentators in the 1890s already regarded companies as 'carefully financed' when they restricted dividends to interest receipts. By this date large offices were expecting their interest earnings to cover most or all of their normal dividend payments and even to offset net underwriting losses.[88] This was not the case before 1850 when the margin between investment income and dividend expenditure was often negative. From the 1790s the Sun's investment income was never large enough to cover all of its annual dividends. In the 11 years when bonuses were paid to shareholders, less than half of the total cost of the dividends was covered by interest earnings.[89] At the Essex & Suffolk office investment income accounted for less than one-third of the dividends paid between 1813 and 1850. By contrast, some companies did aim to pay dividends entirely out of interest earnings. The income from the MFLAC's proprietors' fund proved sufficient to cover the cost of payments to shareholders in normal years, helped by the fact that the office was bound by its deed to pay no more than five per cent in ordinary dividends. It was only in the years of large bonuses to 'with-profits' policyholders that investment income fell short of the sums required to pay both shareholders and policyholders. The Imperial also kept careful control over the finance of its dividends. The £5 per share it paid in 1823, for example, was calculated from a very conservative estimate of the annual amount produced by its stock of £400000 consols yielding three per cent.[90] At many other offices, however, the practice was to lump interest income and underwriting profits together, to set the dividend after expenses and outstanding claims had been allowed for, and to take little or no account of unexpired risks.

The importance of investment income may also be gauged by its ratio to premium receipts and by its contribution to total profits. Average earnings from investments equalled 15 to 20 per cent of the premium income of the Kent Fire Office between 1802 and 1813 and of the Bristol Union and the Salamander during the 1830s. Interest earnings accounted for six per cent of the total receipts flowing into the fire insurance account of the Leeds & Yorkshire between 1843 and 1845, and covered just 14 per cent of the claims paid. The Guardian's investment income during the period 1822-8 was enough to cover 12 per cent of the company's operating costs and ten per cent of the claims paid.[91] For the Phoenix investment income equated to one-quarter of premiums in the 1820s when the high rates on annuity loans temporarily boosted interest earnings. The same ratio at the Sun and the MFLAC was never greater than one-third, at the Imperial it never exceeded seven per cent and at the Essex & Suffolk it never rose above 13 per cent. As the Phoenix and the Sun expanded rapidly through company acquisitions during the second quarter of the century, and as yields on government stock and mortgages remained low, the volume of their premium receipts increased far more rapidly than earnings on investments. Furthermore, the largest offices occasionally made huge bonus payments to their shareholders, which were financed by the sale of assets and which reduced the level of future investment earnings. The 'return of capital' made to the Sun's shareholders in 1825 amounted to £40 per share. This was financed by selling government stock, which reduced its assets by 27 per cent but still left the office with over half a million pounds worth of investments.[92] These figures suggest that investment income was generally less important than underwriting income for most fire offices before 1850. Underwriting surpluses, however, could fluctuate wildly. Thus, when viewed as a proportion of profits, investment earnings varied substantially between offices and within individual offices over time. In good periods when claims were low and growth was rapid, well-managed offices, both large and small, derived the bulk of their profits from underwriting. Investment income amounted to 16 per cent of the Guardian's total profits between 1822 and 1828, and never more than one-third of the profits of the Essex & Suffolk, while at the Sun, the Phoenix and the MFLAC the ratio fluctuated between one-quarter and two-thirds, a range which was probably typical for general insurers as a whole during the nineteenth and early twentieth centuries.[93] Yet there were always outliers. The available figures for the County suggest that severe capital depreciation - not least due to the unwise purchase of South American stock - meant that investments actually reduced profits between 1816 and 1829. The company remained buoyant principally because of its healthy underwriting margins. By contrast, for other companies investments became critical in delivering a profit when heavy losses were incurred in underwriting. The Imperial had a torrid time during the 1820s when interest income just managed to compensate for insurance losses and leave a small profit. When underwriting returned to profitability in the 1830s and 1840s, investments became far less important to the Imperial's profit and loss account.

Table 9.2 estimates average gross profits and returns on capital for three metropolitan and three country fire offices. Discussions of profitability in existing company histories have focused largely on underwriting performance. By contrast, gross profits in table 9.2 are given as the aggregate of average underwriting surpluses (premiums less expenses and claims paid) plus interest earnings on investments, prior to the payment of taxes and dividends.[94] These aggregates were then expressed as percentages of the book value of assets or the stated value of nominal net capital to give annual profit rates.[95] In the absence of a more extensive trawl of the surviving ledgers than is possible here, this table can provide only a few suggestive indicators. First, it seems that there was no relationship between company size and profitability. One of the smaller country offices, the Essex & Suffolk, consistently enjoyed the highest return on capital, several times higher than the profit rates of larger offices such as the MFLAC, the Imperial and the Sun, while another small provincial office, the Salop, returned only a modest four per cent in the 1830s. Second, certain trends are visible in table 9.2 which are also supported by other data. Dickson suggested that the Sun's annual rate of profit declined towards the end of the eighteenth century and that the business 'stagnated'.[96] The spot readings for the Sun in table 9.2 show that the return on

Table 9.2 Gross profits and returns on capital

PR = profit rates/returns on capital (total profits as % of book assets)
GP = average gross (pre-tax, pre-dividend) profits, £

	Mirowski 17 firms	London Assurance	Sun*		Imperial*		Essex & Suffolk*		MFLAC*		Salop*	
	PR	PR	GP	PR	GP	PR	GP	PR	GP	PR	GP	PR
1721-30	1.5	1.2										
1731-40	8.3	4.7										
1741-6	8.1	4.3										
1758-60	11.2	6.3										
1761-70	12.0	3.7										
1771-80	12.3	4.0										
1781-90	15.2	4.2										
1791-1800	19.0	5.9	39602	13.6								
1801-10	17.9	5.0	49954	7.0	8955	6.4	995	28.4				
1811-21	20.0	7.9	49087	6.6	6576	3.7	2529	20.6				
1821-30		9.6	22539	-3.8	1384	0.5	4698	16.7	16871	7.0		
1831-40			51053	5.8	8598	2.9	4367	12.6	26930	7.8	2346	
1841-50			66333		27350	6.6	3698	9.3	30427	6.7		4.1

Notes: *sub-periods as above, except: Mirowski's firm sample, mean profit, 1728-30, 1821-6; Sun, PR for the years 1798, 1805-8, 1816, 1830, 1835 only; Imperial, GP and PR, 1803-10; Essex & Suffolk, PR, averages of 1805, 1807-10, and 1841-4, GP, 1802-10, 1841-4; MFLAC, GP and PR, 1824-30, 1841-3; Salop, GP and PR, average of 1831-6, 1839-40.

Sources: Mirowski, *Birth of the Business Cycle*, table VIII, pp. 209-10, and pp.231-56 (for the London Assurance's profit rates); Trebilcock, *Phoenix Assurance*, vol.I, table 13.7, pp.728-9 (for Sun's asset values). Other sources as in tables 9.1 and 9.3.

capital fell by half between 1798 and 1805-8, and that it remained below seven per cent in 1816 and 1835. Annual average profit rates for the Imperial and the Essex & Suffolk also fell during the early nineteenth century, while the County's average gross profits declined from £13600 in 1816-20 to £8500 in 1821-9. Mirowksi's estimates of the London Assurance's profit rates are the only ones to rise during this period, but these represent rates of return on that corporation's total business, of which the fire insurance branch formed only a small part. During the 1830s there was an improvement in profit margins across the fire insurance industry. Average profit rates for the MFLAC, the Sun and the Imperial rose by comparison with the previous decade, as did the County's net profits.[97] Only the profit rates experienced by the Essex & Suffolk continued to decline (from a very high base). The following decade witnessed a greater divergence of results. Gross profit rates at the MFLAC and the Essex & Suffolk fell, while the Imperial and the County enjoyed an improvement in returns on capital.

Overall, these estimates of profit rates, together with the data on underwriting performance presented in figure 1.5, suggest that the largest variable influencing insurance rates of return during the first half of the nineteenth century was investment income. As figure 1.5 shows, after average premium rates began to fall from their peak in the early 1800s, they followed the long drift of average loss rates downwards, but the gap between the two series remained fairly constant down to 1850. From one perspective this indicates that there were no major efficiency gains in fire underwriting during this period. It also suggests that, given the long-run stability of underwriting margins, any major shifts in profitability were largely due to changes in investment yields. After 1815 there were some one-off capital gains to be realised for insurers selling government securities which they had purchased at low prices in wartime. These may have kept the profit rates of some offices buoyant for several years after the war. However, as yields on the public funds fell during the 1820s, as offices suffered from defaults on mortgages and annuity loans, and as several were caught out by the depreciation of stocks during the crisis of 1825-6, gross profit rates were squeezed for many. During the 1830s and 1840s the increasing diversification of insurance investment helped reduce the risk of capital losses and raise the average yield on investments, especially for those offices - the majority - which had not engaged heavily in annuity lending. The average annual interest realised on the Alliance's capital, for example, rose from 3.86 per cent to 4.23 per cent between 1827-30 and 1837-9, a ten per cent increase during a period when consol yields fell by seven per cent. This contrasts with the average interest earned on its investments by the Phoenix, a major annuity lender, which fell from eight per cent in the 1820s to four per cent during the 1840s.[98]

Table 9.2 also suggests that 'supernormal' or 'economic' profits - were generally low throughout the period. 'Economic' profit is defined as the actual profit rate minus the opportunity cost of not investing in the best alternative investment, which in this case may be taken as the average yield on consols.[99] Clearly some offices made handsome 'economic' profits, notably the Essex & Suffolk, which realised 24 per cent during its first decade of business. For most insurers, however, 'economic profits' were modest, generally in the range of one to four per cent. Table 9.2 also permits some comparison to be made with profitability in other sectors of the British economy. Insurance profits do not appear impressive when placed alongside Mirowski's mean profit indices for his sample of 17 industrial, commercial and financial firms. Profit rates in the textile industries tended to be higher than those in insurance. The average gross returns on capital (profits plus interest less depreciation of assets) ranged between six and ten per cent in the cotton industry during the 1820s, but they had been much higher in earlier decades and continued to be impressive for some of the largest firms. McConnell & Kennedy enjoyed an average return of 19 per cent between 1798 and 1809, while the Gregs received 20 per cent between 1806 and 1815 and 13 per cent between 1820 and 1831. Marshalls, the flax spinners of Leeds and Shrewsbury, averaged 26 per cent in 1825-30, 28 per cent in the 1830s, and 14 per cent in the 1840s, while Fosters, the Bradford worsted spinners, returned 25 per cent during the 1840s.[100] Elsewhere, returns tended to be lower, although they compared with or exceeded the insurance profit rates reported in table 9.2. The Bridgewater canal returned 16 per cent in the early 1820s; commercial property companies in Manchester and Leeds during the 1820s and 1830s returned between five and 15 per cent; and the largest private and joint-stock banks generated profits of between four and nine per cent.[101] There is little in these figures to undermine the assertion made elsewhere, that profit expectations 'were unlikely to have figured heavily' in the decision of businessmen in other sectors of the economy to diversify into insurance during the 1820s, or indeed at any time between 1720 and 1850.[102]

What counted for the less active insurance investor were dividends and the value of his or her shares. Profits, expressed as a return on current capital, could be very different from annual dividend payments expressed as a percentage of the face value of a share. In the nature of the largely unregulated insurance industry, the former were for internal company scrutiny only, with the details often confined to board members. Dividends, on the other hand, were for public consumption, even where insurance shares - the great majority - were not quoted on the official stock exchange. The generosity shown by an office to its shareholders was one of the more visible aspects of its activities and was related to public perceptions of its strength and competitiveness, particularly after 1800, when the number of joint-stock insurance offices increased and when the population of shareholders multiplied to many thousands.

Table 9.3 presents the average annual dividends paid to their shareholders by 15 insurance offices. The dividends are expressed as percentages of the nominal, face or 'par' value of each share, which reflects the original paid-up capital of each company. Trebilcock has rightly noted that this measurement becomes problematic for companies with the greatest longevity, when time could render a 'par' value meaningless.[103] The case of the Sun illustrates this point vividly. The 4800 shares held by the Sun's proprietors from 1728 'were treated as £10 paid', and consequently the 'subscription stock', or paid-up capital, was recorded in the

Table 9.3 Average dividends paid by 15 insurance offices, 1721-1850

(average % p.a. paid on face value of shares)

	Sun	REA	London	Phoenix	Salop	NGA
1721-30	5.7	5.0				
1731-40	9.3	>4.0				
1741-50	10.8					
1751-60		3.3				
1761-70	19.0	3.3	5.0			
1771-80	24.6	4.0	5.6			
1781-90	30.2		6.3	4.1	0.0	7.0
1791-1800	31.8	6.3	7.6	4.6	58.6	7.4
1801-10	42.8	18.0		5.1	88.3	9.8
1811-20	49.9	15.0		21.3	114.0	
1821-30	40.4	29.2		25.3		
1831-40	44.2	8.3		16.6		
1841-50	52.3	8.3		16.5		

	Imperial	County	Globe	Albion	Atlas
1801-10	2.9	0.0			
1811-20	7.2	15.5	6.0	8.8	5.4
1821-30	10.1	25.0	6.8	5.0	4.8
1831-40	11.0	25.0	6.8		9.5
1841-50	21.8		6.0		12.0

	Newcastle	Eagle	NU	MFLAC
1801-10				
1811-20	73.2			
1821-30	45.0	5.0	7.0	3.3
1831-40			8.5	6.9
1841-50			8.1	5.0

Notes: sub-periods as above except: Sun, averages of 1721-2, 1724-5, 1728-9, 1740-42, 1767-70; REA, 1726-8, 1791 and 1798, 1806-10; London, 1762-70, 1791-8; Phoenix, 1786, 1788-90, 1791-3, 1795-1800; Salop, 1811-15; Imperial, 1803-10, 1841-4, 1848-50; County, 1807-10, 1831-4; Albion, 1817-20, 1821-7; Atlas, 1816-20; Newcastle, 1816-17, 1819-20, 1821-2; Eagle, 1821-6; NU, 1823-30; MFLAC, 1825-30, 1841-3. Sun's average for 1821-30 excludes the 'return of capital' @ £40 per share made in 1825. The REA's figures for 1751-70 are the midpoints of the range given by Supple. The REA's figure for 1791-1800 represents the mean of the lowest and highest values given by Supple for that decade. The Imperial's average for 1841-50 excludes the years 1845-7 for which we have no data on bonuses paid. Abbreviations: NGA = Norwich General Assurance, NU = Norwich Union.

Sources: GL Ms 11931/2-8, Sun, GCM, 1721-1800 *passim*; Ms 11933A, Sun, Annual Accounts, 1791-1887; Supple, *Royal Exchange*, pp.72, 399; Gayer, Rostow and Schwarz, *Growth and Fluctuation of the British Economy*, I, table 36, pp.454-5; GL Ms 8728/7-15, London Assurance, DM, 1762-1800 *passim*; CUL, PAA, Phoenix, Dividend Receipt Books, 1783-1850; Trebilcock, *Phoenix Assurance*, vol.I, table 5.10, p.240; Ryan, 'History of Norwich Union', table 35, pp.1018-19; SRO, Ms 3008/1/2/10, Salop, Income and Capital Account Book, 1780-1822; Walford, *Insurance Cyclopedia*, vol.III, p.423 (for the Globe); GL Ms 18274, Imperial, Tabular Statements; County, GCM, 1807-34 *passim*; Raynes, *History of British Insurance*, p.231 (for the Albion); GL Ms 16170, Atlas, DM, 1816-20 *passim*; GPL, CM/4/1-21, Newcastle, Accounts, 1809-22; GL Ms 16223/1, MFLAC, GCM, 1825-46 *passim*.

ledgers as £48000. Thereafter, the number of shares remained unchanged until 1891. In 1741 and 1752, however, a total of £50000 was added to the 'subscription stock' from reserves, increasing the 'par' value of each share to £21. This value then remained unchanged for the next 140 years. It was used by the Stamp Commissioners in 1806 to calculate the 'value' of the office, and it has been used in table 9.3 to calculate its dividends from 1767. With the growth in the Sun's assets this 'par' value was left far behind by the market value of the Sun's shares which reached £200 by 1778. Moreover, by a series of 'repayments' the whole of the original capital of £48000 had been returned to the shareholders by 1756, making the subsequent relationship between dividends and the 'par' value of shares even more artificial.[104] This disjunction between dividends and the original 'par value' of shares is less evident in the new company foundations from the late eighteenth century. With these offices, operating in an increasingly crowded and active investment market, it becomes more meaningful to express the former as a percentage of the latter in the usual manner, permitting a comparison with returns to investors in other contemporary industries.[105]

Table 9.3 shows a rising trend in dividends which peaked during the Napoleonic wars. The unweighted annual average for all offices rose from five per cent in the 1720s to 32 per cent during the first decade of the nineteenth century. Average dividends then fell back to 14 per cent by the 1830s, before recovering to 18 per cent in the following decade. Figure 9.1, a scatter graph of all annual dividend payments recorded for 16 offices, indicates the wide dispersion of dividends around these means, so that to be able to speak of an industry 'average' is itself questionable. The shareholders of the small offices in Shrewsbury and Newcastle, both founded in the 1780s, enjoyed huge annual returns on their original subscriptions, as did the proprietors of the Sun. By contrast, younger offices with large proprietorships, such as the Norwich Union, the Atlas and the MFLAC, struggled to raise their dividends into double figures, and those offices, such as the Albion and the Eagle, who eventually abandoned fire insurance during the 1820s, continued to offer only modest dividends while they still underwrote property against fire. Different companies also experienced different trajectories in their returns to shareholders. The Sun, the Atlas and the Imperial were, on average,

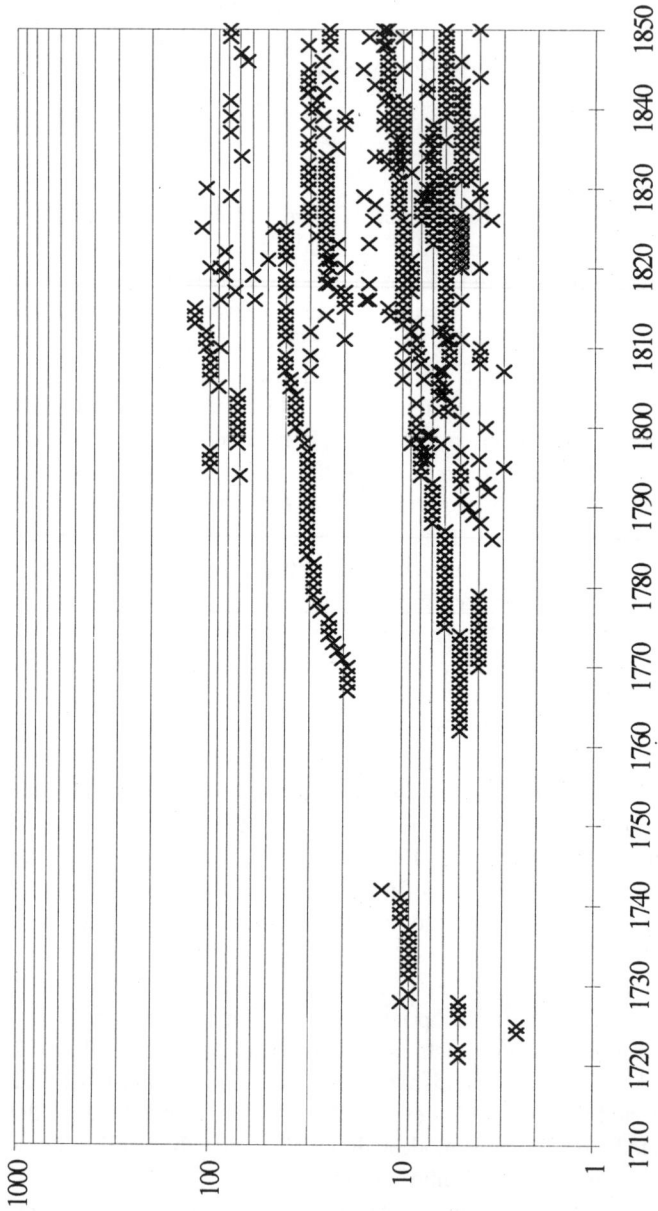

% paid on par value of shares, log scale.

Figure 9.1 Annual dividends: 16 insurance offices, 1721-1850
Sources: see table 9.3.

at their most generous in the 1840s, while the Norwich Union and the MFLAC paid most in the 1830s, and the average dividends paid by the Phoenix and the REA peaked in the 1820s.

We may also ask how generous were insurance companies to their shareholders by comparison with other types of joint stock enterprise? Here, in contrast to profit rates, the comparison is generally favourable to the insurance industry. Some smaller canals of the late eighteenth century, such as Birmingham and Loughborough, paid between 11 and 28 per cent, but longer lines paid less. By 1825 the average dividend on canal shares amounted to six per cent on £13.2m capital, while £3.7m of canal capital paid nothing.[106] Returns on some early railway companies could be impressive. A Scottish investor in 1835 anticipated that railways would pay between seven and 13 per cent. In general, however, only the most successful railways paid over seven per cent, and the average dividend paid by 14 major firms in the 1840s was six per cent, or just one-third of the average insurance dividend in table 9.3.[107] Some of the early dock companies matched the dividends paid by insurers. The Hull Dock Company, 'a resounding success', returned an average of 22 per cent in the period 1780-1800 and 40 per cent in the first years of the nineteenth century. The West India Dock Company paid ten per cent between 1803 and 1829, the maximum permitted by its charter, and eight per cent thereafter.[108] Many banks, water and gas companies, however, returned relatively modest amounts to their shareholders. The average dividend paid by six major joint stock banks in the period 1827-50 fluctuated between four and eight per cent. Average dividends paid by four London water companies rose from two per cent to seven per cent between 1811-20 and 1841-50. 22 gas companies in London and the north-west paid between four and six per cent in the 1820s when insurance offices were paying an average of 17 per cent. Even the most successful property companies usually returned less to their subscribers than the insurance offices. Sheffield's Theatre and Assembly Rooms paid around six per cent in most years between 1795 and 1830, while dividends on Leeds South Market in 1835 and Leeds Central Market in 1829 were just three per cent.[109]

This survey reinforces the picture of an insurance industry relatively generous to its shareholders, profiting from strong volume growth, and commonly dipping into streams of premium income to boost dividend and bonus payments to shareholders. With such generosity, it is little surprise that insurance shares were sought after except in the most difficult financial crises. With small numbers of proprietors and a relatively slow turnover of shares, an excess of demand over supply appears the best explanation for the share price rises enjoyed by most eighteenth-century offices. Over the 70 years between the post-Bubble prices of 1721-4 and the peak of 1792, the market value of shares in the London Assurance rose by 167 per cent, and the REA by 213 per cent. The REA's share price rose by a further 80 per cent before the end of the Napoleonic wars. Thereafter, it declined to the early 1840s, then recovered strongly in the following decade.[110] The shares of both corporations were worth having, whether for the short- to medium-term gains which took place at intervals, or to keep in the family over several generations. The corporations were the only insurance shares traded in Change Alley and recorded in the various stock exchange price lists published before 1810. Trading in their shares became thin by the 1780s and both corporations were eventually dropped from Wetenhall's *Course of the Exchange* in 1802-3. From 1810 insurance shares began to be listed again in increasing numbers. By the end of the decade 19 companies were listed by Wetenhall and prices quoted for ten of these.[111] These shares, on aggregate, rose more modestly than had the shares of the two corporations during the eighteenth century. The share prices of eight of these companies were indexed by Gayer, Rostow and Schwarz (GRS) on the base year 1811. This index rose by 47 per cent between 1813 and 1824, fell back by 28 per cent by 1832, then gradually recovered by mid-century to the level attained in 1824.[112]

The majority of insurance offices, however, seldom or never appeared in the published stock lists for most of this period. Evidence suggests that insurance share transactions outside the Exchange were livelier and that prices were often more dynamic and volatile than the movements suggested by the GRS index. For example, while the coefficients of variation of the share prices of the London Assurance and the REA during the eighteenth century were 0.25 and 0.14 respectively, and that of the GRS index only 0.13, the coefficient for the Phoenix share price was 0.55. Those investors who bought the Phoenix shares low and sold high made handsome gains, doubling their money between 1788 and 1800, increasing it 12-fold between 1807 (the disaster at St Thomas, West Indies) and 1818, or quadrupling it between 1826 and 1841, just before the huge fire at Hamburg sent the Phoenix share price tumbling again.[113] Other offices also experienced substantial increases, and sometimes great fluctuations, in the price of their shares in the private market. The value of shares in the Salop Fire Office rose 28-fold between 1780 and 1820, reflecting Salop's small number of proprietors (30), the restricted access to the shares, the consistently healthy underwriting record, and the growth of capital from £1500 to £40000 during this period. The capital growth of other provincial offices may have also multiplied the value of their shares by similar factors. By 1809, for instance, the 'profits' of the Newcastle Fire Office had added £35000 to its original starting capital of £2100. This probably raised the value of the 21 original £100 shares of 1783 to £1770, a rise over 25 years nearly as impressive as that of the Salop office.

During the first quarter of the nineteenth century insurance shares were lucrative investments for those who could get hold of them. Among the promoters of new offices there was a general expectation that new shares would sell easily, and that, provided the early underwriting performance was satisfactory and funds accumulated, share values would rise quickly. In 1805, after only two years of full trading, the founders of the Suffolk & General County Fire Office remarked upon the growth in its insurances to £1.6m and agreed to pay a dividend of 5.5 per cent. One director, James Oakes, recorded in his diary that 'it was thought probably that [the] shares might now bear a premium'.[114] The Imperial declared in 1818 that its share price had increased by 'nearly 100%', as evidence of the company's prosperity. The Imperial had issued 2400 shares at £50 paid up in 1803. By 1818 the company's capital stood at £233387, implying a share price of £97 which was probably the basis of the board's valuation.[115] The par value of shares in the County Fire Office was £10 when they were issued in the summer of 1808, but within weeks they were already selling at a four per cent premium. In the following year the board fixed £15 as the buying price and £20 as the selling price. In 1821 Barber Beaumont reported that the shares 'sell now at about £40 each'. They rose to £45 by 1837.[116] North of the border shares in the North British and the Hercules offices doubled between 1809 and 1824, and rising insurance share prices and falling yields on existing stock attracted many Scottish investors in the boom of 1824-5. The shares of ten insurance companies were among 50 stock companies traded in Edinburgh by 1825.[117]

Share prices in some fire offices also fell at times of tight credit or following heavy underwriting losses and the depletion of a company's funds, and new issues were not always immediately successful. The level of dividends paid, relative to alternative investments, might also affect an insurance company's share price. The ceiling of four per cent on the dividends which could be paid by the Leeds & Yorkshire may have contributed to the fall in the company's share price after the early upswing of 1824-5. According to an officer of the Sun writing in 1854, the 'mistake' of the small Shropshire & North Wales Fire Office, founded in 1837, had been 'in calling up £12 when £4 would have answered all purposes, and the bulk of their money is in the funds producing only £3% and this beats down their dividends'. As a result, there were 'a good many shares now for sale at £10, and the price last year was £11.10s'.[118]

In general, however, shares in fire insurance offices proved good investments, both for the handsome dividends paid and for the capital gains to be realised over time. This bred public confidence in the industry, which in turn ensured rapid growth after 1815 and buoyant demand for the products of new offices entering the market. It is notable that during the whole period 1720 to 1850, despite the violence of the underwriting cycle and the dramatic changes in the nature of some of the risks insured, fire insurance generally suffered from none of the associations with gambling and speculation which stuck to life assurance for most of the eighteenth century, nor the bankruptcies and public scandals which dogged that branch of underwriting in the early Victorian period. For the most part, investors, borrowers and policyholders regarded fire insurance as a sound, reliable and profitable financial service, a solid contribution to the wealth of the nation.

Notes

[1] Dickens, *Martin Chuzzlewit*, p.324.

[2] John, 'Insurance Investment'; Gayer, Rostow and Schwarz, *Growth and Fluctuation of the British Economy*; Mirowski, 'Rise (and Retreat) of a Market'; *idem., Birth of the Business Cycle*.

[3] Figures for the nominal unredeemed capital of the funded and unfunded debt from Mitchell and Deane, *Abstract of British Historical Statistics*, pp.401-3.

[4] Brewer, *Sinews of Power*; O'Brien, 'Central Government and the Economy'; *idem.*, 'Political Economy of British Taxation'; Dickson, *Financial Revolution*, pp.284-6; Cope, 'Stock Exchange Revisited', p.19; Morgan and Thomas, *Stock Exchange*, pp.66-7.

[5] Roseveare, *Financial Revolution*, p.69; Supple, *Royal Exchange*, p.75; Michie, 'City of London', p.22. My thanks to Michael Turner for the latter reference.

[6] Companies are, of course, normally valued by the current market price of their shares, but this calculation is simply not possible for a period in which most insurance company shares were traded privately, and from which few recorded share values have survived.

[7] Dickson, *Financial Revolution*, p.287, table 40; Carter, 'Analysis of Public Indebtedness'.

[8] GRE archive, REA, Balance sheets, Oct. 1734, Apr. 1760; Supple, *Royal Exchange*, p.75; GL Ms 15042/1, Sun, Quarterly Accounts and Balance Sheets, 1786-1812; Trebilcock, *Phoenix Assurance*, vol.I, p.620.

[9] John, 'Insurance Investment', p.144.

[10] Consol prices fell from high of $70^5/_8$ in 1796 to a low of $47^1/_2$ in 1797. Homer, *History of Interest Rates*, p.162, table 13.

[11] GL Ms 8666/12-13, Hand-in-Hand, DM, 1731-6 *passim*; Ms 11931/7, Sun, GCM, 4 Jan. 1787.

[12] John, 'Insurance Investment', pp.144-5.

[13] This was still true in the 1960s, when one textbook recommended that 26 per cent of the total investments of a general insurer should be held in a highly liquid form, i.e. due to mature within a year. It was also the case, however, that a contemporary study found the practice of insurance investment did not emphasise liquidity as much as theory would expect. Clayton and Osborne, *Insurance Company Investment*, pp.42-3, 83-6.

[14] Dickson, *Sun Insurance*, p.237; GL Ms 14022/11, Union, DM, 21 Mar. 1759.

[15] Dickson, *Sun Insurance*, pp.241-2; GL Ms 11931/6, Sun, GCM, 8 Jan. 1767, 2 July 1772, 2 Apr. 1778.

[16] John, 'Insurance Investment', p.148.

[17] John, 'Insurance Investment', pp.150-51; Dickson, *Sun Insurance*, p.243. The decennial average yield on consols rose from 3.13 in the 1750s to 4.64 in the 1780s, Homer, *History of Interest Rates*, pp.161-2, table 13.

[18] John, 'Insurance Investment', p.157; Dickson, *Sun Insurance*, p.245.

[19] GL Ms 11931/4, Sun, GCM, 8 July 1732; Dickson, *Sun Insurance*, p.244.

[20] Anderson, 'The Attorney and the Early Capital Market', pp.52-3; Allen, 'The Price of Freehold Land', p.49; Holderness, 'Credit in a Rural Community', p.112.

21   John, 'Insurance Investment', p.156; Clark, 'Commons Sense'; Holderness, 'Credit in a Rural Community', p.103; French and Hoyle, 'The Land Market of a Pennine Manor'; Dickson, *Sun Insurance*, p.246.

22   Allen, 'The Price of Freehold Land'; Clark, 'Land Hunger'; Offer, 'Farm Tenure and Land Values'; Homer, *History of Interest Rates*, p.163; SC on the Usury Laws, *PP* (1818) VI, evidence of E. Wakefield, 197; SC into...the Laws regulating the Interest on Money, *PP* (1845) XII, evidence of J.W. Freshfield, 382.

23   The various estimates cited by Mathias suggest there were around 5-6000 lawyers in England and Wales by 1760 (disregarding Joseph Massie's outlier of 12000). Mathias, 'The Lawyer as Businessman', p.157. On local mortgage markets and the role of provincial attorneys, see Anderson, 'The Attorney and the Early Capital Market'; Holderness, 'Credit in a Rural Community', pp.109-12; Miles, 'The Money Market'. For recent contributions to the literature on aristocratic debt, see Cannadine, 'Aristocratic Indebtedness'; Spring, 'Debt and the English Aristocracy'. Even the Springs, sceptical of the notion of the improvident landowner, do not contest the point that debt grew with strict settlement and entailed estates.

24   GL Ms 15042/1, Sun, Quarterly accounts, 1786-1812. For examples of Sun's aristocratic mortgagors, see Dickson, *Sun Insurance*, pp.249-50.

25   Dickson, *Sun Insurance*, pp.251 n1, 257-8; Homer, *History of Interest Rates*, p.161.

26   For example, £20000 was lent by the Sun at four and a half per cent to Patrick Heron on his Lincolnshire estate, valued at over £1700 per annum at five per cent in 1790. The rental, if invested at five per cent, would have taken less than nine years to produce £20000. GL Ms 11931/7, Sun, GCM, 29 July 1790.

27   Dickson, *Sun Insurance*, pp.251-2.

28   GL Ms 11931/7, Sun, GCM, 5 Jan. 1786, 8 Jan. 1789; Ms 11932/5, Sun, CMM, 25 Apr. 1754; Dickson, *Sun Insurance*, pp.254-6.

29   John, 'Insurance Investment', p.147.

30   Calculated from Homer, *History of Interest Rates*, p.163.

31   The secretary of the Albion Fire and Life Office, for instance, told a parliamentary committee that during the war the term mortgage 'had almost become obsolete'. SC on the Usury Laws, *PP* (1818) VI, evidence of W. Phipps, 159.

32   Clay, 'The Price of Freehold Land', pp.186-9; Allen, 'The Price of Freehold Land', p.48.

33   There had been 246 enclosure acts during the 1780s, but some 1.5m acres were enclosed under 921 acts between 1793 and 1804, Mathias, 'Agriculture and Industrialization', p.106.

34   Turner, Beckett and Afton, *Agricultural Rent*, fig.10.5, p.221. I am grateful to Michael Turner for interesting discussions of these points. It should be noted that Offer has performed a similar, though not identical, calculation with different results. Offer's estimates for this period are derived from the rental series of Norton, Trist and Gilbert, which provides a narrower set of values than the new rental index of Turner, Beckett and Afton. Offer, 'Farm Tenure and Land Values', fig.3, p.16.

35   Supple, *Royal Exchange*, pp.312-13; GL Ms 16170/1-2, Atlas, DM, 24 Aug., 28 Sept., 23 Nov. 1809, 30 Sept., 16 Dec. 1813.

36   Buchanan, 'Aspects of Capital Formation', p.82; GPL, CM/4/7, Newcastle Fire, Circular to Proprietors, 16 July 1813.

[37] SRO, Ms 3008/1/2/1, Salop, DM, 11 Feb., 20 Apr. 1792; Ms 3008/1/2/10, Salop, Income and Capital Account Book, 1780-1822.

[38] GPL, CM/4/1-21, Newcastle Fire, Accounts 1809-22; Supple, *Royal Exchange*, p.134n. It is not clear from the Newcastle office's accounts whether the 'money taken upon annuities' referred to purchases of private annuities, or government life annuities on the Sinking Fund, first sold in October 1808. A later reference to these suggests the latter. When the Sun sought to buy the Newcastle Fire in 1836, Charles Ford told John Richards that the Sun could only offer to pay the price for these annuities that would be paid if the Sun had bought them from the Government life office in Old Jewry, 'and that the Newcastle office might do equally well itself'. The inference was that the Newcastle office might as well sell the annuities back to the government rather than sell them to the Sun. Ford added that the Sun would rather avoid taking these altogether, 'and confine itself to the fire business only'. GL Ms 15032/8, Sun, Take over Papers, Newcastle Fire, Ford to Richards, 24 Oct. 1836. For deails of the government scheme, see 'Report of John Finlaison', *PP* (1829) III, 293.

[39] 'The amount lent for industrial purposes in the eighteenth century was negligible', John, 'Insurance Investment', p.157.

[40] Homer, *History of Interest Rates*, table 19, pp.195-9; Supple, *Royal Exchange*, p.313.

[41] Trebilcock, *Phoenix Assurance*, vol.I, p.616.

[42] Supple, *Royal Exchange*, p.312, table 13.1, p.315; Trebilcock, *Phoenix Assurance*, vol.I, table 11.6, p.653, p.732.

[43] Dickson, *Sun Insurance*, p.262; Supple, *Royal Exchange*, pp.314-15.

[44] Supple, *Royal Exchange*, p.313 n2; GL Ms12160A/10, Imperial, DM, 14 May 1828; Ms 12162A/1-2, Alliance, DM, 1828-30 *passim*; Trebilcock, *Phoenix Assurance*, vol.I, pp.659-61.

[45] Dickson, *Sun Insurance*, p.243; SC into the Laws regulating the Interest on Money, *PP* (1845) XII, evidence of G.C. Glyn, 352-3.

[46] GL Ms 12162A/2, Alliance, DM, 22 Feb., 23 May 1832.

[47] GL Ms 12162A/1, Alliance, DM, 28 Jan. 1829.

[48] For a discussion of the annuity loan, see Trebilcock, *Phoenix Assurance*, vol.I, pp.630-43.

[49] Campbell, 'Usury and Annuities', pp.474-5, 485.

[50] 53 Geo. III c. 141, art.III; *House of Commons Journals*, 68 (1812-13), p.661; SC on the Usury Laws, *PP* (1818) VI, evidence of E.B. Sugden, 150-51. The petitions of 30 fire and life offices are listed in the *General Index of the House of Commons Journals*, vols.56-75 (1801-20), pp.379-80. Most of these were in order to sue and be sued in the name of an executive officer, and several included the power to enrol annuities.

[51] SC on the Usury Laws, *PP* (1818) VI, 150-51, evidence of W. Phipps, 160.

[52] Trebilcock, *Phoenix Assurance*, vol.I, p.632.

[53] Calculated from GL Ms 12162A/2, Alliance, DM, 1830-32 *passim*; Ms 14075/1, Alliance, Ledger no.1; Ms 16222/2-4, MFLAC, DM, 1824-30 *passim*.

[54] Trebilcock, *Phoenix Assurance*, vol.I, pp.637, 662-3.

[55] Trebilcock, *Phoenix Assurance*, vol.I, pp.636-43. For examples of pressure to reduce the rate on annuities, see GL Ms 12162A/2, Alliance, DM, 13 Oct. 1830; Ms 14281/3, Guardian, DM, 2 May 1828.

56   GL Ms 14281/3, Guardian, DM, 5 Dec. 1828; Trebilcock, *Phoenix Assurance*, vol.I, p.642, table 11.6, p.653.

57   Dickson, *Sun Insurance*, p.260; Trebilcock, *Phoenix Assurance*, vol.I, pp.642-3.

58   SC on the Usury Laws, *PP* (1818) VI, evidence of J. Gibbs, 161.

59   Supple, *Royal Exchange*, p.320.

60   The Phoenix and the Shropshire figures calculated from Trebilcock, *Phoenix Assurance*, vol.I, table 11.6, p.653; GL Ms 15032/9, Sun, Take over Papers, Shropshire & North Wales, Clarke to Richards, 8 Dec. 1854. The Shropshire & North Wales, founded in 1837, had £33140 lent on mortgages when the Sun investigated in 1844. Clarke's letter indicates that £12 had been paid up on each share. In 1837, 4686 shares had been sold which would have resulted in a capital of £56232. Thus, assuming that no more shares were sold, mortgages accounted for 59 per cent of the original share capital.

61   Noakes, *County Fire*, p.82; GL Ms 16222/2, MFLAC, DM, 7 Feb. 1825.

62   Feinstein, 'National Statistics', table 17.5, p.389, appendix, table XII, p.450; Burnett, *Social History of Housing*, pp.14,16; Parry Lewis, *Building Cycles*, p.35.

63   Supple, *Royal Exchange*, pp.321-3.

64   GL Ms 12162A/1, Alliance, DM, 22 Feb. 1826, 25 Apr. 1827.

65   Supple, *Royal Exchange*, p.324.

66   Ashcrott and Preston-Thomas, *English Poor Law System*, p.39. My thanks to Janet Blackman for this reference.

67   Williams, *From Pauperism to Poverty*, pp.77-81, 218-28; Driver, *Power and Pauperism*, table 5.2, p.78. A parliamentary return of 1876, for example, gave the total expenditure on the erection of pauper establishments since 1868 as £2.1m, of which 81 per cent came from outstanding loans. Ashcrott and Preston-Thomas, *English Poor Law System*, p.299 n3. Feinstein has suggested that £3m was borrowed by all local authorities (for all purposes) before 1851. Feinstein, 'National Statistics', p.376.

68   At 1851-60 prices. Feinstein, 'National Statistics', appendix, table XIII, p.452.

69   37 per cent of railway capital in England and Wales in 1844, for example, was in the form of loans. Daunton, *Progess and Poverty*, p.312.

70   There were no limits on the borrowing powers of English turnpikes under the general act of 1773, although the details of debts had to be returned under the act of 1820 (I Geo. IV c. 95). Savage, *Economic History of Transport*, p.25; Ginarlis and Pollard, 'Roads and Waterways', pp.187, 190.

71   Cf. the reference to the directors' search for higher yields in GL Ms 16223/1, MFLAC, GCM, 4 May 1826.

72   Pearson, 'Collective Diversification', pp.406-12.

73   County, DM, 14 Oct. 1813; GL Ms 14281/3, Guardian, DM, 6 Mar. 1829.

74   GL Ms 12162A/1-3, Alliance, DM, 1825-37 *passim*; Ms 14075/1, Alliance, Ledger no.1.

75   Trebilcock, *Phoenix Assurance*, vol.I, p.656; Supple, *Royal Exchange*, p.328.

76   Supple, *Royal Exchange*, p.315, table 13.1, p.327; Dickson, *Sun Insurance*, p.262; Trebilcock, *Phoenix Assurance*, vol.I, pp.661-2.

77   GL Ms 12160A/14, Imperial, DM, 15 July 1840, 8 Dec. 1841. The Imperial's bill became 5 Vict. c. 66, passed in June 1842.

Insuring the Industrial Revolution

78 Trebilcock, *Phoenix Assurance*, vol.I, pp.737-42.
79 Supple, *Royal Exchange*, pp.309-10.
80 Clayton and Osborne, *Insurance Company Investment*, pp.41-2; Trebilcock, *Phoenix Assurance*, vol.I, p.711.
81 Clayton and Osborne, *Insurance Company Investment*, p.85; Cornell, *Principles and Finance of Fire Insurance*, p.143. Cornell notes that, as late as 1886-95, 2.5 per cent of the premium surpluses in UK fire insurance were allocated towards dividend payments.
82 Trebilcock, *Phoenix Assurance*, vol.I, pp.108-9; GL Ms 12160A/8, Imperial, DM, 2 July 1823.
83 GCA, TD446/5/18/1, North British, DM, Preamble to list of subscribers, 9 Mar. 1809.
84 Dickson, *Sun Insurance*, p.289.
85 Some country banks also began to maintain regular reserve funds at this time, although the practice remained haphazard and intermittent, Pressnell, *Country Banking*, p.229.
86 Dickson, *Sun Insurance*, p.111. On the conventional 40 per cent premium reserve, see Westall, *Provincial Insurance*, p.428, glossary.
87 Clayton and Osborne, *Insurance Company Investment*, p.85.
88 Tipping, 'America as a Fire Insurance Field', p.60; Supple, *Royal Exchange*, p.310; Trebilcock, *Phoenix Assurance*, vol.I, p.617.
89 Calculated from GL Ms 11933A, Sun, Book of Annual Accounts, 1791-1887.
90 The average yield of consols in 1823 was 3.8%, which on £400000 would have secured £6.3 per share. Similarly, the Imperial's valuation of its capital in 1823 was £272798, which represented a price of 68.2 for consols, whereas consols had not been at this price since 1820. GL Ms 12160A/8, Imperial, DM, 2 July 1823.
91 Calculated from CKS, U2593/B16/1, Kent, Secretary's statements, 1806-7; SRO, Ms 3008/1/2/10, Salop, Income and Capital Account Book, 1780-1822; GL Ms 15032/2, Sun, Take over Papers, Bristol Union; Ms 11935E, Sun, Take over Papers, Salamander; Royal Insurance plc, Leeds & Yorkshire, DM, 1 July 1844, 2 July 1845, 6 July 1846; GL Ms 18102/1, Guardian, Annual Account Book, 1822-45. The Guardian's figures relate to its fire business only.
92 GL Ms 11933A, Sun, Annual Accounts, 1791-1887; Dickson, *Sun Insurance*, pp.110-11; Supple, *Royal Exchange*, p.399.
93 The investment earnings of the Provincial Insurance, for example, accounted for 65 per cent of its total profits in 1903-13, and 51 per cent during the First World War. Calculated from Westall, *Provincial Insurance*, table 5.7, p.102, table 8.5, p.157.
94 This can only approximate actual profit/loss totals, for no account can be taken of capital gains or losses through sales of stock, or through mortgages written off. Furthermore, no attempt has been made to capitalise dividend payments, the procedure followed by Westall when estimating the internal rate of return for the Provincial Insurance Company in the early twentieth century. Given the limited survival of accounts for insurance offices in this period, such a calculation would require a great deal of further labour, beyond the scope of this volume. Westall, *Provincial Insurance*, table B.3, p.426.
95 This is the standard procedure, see Mirowski, *Birth of the Business Cycle*, pp.203-4; Westall, *Provincial Insurance*, p.102.

[96] Dickson, *Sun Insurance*, p.74.

[97] The County's average annual net (post-dividend) profits fell from £4766 in 1816-20 to a loss of £1489 in 1821-9, but recovered to £26873 in 1836-9. Calculated from 'Abstract shewing the appropriation of assets 1815-29' and 'Profit/Loss Abstracts 1836-46', in County, Annual Accounts, 2 vols., 1807-46.

[98] Calculated from GL Ms 12162A/1-3, Alliance, DM, 1828-40 *passim*; Homer, *History of Interest Rates*, table 19, pp.195-9. See Trebilcock, *Phoenix Assurance*, vol.I, table 11.2, p.623.

[99] Begg, Fischer and Dornbusch, *Economics*, p.97.

[100] Calculated from Howe, *Cotton Masters*, table 1.4; Boyson, *Ashworth Cotton Enterprise*, pp.29-31; Mirowski, *Birth of the Business Cycle*, pp.253-4; Rose, *Gregs of Quarry Bank Mill*, p.44, table 3.5, p.53; Rimmer, *Marshalls of Leeds*, table 15, pp.322-4; Sigsworth, *Black Dyke Mills*, appendix A, table I, p.226.

[101] Bridgewater canal returns calculated fom Mirowski, *Birth of the Business Cycle*, p.256. Manchester Exchange Rooms were said to have returned seven to ten per cent in 1824. Leeds Bazaar and Shambles yielded five to seven per cent in rents in 1836, while Leeds Free Market let tolls in 1835 for a return of 15 per cent on the original investment of 1827. Grady, 'Georgian Public Buildings', p.74; *idem.*, 'Profit, Property Interests and Public Spirit', pp.188-9. Drummond's bank at Charing Cross returned between four and eight per cent, 1777-1819, calculated from Mirowski, *Birth of the Business Cycle*, pp.247-54. The Provincial Bank of Ireland, averaged five per cent in 1827-30, and less than nine per cent in the 1830s and 1840s, calculated from Gayer, Rostow and Schwarz, *Growth and Fluctuation of the British Economy*, I, p.443.

[102] Pearson, 'Collective Diversification', p.397.

[103] Trebilcock, *Phoenix Assurance*, vol.I, p.237.

[104] Dickson, *Sun Insurance*, pp.47-8; GL Ms 11931/4, Sun, GCM, 9 July 1741, 9 July 1747, 6 Jan. 1749; Ms 11932/16, Sun, CMM, 2 Jan. 1806.

[105] This was also the procedure adopted, *faute de mieux*, by Trebilcock in his comparison of dividends paid by the Sun, the REA and the Phoenix. Trebilcock, *Phoenix Assurance*, vol.I, pp.237-8, 714-16.

[106] Ward, *Finance of Canal Building*, appendix 1. A survey of 1838 suggested that over half of all canal companies paid below the five per cent deemed to be an acceptable return. Jackson, *Development of Transportation*, pp.419-20.

[107] Michie, *Money, Mania and Markets*, p.52. Average railway dividends, 1841-50, calculated from Boot, *Commercial Crisis*, table 2, p.12.

[108] Jackson, *Hull in the Eighteenth Century*, p.247, appendix 34, p.426; Stern, 'First London Dock Boom', p.77.

[109] Gayer, Rostow and Schwarz, *Growth and Fluctuation of the British Economy*, I, pp.427-8, table 33, p.431, 443-50; Wilson, *Lighting the Town*, appendix C, pp.226-7; Grady, 'Georgian Public Buildings', p.75; *idem.*, 'Profit, Property Interests and Public Spirit', pp.186-7.

[110] Mirowksi, 'Rise (and Retreat) of a Market', table 4, pp.569-70; Trebilcock, *Phoenix Assurance*, vol.I, table 13.5, p.720.

[111] Wetenhall, *Course of the Exchange*, 1720-1850 *passim*; Mirowksi, 'Rise (and Retreat) of a Market', p.571; Trebilcock, *Phoenix Assurance*, vol.I, pp.717-19.

112 Gayer, Rostow and Schwarz, *Growth and Fluctuation of the British Economy*, I, table 7, p.361, table 14, p.373.
113 Trebilcock, *Phoenix Assurance*, vol.I, pp.238-9, table 5.10, p.240, p.719.
114 Oakes, *Diaries*, vol.I, p.70, 12 Aug. 1805.
115 GL Ms 12160A/7, Imperial, DM, 23 Sept. 1818.
116 County, DM, 15 Sept. 1808, 15 June 1809; County, Letter Book M, to E. Carrett, 13 June 1821; County, Special Letters, to R. Keyworth, 14 Dec. 1837.
117 Michie, *Money, Mania and Markets*, pp.29-30, 45.
118 GL Ms 15032/9, Sun, Take over Papers, Shropshire & N.Wales, Clarke to Richards, 8 Dec. 1854.

Conclusion

Fire insurance in eighteenth- and early nineteenth-century Britain was an ambivalent business, sometimes dynamic, sometimes static, even laggard. The dynamic face of the industry has been highlighted in several places in this book, most notably by the estimates on volume and long-run growth. Sums insured against fire multiplied by a factor of 24 between 1725 and 1850. The proportion of insurable property covered by insurance more than doubled between 1760 and 1850. At the end of the eighteenth century some 30 fire insurance companies held nearly £3m in assets. By 1850 the number of companies had risen to 70 and assets had grown to over £11m. These figures are impressive even when viewed against the acceleration of the British economy during this period. Insurance output and income grew much faster than GNP before 1780 and after 1810, and faster too than many sectors of manufacturing and commerce. Capital formation in fire insurance expanded three times more quickly than national income during the first half of the nineteenth century. By 1850 the amount of fire insurance sold per caput was about eight times that sold in 1725, in a market only three times as large.

Rapid growth was not the only impressive feature of British fire insurance during the industrial revolution. It also pioneered methods of corporate organisation, particularly those appropriate to stock companies, in an economy in which small partnerships and the self-employed were still predominant. The large capital-rich insurance offices took the committee form of company management, inherited from the great trading corporations of the seventeenth century, and developed it to new levels of sophistication through a process of subdividing and devolving directorial and managerial duties. In few sectors of British business before the railway age were the boundaries between the power of managers and the rights of owners so sorely tested. This led to an area of conflict which was not entirely resolved before 1850. By this date the most prominent company secretaries, such as the Sun's Charles Ford, were already close to attaining the power of a modern chief executive, without ever quite breaking free from the old subservient relationship to their boards of directors. They paved the way for the great insurance autocrats of the late nineteenth and early twentieth centuries, men such as Swinton Boult, Sir Francis Norie-Miller and Sir Edward Mountain, and the gulf between proprietors and managers in the large insurance corporations widened.

Insurance was also at the cutting edge of business development in other areas - marketing, cartel formation, the corporate takeover, and investment strategies. With hundreds of agents by the beginning of the nineteenth century, the sales and marketing systems of the largest fire offices were far more extensive than those of

Britain's biggest merchants and manufacturers.[1] The insurers' cumulative experience of facing monitoring and principal agent problems was second to none. Their failure to resolve such problems, as agency networks grew to unwieldy dimensions, prepared the ground for the development of branch organisations in the second half of the nineteenth century. Equally, the record of the larger insurance offices in creating oligopolistic or collusive arrangements to reduce overt price competition, matched or surpassed that of other industries. The durability and success of the formal tariff organisation that emerged in the 1840s in part reflected the persistence with which different fire offices had sought to cooperate during the previous half century. Perhaps most impressive of all, the tactics and strategies developed in pursuit of corporate acquisitions from the 1820s were unrivalled anywhere else in the economy and had a particularly 'modern' look about them.[2] Finally, the insurance offices pioneered flexible corporate investment strategies and became widely recognised by institutional and private borrowers as major sources of credit. The evidence presented in chapter 9 above indicates that the flight of insurance capital out of gilts and mortgages commenced around 1820, some two decades earlier than previously believed. Some provincial insurers, such as the fire office in Newcastle, were even more precocious by investing in local utilities before 1800.

In all these ways fire insurance presented itself as one of the most advanced sectors of the British economy. There was, however, another side to the business. Underwriting techniques proved slow to develop in the face of rapid changes in the technology, organisation and scale of industrial production and distribution. From the 1780s insurers began to have serious difficulties in assessing factories and warehouses with their new mixtures of goods and manufacturing processes. The struggle to adjust premium rates and policy conditions to these risks continued until the tariff cooperation of the 1840s helped reduce the asymmetry of information and the attendant transaction costs. One important by-product of this struggle was the improvement of data collection and processing by most large offices from the 1820s. Compared to their eighteenth-century counterparts, the fire insurers of 1850 benefited from a far more exact knowledge of the structure and distribution of their liabilities, which, in turn, allowed a more effective spread of risk and helped reduce the impact of sudden losses. Such improvements, however, were a long time coming and the delay arguably raised the cost of fire insurance and hindered its growth for most of this period.

In terms of product design or diversification the fire offices were also remarkably uninnovative over the long run. The only major new product in this period was the bonus policy and, despite the longevity and wealth of some London offices, no effort was made to enter new lines of underwriting such as transport or burglary insurance.[3] A few types of non-standard cover were allowed such as rental, livestock, carriage and bottomry insurance, but these remained at the margins of the staple business of underwriting buildings and their contents against fire. Requests to cover any unusual liability were usually rejected.

Even the impressive long-run growth has to be qualified. Fire insurance grew more slowly than national income and the stock of insurable property between the 1780s and the 1810s, and stagnated in real terms. During this period an increasing number of offices were slicing up the same cake into smaller pieces. After the turn of the century and the break-up of the London cartel this drove down prices to unsustainable levels, especially in areas of industrial underwriting. There is evidence of capacity constraints at this time, partly reflected in attempts by medium-sized and small firms to spread risks through bilateral arrangements. Furthermore, insurance remained disproportionately concentrated in southern England relative to the national distribution of population and taxable wealth. This skewness must have taken some time to correct, particularly given the long period of slower growth. One consequence of this was a lower level of insurance penetration than the economy should have experienced relative to average per caput incomes. During the first half of the nineteenth century the total premium income of British fire insurers, expressed as a percentage of GDP, was comparable to the level found in the poorest developing countries of the late twentieth century, and far behind what it should have been had a log linear relationship existed between real per caput incomes and insurance. Or, to put it another way, Britain was a much wealthier nation in 1850 than the size of its insurance industry would indicate.

Insurance in other nations was bound to catch up with developments in Britain, in the same way as the relative pace of industrialisation in Britain, Europe and North America changed during the course of the nineteenth century. The skewed distribution of property insurance in Britain, however, together with the slowdown in real growth between 1780 and 1815, may have reduced the distance which foreign insurance industries had to travel. Before 1800, although there were thriving marine insurance centres in Amsterdam and Hamburg, there were very few joint-stock fire insurance companies in Europe and no life insurance sold at all. By 1850 there were about ten fire insurance offices in Belgium, around 20 stock offices in France, and 31 stock and mutual offices in Germany.[4] The largest continental stock insurers were already approaching the size of the biggest British firms. The premium income of the leading British fire office (the Phoenix) in 1851 was £223000, compared with the incomes of Germany's major office, the Gotha, at £174000, and France's biggest fire insurer, the CRP, at £146000.[5] Despite lower real per caput incomes, sums insured per caput were actually higher in France in 1850 than in the United Kingdom, and nearly as high in Belgium. Ten years later, per caput sums insured against fire were as high in some parts of Prussia as in Britain.[6]

This is not to say that the position of British insurance as world leader had been lost by mid-century. What was happening was that the native insurance industries of European states were developing quickly in response to the demand created by urban and industrial development and income growth within their territories between 1820 and 1850. In some new lines, notably reinsurance and accident insurance, continental Europe had leapt ahead of Britain by 1850. The British domestic market for property insurance, however, was still the world's largest at mid-century and British domination of the international trade in insurance remained supreme until the First World War. While competition in Europe became much tougher for British firms after 1850, America and other overseas markets provided plenty scope for the growth of British insurance exports during the second half of the century. The fragmented nature of the US market and the relatively small size of its native firms meant that the degree of insurance penetration there remained limited. The average per caput sum insured in the US in 1850 amounted to only £5 compared to £31 in the UK, and most of Europe was also still well behind Britain by this measure of development.[7] As late as 1880 the total net premiums earned by British fire offices were about three times those received by the fire offices of Germany and France, and were only just short of the combined fire and marine income of US insurers.[8]

This kind of comparative analysis is in its infancy. Although it is useful to begin to place the achievement of British fire insurance in an international perspective, it has not been the focus of this book. Instead we have attempted to reveal the character of fire insurance in Britain and to uncover the factors determining its progress. We have also tried to place the industry in its wider domestic context and to examine its impact upon economic and social change. The statistical analysis presented in chapter 1 indicated that population growth was the largest determinant of insurance growth while fire insurance also retained a close association with the building cycle, at least until the end of the eighteenth century. Furthermore, the evidence from company records suggests that the expansion of private housing and non-industrial property were the engines behind the growth in demand for fire insurance. Between 1770 and 1841 the building industry increased its weight in aggregate industrial production from 11 to 24 per cent in response to population growth, family formation, urbanisation, and rising incomes.[9] The high proportion of insurance accounted for by residential property throughout this period provides clear testimony of its continuing significance to most fire offices. 'Ordinary' insurances accounted for 93 per cent of the sums insured by the Norwich Union in 1822, 65 per cent of the REA's fire insurances in 1826 and 68 per cent of the Sun's premiums in 1840. Many smaller offices such as the Westminster, the Essex & Suffolk Equitable and the Sheffield had nearly all of their risks in this category. Thus the direct contribution to the growth of insurance made by demand from manufacturing industry remained limited. 'Tied' insurances in the form of residential property attached to insurances on mills and warehouses, however, were important to the fire offices, as was the necessity of retaining the goodwill of powerful businessmen by insuring their more hazardous properties.

Can it be said, then, that the 'industrial revolution' was insured at all? The answer is a qualified affirmative. On the one hand, large sectors of the British economy were not covered by insurance before 1850. These include much of agriculture, most of the metal working and transport industries, and all capital in mining and quarrying. Forges and foundries, carriers' wagons and canal barges, coal mines and salt quarries were usually deemed uninsurable by underwriters. On the other hand, some manufacturing industries attracted a great deal of fire insurance, notably textiles, sugar refining and brewing. The slower growth of insurance at the end of the eighteenth century, the accompanying capacity constraints as the accumulation of property outstripped the supply of insurance, and the continued insistence of the fire offices on self-insurance by all types of policyholders, meant that the proportion of insurable industrial capital covered by insurance never approached 100 per cent. Nevertheless by 1820 most textile mills were insured for some of their value, and, notwithstanding the sums invested in fireproofing, many manufacturers had come to regard insurance as necessary rather than optional. Furthermore, it can be argued that the exertions of underwriters in refining their risk assessment procedures and classifications of insurable property encouraged higher safety standards in the workplace, warehouse, counting house, shop and home. In turn, this may have contributed to greater efficiency across a range of industrial and commercial activities, although this suggestion remains speculative.[10]

If the industrial revolution was, at least partially, insured, did fire insurance ensure the industrial revolution? The search for the causes or preconditions of the first industrial revolution is an ongoing story of revision and counter revision. Explanations offered have included a better specification of property rights after the Glorious Revolution; Britain's resource endowment of cheap mineral energy; technological innovation, due in part to institutional incentives, such as an effective patent system, helping to lower input costs; an early revolution in agricultural productivity, raising incomes and allowing the release of labour into industry; population growth due to higher earnings and rising levels of marital fertility, which in turn provided an abundant labour supply after c.1760; the accumulation of capital and labour skills in rural 'proto-industry'; lower transport costs due to improvements in shipping and internal water and road networks; an efficient mercantile credit system, based upon a variety of devices, most notably the bill of exchange.[11] The role of all or any of these factors as 'indispensable' antecedents to British industrialisation has rightly been questioned in recent accounts, so much so that attempts to understand the genesis of the industrial revolution are now rarely couched in terms of a list of 'causes'.[12] If such a list still exists, fire insurance may be safely deleted from it. There is no evidence of any manufacturer failing to proceed with an investment in a mill or a piece of machinery because he could not obtain insurance. Fire insurance emerged from the brick and stone terraces of late seventeenth-century London. For much of the eighteenth century its development was focused upon the south-east of England and the industrial regions which most attracted underwriters, East Anglia and the south-west, were those destined for early deindustrialisation. Only in the 1780s did the north-west begin to climb up the Sun's rank order of regions by premium income, and only in the following decade did it become the Sun's second most important source of premiums (table 3.3). The underwriting of northern industrial property, and the cross subsidisation of losses made on mill insurances from profits made on ordinary residential policies, expanded in tandem with the growth of the textile industry, or else followed closely in its wake. Indeed it was the wealth accumulated by sugar refiners and overseas merchants in Bristol and London, by textile merchants and manufacturers in Leeds,

Liverpool and Manchester, and by coal magnates in the north-east, which provided the start-up capital for fire offices in these localities between 1760 and 1830.

Therefore, rather than determining economic development and structural change, much of British fire insurance was shaped by it. Causal forces in history, however, rarely flow in only one direction. There were many ways in which fire insurance might have ensured the general growth of the economy, if not the specific process of industrialisation. The availability of relatively cheap and financially solid forms of insurance offered a greater level of security to the owners of mercantile, manufacturing and residential property in many sectors of the British economy. As indicated in chapter 2, a very high proportion of property in London was already insured by the middle of the eighteenth century, and this service was already being extended, in an uneven way, to towns and villages across the Kingdom. It might be argued that insurance, once familiar, helped reduce the fear of loss and the debilitating effect of uncertainty, and provided an 'institutional incentive' for the accumulation of material goods, investment and innovation. Establishing an evidential link between the expansion of insurance and broad attitudinal changes in a society is extremely difficult. The investment by insurance offices in fire-fighting facilities in dozens of towns, however, must have increased popular awareness of fire prevention, and, perhaps, changed perceptions of the hazard. Fire insurance also played an important role in the financing of infrastructural development. From the 1780s many provincial fire offices were pivotal to local investment flows, channelling capital and credit into turnpikes, canals, wharves, water and gas companies, building projects, manufacturing ventures as well as land. Insurance offices in Newcastle, Liverpool, Manchester, Leeds, Birmingham, Wiltshire, Norwich, Shrewsbury and Bristol belonged to the institutional and associational networks constructed from the late eighteenth century by county and urban elites. Thus, being themselves the product of collective action, and in turn helping to reduce economic uncertainty, the insurance offices formed part of the feedback mechanism by which trust and confidence multiplied within business communities.

It is generally agreed that the 'compelling question in history and economics' is why do some societies increase their material welfare over time while others do not?[13] Can insurance help answer this? Insurance during the British industrial revolution acted to redistribute wealth within a pool from low risk to high risk areas, notably from residential property owners to the owners of hazardous commercial goods and new manufacturing processes. But did it add value? A theoretical case can be made for insurance helping to increase welfare by creating net increments of trust and security, raising confidence to invest, produce and consume. Arguably this was as important as saving or abstinence from consumption, which are the usual means of accumulating capital in market theories of economic change. As William Gordon put it in 1765, when advocating the use of insurance by merchants:

> No profit is equal to the anxiety a man must be under, who hath perhaps as much at risk as he is worth in the world; and this anxiety, supposing in the end his property should be

safe, would introduce such a confusion and disorder in the other parts of his affairs, as would be more than an equivalent for the premium he had saved.[14]

The hope of gain and fear of loss provide incentives and counter incentives for individuals to engage in productive activity. Property insurance helped lift those restrictions on the use of capital which were imposed by the fear of loss, thereby liberating production and removing a constraint on growth. Another way of viewing this is to suggest that insurance helped remove market imperfections by reducing the obstacles strewn in the path of investment and wealth accumulation by uncertainty and fear of sudden loss. Whereas the focus of economic historians, especially the cliometricians, has been on productivity change brought about by innovations, particularly those which reduced the cost of inputs, such incentives to enter the market have often been relegated to 'secondary' factors.[15] Some, however, have recognised that risk aversion may have played a part in determining the rate of technical innovation, and also that inventive talent could respond to positive incentives and supportive attitudes. Forms of quasi-insurance, such as patenting and legal security for property rights, were elements in the appropriate institutional structure for technological development.[16] It could be equally argued that commercial forms of insurance - the well established marine underwriting of cargoes, the tentative attempts by merchants to insure private debt, and, above all, the huge corporate business of insuring property against fire - together provided the kind of institutional foundation which risk taking in the first industrial revolution required.[17]

Notes

[1] Even Josiah Wedgwood, arguably the greatest marketing man of his day, only had five showrooms and three travelling salesmen by the 1790s (although, admittedly, 80 per cent of his wares were exported). McKendrick, 'Josiah Wedgwood', pp.120, 126.
[2] It may be that the contemporary merger movement in banking developed similar tactical devices, but this remains to be investigated by modern research. The only existing monograph does not touch upon such issues. Sykes, *Amalgamation Movement in English Banking*.
[3] Pearson, 'Towards an Historical Model of Services Innovation'.
[4] Brown, 'On the Progress of Fire Insurance in Great Britain'. The German total excludes an unknown number of very small local mutual insurers. I have found no figures for French mutuals, which accounted for just over one-quarter of French fire insurance in 1852.
[5] *Jahrbuch*, 1 (1864), p.24, 2 (1865), p.50; *Assurance Magazine*, III (1853), pp.163-4; Trebilcock, *Phoenix Assurance*, vol.I, pp.165, 694.
[6] Per caput sums insured in 1860 from Pearson, 'Reinsurance Markets in Europe', table 3, p.564. The figures for 1850 are calculated from insurance data in Brown, 'On the Progress of Fire Insurance in Great Britain'; population data in Mitchell, *European*

Historical Statistics; real incomes in Foreman-Peck, *History of the World Economy*, table 2.4, p.47.

[7] US per caput sums insured from Armstrong, 'History of Property Insurance', table VII. On British insurers in the US, see Pearson, 'British and European Insurance Enterprise'.

[8] The data for the US, Germany and France relate to the year 1878, from *Assecuranz Jahrbuch* (1880); Armstrong, 'History of Property Insurance', table VIII. The British figure is for 1882, from *Post Magazine*, 8 Sept. 1883.

[9] O'Brien, 'Modern Conceptions of the Industrial Revolution', p.14.

[10] Cf. Pearson, 'Fire Insurance and the British Textile Industries', p.12.

[11] Wrigley, *Continuity, Chance and Change*; Mokyr, *Lever of Riches*; O'Brien, 'Modern Conceptions of the Industrial Revolution'; Mathias, 'Industrial Revolution: Concept and Reality'; Berg, *Age of Manufactures*; Hudson, *Industrial Revolution*.

[12] Hawke, 'Reinterpretations of the Industrial Revolution'; Mokyr, 'Editor's Introduction'.

[13] Anderson, *Explaining Long-term Economic Change*, p.10.

[14] Gordon, *Universal Accountant*, vol.I, p.9. Cf also Magens, who had argued ten years earlier that the precaution of insurance enhanced a merchant's credit. Magens, *Essay on Insurance*.

[15] O'Brien, 'Modern Conceptions of the Industrial Revolution', p.13.

[16] Mokyr, *Lever of Riches*, pp.11-12, 157-9, 177.

[17] Cf. North, *Institutions*, pp.126-7. Debt insurance awaits its historian, but is briefly discussed in Cullen, *Anglo-Irish Trade*, pp.101-2.

Appendix A

Estimates of total sums insured: English fire offices, 1725-1848

The estimates for 1725-82

For the period before 1782 data on fire insurance can only be compiled from the surviving records of fire offices. Archival data for sums insured against fire are less comprehensive than those for premium income. We have no sums insured for the three London stock companies, the Sun, the REA and the London Assurance. For these offices my estimates are derived from their annual premium figures using notional average rates (premium rates per £100 insured) as multipliers. The latter were derived from scattered references in a range of sources to the sums insured by each office, together with the offices' own premium rate tables for the relevant years. Full details of this mode of estimating sums insured for each office are available from the author. No figures for sums insured are available for any country fire office before 1805. The estimates here are based on the estimated aggregate annual premiums for all country offices multiplied by a notional constant average rate of £0.1% (two shillings per £100 insured). For the estimation of annual premiums, see appendix B. Some confidence in the accuracy of these estimates is gained from Lord North's estimate of £150m sum insured in 1782, a figure compiled 'from pretty accurate information' from the contemporary fire offices, and calculated for the purpose of raising a stamp duty on insurances. The Chancellor's estimate is close to my total of £148.9m for 1782.[1]

The estimates for 1782-1848

From 1782 sums insured can be calculated from the published duty returns. The latter exist as annual aggregates (for England & Wales, Scotland, Ireland, London and Country offices) to 1822, and quarterly by individual office after that date. Various series of returns were produced but there are discrepancies between them. Samuel Brown declared upon inspecting them, that 'scarcely any of the printed totals for any one year precisely agree'. In 1856 George Coode produced a series in his 'Report on Fire Insurance Duties' for the Exchequer.[2] This was reproduced with corrections by Brown in 1858, who also produced his own annual series calculated from the original quarterly returns.[3] Coode, taking Brown's corrections on board, reworked his own figures for his 'Revised Report' of 1863. Finally, the Inland Revenue produced a comprehensive annual series in 1870.[4]

I have recalculated Coode's 1863 revised series for the periods 1790-93 and 1799-1850, using the Inland Revenue series as a check. In doing so I have eliminated several arithmetic errors made by Coode, so that the difference between the two series is less than £1000 for any one year, the product of rounding. For the remaining years, 1783-9 and 1794-8, I have let Coode's 1863 figures stand. His careful reworking of the figures for these years are explained in the annotations to his table. Brown's series correlates closely with my revised version of Coode's 1863 series for the years after 1805. The standard deviations are close for both series, £142.6m and £141.2m respectively, and identical for the five year moving averages calculated from both sets of annual data (£127.4m). In revising Coode's annual figures, I have followed Supple in taking the years 1783-99 as ending 1 August, so that, for instance, the return for 1 August 1783 to 1 August 1784 is labelled 1784.[5] From 180 0 t he r eturns r elate t o ye ars ending 5 January. My labels refer to the preceding calendar year ending 31 December. Thus the return for year ending 5 January 1801 is labelled 1800. Brown also followed this procedure.

Five year centred moving averages

My series for sums insured 1725-1782 derives from annual data. These will be affected by non-collection and delayed payments, so the annual figures have been converted into five year centred moving annual averages. Thus the average sum insured given for 1782 will include some insurances taken out in 1780-82 but not recorded until 1782-5. The 'Revised Coode' series, 1783-1850, has also been converted into five year averages. It is based on annual duty returns which were subject to distortions due to large arrears of payment in any one year. Coode himself argued that 'correct and trustworthy averages of the progress of insurance can be calculated...if series of years sufficiently long are taken for comparison', and that a period of five years 'is always sufficient to eliminate error arising from mere irregularity in the periodical collection of the duty'. Supple also noted the unreliability of the annual data before 1850.[6]

Real sums insured

Probably the greatest element in the inflation of sums insured against fire was the inflation of property prices, which, at least partly, was the result of increases in building costs. It is therefore useful to deflate the five year averages of sums insured by an index of such costs to arrive at estimates of the real value of the property insured. Schumpeter-Gilboy's producers' goods index was spliced with Rousseau's 'principal industrial products' index at 1800 = 100, and the combined index was used to deflate the series of five year moving annual averages of sums insured 1725-1848. Schumpeter-Gilboy and Rousseau contained 12 and 18 commodities respectively, five of which were common to both indices. Both indices also contained commodities directly related to construction; iron, lead and wood in Rousseau, lime, tiles, pantiles, lead, and bricks in Schumpeter-Gilboy. Two alternative deflators were also tried but discarded, O'Brien's index of industrial prices, and his index of construction prices. These made little difference to the long-run growth of real sums insured. The O'Brien indices and the spliced Schumpeter-Rousseau index were closely correlated ($r = 0.96$), and the former had the disadvantage for present purposes of terminating in 1820.[7]

Notes

[1]   Cobbett, *Parliamentary History*, XXII (1781-2), pp.1155-7.

[2]   Coode, 'Report on Fire Insurance Duties', *PP* (1857) III, 643.

[3]   Brown, 'Progress of Fire Insurance'.

[4]   Coode, 'Revised Report on Fire Insurance Duties', *PP* (1863) XXVI, 27; 'Report of the Commissioners of Inland Revenue', *PP* (1870) XX, 193.

[5]   Supple, *Royal Exchange*, p.107.

[6]   Coode, 'Revised Report on Fire Insurance Duties', p.1; Supple, *Royal Exchange*, p.107.

[7]   Mitchell and Deane, *Abstract of British Historical Statistics*, pp.468-9, 471-3; O'Brien, 'Agriculture and the Home Market'.

Sums insured: English fire offices, 1725-1848

Five year centred moving averages
(Deflator based on 1800 = 100)

Year	Current £ insured	Real £ insured	Year	Current £ insured	Real £ insured
1725	31431947	52025291	1763	81621468	115230308
1726	33641609	52656432	1764	86084436	122734245
1727	35677507	52964546	1765	90334263	131395292
1728	37702269	57148702	1766	94308449	137175926
1729	39591065	60011719	1767	98525211	143309397
1730	40909709	60112226	1768	102718650	150933526
1731	41534260	62957194	1769	106117268	166096593
1732	41864474	66983158	1770	110294105	168961182
1733	41927013	70203371	1771	113810036	174347289
1734	41784490	69964727	1772	117251781	172288332
1735	41967633	72811315	1773	120177996	174804358
1736	42525293	74678563	1774	122103092	179416788
1737	43305475	76987511	1775	124623723	183120572
1738	44018528	78255161	1776	126634503	180548202
1739	44933989	74373499	1777	127555140	180077844
1740	45811689	74122283	1778	128818115	178363543
1741	46502851	69035161	1779	132221881	173090463
1742	47053468	69852571	1780	135498920	172671191
1743	47437450	75065855	1781	143796164	188242251
1744	47613166	69962204	1782	148634750	178361700
1745	47740335	84871706	1783	148903862	183266292
1746	47896621	75792455	1784	147408982	196545309
1747	48564520	81317336	1785	145226933	195445593
1748	49691152	80399167	1786	138139734	176036475
1749	51130764	80910220	1787	135690933	176031481
1750	52562924	86012058	1788	137925067	175762918
1751	54505598	92338895	1789	141548253	190494846
1752	56261699	100020798	1790	146582380	197269745
1753	58301238	103646645	1791	155017573	208621781
1754	60377889	97690068	1792	162552040	210878322
1755	62564724	99003519	1793	169598720	196953352
1756	64379550	99684464	1794	176182980	213196211
1757	66249988	101489344	1795	179399922	211750728
1758	68280661	97350646	1796	180696262	188552622
1759	70062798	99891514	1797	184910462	188844728
1760	72183532	101906163	1798	189863582	211940743
1761	75076128	107039232	1799	197026802	221655153
1762	78185791	110379941	1800	206101600	206101600

Year	Current £ insured	Real £ insured	Year	Current £ insured	Real £ insured
1801	216964000	213042964	1825	435904667	587210419
1802	226877200	253294408	1826	449736933	685113272
1803	237272600	238737246	1827	460640000	708342642
1804	247938680	252587530	1828	467832133	747614095
1805	259557080	254866289	1829	475407067	790728080
1806	272563680	261340470	1830	486815733	844159197
1807	287889600	280994041	1831	493275867	828906869
1808	305970080	246896649	1832	501062987	878207171
1809	323020320	229922761	1833	514550018	911648401
1810	339212640	282100308	1834	527415596	826622521
1811	348573600	305470413	1835	543118859	835173340
1812	361454080	316758145	1836	563408493	791686071
1813	368945916	318191451	1837	584199578	889948889
1814	373733196	312402620	1838	603365617	936653291
1815	378203276	375897158	1839	621220258	872921569
1816	386121516	462777993	1840	638124888	904472667
1817	387643516	461210898	1841	651243962	965025144
1818	388939467	459399515	1842	661933804	1078952101
1819	392448933	477381911	1843	672951795	1142616069
1820	396503067	534132230	1844	684392155	1162040846
1821	398937467	565450496	1845	696428140	1146644311
1822	405109067	569248085	1846	707697411	1165198768
1823	415300533	583568853	1847	719607544	1127846440
1824	427611600	571317138	1848	730718399	1294642382

Appendix B

Estimates of total premiums: English fire offices, 1725-1848

Calculating total premium income

Figures for annual premium income have survived in archival records for six out of the seven metropolitan and four out of the 15 English provincial fire offices established before 1799. To construct the annual series of total premiums for all offices, the first step was to sum the original premium data of each fire office, as recorded in the surviving accounts. Second, where premiums were not available, other related data of the office concerned, namely sums insured and average rates, were utilised in order to estimate premiums. Third, where no data at all was available for a provincial office, the volume and trend growth of the Sun's premiums from its nearest local agency were used to create annual 'guesstimates'. Ninety-eight per cent of the total annual premiums in the estimates for 1723-99 were derived from either the first or second modes of calculation. Those whose premium 'guesstimates' before 1800 were partly or largely based on Sun agency remittances were the three Bristol offices, the Old Bath, and the Leeds and Manchester offices.

For the first half of the nineteenth century the principle method of calculating annual totals remained the same, namely to sum all surviving annual premium data of individual fire offices in company records. In total, these data were collected for 36 fire offices across this period. For those offices whose premium figures have not survived, aggregate premiums were estimated from their percentage share of annual stamp duty on sums insured. The annual breakdown by office of duty paid for 1805, 1810 and 1822-50 was supplemented for the other years by the market shares estimated by Trebilcock.[1] The 36 fire offices, whose own data on premiums were utilised, always accounted for more than 70 per cent of total market share in any year between 1800 and 1845.[2] Between 1846 and 1850 internal company data was less complete, and for these years the proportion of total premiums which were estimated rose to 55 per cent. Full sources and methods of estimation are available from the author.

'Premiums' of mutual offices

One difficulty existed with the three London mutual offices, the Hand-in-Hand, the Union and the Westminster. In these offices all policyholders were also members of the society. Policies were taken out for a seven year term and members paid a one-off 'premium' of 2s% (two shillings per £100 insured) plus a 'deposit' (or subscription) of 10s%. This was calculated as 2s% p.a. with the seventh year of insurance discounted.[3] The 'premium' was non-returnable and largely intended to cover the expenses of the office. Annual dividends were paid on the deposits. The deposits were effectively the 'capital' of these societies, invested in the public funds and drawn upon to cover fire losses during the term of a member's insurance, with the balance of the 10s% being returned at the expiry of the insurance. Such 'contributions to losses' were calculated by the directors as a percentage rate of the member's sum insured, with the rate varying each year according to the level of losses.

The nominal 'premiums' of these offices, therefore, were not equivalent to those of the stock offices, and the net cost of an insurance to a member of a mutual office remained unknown until the expiry of his or her policy. In 1783, when responding to members' complaints about the deposit return system, the Union claimed that their aggregated premiums and gross deposits taken for seven year insurances 'are nearly equal to the premium given to other Offices'.[4] Some support for this claim comes from my calculations of average rates for the Union and the Westminster, by dividing sums insured through by their aggregated premiums and gross deposits. The average rates are what one might expect of these offices, given what we know of their premium rates and composition of business, and are similar to those of the non-mutuals. The average rates for 1783-5, for instance, were for the Sun £0.147% (2s 11d% or two shillings eleven pence per £100 insured) and for the London Assurance £0.132 (2s $7^3/_4$d%), while by the above method of calculation they were for the Union £0.114% (2s $3^1/_4$d%). The Westminster's average rate for 1764-6 was £0.103% (2s $0^3/_4$d%).

I have therefore used the aggregated annual 'premiums and deposits received' as a proxy for 'premiums' for the Union and the Westminster offices. Unfortunately no such figures are available for the Hand-in-Hand. The annual 'premiums' for this office have been estimated by applying five year moving annual averages of the 'average rate' for the Hand-in-Hand's sister office, the Union, (i.e. premiums + gross deposits/sums insured x 100), to the annual sums insured by the Hand-in-Hand before 1800. The Union followed the risk classifications of the Hand-in-Hand closely throughout the century, so this seems the most appropriate method to adopt in the absence of other data.

Five year averages

As with sums insured, the premium series was calculated as a five year centred moving annual average in order to account for the problems of non-collection, non-remittance and late payment of premiums. Hugh Watts, secretary of the Sun, in a letter of 1798 to the Chancellor of the Exchequer regarding income tax, remarked that 'the term of three years appears to me too short a period for the forming of an average on the income of fire insurance offices...', and suggested 'three [*sic*.], four, five or seven' years as a basis of calculating an average.[5]

Estimates of real premiums

As with sums insured, it is useful to deflate the premium totals to arrive at the real value of premium income to the fire insurance offices and their policyholders. For this, a consumer rather than a producer price index is the most appropriate, because we are interested in how much bread, butter or coal £1 of premium might buy at any given time. Real values were derived from five year centred moving averages of current premiums deflated by the Phelps Brown and Hopkins index of the price of a composite unit of consumables.[6] The producer price indices considered as deflators for sums insured - namely the Schumpeter-Rousseau spliced industrial index and O'Brien's industrial and construction indices (see appendix A) - were also examined for comparative purposes. The industrial price deflators did produce a higher but less fluctuating rate of real premium growth. Particularly during the period 1780-1801 the violent inflationary swings of food prices had the effect of dampening real premium growth relative to the trend shown by the industrial deflator. Over the whole period, however, the consumables index was closely correlated to these industrial indices (r = 0.99 with Schumpeter-Rousseau), and for the reasons cited above it is preferable as an indicator of the purchasing power of premium income.

Notes

1   Trebilcock, *Phoenix Assurance*, p.461. The first of the returns, quarterly data published annually, was 'An account of all sums paid into the stamp office for duty on insurance from fire', *PP* (1824) XVII, 495.

2   1821 was the sole exception, when, without figures for Norwich Union for that year, the combined market share of those offices with internal premium data fell to 63 per cent.

3   GL Ms 14022/20, Union, DM, 10 Apr. 1793.

4   GL Ms 14022/17, Union, DM, 27 Mar. 1783.

5   GL Ms 11932/15, Sun, CMM, 20 Dec. 1798.

6   Phelps Brown and Hopkins, 'Seven Centuries of the Prices of Consumables'.

Premium income: English fire offices, 1725-1848

Five year centred moving annual averages (£)
(deflator based on 1800 = 100)

Year	Current premiums	Real premiums	Year	Current premiums	Real premiums
1725	35910	92246	1763	115187	276314
1726	38913	95725	1764	123615	272140
1727	41450	108981	1765	130701	277725
1728	43868	105918	1766	137097	287593
1729	45804	105395	1767	142969	283586
1730	47171	123401	1768	148773	298498
1731	47820	135504	1769	152712	333751
1732	48852	137434	1770	157620	345925
1733	50049	144167	1771	162672	328913
1734	51339	155304	1772	167410	305748
1735	52739	156223	1773	171768	314808
1736	53942	156824	1774	174507	316862
1737	55107	148626	1775	179163	344476
1738	55996	155770	1776	181794	357429
1739	57414	164475	1777	183293	361738
1740	59048	143678	1778	185438	351794
1741	60687	133562	1779	191560	397056
1742	61891	153697	1780	196466	421728
1743	62534	169240	1781	195640	403378
1744	62406	188784	1782	193717	391179
1745	62272	184811	1783	192146	346482
1746	62486	164841	1784	189851	340385
1747	64046	174843	1785	187555	350297
1748	66725	174553	1786	193376	361169
1749	70096	180362	1787	201650	378880
1750	73226	194483	1788	210716	380845
1751	76738	209491	1789	221370	405241
1752	79513	207316	1790	232342	418002
1753	82350	220585	1791	245669	442486
1754	85252	217220	1792	260056	461504
1755	88343	239504	1793	275745	475873
1756	91361	237813	1794	289708	464185
1757	94190	201359	1795	303054	435276
1758	97604	209281	1796	314966	425109
1759	99147	231142	1797	326556	489677
1760	101915	248951	1798	339854	521087
1761	105496	270095	1799	356587	486735
1762	110364	271892	1800	375868	375868

Year	Current premiums	Real premiums	Year	Current premiums	Real premiums
1801	406259	363568	1825	706615	790904
1802	436859	507832	1826	709502	840355
1803	460950	569644	1827	707414	896134
1804	490313	586952	1828	705757	920834
1805	510207	525637	1829	721882	951378
1806	520617	561078	1830	741425	1013798
1807	532648	584905	1831	755252	939269
1808	549980	583888	1832	781275	1049064
1809	563512	545413	1833	809301	1157094
1810	587277	551055	1834	834838	1293957
1811	609884	589203	1835	860367	1311474
1812	631721	539165	1836	892633	1225904
1813	648544	540281	1837	921531	1235278
1814	652657	622846	1838	952525	1268145
1815	662485	707644	1839	983456	1220170
1816	666825	777467	1840	1014957	1236732
1817	668227	686181	1841	1064811	1328471
1818	669967	686169	1842	1119404	1510858
1819	677751	711820	1843	1171811	1782745
1820	675420	782249	1844	1221832	1860653
1821	680451	896022	1845	1256213	1824361
1822	690242	1051127	1846	1263754	1764975
1823	703481	1003053	1847	1258510	1568883
1824	705158	926221	1848	1255386	1780262

Bibliography

Manuscript Sources

Blackburn Central Library: *Manchester Fire & Life Assurance,* B368, Blackburn Agency Policy and Endorsement Book, 1830-43.

Bristol Record Office: *Sun Insurance,* Ms 37165 (1/1-2), Bristol Agency Policy Books, 1820-34; Ms 37165 (1/12-13), Bath Sun Policy Books, 1826-44.

Cambridge University Library: Phoenix Assurance Archives, *Phoenix Assurance,* PX 302, Annual Summary, 1783-1877; PX 508, Annual Analysis of Business commencing 1810; PX 509, Statistical Analysis of the Company's Business, 1809-46; PX 1010, Agents' Extra Letter Book A, 1794-1833; PX 1759-73, Take over Files, Berkshire & Gloucestershire Provincial, 1831, East Kent & Canterbury Economic, 1828, Glasgow, 1811, Hertfordshire, Cambridgeshire & General Country, 1824, Metellus (West of Scotland), 1839, Manchester, 1788, Palladium, 1830, Reading, 1841, Salamander, 1835, Worcester, 1817.

Centre for Kentish Studies, Maidstone: *Kent Fire Office,* U2593/B1, Deed of Settlement, 1802; U2593/B6/1-9, Directors' Minutes, 1802-17; U2593/B12, Report of the Committee to investigate the Accounts, 1814; U2593/B15, Financial Summary, 1802-14; U2593/B16/1, Secretary's Statements, 1806-7; U2593/B37, Waste Transfers, 1805-11; U2593/B43, Pencil Copy of List of Statistics, 1815-93; U2593/B125, Rough List of Agents, 1809.

Gateshead Library: Cotesworth Mss, *Newcastle Fire Office,* CM/4/1-21, Accounts, 1809-22.

Guildhall Library, London: *Alliance Assurance,* Ms 12162A1-4, Directors Minutes 1824-49; Ms 12162B/1-4, Index to Directors' Minutes; Ms 14075/1-2, Ledgers, 1824-55. *Atlas Assurance,* Ms 16170/1-5, Directors' Minutes, 1807-36; Ms 16174/2, Ledger no.2, 1839-45. *Essex & Suffolk Fire Office,* Ms 16206/1-3, Minute Books, 1802-45. *Globe Insurance,* Ms 11657, Instructions to Agents, 1857; Ms 11674/1, Ledger, 1803-10; Ms 11679, Policy Register, 1823-7. *Guardian Assurance,* Ms 14281/1-4, Directors' Minutes, 1821-34; Ms 18099, List of Voting Proprietors, 1824; Ms 18100, Register of Probates of Shareholders, 1823-63; Ms 18102/1, Annual Account Book, 1822-45; Ms 18106, Fire Ledger, 1821-67; Ms 18107, Fire Journal A, 1821-32; Ms 18111, Agents' and Local Committees Lists, 1821-62. *Hand-in-Hand Fire Office,* Ms 8670, General Letter Book, 1752-1842; Ms 8666/10-28, Directors' Minutes, 1727-1800; *Imperial Insurance,* Ms 12160A/1-15, Directors' Minutes, 1803-46; Ms 18274, Tabular Statements, 1803-1901. *London Assurance,* Ms 8728/7-15, Directors' Minutes, 1754-1800; Ms 8730/2, General Court Minutes, 1753-98; Ms 8735/1-6, Fire Committee Minutes, 1725-1806; Ms 8744/1, Fire Charter Journal A, 1721-85; Ms 8746A Fire Assurance Annual Account, 1721-1854; Ms 8746/1, Fire Charter Ledger A, 1722-1803; Ms 8747/2, Fire Policy Register, 1760-1; Ms 8749A/2, Fire-Marine Accounts (Balance Sheets), 1727-1834; Ms 8755/2, Out Letter Book, 1751-1805; Ms 15025, Extracts from the Minutes of the Fire Committee, 1725-1824; Ms 18822, Notes and Memoranda concerning the Need to improve the Fire Insurance Business, 1792-1830; Ms 18833,

Miscellaneous Letters, Policies etc, 1745-1830. *Manchester Fire & Life Assurance*, Ms 16217, Deed of Settlement, 1824; Ms 16223/1, General Court Minutes, 1825-46; Ms 16222/2-8, Directors' Minutes, 1825-46. *Sun Insurance*, Ms 11931/2-8, General Committee Minutes, 1715-1808; Ms 11932/1-15, Committee of Management Minutes, 1725-1800; Ms 11933/5, Committee of Accounts Minutes, 1752-62; Ms 11933A, Book of Annual Accounts, 1791-1887; Ms 11935/1-14, Country Committee Minutes, 1730-1839; Ms 11935A/1, Report Books, 1804-47; Ms 11935E, Take over Papers, Old Bath, 1827, Bath Sun, 1827, 1838, Birmingham District, 1837, Bristol Crown, 1829-37, British, 1843, Coventry & Warwickshire, 1839, Glasgow, 1841; Hibernia, 1839, Leicester & Midlands, 1843; North & South Shields, 1836; Preston & North Lancashire, 1848, Salamander, 1835; Ms 11935J, Special Minute Book, 1807-52; Ms 11937/144-88, Fire Policy Registers - Country Series, 1823-30; Ms 11963/2-3 Office Ledgers, 1742-86; Ms 12019B, Accounts of Fire Claims, 1771-87; Ms 14116, Simplified Profit and Loss Accounts; Ms 14386, Agents' Bond Book, 1786; Ms 15032/1-8, Take over Papers, Bristol, 1840, Bristol Union, 1844, Caledonian, 1839, Essex Economic, 1838, Halifax & Bradford, 1845, Hercules, 1848, Liverpool, 1838-9, Newcastle, 1835-6, Newcastle & North of England, 1838, Sheffield, 1858, Shropshire & North Wales, 1844/54; Ms 15033, Take over Papers, East Kent & Canterbury Economic, 1828; Ms 15042/1, Quarterly Accounts and Balance Sheets, 1786-1812; Ms 15045, Duty Papers and Licences, 1782-1871; Ms 15047, Fire Offices discontinued up to Christmas 1848; Ms 18856, Agents' Accounts, 1786; Ms 18858, Notes and Letters concerning Premiums for Fire Insurance on Docks and Warehouses, 1842-70. *Union Fire Office*, Ms 14022/3-26, Directors' Minutes, 1721-1819.

Glasgow City Archives, Mitchell Library, *North British Insurance*, TD446/4/1, Annuity Statements no.1, 1825-45; TD446/4/2/1, Journal no.1, 1809-21; TD446/4/3/1, Ledger no.2, 1822-9; TD446/5/18/1, Directors' Minutes, 1809-21.

Goldsmith's Library, University of London: *West of England Fire Office*, GL 1829, Proposals and Rates, 1829.

GRE Archives, Lytham St.Annes: *Royal Exchange Assurance*, R 001, Early Records of Business, vol.1; R 008, Accountants Book, 1720-66; RED 305, Report of Home (London) Premiums, 1768-1907; REE 105, Accountants Book, 1766-1808; Domesday Book; Manuscript Balances, 1734, 1760.

Liverpool Record Office: Holt & Gregson Papers, Ms 942 Hol/10, Account of whole number of ships arrived at or sailed from Liverpool, 1709-91; Liverpool, London & Globe Archives, *Globe Insurance*, Box file AA, Directors' Minutes, 1799, Letter Book, 1809-10; Globe 1, Box Folder M, F.M. Eden to J. Bentham, 8 Sept. 1802, Prospectus, 1799; Globe 5, Circular, 1803; Globe 11, Box File G, Policy Form 1813.

Manchester City Archives, *Manchester Fire & Life Assurance,* L1/2/1/1-2, Fire Insurance Policy 16437, W. Eckroyd, 1830-31; *Phoenix Assurance*, L1/2/2/2-10, Fire Insurance Policy 461428, W. Eckroyd, 1820-29.

Merseyside Maritime Museum: Earle Papers, *Imperial Insurance*, Proposal Form, 1830.

Norwich Union, Norwich: *Norwich Union*, Directors' Minutes, vol.2, 1821-6.

Oldham Public Library: *West of England Fire Office*, Pamphlet TIV, Insurance Policy, Messrs Yeardley & Sinister, 1823.

Public Record Office: Chatham Papers, 30/8/187, fols.234-9, Hugh Watts to William Pitt, 22 June 1797; 30/8/277, fols.95-109, *Kent Fire Office*, Prospectus, 1802.

Royal Insurance plc, Leeds: *Leeds & Yorkshire Assurance*, Directors' Minutes, vol.2, 1843-55; Resolutions passed at the General Meeting of the Proposed Shareholders, 1824.

Shropshire Record Office: Eyton Collection, Ms 665/339, Eyton, Reynolds and Bishop, Articles of Co-partnership, 1792; Ms 665/476, List of Original Proprietors in the Shrewsbury Canal, 1793. *Salop Fire Office*, Ms 3008/1/1/1-4, Articles of Agreement, 1780-1822; Ms 3008/1/1/58, General Meeting Book, 1780-1858; Ms 3008/1/2/1, Directors' Minutes, 1780-94; Ms 3008/1/2/10-11, Income and Capital Account Books, 1780-1873; Ms 3008/1/4/7, List of Proprietors; Ms 3008/1/4/16/1-225, Share Assignments, 1783-1864; Ms 3008/1/4/17/1-28, Share Transfers, 1803-13, 1837-44; Ms 4791/1/1-2, Policy Books, nos.1-2, 1780-92.

Sun Alliance plc, London: *County Fire Office*, Deed of Constitution, 1808; Instructions to Agents, 1807, 1810, 1824; Agents' Circulars, 1809, 1810, 1811; Order for the Insurance of a Mill (specimen), 1824; Mill Rates, 1809, 1813, 1824; Annual Accounts, 1807-46; Minutes of County Meetings, 1807-25; Bedford Agency Policy Register, 1808-30; Directors' (Fair) London Minutes, vols A-E, 1807-36; Letter Book 'M', 1821-22; Special Letters, 1831-64.

Westminster City Archives, Victoria Library, *Westminster Fire Office*, Ms 343/75-76, General Court Minutes, 1717-98; Ms 343/1, 16-17, Directors' Minutes, 1717-21, 1780-87; Ms 343/81, Day Book, 1790-93; Ms 343/83-6, General Account Books 1759-94; Ms 343/87-8, Account Books, 1782-1855; Ms 343/89, Stock Book, 1812-62; Ms 343/112/2, Rate Book, 1803; Ms 343/112/54, Secretary's Address to the Board of Directors, 13 Dec. 1866.

West Yorkshire Archive Service, Sheepscar, Leeds: *Leeds & Yorkshire Assurance*, acc.3393, box 41, Secretary's Letter Book, 1824-9.

Primary Printed (place of publication London, unless otherwise stated)

Official Publications

Coode, G., 'Report on Fire Insurance Duties', *PP* (1857) III, 643.

Coode, G., 'Revised Report on Fire Insurance Duties', *PP* (1863) XXVI, 27.

Lambert, S. ed., *House of Commons Sessional Papers of the Eighteenth Century* (Wilmington, Delaware, 1975).

'Abstract of the Answers and Returns to the Population Act 41 Geo.III c.1800', *PP* (1801-2) VI, 1.

'Accounts respecting the Income Duty', *PP* (1801-2) IV, 155.

'An Account of all Sums paid into the Stamp Office for Duty on Insurance from Fire, in London and in the Country', 1822/3 to 1845, *PP* (1824) XVII, 495; *PP* (1825) XXI, 105; *PP* (1826) XXII, 21; *PP* (1826-7) XVII, 37; *PP* (1828) XVI, 629; *PP* (1829) XV, 387; *PP* (1830) XXV, 551; *PP* (1831) XVII, 241; *PP* (1831-2) XXXIV, 377; *PP* (1833) XXXIII, 423; *PP* (1834) XLI, 315; *PP* (1835) XXXVII, 691; *PP* (1836) XLV, 223; *PP* (1837) XXXIX, 273; *PP* (1837-8) XXXVI, 297; *PP* (1839) XXX, 375; *PP* (1840) XXIX, 445; *PP* (1841) XIII, 361; *PP* (1842) XXVI, 459; *PP* (1843) XXX, 427; *PP* (1844) XXXII, 353; *PP* (1845) XXVIII, 309; *PP* (1846) XXV, 363.

'An Account showing the Gross produce of the Duties on Stamps on Fire Insurance in Great Britain, 1790-1821', *PP* (1821) XVI, 361.

'Census of Great Britain 1841, Population: Occupation Abstract', *PP* (1844) XXVII, 1.

'Census of Great Britain 1851, Population: Occupations', *PP* (1851) LXXXVIII, part I.

'Census of Ireland for 1851, General Report', *PP* (1856) XXXI, 620.

'Census of Ireland for 1851', *PP* (1852-3) XCI, 44.

'Comparative Account of the Population of Great Britain in 1801, 1811, 1821 and 1831',
   PP (1831) XVIII, 1.

Factory Inspectors' Reports, Report of R.J. Saunders, *PP* (1839), XIX, 442-6.

General Index of the House of Commons Journals, vols.56-75 (1801-20).

House of Commons Journals, 34 (1772-4), 68 (1812-13).

'Report of the Commissioners appointed to take the Census of Ireland for 1841', *PP* (1843)
   XXLV, 1.

'Report of the Commissioners of Inland Revenue on the Duties under their Management',
   PP (1870) XX, 193.

'Report of John Finlaison, Actuary of the National Debt, on the Evidence and Elementary
   Facts on which the Tables of Life Annuities are founded', *PP* (1829) III, 288.

Returns of Mills and Factories, *PP* (1839) XLII, 1.

Royal Commission on the Employment of Children in Factories, *PP* (1833) XX, Leeds
   evidence before Drinkwater, C1, 65-134, Leeds evidence before Power, C2, 29-62; *PP*
   (1834) XX, Supplementary Report, pt.II, C1.

Select Committee to inquire into the Effect of the Alterations made in the Laws regulating
   the Interest on Money, *PP* (1845) XII, 339.

Select Committee on the Usury Laws, *PP* (1818) VI, 139.

Special Reports of the Inspectors of Factories, *PP* (1841) X, 199-274.

Trade Directories

Holden's Triennial Directory of London, 1808.

Kent's Directory for London, 1761, 1763, 1771.

Lewis's Liverpool Directory, 1790.

Pigot's Directory of Manchester and Salford, (Manchester 1838).

Post Office Directory of London, 1807.

Universal British Directory, 1797.

Newspapers and Periodicals

Annual Register, 1758-80, 1805.

Aris's Birmingham Gazette, 1805.

Assecuranz Jahrbuch, vol.1 (Vienna, 1880).

Assurance Magazine, vols. I-XI (1851 - 1863-64).

Bath Herald, 1798.

Berrow's Worcester Journal, 1790.

Billinge's Liverpool Advertiser, 1795.

Cowdray's Manchester Gazette and Weekly Advertiser, 1824.

Gentleman's Magazine, 1731-1841.

Insurance Yearbook, 1981-82.

Jahrbuch für das gesamte Versicherungswesen in Deutschland, vols.1-5 (Frankfurt, 1864-
8).

Kentish Gazette, 1828

Leeds Mercury, 1777-82.

London Magazine, 1732-80.

London Chronicle, 1757.

Manchester Mercury, 1771-88.
Newcastle Chronicle, 1783-84.
Newcastle Courant, 1783-85.
Newcastle Journal, 1783, 1787.
Reading Chronicle, 1841.
Post Magazine and Insurance Monitor, 1883.
Prescott's Manchester Journal, 1777.
Salopian Journal, 1794-6, 1806
Shrewsbury Chronicle, 1779-81.
Sigma, 1973, 1993.
Wheeler's Manchester Chronicle, 1824.
Williamson's Liverpool Advertiser, 1776-95.

Miscellaneous printed primary sources and contemporary (pre-1900) literature

Anderson, A., *An Historical and Chronological Deduction of the Origin of Commerce*, 4 vols., (1764, revised edn., 1787-9).

Angiolini, L., *Lettere sull' Inghilterra* (Milan, 1790).

Anon, *Fire Insurance Guide: An Impartial Guide to the Best and Cheapest Insurance against Fire* (1822).

Anon, 'Observations on the Duties on Insurance', *Edinburgh Review*, 55 (1832), pp.527-30, reprinted in D.T. Jenkins and T. Yoneyama eds., *History of Insurance*, vol.1, (2000), pp.311-14.

Ashcrott, P.F. and Preston-Thomas, H., *The English Poor Law System, Past and Present* (1888).

Ashfield, A. ed., *Romantic Women Poets 1770-1838: An Anthology* (Manchester, 1995).

Association for the Abolition or Reduction of the Duty on Fire Insurance, *The Fire Insurance Duty! History of the Agitation for Abolition or Reduction and Reply to Mr George Coode's Blue-Book Revised Report, Showing the Duty to be Bad in Principle, Obstructive to the Progress of Insurance, and Opposed to the Public Interest* (1863).

Baines, E., *History, Directory and Gazeteer of the County Palatine of Lancaster* (1824, reprinted, Newton Abbot, 1968).

Birmingham Fire Office, *Copy of the Deed of the Birmingham Fire Office*, (Birmingham, 1806).

Blake, W., *The Complete Poetry and Prose of William Blake*, ed. D.V. Erdman (New York, 1988).

Boswell, J., *The Life of Samuel Johnson* (1791, Harmondsworth, 1986).

Boulton and Watt, *The Selected Papers of Boulton and Watt - volume 1, The Engine Partnership, 1775-1825*, ed. J. Tann (1981).

British Linen Company, *The British Linen Company, 1745-1775*, ed. A.J.Durie, Scottish History Society, 5th series, vol.9 (Edinburgh, 1996).

Brown, S., 'On the Progress of Fire Insurance in Great Britain, as compared with other Countries', *Assurance Magazine* , VII (1858), pp.259-72.

Brown, W., *Early Days in a Dundee Mill 1819-23: Extracts from the Diary of William Brown, an Early Dundee Spinner*, ed. J. Hume, Dundee Abertay Historical Society Publication no.2 (Dundee, 1980).

Burke, E., *The Correspondence of Edmund Burke, vol.VII, 1792-4*, eds. P.J. Marshall and J.A. Woods (Cambridge 1968).

Cobbett, W., *Parliamentary History of England*, XXII (1781-2), XXXIII-VI (1797-1803).

Cobbett, W., *Rural Rides* (Harmondsworth, 1967).

Crabbe, G., *George Crabbe: The Complete Poetical Works*, vol.II, ed. N. Dalrymple-Champneys (Oxford, 1988).

Crossley, D. and Saville, R. eds., *The Fuller Letters: Guns, Slaves and Finance, 1728-1755*, Sussex Record Society, vol.76 (Lewes, 1991).

Cunnington, B.H. ed., *Some Annals of the Borough of Devizes: being a Series of Extracts from the Corporation's Records, 1791-1835* (Devizes, 1926).

Defoe, D., *A Tour through the Whole Island of Great Britain* (Harmondsworth, 1971).

Dickens, C., *The Life and Adventures of Martin Chuzzlewit* (1843-4, Thomas Nelson edn., 1912).

Dickens, C., *Sketches by Boz* (Odhams edn., n.d.).

Dickens, C., *Hard Times* (1854, Penguin edn., Harmondsworth, 1969).

Dodson, J., *Arithmetique Made Easie* (1760).

Eden, F.M., *Observations on Friendly Societies* (1801).

Eland, G. ed., *Purefoy Letters, 1735-1753*, 2 vols., (1931).

Engels, F., *The Condition of the Working Class in England* (1844, Panther edn., St Albans, 1969).

English, H., *A Complete View of the Joint-Stock Companies formed during the Years 1824 and 1825* (1827).

George, Prince of Wales, *The Correspondence of George, Prince of Wales, 1770-1812*, vol.VI, ed. A. Aspinall (1969).

Gordon, W., *The Universal Accountant and Complete Merchant*, 2 vols. (2nd edn., Edinburgh, 1765).

Gray, T., *The Letters of Thomas Gray*, ed. D.C. Tovey, 3 vols. (1900-12).

Green, V., *The History and Antiquities of the City and Suburbs of Worcester* (1796).

Grindon, L.H., *Manchester Banks and Bankers* (Manchester, 1878).

Hamon, G., *Histoire Générale de l'Assurance en France et à l'Étranger* (Paris, 1896).

Hatton, E., *A New View of London*, 2 vols. (1708).

Hoyle, E., *An Essay Towards Making the Doctrine of Chances Easy to Those Who Understand Vulgar Arithmetic Only* (1761).

Hutton, C., *The Schoolmaster's Guide: or, A Complete System of Practical Arithmetic* (2nd edn., Newcastle, 1766).

Laxton, P., *The A to Z of Regency England* (Lympne Castle, 1985).

Lonsdale, R., *The New Oxford Book of Eighteenth Century Verse* (Oxford, 1984).

Magens, N., *Essay on Insurance* (Hamburg, 1755).

Marshall, S., *A Treatise on the Law of Insurance* (1st American edn., Boston, 1805).

Mortimer,T., *Everyman his own Broker* (1761, 13th edn., 1801).

Oakes, J., *The Oakes Diaries*, 2 vols., (Suffolk Record Society, 1990), ed. J. Fiske.

Park, J.A., *A System of the Law of Marine Insurances with Three Chapters on Bottomry; on Insurances on Lives; and on Insurances against Fire* (1786, 4th edn., 1800).

Peet, H. ed., *Liverpool Vestry Books*, vol.1, *1681-1834* (1912).

Phillips, M., *A History of Banks, Bankers and Banking in Northumberland, Durham and North Yorkshire* (1894).

Place, F., *The Autobiography of Francis Place* ed. M. Thale (Cambridge, 1972).

Relton, F.B., *An Account of the Fire Insurance Companies, Associations, Institutions, Projects and Schemes established and projected in Great Britain and Ireland during the 17th and 18th Centuries* (1893).

Sheridan, R.B., *The Letters of Richard Brinsley Sheridan*, vol.III, ed. C. Price (Oxford, 1966).

Sinclair, J., *A History of the Public Revenue of Great Britain*, vol.III (1784).

Smith, A., *An Inquiry into the Nature and Causes of the Wealth of Nations*, 2 vols., eds. R.H. Campbell und A.S. Skinner (Oxford, 1976).

Smith, F.G., *Practical Remarks on the Present State of Fire Insurance Business* (Edinburgh, 1832).

Smith, J.T., *Nollekens and his Times* (1828, reprinted 1949).

Smollett, T., *The Expedition of Humphrey Clinker* (1771, Oxford, 1966).

Southey, R., *Letters from England*, ed. J. Simmons (1951).

Stevens, R., *Essay on Average* (1822), reprinted in D.T. Jenkins and T. Yoneyama, eds., *History of Insurance*, vol.2, (2000), pp.3-158.

Sun Fire Office, 'Instructions for the Agents of Sun Fire Office' (1807), reprinted in D.T. Jenkins and T. Yoneyama, eds., *History of Insurance*, vol.1, (2000), pp.251-93.

Tipping, W.A., 'America as a Fire Insurance Field', *Transactions of the Insurance and Actuarial Society of Glasgow*, 4th series, no.3 (1897), pp.54-70.

Tocqueville, A.de., *Democracy in America*, ed. R. Heffner (New York, 1956).

Torrington, *The Torrington Diaries: containing the Tours through England and Wales of the Hon. John Byng between the years 1781 and 1794*, ed. C.B. Andrews, 4 vols. (1934-8).

Walford, C., *Insurance Cyclopedia*, vols.I-V (1871-8).

Walford, C., 'Fires and Fire Insurance Considered under their Historical, Financial, Statistical and National Aspects', *Journal of the Royal Statistical Society*, (Sept. 1877), pp.347-432.

Walpole, H., *The Yale Edition of Horace Walpole's Correspondence*, ed. W.S. Lewis (1967).

Wetenhall, J., *The Course of the Exchange* (1720-1850).

Secondary Literature (post-1900) (place of publication London, unless otherwise stated)

Alford, B.W.E., *W.D. & H.O. Wills and the Development of the UK Tobacco Industry, 1786-1965* (1973).

Alford, B.W.E. and Barker, T.C., *A History of the Carpenters Company* (1969).

Allen, R.C., 'The Price of Freehold Land and the Interest Rate in the Seventeenth and Eighteenth centuries', *Economic History Review*, XLI (1988), pp.33-49.

Anderson, B.L., 'The Attorney and the Early Capital Market in Lancashire', in J.R. Harris ed., *Liverpool and Merseyside: Essays in the Economic and Social History of the Port and its Hinterland* (1969), pp.50-77.

Anderson, B.L., ''Financial Institutions and the Capital Market on Merseyside in the Eighteenth and Nineteenth Centuries', in B.L. Anderson and P.J.M. Storey eds., *Commerce, Industry and Transport: Studies in Economic Change on Merseyside* (Liverpool, 1983), pp.26-59.

Anderson, J.L., *Explaining Long-term Economic Change* (Cambridge, 1995).

Archer, I.W., *The History of the Haberdashers' Company* (Chichester, 1991).

Archer, J.E., *By a Flash and a Scare: Incendiarism, Animal Maiming and Poaching in East Anglia, 1815-1870* (Oxford, 1990).

Armstrong, D., 'A History of the Property Insurance Business in the United States prior to 1890', (unpublished D.Phil. thesis, New York University, 1971).

Arnold, D., 'Hunger in the Garden of Plenty: The Bengal Famine of 1770', in A. Johns, ed., *Dreadful Visitations: Confronting Natural Catastrophe in the Age of Enlightenment* (1999), pp.81-111.

Arps, L., *Auf Sicheren Pfeilern: Deutsche Versicherungswirtschaft vor 1914* (Göttingen, 1965).

Arrow, K.J., 'The Economics of Moral Hazard: Further Comment', *American Economic Review*, 58 (1968), pp.537-9.

Ashton, T.S., *Iron and Steel in the Industrial Revolution* (1924, 4th edn., 1968).

Ashton, T.S., *Economic Fluctuations in England 1700-1800* (Oxford, 1959).

Ashworth, W., *The Genesis of Modern British Town Planning* (1954).

Ayres, J., *Building the Georgian City* (New Haven, 1998).

Baer, M., *Theatre and Disorder in Late Georgian London* (Oxford, 1992).

Bagwell, P.S., *The Transport Revolution from 1770* (1974).

Baker, A.M., 'Liberalization of Trade in Services - The World Insurance Industry', in O. Giarini ed., *The Emerging Service Economy* (Geneva, 1987), pp.193-211.

Baranoff, D., 'Principals, Agents and Control in the American Fire Insurance Industry, 1799-1872', *Business and Economic History*, 27 (1998), pp.91-101.

Barker, T.C., *Pilkington Brothers and the Glass Industry* (1960).

Barnett, D., *London, Hub of the Industrial Revolution: A Revisionary History, 1775-1825* (1998).

Beaumont, D.A., *Barber Beaumont* (1999).

Beck, U., *Risikogesellschaft: Auf dem Weg in eine andere Moderne* (Frankfurt/Main, 1986).

Beckett, J.V., *The Aristocracy in England 1660-1914* (Oxford, 1986).

Begg, D., Fischer, S. and Dornbusch, R., *Economics* (6th edn., Maidenhead, 2000).

Beresford, M.W., *The Leeds Chambers of Commerce* (Leeds, 1951).

Beresford, M.W., 'The Back to Back House in Leeds, 1787-1937', in S.D. Chapman, ed., *The History of Working Class Housing: A Symposium* (1971), pp.93-132.

Beresford, M.W., 'The Making of a Townscape: Richard Paley in the East End of Leeds, 1771-1803', in C.W. Chalklin and M.A. Havinden, eds., *Rural Change and Urban Growth 1500-1800* (1974), pp.281-320.

Beresford, M.W., 'The Face of Leeds, 1780-1914', in D.Fraser, ed., *A History of Modern Leeds* (Manchester, 1980), pp.72-112.

Beresford, M.W., 'Prometheus Insured: The Sun Fire Agency in Leeds during Urbanisation, 1716-1826', *Economic History Review*, XXXV, (1982), pp.373-89.

Beresford, M.W., 'East End, West End: The Face of Leeds during Urbanisation 1684-1842', *Publications of the Thoresby Society*, LX & LXI, nos.131-2, (1985-6).

Berg, M., *The Age of Manufactures, 1700-1820* (1985).

Berg, M., 'Commerce and Creativity in Eighteenth-Century Birmingham', in M. Berg, ed., *Markets and Manufacture in Early Industrial Europe* (London, 1991), pp.173-204.

Bernstein, P.L., *Against the Gods: The Remarkable Story of Risk* (New York, 1996).

Blackstone, G.V., *A History of the British Fire Service* (1957).

Boot, H.M., *The Commercial Crisis of 1847*, University of Hull, Occasional Papers in Economic and Social History, no.11 (Hull, 1984).

Boot, H.M., 'Real Incomes of the British Middle Class, 1760-1850: the Experience of Clerks at the East India Company', *Economic History Review*, LII (1999), pp.638-68.

Borch, K., *The Mathematical Theory of Insurance* (Lexington, Mass., 1974).

Borch, K.H., *Economics of Insurance* (Amsterdam, 1990).

Borsay, P., *The English Urban Renaissance: Culture and Society in the Provincial Town, 1660-1770* (Oxford, 1989).

Boyd, W., *An Ice-Cream War* (Harmondsworth, 1983).

Boyson, R., *The Ashworth Cotton Enterprise* (Oxford, 1970).

Brett, P.D., 'The Newcastle Election of 1830', *Northern History*, 24 (1988), pp.101-23.

Brewer, J., *The Sinews of Power: War, Money and the English State, 1688-1783* (1989).

Brewer J. and Porter, R. eds., *Consumption and the World of Goods* (1993).

Brown, P.C., 'Fire Insurance in Liverpool', *Transactions of the Historic Society of Lancashire and Cheshire*, 78, n.s. vol.42 (1926), pp.3-20.

Buchanan, B., 'Aspects of Capital Formation: Some Insights from North Somerset, 1750-1830', *Southern History*, 8 (1986), pp.73-93.

Burnett, J., *A Social History of Housing 1815-1985* (2nd edn, 1986).

Butt, J., 'The Scottish Cotton Industry during the Industrial Revolution, 1780-1840', in L.M. Cullen and T.C. Smout, eds., *Comparative Aspects of Scottish and Irish Economic and Social History 1600-1900* (Edinburgh, 1975), pp.116-28.

Butt, J., 'Housing', in R.A.Cage, ed., *The Working Class in Glasgow 1750-1914* (1987), pp.29-55.

Cain, P.J., and Hopkins, A.G., *British Imperialism: Innovation and Expansion 1688-1914* (1993).

Cairncross, A.K. and Weber, B., 'Fluctuations in Building in Great Britain, 1785-1849', in E.M. Carus-Wilson, ed., *Essays in Economic History*, vol.3, (1962), pp.318-33.

Cameron, R., 'England', in R. Cameron, ed., *Banking in the Early Stages of Industrialisation* (1967), pp.15-59.

Campbell, S., 'Usury and Annuities of the Eighteenth Century', *Law Quarterly Review*, CLXXVI (1928), pp.473-91.

Campbell, W.A., 'Gas Lighting in Newcastle', *Archaeologia Aeliana*, 5th series, XIII (1985), pp.197-201.

Cannadine, D., 'Aristocratic Indebtedness in the Nineteenth Century: The Case Re-Opened', *Economic History Review*, XXX, (1977), pp.624-50.

Carter, A., 'Analysis of Public Indebtedness in Eighteenth-Century England', *Bulletin of the Institute of Historical Research*, 24 (1951), pp.173-81.

Carter, R.L., 'The Economics of Insurance', *CII Journal*, 65 (1968), pp.193-223.

Cato Carter, E.F., *Order out of Chaos: A History of the Loss-adjusting Profession, part I* (Chartered Institute of Loss Adjusters, 1984).

Chalklin, C.W., *The Provincial Towns of Georgian England: A Study of the Building Process 1740-1820* (1974).

Chalklin, C.W. and Havinden, M.A. eds., *Rural Change and Urban Growth 1500-1800* (1974).

Chaloner, W.H. and Marshall, J.D., 'Major John Cartwright and the Revolution Mill, East Retford, Nottinghamshire, 1788-1806', in N.B. Harte and K.G. Ponting, eds., *Textile History and Economic History* (Manchester, 1973), pp.281-303.

Chambers, J.D., 'Three Essays on the Population and Economy of the Midlands', in D.V. Glass and D.E.C. Eversley eds., *Population in History* (1965), pp.308-53.

Chapman, S.D., 'Fixed Capital Formation in the British Cotton Industry, 1770-1815', *Economic History Review*, 23 (1970), pp.235-66.

Chapman, S.D., 'Fixed Capital Formation in the British Cotton Manufacturing Industry', in J.P.P. Higgins and S. Pollard eds., *Aspects of Capital Investment in Great Britain 1750-1850* (1971), pp.57-119.

Chapman, S.D. ed., *The History of Working Class Housing: A Symposium* (1971).

Chapman, S.D., 'Working Class Housing in Nottingham during the Industrial Revolution', in S.D. Chapman, ed., *The History of Working Class Housing: A Symposium* (1971), pp.135-63.

Chapman, S.D., 'The Devon Cloth Industry in the Eighteenth Century: Sun Fire Office Inventories of Merchants' and Manufacturers' Property, 1726-1770', *Devon and Cornwall Record Society*, n.s., 23 (1978).

Chapman, S.D. and Butt, J., 'The Cotton Industry 1775-1856', in C.H. Feinstein and S. Pollard, eds., *Studies in Capital Formation in the United Kingdom 1750-1920* (Oxford, 1988), pp.105-25.

Chapman, S.D. and Chassagne, S., *European Textile Printers in the Eighteenth Century* (1981).

Clark, G(eoffrey), *Betting on Lives: The Culture of Life Insurance in England, 1695-1775* (Manchester, 1999).

Clark, G(regory)., 'Commons Sense: Common Property Rights, Efficiency and Institutional Change', *Journal of Economic History*, 58 (1998), pp.73-102.

Clark, G(regory)., 'Land Hunger: Land as a Commodity and as a Status Good, England, 1500-1910', *Explorations in Economic History*, 35 (1998), pp.59-82.

Clark, P. and Hosking J. eds., *Population Estimates of English Small Towns 1550-1851*, University of Leicester, Centre for Urban History, Working Paper no.5, (revised edn., Leicester, 1993).

Clarke, L., *Building Capitalism: Historical Change and the Labour Process in the Production of the Built Environment* (1992).

Clark-Kennedy, A.E., *The London: a Study in the Voluntary Hospital System, vol.1: 1740-1840* (1962).

Clay, C., 'The Price of Freehold Land in the later Seventeenth and Eighteenth Centuries', *Economic History Review*, XXVII (1974), pp.173-89.

Clayton, G., *British Insurance* (1971).

Clayton, G. and Osborne, W.T., *Insurance Company Investment: Principles and Policy* (1965).

Cockerell, H.A.L. and Green, E., *The British Insurance Business: A Guide to its History and Records* (1976, 2nd edn., Sheffield, 1994).

Coleman, D.C., *The British Paper Industry 1495-1860: A Study in Industrial Growth* (Oxford, 1958).

Colley, L., *Britons: Forging the Nation, 1707-1837* (1996).

Cope, S.R., 'The Stock Exchange Revisited: A New Look at the Market in Securities in London in the Eighteenth Century', *Economica*, 45 (1978), pp.1-21.

Corfield, P.J., *The Impact of English Towns 1700-1800* (Oxford, 1982).

Cornell, F.W., *The Principles and Finance of Fire Insurance* (1930).

Crafts, N.F.R., *British Economic Growth during the Industrial Revolution* (Oxford, 1985).

Crafts, N.F.R. and Harley, C.K., 'Output Growth and the Industrial Revolution: A Restatement of the Crafts-Harley View', *Economic History Review*, 45 (1992), pp.703-30.

Crick, C., 'The Origins and Development of Wallpaper', in *Historic Wallpapers in the Whitworth Art Gallery* (Exhibition Catalogue of the Collection of the Wallpaper Manufacturers Limited, Manchester, 1972), pp.6-14.

Cromar, P., 'The Coal Industry on Tyneside, 1715-1760', *Northern History*, 14 (1978), pp.193-207.

Cullen, L.M., *Anglo-Irish Trade, 1660-1800* (Manchester, 1968).

Cullen, L.M., 'Eighteenth Century Flour Milling in Ireland', *Irish Economic and Social History*, 4 (1977), pp.5-25.

Cullen, L.M. and Smout, T.C. eds., *Comparative Aspects of Scottish and Irish Economic and Social History 1600-1900* (Edinburgh, 1975).

Daston, L.J., 'The Domestication of Risk: Mathematical Probability and Insurance 1650-1830', in L. Krüger, L.J. Daston and M. Heidelberger, eds., *The Probabilistic Revolution, Volume 1: Ideas in History* (Cambridge, Mass., 1987), pp.237-60.

Daston, L.J., *Classical Probability in the Enlightenment* (Princeton, 1988).

Daunton, M.J., *Progress and Poverty: An Economic and Social History of Britain 1700-1850* (Oxford, 1995).

Davies, E.A., *An Account of the Formation and Early Years of the Westminster Fire Office* (1952).

Davison, C., *A History of British Earthquakes* (Cambridge, 1924).

Deane, P. and Cole, W.A., *British Economic Growth 1688-1959* (1962, 2nd edn., Cambridge 1967).

Deerr, N., *The History of Sugar*, 2 vols. (1950).

Devine, T.M., *The Tobacco Lords: A Study of the Tobacco Merchants of Glasgow and their Trading Activities, c.1740-90* (Edinburgh, 1975).

Devine, T.M., 'The Colonial Trades and Industrial Investment in Scotland, 1700-1815', *Economic History Review*, XXIX (1976), pp.1-13.

Dickson, P.G.M., *The Sun Insurance Office 1710-1960* (1960).

Dickson, P.G.M., *The Financial Revolution in England* (1967).

Dictionary of National Biography, vols.VI, IX, (1921-2).

Dietz, V.E., 'The Politics of Whisky: Scottish Distillers, the Excise, and the Pittite State', *Journal of British Studies*, 36 (1997), pp.35-69.

Donnachie, I., 'Sources of Capital and Capitalization in the Scottish Brewing Industry, c.1750-1830', *Economic History Review*, 30 (1977), pp.269-83.

Drew, B., *The London Assurance: A Second Chronicle* (1949).

Driver, F., *Power and Pauperism: The Workhouse System, 1834-1884* (Cambridge, 1993).

Dubois, A.B., *The English Business Company after the Bubble Act, 1720-1800* (New York, 1938).

Dunning, J.H., *Insurance in the Economy*, Institute of Economic Affairs, occasional paper, 34 (1971).

Dyer Simpson, J., *1936 Our Centenary Year* (privately printed, Liverpool, London & Globe Insurance Company Ltd, 1936).

Dyos, H.J. and Aldcroft, D.H., *British Transport: An Economic Survey from the Seventeenth Century to the Twentieth* (Leicester, 1969).

Earle, P., *The Making of the English Middle Class: Business, Society and Family Life in London, 1660-1730* (1989).

Falkus, M.E., 'The British Gas Industry before 1850', *Economic History Review*, XX (1967), pp.494-508.

Feinstein, C.H., 'National Statistics 1760-1920', in C.H. Feinstein and S. Pollard eds., *Studies in Capital Formation in the United Kingdom 1750-1920* (Oxford, 1988), pp.258-471.

Fisher, D., *The Industrial Revolution: A Macroeconomic Interpretation* (Basingstoke, 1992).

Flinn, M.W., *The History of the British Coal Industry, vol.2: 1700-1830, The Industrial Revolution* (Oxford, 1984).

Floud, R., and McCloskey, D.N., eds., *The Economic History of Britain since 1700*, 2 vols., (2nd edn., Cambridge, 1994).

Foreman-Peck, J., *A History of the World Economy* (Brighton, 1983).

Fowler, J. and Cornforth J., *English Decoration in the Eighteenth Century* (2nd edn., 1978).

Fraser, D. ed., *A History of Modern Leeds* (Manchester, 1980).

French, C.J., 'London's Overseas Trade with Europe 1700-1775', *Journal of European Economic History*, 23 (1994), pp.475-502.

French, H.R. and Hoyle, R.W., 'The Land Market of a Pennine Manor: Slaidburn, 1650-1780', *Continuity and Change*, 14 (1998), pp.349-84.

Frost, L., 'Coping In Their Own Way: Asian Cities and the Problem of Fires', *Urban History*, 24 (1997), pp.5-16.

Fukuyama, F., *Trust: The Social Virtues and the Creation of Prosperity* (Harmondsworth, 1996).

Gatrell, V.A.C., 'Labor, Power, and the Size of Firms in Lancashire Cotton in the Second Quarter of the Nineteenth Century', *Economic History Review*, XXX (1977), pp.95-129.

Gauldie, E., *Cruel Habitations: A History of Working Class Housing 1780-1918* (1974).

Gayer, A.D., Rostow, W.W. and Schwarz, A.J., *The Growth and Fluctuation of the British Economy 1790-1850*, 2 vols. (Oxford, 1953).

George, M.D., *London Life in the Eighteenth Century* (1966 edn.).

Gesellschaft für feuerversicherungsgeschichtliche Forschung, *Das Deutsche Feuerversicherungswesen*, 2 vols. (Hannover, 1913).

Gibb, A., *Glasgow: The Making of a City* (1983).

Ginarlis, J. and Pollard, S., 'Roads and Waterways, 1750-1850', in C.H. Feinstein and S. Pollard eds., *Studies in Capital Formation in the United Kingdom 1750-1920* (Oxford, 1988), pp. 182-224.

Grady, K., 'Profit, Property Interests, and Public Spirit: the Provision of Markets and Commercial Amenities in Leeds, 1822-29', *Publications of the Thoresby Society,* LIV (1976), miscellany 16, part 3, pp.165-95.

Grady, K., 'The Georgian Public Buildings of Leeds and the West Riding', *Publications of the Thoresby Society*, LXII, no.133 (1987).

Green, D.R., *From Artisans to Paupers: Economic Change and Poverty in London 1790-1870* (Aldershot, 1995).

Hadfield, C., *British Canals: An Illustrated History* (1950).

Hammond, J.L. and Hammond, B., *The Village Labourer, 1760-1832* (6th edn., 1978).

Hammond, J.L. and Hammond, B., *The Skilled Labourer* (2nd edn., 1979).

Hannah, L., 'Mergers in British Manufacturing Industry, 1880-1918', *Oxford Economic Papers*, 26 (1974), pp.1-20.

Harris, J.R., *The British Iron Industry 1700-1850* (1988).

Harris, J.R. and Roberts, R.O., 'Eighteenth Century Monopoly: The Cornish Metal Company Agreements of 1785', *Business History,* 5 (1962), pp.69-82.

Harris, R., *Industrializing English Law: Entrepreneurship and Business Organization, 1720-1844* (Cambridge, 2000).

Harrison, R.S., *Irish Insurance: Historical Perspectives, 1650-1939* (Skibbereen, 1992).

Harte, N.B. and Ponting, K.G. eds., *Textile History and Economic History* (Manchester, 1973).

Harvey, C., Green, E.M. and Corfield, P.J., 'Continuity, Change, and Specialization within Metropolitan London: the Economy of Westminster, 1750-1820', *Economic History Review*, LII (1999), pp.469-93.

Hawke, G., 'Reinterpretations of the Industrial Revolution', in P.K. O'Brien and R. Quinault eds., *The Industrial Revolution and British Society* (Cambridge, 1993), pp.54-78.

Hay, D., 'The State and the Market in 1800: Lord Kenyon and Mr Waddington', *Past & Present*, 162 (1999), pp.101-62.

Hay, D. and Snyder, F. eds., *Policing and Prosecution in Britain, 1750-1850* (Oxford 1989).

Hedley, W.P., *Northumberland Families*, 2 vols. (Society of Antiquaries, Newcastle, 1968).

Hobsbawm, E.J. and Rude, G., *Captain Swing* (1969).

Hodgson, J., 'Thomas Slack of Newcastle, Printer, 1723-1784, Founder of the "Newcastle Chronicle" ', *Archaeologia Aeliana*, 3rd series, XVII (1920), pp.145-52.

Holderness, B.A., 'Credit in a Rural Community, 1660-1800', *Midland History*, III (1975-6), pp.94-115.

Holdsworth, W.S., *A History of English Law*, vol.VI (1924).

Homer, S., *A History of Interest Rates* (New Brunswick, N.J., 1963).

Hope-Jones, A., *Income Tax in the Napoleonic Wars* (Cambridge, 1939).

Hoppit, J., *Risk and Failure in English Business 1700-1800* (Cambridge, 1987).

Hoppit, J., 'Political Arithmetic in Eighteenth-Century England', *Economic History Review*, XLIX (1996), pp.516-40.

Hoskins, W.G., *Industry, Trade and People in Exeter 1688-1800* (Manchester, 1935).

Howe, A., *The Cotton Masters, 1830-1860* (Oxford, 1984).

Hudson, P., 'The Regional Perspective', in P. Hudson ed., *Regions and Industries: A Perspective on the Industrial Revolution in Britain* (Cambridge, 1989), pp.5-38.

Hudson, P., *The Industrial Revolution* (1992).

Hunt, B.C., *The Development of the Business Corporation in England 1800-1867* (Cambridge, Mass., 1936).

Hurren, G., *Phoenix Renascent* (1973).

Hussey, C., *English Country Houses: Mid-Georgian 1760-1800* (Revised edn., 1963).

Hyde, F.E., *Liverpool and the Mersey: An Economic History of a Port, 1700-1970* (Newton Abbot, 1971).

Iredale, D.A., 'John and Thomas Marshall and the Society for Improving the British Salt Trade: An Example of Trade Regulation', *Economic History Review*, XX (1967), pp.79-93.

Jackman, W.T., *The Development of Transportation in Modern England* (1962).

Jackson, G., *Hull in the Eighteenth Century: A Study in Economic and Social History* (1972).

Jackson, J.F., *A Short History of the Newcastle upon Tyne and Gateshead Gas Company* (Newcastle, 1945).

Jackson, T.V., 'Personal Wealth in Late-Eighteenth-Century Britain', *Economic History Review*, 44 (1991), pp.319-27.

James, J.A., 'Personal Wealth Distribution in Late-Eighteenth-Century Britain', *Economic History Review*, 41 (1988), pp.543-65.

Jarvis, A., 'James Cropper, Liverpool Docks and the Liverpool & Manchester Railway', *Journal of Transport History*, 19 (1998), pp.18-32.

Jenkins, D.T., 'The Validity of the Factory Returns 1833-50', *Textile History*, 4 (1973), pp.26-46.

Jenkins, D.T., *The West Riding Wool Textile Industry 1770-1835: A Study of Fixed Capital Formation* (Edington, 1975).

Jenkins, D.T., 'The Practice of Insurance against Fire 1750-1840, and Historical Research', in O.M. Westall ed., *The Historian and the Business of Insurance* (Manchester, 1984), pp.9-38.

Jenkins, D.T., 'Indexes of the Fire Insurance Policies of the Sun Fire Office and the Royal Exchange Assurance, 1775-1787', (Economic & Social Research Council, mimeo, 1986).

Jenkins, D.T., 'The Wool Textile Industry 1780-1850', in C.H. Feinstein and S. Pollard eds., *Studies in Capital Formation in the United Kingdom 1750-1920* (Oxford, 1988), pp.126-40.

Jenkins, D.T. and Yoneyama, T. eds. *History of Insurance*, 8 vols. (2000).

John, A.H., 'Insurance Investment and the London Money Market of the 18th Century', *Economica*, 20 (1953), pp.137-58.

Johns, A. ed., *Dreadful Visitations: Confronting Natural Catastrophe in the Age of Enlightenment* (1999).

Jones, E.L. and Falkus, M.E., 'Urban Improvement and the English Economy in the Seventeenth and Eighteenth Centuries', *Research in Economic History*, 4 (1979), pp.193-233.

Jones, E.L., Porter, S., and Turner, M., *A Gazeteer of English Urban Fire Disasters, 1500-1900*, Historical Geography Research Papers no.13, (Norwich, 1984).

Jones, S.R.H., 'Price Associations and Competition in the British Pin Industry, 1814-40', *Economic History Review*, XXVI (1973), pp.237-53.

Jourdain, M., *English Interiors in Smaller Houses 1660-1830* (1923).

Keeson, C.A.G.C., 'Barber Beaumont', *East London Papers*, 3 (1960), pp.13-21.

Kendrick, T.D., *The Lisbon Earthquake* (1956).

King, P.J.R., 'Prosecution Associations and their Impact in Eighteenth-Century Essex', in D. Hay and F. Snyder eds., *Policing and Prosecution in Britain, 1750-1850* (Oxford, 1989), pp.171-207.

Knight, F.H., *Risk, Uncertainty and Profit* (1921, reprinted New York, 1964).

Knowles, C.C. and Pitt, P.H., *The History of Building Regulation in London, 1189-1972* (1972).

Kravis, I.B., Heston, A.W. and Summers, R., 'Real GDP Per Capita for more than One Hundred Countries', *Economic Journal*, 88 (1978), 215-42.

Kynaston, D., *The City of London: volume I – A World of its Own, 1815-1890* (1994).

Langford, P., *A Polite and Commercial People: England 1727-1783* (Oxford, 1989).

Langford, P., *Public Life and the Propertied Englishman, 1689-1798* (Oxford, 1991).

Langton, J., 'The Industrial Revolution and the Regional Geography of England', *Transactions of the Institute of British Geographers*, new series, 9 (1984), 145-67.

Law, C.M., 'Some Notes on the Urban Population of England and Wales in the Eighteenth Century', *Local Historian*, X (1972), 13-26.

Lawton, R., 'Population Mobility and Urbanization: Nineteenth-Century British Experience', in R. Lawton and R. Lee eds., *Urban Population Development in Western Europe from the Late Eighteenth to the Early Twentieth Century* (Liverpool, 1989), pp.149-77.

Lee, C. 'The Service Industries', in R. Floud and D.N. McCloskey eds., *The Economic History of Britain since 1700*, vol.2 (2nd edn., Cambridge, 1994), pp.117-44.

Lee, C.H., *The British Economy since 1700* (Cambridge 1986).

Lemaire, J., 'Borch's Theorem: A Historical Survey of Applications', in H. Loubergé ed., *Risk, Information and Insurance: Essays in Memory of Karl H.Borch* (Boston, Mass. 1991).

Levy, H., *Monopolies, Cartels and Trusts in British Industry* (1909, 1st English edn., 1927).

Lippman, S.A. and McCall, J.J., 'The Economics of Uncertainty: Selected Topics and Probabilistic Methods', in K.J. Arrow and M.D. Intriligator eds., *Handbook of Mathematical Economics*, vol.1 (Amsterdam, 1981), pp.211-84.

Little, A.J., *Deceleration in the Eighteenth Century British Economy* (1976).

Lloyd, S., '"Pleasure's Golden Bait": Prostitution, Poverty and the Magdalen Hospital in Eighteenth-Century London', *History Workshop Journal*, 41 (1996), pp.51-70.

Lloyd-Jones, R. and Lewis, M.J., *Manchester and the Age of the Factory* (1988).

Maddala, G.S., *Introduction to Econometrics* (2nd edn., Englewood Cliffs, New Jersey, 1992).

Mansel, P., *Constantinople: City of the World's Desire, 1453-1924* (Harmondsworth, 1995).

Marshall, J.M., 'Insurance Theory: Reserves versus Mutuality', *Economic Inquiry*, 12 (1974), pp.476-92.

Mathias, P., *The Brewing Industry in England 1700-1830* (Cambridge, 1959).

Mathias, P., *The First Industrial Nation: An Economic History of Britain 1700-1914* (1969).

Mathias, P., *The Transformation of England: Essays in the Economic and Social History of England in the Eighteenth Century* (1979).

Mathias, P., 'The Lawyer as Businessman in Eighteenth-Century England', in D.C. Coleman and P. Mathias eds., *Enterprise and History: Essays in Honour of Charles Wilson* (Cambridge, 1984), pp.151-67.

Mathias, P., 'The Industrial Revolution: Concept and Reality', in P. Mathias and J.A. Davis eds., *The First Industrial Revolutions* (Oxford, 1989), pp.1-24.

Mathias, P., 'Agriculture and Industrialization', in P. Mathias and J.A. Davis eds., *The First Industrial Revolutions* (Oxford, 1989), pp.101-26.

McKendrick, N., 'Josiah Wedgwood and the Commercialization of the Potteries', in N. McKendrick, J. Brewer and J.H. Plumb, *The Birth of a Consumer Society: The Commercialization of Eighteenth Century England* (1982), pp.100-45.

McLynn, F.J., *The Jacobite Army in England, 1745: The Final Campaign* (Edinburgh, 1983).

Michie, R.C., *Money, Mania and Markets: Investment, Company Formation and the Stock Exchange in Nineteenth-Century Scotland* (Edinburgh, 1981).

Michie, R.C., *The London and New York Stock Exchanges, 1850-1914* (1987).

Michie, R.C., 'The Rise and Rise of a Global Financial Centre: The City of London since 1700', (Inaugural lecture, University of Durham, Dept. of History, 25 Nov. 1999).

Middlebrook, S., *Newcastle upon Tyne: Its Growth and Achievement* (Newcastle, 1950).

Miles, M., 'The Money Market in the Early Industrial Revolution: The Evidence from West Riding Attorneys, c.1750-1800', *Business History*, XXIII (1981), pp.127-46.

Minchinton, W.E., *The Trade of Bristol in the Eighteenth Century*, Bristol Record Society Publications, vol.XX (Bristol, 1957).

Minchinton, W.E., 'The Economic History and Industrial Archaeology of Devon since 1700', in F. Barlow ed., *Exeter and its Region* (Exeter, 1969), pp.175-93.

Mirowski, P., 'The Rise (and Retreat) of a Market: English Joint-Stock Shares in the Eighteenth Century', *Journal of Economic History*, 41 (1981), pp. 559-77.

Mirowski, P., *The Birth of the Business Cycle* (New York, 1985).

Mitchell, B.R. and Deane, P., *Abstract of British Historical Statistics* (Cambridge, 1962).

Mitchell, B.R., *British Historical Statistics* (Cambridge, 1988).

Mokyr, J., *The Lever of Riches: Technological Creativity and Economic Progess* (Oxford, 1990).

Mokyr, J., 'Editor's Introduction: The New Economic History and the Industrial Revolution', in J. Mokyr ed., *The British Industrial Revolution: An Economic Perspective* (Boulder, 1993), pp.1-131.

Morgan, C.J., 'Demographic Change 1771-1911', in D. Fraser ed., *A History of Modern Leeds* (Manchester, 1980), pp.46-71.

Morgan, E.V. and Thomas, W.A., *The Stock Exchange: Its History and Functions* (1962).

Morris, R.J., *Class, Sect and Party: The Making of the British Middle Class, Leeds 1820-1850* (Manchester, 1990).

Mulhearn, R.M., 'Police and Pilferers at the Port of Liverpool, 1800-1850', *International Journal of Maritime History*, 11 (1999), pp. 149-61.

Neal, L., 'The Finance of Business during the Industrial Revolution', in R. Floud and D.N. McCloskey eds., *The Economic History of Britain since 1700*, vol.1 (2nd edn., Cambridge, 1994), pp.151-81.

Neal, L., *The Rise of Financial Capitalism: International Capital Markets in the Age of Reason* (Cambridge, 1990).

Neale, R.S., *Bath 1680-1850: A Social History* (1981).

Noakes, A., *The County Fire Office 1807-1957: A Commemorative History* (1957).

North, D.C., *Institutions, Institutional Change and Economic Performance* (Cambridge, 1990).

North, D.C., *Understanding the Process of Economic Change*, IEA, occasional paper 106, (1999).

O'Brien, G., *The Economic History of Ireland in the Eighteenth Century* (1st edn. 1919, reprinted Philadelphia, 1977).

O'Brien, P., 'Agriculture and the Home Market for English Industry 1660-1820', *English Historical Review*, C (1985), pp.773-800.

O'Brien, P.K., 'British Incomes and Property in the Early Nineteenth Century', *Economic History Review*, XII (1959), pp.255-67.

O'Brien, P.K., 'The Political Economy of British Taxation, 1660-1815', *Economic History Review*, XLI (1988), pp.1-32.

O'Brien, P.K., 'Introduction: Modern Conceptions of the Industrial Revolution', in P.K. O'Brien and R. Quinault eds., *The Industrial Revolution and British Society* (Cambridge, 1993), pp.1-30.

O'Brien, P.K., 'Central Government and the Economy, 1688-1815', in R. Floud and D.N. McCloskey eds., *The Economic History of Britain since 1700*, vol.1 (2nd edn., Cambridge, 1994), pp.205-41.

Offer, A., 'Farm Tenure and Land Values in England, c.1750-1950', *Economic History Review*, XLIV (1991), pp.1-20.

Orbell, J., 'The Corn Milling Industry 1750-1820', in C.H. Feinstein and S. Pollard eds., *Studies in Capital Formation in the United Kingdom 1750-1920* (Oxford, 1988), pp.141-63.

O'Shaugnessy, A.J., 'The Formation of a Commercial Lobby: The West India Interest, British Colonial Policy and the American Revolution', *Historical Journal*, 40 (1997), pp.71-95.

Pares, R., 'The London Sugar Market, 1740-1769', *Economic History Review*, IX (1956-7), pp.254-70.

Parry Lewis, J., *Building Cycles and Britain's Growth* (1965).

Paulsen, R., *Hogarth: His Life, Art and Times*, 2 vols. (New Haven, 1971).

Pauly, M.V., 'The Economics of Moral Hazard: Comment', *American Economic Review*, 58 (1968), pp.531-7.

Pauly, M.V., 'Overinsurance and Public Provision of Insurance: The Roles of Moral Hazard and Adverse Selection', *Quarterly Journal of Economics*, 88 (1974), pp.44-62.

Pearson, R., 'Collective Diversification: Manchester Cotton Merchants and the Insurance Business in the Early Nineteenth Century', *Business History Review*, 65 (1991), pp.379-414.

Pearson, R., 'Fire Insurance and the British Textile Industries during the Industrial Revolution', *Business History*, 34 (1992), pp.1-19.

Pearson, R., 'Taking Risks and Containing Competition: Diversification and Oligopoly in the Fire Insurance Markets of the North of England in the Early Nineteenth Century', *Economic History Review*, XLVI (1993), pp.39-64.

Pearson, R., 'Capital Formation in the Industrial Revolution Revisited: Insurance Valuations and Some New Sectoral Estimates', *Explorations in Economic History*, 30 (1993), pp.450-69.

Pearson, R., 'The Development of Reinsurance Markets in Europe during the Nineteenth Century', *Journal of European Economic History*, 24 (1995), pp.557-71.

Pearson, R., 'Towards an Historical Model of Services Innovation: the Case of the Insurance Industry, 1700-1914', *Economic History Review*, L (1997), pp.235-56.

Pearson, R., 'British and European Insurance Enterprise in American Markets, 1850-1914', *Business and Economic History*, 26 (1997), pp.438-51.

Pearson, R., 'John Thomas Barber Beaumont (1774-1841)', *Oxford Dictionary of National Biography* (forthcoming).

Pearson, R., 'Charles Bell Ford (1784-1860)', *Oxford Dictionary of National Biography* (forthcoming).

Pearson, R. and Richardson, D., 'Business Networking in the Industrial Revolution', *Economic History Review*, LIV (2001), pp.657-79.

Pemberton, H., 'Two Hundred Years of Banking in Leeds', *Publications of the Thoresby Society*, XLVI (1963), miscellany 13, pp.54-86.

Pevsner, N., *The Buildings of England: Essex* (1954).

Pevsner, N., *The Buildings of England: Hertfordshire* (1953).

Pevsner, N., *The Buildings of England: Bedfordshire and the County of Huntingdon and Peterborough* (Harmondsworth, 1968).

Pevsner N. and Cherry, B., *The Buildings of England: Devon* (Harmondsworth, 2nd edn., 1989).

Phelps Brown, E.H. and Hopkins, S.V., 'Seven Centuries of the Prices of Consumables, Compared With Builders' Wage Rates', in E.M. Carus-Wilson ed., *Essays in Economic History*, vol.2 (1962), pp.179-96.

Philips, D., 'Good Men to Associate and Bad Men to Conspire: Associations for the Proscecutions of Felons in England 1760-1860', in D. Hay and F. Snyder eds., *Policing and Prosecution in Britain, 1750-1850* (Oxford 1989), pp.113-70.

Pollard, S., *Peaceful Conquest: The Industrialization of Europe 1760-1970* (Oxford, 1981).

Pollard, S., 'The Insurance Policies', in C.H. Feinstein and S. Pollard eds., *Studies in Capital Formation in the United Kingdom 1750-1920* (Oxford, 1988), pp.225-56.

Pollard, S., 'Entrepreneurship, 1870-1914', in R. Floud and D.N. McCloskey eds., *The Economic History of Britain since 1700*, vol.2 (2nd edn., Cambridge 1994), pp.62-89.

Pollins, H., 'The Marketing of Railway Shares in the First Half of the Nineteenth Century', *Economic History Review*, 2nd series, VII (1954-5), pp.230-39.

Porter, R., *English Society in the Eighteenth Century* (Harmondsworth, 1982).

Porter, S., 'Fires and Pre-industrial Towns', *Local Historian*, 10 (1973), pp.395-7.

Porter, S., 'The Great Fire of Gravesend, 1727', *Southern History*, 12 (1990), pp.19-33.

Pressnell, L.S., *Country Banking in the Industrial Revolution* (Oxford, 1956).

Raynes, H.E., *A History of British Insurance* (1948).

Redford, A., *Manchester Merchants and Foreign Trade 1794-1858* (Manchester, 1934).

Reed, H.F., *Some Notes on the Early History of the Kent Insurance Company 1802-1952* (Maidstone, 1952).

Rennison, R.W., 'The Supply of Water to Newcastle upon Tyne and Gateshead, 1680-1837', *Archaeologia Aeliana*, 5th series, V (1977), pp.179-95.

Richardson, P., 'The Structure of Capital during the Industrial Revolution Revisited: Two Case Studies from the Cotton Industry', *Economic History Review*, XLII (1989), pp.484-503.

Rimmer, W.G., *Marshalls of Leeds, Flax-Spinners, 1788-1886* (Cambridge, 1960).

Rivett, G., *The Development of the London Hospital System 1823-1982* (1986).

Roberts, P., 'Agencies Human and Divine: Fire in French Cities, 1520-1720', in W.G. Naphy and P. Roberts eds., *Fear in Early Modern Society* (Manchester, 1997), pp.9-27.

Rodger, R., 'The Victorian Building Industry and the Housing of the Scottish Working Class', in M. Doughty ed., *Building the Industrial City* (Leicester, 1986), pp.151-206.

Rose, M.B., *The Gregs of Quarry Bank Mill: The Rise and Decline of a Family Firm, 1750-1914* (Cambridge, 1986).

Roseveare, H., *The Financial Revolution 1660-1760* (1991).

Rubinstein, W.D., 'The Victorian Middle Classes: Wealth, Occupation, and Geography', *Economic History Review*, XXX (1977), pp.602-23.

Rubinstein, W.D., 'Wealth and the Wealthy', in J. Langton and R.J. Morris eds., *Atlas of Industrializing Britain 1780-1914* (1986), pp.156-9.

Rubinstein, W.D., *Capitalism, Culture and Decline in Britain 1750-1990* (1993).

Rude, G., *Hanoverian London 1714-1808* (1971).

Ryan, R., 'The Percentage Duty on British Fire Insurance 1782-1869', *Journal of the Chartered Insurance Institute*, 6 Jan. 1981, pp.55-7.

Ryan, R., 'The Norwich Union and the British Fire Insurance Market in the Early Nineteenth Century', in O.M. Westall ed., *The Historian and the Business of Insurance* (Manchester, 1984), pp.39-73.

Ryan, R.J., 'A History of the Norwich Union Fire and Life Insurance Societies from 1797 to 1914' (unpublished Ph.D. thesis, University of East Anglia, 1983).

Savage, C.I., *An Economic History of Transport* (2nd edn., 1966).

Schofield, R., 'British Population Change, 1700-1871', in R. Floud and D.N. McCloskey eds., *The Economic History of Britain since 1700*, vol.1 (2nd edn., Cambridge, 1994), pp.60-95.

Schooling, W., *Alliance Assurance 1824-1924* (1924).

Schwarz, L.D., 'Occupations and Incomes in Late Eighteenth Century East London', *East London Papers*, 14 (1972), pp.87-100.

Schwarz, L.D., *London in the Age of Industrialisation: Entrepreneurs, Labour Force and Living Conditions, 1700-1850* (Cambridge, 1992).

Schwarz, L.D. and Jones, L.J., 'Wealth, Occupations and Insurance in the Late Eighteenth Century: the Policy Registers of the Sun Fire Office', *Economic History Review*, 36 (1983), pp.365-73.

Shammas, C., 'Changes in English and Anglo-American Consumption from 1550 to 1800', in J. Brewer and R. Porter eds., *Consumption and the World of Goods* (1993), pp.177-205.

Shannon, H.A., 'Bricks - A Trade Index, 1785-1849', in E.M. Carus-Wilson ed., *Essays in Economic History*, vol.3 (1962), pp.188-201.

Shavell, S., 'On Moral Hazard and Insurance', *Quarterly Journal of Economics*, 93 (1979), pp.541-62.

Sheppard F., Belcher, V. and Cottrell P., 'The Middlesex and Yorkshire Deeds Registries and the Study of Building Fluctuations', *London Journal*, 5 (Nov. 1979), pp.179-217.

Sigsworth, E.M., *Black Dyke Mills: A History* (Liverpool, 1958).

Smail, J., 'The Sources of Innovation in the Woollen and Worsted Industry of Eighteenth-Century Yorkshire', *Business History*, 41 (1999), pp.1-15.

Smith, B.D. and Stutzer, M., 'A Theory of Mutual Formation and Moral Hazard with Evidence from the History of the Insurance Industry', *Review of Financial Studies*, 8 (1995), pp.545-77.

Smith, D., *Conflict and Compromise: Class Formation in English Society, 1830-1914* (1982).

Smith, P.F., *Economics of Financial Institutions and Markets* (Homewood, Ill., 1971).

Smout, T.C., *A History of the Scottish People 1560-1830* (1985).

Spring, D. and Spring, E., 'Debt and the English Aristocracy', *Canadian Journal of History*, XXXI (1996), pp.377-94.

Stern, W., 'The First London Dock Boom and the Growth of the West India Docks', *Economica*, (Feb. 1952), pp.59-77.

Stevenson, J., 'Food Riots in England, 1792-1818', in R. Quinault and J. Stevenson eds., *Popular Protest and Public Order: Six Studies in British History, 1790-1820* (1974), pp.33-74.

Stobart, J. and Owens, A. eds., *Urban Fortunes: Property and Inheritance in the Town, 1700-1900* (Aldershot, 2000).

Stone L. and Stone, J.C.F., *An Open Elite? England 1540-1880* (Oxford, 1984).

Summerson, J., *Georgian London* (Harmondsworth, 1962).

Supple, B., *The Royal Exchange Assurance: A History of British Insurance 1720-1970* (Cambridge, 1970).

Sweezy, P.M., *Monopoly and Competition in the English Coal Trade 1550-1850* (Cambridge, Mass., 1938).

Sykes, C.S., *Private Palaces: Life in the Great London Houses* (1989).

Sykes, J., *The Amalgamation Movement in English Banking, 1825-1924* (1926).

Tann, J., *The Development of the Factory* (1970).

Thomas, D. and Hare, A., *Theatre in Europe: A Documentary History. Restoration and Georgian England, 1660-1788* (Cambridge, 1989).

Thomas, K., *Religion and the Decline of Magic* (Harmondsworth, 1973).

Thompson, E.P., *The Making of the English Working Class* (2nd edn., Harmondsworth, 1968).

Trainor, R.H., *Black Country Élites: The Exercise of Authority in an Industrialized Area 1830-1900* (Oxford, 1993).

Trainor, R.H., 'The Élite', in W.H. Fraser and I. Maver eds., *Glasgow: volume II: 1830-1912* (Manchester, 1996), pp.227-64.

Trebilcock, C., *Phoenix Assurance and the Development of British Insurance*, vol.I, 1782-1870 (Cambridge, 1985).

Treble, J.H., 'Liverpool Working Class Housing, 1801-1851', in S.D. Chapman ed., *The History of Working Class Housing: A Symposium* (1971), pp.167-213.

Turner, M., 'Corn Crises in Britain in the Age of Malthus', in M. Turner ed., *Malthus and His Time* (1986), pp.112-28.

Turner, M.E., Beckett, J.V. and Afton, B., *Agricultural Rent in England, 1690-1914* (Cambridge, 1997).

Union Assurance Society, *Bicentenary History 1714-1914* (privately printed, 1914).

Utton, M.A., *Diversification and Competition* (Cambridge, 1979).

Walker, C.F., 'Shaking the Unstable Empire: The Lima, Quito and Arequipa Earthquakes, 1746, 1783 and 1797', in A. Johns ed., *Dreadful Visitations: Confronting Natural Catastrophe in the Age of Enlightenment* (1999), pp.113-44.

Waller, P.J., *Town, City and Nation: England 1850-1914* (Oxford, 1983).

Ward, J.R., *The Finance of Canal Building in Eighteenth Century England* (Oxford, 1974).

Wasow, B. 'Determinants of Insurance Penetration: A Cross Country Analysis', in B. Wasow and R.D. Hill eds., *The Insurance Industry in Economic Development* (New York, 1986), pp.160-76.

Weatherill, L., 'The Meaning of Consumer Behaviour in Late Seventeenth- and Early Eighteenth-Century England', in J. Brewer and R. Porter eds., *Consumption and the World of Goods* (1993), pp.206-227.

Weiler, K.J. and Mirowski, P., 'Rates of Interest in 18th Century England', *Explorations in Economic History*, 27 (1990), pp.1-28.

Wells, R., *Wretched Faces: Famine in Wartime England, 1793-1801* (Gloucester, 1988).

West, S., 'Wilkes's Squint: Synecdochic Physiognomy and Political Identity in Eighteenth Century Print Culture', *Eighteenth-Century Studies*, 33 (1999), pp.65-84.

Westall, O.M. ed., *The Historian and the Business of Insurance* (Manchester, 1984).

Westall, O.M. 'The Assumptions of Regulation in British General Insurance', in G. Jones and M. Kirby eds., *Competitiveness and the State: Government and Business in Twentieth Century Britain* (Manchester, 1991), pp.141-60.

Westall, O.M., *The Provincial Insurance Company 1903-38: Family, Markets and Competitive Growth* (Manchester, 1992).

Westall, O.M., 'Marketing Strategy and the Competitive Structure of British General Insurance, 1720-1980', *Business History*, 36 (1994), pp.20-46.

Westall, O.M., 'Invisible, Visible and "Direct" Hands: An Institutional Interpretation of Organisational Structure and Change in British General Insurance', *Business History*, 39 (1997), pp.44-66.

Westerfield, R.B., *Middlemen in English Business, 1660-1760* (1915, reprinted New York, 1968).

Williams, D.E., ' Were "Hunger" Rioters Really Hungry? Some Demographic Evidence', *Past & Present*, 71 (1976), pp.70-75.

Williams, D.M., 'Liverpool Merchants and the Cotton Trade, 1820-1850', in J.R. Harris ed., *Liverpool and Merseyside: Essays in the Economic and Social History of the Port and its Hinterland* (1969), pp.182-211.

Williams, K., *From Pauperism to Poverty* (1981).

Williams, R., *The Country and the City* (St Albans, 1975).

Wilson, J.F., *Lighting the Town: A Study of Management in the North-West Gas Industry 1805-1880* (1991).

Wilson, R.G., *Gentleman Merchants: The Merchant Community in Leeds 1700-1830* (Manchester, 1971).

Wilson, R.G. and Mackley, A.L., 'How Much Did the English Country House Cost to Build, 1660-1880?', *Economic History Review*, LII (1999), pp.436-68.

Woods, R., 'Population Growth and Economic Change in the Eighteenth and Nineteenth Centuries', in P. Mathias and J.A. Davis eds., *The First Industrial Revolutions* (Oxford, 1989), pp.127-53.

Woodward, J., *To do the Sick no Harm: a Study of the British Voluntary Hospital System to 1875* (1974).

Wrigley, E.A., *Continuity, Chance and Change: The Character of the Industrial Revolution in England* (Cambridge, 1988).

Wrigley, E.A. and Schofield, R.S., *The Population History of England, 1541-1871: A Reconstruction* (1981).

Youngson, A.J., *The Making of Classical Edinburgh 1750-1840* (Edinburgh, 1966).

Index